C000010928

BROMLEY, KENT

THE OLD COTTAGE, WIDMORE.

From a water-colour drawing by Thos. Girtin. *By the kind permission of R. W. Lloyd, Esq., and " The Studio, Ltd."*

Frontispiece]

THE BACK OF THE BELL HOTEL, 1896.

From a water-colour drawing by Mr. Philip Norman. *By kind permission of Mrs. Hamilton.*

BROMLEY
KENT

FROM THE EARLIEST TIMES TO THE PRESENT CENTURY

COMPILED FROM MATERIALS COLLECTED FROM
ORIGINAL SOURCES BY VARIOUS HANDS

BY

E. L. S. HORSBURGH, B.A., F.R.Hist.S.

LATE EXHIBITIONER, QUEEN'S COLLEGE, OXFORD; EX-PRESIDENT OXFORD UNION SOCIETY

WITH A CHAPTER ON

THE MANOR AND THE PALACE

BY

PHILIP NORMAN, LL.D., F.S.A.

PUBLISHED FOR THE "HISTORY OF BROMLEY" COMMITTEE BY

HODDER AND STOUGHTON Ltd.

MCMXXIX

This is a reproduction of the original edition published by Hodder and Stoughton Ltd. but for economy the type area has been slightly reduced and the blank pages deleted. The effect of the latter has been to break the convention that even and odd numbered pages are always on the left and right respectively.

The publishers wish to express their grateful thanks to the London Borough of Bromley and the staff of the Central Library, Bromley, for their co-operation and assistance.

© LONDON BOROUGH OF BROMLEY
February 1980
ISBN 0850770688

LODGEMARK PRESS LIMITED
Bank House, Summerhill, Chislehurst,
Kent, BR7 5RD, England

The reprinting of this book is hopefully one step in the publication of a local history series on south-east London and north-west Kent. We have already produced "Penge" and titles on the Marian Vian School at Elmers End, "Ruxley Manor", "Knockholt" and the W.W.II experiences at Burnt Ash, are in course of preparation. To be kept informed as to details, availability and price etc., please contact us giving your name and address requesting that you be added to our local history list. As they appear new titles should be available from booksellers in the area.
Lodgemark Press Ltd., Bank House, Summerhill, Chislehurst, Kent, BR7 5RD. Tel: 01-467 6533.

Printed by T. J. Press (Padstow) Ltd., of Padstow, Cornwall.

PREFACE

FOR the last twenty or thirty years antiquaries, enthusiasts, patriotic townsfolk, and others have been engaged in collecting materials for a detailed History of Bromley.

The old Bromley, which had existed with comparatively little change for hundreds of years, was visibly passing away before their eyes. The picturesque country town, centring round the Palace of the Bishops of Rochester, and containing some four or five thousand inhabitants, which was Bromley within the memory of some who are still living, was rapidly converting itself into a large, populous modern town, which from its proximity to London was more and more in danger, with each succeeding year, of being absorbed into the great vortex of Metropolitan suburbs.

While memories of the past still continued to survive, it was felt to be desirable that the records should be brought together in a convenient form, so that a History of Bromley might make a link between the vanishing and the coming generations. Thus newcomers would be better able to understand the devotion and enthusiasm with which native residents regard their town, and would themselves be led to realise that they are " citizens of no mean city," but of one that has behind it a thousand years of close association with our national life.

With this end in view an immense mass of material was gradually brought together, and many hands were engaged in the work of collection. There was, moreover, one man most eminently fitted by his attainments, and by his long family connection with the town, to co-ordinate all this miscellaneous information, much of which he had himself collected, and to mould it into the form of a worthy historical memorial of his native place. It was confidently hoped that Mr. Philip Norman, LL.D., would accept the position of Bromley's Historian. The pressure of years and circumstances has unfortunately disappointed this hope, and it seemed for a time that so much preliminary labour had been expended in vain.

But there was in the town a resolute determination on the part of a few ardent spirits that the project should not be allowed to drop. Among these was Mr. W. J. Harris, Bromley's Public Librarian, and it was due to his initiative that early in 1908 a Committee was formed to consider the question of publishing a History of Bromley. This Committee consisted of Mr. W. Baxter, Dr. H. J. Ilott, Mr. Philip Norman, Miss E. O. Parr, Mr. George Smith, the Rev. Donald Tait, Vicar of Bromley, Mr. Alfred Wright, with Mr. Harris as Honorary Secretary.

As a result a fresh stimulus was given to the accumulation of material, especially by Mr. Norman, who at that time was prepared to undertake the office of Historian. He found a zealous assistant in Mr. George Clinch, and special branches of investigation were allotted to each member of the

v

Committee and to others outside it. All this necessary preparatory work was well advanced towards completion when the outbreak of the Great War in 1914 brought the projected History to a standstill. Mr. Norman reluctantly abandoned the task he had originally undertaken, and all the materials were deposited in the Public Library, where they lay till 1921.

In September of that year Mr. Percival Ashton resuscitated the proposal, and once more a committee was formed—the History of Bromley Committee—with Mr. George Weeks, at that time Alderman and ex-Mayor, as Chairman and Treasurer. Supporting him on that Committee were Mr. P. J. Ashton, Mr. E. G. Atkinson, Mr. W. Baxter, Dr. H. J. Ilott, Mr. Edward Latter, Miss E. O. Parr, Col. Edward Satterthwaite, Mr. Alfred Wright, with Mr. H. Alderton, the Public Librarian, as Hon. Secretary.

The first effort of the Committee was to secure some suitable individual who could undertake the task which Mr. Norman had felt compelled to relinquish. Several attempts in promising directions only ended in failure, and at last Mr. George Weeks, on behalf of the Committee, and on the recommendation of my old pupil, Sir Ernest Hodder Williams, approached me, as an old friend of his, and as one who had resided in Bromley in days gone by, and I consented to undertake the work. Unfortunately it has only been possible for me to devote to this enterprise a portion of the very limited amount of leisure allowed me from the claims of a busy life, and hence a task which could easily have been accomplished, by a man devoting himself exclusively to it, within a year has been protracted over a period of more than five years. No one has regretted this more than I have myself, but it was quite unavoidable.

It must be clearly understood by every reader of this book that I am not myself an authority on the history of Bromley, and that I am not personally responsible for the accuracy of the statements made in this volume. My business was simply to take the materials supplied to me and to work them up, to the best of my ability, into a readable narrative. Thus, while practically every sentence in the volume has been written by me, except in the case of the Itinerary, which is the joint work of Mr. W. Baxter and Mr. G. Weeks, the statements which the sentences contain have been supplied to me. I am prepared to face the full blast of criticism on questions of style and composition, but this is the limit of my liability.

The credit for this volume as an historical record does not therefore rest with me, but with those who have worked so long and so assiduously in gathering the materials of which it is composed. Of these perhaps the first in order of time is the late Mr. Coles Child, who acquired the manor of Bromley in 1845. He was immensely interested not only in the venerable traditions associated with his property, but in everything which concerned the town in which that property was situated. Mr. Coles Child, both personally and through the medium of his agents, made extensive researches into old records, and left behind him voluminous and well-authenticated notes, of which ample use has been made in this volume.

At the same time, as has been said, Mr. Philip Norman was accumulating a large body of material bearing upon almost every period and aspect of Bromley life, and some sections of this volume are practically transcripts from Mr. Norman's MS., one most important chapter being his exclusive work.

Of Mr. W. Baxter it is not too much to say that Bromley, past and present, has been the passion of his life. No living man can be so intimately acquainted with every detail of Bromley life throughout the ages as is Mr. Baxter. For many years it has been his custom to contribute valuable articles on various questions connected with the history of the town to the *District Times*, and it is to his indefatigable researches that Bromley owes the preservation of many ancient documents of great importance and interest which, but for him, would have been left to moulder in decay. Throughout the compilation of this volume it has been necessary for me to keep in constant and close touch with two men who could clear up ambiguities, supply information, correct errors in my version of the story, and generally supervise my conduct of the enterprise. One of these coadjutors is Mr. William Baxter, the other is Mr. George Weeks, Chairman of the History Committee.

Perhaps between Mr. Baxter and Mr. Weeks there may exist a friendly rivalry as to which of the two is the better acquainted with everything connected with their native town. To which of the two I am the more indebted it would be difficult to say, and it has been from the first a matter of regret to me that neither of them could be induced to undertake the task which has fallen to far less competent hands. The position of Mr. Weeks as Chairman of Committee has been, I fear, a thankless one. He has had to endure over a course of several years not only the procrastination and delay incident to my conduct of the work, but also the burden of almost continuous correspondence upon every point of doubt or difficulty which has arisen in the compilation of the narrative. It is due to his invariable courtesy and encouragement that I have been induced to persevere to the end.

Foremost among others to whom the Bromley public and the readers of this volume are indebted is Mr. Bernard F. Davis, the son of one who was so long, so honourably, and so usefully associated with the town. That which is a toil to most men is to him a recreation, for he devotes much of his leisure to delving in the musty records of the British Museum, the Rochester archives, the Record Office, and other depositories of the memorials of the past. Though only professing to be an amateur in deciphering old documents, a keen flair and much practice have given to his investigations and conclusions an authority which professional researches have only succeeded in confirming. Thus it is entirely due to Mr. Davis that the quite erroneous statements of previous historians as to Simpson's

Place are here corrected, and what is believed to be a true narrative sub-stituted for them. But this is only one example of the many services, in connection especially with the remote and mediæval history of Bromley, which Mr. Davis has rendered to historical truth. Wherever his authority for any statement in this volume is cited, the reader may rest assured that his sources have been explored with scientific accuracy.

The Committee are also much indebted to Miss E. O. Parr, whose knowledge of certain portions of the Parish is unrivalled, and who has shown herself ready at all times to undertake investigations, and to assist, in every way possible, in the conduct of this enterprise.

Several of the illustrations are from photographs, taken by the late Mr. R. V. Harman, lent by Mr. H. G. Dunn and members of his family; others have their source indicated upon them, and some are printed from blocks lent by Mr. H. C. Bush, for all of which thanks are due and are here tendered.

The Committee gratefully recognise the generous assistance afforded by the Publishers in the production and publishing of the book.

In like manner the help of the Grout Engraving Company is similarly acknowledged for technical advice and for the provision of blocks for the illustrations at cost price.

It must be understood that this History can only claim to be complete up to the incorporation of the Borough in 1903. Indeed, the original plan was to stop at this date. To adhere strictly to this plan was not found possible in practice, and references occasionally appear to events even as late as the current year. These casual references, however, do not pretend to constitute a full history of the town from 1903 onwards. It will be for the Historian of the future to take up the narrative of Bromley as a Borough, and to give that prominence to the period of the Great War and the troubled years which followed it which have only been slightly touched upon in this volume.

E. L. S. H.

Christmas, 1928.

FOREWORD

ALL these things, . . . we will assay to abridge in one volume.
For considering the infinite number, and the difficulty which they find that desire to look into the narrations of the story, for the variety of the matter, we have been careful, that they that will read may have delight, . . . and that all into whose hands it comes might have profit.

Therefore to us, that have taken upon us this painful labour of abridging, it was not easy, but a matter of sweat and watching; even as it is no ease unto him that prepareth a banquet, and seeketh the benefit of others: yet for the pleasuring of many we will undertake gladly this great pains; leaving to the author the exact handling of every particular and labouring to follow the rules of an abridgement.

    .   .   .   .

To stand upon every point, and go over things at large, and to be curious in particulars, belongeth to the first author of the story.

But to use brevity, and avoid much labouring of the work, is to be granted to him that will make an abridgement.

Here then will we begin the story: only adding this much to that which hath been said, that it is a foolish thing to make a long prologue, and to be short in the story itself.

(2 Maccabees ii. 23–32.)

CONTENTS

Contents

LIST OF ILLUSTRATIONS

COLOURED PLATES

BLACK-AND-WHITE PLATES

List of Illustrations

List of Illustrations

ILLUSTRATIONS IN THE TEXT

Chapter I

FROM PREHISTORIC TIMES TO DOMESDAY

THE parish of Bromley, consisting of between four and five thousand acres of land, was, to the extent of one-fifth of it, nothing but woodland and waste even as late as the close of the eighteenth century (1798). It may be reasonably inferred that in prehistoric times the whole district in and around the modern town of Bromley was covered by woods and undergrowth. Very conspicuous among its flora was the common broom, and from this feature of the landscape the name Bromleag, or, in Latin form, Bromlega, was ultimately derived, meaning the heath where the broom grows.

Neolithic man seems to have found a home there, attracted doubtless by the presence of a river and numerous springs, for neolithic implements have been unearthed at so many places in and near Bromley as to afford conclusive proof that the district had a considerable population during the later part of the Stone Age.

Of the conditions in succeeding ages nothing is known until we reach the period of the Roman occupation of Britain. The discovery at Widmore in 1864, in the grounds of Beechfield, the residence of Mr. James W. Ilott, of the remains of several Roman cinerary urns, is evidence that the Romans were there, and that some Romans cremated their dead there, but these facts are insufficient to justify a theory that there was any considerable Roman settlement within the present parish of Bromley. The great main Roman road, Watling Street, ran at some distance to the north, and, though Bromley may have been connected with Watling Street by a cross-road, no traces of such a connection have been discovered.

The earliest definite reference to Bromley is found in a charter, dated A.D. 862, preserved in the British Museum. It records that Ethelbert, King of Wessex and Kent, grants to Dryhtwald, his minister, ten ploughlands at Bromleag. In the deed of gift the boundaries of these lands are precisely defined, and within the uncouth spelling of the Anglo-Saxon scribe it is still possible to identify the familiar localities of to-day. Thus ' Langanleage ' is Langley ; ' liofshema ' is Lewisham ; ' modingahema mearce ' is Mottingham, just as ' bromleaginga mearc ' is the ' mark,' or boundary, of the Bromley people. Farnborough, Keston, Cray, Wickham, are also capable of identification.

But the history of Bromley may be said to begin only when it became connected with the see of Rochester. Precisely when this connection was established is uncertain. The statement by Hasted in his *History of Kent* that Ethelbert, King of Kent, gave to Bishop Eardulf and the Church of St. Andrew at Rochester six sulings, or ploughlands, in Bromley, rests upon a document which is no longer to be found. Mr. George Clinch, after careful

GRANT BY KING EADGAR TO AELFSTAN, BISHOP OF ROCHESTER, OF LAND AT BROMLEY, KENT.

Photographed from the original in the British Museum.

investigation, thought that no King of Kent named Ethelbert was even a contemporary of Bishop Eardulf of Rochester, and that the grant, if made, was by King Eadbert, who ruled in Kent from A.D. 725 to 760. A gift of land, which subsequently included the manor of Bromley, is recorded by Dugdale in his *Monasticon* as having been made in A.D. 747 as the joint donation of the Kings of Mercia and Kent. But until the time of King Eadgar, in the tenth century, the history is obscure. Kent was subject to frequent ravages by the Danes. The whole county, which included the see of Rochester, was for the most part in a deplorable condition ; even the list of Rochester's Bishops is, during this period, at times imperfect, and there is, therefore, no sure footing on which a definite assertion may be based.

Though there can be little doubt that the connection between Bromley and the domains of the Bishops of Rochester was of early origin, no record which can be regarded as indisputably authentic is available till the tenth century. Two donations of Bromley land were then made to the see of Rochester, or rather two donations of the same land, one by a certain Byrhtric of Meopham, who, with Ælswyth his wife, bequeathed land at Bromley to St. Andrew's Priory, Rochester, when Ælfstan was Bishop. This gift, however, as the testators expressly state, was not an original grant, but only a confirmation of a grant previously made by members of the same family. We learn, however, from the Rochester Registers that after Byrhtric's death the deeds of the land were either stolen from the monks or were never delivered. The Bishop took the case before the King and his Witan, with the result that on receipt of certain moneys, mentioned both in the charter and in the Registers, King Eadgar granted the lands in question " to the venerable Apostle of Christ, Saint Andrew, and, for propitiatory money, to Ælfstan, priest of the Church of Rochester."

The original charter thus granted by King Eadgar is in the British Museum, and, by the courtesy of the Museum authorities, a photographic facsimile is here given. It is in Latin, and confers upon the Church of Rochester " ten measures, which the inhabitants of Kent call ten ' sulings,' [1] in that place where the tillers of the soil have already given the name Bromley." It is given in perpetuity, and free from all restrictions or reservations, except only " the case of (military) expeditions and the building of a bridge or fort." " And if any man should presume in his audacity to lay violent hands on it, let him know of a surety that he, quaking and trembling, will give an account of his actions before the local Judge, unless he shall previously have preferred to give worthy recompense."

At the end of the actual charter is a paragraph in Anglo-Saxon stating the boundaries of the land, which may be rendered as follows : " First on

---

[1] *Suling*—a word peculiar to Kent. It represented as much land as a yoke of oxen could plough in a year. It is equivalent to about 180 acres.

" In communi terra Sancti Martini sunt CCCC acrie et dimidia quæ finut 2 *solinos* et dimidium."—Domesday Book.

the east, the boundaries of Chiselhurst, then to the boundaries of Crofton ; then from there to the boundaries of Rugebeorg ; then, on the south side, the boundaries of Keston, and onwards by the Guard-place ; then, on the west, the boundaries of Wickham, and the boundaries of ' Beohhaham ' [Becham] ; then, on the north, the boundaries of Beringaham, and the boundaries of Mottingham, and thence, east again, on to the King's boundaries ; then to Chiselhurst. This is the charter of the ten sulings that Eadgar the King gave to Saint Andrew, Christ's Apostle, as a heritage for ever."

The charter states that the said gift was made " in the 955th year from the incarnation of our Lord Jesus Christ," and therefore the charter itself is commonly dated A.D. 955. This date, however, applies to the gift, and not necessarily to the charter, and may refer to the original gift by Byrhtric. As Eadgar did not become King until 957 at the earliest, and as the charter is signed by Dunstan in his capacity of Archbishop of Canterbury, an office to which he did not succeed until after 959, it is clear that Eadgar's charter is of later date than 955.

The land, however, was not long permitted to remain in the quiet possession of the monks of Rochester. On the death of King Eadgar, the widow of Byrhtric, who retained the lands on lease, was induced by her kinsmen to possess them by violence. With the assistance of the alderman Eadwin, and " the folk that was God's adversary," they compelled the Bishop, on peril of all his property, to give up the charters. The movement was encouraged, if not instigated, by King Ethelred, who was at this time at enmity with the monks of Saint Andrew. The identical land, defined in the charter of 862, was given by Ethelred to his minister Æthelsig in 987. A few years later, however, in 998 Ethelred became friendly to the Church and reconciled to the Rochester monks. The greater part of the lands were duly restored to them (six sulings), and from this time forward there is no record of any further disturbances. A year or two later the Danes sailed up the Medway, made themselves masters of Rochester, defeated the Kentish forces, and for the time being " ruined everything."

In the troublous times which followed, the history of Bromley is a blank until after the Norman Conquest. The Conqueror signalised his triumph by creating his half-brother Odo Earl of Kent. Odo, already Bishop of Bayeux, was singularly deficient in a sense of ecclesiastical fitness, for he took advantage of the destitution and demoralisation of the Church by appropriating various estates belonging to the see of Rochester, including the episcopal domain in Bromley. But he soon found himself confronted by a man of character, wielding an influence over the Conqueror superior to his own. Lanfranc was now Archbishop of Canterbury, and in 1077 Lanfranc had installed his friend Gundulf as Bishop of Rochester, the bishopric being still a feudatory of Canterbury, and thus in a position to benefit by the support and assistance of the Primate. Lanfranc, once firmly seated upon the metropolitan chair—appointed by the Pope, and in favour with the King, to whose son he was preceptor—determined to attempt to recover the possessions belonging by right to the sees of Canterbury and Rochester.

He laid his grievances before the throne, and, as a consequence, the King convened a solemn assembly of the whole county at Penenden Heath, near Maidstone. To that assembly those who were known to be most learned in the ancient laws were specially summoned. The Bishop of Constance, Gosfridus, presided over the deliberations, and, after three days of disquisition and consultation, it was determined that Odo should make restitution of much of that which he had appropriated, among the lands thus returned to Rochester being at any rate a part of the manor of Bromley. In the Registrum Roffense the date of the assembly on Penenden Heath is given as A.D. 1076, but a somewhat later date, which will coincide with Gundulf's tenure of the see (consecrated March 19th, 1077), is more probable.

It was while Gundulf held the see of Rochester that the great Domesday Survey was completed. What it tells about Bromley is not much, but the little that there is is of special interest. The entry, as it stands in the original, must be quite unintelligible to all but experts, but its importance demands a place for it in a history of Bromley. It runs as follows :

" *Terra epi Rovcestre.*

" Isde' eps' ten' Bronlei in Bronlei Hund. p. vi solins se defd. T.R.E. & mo' p. III Tra'e XIII car'. In dno sunt. II car & XXX uilli. cu' XXVI bord. hnt XI car Ibi I mold de IV sold. & II. ac' pti Silua c porc. T.R.E. et post' ualuit XII lib. & X sol. modo XVIII lib. & tam' reddit XXI lib. II solid. minus."

Expanding the contractions and abbreviations, the document stands :

" *Terra episcopi Rovcestre.*

" Isdem episcopus tenet Bronlei, in Bronlei Hundredo, pro vi solins se defendebat, tempore Regis Edwardi. Et modo pro tribus. Terra est XIII carucarum. In dominio sunt II carucae ; et XXX villani cum XXVI bordariis habent XI carucas. Ibi I molendinium de IV solidis et II acrae prati. Silva c porcorum. Tempore Regis Edwardi, et post valuit XII libras et X solidos ; modo XVIII libras, et tamen reddit XXI libras II solidos minus."

Translated into English, we have a series of solid facts which throw considerable light on the extent, population, and general character of the district in 1086 :

" *Land of the Bishop of Rochester, in the Hundred of Bromley.*

" The same Bishop holds of Bromley, in the Hundred of Bromley, for six sulings in the time of King Edward (the Confessor). And now for three.

There is the arable land of thirteen plough-teams. In demesne there are two plough-teams. And thirty villeins with twenty-six borderers have eleven teams. There is one mill of 4s. and two acres of meadow. Wood for one hundred hogs. In the time of King Edward and after it was worth £12 10s. Now £18, and yet it renders £21, less 2s."

From the text of the entry we pass to its actual content. What are the essential facts which we learn from Domesday ?

The Manor of Bromley in A.D. 1086 was in the possession of the Bishops of Rochester. The extent of the manor had diminished, since the time of Edward the Confessor, being now assessed on the basis of three sulings instead of six. The inference is that much of the land had gone out of cultivation since the Confessor's time if the assessment for Danegelt was only half of what it had been.

The arable land, amounting in all to thirteen carucates,[1] or the equivalent of what thirteen teams of eight oxen apiece could plough in a year, was cultivated partly by the actual lord, i.e. by the Bishop directly. This is the meaning of the Latin word *dominio*, rendered in the translation *demesne*. The lord retained in his own possession two carucates. The remaining eleven were cultivated by villeins and borderers, of whom the former numbered thirty, the latter twenty-six. Villeins were so called because they belonged to the *vill*, or manor, on which they were born ; and although attached to the soil as serfs, and capable of being sold as an integral part of the land, they yet enjoyed certain privileges which differentiated them from slaves.

Bordarii, or borderers, were villeins of a lower class, whose services to their lord were of a more menial character. Adopting the common estimate of five to a family, the thirty villeins and twenty-six borderers may approximate to a total population of between two and three hundred people.

The mill mentioned was a water-mill, worked no doubt by the water of the river Ravensbourne, for windmills were not introduced into the country until later. Traces of an old mill were to be found in comparatively modern times. The woodland was evidently rich in oak trees, affording an abundant supply of acorns for pigs.

The last notable fact is that, though the dimensions of the manor had shrunk since the times of the Confessor, its taxable value had very considerably increased. Bromley, for reasons unexplained, ran contrary to the

---

[1] Assuming the carucate to be equivalent to the suling, as seems to be the case—viz. 180 acres—the extent of the Manor in 1086 was as follows :

Lord's demesne . . .	360 acres
Meadow	2 „
In occupation of villeins, etc.	1,980 „
Waste, wood, common, etc.,.	2,364 „

Total 4,706 the area in 1871.

general rule, for Domesday shows the taxable value of land to be generally less in 1086 than it was in the days of the Confessor.

Hasted has credited Bishop Gundulf with the first foundation of the episcopal palace at Bromley. From the fact, however, that Gundulf was a great and durable builder, and that the palace at Bromley was a dilapidated ruin within less than a hundred years of Gundulf's death, and from the further consideration that a manor connected so closely from very early times with the see of Rochester was likely to have contained almost from the first some sort of residence for the Bishop, the attribution of the palace, in its first foundation, to the architectural genius of Gundulf must be received with caution. But the express mention of the Bishop's demesne in Domesday may be taken with some confidence as implying a residence of some sort, even if we reject the statement of Hasted as being improbable.

We have now arrived at what may be called the first landmark in the history of Bromley—the period of Domesday Survey—and we may conveniently at this point endeavour to form some sort of picture of the Bromley of that day.

It was an episcopal manor, much reduced in extent from what it had been at an earlier day, consisting of a fair proportion of ploughland, but for the most part thickly wooded or lying as waste. Rude cottages, scattered here and there in isolation one from another, sheltered some fifty or sixty families, of which all the members, in a greater or less degree, were the serfs of the episcopal overlord.

The principal building was probably the residence built at some time for the accommodation of the overlord himself on the occasions of a visit to his manor, and it may be that something in the nature of a chapel, attached to the residence, did duty for a church. For Domesday, notwithstanding its particularity about villeins and hogs, makes no mention of a church. This omission, however, is by no means fatal to the supposition that a church was then in existence.

The whole presents a picture of nothing else, I am afraid, than of a straggling and rather miserable little place, with no signs of a commodious, far less of a cultured, existence—a handful of rude peasantry in their necessities, their monotony, and their routine not far removed from the animals which they tended or from the earth on which they expended their daily toil. Such was in all probability the Bromley of A.D. 1086, and yet not less—possibly, from the presence of an episcopal residence, rather more—advanced than the generality of similar manors.

Chapter II

BROMLEY IN MEDIÆVAL TIMES, 1086—1485

THE years which immediately followed the Domesday Survey are marked by very considerable changes in the general character of Bromley.

Whereas, at the time of Domesday, it does not appear that there existed a single family above the rank of villein, we find within a century from that time various persons holding estates in and about Bromley by Knight's service to the Bishop. We find definite evidence of the existence of a church in Bromley, some of its Rectors being destined to cut a considerable figure not only in the history of Bromley but in the diocese of Rochester. One Bromley Rector becomes Bishop of Rochester. A Bishop of Rochester secures from King John a charter for the holding of a market in Bromley, in itself clear evidence of the increasing population and importance of the place. We have numerous inquisitions on the part of the Crown as to the tenure of land and the rights of proprietors. We have records of sub-infeudation ; the Rectors of Bromley holding Manorial Courts as being themselves invested with practically all the rights of a lord of the manor, and we have, sometimes, violent and unseemly disputes between Bromley Rectors and Lord Bishops of Rochester.

Such are the main features in the growth and development of Bromley which it is the purpose of the present chapter to present in detail.

The practice of sub-infeudation, or the sub-letting by the superior overlord of a portion of his estates to an inferior holder on terms of some sort of service or payment, was an early development in the system of feudal tenure. In accordance with this practice the Bishops of Rochester, within a century of Domesday, had made grants of land out of the domains of the bishopric to no less than twenty-seven persons who held of the Bishop by Knight's service. Among the number was a certain " Welfgert de Bromlega " for one-sixth part of a Knight's Fee, or £3 6s. 8d. This transfer dates from before A.D. 1189. Within the next thirty years the number of sub-tenants of the bishopric had increased to thirty-one, as is shown by an inquisition made by command of King John (A.D. 1210–12). Included among these are the names of " Galfredus de Sundresse, dim. f." and " Walterus de Braibroc 6ᵐ partem." This is the first mention of Sundridge as a separate estate, and we may conclude that the Manor of Sundridge, if indeed it ever was in a strict sense a manor, came into existence, as distinct from the Manor of Bromley, somewhere between the death of Henry II in A.D. 1189 and the date of John's inquisition. The name of " de Banquel " also appears as the owner of an estate which has been commonly supposed to include " Simpson's Place." This, and other misconceptions concerning Simpson's, will be dealt with in the chapter devoted to that estate.

This process of sub-infeudation, however, was found to encroach upon and to diminish the sovereign rights of the Crown. The Statute of " Quia Emptores " in 1290, though its primary aim was to define precisely the sovereign rights of the superior overlord, resulted in effect in putting a stop to the creation of these inferior manors.

It has been seen that in Domesday no mention is made of the existence of a church in Bromley. Leaving for full consideration in a subsequent chapter the question as to whether the silence of Domesday is conclusive against the existence of such a church in A.D. 1086, we have documentary evidence that within forty years of the great Survey there was a church in Bromley. In the Registrum Roffense several grants are recorded as having been made by Walter, Bishop of Rochester, to Hugone de Bromleghe, who in one of them is described as " Presbiter de Bromleghe." This is the first documentary record of a priest attached to a church in Bromley. Exact dates are not available, but the grants were made between the years A.D. 1148 and 1182.

The same register—Registrum Roffense—contains an entry of the sum of ninepence paid by the parish of Bromley for ' chrism rent.' This rent was payment made to the bishop for the consecrated oil used in the baptismal service. This beautiful service in which the child was invested with the white robe of innocency—the chrisome—was retained in the Church even as late as Edward VI's First Prayer Book of 1549. " A made a finer end," says Mistress Quickly of the dead Falstaff, " and went away an it had been any christom child." If a rent for chrism oil jars upon the susceptibilities of a modern day, yet one may regret that the innocent symbol of the chrisome robe should have been lost to our Baptismal Service since 1552.

A further indication of the progressive development of Bromley in little more than a century after Domesday is provided by the activities of Gilbert de Glanvill, who was consecrated Bishop of Rochester in 1185. This prelate, who had been at one time attached to the household of Thomas à Beckett, signalised his accession to the see by a thorough restoration of three of his episcopal residences. He built, we are told, houses " more congruous than those already existing." One of his restorations was the Bishop's Palace at Bromley, which had fallen into a ruinous condition—a circumstance which militates against the assumption that it had been built scarcely a century before by Bishop Gundulf. From these activities the inference may possibly be drawn that Bromley had now become of sufficient importance for the Bishop to desire to have a suitable residence there, but more substantial evidence of the progress of the manor is afforded by Glanvill's application to the Crown for the grant of a weekly market, the grant being conceded on July 19th, 1205, in the following terms :

" The King (John) to the Sheriff of Kent etc.—Know ye that we have granted to our venerable Father G. Bishop of Rochester that he may have a Fair at Strode every year to continue for two days, to wit, on the Feast of the Assumption of the Blessed Virgin, and the day following, and that he may have a market at Brumlegh every Tuesday throughout the year, so nevertheless that such Fair and Market be not to the injury of the neighbouring Fairs and Markets. And therefore we command that you cause the same to be proclaimed throughout your Bailiwick.

" Witness ourself at Canterbury, the 19th day of July. By the Justiciar."

At the beginning of the thirteenth century therefore Bromley is a market town, containing a newly restored episcopal palace, a church of such importance as shortly to supply a Bishop to the see of Rochester, and several manorial tenants, holding in fief, by Knight's service, to the Bishop, in contradistinction to the total absence a century earlier of any families of gentle blood.

In A.D. 1227 two other families come upon the scene in the persons of Adam le Blund, who acknowledges the right of Gilbert de Helles to " ten solidates of rent with the appurtenances at Sundresse " (Sundridge), and agrees that he and his heirs should render from thenceforth to the said Gilbert and his heirs five shillings sterling for one Ing (meadow) of land which he holds from him in Sundridge. The Le Blund family is found at Sundridge for many years. In 1255 a certain Peter le Blund became Constable of the Tower of London. In 1272 the le Blund of that day, Robert, acknowledges the right of Olivia le Champeneys, and Roesia de Berkhampstead, to two messuages, one carucate of land, and ten acres of meadow with appurtenances at Sundridge.

In the years immediately preceding the year 1235 Richard de Wendover was Rector of Bromley. In that year the monks of the Priory and Cathedral of St. Andrew at Rochester chose Richard de Wendover as Bishop of Rochester, and he was presented for confirmation to the Archbishop. The Archbishop, however, declined to confirm the election by the monks, really upon the plea that the prerogative of nomination to the vacant bishopric lay with the Archbishop himself. The Archbishop actually based his refusal upon the contention that de Wendover was ignorant and illiterate, and in every respect unworthy of so great an office. The monks appealed to Rome, and, after a contest lasting three years, during which time the see of Rochester was vacant, they triumphantly carried at Rome their claim to elect. Wendover was consecrated in 1238 and held the see for twelve years. He is said to have been buried in Westminster Abbey by special command of the King. According to Weever's *Ancient Funerall Monuments*, his portrait was to be found at one time in Bromley Church. Weever's words are : " In the Church wall at Bromley lyeth the portraiture in stone, as I learne by tradition, of Richard Wendover, Bishop of Rochester, and parson of this Town. . . . He was accounted a very holy and virtuous man which I cannot much contradict."

Notwithstanding the progressive growth, both in population and importance, of Bromley in the years which followed Domesday, the taxable value of the manor was very little greater in 1255 than it was in 1086. A Commission appointed in 1255 to determine, in the interests of the Crown, the value of manorial properties, declared on oath that the yearly rent of the Manor of Bromley amounted to £23, and that, owing to the sterility of the soil, the produce derived from the arable land was insufficient even to cover expenses, much less to maintain the buildings upon it, which therefore were a charge upon the manorial rents to the amount of sixty shillings per annum.

Some twenty years later, according to Charles Freeman in his *History of Bromley* (1832), an inquiry instituted by the Papal legate, on behalf of the Pope, was made as to the value of the Bishop of Rochester's Manors. His manor of Bromley was then estimated to bring in from all sources, money, hens, eggs, and ploughshares, the total sum of £29 3s. 6d. Still later, in 1291, a Royal Commission estimated the value of the manor as a total sum of £32 11s. 2d., made up, among other items, from 12s. 6d. from hens, 1s. from eggs, £23 10s. in rents of assize, and " 40s. from two mills " (whereas, in the time of Domesday, there was only one mill), the total value amounting to £32 11s. 2d.

Among the Cottonian manuscripts there is one, apparently dating from about 1320, which states the amount of stock, utensils, etc., which ought to be found upon the Manor of Bromley whenever it changed hands through the death or translation of its episcopal overlord :

" There ought to remain at Bromleghe, on the Bishop's Manor, 1 cart horse, value 13s. 4d. ; 16 oxen ; 4 stallions ; 8 cows ; 1 bull ; 100 ewe sheep ; 5 rams ; 2 boars ; 25 hogs of one year old ; 3 barrels ; 1 brass pot ; 1 porridge pot ; and 1 table. . . . But these things were, during the vacancy of the See, either destroyed or lost : and now, by the long vacancies of the See, or the reservations of the See of Rome, they will be all made away with or lost, and the buildings themselves will probably run to ruin, the temporals be diminished, and the woods destroyed."

It appears, however, that the manor to which all the particulars given above apply was no longer the same manor as that which is defined in Domesday. Instead of being in the sole possession of the Bishops of Rochester, a considerable part of it was claimed by the King. Commissioners, appointed about 1274, by Edward I, on his return from the Holy Land to take up the duties of his kingly office, to ascertain in every county what royalties and privileges had been encroached upon during his absence, declared that " half of the Hundred of Bromley is in the hands of the Lord the King." Eighteen years later, in 1292, by a writ of ' Quo Warranto,' the then Bishop of Rochester, Thomas de Wouldham, was required to justify his claims to jurisdiction in the King's manor of Bromley. The Bishop, however, succeeded in justifying his claims on the ground that he and his predecessors had possessed the liberties of the manor beyond the time of memory, and had enjoyed them without interruption. Whereupon the jurors found for the Bishop. Whether this decision applies to the manor as a whole, or only to a part of it, does not appear.

Apart from a few transactions relating to the transfer of land within the manors of Bromley and Sundridge, there is little to record during the remainder of the thirteenth century until the accession of Thomas de Wouldham to the chair of Rochester in 1292.

A bare entry in Willis's *Mitred Abbeys* has given rise to the story of a tragedy enacted at Bromley in 1261. It states that " Roger Forde, Abbot of Glastonbury in Somerset, was killed at the Bishop of Rochester's Palace at Bromley in Kent, on a journey which he took to defend the rights of his church, 6th October, 1261, and was buried in Westminster Abbey." Contemporary authorities, however, as Mr. Norman shows in his chapter on the Manor, merely state that Roger Forde died suddenly at Bromley, and Willis's modern rendering of " died suddenly " into " was killed " is without authority.

The episcopate of Thomas de Wouldham is notable, so far as Bromley is concerned, for a dispute between the Bishop and the Rector of the parish. By this time the Bromley parson was beginning to become a personage of considerable importance. We shall find him later in the full exercise of the rights of a manorial lord, holding his court with tenants performing their suit. The parson in 1292 was Abel de Sancto Martino, who claimed as the ' liberties,' or rights, of the Rector of Bromley the same liberties as were claimed by the Bishop. These liberties were " the return of the King's writs, assize of bread and ale, view of Frankpledge, and pleas of Withernam in the Manor of Bromley," all of which means that tenants were fined for any breach of the regulations governing the size, weight, and dimensions of certain commodities such as the loaf of bread, or the measure of ale, for breach of a pledge or security given for the behaviour of a freeman, or for unlawful reprisals in the seizure of cattle or goods.[1]

The unfortunate tenants of the parties were the suffering *tertium quid* in this controversy, for both Bishop and parson indifferently levied fines upon

---

[1] Pleas of Withernam. " Placito de vetito namio, or Plea concerning forbidden . . . " defined, or rather still further obscured, by Freeman as " the taking, or driving a distress to a hold, or out of the county, so that the sheriff cannot upon *replevin* make delivery thereof to the party distrained."

Defined by Clinch as " a taking or reprisal of other cattle or goods in lieu of those that were formerly unjustly taken, or eloigned, or otherwise withholden."

defaulters, with the result that they were compelled to pay twice over. The matter was ultimately settled by a sworn jury which decided that the Bishop had a right to those liberties, and that he found them in the possession of his church upon his coming to it. Whereupon the parson submitted, and was fined half a mark (or 6s. 8d.).

It was, however, at this point that the King stepped in, under the writ of ' Quo Warranto ' before noted, demanding of the Bishop that he should show cause why he made his various claims in the King's Manor of Bromley. The Bishop was able to establish his rights, which were still further exemplified and confirmed more than half a century later by a patent roll of Edward III dated July 13th, 1356.[1]

A grant of 1310 to William de Bliburgh, clerk, permits him " to strengthen with walls of stone and cement and embattel his mansion of Bromle." From the use of the word ' clerk ' it has been generally supposed that de Bliburgh was a cleric, or even a Rector of Bromley. The term ' clerk,' however, had then, as now, a lay as well as an ecclesiastical significance, and this de Bliburgh was, whether cleric or layman, a landed proprietor in possession of a fairly extensive estate of about thirty-six acres with a quit-rent to the Bishop of 5s. on the property. The estate ultimately descended to a certain Richard de Doulee. Mr. Coles Child believed that the de Bliburgh estate was at the corner where the road leads off from Bromley to Shortlands, the land being eventually held by Messrs. Mumpesson Peach & Waller, but it certainly included Simpson's Place.

In 1312 Cicely, the wife of John de Banquel, was able against the King to produce a charter, granted to her and her heirs for ever by Edward I, which gave her the right of free warren—i.e. the sporting rights—over her demesne lands in Lee, Lewisham, and Bromley ; a charter which was subsequently confirmed in 1391 in favour of Sir Richard Stury, a charge of half a mark being paid for such confirmation.

In 1316 Bishop Thomas de Wouldham died at Bromley, the fact of his death being, for some unknown reason, concealed for three days. It is stated in the Canterbury Archives that there had been enmity and ill-feeling between the Bishop and Hamo de Hethe, Prior of St. Andrew at Rochester. But Hamo, hearing of the Bishop's illness, hurried to Bromley, and falling prostrate before the dying man, begged forgiveness and absolution. Thus the two chief ecclesiastics of the diocese parted in a spirit of Christian peace.

One of the executors of the Bishop's will was John de Frendsburie, Rector of Bromley. Frendsburie was the successor in the rectory of Abel de Sancto Martino, the hero of the struggle over Pleas of Withernam. Frendsburie was evidently the Bishop's friend and confidant. His attachment, however, was rather to the man than the Bishop, for we soon find him in violent altercation with de Wouldham's successor.

This successor was Hamo de Hethe, or Hythe (Kent), who, in 1319, was

---

[1] Not July 10th, 1355, as stated by Dunkin, and others who have followed him.

elected Bishop by the monks of St. Andrew, and confirmed by the Archbishop. The Pope, however, declined to recognise the appointment, and " out of his paternal care " he granted the see to John de Puteoli, Confessor to Queen Isabella. Long and costly negotiations followed, which ended by the Pope giving way and confirming Hamo's election. But the resources of Hamo and of the see were so exhausted by the contest that the Bishop had to be supported by contributions in money and kind from his clergy, and, in 1320, he sold Elmstead woods for a sum of 200 marks, or £133 6s. 8d.

His own necessities did not, however, entirely paralyse his efforts on behalf of the diocese. He exerted himself to obtain money for the repair of the church in Bromley, which had apparently fallen almost into ruin, the grant in aid being obtained " by the consent of the Prelates and other Nobles of the Kingdom," a phrase which seems to imply something in the nature of a Parliamentary grant. The entry, however, in *Anglia Sacra* which records the fact is obscure and corrupt to the point of being almost unintelligible.

In the same year, 1327, probably for the same purposes, subsidies were levied upon the residents of the manor. A list is still extant among the Exchequer Rolls which is of more than ordinary interest because it contains the names of fifty-two of the then residents in Bromley. We find among them a Payn, a Blunt, a Pot, a Webbe, and a Chapman. The names of Hunt, Yonge, Baker, Paul, Gilbert, de Blakebrook (or Blackbrook) also appear, together with those of two clerics, Abel and Thomas, though neither of them were Rectors of the parish, and both were probably lay clerks.

The Rector at this time, as has been seen, was John de Frendsburie, the executor of the late Bishop's will. This office involved him in a violent dispute with the existing Bishop Hamo, who sued him for damages in the Court of Arches in connection with the loss of implements and utensils, property belonging to the episcopal residence. A verdict for the Bishop to the amount of £200, an immense sum in those days, seems to have soured the Rector, and made him contumacious. In 1329 he was deprived of his benefice for disobedience, and Hugh de Penebregge was appointed in his place. But upon attempting to take possession de Penebregge was forcibly expelled by de Frendsburie, who followed up this violent measure by sending his chaplain to Rochester, who, at the high altar of the Cathedral, excommunicated the Bishop in due form with bell, book, and candle. De Frendsburie was evidently a man of decision, and we should like to know more of this battle royal between Rector and Bishop than the bare fact that the excommunication was revoked, and the rash priest severely punished.

Apart from a few references to the tenure of land in the manor, and to aids demanded from those holding land by Knight's service on the occasion of the knighting of the Black Prince, the history of Bromley becomes a blank for nearly a century. There are no documents, nor have we any particulars whatever as to how Bromley was affected by that greatest of all calamities hitherto recorded—the Black Death. The economic effects which followed generally from an epidemic which cut off more than one-half of the population doubtless followed in Bromley also—a largely increased demand for labour, the consequent demand for higher wages, the imposition by Parliament of limiting Statutes designed to maintain wages at their original level, all culminating in Wat the Tyler's rebellion. In that rebellion men of Kent were active, and doubtless some men of Bromley too, as we know to have been the case later in the insurrection of Jack Cade. But the records of Bromley are silent on the whole of this period.

Nor is the fifteenth century very rich in documents relative to Bromley. The most interesting records are those which refer to the manorial courts of the Bromley ' parsons,' or Rectors, but before dealing with them it will be well to note the one or two circumstances concerning the town which have come down to us.

In 1422 the then Bishop of Rochester, John Langdon, practically alienated from the see some acres of woodland in Bromley by granting a lease for that land for a term of 419 years. It was felt that such a lease was in excess of the rightful powers of the Bishop, and Bishop Wells, who almost immediately succeeded, made a determined and eventually successful effort to secure its revocation.

In 1477 Bishop John Lowe obtained from the Crown a charter, confirming all previous charters and liberties granted to the see, and, in addition, the right to hold a market on Thursday in every week,

" and a Fair in the street, with toll and pickage of the same in every year, to last for three days, to wit, on the vigil, the day, and on the morrow of St. James the Apostle, notwithstanding that, within the aforesaid Manor, he may hold another Fair on the day, and on the morrow of St. Blaise, provided nevertheless that the said Market and Fair be not to the detriment of other Markets and Fairs." (*Translation of the clause from the Latin charter.*)

The effect of this grant was to change the market-day originally assigned by the charter of 1205 from Tuesday to Thursday, and to establish annual fairs upon the saints' days of St. James (July 25th) and of St. Blaise (February 3rd). It eventually became the custom for the Bishops to let on lease both the market and the fairs, the last of such leases expiring in 1862.

The St. James's Fair was suppressed in quite modern times (1865) by the Lord of the Manor, Mr. Coles Child, acting in the general interest of the inhabitants, to whom it had become a source of annoyance. The ingenious method adopted for its suppression is detailed elsewhere.

It was during the episcopate of Bishop Lowe that there occurred the great political and social uprising which is known as Jack Cade's rebellion (1450). It was essentially a Kentish movement, initiated by the ' Commons of Kent,' and enacted chiefly on Kentish soil. That it secured partisans among the men of Bromley and its district is proved by the pardons subsequently granted to " Rob^tus Payn de Bekenam, Andreas Woodcock de Bromley," and one " Hund, de Bromley et Bekenham." But, apart from these pardons, we have no record of Bromley's share in Cade's insurrection.

The same Bishop was accustomed to impose, among other penances pronounced against culprits, the obligation of presenting at the shrine of St. Blaise in Bromley, in one case, a wax taper of a pound in weight, in another a torch to the value of 6*s*. 8*d*.

It is at this period also that we have definite and detailed evidence that the Rectory of Bromley, though subordinate to the Bishop, yet claimed and sometimes exercised the rights of an independent manor. Various Rectors in the middle of the fifteenth century are found holding rectorial, or manorial, courts, with all the power, authority, and prestige which attached to a Manorial Lord. The Court Rolls which record these proceedings indicate that at an early period an allotment of land had been made for the support of the parish church, and that thus a manor had been created within the episcopal manor. Not only do we find a Rector of Bromley holding his court, and levying quit rents and heriots in the same manner as the superior lord, but on one occasion he was able to recover by escheat the land of a tenant who died without heirs.

To these rectorial courts the tenants of the Rector were accustomed to come in order to settle their relations to one another, and the rights and privileges attaching to their own tenements.

Thus, for example,

" Bromlegh Court of Richard Fryston, clerk, of his Rectory of Bromlegh, held there on Tuesday next after the Feast of the Conception of the Blessed Mary, in the thirty-second year of the reign of King Henry VI (1453).—At this Court came Robert Blondell as a tenant of the Lordship aforesaid, and acknowledged himself to hold of the Lord of the aforesaid lordship one virgate of land, lying in one parcel of land called Prynnes Knoll by the rent of three pence at the Feast of St. Michael annually to be paid— and he performed his fealty to the Lord in full Court."

" Bromlegh Court held there on Tuesday next after the Feast of St. Luke the Evangelist, in the thirty-fifth year of the reign of King Henry VI. At this Court came Robert Burbage, Thomas Bernes, Robert Woodder, Alex^r Curteys and Robert Curteys, tenants and suitors at this Court, and performed their suit.

" And they presented that William Bernard and his family broke the fences of the Lord, and cut the Lord's wood in his grove, and he places himself at the mercy of the Lord.

" And that Thomas Merston occupied the pasture and wood of the Lord with his own cows pigs and sheep against the will of the Lord, and he places himself at the mercy of the Lord."

No other facts relative to Bromley in the fifteenth century have come down to us, save that by this time the estate of Sundridge had passed into the hands of a family named Booth, and that the estate, previously mentioned as belonging to the family of de Banquel, had now passed into other hands, but the facts connected with this last transaction will most fitly find their place in the chapter specially devoted to the history of " Simpson's Place."

Chapter III

TUDOR, STUART, AND EARLY GEORGIAN TIMES, 1485—1730

"HAPPY," it is said, "is the nation that has no history." But unhappy is the historian who, when called upon to record the history of Bromley in the sixteenth and seventeenth centuries, discovers that there is little history to record ! And this is very much the present case, not, I think, because records have been lost, documents destroyed, or through such mischances as have obliterated the annals of past ages, but simply because the town of Bromley for many centuries pursued " the noiseless tenor of its way," unaffected to any recorded extent by the current of events or changing circumstances. A few hundreds of people had their dwellings there ; lived, loved, and died in a simple unrecorded way, and have left to posterity little more than the shadow of a name.

One development, however, stands out clearly in Tudor times. Bromley was then offering considerable attractions to wealthy men who bought property within the parish, built substantial residences thereon, lived therein, and were buried in the parish churchyard.

An investigation of old wills in Somerset House discloses the names of Thomas Frenche of Plasto, 1535, of Richard Hendrie of Wigmore Farme, 1549, of Thomas Harris of the Parke of Bromley, of Anthony Calthrope of the Mansion-house on Mason's Hill. The names of Draper, Bedle, Shotte, King, Style, Richbell, all indicate substantial landowners in Southborough, Plaistow, Bromley Common, Sundridge, or Bromley itself, and all of these names appear within a century from about A.D. 1500 to 1600.

But the fact of their existence as residents and property holders contributes but little material to the historian. We know nothing of any real importance concerning them. Indeed, the evidence is both ample and remarkable on which we may rest the conclusion that for several centuries Bromley presented no marked features of change. Curious investigations have recently been made into the lists of those assessable to lay subsidies in the parish of Bromley in the Middle Ages. These investigations show that the numbers thus assessable between the years 1332 and 1535 varied little between the figures 60 and 70. Regarding each name assessed as representing a family of five, we have a ' landed ' population of between 300 and 350, and, adding as many again for those not assessable for subsidies, we have a total population for the centuries in question of less than 700.

In 1662, a hundred years later, there is extant a detailed list of the inhabitants of the parish of Bromley possessing " hearths and stones." The total number for Bromley, Plaistow, Sundridge, Sideborough, the Common, Mason's Hill, and Wigmore is 129. Again assuming a family of five for each name enumerated, we have a total population of less than 700.

JOHN WARNER *BISHOP of ROCHESTER*.

& Founder of Bromley College.

Pub.d Dec 21. 1796. by Cadell & Davis Strand.

Just a century later, in 1771, an assessment for land tax enumerates all the proprietors of land in the parish together with the tenants in occupation. Of the latter there are 251. To these must be added about 150 " proprietors," representing a population of about 1,400. The same assessment, on the opposite leaf, gives the names of all occupiers of houses, and their liability under the window tax. The number is 272 representing a population of about 1,360.

These comparative records, therefore, show very conclusively that to the end of the seventeenth century the population remained stationary in the neighbourhood of about 700 ; in the eighteenth century the population about doubled itself. But in the course of some twenty years, from 1790 to 1810, that figure was again doubled. Dunkin, writing in 1815, is able to quote the official returns of 1811 which show that Bromley then possessed 472 inhabited houses, 634 families of which 207 were employed in agriculture, 213 in trade and manufactures, and 214 " not comprised in the preceding classes, the total population numbering 2,965, of which 1,431 were males and 1,534 females."

The general conclusions derived from the various records quoted are strikingly confirmed by the entries in the Parish Registers of baptisms and deaths. From 1580 to 1589 the averages respectively were 24 and 19 ; from 1680 to 1689 the averages are 34 and 38 ; from 1730 to 1739 they are 43 and 47. Then in the last decade of the century the figures show a notable increase, being respectively from 1790 to 1799, 83 and 66.

The history, therefore, of Bromley from the accession of the Tudors to mid-Georgian times, as far as it is connected with events of national importance, is centred not so much in the town itself as around the palace and the successive Bishops of Rochester, and this history is contained in Mr. Philip Norman's chapter upon the Palace and Manor. It only remains, therefore, here to pick up such unconsidered trifles as may have come down to us, and to form, as far as may be, a mental picture of what old Bromley was in what I will call its stationary period.

The first great change notable in the sixteenth century was the loss by the Church of Bromley of its rectorial status. It has been seen that in the Middle Ages the Church had succeeded in securing what almost amounted to distinctive manorial rights which sometimes brought the Rectors of Bromley into direct conflict with the Bishops of Rochester.

In 1536 the then Bishop of Rochester, John Hilsey, received from the Crown, for himself and his successors, a grant of the advowson and patronage of the rectory after the death of the existing Rector. The rectory, in other words, was appropriated to the bishopric, and the independent manorial jurisdiction of the Rectors of Bromley was finally extinguished, and Rectors of Bromley ceased to exist. From that time the appointment of the minister was in the hands of the Bishop, he being bound by the terms of the appropriation deed, to provide for the ' curate-in-charge ' an adequate stipend of a fixed amount.   This arrangement, as time went on, proved as disastrous to the minister as it was profitable to the Bishop, for the stipend being fixed while the value of money was continually changing, the curate-in-charge, or Vicar of Bromley, found himself, in the course of time, miserably under-paid.

In the meantime the Bishop proceeded to grant leases for long terms of the rectorial property appropriated to him.   The first of such leases was apparently in 1639 when George Buckeridge " of Lewisham Gent," became the lessee for a term of twenty-one years, at a yearly rental of £60 and forty quarters of oats.   This arrangement, however, was violently dislocated by the sweeping changes in the world of ecclesiastical affairs consequent upon the Civil War between King and Parliament.

The Civil War was, on the part of Parliament, as much a struggle against episcopacy as against the arbitrary prerogative of the Crown.   The successes of the Parliamentary armies in 1645 were followed in 1646 by a Bill in Parliament providing for the total abolition of episcopal government in the Church, and on October 9th the Bill became an Act.   Provision was then made for the sale of the estates hitherto attached to the various bishop-rics, the episcopal manor of Bromley being sold to Augustine Skinner on March 1st, 1647, for a sum of £5,665 11s. 11d.   Skinner was one of the Commissioners appointed to carry out the orders of Parliament in the County of Kent, and he seems to have taken advantage of his official position to secure the manor of Bromley for himself.   Considerable difficulty, however, was experienced in ejecting the Bishop from his palace, and securing possession for the new owner.   In the Journals of the House of Lords under date April 20th, 1648, it is recorded that by the authority of the Lords and Commons an order had been issued to the High Sheriff of Kent :

" to remove Dr. Warner, late Bishop of Rochester, and all other persons whom he shall find in possession of the Manor House of Bromley in Kent, out of the said House ; and to deliver the possession of the said Manor House with the appurtenances and other lands there unto Augustine Skinner, Esquire, or to such persons as he shall authorise under his hand and seal, to receive the same, who hath purchased the said Manor . . . according to the Ordinances of Parliament . . . and to give an account hereof to the Houses within Four Days from the date hereof."

Whether the High Sheriff was lukewarm in the execution of his duty or whether the resistance put up by the Bishop was too strong to be overcome is uncertain.   What is clear is that the Bishop still remained in possession, Skinner in the meantime protesting to Parliament against the denial of his rights, and perhaps against the procrastination of the High Sheriff.   For on

May 16th a further order was issued by the joint authority of both Houses, allowing to the Sheriff :

" Three days longer to put Captain Skinner into possession of Bromley House lately belonging to the Bishop of Rochester, and he is enjoined to put him into possession by that time according to former Order made in that behalf."

This order was effective, and Augustine Skinner was duly installed in Bromley Palace as Lord of the Manor of Bromley, and remained in possession until the Stuart Restoration in 1660.

Throughout these troublous times of the Civil War and the Commonwealth when thrones, ecclesiastical and regal, were being shattered into fragments, we have no record of how the minister and the ministry of Bromley Parish Church fared until 1653. In that year a Mr. Henry Arnold was appointed as Vicar of Bromley. Though a Churchman, his theological views were to such an extent in harmony with those of the successive predominant factions that neither Presbyterians, Independents, Major-Generals, nor Triers found it necessary to eject him. Indeed, so acceptable was he to the Government of Cromwell that a special order, dated December 25th, 1655, was issued increasing Arnold's stipend of £60 by £22 10*s*. " His Highness and the Counsell have approved thereof and that the same be from time to time paid unto the said Mr. Arnold, approved by the Counsell on approbation of publique parishioners [1] for such time as he should continue Minister there." After the Restoration Arnold continued in his position as Vicar of Bromley, and retained it until 1662, when a stringent Act of Uniformity enacted that every clergyman, schoolmaster, or Fellow of a College should accept, before the Feast of St. Bartholomew, August 24th, everything contained in the Book of Common Prayer as the sole medium of public worship. Any clergyman refusing to do so was *ipso facto* and forthwith to be deprived of his benefice without provision for his future maintenance. Henry Arnold, of Bromley, was one of the two thousand ministers in the Church of England who were the victims of what is known as Clarendon's " Massacre of St. Bartholomew." The few available details here recorded of his life and ministry are insufficient to put an authentic stamp upon the character of the man, but they allow us to picture him as one fit to be enrolled among the worthies of Bromley, a man who was no Vicar of Bray, ready to trim his theological sails to every wind of doctrine, but rather one whose life corresponded to the loftiest Puritan ideal of conscience as the prime governor of action, and who sought to find the sanctions of conduct " as ever in his great Taskmaster's eye."

---

[1] The word here rendered ' parishioners ' is, in the original order in Lambeth Palace Library, almost illegible. ' Parishioners ' seems to be the only word corresponding to the general sense and such letters as can be deciphered.

The restoration of the Stuart Monarchy in 1660 involved the restoration of the old order both in State and Church.   Episcopacy was re-established. The sequestered estates of the various dioceses were given back to them, and eight bishops who had survived throughout the troubled years of war and Commonwealth personally re-entered into possession of the office and property from which they had been ejected.   Among these was John Warner of Rochester, now an old man of seventy-nine, whose closing years of peaceful activity in his see are in striking contrast with the stormy days of wanderings and exile which immediately preceded them.   Warner died in Bromley in 1666, and in the history of Bromley his noble legacy of £8,000 for the foundation of the College takes a prominent place.   The reader, however, will be content here with a mere casual allusion to this benefaction, the full story of Warner and Bromley College being contained in a subsequent chapter.

In the years which followed Warner's tenure of the bishopric, Bromley is connected with important national events through Francis Turner, Bishop of Rochester, one of the famous Seven Bishops who were imprisoned in the Tower by order of James II for refusing to read the Declaration of Indulgence : through Thomas Sprat and the ' Flower-pot Plot,' of which Sprat himself, Lord Macaulay, and Mr. Norman in this book, have given such a full account ; and through Francis Atterbury, wit, politician, intriguer, the friend of Pope and the Pretender, the inveterate and exiled enemy of the House of Hanover.[1]   But apart from the vicissitudes of Bishops resident in Bromley, which belong rather to the history of the palace than of the town, the records of Bromley are practically a blank until the eighteenth century is well advanced.

At this point, therefore, an endeavour may be made to form some sort of picture of old Bromley as it was in the period covered by this chapter— a period extending over two centuries and a half in time, but marked apparently by very little change in the general character either of the town or of its population.

The town itself, situated at a distance of ten miles from London Bridge, on the main road between the Metropolis and Tonbridge and Hastings, and containing one of the principal residences of a Bishop, was doubtless at all times a place of some consideration.   It was no unfrequented backwater of civilisation, but in the main stream of communication between important centres, and the inhabitants were probably well alive to what was passing in the world around them.   But none the less it was for many centuries little more than a hamlet, enclosed all around by depths of wood and field and heath which provided occupation and a livelihood for the ' colyers,' or charcoal-burners, who figure largely in the lists of the inhabitants.

The town consisted of a single street stretching, as the High Street

---

[1] All of this is fully treated in the chapter on the Palace and the Manor.

does to-day, from the neighbourhood of the College to the market-place, and somewhat beyond it. This extension of the road beyond the market-place has been dignified by some historians with the name of a separate street; but, says Freeman: " Where they found two streets I am unable to imagine." Yet, ' Up Town ' and ' Down Town,' as indicating separately the entrance to and exit from the town, were old-time expressions with which Freeman must surely have been familiar.

The beauty of the surrounding country, the pleasant, healthy air, and the vicinity of London had already, as has been shown, attracted a few substantial families to Bromley to swell the number of such families already established there. To the names given at the beginning of this chapter may be added those of the Knights and Thornhills—owners of broad acres and commodious residences which combined with the Bishop's palace to give distinction to the town. But apart from such residences, to which special reference will be made later, the houses which flanked the main street were such small and poor dwellings as consorted with the condition of a population mainly engaged in trade and agriculture, dwellings of course, as was the case everywhere at the time, from which the first elementary principles of sanitation were totally absent; externally picturesque no doubt, but internally little better than death-traps. The periodic visitations of the Plague did not pass Bromley by. We read of the Bishop in 1630 being turned out of his palace by the Plague. In this year sixty-two burials are recorded in the Parish Registers as against an average of less than thirty. Five years earlier, in 1625, one hundred and eleven burials are entered. These were plague years, and the exceptional mortality was unquestionably due to that scourge. In 1665, the year of the Great Plague, we have under the general entry " died of the Plague " the following items :

> " 14 August　old Thomas Hunt."
> "　5 August　Mary, the wiffe of Thomas Haloway."
> " 22　　„　　A strange woman at the Windmill."
> " 26　　„　　A daughter of the strange woman's."

and several more entries for the autumn and winter months.

By 1693 a Pest House had come into existence in Bromley as an established institution, for under date April 29th of that year the burial is recorded of " Ye daughter of Goody Bate of the Pest House," and under date December 10th, 1698, " Holloway, widow of the Pest House." This Pest House was situated nearly opposite the existing gates of Bromley College, and was still there until about 1794.

It is not, however, to be inferred from what has been said as to the insanitary condition of its houses, or from the references to the ravages of plague, that Bromley was behind other places in its notions of sanitation, or that the mortality was greater there than elsewhere. On the contrary, owing to its elevated position and the purity of its air, it is probable that Bromley suffered less from epidemic diseases than towns less favourably situated. But in existing conditions it was impossible that plague, which had its origin in squalor and found its nutriment in garbage and filth, could leave Bromley altogether unaffected. All places, even the healthiest, must suffer the penalties of ignorance and neglect.

Among the plague entries noted is that of the death of " a strange woman at the Windmill." This windmill came into existence about 1600 by the act of Edmund Style, who, in his will, dated 1614, speaks of " a Mill I have erected in the Parish of Bromleighe." There were at one time several windmills in the neighbourhood of Bromley, all of which, except the fine old relic at Keston, have entirely disappeared. The particular windmill in question stood a short distance west of the London Road, and about a quarter of a mile north-west of the College—its position is marked in Rocques' Map of 1763. The mill not only survived but continued in active use until the nineteenth century was well advanced. Somewhere between 1835 and 1840 it was demolished and the field on which it stood enclosed. Quite a number of deaths at the windmill are recorded in the registers, showing that there must have been a residence of some kind attached or contiguous to the mill. Thus we have : " Dec. 3, 1669, a man child that the windmiller nursed " (it is suggested that this entry adds a new word to the language); " 23 Ap. 1676 : Matthew Janwood of the Windmill " ; and again in 1704 and 1726 the burials are recorded of Willm Lets, and Sarah, the daughter of William Bar " from the windmill."

It is from the Parish Registers that we gain our first authentic information as to the existence of inns in Bromley. Under date March 30th, 1652, occurs the entry recording the burial of " Daniell, the sonne of Daniell Gyles of the bell " ; followed on August 21st, 1668, by " Joseph, the sonne of Daniell Gyelles of the belle." It was at the Bell in Bromley that the Parliamentary survey of the manor was started in 1696. Almost immediately preceding the last entry the burial of " Robert Kinge of the Cross Keyes in Bromley " is recorded under date April 13th, 1668. In 1725, February 1st, that of " Benjamin the son of Charles Allen drawer at the White Hart."

The Rose and Crown, dating from 1588, " The Golden Lyon at Mason's Hill," the Queen's Arms, the Queen's Head, the King's Arms, the Tiger's Head, the Red Lyon, the Plough, the Crooked Billet, " The White Horse in Wigmore Lane," all occur as the names of inns existing in Bromley between the dates 1671 and 1736. Of several of these nothing is known beyond the bare fact that once they existed, but some are of course historic, notably the White Hart and the Bell.

The origin of these two famous hostelries is lost in the mists of time. It is therefore impossible to say how long their rivalry for pre-eminence has lasted. The first documentary records which we have show " The Bell " as an established institution by the middle of the seventeenth century, and, for all we know, it may have come into existence a century, or even centuries, before that time. The first entry in the Parish Registers relative to " The White Hart " is dated 1725, but that it was at least coeval with " The Bell " is proved by the existence of two copper tokens bearing the names of two successive landlords of the inn, the later of these tokens bearing the date 1664. Between the years 1648 and 1672 the country was suffering from the lack of small change, and as a consequence innkeepers and other tradesmen were authorised to issue tokens which would pass for small currency. The earlier of these tokens bears the name of Michael Lee, and runs thus : upon the obverse, " MICHAEL. LEE. AT WHITE — (a hart lodged)," and on the reverse, " IN BRUMLEY, 1664 — M.E.L." The E. in these initials being that of his wife. The later one bears upon the obverse the name of Thomas Ghost, landlord of the White Hart, together with a representation of a hart. Thus : " THOMAS. GHOST. AT. THE — (a hart lodged)," and upon the reverse : " IN. BROMLEY. IN. KENT. — HIS HALF. PENY." (There are three other tokens. All of them will be referred to in a later chapter and are illustrated.)

It is only within comparatively recent time, that is, within a century, that the White Hart has assumed its present form. Originally its front extended to the roadway, keeping line with the shops on either side of it, the whole building being thus actually larger in bygone centuries than it is to-day.

We are, however, concerned in this chapter with Bromley as it was up to the middle of the eighteenth century, and must, therefore, be content for the present with merely marking the existence of these, and other hostelries as prominent features of the old town. Little or nothing, beyond bare entries in the Registers, is known of them or of their activities until a much later date. Further references, therefore, to the part played by these old inns in the history of the town are reserved for a chapter which follows.

Our picture of old Bromley in Tudor, Stuart, and earlier Georgian times embraces only a single street, flanked on each side by old, doubtless picturesque, but always, from a modern point of view, insanitary houses, a block of shops alternating with a block of cottages, with larger private dwellings intervening, and here and there an inn. The tradesmen's shops, of which the first floor sometimes projected, showed bow-fronted windows with small panes of glass. The customer, in entering, had either to take a step or two up or a step or two down in order to reach the floor of the shop.

The street debouched on to the market square, conspicuous for its old Market House crowned by a cupola and terminating in a vane. It was a tiled and boarded building with three windows facing the street. On market days (Thursdays) and fair days (the Feasts of St. James and St. Blaise) the market square was, for many centuries, the centre to which the whole population gravitated. Here James II was duly proclaimed King on

WIDMORE LANE FROM THE MARKET PLACE,

Showing the Parish Fire-engine House and, beyond it, the Cage (1860).

February 10th, 1685, by the sheriff of the county, William Rooke of Canterbury.

In John Evelyn's diary, under the date of February 10th, 1685, is the following :

" Being sent to by the Sheriff of the County to appear and assist in proclaiming the King, I went the next day to Bromley, where I met the Sheriff and the Commander of the Kentish Troop, with an appearance, I suppose, of above 500 horse, and innumerable people, two of his Majesty's trumpets and a Sergeant with other officers, who having drawn up the horse in a large field near the town, marched thence, with swords drawn to the market place, where, making a ring, after sound of trumpets and silence made, the High Sheriff read the proclaiming titles to his bailiff, who repeated them aloud, and then, after many shouts of the people, his Majesty's health being drunk in a flint glass of a yard long, by the Sheriff, Commander, Officers and Chief Gentlemen, they all dispersed, and I returned."

Near the market square in Widmore Lane was the Cage, a small square brick building which served as a place of detention for accused persons, with a central door and two cells right and left for the accommodation of male and female culprits. Each cell had an iron grating in front, so that any tall person standing on a little elevation could see and converse with its occupant. In the days before police the Cage was a substitute for the modern police-station, but without its amenities. Entirely destitute of any warming apparatus, the unfortunate inmates were exposed practically to the elements during their period of detention, which might extend over Saturday and Sunday nights. From the Cage they were conducted, handcuffed, before the magistrates, and then were usually consigned to Maidstone Gaol.

Possibly it was hard by the Cage that the stocks and the whipping-post stood, though their position cannot be definitely fixed. One feels, to make things complete, there ought to have been a ducking-stool somewhere handy, and we find that there was one associated with the pond at Widmore.

Below, on the west side of the town, ran the River Ravensbourne, a rippling, purling stream, not only within the period under consideration, but within the memory of some who are still living. Between Martin's Hill and the river wild duck, snipe, kingfishers, moorhens, and dabchicks were wont to disport themselves, while speckled trout, dace, and roach swam in the crystal waters of the burn, and even to-day wild duck and moorhens are to be found within a mile of the market-place.

Any imaginary picture of old Bromley in the bygone centuries must necessarily be dim and incomplete for want of the detailed and exact information which alone could give it actuality. The picture, however, which I have here attempted to draw can be invested with some degree of actual life through our knowledge of some of the principal residents who owned mansions and estates within the town.

The estate of Simpson's Place was of such importance that it is treated separately in a chapter to itself. We will therefore pass Simpson's over here, and come to an estate lying on the left-hand side as you enter the town coming from London.

This estate, at some time known as The Grete House, extending over thirteen acres in the town itself, seems to have comprised the whole east side of the High Street from the Bell Inn towards the north, including at any rate a part of the site on which the college now stands. The first authentic document relating to this estate is a marriage settlement of 1532, by which we learn that the then owner was a certain Thomas Knight, a Pandoxator, or brewer, of the City of London. In addition to his town property in Bromley he also owned ninety-four acres of land in the neighbourhood of Bromley Common, known under the general name of ' Goodwyns.' Dr. Beeby, who has written an account of the Knight estate in *Archæologia Cantiana* (Vol. XIII, 1880), identifies this property with what is now known as Cooper's Farm and Turpington Farm, near Blackbrook, but more recent researches by Mr. B. F. Davis have shown that Oakley, not Cooper's Farm, was the original Goodwyns.

Thomas Knight was evidently a man of substance, and that he was also a man of taste is in evidence to-day. For in the hall of Mr. Edward Latter's house, Pixfield, is preserved a part of the panelling with which Thomas Knight decorated one of his apartments. The panels, rescued from destruction by Mr. Robinson Latter, and relieved by him with infinite care and exertion of several thick coatings of paint, disclose examples of delicate carving of rare beauty and workmanship. My own inspection of them led me to think that they were worked by Italian craftsmen, the figures of angels, frequently repeated, being decidedly Florentine in design. The carvings, deep and some of them in high relief, include the badges of Henry VIII and Catherine of Aragon ; the Royal Arms supported by a dragon and a greyhound ; the coat-of-arms of Warham, Archbishop of Canterbury, twice over ; the ecclesiastical symbol I.H.S., with the five wounds encircled by a crown, the Tudor rose, numerous figures of supporting angels, and panels with the initials T. K. constantly recurring. Dr. Beeby was inclined to think, from the ecclesiastical and sacred character of some of the carving, that the panels had originally been a part of the rood-screen in the church, but expert opinion is against him. In the will of a subsequent owner special mention is made of " the wainscott " in the mansion. It may be asserted with confidence that the wainscot in question consisted of the panels installed in his house by Thomas Knight purely as a domestic decoration.

We have, then, living in Bromley, quite early in the sixteenth century— for the Star of Catherine of Aragon was still in the ascendant—a rich landowner who had made his money in London from beer, and yet a man with

CARVED PANELS FORMERLY (1532) IN THOMAS KNIGHT'S HOUSE, HIGH
STREET, BROMLEY. NOW AT "PIXFIELD."

artistic instincts which he was prepared to gratify by the employment of craftsmen of rare distinction for the decoration of his house.   His son and successor, Robert Knight, is known to us only by his contribution of twenty marks to the loan raised by Henry VIII in 1542.

On the death of Robert's wife, Alice, the estate was held in trust for Robert Knight's sons, and it was sold by the trustees to Richard Thornhill in 1577.   The deed of conveyance is still extant, in the possession of the Latter family, under which the estate changed hands.   The fact that the deed of sale contains the signature of Sir Edmund Style has been erroneously supposed to show that somehow the estate had been acquired and then sold by him.   Sir Edmund, in fact, only signed the deed in his capacity of trustee of the Knight marriage settlement.

The Thornhill family, thus established in Bromley in Elizabeth's reign, had been, according to Burke's *General Armoury,* connected with the island of Barbadoes, and in some way or another had acquired great wealth. Richard Thornhill, apart from the property in Bromley, owned land at Bapchild, Navington, and Borden, and a mansion, Mere's Court, near Rainham.   In the list of subscribers to the Armada loan Thornhill's name appears for £100, only thirteen other persons in the whole county of Kent being called upon to contribute as much.   Here it may be incidentally noted that Thornhill was not the only Bromley man who contributed to the Armada loan.   The name appears of " John Scott of Bromley, Gent. £25." and also of " Timothie Lowe, of Bromley, Gent." for the same amount.   One would like to know who these gentlemen were, and where they lived in Bromley in Armada days, but no further information regarding them is available.

Returning to Thornhill, Richard died on February 15th, 1600, and a very fine brass to commemorate him and his family is one of the most distinctive features in Bromley Church.   In the chapter on the church this brass is fully described.   He was twice married, first to Margaret Mills of Chevening, by whom he had two sons and three daughters, and second to Elizabeth Watson with issue two sons and one daughter.   The effigies of Thornhill himself, his two wives, and all the children appear upon the brass, together with the family arms, and a rebus.   By his will, proved on March 17th, 1600, and still preserved in Somerset House, he left " to the clercke and sexton of Bromeley . . . twoo clokes or twoo cotes at the discretyon of my executors, Item, what workmanshippe may be done to my grave stone [and by this presumably the brass is meant].   I would have it don with the advise of Mr. Smithe, harralde, and to be layde at the discretyon of my executors, by the license of my Lord Bishoppe of Rochester.   To the poore in Bromley, in money to be disposed by the discretyon of my executors, not exceeding tenne poundes."

A still more important section of the will refers to his " capital messuage with the appurtenances in Bromeley, and all " his " landes and tenements there with all the leades, cesternes of leade, glass, wainscott," etc., which he leaves in trust for his grandson and heir Timothy, and, failing him, to John, Timothy's younger brother. Originally the property had been settled on the testator's son, Samuel Thornhill, the father of Timothy and John, but as Samuel died before his father, fresh dispositions were necessary. The will also enacted that during the minority of Timothy the house should be occupied and maintained at an annual rent of £20 by Jane, a daughter of the testator. This Jane was married to Richard Smythe, who may have been the " Mr. Smithe, harralde," who was to be the advisor as to the workmanship of the gravestone.

In due course Timothy Thornhill succeeded to the estate, and was knighted by James I at Theobalds in January 1619. The date, however, does not accord with an entry in the Parish Register under September 29th, 1615, which records the baptism of " Thomas ye sonne of Timothye Thornill *Knight*." It would appear then either that Timothy Thornhill was knighted at an earlier date than 1619, or that there were two Timothy Thornhills in Bromley, one already a Knight in 1615, and the other becoming a Knight four years later. It is clear that knighthoods became almost an hereditary appanage of the family, for John, the other grandson of the original Richard, also became a Knight, or, at any rate, *a* Sir John Thornhill is found flourishing in Bromley between the years 1634–47.

In the church two Thornhill monuments relative to Sir John Thornhill at one time existed, though they exist no longer, pathetically recording the deaths of the infant children of Sir John Thornhill. The first, which bore the date 1640, records that :

" Hic requiescit Francisca, Johannis Thornehiil, equitis aurati, per Aliciam uxorem ejus infantula, quae languentes horas cum aeterna commutavit gloria."

(Here lies Francisca, the infant daughter of John Thornhill, Knight, by Alice his wife, who exchanged her languishing hours for eternal glory.)

Upon the other the inscription ran :

" Hic Jacet Samuel Thornhill quartus, Johannis Thornhill, nuper de Bromley, in comitatu Cant. militis, filius, qui anno aetatis suae primo, menseque nono, ex hac vita, flosculus tanquam, dicessit vicessimo quarto Junij 1647."

(Here lies Samuel Thornhill, the fourth son of John Thornhill, Knight, late of Bromley in the county of Kent, who in the first year and ninth month of his age, departed this life, like a little flower, on the 24th June 1647.)

The Parish Registers record the burial of these little children in 1640 and 1647 respectively, and between them comes the entry, August 7th, 1646, of the burial of Sir John Thornhill himself. Hence the phrase " nuper de Bromley " in the inscription quoted above.

With the death of Sir John the connection of the Thornhill family with Bromley seems to have come to an end.   No further references to any Thornhills appear in the Parish Registers, nor is there anything of interest to record concerning the estate, the mansion, or its occupants for just about a century.   A portion of the estate was secured by the executors of Bishop Warner for the purposes of the College, by deed from John Baynes in 1669, John Baynes having purchased the entire estate in 1665.   The house, and presumably what remained of the property, came at some time into the possession of one William Scott—a descendant possibly of the Scott of Armada times—who leased the domain for £35 a year to Dr. John Hawkesworth, whose tenure dates from about 1751.

We are thus brought to a new period in the history of Bromley, when comparatively familiar figures such as Dr. Hawkesworth, for example, present themselves to the view.   A final word, to close this chapter, may, however, be said of an interesting discovery in the spring of 1898.   At that time excavations were being made, for the purposes of the electric light works, a short distance behind the premises of the late Mr. Daniel Grinsted, premises which are themselves supposed to occupy the site on which the forecourt of the Thornhill mansion had stood.   In the course of these excavations the foundations of the old house were laid bare, and farther back a massive garden wall was discovered, with a succession of small arched recesses about two feet high, a foot and a half wide, and nine or ten inches deep.   The brickwork dated apparently from Tudor times, and there is little doubt that the wall itself was the original wall of the Thornhill garden.

There has been much speculation as to the uses to which the small recesses were put, some maintaining that they were merely decorative, others that they were receptacles for bee-hives, or for statuettes, or for lanthorns. Mr. George Clinch discovered a passage in William Lawson's *New Orchard and Garden*, published in 1649, in which the writer speaks of " seats in the stone wall of the orchard or garden, which is good, but wood is better," and from this passage Mr. Clinch surmised that the recesses were used as seats.   This, however, is a question for antiquaries and experts.   Anyone who feels competent to express an expert opinion can still see one of these recesses and form his own judgment, for Mr. Grinsted transferred one of them to his own residence at 20 Widmore Road, and reconstructed it in his garden, where it is to be seen to-day.

Our picture of old Bromley would be much more complete if we were better informed as to the other considerable families who were living in the town and its immediate neighbourhood.   But of these, apart from the possessors of adjoining manors which are dealt with separately, we have little or no information.   The history of Bromley in the period covered by this chapter is largely lost in shadow.   During the years which follow the shadows begin to clear, and modern Bromley gradually emerges into view.

Chapter IV

BROMLEY FROM THE EIGHTEENTH CENTURY
TO THE COMING OF THE RAILWAYS

THE history of the town of Bromley during the last two centuries presents to the observer two distinct and clearly marked epochs, which do not by any means coincide with the centuries themselves, but which are separated, one from the other, by an event of the first magnitude in the general, social, and economic development of the country. This event was the coming of the railway. Thus the first epoch covers about one hundred and fifty years, roughly speaking to 1860. The second epoch covers the period from 1860 to the present time.

The contrast between these two periods is certainly striking. In the first, the Bromley of old times still continues its placid and somewhat uneventful course of slow and gradual development. If an inhabitant of the town in 1700 could have come to life again in 1850, he would have been scarcely conscious of any very material changes. The aspect of the town, and of the adjoining country, would have seemed to him much the same, but for the addition of a few large houses and residential estates which were not there in his day, and for alterations consequent upon enclosures of waste land and of parts of the Common. He would not have been astonished by any marked increase in the population, nor would he have noticed any notable alterations in the methods of government and administration.

But if our hypothetical inhabitant of 1700 could come to life again to-day he would be hard put to it to recognise in the modern town any of the features of the Bromley which he knew. He would find himself confused by a teeming population of about 35,000 souls, where only some 2,000 had flourished in his time. The main features of the College and the Church Tower would be familiar to him ; he would recall the *names* of the White Hart and the Bell, though they would be little more to him than the shadows of a name. Apart from these, he would find himself in a new world of streets and habitations and of a ceaseless traffic as dangerous as bewildering. A Mayor and Corporation and all the appurtenances of an elaborate system of local administration would impose themselves upon his view, and the whisper of an income tax at 4s. 0d. in the pound would probably precipitate his immediate departure to the happy land of shades from which he had incautiously emerged.

It is undoubtedly the coming of the railway which has brought about this complete transformation, and it is the aim of the present chapter to bring the history of slow and gradual development in the town of Bromley up to that time. A concluding chapter in this section will summarise the changes of the last sixty years, and so will present, it is hoped, a faithful picture of Bromley as it is to-day.

The foundation of the College by Bishop Warner in the last quarter of the seventeenth century naturally resulted in bringing a permanent element into the population of the town which had previously been non-existent; and such an institution, in its architectural design, in its moral purpose, and in the distinguished patronage under which it flourished, increased the reputation and added to the prestige of Bromley.   Provision was then made for the maintenance of the widows of clergymen of the Church of England, a provision which is in itself symptomatic of a changing attitude towards social requirements.

Early in the new century there was a growing sense that something ought to be done for the education of the children of the parish, who up to that time had been without any systematised form of instruction.   In 1716 this sentiment took shape in the drafting of a bond, drawn up on November 11th of that year, by which certain charitably disposed persons undertook, according to their means and inclination, to pay an annual subscription " for the setting up of a Charity School," with the result that such a school was forthwith established.

A full history of the development of education and of schools in Bromley is reserved for a special chapter, in which all the necessary details in regard to the Charity School will be given.   We are concerned here only with its foundation early in the eighteenth century and its continued existence throughout that century, as proofs that a new spirit was now beginning to make itself manifest towards the question of education for the poorer classes of the people; that a faint and glimmering appreciation of a great fact was beginning to dawn—the fact that the moral standard of a nation is closely associated with the standard of its education.

The foundation of a charity school was followed a few years later by the erection of a workhouse, on land leased to the Churchwardens and Overseers of the parish by Joseph Wilcocks, Bishop of Rochester.   The lease is dated October 7th, 1732, and by that date the structure was completed.   It stood on the London Road, on the opposite side to the College, and some little distance north of that institution.

We may, I think, link together these three events, which appear to be entirely dissociated, as proceeding from one common impulse now beginning actively to operate: the foundation of the college for friendless widows, the foundation of a charity school for poor children, and the erection of a workhouse for the homeless and the destitute.   All alike display the germs of that spirit of philanthropy, that consciousness of the common humanity of all, that desire to alleviate distress, and improve the individual, which later found such triumphant expression in the missionary zeal of Wesley, Howard, Mrs. Fry, and Thomas Raikes.

There is now a blank in the records extending over a period of more than twenty years.   Nothing of any importance bearing upon the development of the town seems to have happened, or, if any such event happened, it has not been recorded. I can only fill up this gap by inserting here an interesting discovery which was made in 1733, and which has much exercised the learning and ingenuity of antiquaries.

In 1747 a letter appeared in *The Gentleman's Magazine*, signed " E. S. of Bromley in Kent," in which the writer, Edward Steele, discourses learnedly on " Burial Garlands." In support of his general contention he relates that " in the year 1733, the Parish Clerk of Bromley Church, when digging a grave in the churchyard, close to the east end of the chancel wall, dug up one of these crowns or garlands." The writer had evidently not only seen this curiosity, but retained a portion of it in his own possession " as a choice relic of antiquity." His description of it therefore has the authority of an eye-witness. He describes it as " artificially wrought in filagree work in gold and silver wire, in resemblance of myrtle (with which plant the funebrial garlands of the ancients were composed) whose leaves are fastened to hoops of larger wire of iron, now something crowded with rust, but both the gold and silver remains to this time very little different from its original splendour. It was also lin'd with cloth of silver."

The custom of hanging up garlands, or ' crants,' made of white paper, in the church on the occasion of a young girl's funeral was a very ancient one. It is referred to by Shakespeare in *Hamlet*, Act. V, Sc. i, l. 225, where the officiating priest at the funeral of Ophelia begrudges her the rites of Christian burial. The circumstances of her death so strongly suggested suicide that—says the churlish priest—

> " She should in ground unsanctified have lodg'd,
> Till the last trumpet ;
> Yet here she is allow'd her virgin crants,
> Her maiden strewments, and the bringing home
> Of bell and burial."

The passage adds strength to the contention of E. S. that these garlands symbolised the virginity of the deceased person, and the fact that in the particular case the wreath was elaborately worked in gold and silver filigree, instead of common paper, seems to imply the death and interment of some maiden of wealth and social consideration. The further fact that the garland was buried with the corpse, and not hung in the church, is an indication of comparatively recent burial, for it was only, says E. S., writing in 1747, within " about the last forty years that these garlands grew much out of repute, and were thought by many as very unbecoming decorations for so sacred a place as the church, . . . yet, notwithstanding, several people, unwilling to forsake their ancient and delightful custom, continued still the making of them, and they were carried at the funerals, as before, to the grave, and put therein upon the coffin, over the face of the dead. This I have seen done in many places."

It is unfortunate that so interesting a discovery should have been made in an age so singularly indifferent to antiquity and the relics of the past. This garland, instead of being added to the treasures of the church and carefully preserved, was allowed to disappear except for such part of it as, apparently without protest, E. S. was permitted to retain for himself.

About twenty years later a discovery of quite another character might have had consequences for Bromley of the first importance. In 1754 Mr. Harwood, Domestic Chaplain to Bishop Wilcocks, noticed that a thin stream of water flowing into the palace moat, which for some reason had been drained, left in its tract a yellow ochrey sediment. Tracing back this stream, it was found to have its source in a spring, situated a very small distance eastward of the Bishop's Palace. An analysis of the water from this spring showed that it was a chalybeate water, similar to, though even stronger than, the chalybeate water of Tunbridge Wells. A surgeon living at Bromley, Mr. Thomas Reynolds, conducted a series of experiments—no less than twenty-nine in all—to test the medicinal qualities and value of this newly found spring, and published the results of his investigations in a pamphlet, now very rare, entitled, " Some experiments on the Chalybeat water, lately discovered near the Palace of the Lord Bishop of Rochester at Bromley in Kent, &ct., &ct., by Thomas Reynolds, Surgeon, *'with such doth He heal men, and taketh away their pain.'* Eccles. XXXVIII. 7. London, 1756."

The reader will find a full account of this spring and its relation to the well of St. Blaise given in Mr. Norman's chapter on the Palace. This brief mention of it here will therefore be sufficient.

In the same chapter Mr. Norman traces in detail the various changes and additions made by successive Bishops to the actual structure of the Palace and to its demesne. The importance of the work done by Bishop Thomas may be accentuated here, for, finding upon his appointment that the building was in a dilapidated condition and, in his opinion, beyond repair, that Bishop demolished the old Palace in its entirety and erected in its stead the Palace much as it is to-day. The new building bears the date 1775, and displays the arms of Bishop Thomas quartered with those of the see of Rochester, these escutcheons being repeated on the chimneypiece of the library. Such additions to the Palace as were made by Mr. Coles Child, on becoming possessed of the property in 1845, have in no way encroached upon or impaired Bishop Thomas's original design.

The bishopric of Rochester carried with it, as has been seen, the lordship of the Manor of Bromley, and the rectorial rights over the parish and the parish church. Within that manor and parish were certain common lands and meadow grounds known as ' half-yearly lands ' over which the freeholders and inhabitants of the parish held common rights—" right of Common or Common of Pasture—from the 10th of October to the fifth of April every year."

A lease of these common lands had been granted by Bishop Zachary Pearce to a certain William Scott, who felt that it would be much to his advantage if the common rights over these lands could be extinguished. I surmise that this gentleman's family had been established at Bromley for some centuries. Among the contributors to the Armada loan in 1588 appears the name of " John Scott of Bromley, gent.," with a subscription of £25. Whether William Scott of the eighteenth century was a descendant of John Scott of the sixteenth is a matter of conjecture, but he was evidently a highly influential person, for he was successful in securing the passage through Parliament of a private Act, whereby the common rights of the freeholders and parishioners over the lands he held on lease were for ever extinguished from June 24th, 1764.

In compensation he, and all future possessors of those lands, were to pay, for ever, a sum of forty pounds per annum, clear of all deductions whatsoever, to the Churchwardens and Overseers of the Poor for the parish of Bromley. In default of such payment, the Churchwardens and Overseers were empowered to exercise the rights enjoyed by landlords in Common Law for the recovery of arrears of rent, either by distraint or otherwise as circumstances might dictate.

There is in the Act of Parliament, which is before me as I write, no specification of the exact position of the lands in question. Doubtless the Act was accompanied by a plan, but there being no plan attached to the Act now in my possession, it is impossible to locate exactly the property to which it applies.

About the time at which we have now arrived, Bromley became the poorer by the loss of one of its most prominent and celebrated residents. A monument in the parish church bears the inscription :

" To the Memory of
John Hawkesworth, LL.D."

Dr. John Hawkesworth, who died on November 17th, 1773, at the age of fifty-eight, had, for many years, lived in the old Knight-Thornhill mansion or " Grete House," which lay back from the east side of Upper High Street. There his wife had set up a boarding school for girls. As a man of letters he had early formed the acquaintance of Dr. Johnson, and this association developed into an attachment—the attachment of a disciple to his master. Hawkesworth was an original member of the first literary club formed by Johnson to distract the monotony of dictionary making. It met in Ivy Lane, Paternoster Row, and was the prototype of the more famous Turk's Head Club of 1764, of which Hawkesworth was not a member. It was the ambition of the pupil to assimilate his own style of composition as far as possible to that of Johnson, and Boswell asserts that " Hawkesworth's imitations of Johnson are sometimes so happy that it is

JOHN HAWKSWORTH
L.L.D.

E. Arthur Reynolds. pinx.   J. Hall sculp.

Done from an Original Picture in the possession
of the Hon.ble Mr. Fitzmaurice.

Publish'd according to Act of Parliament Jan.ry 1st 1775.by T: Cadell in the Strand.

From the collection of engravings at the National Portrait Gallery.

extremely difficult to distinguish them with certainty from the compositions of his great archetype "—a pronouncement endorsed by Courtenay in his *Moral and Literary Character of Dr. Johnson* :

> " Ingenious Hawkesworth to this school we owe,
> And scarce the pupil from the tutor know."

Among Hawkesworth's many literary ventures *The Adventurer* takes a prominent place.   Of this publication he was editor, and its principal contributor.   Naturally he sought to secure the assistance of Johnson, and was successful in obtaining from him, not only some valuable essays, but also his active co-operation and support.   It was as a consequence of Johnson's personal solicitation that Dr. Joseph Warton was induced to write for *The Adventurer*, and at this period, about 1753, it is clear that the intimacy between Johnson and Hawkesworth was at its height.   It was doubtless the attraction of Hawkesworth which led Johnson to bury his wife, who died in 1752, in Bromley Parish Church, and Hawkesworth is mentioned by Boswell as one of the friends who visited him at Gough Square in his affliction.   The circumstances which subsequently led to an estrangement between them I have not been able to discover.

Unquestionably it is his association with Johnson which has kept Hawkesworth's memory alive.   And yet in his own day he was regarded as in the first rank of literary men, and the contemporary laudations of his work seemed not extravagant in their day.   The monument erected to his memory on the north wall of the church is inscribed with a lengthy quotation from one of his own ' Adventurers,' and doubtless records the current impression of his value as a man of letters in that " He lived useful and ornamental to Society in an eminent degree ; was among the boasted felicities of the present age, and that he laboured for the benefit of posterity."

Apart from *The Adventurer* he was connected, as editor, with *The Gentleman's Magazine*.   He wrote Eastern tales, fairy-tales, dramatic pieces, a translation of Fénelon's *Télémaque*, and made himself responsible for the issue of a narrative of the first voyage to the South Seas.

A study of the social records of this period brings forcibly into prominence the wide gulf which separates us who live to-day from the life of a hundred and fifty years ago.   The human intercourse, the occupations, the amusements, the crimes, the punishments of those times seem scarcely to be related to society as we know it.   Not that human nature has undergone any material change in this interval of time, so comparatively short a period.   Human nature indeed may be regarded as constant throughout recorded time.   But changes in environment and conditions are soon reflected by corresponding changes in the manner in which human nature manifests itself.   Bromley, though so close to London, was little more than a country village. Its only means of communication with the outside world was by coach, or on horseback, or on foot. After sunset the whole town was in darkness, save for some feeble flicker in front of the various inns. A solitary parish constable seems to have been the only representative of anything in the nature of a police force. Smuggling was a recognised and flourishing business. Highwaymen infested the coach routes, not only to the south beyond the town : even the short journey of ten miles between Bromley and London was fraught with terrors to the traveller, for on Blackheath the " Gentlemen of the Road " were specially active and formidable.

In such conditions crimes of violence—robberies, murders, and hold-ups—were of frequent occurrence, and the records of some of these throw a strange light upon the manners of the time. Thus in the accounts rendered by the parish constable in July 1766 there is the following entry :

" For attending of the tryall of George Allen, Highwayman, taken at Bromley at the Assizes at Maidstone :

" Paid for Hors-hire for two days at 3*s*. pr. .	o 6 o	
" For myself and expences for my Hors for two days . . .	o 16 o	
	£1 2 o "	

The vestry to which this account was rendered was evidently not prompt in payment, for it is only in February 1768, eighteen months after the event, that " Sam¹ Millen, Constable of Bromley," acknowledges the receipt of the contents in full.

The manners of the highwaymen towards their victims exhibit the variety which is characteristic of their class. Occasionally they were not unkindly. Thus, in a newspaper of 1773, it is recorded that :

" Last night Mr. Delver, whalebone merchant, being taken ill at Hayes, and coming to town in a postchaise, was stopped by a highwayman who robbed him of his money ; but finding him greatly indisposed, and not able to help himself, civilly wrapped him up warm, wished him better health and a good evening, gave the postboy a shilling, and ordered him to drive gently on."

Mr. Philip Norman records that his grandmother was stopped at the bottom of Chislehurst Hill and robbed by highwaymen in 1793, one of them insisting on shaking hands with her, after relieving her of her purse.

In cases of murder, and crimes of violence punishable by death, it was not unusual for the extreme penalty to be exacted as near as possible to the scene of the crime. Thus John Clarke, gardener to Mr. Charles Long (afterwards Lord Farnborough) at Bromley Hill, was hanged on Bromley Hill for the murder of a fellow-servant.

Near the end of the eighteenth century a man was hanged in chains for robbing the mails, the scene of his execution on a bit of the old road, not far from Green-Street-Green, being the place where the robbery was committed.

In the case of Philip Nicholson, however, who murdered Mr. and Mrs. Bonar of Camden House in 1810, a different procedure was adopted. " It may be mentioned," writes Mr. Henry H. Drake in his *History of the Kent Hundred of Blackheath* :

" as an instance of an obsolete mode of carrying out the extreme penalty of the law that a hurdle or sledge—a shallow box about 6 ft. by 3 ft.—was provided : at each end was a seat just capable of accommodating two persons. The murderer, doubled-ironed, was first placed in it with his back to the horses : he was also pinioned with ropes, and round his shoulders was placed the fatal cord. By his side sat the executioner : opposite, the Rev. Mr. Bramston, a Catholic, and by his side sat one of the Maidstone Jailors with a loaded blunderbuss. The procession proceeded at a very slow pace from Maidstone to Penenden Heath,"

where the capital sentence was carried into effect. The body was then driven in a postchaise to Bromley, and delivered over to Mr. James Scott, surgeon, for dissection. Nicholson's skull, remarkable for an extremely fine set of teeth, is still, or was until quite recently, in the possession of Dr. H. J. Ilott.

In 1791 a robbery was successfully accomplished which disastrously and permanently affected the parish of Bromley, for on April 13th of that year an entry was made into the vestry of the church with results thus recorded on the fly-leaf of the Church Register by Dr. Henry Smith, the incumbent at the time :

" On the night of the 13th of April of this year, 1791, the vestry-room door was broken open, and the chest of deal, in which the plate was kept, was robbed of the following articles : one large flagon with lid fixt ; one quart chalice, one rich chased chalice and loose cover, with a straining spoon, one large paten and one small paten ; the above were all gilt : the gold fringe from the pulpit and the Communion hangings ; one large damask table cloth, and two damask napkins.

" It appears, from every observation, that the perpetrators of this sacrilegious deed must have secreted themselves in the Church during the morning service, for there were not the least traces of violence upon the doors, wall, or windows. They let themselves out of the Church by unscrewing the locks of the doors leading to the gallery at the East [*sic*—really west] end, which must be done on the inside.

" A bottle of Tent wine was taken out of the cupboard and drunk, which makes me think there were more than one, and I indeed can hardly imagine *one* person to have courage sufficient to carry him through such a Diabolical Enterprize.

" H^y Smith, Minister."

Some years before this event, in October 1770, a curious spectacle might have been seen in Bromley Church—the penance of Ann Chapman. Ann Chapman, a widow who had fallen into loose ways of life, was enjoined by the Worshipful Francis Simpson, Doctor of Laws, the lawfully constituted official for the whole Archdeaconry of Rochester, to do penance in Bromley Parish Church. The document, secured by Mr. Norman, though long, is so rare, and affords so curious an illustration of the change in manners since its time, that it deserves quotation in full. After citing the authority under which the order was issued, the document runs :

" The said Ann Chapman, widow, shall come to the said Church on Sunday, the twenty eighth day of October in the year of our Lord one thousand seven hundred and seventy at the tolling of the second bell to morning prayers, and shall stand in the porch of the said Church from the tolling of the said second bell until the second Lesson be ended, Bare headed, bare legged and bare footed, having a white sheet over her wearing apparel, and holding a white rod of an Ell long in her hand after the manner of a penitent sinner, and the second Lesson being ended, she shall come into the said Church and stand in some convenient place near the Minister's Reading desk (arrayed as before) during all the time of Divine Service and . . . Sermon, and . . . immediately . . . after the reading of the Nicene Creed shall make an humble confession of her fault, saying after the Minister with an audible voice as followeth to wit :—

" I Ann Chapman do in the presence of Almighty God and this Congregation humbly and penitently confess and acknowledge that having not the fear of God before my eyes, and being seduced by the Temptations of the Devil and my own Lusts have lived incontinently and committed the foul sin of Fornication, having had a bastard or base begotten child born of my body whereby I have greatly offended Almighty God, endangered my own Soul, and given an Evil example and scandal to all good Christians for which Offence I am heartily sorry, and do humbly beg pardon of God and this Congregation for the same, and do promise (God assisting me with His Grace) never to offend in the like manner again, and I beseech this Congregation to pray for me and with me to say Our Father which art in Heaven and so forth.

" The said Ann Chapman shall duly certify her due performance thereof under the hands of the Minister and Churchwardens of the said parish, and return this Schedule into the Registry of the Archdeaconry of Rochester on or before Wednesday, the 7th day of November, in the year of Our Lord 1770.

Signed Rog^r Altham.   Dep^{ty} Reg^r."

Appended under date October 28th, 1770, is the following certificate :

" This pennance was then duly performed by the said Ann Chapman widow as herein directed in the presence of

> Tho. Bagshaw, Min^r.
> John Brett, Curate.
> Samuel Cutson, Overseer of ye Poor."

" To stand in the white sheet " has become a proverbial expression. Here we have an authentic official record of what that ceremony precisely implied.

Such a spectacle as the penance of Ann Chapman must have afforded a pleasurable relief to the dull monotony of life in the town.   For Bromley, according to Thomas Wilson, who wrote in 1797, was singularly deficient in the supply of any form of organised entertainment or amusement for its inhabitants.

" Here," says Wilson, " are but few amusements ; the community is too small to support expensive ones ; therefore the whole of them consist of a very respectable subscription concert, and one circulating library."

The very sentence seems to express dullness personified.   But the human spirit craves for sensation and excitement in some form, and where that spirit has never been led to rise much above its primitive level, it will find its satisfaction in primitive forms of recreation.   Among these forms must be reckoned the eating matches, records of which extend back as far as 1726. In that year one of the attractions of the Bromley Fair, held on St. James's Day, was :

" A strange eating worthy, who is to perform a Tryal of Skill, for a wager of Five guineas—viz. he is to eat four pounds of bacon, a bushel of French beans, with two pounds of butter, a quartern loaf, and to drink a gallon of small beer."

This, however, is but a variation upon the fat ladies and strong men who still survive as recognised institutions at a country fair.

A more recent performance of the same character was that of Peter Nesbit, the carrier between Bromley and Beckenham, who, on the occasion of the marriage of the Prince of Wales to Princess Alexandra of Denmark (March 10th, 1863), consumed in public, at a table placed in the recess fronting the White Hart, an enormous pie, labelled " All for Me," planned by Mr. W. W. Baxter's assistants and specially prepared for the occasion by his cook. The pie consisted of 5 lb. of rumpsteak, 4 lb. of flour, 1 lb. of lard, and four of the largest potatoes procurable, to be washed down in half a gallon of ale. Being primed, as a start, with a supply of gin and bitters, Peter commenced operations on the pie as the festal procession arrived abreast of his table, and in spite of jests and rough remarks, he finished it. It did not, as might be expected, finish him, for Peter Nesbit survived the performance of this gastronomic feat for four years, and ultimately died, from other causes, August 12th, 1867.

The record of Peter's gormandising exploit has carried me beyond the period with which I am now dealing, and I have only inserted it as an illustration of manners, and because it appeals to the memory of some of the inhabitants of Bromley who are still living. Man must always, at any period, find some outlet for his animal instincts, and the close of the eighteenth century afforded a worthy occasion for the manhood of Bromley to assert its primitive energies in national and patriotic activities. In 1793, after the execution of Louis XVI of France, our country was drawn into the war of the French Revolution, which developed, under Napoleon, into a general European War, in which the conservative forces of the age were ranged in deadly opposition to the new spirit which the Revolution had generated among men.

Already, in 1792, some months before the actual declaration of hostilities, a meeting was called, at Bromley, of the inhabitants of the district with the purpose of forming an association, the members of which should declare their attachment to—

" our present excellent form of Government, should endeavour to impress their fellow-subjects with the same sentiments of loyalty to His Majesty, and the same reverence for our Constitution as it was established by the glorious Revolution of 1688."

To give practical effect to these sentiments, the members of the Association—

" solemnly pledge ourselves to maintain the Public Tranquility, by bringing to justice all persons who by inflamatory writings and conversation attempt to excite His Majesty's subjects to Riots and Insurrections, and by standing forth to assist the Civil Magistrate upon all occasions when the Public Peace is threatened with danger."

This meeting on December 13th, 1792, under the chairmanship of

Mr. Charles Townshend, was presumably held at the White Hart Inn, for it was resolved that—

" a Book containing the above Declaration be left at the White Hart Inn in Bromley till Thursday fortnight inclusive in which all friends of the Constitution be invited to set their names."

As a result 326 names were inscribed, representing not Bromley alone, but Beckenham and the surrounding district.   Of Bromley names those of George Norman, R. Rawes, J. Pieters, E. Latter, and Peter Thellusson are familiar.   William Whitwele, " Bailif to the Right Honble Willm Pitt, Hollwood " also signed.

From the Articles of Association it is clear that this organisation was not founded on military lines. It was a protest against revolutionary doctrines which seemed to the members to threaten danger to the State.   Still, it may be considered as the forerunner of a distinctively military Association which resulted, six years later, in the formation of the Bromley volunteers.

The West Kent Yeomanry, including a Chislehurst troop, was formed between 1794 and 1797 and remained in being after the disbandment of the emergency troops of the Napoleonic wars, and did good service in the South African War and in the Great War before being converted into the 387th (Queen's Own Yeomanry) Battery 97th Kent Brigade R.A.   The Bromley Squadron was always to the fore.

By 1798 the successes of the French, and especially the triumphant conquests of Napoleon in Italy, had aroused a general feeling of alarm throughout the country.   A call was made for a large volunteer force to supplement the regular army by undertaking the duties of home defence. On May 3rd, 1798, a number of the young men of the parish assembled at the church, and formed an " Armed Association."   A paper was drawn up for signature by which—

" We whose names are hereunto subscribed do hereby enroll ourselves to serve personally in the Bromley Armed Association according to the terms of the Resolution made and signed by the Committee of the said Association held at the Church in Bromley the third day of May, 1798."

Seventy signatures were appended, the first being that of George Norman, who became Captain of the force, and remained so during its existence.   The document itself was preserved until quite recently in a room attached to the Drill Hall, but when, in 1921, Major E. H. Norman, as Brigade Major of the Kent Territorials, desired to see it, it could not be found. It has, however, been retrieved, and is now in the Public Library.

Preserved in the Record Office are the " Bromley Volunteer Muster Rolls from 1803–1807 " giving lists of the officers and privates.   In 1803 the force consisted of its officers and sixty-seven non-commissioned officers and men. To these sixty-seven payment was made by Government for "attendance on 20 days of exercise," with a further allowance of £1 per man for uniform and equipment. On November 3rd, 1803, the bursting of a musket killed one man and knocked down two others. It was found that, through the carelessness of the owner, no less than six cartridges were in it at the time of its discharge.

The date when the force was disbanded is uncertain. Apparently it was in 1807, as the Muster Rolls cease in that year, but for some years previous to that date enthusiasm seems to have cooled, and Government became indifferent. The Rev. John Till, writing in October 1804 to his late pupil Lord Lewisham, at Oxford, complains that :

"We are, I think, not very alert in our preparations and the late measures of Government have proved so refrigerent that I fear the volunteering spirit is a good deal chilled.—In Bromley Mr. Norman had no sooner sounded the trumpet than two hundred volunteers enlisted themselves under his banner ready to follow him wherever he pleased. These were afterwards cut down to a hundred and twenty, and since then, I am told, to sixty. I should much fear that these repeated loppings off of excrescences might be apt to cut to the quick and endanger the vital process."

Some fifty years later, in 1859, under the repercussion of another national crisis—the Crimean War—Infantry Volunteers were again called for.

Bromley answered the appeal of the Lord-Lieutenant of that day, Viscount Sydney, of Frognal, Chislehurst, and as a result of meetings held in June and December of that year the Rifle Corps, which was afterwards known officially as the 18th Kent, was formed. Later the different corps (or companies) in the neighbourhood were consolidated into the 1st (Administrative) Battalion Kent Rifle Volunteers, which became successively the 3rd Kent (West Kent Rifles) and the 2nd V.B. The Queen's Own (Royal West Kent) Regiment. This battalion was the parent of the 5th Battalion R.W. Kent and the 20th Battalion London Regiment of the Territorial Army.

At first the drills took place in the various parks surrounding the town, and when the Town Hall was built, in the basement of that building. The Drill Hall, which still bears on its façade the name of the XVIII Kent, was built in 1872 and is still serving its purpose.

Efficiency in marksmanship was essential and formed an important feature in the training. A rifle range on the Chin Brook between Grove Park and the Chislehurst Tunnel was opened in 1861, but had to be closed when the South-Eastern main line via Chislehurst was built. A new range was obtained at Southend from which Rangefield Road on the Downham Estate takes its name.

The most celebrated of Bromley marksmen was Corporal Percy Oliver, who went to America to represent the English Volunteers at an international match against the National Guard of the United States.

The 18th Kent Volunteer Corps, commanded by Lieutenant Satterthwaite, was present at the first great Volunteer Review, before Queen Victoria, held in Hyde Park on June 23rd, 1860.

The Kent Companies were highly commended by H.R.H. the Commander-in-Chief, for the admirable precision of their forming and marching.

The Corps also attended the first great Volunteer sham-fight in Camden and Bickley Parks in 1860, and many subsequent reviews in Hyde Park, at Windsor, Wimbledon, and Aldershot, besides the Easter Reviews at Brighton, Dover, etc.

The Battalion first went into camp in Camden Park in 1874 and this useful training was continued almost every year.

The first Commander was Captain Bowden of Chislehurst, where there was a subdivision of the Corps. He, after a brief tenure, resigned in favour of Captain Clement Satterthwaite, who retained the command as Captain and Major until 1876, when he was succeeded by Captains R. Sneade Brown, Edward Satterthwaite, Edward and Bertram H. Latter, C. F. Hichins, and F. C. Selby.

The subaltern ranks included members of the Norman, Charrington, and Wathen families.

Its members first saw active service in the South African War, when one of the three companies sent out by the Battalion was commanded by Captain B. H. Latter.

The organisation was in 1908 merged in the Territorial Force, and the Battalion did good service during the Great War in India and Mesopotamia. An extract has been quoted on page 44 from a letter by the Rev. John Till. From that letter it would appear, if Mr. Till was not writing in the language of hyperbole, that at the call for volunteers, two hundred of the able-bodied men of Bromley were eager to serve under Mr. Norman's banner. This number corresponds to between one-sixth and one-seventh of the total male population at the beginning of the nineteenth century. In 1801, in accordance with the Act of Parliament, the first Census of the people was taken, and the original record for Bromley is before me. The total number of inhabited houses on March 10th, 1801, was 415, and they contained 538 families. Of these families 1,340 were males and 1,360 were females, making a total population of 2,700 " excluding soldiers and sailors." The reference here is to the establishment of military camps in the vicinity of the town—a practice which dates far back into the eighteenth century, the men being billeted, either all or in part, upon the householders, for there is no record of anything in the shape of barracks existing for their accommodation. The figure 2,700 therefore represents

COMMANDING OFFICERS, 18TH KENT RIFLE VOLUNTEERS.

Major Clement Satterthwaite, 1860–1876 (seated).
Captain R. Sneade Brown, 1876–1880 (standing, centre).
Colonel Edward Satterthwaite, 1880–1888 (standing, right).
Major Edward Latter, 1888–1894 (seated on ground).
Captain Bertram Latter, 1894–1902 (standing, left).

the actual *bona fide* residents in the town. Of the male population, 277, or almost exactly one in five, were engaged chiefly in agriculture; 254 were mainly engaged in trade, handicrafts, or manufacture of some kind, leaving just about 800 males who were "not so employed." For purposes of immediate comparison it may be convenient to state here the figures of the census of 1901—a century later. The number of houses in 1901 was 5,524 as against 415; the number of inhabitants 27,354 as against 2,700. The census of 1921 shows a still further increase, of houses to 7,586, of population to 35,070.

A fair proportion of the 800 males not recorded as being engaged in any form of employment may be accounted for by the fact that Bromley, and its neighbourhood, was now being recognised as a very desirable residential situation. Commodious houses, enclosed in parks and ornamental gardens, were springing into existence, notably the splendid estate of Mr. Charles Long at Bromley Hill, who was doubtless affected, in his choice of a residence, by the proximity of his friend, the Prime Minister, at Holwood. The attachment of the Pitt family to the neighbourhood dates back to Lord Chatham's purchase of the mansion at Hayes, known as Hayes Place. William Pitt was born there. On becoming Prime Minister, he purchased the Holwood estate, which became the favourite resort for his scanty hours of leisure. There Pitt sat with Wilberforce beneath the oak, and contemplated the emancipation of slaves. Bromley and its neighbourhood was by way of becoming fashionable, and there grew up around it a leisured class of wealthy and more or less distinguished men. But an even stronger attraction was the establishment in Bromley of the famous surgeon, Mr. James Scott, whose reputation was more than national; it was European; and apart from the numbers who came to Bromley as visitors to consult him, account must be taken of those who settled in Bromley as residents in order that they might be permanently and conveniently under his care. As in one of the chapters of this history James Scott and his achievements will figure prominently, it is sufficient here to note him as the magnet which, from the time of Scott's first settlement in Bromley, about 1794, until his death in 1848, drew an ever-increasing number of residents to the town.

Yet another circumstance still further tended in the same direction:

In 1822, by an Act of Parliament passed the previous year, a considerable portion of Bromley Common was enclosed, and passed into the hands of private owners. The property was gradually developed as a building estate with the results now visible. Before enclosure, Bromley Common was what its name implies, a stretch of unproductive land thickly covered with gorse, "and," complains Freeman, "from the Plough Inn there was scarcely a house to be seen to cheer the benighted traveller." Dunkin, writing in 1815, speaks of twenty-five houses on the Common, meaning probably upon its borders. After the enclosure Bromley began to spread itself out towards the south, and found on the old Common land adequate and satisfactory accommodation for its increasing population. By 1850 that population had increased from 2,700 to rather more than 4,000.

The only other event which figures in the records in the first half of the nineteenth century was the passing of the Palace from the possession of the Bishops of Rochester. The see of Rochester had always been a poor one, and in 1845 the financial position of the diocese came under the serious consideration of the Ecclesiastical Commissioners. Among their recommendations was a proposal to sell the Palace and Manor of the Bishops of Rochester in Bromley. The property was acquired by Mr. Coles Child, in whose family it still remains. Thus was severed a connection between the town and the see of Rochester which had continued without intermission for at least a thousand years. An immemorial link with the past was violently broken. But by this time the past, which for so many centuries had been practically the present, was indeed the past. The modern world was emerging. The pastoral echoes of a bygone day were being rapidly drowned in the roar of the locomotive.

Chapter V

MODERN BROMLEY

MODERN Bromley is the creation of the last seventy years. It has been called into existence by the coming of the railway. Before that period the only organised means of communication between Bromley and the outside world was the stage coach, which at the end of the eighteenth century ran twice a day between the town and the Metropolis. At 9 a.m. every week-day a coach left Bromley for the Boar's Head, Fleet Street, and at the same hour a second coach left for the Spread Eagle, Gracechurch Street. The return journeys started from these respective hostelries in the summer at 4 o'clock in the afternoon, in the winter at 3. On Sundays travellers had need to be early risers, for the coaches started at 7 a.m., returned, and made another journey on the same day.

In course of time the service was extended to four coaches a day, two to Charing Cross and two to Gracechurch Street, and these facilities continued until extinguished by the railway. Apart from these public conveyances a constant stream of horse-drawn traffic was continually passing through, Bromley lying, as it did, on the main road between London, Tunbridge Wells, and Hastings, and the fame of its great posting houses, the White Hart and the Bell, extended far beyond its boundaries—that of the Bell even as far as the secluded ears of Jane Austen writing *Pride and Prejudice* in the recesses of a Hampshire village. A hundred horses, it was said, could be stabled at the White Hart alone, and the accommodation at the Bell was hardly, if at all, inferior.

The commercial interests of the town were served by two carriers' carts which went to London and returned every week-day. This method of receiving and dispatching goods was more popular than the railway even as late as 1884.

For the first few years after the introduction of the steam-driven locomotive on rails but little change was produced in Bromley. It continued to retain its essentially rural aspect, and how rural that was it is almost impossible for the modern dweller in Bromley to conceive without some pictorial aid which will visualise his imagination. The population in 1801, as we have seen, was only 2,700, ten years later it showed an increase of but 265. In the succeeding decade—1811 to 1821—the increase was even less than in the previous decennial period, being 182 in all. In 1821 therefore the total inhabitants only numbered 3,147. Then a marked increase becomes noticeable, due very largely to the numbers of people attracted as residents to Bromley in order to be under the care and continuous supervision of the famous surgeon, Mr. James Scott. In 1831 the population had mounted to 4,002, an increase of 855. For ten years no very perceptible change is to be noted, the numbers in 1841 being 4,325, and the succeeding Census showed a positive decline from 4,325 to 4,127. This decade is the only one in the history of the town which, in recorded times, shows a decrease. The causes of this decrease are to be found in particular circumstances affecting the town itself, and in the general, social, and economic conditions which prevailed throughout the country.

The magic of James Scott's name had long ceased to operate, for he had retired, with an ample fortune, to Clay Hill, Beckenham, in or about 1829. Residential patients therefore were no longer attracted to the place, and in 1845 a crisis occurred in the history of the town which was judged by many to be nothing short of catastrophic. Bromley Palace, the residence for centuries of the Bishops of Rochester, was sold by the Ecclesiastical Commissioners to Mr. Coles Child, and the age-long association between Bromley and the Bishops was abruptly terminated. This in itself was thought to be a blow from which recovery was impossible, but the blow was intensified by the character and personality of the particular prelate who, at the time of the migration, occupied the see of Rochester. Bishop Murray was something more than a Bishop. He was a man living and having his being among his fellow-men. His interests extended not only to the spiritual but to the temporal interests of the people around him, and his departure seemed to foreshadow the ruin of Bromley. Many of the tradesmen, we are told, left the town, and some retired to the outskirts on their savings rather than risk business any longer in a place that appeared to be doomed. The Rev. Thomas Scott, Chaplain to the College, and local poet, composed some lines which he entitled : " Bromley bewailing her lost Bishop," in which, in strains of sincere feeling—however deficient in poetic inspiration—he deplores the passing of the Palace :

> " For now, alas ! Palace—it is no more,
> No Bishop dwells in it as heretofore !

> " Toll we our bell ! our Bishop we deplore !
> Bromley can boast her Bishop now no more.

> " And Murray now, the last upon the list,
> But not the least—at Bromley will be missed,
> And much lamented ! Bishop here the last
> Of near a hundred Bishops that have passed."

But much as the townspeople bewailed their loss, their gloomy anticipations were happily without any solid foundation. The Lordship of the Manor had passed, it is true, from ecclesiastical into secular hands, but the social consequences to the town were destined to prove by no means deleterious. There may have been some immediate and quite temporary results contributing to the check upon the prosperity of Bromley, but the more important causes of a decline in population are to be found not in local but in national conditions.

The decade of decline was that between 1841 and 1851 : the " Hungry Forties," in fact, a period when the country as a whole reached perhaps its lowest point of demoralisation, distress, and discontent.   The pressure of the Corn Laws reduced vast numbers of the people almost, if not quite, to the point of starvation.   The universal misery led to a widespread belief that in some readjustment of the machinery of government alleviation was to be found, a belief which gave rise to the Chartist movement with its sixfold demand.   The repercussions of national disturbance manifested themselves at Bromley as elsewhere.   It is in the memory of those alive quite recently that bread was openly looted in Bromley market-place, and at least one prominent townsman was an active member of the Chartist organisation. When there is added to this catalogue of public distress the consequent increase in emigration, the fascination of the Californian gold rush of 1849, and the incidence of excessive rates, we have a sufficient explanation, apart from local circumstances, of Bromley's decline during the " Hungry Forties."

But such is the paradox in human affairs that at this moment Bromley was on the verge of an unparalleled expansion.   Between 1851 and 1861 the Census showed an increase of 1,738 : the number of inhabited houses had risen in ten years by about 250, and the proportion of males to females shows that excess in the number of the latter which is a constant element in the national statistics of population.   (The actual numbers in 1861 being 2,515 males and 2,990 females.)   It was in this decade that the railway became actively operative in the Bromley district, and with the coming of the railway the modern epoch of expansion began.   The development now becomes nothing less than extraordinary, and it can perhaps best be expressed by the bald figures of a statistical table :

Year.			Total. Population.	Males.	Females.	Inhabited Houses.
1861	.	.	. 5,505	2,515	2,990	1,090
1871	.	.	. 10,674	4,792	5,882	1,946
1881	.	.	. 15,154	6,892	8,262	2,684
1891	.	.	. 21,684	9,541	12,143	3,907
1901	.	.	. 27,397	11,957	15,440	5,131
1911	.	.	. 33,646	14,448	19,198	6,776
1921	.	.	. 35,070	15,273	19,797	7,586*

* Including 246 vacant.

In proportion to the increase in railway facilities, so has the population of the town advanced, to the point that now the one-time rural aspect of Bromley has disappeared ; the features of old Bromley have been merged in a populous suburb, and the greedy eyes of the London County Council are already contemplating, as a possibility happily remote, the absorption of Bromley into the vast and incoherent expanse of the metropolitan area. Though the first railway in England was opened in September 1825, and though the "Railway Mania" was at its height in 1845, Bromley remained for many years quite untouched by railway enterprise, the nearest railway station to the town, up to 1858, being at Greenwich. In that year, however, a line of railway known as " the West End and Crystal Palace Railway " was extended as far as Shortlands, and on May 3rd a large and matutinal crowd assembled on Martin's Hill to witness the departure at 8.40 a.m. of the first train dispatched from Shortlands Station to its destination at the Company's London Terminus at Pimlico. Almost immediately the Mid-Kent Railway Company opened up a route to Beckenham and subsequently via Bromley to St. Mary Cray, and this route became available for traffic in July 1858. This involved the construction of a station at Bromley, the site selected being that on which the South Station still stands, the Charity Schools which had previously occupied the position being transferred in 1855 to land adjacent to the College Field. Two years later the East Kent Railway Company connected up their system with the existing lines.

This multiplication of small companies afforded a favourable opportunity for an amalgamation, and on November 1st, 1861, the London, Chatham, and Dover Company secured a practical monopoly over the line running through Shortlands and Bromley to Chatham, Faversham, and Dover.

In the meantime the South-Eastern Company had constructed their line from Charing Cross, via Croydon and Tonbridge, to Ashford and Dover. In 1868 a new and more direct line to these places, via Chislehurst and Sevenoaks, was constructed by them, but it was of small service to Bromley as long as no line existed connecting Grove Park with the town. The branch line from Grove Park to Bromley, largely initiated by Mr. W. D. Starling, was completed and opened on January 1st, 1878, and thus a far more convenient access to their offices in the city was offered to business men. A construction which can only be called an apology for a station was hastily thrown together and served as the terminus at Bromley till 1926. But, however inadequate both station and service might be, yet from 1878 onwards residents in Bromley could profit by two important lines of railway, the London, Chatham, and Dover, and the South-Eastern, which, between them, afforded a convenient approach to almost any part of the Metropolis.

Bad, beggarly, and unpunctual as the service of both these lines originally was, yet the fares were moderate, and, indeed, considerably less than they are at the present time. The price of a first-class return ticket from Bromley to London was 2s. 3d., the third-class fare for the same journey being one shilling less.

The effect of railway facilities was immediately apparent in the Census Returns. A reference to the table will show that from 1861 onwards the population leapt up by decennial increases of about five thousand, so that a population of 5,505 in 1861 had grown to 33,646 in 1911. Necessarily the whole face of things in Bromley and all the conditions of life underwent in those years a radical and profound alteration. In its structure, in its system of local government, in its general atmosphere, the Bromley of to-day bears little resemblance to the old and somewhat sequestered township of seventy years ago.

In regard to structure, one very important and salutary improvement has to be recorded long before the coming of the railway. In 1832 what was popularly known at the time as the " New Cut " immensely relieved the congestion and awkward angularity of the main thoroughfare through the town. The coach road from London used to bend sharply to the left at the Bell, and then sharply to the right through the market-place, the line of shops and houses which still exists forming the western boundary of the route. Behind these houses there ran a narrow and squalid lane, known as " the Back Alley," bounded by a deep declivity with undeveloped lands stretching away from its summit towards the church. In 1832 this lane was converted into a road, which, in coaching days, was wide and convenient enough, and in due course sightly and substantial premises replaced the barren squalor of the past—premises which in the hands of Messrs. Medhurst and others have gradually acquired their present imposing form and manifold utility.

But perhaps the most important structural change, in the period now under consideration, was the building of a new Town Hall between 1863 and 1864. Reference has already been made on pages 47 and 49 to the purchase of the manor of Bromley by Mr. Coles Child in 1845. In due course the new Lord of the Manor announced his desire and intention to substitute a more commodious building for the Old Market House, which had stood for generations in the market-place. Our illustrations present an adequate and faithful view of the general construction and appearance of this old building. As compared with the existing mass of masonry it occupied a comparatively small space, and thus left ample room for all the numerous activities connected with the Bromley fairs. It was certainly picturesque, and added an old-world flavour to the town, but as a centre of municipal life it left much to be desired. In 1863 the intentions of Mr. Coles Child were carried into effect and took shape in a new Town Hall, which still stands, though now diverted from its original uses. Thus the whole character of the original market-place was completely changed. The sense of space was now dwarfed by a structure which, however architecturally imposing, and however convenient internally, is yet scarcely adapted fittingly to adorn the surrounding area. Indeed, the existing building dominates rather than adorns, and should deliberation, or the accident of circumstances, lead at any time to its ultimate disappearance, Bromley will be the richer in the opportunity for restoring to its old market-place a more appropriate setting.

The erection of the Town Hall in Market Square was closely followed by the suppression and extinction of the Bromley fairs, which for generations had been a distinctive feature in the life of the town. It was doubtless to some extent a case of cause and effect, for the reduced dimensions of the

THE MARKET PLACE, SOUTH SIDE, 1860.

open space in the square no longer afforded the same facilities for such functions. But the fairs had been for a long time a source of more demoralisation than advantage, and now a favourable opportunity was afforded for their abolition. The method by which they were suppressed was very ingenious.

The Bromley fairs, the proceedings and character of which are described in detail elsewhere in this book, dated back to 1447, when a charter was granted by King Henry VI to the Bishops of Rochester, as Lords of the Manor, granting them the privilege of holding a fair twice a year in Bromley on the Feasts of St. James, July 25th, and St. Blaise, February 3rd, but since the reform of the Calendar in 1752 the fairs were held on February 14th and August 5th. The chartered rights of the Bishops descended with the manor to Mr. Coles Child, and, as Lord of the Manor, the fairs were held under his sanction and authority. When, therefore, an opinion began to prevail among the responsible authorities that the time had come to put an end to the fairs it was easy, by means of an ingenious collusive action, to give effect to that opinion. In February 1865 a summons was taken out, by order of the magistrates, against Mr. Coles Child requiring him to show by what right a fair was held in Bromley. Mr. Coles Child on his part failed to appear in answer to the summons, or to produce any authority vested in him for holding a fair. The magistrates therefore decided that the fairs were held under no duly constituted authority, and issued an order for their suppression.

In this simple way a practice which had survived in Bromley for more than four centuries was noiselessly swept away with satisfaction to all soberminded people and with regret from few. The original uses of the fairs as a means of interchange for horses, cattle, and agricultural produce had practically disappeared, and the fairs had come to mean little more than boisterous and vulgar carousings in the market-place. " They had become no better than a ghost of the fairs of old."

Another institution, still flourishing in Bromley, and dating back to the days of John, was also on the verge of extinction a few years previous to the extinction of the fairs. The present Bromley market is held weekly under a charter originally granted to the Bishop as Lord of the Manor in 1205, under condition that it should be held weekly on Tuesdays without any intermission. This charter was confirmed in 1447 by Henry VI, the day being then altered from Tuesday to Thursday. Any failure to hold the weekly market imperils, if it does not actually annul, the charter under which it is authorised. Thus, even if a Thursday should be Christmas Day, some formal show of a market must be made. This has been done by setting up a single stall for an hour or two as a symbol that a market is being held.

At some time, probably in January 1859, for reasons which have not come down to us, the Bromley market was intermitted for a brief period, and the charter ceased to be valid. But it was at once revived by a special permit from Queen Victoria, and it is by virtue of that permission that the market still survives.

Before proceeding to trace the further structural development of the town it may be well here, even at the risk of some repetition as the book proceeds, to endeavour to form some mental picture of what the town of Bromley was really like about 1850. The old market-place is made actually visible to us through photographic reproductions, but no illustration can adequately show the exit from the square into Widmore Road as it was seventy years ago. The east side of the square itself was bounded by a row of antiquated though picturesque cottage buildings which served the purpose of shops. A sharp turn to the right led into the thoroughfare now known as Widmore Road, but then as Widmore Lane, and immediately a somewhat rural aspect presented itself to the view. Apart from some wooden cottages and the Three Compasses Inn on the right, there were as yet no business premises, nor did East or West Streets exist. This exit from the centre of the town was extremely constricted, and, as such, was a growing source of danger as population and traffic increased.

At the back of Messrs. Crowhurst's premises in the market-place lay a spacious garden, conspicuous for its masses of flowering shrubs and a wealth of umbrageous trees. To the south the town ceased to be a town about the point where the Public Library now stands, the main road as far as the South Station being entirely destitute of houses on the west side, with the exception of Bromley House. On the east Bromley Lodge—now the Constitutional Club—with its demesne of gardens and park occupied all the space now filled by Holwood, Elmfield, and the adjoining roads.

Where Ethelbert, Ringers, and Ravensbourne Roads now stand there was a wild piece of spinney, with bracken, blackberries, violets, and ferns growing at random, and in the centre of this waste, approachable through rough paths, lay Simpson's Place.

To the north of the town there was practically open country immediately beyond the College and from College Field—that is, from any spot in what is now the southern end of College Road—an uninterrupted view, extending to the church in the distance, could be obtained of stiles and meadows, shrubs and trees.

Such was Bromley seventy years ago, a country town in process of transformation into the Bromley of to-day. My own acquaintance with Bromley began in 1881. By that time it had assumed most of the general features it now wears. Thus a period of thirty years was enough to convert this rural market town into a flourishing borough capable of housing and supporting a population of 35,000 people.

The first widening of the narrow entrance from Widmore Lane into the Market Square was not accomplished till 1883. It constituted a death-trap in the heart of the town, and, as such, was repeatedly the subject of agitation, but nothing was done until a Mr. Payne was knocked down here in 1879. The authorities then began to stir, and after some dispute and an arbitration inquiry as to the value of the land required, a price of £2,502 10s. was agreed upon. Tenders were then invited, first for possession of the new corner on the east side when built, then for rebuilding. In the first Mr. H. Collins was successful, for a price of £1,820 ; in the second Mr. H. Balding secured the commission, his tender being £2,818. Thus the first widening of this corner was effected in March 1883, to be supplemented, thirty years later, by those further extensions on the other side with which we are now familiar.

It would be as tedious as unnecessary to relate in detail the various transformations which little more than half a century has witnessed, for every resident in Bromley is familiar with the main features of his own town. The essential point to keep in mind is what the town was only a comparatively short time ago. The Broadway, with its fine row of shops extending on one side of the main road to the South Station, is a modern improvement of which there was no trace in my time. The Bromley Lodge estate became converted, in the early seventies, into the various roads, such as Holwood and Elmfield, which intersect that area. In 1881 the Bromley Lawn Tennis Club had its courts on land immediately behind the last houses in Holwood Road, but the Club was compelled in the course of a few years, under the invasion of the builder, to transfer its activities to South Hill. On the west side of the main road there sprang into existence all that populous residential area served by Ringers, Ethelbert, and Ravensbourne Roads, and all traces of the original rural waste were lost, or improved away, by commodious dwelling-houses set, for the most part, in convenient gardens. Nearer to the town, on the same side, the construction of the Public Library on the site of the Neelgherries marks an epoch in the history of the town which will require full consideration in a later portion of this chapter. At this point a mere mention will suffice.

In the centre of the town the work of development was simultaneously in progress. In 1871–2 East Street and West Street were in the making— the Drill Hall was built, and the way was paved for those further extensions which naturally followed on the opening of the North Station in 1878. Between 1881 and 1891 Tweedy Road began to assume its present form, though nearly the whole area to the north of it, now intersected by the various roads which lead towards Plaistow and Sundridge Park Station, still retained for a few years its rural aspect. Immediately adjoining Plaistow Church the large cricket field of the Plaistow Cricket Club was used by the boys of Quernmore School when not required for more serious games, the approaches to it from the town still leading through a footpath and a cornfield, now absorbed into College Road.

This process of rapid extension in the decades which immediately followed the coming of the railways had the effect, among many others, of very considerably increasing the value of land. Apparently waste lands which had long lain idle and unregarded now assumed potentialities of wealth as residential areas. Not unnaturally an epoch of encroachments accompanied an epoch of expansion, and those who were in any position to do so sought by the erection of fences to secure quiet possession of disputable property. In 1872 Mr. W. D. Starling erected an oak fence, six feet high and correspondingly substantial, enclosing a considerable stretch of the waste land bordering the London Road from its junction with the High Street to about the present position of Blyth Road. Mr. Starling was reported to have obtained the consent of the local authorities before erecting the fence. At any rate, indignation meetings and appeals to the Local Board were without effect.

At this juncture Mr. C. W. Gedney stepped into the breach, and raised the whole question of the legality of Mr. Starling's proceedings by the summary process of demolishing the fence. In conjunction with Mr. E. Tuck, Mr. Gedney hired a gang of Beckenham navvies, who, appropriately armed, and encouraged by the applause of an appreciative gallery, soon made short work of the fence. Mr. Gedney and Mr. Tuck and others were summoned to appear before the magistrates on the charge of convening a riotous assembly, but on a cross-summons Mr. Starling was indicted for unlawful encroachment upon public land. As a result the defendants were acquitted, and it was the prosecutor who lost his case. The cost of these 'village Hampdens' was defrayed by public subscription, and the town continues to owe to Mr. Gedney and his fellow ' rioters ' the substantial debt that the London Road is, at the point in question, some six to eight feet wider than, but for them, it would have been. This is the visible debt, but perhaps the invisible one is even greater, for at a time when the spirit of encroachment was actively abroad, Mr. Gedney's summary but most salutary procedure compelled that spirit to fear, to tremble, and to desist.

Exactly in proportion as the town grew to dimensions undreamed of in all the centuries past, so there grew up a multiplicity of needs to satisfy the new conditions—the need for open spaces and public recreation grounds, for an adequate lighting system, for protection of property against fire—for the protection of the public by an efficient police force—for an organised form of local government, and for such facilities for education, amusement, and the pursuit of business, as newspapers, banks, and a postal system can supply. I now propose therefore to examine each of these needs in turn, and the result should be a fairly complete narrative of how modern Bromley has come into being.

The feverish activities of the architect, builder, and engineer in transforming a town of 4,000 inhabitants (1851) into a town of 15,000 inhabitants (1881) and of 35,000 in 1921, naturally constituted a serious menace to any open space which might prove suitable and available for building. At its centre Bromley was fairly secure, for behind the White Hart Hotel was the

White Hart field, the property of the Lord of the Manor, and as long as Mr. Coles Child lived it was known that there was little probability of this fine expanse being exploited for purposes of gain. But away beyond the church there lay one of the finest prospects which the county of Kent affords—Martin's Hill—with all the ground sloping down to the Ravensbourne towards Shortlands, a natural pleasure-ground, and yet affording strong temptations to building enterprise. Early in the sixties ominous rumours began to spread that the ' eligibility ' of the site had already attracted the notice of prospectors. The townspeople showed at once a proper spirit by a violent agitation in favour of securing Martin's Hill for the town. Letters and rhymes appeared in the lately established newspaper, the *Bromley Record*.

> " On this, the people's piece of land,
>   May builder never ply his skill.
> May never innovating hand
>   Deprive the town of Martin's Hill."

So sang one of the local poets of the time, disguising his identity under the pseudonym of " Bromleyite."

A hot controversy arose as to the ownership of the land, and, while it was admitted that the freehold belonged to the Manor, it was contended that long enjoyment and use, probably since the days of King Ethelbert, had established a ' custom ' which conferred rights upon the community. None the less it was shown that considerable portions of the original space towards Beckenham Lane had already passed by purchase into the hands of private owners. It became apparent that if Martin's Hill was to be secured to the town it must be paid for. An attempt to raise the purchase money by public subscription proved abortive ; the agitation died down, and for some years the question was shelved.

In June 1878, however, a rumour ran that the Martin's Hill site could be purchased for £4,000. Mr. T. Davis therefore immediately gave notice that at the next meeting of the Local Board he would move a resolution. At that meeting, held on June 17th, 1878, a resolution proposed by Mr. R. Sandon was promptly carried to the effect that the Chairman should negotiate with the Ecclesiastical Commissioners, into whose hands the hill had now fallen by an Act of 1836, and an influential deputation consisting of Lord Kinnaird, the Rev. A. G. Hellicar, Mr. Robinson Latter, and others [1] was so successful in its representations that the Commissioners offered the site for £2,500. The offer was immediately accepted and Martin's Hill was won for the public.

This purchase, however, by no means represents the whole area which

---

[1] The names of all those forming this deputation should be preserved. They were, in addition to those mentioned, the Chairman of the Local Board (Archibald Hamilton), Major Babbage, and Messrs. S. P. Acton, S. Baddeley, T. Davis, J. W. Ilott, R. Sandon, and J. B. Walter.

MARTIN'S HILL, 1875.

From a pencil drawing by W. Willis.

is now generally known as Martin's Hill. It included nothing but the actual hill. It was the occasion of Queen Victoria's Jubilee in 1887 which gave the opportunity of acquiring not only the Hop Garden which extended from the lower slopes to the river, but also the meadow beyond it, now known as Queen's Mead. The inclusive cost of this additional land was £4,600, and a further sum of £1,650 was expended in forming a road to connect Glassmill Lane with the Shortlands main road, in laying out the ground for purposes of recreation, and in the necessary fences. No more admirable method of celebrating the Queen's reign could have been devised than this purchase, and now Martin's Hill has become the glory of the town. Later improvements on the lower levels have added to the amenities of the property, and to the facilities for recreation, while on the summit of the hill itself the imposing War Memorial testifies far and wide to the valour and devotion of Bromley's sons in the Great War.

Queen Victoria's Diamond Jubilee in 1897 was made the occasion of a splendid gift by the Lord of the Manor. Mr. Coles Child, to show at once his loyalty to the throne and to Bromley, presented to the town the larger part of the White Hart field on condition that it should be converted into a public garden. From time immemorial this fine open space, consisting of nearly four acres, was part and parcel of the life of the town, and many famous exploits of the Bromley Cricket Club were performed upon its surface. The remaining portion of it was appropriated to the erection of the Phillips Memorial Hospital, and for the construction of Lownds Avenue. The lay-out of the gardens, known originally as Victoria, but now as Queen's Garden, was entrusted to the Borough Engineer, Mr. Stanley Hawkings, and it is to his taste and discretion that the existing design is due. The gates at the town end, at one time the gates of Plaistow Lodge, were presented by the Kinnaird Park Syndicate. They were reputed to be the gates attached to the railings round St. Paul's Churchyard, and their design was attributed to Sir Christopher Wren, but further investigations have proved these suppositions to be untenable. In the chapter of this book dealing with Plaistow the whole question of the gates is discussed in detail, and thus a bare reference will suffice here.

The latest additions to the amenities of Bromley are the house and grounds known as " Neelgherries," which were bequeathed to the town by the will of Mrs. Emily Dowling, who died at a very advanced age in 1900. The property for many years had been in the possession of Mr. George Sparkes, who, upon his death in January 1878, left all his estate to his widow. This lady in course of time married again, and became Mrs. Emily Dowling, and it is to the Dowling bequest that Bromley owes " Neelgherries."

The gift came at a psychological moment, for the rapid extension of the town had, for some time past, been calling for a corresponding extension of facilities for intellectual culture. The advantages of the Literary Institute were confined exclusively to its members, and great as its activities had been in providing intellectual resources, and in forming a library, it was none the less by this time quite unequal to serving the needs of a population of 27,000 people. The widespread munificence of Mr. Andrew Carnegie, coupled with the possession of a most appropriate site, combined to suggest the transference of the Public Library from the Science and Art School as the best purpose to which the Dowling bequest could be devoted. Accordingly the house was removed and its site was used for the erection of that Library which is in every sense an adornment to the town. Its position is central, its frontage to the street is architecturally suitable, the whole building being to the design of Mr. Evelyn Hellicar, A.R.I.B.A. Its arrangement for borrowers and readers is convenient, and its large lecture halls and committee room upstairs give to the people ample facilities for amusement and edification. The Public Library has become one of the institutions of Bromley, and as such receives fuller notice in a later chapter. Here we merely call attention to the erection of this building as being one of the most notable landmarks in the history of the town.

The adjoining grounds were converted into the Neelgherries or Library gardens and here, as at Martin's Hill, the genius of Mr. Miles has asserted itself. It would indeed be difficult to conceive how the given space could have been laid out to better purpose. In the variety of trees and shrubs which are permanent, in the ever-varying beauty of the flower beds, and, best perhaps of all, in the design and contents of its rockwork, the Library gardens are indeed a joy for ever, the comparative poverty of the approach providing precisely that element of surprise, of the unexpected, which is a distinguishing mark of the best horticultural art.

From horticulture to the lighting system is not so violent a transition as might appear, for nothing adds to the amenities of a town more than an adequate and effective system of illumination. And not to the amenities only. The protection of life and property, the execution of law, the facilities for amusement and education, the general convenience of the public, and the conduct of business are all intimately bound up in the matter of light. It is difficult to realise that less than one hundred years ago the streets of Bromley, after nightfall, were totally devoid of illumination save for the lamps, filled with colza oil, which hung up in front of the principal inns, and perhaps a few of the principal shops. The lighting restrictions imposed during the Great War enable us, who experienced them, to form some conception of how our grandfathers permanently existed up to so comparatively short a time ago as 1836.

On April 18th in that year the Bromley Vestry applied to Parliament for an Act to establish and regulate a proper system of lighting and paving for the town. In the following year a Mr. Jonathan Hutchison, apparently on his own initiative, introduced gas into Bromley, and carried on the industry for nearly twenty years, in his own private interest. In March 1854 Mr. Hutchison disposed of his works to the Bromley Gas Consumers

Company, with its factory and offices in Farwig Lane. By this time the population had increased to between five and six thousand, the number of houses to about nine hundred, and the demand for the new illuminant exceeded the means of supply. Accordingly the original pipes were taken up and replaced by larger ones ; the system was extended throughout the town, and as far as the eleventh milestone on Bromley Common, and the Company flourished amain.[1]

At its first installation gas was regarded by the old inhabitants with mingled feelings of suspicion, apprehension, and curiosity. Mr. John Cooper was one of the first to introduce gas into his workshop. His premises were visited by all and sundry who came and asked ' to see it burn,' and ' was it safe ? ' and there was much shaking of venerable heads, and many serious warnings against the risks and dangers involved in so hazardous an experiment. But when gas came it came to conquer. The system was soon extended as far as Bickley and Chislehurst. Extensive works midway between Bromley and Bickley were in due course constructed, and gas reigned without a rival until the coming of electricity in comparatively recent times. Mr. W. Baxter was the first man in Bromley to experiment for business purposes with this new illuminant. He contrived a series of batteries supplying power to three lamps, and lit up one window of his father's shop at 41 High Street. But in less than one hour there was what Mr. Baxter describes as ' a grand smash-up,' and the experiment was abandoned.

Notwithstanding such catastrophes, which were common enough in the inception of this great and beneficent advance, electricity has won its way to the first place as a safe and convenient illuminating power, and the works established in West Street in 1897–8, with their numerous extensions, now minister under public control to the necessities and comfort of the whole surrounding district.

For the adequate protection of life and property something more is needed than an efficient lighting system. Protection against fire is as necessary as protection against crime. In Bromley the methods adopted to afford such protection correspond in sequence and character with those generally adopted throughout the country. Down to the end of the seventeenth century no organised precautions against fire, and nothing in any way adapted to extinguish it, seem to have existed. In Holland, in 1670, Jan Van der Heide invented a manual fire-engine with flexible hose attached, and this engine, with the improvements introduced by Newsham, an Englishman, some fifty years later, remained until quite recent years as the accepted standard for fire-engines. As early as 1708, by a statute of Queen Anne, each parish was obliged to provide and maintain two engines

---

[1] The price of gas for about twenty years after its installation was 15*s*. per thousand feet. In 1854 it dropped to 8*s*. From 1868 to 1879 it was from 5*s*. to 6*s*. From 1879 onwards it was between 3*s*. and 4*s*.

2. Mackrell Smith.
3. John Cooper.
4. Sir John Lubbock, Bart.
5. Robinson Latter.
6. John Aird (the Contractor).

7. Jas. W. Ilott.
10. The Architect.
11. H. C. Lukey.
13. H. W. Amos.
14. G. H. Osborn (the Manager).

1. G. H. Osborn.
2. Jas. Spink.
3. S. J. Wilde.
4. Thos. Morley.
5. Bertram Latter.
6. Edward Porter.
7. H. W. Amos.
8. Wm. Sutton.
9. C. W. Gedney.
10. Miss G. Nesbitt.
12. Miss M. Nesbitt.

13. Miss M. Latter.
14. G. Wicks.
15. H. Matherson.
16. Robinson Latter.
17. John Aird.
18. S. P. Acton.
19. Sir John Lubbock, Bart.
20. J. W. Ilott.
21. H. Brothers.
22. R. Ritchie.

Opening of the First Retort House, Homesdale Road, 1864.

Laying the Foundation of New Retort House, 1879.

BROMLEY GAS WORKS.

with ladders and equipment, the expense to be borne by the rates, and under this statute Bromley in due course became possessed of two machines. Later on one of these, if not both, was housed in a shed adjacent to the Cage, in Widmore Road, and was popularly known as 'the Squirt.'

On July 1st, 1828, a disastrous fire at Messrs. Isard's premises in Market Square tested to the full the capacity of such extinguishing apparatus as the town possessed, and the nature of the business

ANCIENT BROMLEY FIRE ENGINE, EARLY EIGHTEENTH CENTURY

perhaps explains the coincidence that at the same premises a fire should have raged, threatening disastrous consequences, nearly a hundred years later (July 1921).

With the rapid development of the town between 1860–70 it became apparent that the existing protection against fire was totally inadequate. A movement was started for forming on organised lines a Volunteer Fire Brigade which took shape at a public meeting held in the Town Hall in March 1868, and though at first the necessary voluntary subscription fund rather languished, a vigorous effort by Mr. W. Pawley enabled the brigade to be formed and an up-to-date engine to be purchased. On November 14th, 1868, the new manual engine arrived and was escorted through the town with much pomp and ceremony, quarters being provided for it at the White Hart by the courtesy of Mr. Lownds, who also undertook to provide horses. The first officers of the Bromley Volunteer Fire Brigade were: Captain, or Superintendent, C. Satterthwaite; Deputy Superintendent, R. V. Harman; J. Dunn, Foreman; J. Eldridge, Engineer; and S. Chitty, Sub-engineer. The first Firemen were G. Amos, E. Ayling, J. Banks, J. Burgess, T. Heaysman, J. Hopton, J. Ingles, M. Keer, C. Knight, and G. H. Payne, the personnel being largely drawn from the 18th Kent Rifle Volunteers.

In 1873 the office of Captain devolved on Mr. Conrad Nickalls, brother of Sir Patteson Nickalls of Chislehurst, and under his command for fourteen years, very largely by reason of his own assiduous labours, the Bromley Fire Brigade became one of the most efficient in the country. Striking proof of this was given by the open competition held at the Crystal Palace in 1874, when the four-man Drill Championship was won by Bromley against the competition of all England, and this high state of efficiency was maintained throughout the Captaincy of Mr. Nickalls and that of Mr. J. Hopton, who succeeded him in 1887.

In 1897 the Brigade was taken over by the Urban District Council. A permanent station, adequate to the existing needs, was established in West Street, a 'steamer' engine was purchased in 1897, and Mr. J. Ingles was appointed Captain in July 1900.

In 1904, however, Bromley had become an incorporated town with nearly 30,000 inhabitants and over 5,000 houses. The members of the Voluntary Brigade were now, most of them, advanced in age, and Mr. Ingles himself resigned his position as Captain. It was felt generally, and not least by the Town Council, that the time had come to terminate the voluntary system, and to place the town under the protection of a permanent force of duly qualified experts. In March 1904 Mr. Samuel Manning, of the London Fire Brigade, was appointed Chief Officer, to be succeeded in turn by Mr. Charles Norton and Mr. Charles Dixon, with Mr. A. C. Smith as Second Officer, a position which he still holds. In 1910 the old Fire Station in West Street was supplanted by the present up-to-date and commodious quarters designed by Mr. Stanley Hawkings, the Borough Engineer, at a cost of £5,191 12s. 8d. The system of horse traction has, of course, given way to motor traction, and, speaking generally on the subject of equipment, the inhabitants of Bromley can sleep quietly in their beds fortified by the knowledge that all that science, skill, and enterprise can do to secure them against fire has been done and is at their disposal. I desire here to acknowledge the courtesy of Mr. Dixon, who not only allowed me to make a thorough inspection of the station, but also provided me with a demonstration of the truly marvellous celerity with which his men are able to come into action. The operation on this occasion took eight-and-a-half seconds.

In the foregoing pages frequent reference has been necessary to the Vestry, to the Local Board, the Urban District Council, and to the Town Council of the Borough. The names themselves imply some of the various systems of Local Government under which the town has been organised from ancient times to the present.

As a complete chapter of this book is devoted to Local Government, full particulars in regard to it are reserved for that chapter. Thus it will only be necessary here, as incidents in the history of the town, to indicate the nature and character of its Local Government from time to time, and the dates when changes in the system were made.

Originally the manorial system was that under which a Manor was governed. Bromley was the Manor of the Bishops of Rochester, and therefore the Bishops, as Lords of the Manor, were responsible for the government and general well-being of the town and its inhabitants. But with the seventeenth century the jurisdiction of the manorial overlord began to decline, and the Parish Vestry began to assume its office. The Vestry was a meeting of the parishioners held from time to time, and, at any rate in theory, the task of carrying on the government of the town, in regard to all matters not already prescribed by law, was in the hands of the people themselves. The minute-books of the Bromley Vestry are fairly complete from 1703 up to the present day.

In 1867 a town meeting was called to consider the Local Government Act of 1858, and under the provisions of that Act it was resolved to set up a Local Board, consisting of twelve members, which should be responsible for the government of the town. In 1889 the duties of the town in the matter of education were transferred to a School Board.

In 1894, under the Local Government Act of 1888, the Local Board was superseded by the Urban District Council, and in 1902 School Boards were abolished, the control of education being placed largely in the hands of the County Councils. In the case of towns, however, with the necessary qualification they were allowed under the terms of the Act of that year to form their own Education Committees, and, as far as elementary education was concerned, to manage their own affairs. Accordingly the first Education Committee for the town of Bromley was formed in June 1903.

On August 25th, 1903, Bromley received from the Crown its Charter of Incorporation. Its local government became the duty and the business of the Mayor and Corporation, and thus Bromley assumed the dignity and status which befitted its rapid development in less than seventy years from a small market town into a vigorous and thriving one of little, if anything, less than 40,000 people.

Almost from the first beginnings of this vigorous growth the great London Banks began to cast their eyes on Bromley as a promising field for enterprise. The London and County Bank was the first to realise the project, a branch of that bank being established in 1865, and thus the existing Westminster Bank is entitled to boast that it is the premier bank in the town. The need for such an institution was pressing, for, previous to its advent, such facilities for banking as existed were provided by one or two prominent tradesmen, such as Mr. Benjamin Nash and Mr. H. C. Lukey, who missed the opportunity of themselves establishing a flourishing local bank. It is true that since 1816 there had existed a Savings Bank for all the seventeen parishes of the Union, which, by its success, had proved itself of value to the town, but the disappearance of the Actuary in 1856 with nearly £1,000 of the bank's money shook public confidence, notwithstanding the fact that the loss was promptly made good by public subscription. But by 1865 the town had completely outgrown such crude and elementary methods as had previously existed of serving the financial and business requirements of the community, and therefore the coming of the London and County Bank, with all the conveniences and security it brought with it, may legitimately be regarded as a landmark in the history of the town.

So, too, with the postal system ; though in this respect development proceeded on national and not on local lines. The transport of letters in this country was placed under the supervision of a " Postmaster-General " by an Act of Queen Anne (1710), which superseded the farming out of the posts to private individuals—the system which had previously prevailed. Mail coaches were instituted in 1783, and continued to be the chief agents of the postal service until the coming of the railways. But a comparatively small population of scarcely ten millions in 1800, the primitive conditions of national education, and the high charges—fourpence for fifteen miles and *pro rata* for a single sheet—contributed to make the postal services a comparatively simple business until the coming of the penny post in 1840. This, coupled with the invention of adhesive stamps (which, however, were not, until much later, perforated, but had to be cut from a sheet with scissors), enormously increased the circulation of letters. In ten years the number dispatched through the post rose from 76 millions in 1840 to 337 millions in 1850, and by the latter date the railways were beginning to be in a position to take over much of the work of transport which had been done by the mail coaches.

In Bromley, previous to 1784, letters were dispatched by any method which might come conveniently to hand—horse carriers, privately owned coaches, carriers' carts, or anyone or anything which happened to be going to the place to which a letter was addressed. The institution in 1784 of John Palmer's Royal Mail Coaches introduced some order, method, and regularity into the dispatch and delivery of letters. It is probable that in Bromley, as elsewhere, a postmaster was appointed about this time, the first reference to such an official indicating Hugh Hair as Postmaster some time prior to his death in 1802. In 1812 a wine merchant, John Acton, who lived where Messrs. Pamphilon's premises now stand, was appointed Postmaster, an office which he held until his death in 1839. He was succeeded by his son, Samuel Poole Acton, whose tenure only ceased with his retirement in 1857. From this date till 1876 Mr. Joseph B. Shillcock was Postmaster.

Since this passage was written, special inquiries addressed to the Postmaster-General as to Hugh Hair have elicited from the Post Office the following facts, hitherto entirely unknown and unsuspected. It is now possible to give here a complete list of Bromley Postmasters since the year 1685.

1685–1687	Wm. Crumpe	. .	Who lived near the Bell Inn.
1687–	Thos. Bennett	. .	Landlord of the White Hart Inn.
1688–1692	Thos. Godden	. .	Who appears in the rate books.

1693–1695	Edmund Millington	.	Parish Clerk.
1696–1720	William Waldron .	.	Lived where Westminster Bank stands.
1721–1727	Mrs. Ann Bartlett .	.	Her husband appears in the rate books.
1728–1735	J. Lawson .	.	Styled " Mr." Lawson in rate books.
1736–1752	Wm. Wood.		
1752–1753	Martha Wood.		
1753–1774	Wm. Stich .	.	Large owner of property in the town.
1775–1783	John Phillips	.	Landlord of White Hart Inn.
1784–1786	Thomas Palmer .	.	Ditto.
1787–1788	James Wilson	.	Landlord of the Bell Inn.
1789–1796	Wm. Francis Peachey.		
1796–1802	Hugh Hair .	.	Draper in market-place. Wine merchant in High Street.
1802–1811	Ann Hair .	.	Hugh Hair's widow.
1812–1839	John Acton .	.	Succeeded Hair as wine merchant.
1839–1857	Samuel Poole Acton	.	Son of John.
1857–1876	Joseph Bradley Shillcock		Chemist, High Street.
1876–1890	Wm. Hewick.		
1891–1897	Wm. Beale.		
1898–1902	John Peach.		
1902–1909	James Harris Ayers.		From 1876 onwards the appointment as Bromley Postmaster was separated from any other occupation.
1909–1913	Fredk. N. Crabtree.		
1913–1915	John Compton.		
1915–1927	Samuel J. Holloway.		
1927	H. F. Peake.		

The system of delivery and the methods of business were, during the greater portion of this period, both primitive and casual. For example, the mail coach returning from Sevenoaks to London was timed to pass through Bromley at 4 a.m. The sleep of the Postmaster was thus liable to be disturbed at a very untimely hour. To obviate this, the mail-bag was entrusted to a person commonly known as ' Charley,' who lived in the vicinity of the Swan Inn. On reaching the neighbourhood of Charley's domicile the guard of the coach would blow a few vigorous blasts upon his horn. Whereupon Charley opened his window, threw out the mail-bag, received another, and the coach proceeded on its way to London.

At the post office itself a trap-door in the front window of the premises was fitted with a knocker. On plying the knocker the window, in due course, might open and business be done. Modern methods may somewhat differ in detail, but it will be observed that they adhere to original principles. The business might be the handing in of a letter for dispatch, or the purchase of stamps, which were cut, in required quantity, from the sheet with the office scissors. Letter boxes, wall boxes, perforated stamp-sheets were things of the future, but the postman already existed as an institution. The Bromley postman of the mid-nineteenth century period was a well-known figure, commonly known as ' Trusty,' whose daily round included Widmore, Southborough, and Bromley Common. ' Trusty's ' daughter married Mr. George Spooner, whose *Reminiscences of*

Old Bromley have provided valuable material for this, and other chapters, of this work.

With the coming of the railways the primitive methods of the past to some extent disappeared. The mail coach was displaced by the mail train. The postal service was accelerated, and with greater facilities for the receipt and dispatch of letters the use of the service was largely increased. More especially was this the case from 1870 onwards, for in that year both postal telegrams and halfpenny postcards were introduced. And yet, in 1882, there was one delivery *less* in Bromley than in 1858, and at the end of the century six dispatches and four deliveries to and from London showed little advance on the four deliveries and four dispatches of 1858.

On the retirement of Mr. Shillcock in 1876, premises were secured for the exclusive use of the Bromley Post Office. The premises originally taken, on the east side of the market-place, were, however, only a temporary makeshift till more suitable quarters could be secured. In 1877 the Post Office was established on the west side of the market-place, in Middle Row, and there it remained until 1897. By this time the rapid expansion of the town had completely outgrown its Post Office accommodation. A new and up-to-date office was imperatively required. The nucleus of the present building in East Street was occupied in 1897 by Mr. Beale and his staff, and in due course the existing premises, which both in situation and structure are worthy of the town, were called into being. The growth of business in the course of a few years may be gauged by a comparison of the staff employed in 1879 and 1909. In 1879 the staff consisted of three indoor postal servants, sixteen outdoor, and three telegraph boys. In 1909 of twenty-four, eighty-five, and fifteen respectively.

Coincident with the expansion of Bromley into a populous town came the newspapers, or rather, to start with, the newspaper. It was in June 1858, the year of the opening of the railway, that Bromley's first newspaper came into being, entitled *The Bromley Record and Monthly Advertiser*. As its name implies, it was, at first, issued monthly, from an office in Lower High Street, the founder of the enterprise being Mr. Edward Strong, whose primary aim was to make the paper a medium for advertisement. The first number, published on June 1st, consisted of eight pages containing a summary of local news, and also time-tables for trains and omnibuses, notices of sale, and tradesmen's advertisements. It proved such an immediate success that, in its third year, its size was doubled, and under its original title it enjoyed a prosperous existence for fifty-five years, finally ceasing to exist in 1913.

The Public Library possesses a complete file, conveniently bound, of the *Bromley Record* from its inception. An index is all that is necessary to complete its value, for, with the aid of an index, it would be easy to refer to almost any point of interest in the history of Bromley for a period of over half a century. The paper throughout its career rendered valuable service to the town, and it is fitting that the energy, enterprise, and perseverance of Mr. Strong and his family should here receive a grateful recognition.

In 1865 the *Bromley Telegraph* was established by Charles W. Gedney as editor and proprietor. In 1902 Mr. Gedney retired, having personally conducted his paper for thirty-seven years. During that time he, with his paper, may be termed the stormy petrel of Bromley politics.

The key-note of the *Telegraph* was criticism, pungent and outspoken, which earned for it a general though apprehensive popularity. Everyone took the *Scorpion*, as it came to be called, either to see if perchance the reader was himself assailed, or to enjoy assaults upon his neighbours and acquaintances. Mr. Gedney utterly declined to accept the doctrine that everything he found existing was for the best in the best of all possible towns. He had no reverence for established institutions where he considered them to be effete, and was no respecter of persons where he deemed them inefficient. Local Boards, Boards of Guardians, *et hoc genus omne*, trembled at the *Telegraph* frown, and all encroachers upon public rights felt the weight of his organised powers of destruction.

As a journalist he was absolutely fearless, and generally in the right. His trenchant attacks on men and institutions subjected him to twenty actions in the High Court, and on eighteen such occasions he was successful. His own humorous comment on these proceedings was that the two actions which he lost he ought to have won, and that another which he won he ought to have lost. The official mind, and indeed that of the general public, was quite unaccustomed at this early date to journalistic attacks, which indeed were regarded as so presumptuous as to be almost blasphemous. I well remember, when I first came to Bromley in 1881, that Mr. Gedney was represented to me as a dangerous iconoclast, and doubtless would have been dubbed a Bolshevist had such an appellation at that time existed. But, in fact, the causes which moved Mr. Gedney's enthusiasm were the causes of the poor, the destitute, the orphans, and the children, and for such causes, both in and out of his newspaper, he fought consistently, valiantly, and successfully.

On Mr. Gedney's retirement his paper was taken over by the proprietors of the *Bromley Chronicle*, the original title being retained, in conjunction with the *Chronicle*, until 1912.

This paper was launched in 1891, and enjoyed a prosperous life for thirty years. It was especially notable for its admirable illustrations, and for the quality of its leading articles. It catered not only for Bromley, but the surrounding district. In 1921 the *Chronicle* was merged in the *Bromley Mercury*, established in Bromley in 1919. It was, however, scarcely an entirely new venture of that date. It was rather an extension of the *Kentish Mercury* which, since 1833, had commanded a large circulation throughout the county. The *Mercury* therefore was able at once to take its place as a leading newspaper, and to share with the *District Times* a practical monopoly of public support.

In much the same way as the *Mercury*, the *Bromley and District Times* was started in 1881. The Kentish District Times Company already published some dozen papers circulating in north and west Kent, the *Bromley District Times* merely adding one more to the number. It was thus able to assume from the first a commanding position, and soon came to be recognised as Bromley's principal newspaper. That position, though challenged by the *Mercury*, it still retains.

The only other newspaper which maintained a circulation for a considerable length of time was the *Bromley Journal*, established in 1864. It was owned and edited by Mr. E. Rowe, and appeared weekly on Fridays. Published in the Conservative interest, it enjoyed a circulation beyond the limits of the town, and survived till about 1900.

The history of Bromley newspapers establishes the fact that a well-conducted journal stands a good chance of a continued and prosperous existence. It also affords instances of papers started which have had probably the shortest existence on record. The *Bromley and County Independent*, promoted by Mr. Henry Nye, is catalogued in the British Museum as consisting of one issue, that of September 4th, 1889 ; while the *Scribbler*, published in March 1894, came to an untimely end with the publication of its fifth number.

In proportion as a community advances in civilisation, it acquires a social sense, a feeling that the interests of the individual are closely linked with those of the society of which he forms a part, and a growing conviction of the importance of law and order to the general well-being. The protection of life and property becomes a matter of the first consideration, and the machinery by which that protection may be ensured is gradually evolved from crude beginnings up to the modern system of police. In Anglo-Saxon times, by the system known as Frankpledge, the community of freemen was organised in families, and one man for each ' tithing,' or group of ten families, was elected as a surety for the rest. This individual was known as a ' Borsholder,' a term which continued to survive in Bromley as late as the early nineteenth century. A group of ten tithings constituted a Wapentake or Hundred, for which one individual stood as head or security. Three or four of these Hundreds constituted what was known in Kent as a ' lathe,' and an association of ' lathes ' constituted the shire, under its Reeve, Shire-reeve, or Sheriff. Thus Bromley was in the Hundred of Bromley and Beckenham in the Lathe of Sutton-at-Hone, in the Shire or County of Kent.

By the Statute of Winchester, 1285, the term ' petty constable ' was substituted for that of ' Borsholder,' though the old name continued to persist. The provision in the Statute that ' Justices assigned ' shall present to the King such default as they may find marks a stage in the evolution of Justices of the Peace, the Statute as a whole, in the words of Professor Stubbs, being " a monument of the persistence of primitive institutions working their way through the superstratum of feudalism, and gaining strength in the process."

But the persistence of primitive institutions throughout the succeeding centuries tended to maintain a system which was no longer adequate to its purposes. In the days of the early Stuarts the forces of crime and disorder were more than a match for the organisation in existence to repress them, and on the accession of Cromwell to power the country was divided into twelve police districts, of which Kent and Surrey were number one, and the creation of ' Bellmen '—known after the Restoration as ' Charlies ' in honour of the monarch—provided for each township one or more guardians, whose authority and efficiency, however, do not seem to have been much in advance of that of Dogberry and Verges in Elizabethan days.

The functions of the ' Charlies ' seem to have been confined chiefly to the hours between sunset and sunrise, their duties being to perambulate the town every hour, armed with a lantern, stick, and rattle, and to call out the time and the state of the weather. Sentry boxes for their accommodation in intervals of inaction were set up at fixed spots, one such box being placed nearly opposite the site of Mr. Grinsted's shop in High Street.

In addition to this regular force, a High and a Petty Constable were yearly chosen from among the townsfolk, who, when nominated, were compelled to serve under a penalty of a fine of ten pounds. These constables were generally responsible for the peace of the town, while special officers such as ' Ale-Conners ' and ' Leather-sealers ' were a guarantee for the purity of the ale and the quality of the articles of commerce.

Such, in outline, were the primitive methods deemed sufficient until 1829 for the protection of life and property and the maintenance of law and order. In that year Sir Robert Peel established the Metropolitan Police Force, the Act authorising the levy of a police rate not exceeding eightpence in the pound. Under this Act Bromley fell into the P Division of the Metropolitan Police Area, the local authorities being thus relieved of all responsibility to provide for the security of the inhabitants.

As the town grew in importance and population each successive Police Station became inadequate to its requirements. After various migrations, in 1841 and in 1865, the present handsome and complete establishment in Widmore Road was erected in 1914.

It is an interesting commentary on the growth of Bromley since the coming of the railway that, in 1861, the total police force allotted to the town, with 5,500 inhabitants, was six, the constables, still known as ' bobbies,' or ' Peelers,' wearing tall hats and carrying rattles. In 1924, with a population of over 35,000, the town required one Sub-divisional Inspector, two Station Sergeants, two Inspectors, nine Sergeants, and eighty-seven Constables.

In the course of this historical survey no reference has so far been made to the Parliamentary history of Bromley, to the various elections in which it has been concerned, and to the successive members who have represented it in the House of Commons.

The electoral methods of the past which have been faithfully presented to us, rather than caricatured, in the pages of *Pickwick* were in active operation in Bromley. Excitement centred in the old Market Place, where, on the south side of the Market House, the Hustings were erected, and the public gathered in strength around and below them. On this raised platform the formal nominations were announced, the candidates harangued the assembled people, and the voters publicly recorded their votes. There was usually much rough horseplay, and a great parade of colours and of emblems intended to be derogatory to the respective candidates.

At the election of 1868, the last before the Ballot Act of 1872, local feeling ran particularly high. All the candidates were men well known in the neighbourhood, William Angerstein hailing from Blackheath, Sir John Lubbock from Farnborough, Charles Mills from Sevenoaks, and J. G. Talbot from Edenbridge.

The crowds which flocked into Bromley were very great, and the conflicts between the rival partisans were so violent that the shopkeepers were compelled to put up their shutters, and one old labourer who had come in from the country was knocked down and trampled to death. In 1872, however, the introduction of the Ballot Act abolished the public nomination of candidates and the polling of voters at the Hustings, and the violence and disturbance which had characterised elections hitherto were sensibly diminished as a consequence of that Act.

In recording the actual share of the town of Bromley in Parliamentary elections it is unnecessary to go farther back than the great Reform Act of 1832, which gave such striking effect to the democratic aspirations which were beginning to make themselves felt. This Act took away the right of representation from a large number of close boroughs, and greatly increased the representation of the counties and large towns.

The county of Kent was split into three divisions—East, Mid, and West Kent—each with two members, Bromley naturally falling into the West Kent Division. The Reform Act remained in operation until 1867, and in the interval of thirty-five years there were twelve elections in West Kent, resulting in the return of twelve Conservatives and eight Liberals. Among these Sir E. Filmer held a seat in the Conservative interest from 1838 until his death in 1857, and Mr. T. L. Hodges held his as a Liberal from 1832 until 1852, with the exception of the years between 1841 and 1847.

Between 1867 and 1885 there were three elections, the successful candidates being C. H. Mills, afterwards Sir Charles Mills, and subsequently Baron Hillingdon of Wildernesse House, Sevenoaks, J. G. Talbot, and Viscount Lewisham. The defeated Liberals at these elections were Sir John Lubbock, afterwards Lord Avebury, William Angerstein, Archibald Hamilton of Southborough, E. Marjoribanks, and H. M. Bompas, Q.C.

In 1885 the Representation of the People Act divided Kent into eight divisions, with one member each, Bromley being included in the Sevenoaks Division, and this distribution of seats remained in operation till 1918. In this period of thirty-three years the Sevenoaks Division was represented by only two members, C. W. Mills, son of Sir Charles Mills, holding the seat till 1892, when he was succeeded by H. W. Forster, of the Hall, Southend. When Mr. Forster was raised to the Peerage in 1919 he had contested five elections in the Sevenoaks Division, and was twice returned unopposed.

Under the Representation of the People Act of 1918 Bromley was created a Parliamentary Borough with one member. The constituency includes the Urban Districts of Beckenham and Penge. Three elections have taken place since this last change, and in each case the Hon. Cuthbert James has won the seat in a three-cornered contest.

Some indication of the extent to which the franchise has been increased since the great Reform Bill may be gathered by comparing the number of voters recording their votes at the elections of 1832 and of 1924 respectively. In 1832, when the constituency included the whole Western Division of the county, a total of 8,983 votes was recorded for the three candidates, two of whom were elected. The actual number of voters was rather less than 6,000. In 1924, when the constituency only included the Parliamentary Borough of Bromley, the total votes cast for the three candidates numbered 37,728, each vote representing a voter.

For the convenience of reference a full list of all the elections and of the candidates, since 1832, is given in Appendix D at the end of the volume.

I close this chapter by calling to the memory of the reader the essential purpose which it is intended to serve. And that is to trace through various phases the progressive development of the town during the last sixty or seventy years.

Chapter VI

BROMLEY AND THE BISHOPS OF ROCHESTER TO THE END OF THE FIFTEENTH CENTURY

PART of this chapter appeared in the *Archæological Journal* for 1920, but it has been rewritten with additions and corrections, for several of which I take the opportunity of thanking Mr. W. Baxter. In my efforts to ascertain the main facts I owe much to the able account of Bromley, still in manuscript, which was compiled by the late Mr. Coles Child with the help of various experts. It formed the basis of the paper in *Archæologia Cantiana*, Vol. XIII, 1880, called " The Church and Manor of Bromley," by the late Dr. W. T. Beeby.

The origin of Bromley as a place of habitation need here only be referred to in the briefest way. The story of its connection with the Saxon Bishops of Rochester is rather difficult to follow. In Dugdale's *Monasticon*, with additions, ed. 1830, Vol. I, p. 154, it is said that " Offa, King of Mercia, gave jointly with Sigered, King of Kent A.D. 747, Frindsbury and Wickham to this church (Rochester) to which was soon after added the manor of Bromley." Another early reference occurs in Hasted's *History of Kent*. He tells us that " Ethelbert, King of Kent, gave to Bishop Eardulph and the church of Rochester, land in Bromley containing six sulings,"[1] but his authority, given as ' Apograph,' Dering Library, is a doubtful one. Unquestionably, A.D. 966 or 967, King Eadgar granted to the church of Rochester " ten hides (of land), called by the Kentishmen sulings, with all liberties and emoluments—except repelling invasions and the repairing of bridges and fortifications, which privileges were granted on account of the great price which Bishop Alfstan had paid for this land ; being no less than eighty marcs of the purest gold, and six pounds of fine silver, and thirty marcs of gold besides to the king's praefect." [2] The King's son Ethelred seized the land and gave it to his minister, Ethelsine, but afterwards repenting, in 998, he restored six out of the ten sulings to the see of Rochester with privileges over woods in the Weald.[3] Again, according to Hasted, a Saxon nobleman by name Birtrick (or Byrhtric), with Elfswith his wife, in a will made during the lifetime of Bishop Alfstan, left their land at Bromley to St. Andrew's Priory, Rochester, after the death of one Britware. We do not know if the Saxon Bishops ever lived here, but their ownership of a considerable amount of land rather suggests a dwelling.

[1] E. Hasted, *Hist. Kent*, ed. 1797, Vol. I, p. 552.
[2] Ibid., p. 553.
[3] Ibid., p. 554, and *Text. Roff.*, p. 130. The Weald of Kent, in ancient times part of the forest of Andredsweald, is a large wooded district between the chalk downs. In former times it had few inhabitants. Those with the necessary privileges turned out swine and cattle to feed there.

THE BISHOP'S PALACE, BROMLEY, 1756.

From an engraving in the folio edition of Hasted's "History of Kent."

After the Conquest Odo, Bishop of Bayeux, the King's half-brother, seized on the possessions of the church of Rochester at Bromley, but Lanfranc, Archbishop of Canterbury, recovered them at a memorable assembly on Penenden Heath in 1076, and restored them to Bishop Gundulf.[1]

Passing on to the time of Domesday, finished A.D. 1086, we are told that the Bishop of Rochester then held Bromley as Lord of the Manor, but, although it answered for six sulings in the time of Edward the Confessor, the amount of land had been reduced to three sulings. There were thirty villeins (villani) and twenty-six cottiers (bordarii), which, allowing for their families, might imply a population of over two hundred.

There was a mill, no doubt a water-mill, where corn was ground for the manor, windmills apparently not coming into use in England until nearly the end of the twelfth century. No church was mentioned ; if the Bishops had a house they had a chapel, which perhaps afforded accommodation enough. But between 1115 and 1124 there *was* a church.[2] Domesday records no landowner except the Bishop. This state of things, however, did not last long. Shortly afterwards, as Dr. Beeby, quoting from Mr. Coles Child's manuscript, remarks : " There can be little doubt that the Bishops of Rochester, with or without permission from the Crown, had converted portions of their land in Bromley and elsewhere into knights' fees, in like manner as the Archbishop had been authorised to do " ; and from the same source he adds, to our surprise, that " in less than a century after the Domesday Survey twenty-seven persons held of the Bishop by military service." [3] It is generally agreed that there was considerable subdivision of land in Bromley. At least one dependent manor was carved out, namely, the rectorial manor, and entries from the court roll of this have survived. Another property which has been called a manor by Hasted and Lysons is Sundridge, as were Simpson's and Blackbrook. These and other ancient Bromley estates are fully dealt with elsewhere.[4]

One of the most famous Bishops of Rochester was Gundulf (1077–1108), and Hasted thought that he built the palace or episcopal manor house. Mr. Coles Child believed it to have been older, arguing that a structure for which

[1] E. Hasted, *Hist. Kent*, ed. 1797, Vol. I, pp. 554–5. *Reg. Roff.*, p. 442.

[2] In the *Registrum Roffense*, mention is made of a church being reclaimed with the manor from Odo of Bayeux in 1076. This, however, was written a long time afterwards. In *Arch. Cant.*, Vol. XIII, p. 158, Dr. Beeby records payment for chrism about forty years after the Domesday account. The basin of the font is Norman.

[3] *Arch. Cant.*, Vol. XIII, p. 147.

[4] Sub-infeudation was prohibited under the statute beginning " Quia Emptores," 18 Edward I, A.D. 1289, and no manor could be created afterwards, therefore all manors date from before that year. The fact that a piece of land was held by knight service did not make it a manor. As Dunkin says in his *Outlines of the History of Bromley*, 1815, to the grant must be annexed a certain degree of jurisdiction, as court, baron, etc.

Gundulf was responsible could hardly have become ruinous in the course of a century, because architectural works with which his name has usually been associated—for instance, the keep of the Tower of London, and that of Rochester Castle—seem almost imperishable. We know that A.D. 1184, Bishop Gilbert de Glanvill, who had been one of Becket's scholars, found his house at Bromley so inconvenient and so out of repair that he rebuilt or thoroughly restored it. We may, however, bear in mind that de Glanvill seems to have had a taste for such expenditure ; because he also rebuilt or repaired his palace at Rochester, and the manor houses of Lambeth, Halling, Stone, and Trottescliffe.

In 1203 this prelate obtained from King John a grant of a weekly market at Bromley on Tuesdays throughout the year, an indication perhaps that the inhabitants had increased in numbers. There was protracted strife between him and the Prior and monks of Rochester. He is said to have plunged them into such costly litigation that they were obliged to turn into money the silver shrine of St. Paulinus which dated from the time of Archbishop Lanfranc, and had been much resorted to by pilgrims. Gilbert de Glanvill died in 1214, and, in spite of their opposition, was buried in Rochester Cathedral, where, on the north side of the presbytery opposite the sedilia, is a fine tomb generally believed to be his.

To vent his wrath, one of the monks was said to have composed the following Latin doggerel about the Bishop :

> " Glanvill Gilbertus, nulla bonitate refertus,
> Hic jacet immitis, et amator maxime litis.
> Et quia sic litem dum vixit solet amare,
> Nunc, ubi pax nulla est, est aptior inhabitare." [1]

Of these lines the following translation is suggested :

> " Here Gilbert Glanvill lies, who in his life
> Was harsh, unfriendly, loving legal strife.
> Since peace he hated, now in lowest—well !
> Where there is no peace let him aptly dwell."

In spite of the monument, according to a chronicler, he was buried like Jews and heretics, without the divine office. [2]

From the Calendar of Close Rolls, 1231–4, p. 371 (where the rolls are printed in full), we get the following glimpse of the distracted state of the country during the reign of King John. The Bishop in 1232 (16 Henry III), having shown the King, " that whereas it was the custom to hold a certain market at the said Bishop's manor of Bromlegh on Tuesday in every week,

---

[1] *History of Rochester*, by W. Shrubsole and the Rev. J. Denne, D.D., 2nd ed., 1817, p. 120.

[2] *Cott. MS.*, Nero D2, f. 127 *b*, and Wharton's *Anglia Sacra*, Vol. I, p. 347.

that market was afterwards interrupted by the destruction of the said manor ; which took place on occasion of the war waged between King John and his barons of England. Thereupon the King granted that, if such were the case, that market should again be held in the same manner every week on Tuesday, as formerly had been the case. And the Sheriff of Kent was directed to cause the said market to be proclaimed through the bailiwick, and to be held as aforesaid."

In 1235 Richard de Wendover, Rector of Bromley, was elected Bishop of Rochester by the monks. The Archbishop of Canterbury refused to confirm the election, declaring him to be ignorant and in every way unworthy. The real ground of his refusal seems to have been that he himself claimed the right of naming the Bishop. The monks appealed to the Pope, who, after three years, confirmed the election. He was the only Rector of Bromley who reached this dignity. He died October 12th, 1250, and by the King's command was buried in Westminster Abbey.

A.D. 1255 (40 Henry III), when his successor Lawrence de St. Martin was Bishop, the small value of Bromley Manor, and the unproductive nature of the soil, are referred to in the *Registrum Roffense*, p. 63, thus :

" The sworn valuers of the manor of Bromleghe say that the yearly rent there amounts to £23, and no more, and they say that the buildings there cannot be sustained except from the rent, because the arable lands do not repay the necessary expences each year made about the same. The valuers say that the buildings there require yearly 60*s*."

On October 6th, 1261, Roger Forde, Abbot of Glastonbury, died suddenly [1] at Bromley Palace, he being then on a journey to defend the rights of his church. He is said to have been a man of great learning and eloquence, and was buried in Westminster Abbey. Lawrence de St. Martin was then Bishop of Rochester.

When Thomas de Inglethorp, who was consecrated Bishop of Rochester in 1283, died May 1291, it appears, from a taxation of the episcopal manors, that he had at Bromley in rents of assize £23 10*s*. etc. There were then two mills valued at forty shillings a year. We may, I think, assume that the first (mentioned in Domesday) was by the mill-pond on the Ravensbourne, now included in the grounds of the house called Mill Vale, but where was the second ?

The next Bishop of Rochester was Thomas de Wouldham or Woldham (1292–1316–17), who, according to Hasted,[2] in the twenty-first year of King

---

[1] *Historia de rebus gestis Glastoniensibus*, by Adam of Domerham (a contemporary), T. Hearne's ed., 1727, Vol. II, p. 545. John of Glastonbury (fl. 1400) gives a similar account. Lysons, in his *Environs of London*, 1797, wrongly assumes that Abbot Forde was killed, giving Willis's *Mitred Abbeys*, Vol. I, p. 91, as his chief authority, and other writers have followed him.

[2] E. Hasted, *Hist. Kent*, ed. 1797, Vol. I, p. 556. See also *Reg. Roff.*

Edward I (that is, the year of his election) claimed certain liberties, viz. the return of the King's writs, assize of bread and ale, view of frankpledge, and pleas of withernam, in his manor of Bromley, as well of his own tenants as of those of Abel de St. Martin, Rector of the parish. And he complained that the Rector caused, in like manner, amerciaments to be made of the tenants of his church at the Bishop's view of Bromley for breaking the assize. Notwithstanding which, the Bishop causing the same to be levied by his bailiffs too, the tenants were twice punished for the same default. Whereupon the jury found upon oath that the Bishop had a right to those liberties, and that he found his church possessed of them upon his coming to it. Upon which the parson submitted and was fined half a marc.[1] The *Textus Roffensis* is authority for this statement. To give the gist of the matter in clear language, the Bishop succeeded in asserting his rights as superior lord, above the holder of the rectorial manor.

Thomas de Wouldham died at Bromley February 28th, 1316–17, and from some motive of policy his death was kept secret for three days. A copy of his will, dated 1316, is given in the *Registrum Roffense*, p. 113. Among his executors he names John de Frendsburie, Rector of Bromley, who had succeeded Abel de St. Martin, and who afterwards got himself into trouble by contumacious behaviour to Bishop Hamo de Hethe. It seems that in 1329 he was deprived, and Hugh de Penebregge collated in his stead, but de Frendsburie sent his chaplain to Rochester, and at the high altar with bell and candle excommunicated his Bishop; which excommunication was afterwards revoked, and, at a subsequent visitation of the diocese by the Archbishop, the rebellious Rector was severely punished.[2] Nevertheless he kept or eventually regained the living.

Hamo de Hethe, so named from Hythe his birthplace, was Bishop for thirty-three years, namely, from 1319 to 1352, had been chaplain to Thomas de Wouldham, whom he succeeded,[3] and then Prior of St. Andrew's, Rochester. The day before the death of de Wouldham he came to Bromley, and asked on his knees and obtained forgiveness for having done him some wrong. De Hethe was chosen by the monks with the consent of the Archbishop. The Pope, however, refused to confirm their choice, and appointed John de Puteoli, Confessor to Queen Isabella, wife of Edward II. After more than two years Hamo was confirmed, but not without heavy payment to the Pope. This was probably the cause of his getting into financial difficulties, and having to sell the wood at Elmstead, which he did for 200 marcs.[4] In 1337 he spent a considerable sum on the farm buildings

---

[1] Dr. Beeby in *Arch. Cant.*, Vol. XIII, p. 158.

[2] *Arch. Cant.*, Vol. XIII., p. 158.

[3] The Rev. C. H. Fielding, in *Records of Rochester Diocese*, 1910, p. 11, says that Thomas de Wouldham desired to be buried " in ecclesia Cathedrali Roffensi, vel alibi pro disposicione executorum meorum," but that he was not buried in the cathedral.

[4] Hasted, *Hist. Kent*, ed. 1797, Vol. I, p. 557.

at Bromley which had become dilapidated.   Among the Cottonian manuscripts in the British Museum there is an account, dating probably from his
time, of the stock that ought to be left at Bromley on the death of a bishop.
After enumerating one cart horse value 13*s.* 4*d.* (a mark), sixteen oxen, four
stallions, one hundred ewe lambs, etc., it descends to such minutiæ as three
barrels, one table, one brass pot, and one porridge pot.

William Dene, the Bishop's notary public, wrote a life of Hamo de
Hethe with much detail, which is printed in Wharton's *Anglia Sacra.*   He
repaired and enlarged his manor houses of Halling and Trottescliffe in Kent,
and resided at both places.   In 1325, from his vineyard at Halling, he sent
presents of grapes to the King.   As a decrepit old man he was at Trottescliffe
during the ' Black Death,' 1349, and had an appalling experience.   We are
told that

" From his moderate household he lost four preiests, five squires, ten
serving men, seven young clerks and six pages, so that no one remained to
serve him in any office.   In every manor of the bishopric buildings and walls
fell to ruin, and that year there was hardly a manor that returned a hundred
pounds."

No doubt Bromley suffered with the rest.

Hamo de Hethe was succeeded by John de Sheppey (1352–60), who had
been sent as envoy to Spain in 1345, was treasurer of England in 1356–8, and
left a reputation as a great preacher.   There is a fine tomb commemorating
him in Rochester Cathedral.   We are not, however, aware of his having
been specially connected with Bromley, and this is the case with the two
leading men who come next on our list.

The next Bishop, William de Whittlesey, nephew of Simon Islip, the
Archbishop—not to be confused with John Islip of Westminster—was noteworthy, but he only held the see for two years, becoming Bishop of Worcester
in 1364 and Archbishop of Canterbury in 1368.

More famous was John Kempe, Bishop of Rochester from 1419 to
1421, who was much employed as a diplomatist by Henry V.   The high
offices held by him at various times are enumerated in the *Dictionary of
National Biography.*   Among the rest he was Chancellor of England,
Archbishop of York, Archbishop of Canterbury, and was appointed Cardi-
nal-Bishop by Pope Nicholas.

In 1422 John Langdon, Sub-Prior of Christchurch, Canterbury, was
consecrated Bishop of Rochester.   He had been one of twelve Oxford
scholars appointed in 1411 to inquire into Wycliffe's doctrines, and appears
to have been assiduous in persecuting Lollards.   In 1434 he was engaged in
an embassy to France, and he died and was buried at Basel.   During his
episcopate he granted a lease of some woodlands in Bromley Manor for
419 years, which was with difficulty revoked by Bishop William Wells.

We are told that Thomas Browne (or Brouns) (1435–6), the Bishop preceding Wells, resided much at Bromley during his short tenure of office. He was afterwards translated to Norwich, and was Ambassador to France in 1439.   Like so many of his predecessors I cannot connect Bishop Wells especially with our town and manor.   In 1447 (25 Henry VI) his successor, Bishop John Lowe, obtained from the King a charter for a market once a week, a renewal apparently of that granted in the time of Henry III, and for an annual fair, in addition to that already established.   These are referred to elsewhere.   My only other reference to Bromley during the remainder of the fifteenth century in connection with the Bishops of Rochester is that Bishop Richard FitzJames (1496–1503) held an Ordination there December 23rd, 1497.   He became Bishop of Chichester in 1503, and succeeded Dr. Barons as Bishop of London in 1506.   The oldest portion of Fulham Palace or Manor House dates from his time ; his arms are on the southern face of the west court of the building.

BROMLEY, THE BISHOPS AND THE PALACE FROM THE REFORMATION ONWARDS

ALTHOUGH the dwelling of the Bishops of Rochester at Bromley was called for centuries ' the Palace,' it was, in fact, an episcopal manor house, for, as the late Canon A. J. Pearman remarked in his paper entitled *Residences of the Bishops of Rochester*, " Palace in strictness applies only to a Bishop's house situated in his cathedral city." [1]   In medieval times the Bromley mansion ranked with other episcopal manor houses in Kent, at Halling, Stone, and Trottescliffe.   According to Hasted the Bishops continued occasionally to make their home at least in two of them " until some years after the Reformation; about which time these, as well as the rest of their ancient manors and mansion houses in this county excepting Bromley, were leased out by them for lives or years to different tenants." [2]

Not much of interest directly connecting the Bishops with Bromley in Tudor times has come to light.   In 1504, when John Fisher was appointed Bishop, the income attached to the see appears to have been about £500 a year.   Incidentally we know that he lived for a time in the palace at Rochester, and that when he was suffering from illness there Erasmus wrote regretting its unwholesomeness.   He also stayed at Halling, and ' La Place,' then the house of the Bishops at Lambeth, where a cook, while trying to poison him, killed various people and was barbarously executed in consequence.   It is worth while to mention that in 1507 Bishop Fisher received in Bromley parish church an act of abjuration of certain heresies and errors by one Richard Gavell from Westerham.   In 1532, three years before Fisher gained a Cardinal's cap and lost his head, a bailiff's account tells us that Bromley Park was let for no more than £6 13s. 4d. a year, and the warren produced 165 couple of rabbits valued at £8 12s.   The farmer of the estate was David Fisher, perhaps a relation of the Bishop.

In 1533 Henry VIII presented Emery Tukfold (or Tuffelde) to the rectory of Bromley, and in 1536, as appears from a patent roll, in consideration of the sum of £40, he granted to Bishop Hilsey, who had succeeded Fisher, the advowson and patronage of the rectory.   From that time the church manor, in which the Rectors as lords had held their courts, ceased to have a separate existence.

In 1550 John Poynet (or Ponet) succeeded the famous Ridley, who had been installed Bonner's successor in the bishopric of London and was martyred in 1555.   Poynet, at one time Cranmer's chaplain, was allowed to hold with his see his other church preferments, an exception being made in his favour by an order of Council dated June 29th, 1550, that is the year of his appointment, " upon consideration that he hath no house to dwell

---

[1] *Arch. Cant.* Vol. XXXIII, p. 131, 1918.
[2] E. Hasted, *Hist. Kent*, ed. 1797, Vol. IV, p. 552.

upon," [1] that in Bromley being presumably out of repair. He was translated to Winchester in 1551, and deprived on the accession of Mary, when he fled to the Continent. A supposed scandal about his marriage or marriages has come down to us, some particulars of which are given in *Notes and Queries* for June 27th, 1914.

The next Bishop, John Scory, consecrated in 1551, had been a Dominican friar, then chaplain to Cranmer, and then examining chaplain to Ridley. On his translation to Chichester, the see remained vacant for two years. Scory, being " not an oak, but a willow," recanted under Mary, but under Elizabeth he again became a Protestant, and died Bishop of Hereford.

Scory's successor at Rochester, Maurice Griffith, was recommended to the see by Queen Mary, and justified the recommendation by an active persecution of Protestants. In 1558 he died at his episcopal house in Southwark, which, when Stow wrote, forty years later, was lying " ruinous for lack of reparations."

Of John Piers, consecrated Bishop of Rochester in 1576, translated to Salisbury in the following year, Canon Pearman records that he held fourteen ordinations at Bromley.[2] He finally became Archbishop of York.

In the latter part of the sixteenth century there is nothing special to record about the mansion in our town, which, as may be gathered from what precedes, became soon after the Reformation the chief home of the Bishops of Rochester. John Yonge died there on April 10th, 1605, after holding the bishopric for twenty-seven years. The parish register gives the date of his burial, and a brass on the floor of the church nave near the pulpit has an inscription to his memory. His arms impaled with those of the see were formerly there, but have disappeared. John Buckeridge, who became Bishop of Rochester in 1611, being translated to Ely in 1628, was also buried in Bromley church. There is now no inscription to his memory, but Mr. Coles Child, in his manuscript account, gives a copy of one from the *Registrum Roffense*. The following is an extract from the burial register :

" The last of May. The Right Reverend Father in God John Buckerridge, the Lord Bp. of Ely sometime Bp. of Rochester. He left £20 for the benefit of the poor of Bromley parish."

December 14th, 1629, John Bowle was elected Bishop, and in the following year a letter among the State Papers supplies the information that " Rochester was in the summer beat from his house at Bromley by the Plague, but the Archbishop sent for him up out of Berkshire." Elsewhere in this volume mention is made of the fatalities at Bromley from that disease in the great epidemic of 1665. We are told in the *Dictionary of National Biography*, but I have not found the contemporary reference, that Bishop Bowle died

---

[1] Strype, *Eccles. Mem.*, Vol. II, p. 524.
[2] *Arch. Cant.*, Vol. XXXIII, p. 147.

" at Mrs. Austen's house on the Banckside, the 9th of October, 1637, and his body was interred in St. Paul's Church London in the moneth following." The lady must have been Anne, widow of William Austin, who died in 1633, and to whose memory there is a fantastic monument in Southwark Cathedral, then St. Saviour's parish church, also commemorating his mother, Lady Clarke. A return made by Archbishop Laud to Charles I in 1634 seems to imply censure of this prelate for remissness in the discharge of his episcopal office.[1]

We now reach a period when sources of information become much fuller than has been so far the case. From the local point of view, perhaps the most popular, at any rate the best remembered, of our Bishops from the time of the Reformation was John Warner, a native of London, son of Harman Warner, merchant tailor, who, after holding several livings, among them those of St. Michael, Crooked Lane and St. Dionis Backchurch, London, became chaplain to King Charles I, and Dean of Lichfield, and was consecrated Bishop of Rochester in 1638. The Primate, Laud, having requested a copy of a sermon by Warner, he addressed a letter to Laud from " Bromleigh " March 8th, 1639-40. Being an active loyalist, he was ejected from his see, his goods were sequestered, and, after keeping the palace against the sheriffs for some time, he had to leave Bromley in disguise. A survey of the manor, taken in 1646-7, describes the palace room by room. This will be referred to on a later page. The sequestration of Warner's property was the result of an ordinance by which the estates of Bishops, Deans, and Chapters were forfeited, and, as Mr. Child pointed out, among the Commissioners named to enforce the orders of Parliament in Kent was Augustine Skinner,[2] who, on March 1st, 1647-8, purchased the manor of Bromley. He therefore appeared in the double capacity of seller and buyer. The price paid by him was £5,665 11s. 11d.

After the Restoration Warner was one of eight surviving Bishops who again took possession of their dioceses. He was then about seventy-nine years old, having been born in 1581. According to Dr. J. R. Bloxam's *Register of Residents, etc., St. Mary Magdalen College, Oxford* (1873), p. 65, he died at Bromley Palace, October 14th, 1666, aged eighty-six. The anniversary of his death is kept at Magdalen College on the 14th, and Lee-Warner mentions that as the day " according to most accounts." On the other hand, Thomas Shindler, in his *Register of the Cathedral of Rochester* (1892), p. 65, says that the death occurred on October 21st. He was buried in St. John's Chapel, Rochester Cathedral, on the 31st; his monument there mentions the year only.

Warner, who had large private means, left by will £8,500 for the erection of the buildings of Bromley College, and a rent-charge on the

---

[1] *History of Rochester*, by W. Shrubsole and the Rev. S. Denne, 2nd ed., 1817, p. 151.

[2] Called Captain Skinner in the *Journal of the House of Lords*, Vol. X, p. 263, May 16th, 1648.

manor of Swaton in Lincolnshire (spelt by him Swayton) to provide pensions and a stipend for the chaplain.　This noble foundation is described elsewhere.　Bishop Warner also left £800 for the repair of the palace.

He had been married, but left no children, and the name of his wife is at present unknown.　Although rather outside our limitations it seems worth while to say a few words on this subject.　It has been asserted that she was Bridget, widow of Robert Abbot, Bishop of Salisbury, who died in 1617, and according to another account she was widow of George Abbot, Archbishop of Canterbury, who died in 1633 ; each statement has, however, been altogether disproved in *Notes and Queries*.　The passages are too long to quote, but the former is in the issue of August 20th, 1898, and the latter in that of December 24th of the same year.　Record Office papers show that Bishop Warner's wife was alive on December 4th, 1643, also that during his wanderings in the west country, 1643–6, he went to stay with his " wife's nearest kindred " then living at Bromfield, Shropshire, and thence with them to Ludlow, until his " new coming to London after a dangerous sickness."　On October 31st, 1908, a query appeared in *Notes and Queries*, wherein the following words are quoted from the *Diary of Dr. Thomas Foxe* [1] : " 1648, May 26th, my dear wife Ann Honywood (her maiden name, and born at Pett near Charing in Kent on Nov. 26, 1588) died at my cousin Ursula Warner her house at Bromley."　The writer, who " has reason to suspect " that this lady was the wife of the Bishop, asked for information about her, but there was no reply.

Warner's successor in the bishopric, by name John Dolben, had served first as an ensign in the King's army.　He had fought and been wounded at the battle of Marston Moor, and was afterwards so badly wounded at the siege of York that he kept his bed for a twelvemonth.　At the end of his military career he had reached the rank of major.　Having been ordained in 1656, after the Restoration he soon made his mark as an ecclesiastic, holding various important offices, among them the deanery of Westminster, which he was allowed to retain after his consecration as Bishop of Rochester in 1666.　There is a quotation in Mr. Child's manuscript describing him as " an extraordinary comely person, though grown too fat, dauntless in parliament and a fine extempore preacher."　Dolben restored Bromley Palace, doubtless applying the money left by his predecessor for that purpose. John Evelyn in his *Diary*, August 23rd, 1669, writes : " I went to visit my excellent and worthy neighbour the Lord Bishop of Rochester, at Bromley, which is now repairing, after the dilapidations of the late Rebellion."　In 1683 Dolben became Archbishop of York, being succeeded at Rochester by Francis Turner, who was translated to Ely in the following year, and was one of the seven prelates imprisoned by James II.

The next Bishop of Rochester was the well-known Thomas Sprat, appointed in 1684, who had written a history of the Royal Society which

[1] *Royal Hist. Soc. Trans.*, 1877, Vol. V, p. 58.

first appeared in 1667, and was often re-published, and an account of Cowley, the poet, for whose monument he composed the inscription. A noteworthy work of his was his reply to Sorbiere's remarks on England, 1664. Various letters addressed by him to Sir Christopher, then ' Dr.' Wren, are printed in the *Parentalia*, and as a versifier he figures in Johnson's *Lives of the Poets*. This prelate, while residing at Bromley in 1692, was the victim of a strange conspiracy, being suddenly arrested on the information of a rascal named Robert Young, who, when imprisoned in Newgate, in order to ingratiate himself with the authorities by the pretended discovery of a plot, drew up a paper for the restoration of King James, to which he appended the forged signatures of Sprat, Sancroft, Marlborough and others. He employed as his emissary one Stephen Blackhead, who took the Bishop at Bromley a letter forged by Young which purported to come from a Doctor of Divinity. Sprat was for the time deceived, and Blackhead, not being carefully watched, contrived to drop the letter into a flowerpot in a disused parlour. Young soon afterwards asked to be heard before the Privy Council on a matter of urgent importance. He told the story of the alleged plot, and messengers were sent to Bromley on May 7th, 1692, with a warrant to arrest the Bishop. The latter afterwards gave an account of the whole affair,[1] wherein he graphically described how, immediately before his arrest, he " was walking in the orchard at Bromley meditating on something " he " intended to preach the next day," when he " saw a coach and four horses stop at the outer gate, out of which two persons alighted." He was taken into custody, and his rooms were searched for the incriminating document. Young asked especially that they should examine the flowerpots. It was not then found, and after ten days he was allowed to return home. Meanwhile Young had sent Blackhead to recover the paper, which he contrived to do, and which Young's wife passed on to the Government with a cunning explanation. The Bishop was recalled, examined before the Council, and confronted with Blackhead, whom he drove to confess the truth. In consequence, Sprat was set at liberty on June 13th, 1692, and during the rest of his life he kept the anniversary as a day of thanksgiving for his deliverance. Blackhead absconded and Young was sentenced to stand thrice in the pillory. Some years afterwards he was hanged for coining. Bishop Sprat died of apoplexy at Bromley on May 20th, 1713. He was also Dean of Westminster, and was buried in the chapel of St. Nicholas, Westminster Abbey, but his monument was moved to make way for the Northumberland tomb.

Sprat was followed in the bishopric by another historic personage,

[1] It is called " A Revelation of the wicked Contrivance of Stephen Blackhead and Robert Young against the lives of several Persons, by an Association under their Hands," 1692. Macaulay says of it, " There are very few better narratives in the language, and in *Arch. Cant.*, Vol. XIII, pp. 165, 166, Dr. Beeby quotes the Bishop's account of his arrest.

P. Lely Eques Pinx. M. V. Gucht Sculp.

The Lord Bishop of Rochester

THOMAS SPRAT.
Resided at Bromley 1684–1713.

Francis Atterbury, a favourite of Queen Anne, and during the last four years of her reign one of the leading public men in England.   With the see he was allowed, like so many of his predecessors, to hold *in commendam* the deanery of Westminster ; and here it may be remarked that our Bishops often, indeed nearly always, had other preferment, the reason being that, until the readjustment of episcopal revenues by the Ecclesiastical Commissioners appointed in 1834, the see of Rochester was not only the smallest in the kingdom, but also the most poorly endowed.   I would add that the feeling against pluralities is to a large extent of modern growth.   In 1720 this prelate was imprisoned during seven months for his supposed connection with an attempt to restore the Stuarts.   On his release he was deprived of all ecclesiastical offices and banished from the realm.   He left England on June 18th, 1723, never to return.   Among Pope's miscellaneous writings are lines " on Dr. Francis Atterbury, Bishop of Rochester, who died in exile at Paris, 1732, his only daughter having expired in his arms, immediately after she arrived in Paris to see him."   In fact, he died February 17th, 1731–2 ; his body was brought to England, and privately buried in Westminster Abbey on May 12th following, in a vault which had been prepared by his direction in 1722.[1]

Atterbury's correspondence with leading literary men gives interesting glimpses of his life in Bromley.   He seems to have passed much of his time at the palace, and to have been greatly attached to it.   Writing to Pope from Bromley, May 25th, 1712, he says : " You know the motto of my sun-dial. I will, as far as I am able, follow its advice."   This motto was " Vivite, ait, fugio," and elsewhere he makes it the theme of the following Latin epigram :

> " Labentem tacito quisquis pede conspicis umbram,
>   Si sapis hæc audis : ' Vivite nam fugio.'
> Utilis est oculis, nee inutilis auribus umbra,
>   Dum tacet, exclamat, ' Vivite nam fugio.' "

The translation given by Canon Pearman falls far short of the original ; it is as follows :

> " Whoso on hushed foot mark'st the gliding shade,
>   If wise thou hearest, ' Live ye for I fly ' ;
> To eyes and ears the shadow lends its aid,
>   Silently crying, " Live ye for I fly.' " [2]

In a letter addressed to Matthew Prior, August 26th, 1718, Atterbury writes :

" My peaches and nectarines hung on the trees for you till they rotted."

[1] *History of Rochester,* by W. Shrubsole and the Rev. S. Denne, 2nd ed., 1817, p. 175.
[2] *Arch. Cant.*, Vol. XXXIII, p. 149.

In another, to Pope from Bromley, September 27th, 1721, is the following passage :

"I am now confined to my bedchamber, and the matted room where I am writing, seldom venturing to be carried down to the parlour to dinner."

He also writes to the same correspondent :

"I never part from this place [Bromley] but with regret, though I usually keep here what Mr. Cowley calls the worst of company in the world, my own."

After his imprisonment in the Tower he defended himself at the Bar of the House of Lords.   In his speech he referred to the palace incidentally thus :

"Out of a poor bishopric of £500 a year, for it was clearly worth no more to me, I did in eight years lay our £2,000 upon the house and other appurtenances, because I knew the circumstances in which my predecessor left his family I took not one shilling for dilapidations from his executors."

In the registers of Bromley parish church the burial is recorded of "Sarah Atterbury from ye College aet 83, on January 11th, 1789," and in the churchyard is the following monumental inscription :

"Sarah Atterbury, relict of the Rev. Osborn Atterbury, rector of Ox Hill, co. Warwick, died 5th January 1789, in the 88th year of her age, also Sarah Atterbury, daughter of the above, died 16th June 1820, aged 80."[1]

These were respectively daughter-in-law and granddaughter of the ill-fated Bishop.

In 1731 Joseph Wilcocks, who had been Bishop of Gloucester, succeeded Samuel Bradford as Bishop of Rochester, being installed Dean of Westminster on the same day.   It is noteworthy that later he refused the Archbishopric of York, the reason given by him being that "this church is my wife, and I will not part from her because she is poor."   In this he almost repeated expressions that had been used long before by Bishop Fisher. We are told that his "reparation of the buildings [at Bromley] and improvements of the garden and grounds, were executed with no small cost and elegance," and elsewhere that "he kept the house and gardens in remarkable neatness.   That was his constant amusement even when drawing near his end."   There is a memento of his residence there in the form of a lead cistern, having on it his name and arms, and the date 1732, which is now in

---

[1] *Monumental Inscriptions of Bromley*, by R. Holworthy, F.S.G., 1921.   The name of the parish in Warwickshire is now written Oxhill.

the garden of the present house. Wilcocks was Dean of Westminster when the upper portion of the western towers of Westminster Abbey were being built, partly from the designs of Sir Christopher Wren, supplemented by Hawksmoor. A representation of them was placed on his monument in the Abbey, his grave being under the south-west tower. His son Joseph Wilcocks was a benefactor to Bromley College.

The next Bishop was Zachary Pearce, translated from Bangor to Rochester in 1756, who also became Dean of Westminster, and with difficulty obtained leave to resign that office when, through old age, he could not satisfactorily perform the duties of both. It was said that this was the first occurrence of the kind. He wrote a poem called " The Wish, 1768, when I resigned the Deanery of Westminster." In 1761 he had also declined translation to the see of London. The late George Warde Norman recorded that Bishop Pearce used to have public days at the palace, where he entertained those of his friends and neighbours who cared to be present. A similar custom was kept up at Lambeth Palace until Archbishop Howley died in 1848, and within the present writer's memory at Wentworth Woodhouse, Yorkshire, the home of the Earl Fitzwilliam. In 1764 an Act of Parliament was passed " for extinguishing the right of common in over and upon certain commonable lands and grounds within the manor and parish of Bromley whereon the freeholders and inhabitants had right of common or common of pasture from the 10th of October to the 5th of April in every year." Mr. William Scott then held them by lease from the Bishop, and they were to be granted to him, " and all and every other person and persons who shall or may be possessed thereof," on payment of £40 a year " to the churchwardens and overseers of the poor of the parish in the porch of the church by half-yearly payments." Bishop Pearce resided occasionally at Ealing in a house which he had inherited from his father, Thomas Pearce, a retired distiller, to whose memory there is a monument in Ealing parish church. The Bishop had begun his education in a private school there.[1] He died at Ealing in 1774, aged 84, and was buried at Bromley parish church by the side of his wife, who had predeceased him. His monument is on the south side of the chancel; there is also one to him in Westminster Abbey. He left £5,000 to Bromley College. His portrait, dated 1768, by an artist named Penny, is in the college chapel. It should have been mentioned earlier that he published various theological and classical works.

In 1774 Bishop Pearce was succeeded by John Thomas, who had been chaplain to George II and George III and was already Dean of Westminster. He married first Lady Blackwell, daughter of Sir William Clayton, in whose house he had been tutor, and secondly Lady Yates, widow of a judge. Finding the old palace much dilapidated in spite of Bishop Wilcocks' repairs, he pulled it down and built the present structure in 1775–6. A tablet, dated 1792, is at the west end of the north aisle of the parish church, with an

[1] *History of Brentford, Ealing and Chiswick*, by Thomas Faulkner, 1845, pp. 200, 249.

inscription that he gave £500 towards the cost of that part of the building which was then added. Having been Rector of Blechingley in Surrey for thirty-six years (1738–74), he was buried there, and in the church register is the following entry :

" John Thomas, LL.D., Lord Bishop of Rochester, Aug. 30th, 1793."

The bust to his memory in Westminster Abbey is copied from a portrait by Sir Joshua Reynolds.

His successor was Samuel Horsley, who, besides holding various clerical offices, was Secretary of the Royal Society in 1773, became Archdeacon of St. Albans in 1781 and Bishop of St. David's in 1788, whence he was translated to Rochester with the Deanery of Westminster in 1793. He had been a friend of Dr. Johnson, a member of his Essex Head Club, and attended his funeral. He wrote a version of the Psalms, and commentaries on Isaiah and Hosea. We are told that during Horsley's residence at Bromley palace his favourite exercise was rowing, presumably in the existing pond, once part of the moat. In 1802 he was translated to St. Asaph, and he died at Brighton in 1806. It is remarked about Horsley in Birkbeck Hill's edition of Boswell's *Life of Dr. Johnson* that Gibbon " makes splendid mention of him." On the other hand, in the diary of William Windham, published in 1866, it is said that he " had his thoughts wholly turned on church preferment." That he was careless in money matters is indicated by the fact that he let a life policy of insurance for £5,000 lapse two days before his death. He spent thoughtlessly, neglected his private affairs, and accused himself of indolence. According to one critic, he had a coach with four horses, which seems extravagant, but the roads were very bad in those days.

The next Bishop was Thomas Dampier (1802), who had been Dean of Rochester for twenty years, and was translated to Ely in 1808. Educated at Eton and King's College, Cambridge, he was distinguished by his love of literature, and collected a fine library and many fine prints.

Dampier was followed by Walker King, in whose time Bromley Common was enclosed under an Act of Parliament, April 6th, 1821, which completed what had been begun in 1764. This Act, although modern feeling would be altogether against it, seems not to have been unpopular at the time. It is elaborate, containing more than eight thousand words, and has never been published, but a transcript of it was made for the present writer. The extent to be dealt with is described as about three hundred acres of " commons and waste lands," and " a certain tract of commonable or half year land called the Scrubs, containing by estimation fifty acres or thereabouts," which, for some unexplained reason, had been omitted from the previous Act. The award map and the various awards, completed and signed March 30th, 1826, are now in the parish vestry, and the municipal buildings contain duplicates. A paper on the subject entitled " Bromley

Common" appears in *Arch. Cant.*, Vol. XXXIII. The map accompanying it is being republished in the present volume. The Act fully recognises the manorial rights of the Bishop.

Another noteworthy event during Bishop King's time is that he bought for his own family a lease on lives of the rectorial manor of Bromley with the glebe and church-house, superseding George Norman, to whose father, James, it had come by marriage with Eleonora Innocent, her father having obtained them by marriage with Elizabeth, daughter of William and Eleanor or Elenor Emmett. That family had been for many years at Bromley ; I notice in the church register, among the christenings : 1668, October 18th, Thomas, son of Tho⁵ Emmett, and among burials :

"1670. April 26, Thomas the sonn of Thomas Emmett ; and 1670, Jan. 11, Thomas Emmet [*sic*] of ye Towne of Bromley."

An interesting baptism is that (November 19th, 1731) of John, son of Basden Drury Tytheman to Mr. Emmett.

Bishop King had considerable differences of opinion with parishioners about the workhouse and on other local matters, but I have not made a special study of this subject. According to Freeman the grounds of the palace were reduced to a disordered state in consequence of his seldom visiting it.[1] In 1823 he gave £3,000 to the College, with the object of paying pensions to three widows. He died at Wells, February 22nd, 1827. His descendants retained an interest in the tithes for many years and were compensated or bought out by the Ecclesiastical Commissioners. There is an inscription in Bromley church to a son and daughter of his, both of whom died young. A grandson was Edward King, Archdeacon of Rochester. Another descendant, the Rev. James King, has been described as " an excellent parish priest, albeit a hunting man."

The next Bishop of Rochester, by name Hugh Percy, who has a short notice in the *Dictionary of National Biography*, only held the bishopric for a few months, being translated to Carlisle.

In October 1827 Percy was succeeded by George Murray, who had been Bishop of Sodor and Man and who became ninety-sixth in the list of the Bishops of Rochester, and the last residing at Bromley Palace. He was grandson of the third Duke of Atholl, and son of Lord George Murray, Bishop of St. David's. As remarked again and again, the bishopric of Rochester was a very poor one, and Murray, according to the then custom, held another ecclesiastical office, being nominated Dean of Worcester in 1828 ; he generally spent part of the year in Worcester. He married Lady Sarah Maria Hay, daughter of the ninth Earl of Kinnoull, and had a large family. One of his sons was the late Canon Francis Henry Murray of Chislehurst, another was that distinguished public servant Sir Herbert

[1] *History of the Parish of Bromley*, by C. Freeman, 1832, p. 16.

Harley Murray, K.C.B., sometime Governor of Newfoundland. Among the Bishop's descendants are the Marquess Camden, Lord Hampton, and the Rt. Hon. Sir George Herbert Murray, G.C.B. It may be mentioned without offence, as a record of conditions that have long ceased, that when the third Duke of Atholl disposed of his sovereignty or lordship of the Isle of Man to the Crown, he retained the right of nomination to the bishopric of Sodor and Man. It became vacant when George Murray was twenty-nine and a half years old. According to the ordinal in the Book of Common Prayer, " Every man which is to be ordained or consecrated Bishop shall be thirty years of age," and in 1814 he was appointed by his cousin the fourth Duke. I would add that he was a man of fine presence and much beloved, who acquired great influence which he always exercised for good.

In 1845 a scheme was launched by the Ecclesiastical Commissioners involving drastic changes in the diocese of Rochester. The Commissioners recommended the purchase of an estate at Danbury near Chelmsford in Essex for the future residence of the Bishops, and the sale of the manor and palace of Bromley of which, as mentioned elsewhere, the late Mr. Coles Child became purchaser, with fairs, market and other franchises, as well as the greater part of the demesne lands which had hitherto been held by the Bishops. In the *History of Bromley*, published by E. Strong in 1858, the writer describes " the despair that pervaded the town at the time it was first known that the Bishop of Rochester [1] was about to leave the Palace," and alludes to " the fatherly interest " which he took " in the temporal " and " spiritual welfare of the people of Bromley," the benefit to trade by the numerous visitors to the palace being also enlarged on. The Rev. Thomas Scott, chaplain of the College, bewailed *the lost Bishop and his deserted Palace*, in a rhymed effusion published on All Saints' Day, 1845, which marks equally his regrets and his utter lack of any poetic gift. Our readers perhaps will need no more than the following extract, a fair sample of the whole :

> " Toll we our bell ! our Bishop we deplore !
> Bromley can boast her Bishop now no more.
> No longer now we see our Bishop's face
> Our shops and streets with friendly smiles to grace."

Bromley was for a time excluded from the diocese of Rochester, and joined to that of Canterbury, but was afterwards restored. The Bishops have changed their dwelling again and again since they left a place with which they had been associated since Saxon times.

---

[1] Murray was one of the last of the Bishops who wore an episcopal wig ; he died in 1860. A portrait of him with a wig appeared in the *District Times*, February 12th, 1920. Archbishop Sumner is known to have preached in one as late as 1859 ; Mr. Weeks remembers his doing so in Bromley church.

GEORGE MURRAY, LORD BISHOP OF ROCHESTER 1827-1860.
From the collection of engravings at the National Portrait Gallery.

WHAT precedes has related chiefly to the connection of the Bishops with the palace and manor of Bromley. I will now mention a few facts about the actual building, which, as recorded elsewhere, before the Reformation, and for the first few years afterwards, was merely a manor house, occupied from time to time like others in the diocese. Whether there had been an episcopal residence here from Saxon times onwards, or if it had been first built by Gundulf, is mere matter of conjecture. We know that it was reconstructed by Bishop Glanvill towards the end of the twelfth century, and that in 1550 it was not thought suitable to dwell in, but no detailed account of the structure has come to light before the Parliamentary Survey of 1646–7. A copy of this was lately given by Mr. E. Latter to the Bromley Public Library, and Mr. Baxter supplied interesting extracts from it to the *Bromley District Times* of January 7th, 1927. For the present purpose it is advisable to transcribe verbatim the description of the palace, and the building and lands immediately attached to it, with a few supplementary references.

The Survey was made or completed on February 22nd, 1646–7,[1] by " Edward Boys Esqre, Daniel Shettenden Esqre, Ralph Watts Gent^n, and George Northcott Gent^n," with the assistance of a jury of fifteen, and from it we learn that the " Manor or Manson House " then contained :

" belowe stayres one greate new Hall being builte parte of Bricks parte of timbre, one Little Hall, one Wainscott parlour, Two Studyes, One Buttery, Two Kitchings, One Larder, and three other Roomes adjoyninge, being builte parte of flinte parte of Timber and Morter, Above the staires seaven lodging roomes and one faire Dyning Roome with six garretts above. Item one washhouse with two chambers over it. Two Barnes thatched, One Outhouse contayninge one wainscott Chappell one Lower roome & two Chambers overhead.

" Item one Courte yearde at the entry into the mansion house encompassed East and West with a Brick wall North & South with the Mansion House & Chappell. All which premises are in reasonable good reparation except the Stables & Barnes which wanted a little Tyling & Thatching.

" Item, one Orchar & Garden belonging thereunto. All which premises are moated & paled about, All within the moate contayninge Two acres or thereabouts. Item one Greate Barne thatched with a yard before it paled about, fower fish ponds at the heade of each other with a continuall springe to feede them."

[1] The document is dated 1646. This was according to the " Old Style," when the year began on March 25th. The " New Style " (or Gregorian Calendar, so called after Pope Gregory XIII), with the year beginning on January 1st, was not adopted in England until 1752. Obviously according to this—our modern method of reckoning—the date of the Survey was 1647.

Further we are told that the house is less than a quarter of a mile from Bromley, a market town through which a great road runs from London to Rye, and " that it is usually the summer seate of the Bishopps of Rochester." There is a row of walnuts before it, and all this is valued at an annual rent of £25. Then follows a valuation of other portions of the manor, which were, or had been, privately occupied by the Bishop. For instance, " one parke before the House contayninge by estimason beside the fish ponds sixteen acres " ; the Middle park of thirty acres, the Tower fields of thirty acres towards Mason's Hill, and " the Beechfield containing seventeen acres or thereabouts " ; all described as " gravelly and broomy," recalling the plant which gave a name to our manor. It still grows on the banks of the railway cutting by the South Bromley Railway Station.

In that portion of the Survey which is fully quoted above there are two or three rather important items. The description of the house indicates that it was a large one, in all likelihood considerably larger than the present building, and we may assume that it stood in part at least more to the south, where, as will be mentioned later, various foundations of chalk and flint have been found. Again, here is contemporary evidence that the moat still existed, enclosing a space of about two acres. We learn also that there was a forecourt, with a wall on each side, the chapel opposite to the mansion, and the rooms connected with it, forming no doubt a gatehouse, approached originally by a drawbridge, the foundations of which, consisting of a rude mass of flint and chalk cemented together by hard mortar, were found by Mr. Child " about forty-five yards north of the present house." [1] At the end of the Survey of the mansion and the part of the manor specially attached to it, the precise dimensions of which are given, we are told that all the " said several pieces or parcells of land are in the tenure or occupation of the said Bishop of Rochester, or in the occupation of the Sequestrators for the Lathe of Sutton at Home [*sic*]."

It has been pointed out by Hasted that generally, not long after the Reformation, the episcopal manors and manor houses in the Rochester diocese " were leased out for lives or years to different tenants." [2]

Although the mansion at Bromley continued to be occupied by the Bishops, this Survey also shows that in 1646–7 outside his precinct no less than three hundred acres of manorial land were held by John Younge of Milton in Oxfordshire, having been leased on three lives to his father, of the same Christian name, by Bishop Warner's predecessor. It was to Younge that a number of persons described as freeholders paid their annual quit rents, among them (to descend to minutiæ) Sir Humphrey Style "for Simpson's Place one pound six shillings and two pence halfpenny," and " for the Bell in the use of Daniel Giles, three shillings and four pence." Mr. William Scott appears to have been in a similar position when the Bromley Common Act

---

[1] *Arch. Cant.*, Vol. XIII, pp. 153, 154.
[2] E. Hasted, *Hist. Kent*, ed. 1797, Vol. IV, p. 552.

of 1764 was passed. It is an interesting fact that among the jurors was 'Mich. Warner, Gent,' perhaps related to the Bishop. Another possible relative, Ursula Warner, is mentioned as residing in Bromley, on page 85 of this volume.

It has been pointed out that in March 1647–8 the episcopal property was sold to Augustine Skinner; but, by some means, Bishop Warner stayed on for nearly a year afterwards, or somehow kept his hold of the mansion, in spite of his wanderings, about which we are told elsewhere, for, according to an order of the Lords and Commons, reported in the *Journal of the House of Lords*, Vol. X, p. 217, on April 20th, 1648, the sheriff of Kent was enjoined to remove the Bishop from the manor house, and to deliver it to Skinner. From this and from the statements of Hasted and other writers on Bromley it seems clear that the last-named bought the whole estate, and the bulk of it remained in his hands, or in those of his family, till the Restoration, but Mr. Lee-Warner records that, in compliance with "an ordinance of Parliament A.D. 1648," the *palace* was sold on September 27th, 1649, for £557 to C. Bowles and N. Andrews.[1] The original purchaser must therefore have resold this part of the property. There is then another reference to the rooms there, which does not altogether agree with the report of the Survey of 1646–7, or supplements it. Mention is made of

" one great messuage where the Court is held, four rooms, a gallery divided into two rooms, four chambers, the ward, a prison, washhouse, kitchen and three rooms, with an orchard and garden."

This does not tell us much, but the existence of a prison and of what had been a long gallery are interesting. There was a prison attached to the episcopal palace at Rochester, and the Rev. T. S. Frampton in *A Glance at the Hundred of Wrotham*, 1881, mentions a prison that belonged to the Bishops at Halling. Details of the repair by Bishop Dolben cannot now be found.

In 1699 Bishop Sprat obtained leave from the Archbishop of Canterbury to demolish the chapel and gatehouse of the palace, and they are thus reported on:

" It is an old piece of building which is the gatehouse to the said house, and at the entrance on the left hand is a roome which hath been used for the Chappell, which Chappelle is in length, including the outward roome at the entrance—24 feete and in bredth including a closett on the south side— used for servants, 18 feet. The said Chappell is wainscotted 8 foote high with oake wainscott, with old fashioned little pannells. The roof of the

---

[1] *Life of John Warner, Bishop of Rochester*, by Edward Lee-Warner, 1901, p. 38. It is worth while to note that in the same year (1649) the same pair, Bowles and Andrews, bought the Bishop's palace at Rochester for an almost identical price, namely, £556 13s. 4d. See *Arch. Cant.*, Vol. XXXIII, p. 133.

chappell, by reason of the Gatehouse, is uneven, not all of a higth. On the right of the entrance at the Gate is a roome used for a porter or a gardener. There is no chimney in the said Building, and the dwellinghouse is distant from the said Building the length of the Courtyard." [1]

It is evident from this report that the chapel must have been extremely cold in winter. Query, were some of the " little pannells " afterwards used in the hall or passage and one room of the house lately occupied by Dr. Herbert Ilott at the north corner of Bromley High Street and Church Road, now pulled down ? They belonged to the late sixteenth or early seventeenth century.

The Bishop proposed to make a new chapel in the house " one pair of stairs high," which must surely mean on the first floor. The suggested chapel was viewed and found to be 39 feet long, " divided by a partition which makes the inner chapel to be 25 feet 6 inches long, and the outward chappell for servants 13 feet 6 inches long," the whole being 20 feet wide. The chapel was to be made " very decent " with an altar and rails. We are told that " the inner part is wainscotted the higth of the wall." The Bishop intended to panel the outer or ante-chapel with wainscot (presumably the small panels) from the old chapel. Mr. George Oxenden, who drew up the report to the Archbishop, said that in his opinion this would be much more convenient than the old chapel, which being detached could not suitably be used in bad weather, and also hindered the view from the main building. The last remark, by the by, would apply to any gatehouse.

Our engraving of the old palace as it was before 1756, reproduced from that in the folio edition of Hasted's *History of Kent*, shows an irregular building of various ages, the greater part of it, to judge from the mullions and transoms of the windows, being perhaps Tudor. A gabled portion to the left, its gable and pilasters being surmounted by vase-like ornaments, appears to be more modern or reconstructed. The upper part of this may quite likely be Bishop Sprat's chapel approved by the Archbishop and consecrated in 1701. On the opposite side of the house is an avenue which would lead to the main entrance. In the foreground to the left are figures, one of which is perhaps meant for the then Bishop.

If Horace Walpole may be believed, the structure in its last years was not an imposing one, but he is hardly a safe guide. On August 5th, 1752, being then at " Battel," he writes as follows to Richard Bentley, son of the famous scholar :

" While they were changing horses at Bromley we went to see the Bishop's palace, not for the sake of anything that was to be seen, but because

---

[1] Copied from *Tenison's Register*, Vol. I, ff. 126, 127. Lambeth College Library. See also Dr. Beeby's paper, *Arch. Cant.*, Vol. XIII, p. 155, where, however, the report is not given verbatim.

there was a chimney in which had stood a flower-pot, in which was put the counterfeit plot against Bishop Sprat. 'Tis a paltry parsonage, with nothing but two panes of glass purloined from Islip's chapel in Westminster Abbey, with that Abbot's rebus, an eye and a slip of a tree. In the garden there is a little clear pond teaming with fish. The Bishop is more prolific than I." [1]

Another pane of glass with the Islip rebus is, or was, at Cassiobury House, Herts, the seat of the Earls of Essex. It is mentioned in *Notes and Queries*, March 10th, 1923.

The present brick mansion with stone dressings is a good example of a building of Bishop Thomas's time. On the pediment in front are the Bishop's arms impaling those of the see, and the date 1775. The chimney-piece in what was the library also has these arms. It has been thought, by Canon Pearman [2] among others, that the chapel to the left of the main entrance of the present house has survived from the former building, but the fact that it is on the ground floor is against this idea, and it does not agree in any way with the chapel consecrated in 1701, as described in Mr. Oxenden's report. Its north or outer wall, with sash windows, is externally like the rest of the building, nor does the inside show any sign of being older than the latter half of the eighteenth century. The existing colonnade or verandah at the back of the house, facing the ornamental water, was added by the late Mr. Coles Child, also a porch containing modern stained glass and a kitchen. There is a pretty dovecote in the garden apparently of the date of Thomas's rebuilding.

It would probably now be impossible to make out the plan of the old palace, which must have been rebuilt or added to again and again. All information available has already been given about the forecourt, the former chapel, and drawbridge in front. Mr. Coles Child found, not long after he became owner, that " it was impossible to open the ground to the south without meeting with foundation walls, the lower portions of which were constructed of blocks of chalk." [3] Relics, maybe, of the time of de Glanvill, of Gundulf, possibly in part of even earlier occupation.

It was surrounded by a moat, which, towards the end of the seventeenth or in the early eighteenth century, was partly filled up, what remained being widened, and formed into an ornamental pond. Through a valley near the house flows a branch of the Ravensbourne, once nearly as important as the main stream, although, as far as I am aware, it never had a name. Its sources are chiefly in Holwood Park, it flows through the garden of the house called Hollydale, and the ponds of the Plough Inn and the Cherry Orchard, and it used to have some accession from the Crofton Woods and from Blackbrook. It receives the overflow from the palace pond, and,

[1] *Letters of Horace Walpole, fourth Earl of Orford*, edited by Peter Cunningham, chronologically arranged, 1891, Vol. II.
[2] *Arch. Cant.*, Vol. XXXIII, p. 146.   [3] *Arch. Cant.*, Vol. XIII, p. 153.

North Front.

South Front.

THE BISHOP'S PALACE, BROMLEY.
Built by Bishop Thomas, 1775.

after passing under the high road between Mason's Hill and Bromley, joins the Ravensbourne a little farther south-west. The point of junction is now covered over, and both watercourses have sadly degenerated. The park or paddock to the north, as well as the farm and its lands on the south and south-east, which were lately attached to the palace, are now being built over, but the mansion itself, with the garden and some acres, remains intact, and is now used for the purposes of a girls' school, the head mistress being a Belgian lady, Mlle. Rossignon.

ST. BLAISE'S WELL, BROMLEY

AS to the famous well associated with the palace, Hasted says [1] :

"There is a well in the bishop's grounds near his garden called St Blaze's well, which, having great resort to it antiently, on account of its medicinal virtues, had an oratory attached to it dedicated to that saint. It was particularly frequented at Whitsuntide on account of forty days injoined penance, to such as would visit this chapel, and offer up their orisons in it, the three holy days of Penticost. This oratory falling to ruin at the Reformation, the well too came to be disused, and the scite of both in process of time became totally forgotten."

The well of chalybeate water close to the pond was described in 1756 by Thomas Reynolds, surgeon. His pamphlet, now of great rarity, of which I have a copy, is mostly devoted to an analysis of the water and an account of various experiments connected with it, but gives the following details :

"It was discovered in September, 1754, by the Reverend Mr. Harwood, his lordship's domestick chaplain, by means of a yellow ochrey sediment remaining in the track of a small current leading from the spring to the corner of the moat, with the waters of which it used to mix. It is very probable that this spring has been formerly frequented, for in digging about it there were found the remains of steps leading down to it made of oak plank, which appeared as if they had lain underground a great many years. "When his Lordship was acquainted that the Water of this Spring had been examined and found to be a good Chalybeat, he, with great humanity, immediately ordered it to be secured from the mixture of other waters, by skilful workmen, and enclosed in a circular brick-work [2] like the top of a well ; in hopes that it might prove beneficial, as a medicine, to such as should think fit to drink it. This order was speedily and effectually executed, and the Water not only secured but the access to it made very commodious to the Public, by the generous care, and under the inspection of Mr. Wilcox his Lordship's son. And their benevolent intentions have already been answered with success : for great numbers of people, of all conditions, but chiefly of the midling and poorer sort, drink daily of this excellent Water, many of whom have been remarkably relieved from various infirmities and diseases, which were not only afflicting but dangerous."

Hasted also mentions the steps leading down to the well, perhaps copying from Reynolds. The latter gave up his profession, and lived in the

---

[1] E. Hasted, *History of Kent*, I, 551, ed. 1797. Lysons in his *Environs of London* adds that the remittances of penance were granted by Lucas, legate of Pope Sixtus IV (1471–84).

[2] In the list of " typographical errors " he alters this to " stone-work."

neighbourhood of Bromley for the express purpose of drinking the waters instead of those of Tunbridge Wells, which place he had before been in the habit of visiting.

Hone's *Table Book*, 1827–8, Vol. II, pp. 65–8, contains an account of what he calls the " Bishop's Well." He describes it as trickling through an orifice at the side to increase the water of a moat or small lake. Above the well was then a roof of thatch supported by six pillars, of which he gives an illustration. Mr. Coles Child replaced it by a tiled roof which was broken down in a snowstorm of 1887. The well remains intact, but the overflow of water is hardly perceptible ; the existence of iron in it is shown by a yellowish deposit. Following the line of the last pond filled up by Sir Coles Child, namely, that nearest the moat, is a ditch running more or less north and south, along which clean surface-water occasionally flows. When I visited the palace grounds on April 13th, 1928, this was trickling over artificial rock-work close to the head of the moat into which it found its way. Hard by is St. Blaise's well so called, and from a westerly direction water with a yellow tinge was also percolating ; although from quite another source, it looked like that of the well.

St. Blaise, with whom the well is commonly associated, was, according to tradition, Bishop of Sebaste in Armenia, and was martyred in 316 during the persecution of Licinues. He was patron saint of wool-combers because his flesh was said to have been torn by iron combs. A paper on him was read by Mr. H. Ling Roth before the Society of Antiquaries, December 3rd, 1914, and is printed in their *Proceedings*, 2nd ser., Vol. XXVII, with many illustrations. The late Mr. Leland L. Duncan, F.S.A., M.V.A., mentioned the image of St. Blaise in Bromley Church in his *Churches of West Kent, their Dedications, Altars, &c*. In 1456 Thomas Ferby, for promoting a clandestine marriage in St. Paul's Cray Church, was excommunicated, and had to present a wax taper of a pound weight at the image of St. Blaise in Bromley Church and in Chislehurst Church, and for two years to allow exhibitions to two scholars at Oxford. Again, in 1458, Walter Crepehog, who had promoted an illegal marriage, was ordered to be whipped three times round the market-place at Rochester, and, with other penalties, to present a torch to the value of 6s. 8d. to the image of St. Blaise at Bromley.

An early connection of St. Blaise with our town is set forth in a Charter Roll, 25 and 26 Henry VI, No. 22. A translation of it is given in another part of this volume, but it may be well to remind our readers that a fair " on the vigil the day and the morrow of St. James the Apostle " was then established, notwithstanding the fact that there was already a fair on " the day and morrow of *St. Blaise*."

The saint was popular in Kent, which was a wool-producing county. There are still slight remains of a church, or rather chapel, dedicated in his honour in a detached portion of Aylesford parish, and Mr. Duncan found that at least thirteen churches contained images or altars associated with him

ST. BLAISE'S WELL.

COTTAGES, WIDMORE LANE.
In 1761 part of the White Horse Inn.

in our side of the county. The tradition that the parish church (of St. Peter and St. Paul) at Bromley was originally dedicated to St. Blaise appears to be quite unfounded.

The ancient chapel of St. Blaise in the south transept of Westminster Abbey was once famous. It was used as a vestry, and for other purposes after the Dissolution and finally destroyed. An informing article about this chapel by Henry Poole, master mason of the Abbey, is in *The Antiquary*, Vol. III, p. 241. His plan shows it immediately north of the chapel of St. Faith, with which it is still sometimes confused. An early fourteenth-century stained-glass window with the head of St. Blaise is in Wells Cathedral.

Many years ago there was a controversy about the true site of St. Blaise's well. On June 14th, 1862, the late Mr. Robert Booth Latter, a much-respected inhabitant of Bromley, who had no mean claims as an archæologist, in agreement with others published a letter to the effect that he could find nothing in any history to warrant the conjecture that the chalybeate spring close to the pond was St. Blaise's well, and he believed that the true site was " at the head of the large upper pond now drained off, in springy ground, not far south of the huge oak tree blown down about three years since in the paddock in front of the palace." He also spoke of " about four courses of circular brickwork," indicating apparently the top of a well, having been removed from there some time previously by Mr. Child. The latter replied contending that the well near the moat has curative properties, and that the description of old oak steps found in 1754 justifies the belief that it was ancient. The other well was " 317 yards away and contained perfectly pure water." He also quoted John Dunkin, who, in his *History of Bromley*, 1815,[1] after mentioning that, in spite of what had been written by Reynolds and Hasted, St. Blaise's well was believed by Wilson [2] to be about 200 yards N.W. of the mineral spring in a field near the road with eight oak trees in a cluster, on an elevated spot of ground adjoining," wrote as follows: " I have been informed that the present Bishop is of the same opinion, *though to me this well appears to have been originally designed to supply the adjoining moat.* Besides I conceive an additional argument in favour of the mineral well may be drawn from the ignorance of the age, as the clergy could not fail to ascribe any benefit derived from this water to the special interference of the saint." It should be added that the late Canon Francis H. Murray of Chislehurst, who had passed much of his boyhood at the palace, in a note addressed to the *Bromley Record* expressed his agreement with Mr. Latter, but without strengthening his case by producing any fresh evidence.

On May 12th, 1916, through the kindness of Sir Coles Child, I had the opportunity of examining a brick reservoir in the paddock some distance north of the palace, which formerly supplied the ornamental pond or moat with pure water. It was rather below the present ground-level, and was

---

[1] *History and Antiquities of Bromley*, by J. Dunkin, 1815, p. 14, note.
[2] *Bromley and Five Miles Round*, by Thomas Wilson, 1797, p. 24.

then roofless and dry. The measurements were: length about ten feet, width four feet, and depth eight to nine feet, the ground plan being oblong. The bricks composing the upper part were of no great age, those below looked older, perhaps from being covered with a mossy growth. Sir Coles Child pointed out more than one inlet which had communicated with springs in the neighbourhood, and an orifice for the outlet, whence, as he assured me, the water formerly flowed by a pipe into the uppermost of three ponds on the north, within the palace grounds. These were connected, and the lowest fed the moat. He believes that they were all in a direct line between the moat and Widmore Road. The uppermost or most northern pond had been filled in before his time, but there is, or was, a depression in the ground which he has always thought to have marked the site. Sir Coles Child himself filled in the others. The pond nearest the moat is shown in the Ordnance Survey plan of 1898. It seems almost certain that in medieval times these ponds had supplied fish for the mansion. In 1918 the Rector of Trottescliffe, in answer to an inquiry, wrote telling me of " tench ponds " remaining near what appears to be a seventeenth- or early eighteenth-century structure, now a farmhouse, on the site of the episcopal manor house at Trottescliffe. It will be recalled that in the Parliamentary Survey of Bromley palace and the grounds attached to it, which took place in 1646, *four* fishponds are mentioned.

Many years ago, building operations having taken place on the Widmore Road, to the north, the water from the reservoir partially failed. To supplement it a well was then sunk nearer the Widmore Road. When. later, the road was widened, the modern well was inadvertently filled up by the Borough Council. They cleared it at the request of the owner, and it then continued to supply the moat through a pipe following the line of the old ponds, and produced a flow of fresh spring water, even in the driest season. What has happened since the present operations began I am not in a position to record. The brick reservoir which I saw has been obliterated.

The question still unsolved is the original site of St. Blaise's well and oratory. I have merely put together what I can find of existing evidence. It is inadequate, as there is no contemporary record helping us as to its exact position, and the foundations of the chapel or oratory have never been found; but perhaps most people will share the late Mr. Coles Child's belief, and that of John Dunkin, in the existing well by the moat, or at least that the spring was of similar kind, on account of its curative properties. Perhaps what appears to have been a well on the site indicated by Mr. R. B. Latter had at one time helped to supply water to the ponds which in turn fed the moat.

BROMLEY PARISH CHURCH, FROM S.W.

Chapter VII

EXCURSUS ON THE DATE OF ITS FOUNDATION

BEFORE tracing the history of Bromley Parish Church, something in the nature of an excursus seems to be required on the question of the original foundation of a church in Bromley. Did any such church exist in pre-Norman times ? Or was it originally a Norman structure dating from a time subsequent to the Domesday Survey (1086) ?

It is natural that those who are most keenly interested in the antiquities of the town should desire to establish the existence of a church at the earliest possible date. Those, on the other hand, who can only see their way to rely upon unquestioned documentary evidence accept the silence of Domesday Book as to a church in Bromley as sufficient proof that at the time of the Domesday Survey no such church existed.

These contending views not only afford an interesting subject of antiquarian controversy, but they open up also a field of investigation into early church history. The aim of this excursus is merely to present the arguments on both sides, leaving it to the reader to form his own judgment from such materials as are available.

The first documentary indication that a church existed in Bromley is to be found in a record that, about forty years after Domesday, Bromley was assessed in the sum of nine pence for Chrism rent, this being a tribute paid by a parish church to the Bishop of the diocese in return for the consecrated oil used for baptisms. The payment of such a rent therefore implies the existence of a parish church in which baptisms were administered.

As no mention of such a church occurs in Domesday, the inference may be drawn that Bromley Church originated somewhere within the period of forty years following the Domesday Survey.

The supporters of an earlier date, however, can bring forward conclusive proof that, in the county of Kent alone, several churches existed before Domesday which are not mentioned in that Survey. East Peckham, Barfreston, Darenth, and Ville of St. Martin, Canterbury, are instances in point, attested by the authority of the Rev. S. W. Wheatley, F.S.A., Vicar of St. Margaret's, Rochester. Therefore the silence of Domesday cannot be regarded as conclusive against the existence of a parish church in Bromley in pre-Norman times.

It is further urged that Bishop Gundulf, who built himself a palace at Bromley, and whose architectural enthusiasm still finds expression in the Tower of London, Rochester Castle, and other buildings, would scarcely have been contented to leave his manor of Bromley without a church. Moreover, churches commonly originated in connection with manors. The manor of Bromley dates back to at least A.D. 967. Is it likely to have been without a church for nearly a century or even longer ? On the other hand, the population of Bromley in Gundulf's time was very small, and if, as is asserted, there was already a chapel, dedicated to St. Blaise, within the precincts of the Bishop's palace, is it not probable that all the devotional requirements of the people were amply satisfied by the existence of that chapel ? This suggestion carries with it the authority of Dr. W. T. Beeby. If, however, the contention that the supposed chapel was only a shrine is correct, Dr. Beeby's suggestion falls to the ground.

Fresh light has recently been thrown upon this question by the recent investigations of Mr. B. F. Davis among the records at Rochester. Mr. Davis asserts that the fact that the Bishop's palace at Bromley did at one time possess a chapel dedicated to St. Blaise is irrefutably established by reference to the *Registrum Roffense*, or Register of the Bishops of Rochester. The early Registers were destroyed in the thirteenth century, but are complete from 1310 onwards. From them we learn that Bishop Hamo de Hethe had "his chapel of St. Blaise in his Manor of Bromley" wherein he held ordinations, ordinary services, and from which he issued decrees. The Church of St. Peter and St. Paul at Bromley is also mentioned at the same time in connection with ordinations held by the Bishop.

In September 1332 there is reference to a Mass celebrated in the chapel of the manor.

The phrase " in capella sua (Sancti Blasii) in manerio suo de Bromlegh " often occurs, sometimes the name of the saint being added, sometimes omitted.

If, then, the Register, from the moment it is available, affords conclusive proof that a chapel of St. Blaise existed, it is not unreasonable to surmise that the earlier Registers, which were destroyed, would have proved its existence from very early times. And, as we know that it was used for ordinary services, the celebration of Mass, and for ordinations from the time we first hear of it, we may suppose that it always had been so used in the days of which the record is missing.

Such a chapel might well have served in lieu of a church while Bromley was sparsely populated, and generally in a very primitive state.

There still remains to be considered a further argument, based upon the investigations of Bishop Browne, late Bishop of Bristol, and President of the Society of Antiquaries, and drawn from the dedication of Bromley Church to the joint saints, Peter and Paul.

In a series of lectures, published by the S.P.C.K. in 1919, Bishop Browne included two on " The Cultus of St. Peter and St. Paul." In these two lectures the Bishop set out to show that the peculiar cultus of St. Peter as the sole and superior founder of the Catholic Church was not definitely established until the ninth century. The peculiar boast of the Roman Church in early centuries was that it alone, among primitive churches in the West, could claim two apostles, and those the greatest, St. Peter and St. Paul, as joint founders, that Rome was the scene of the martyrdom of both, and still contained the sepulchres in which their martyred bodies were entombed. Accordingly, until the eighth and ninth centuries, when the claim of the Popes to universal supremacy over the Church grew to be generally accepted in the West—a claim based on the promises and charges given by Christ to St. Peter—St. Peter and St. Paul figured as of equal dignity and importance in the estimation of the Roman Church. Dedications of churches in their joint names were frequent, while dedications to either of the two singly were rare. With the publication of the False Decretals a tendency gradually grew to drop St. Paul from his position of joint dignity with St. Peter, and dedications to the two saints in combination became much less frequent. By an investigation of 433 dedications of ancient churches in the county of Kent, Bishop Browne established his contention by some remarkable figures. Of these churches, he found 101 dedicated to the Virgin, 61 to St. Peter and St. Paul jointly, and only 1 to St. Peter singly, and 1 to St. Paul singly.

From the facts thus collected an inference may be drawn that a joint dedication indicates an early foundation. But Bishop Browne has been careful, in a private letter to the writer, to insist that an inference is not a certainty. " The nearest answer I can give," says the Bishop, " to your leading question is that a dedication to St. Peter and St. Paul, as also a dedication to All Saints, is in itself a strong suggestion of pre-Norman date." He is also of opinion that the absence of record, in Domesday, of a church at Bromley is not conclusive against there being a Peter and Paul there before the Conquest—but, continues the Bishop, " ' *Sub judice lis est*,' and I doubt if there is a Judex."

The question, however, has been raised whether the original dedication of Bromley Church was to St. Peter and St. Paul. In Wilson's *Description of Bromley*, published in 1797, he states that he had met with a very old account which says the church was originally dedicated to St. Blaise, while another authority, Bishop Thomas Dampier, maintained that the original dedication was to St. James, in view of the fact that the ancient Bromley Fair was fixed to be held on St. James's Day. Dunkin, in his *History of Bromley*, regrets that Wilson has not named the authority for the supposition of a dedication to St. Blaise, as he himself in his investigations had never come across anything to support it. As for Bishop Dampier's contention, " I consider," says Dunkin, " the mode of arguing very inconclusive."

The arguments, therefore, when summarised, stand thus :

1. No church at Bromley is mentioned in Domesday ; therefore no church existed at that time.

But many churches are known to have existed in pre-Norman times which are not mentioned in Domesday. Therefore the silence of Domesday is not a conclusive proof that there was no church in Bromley before the Conquest.

2. Gundulf, with his enthusiasm for building, was not likely to have allowed Bromley to remain without a church.

But Gundulf built a palace at Bromley, which very possibly included within its precincts a chapel affording sufficient accommodation for the public worship of those times.

3. The joint dedication to St. Peter and St. Paul may be taken to imply, on ecclesiastical grounds, a pre-Norman origin for Bromley Church.

But it is asserted that the original dedication was not to St. Peter and St. Paul, but to some other saint—St. Blaise, or possibly St. James. For this assertion, however, no evidence is forthcoming. "*Sub judice lis est.*" But the final "*Judex*" has yet to appear.

SECTION I. THE STRUCTURE

THE existing parish church of Bromley, though suggestive by its appearance, apart from its massive tower, of a comparatively modern date, yet bears traces, both external and internal, of an ancient lineage. It is in fact the direct descendant of a previous church, possibly Norman, erected on the same site. There is no reason to doubt the truth of the tradition that from the first the church at Bromley was dedicated jointly to St. Peter and St. Paul, but when a church was first erected remains a matter of controversy. If any church existed in Saxon times no visible traces of it remain, though excavation and a close examination of the masonry might make visible much which is now hidden.

And even of the supposed original Norman church nothing survives except the basin of the font, an ancient block of carved Bethersden marble in which for more than seven hundred years the children of Bromley have been baptised. The church, being regarded as an appendage to the Bishop's manor of Bromley, was doubtless served from the first by Rectors appointed by the Bishops of Rochester, but the first recorded Rector of Bromley was Richard de Wendover, who held that office from 1226 to 1238. By that time the position of Rector of Bromley was evidently one of some importance and carried with it an augury of further distinction. For Wendover left Bromley in order to become himself Bishop of Rochester, and upon his death, in 1250, his body, by the King's express command, was buried in Westminster Abbey.

It is generally assumed that the church in which Richard de Wendover ministered was the Norman structure, the existence of which is presupposed. It must, however, be emphasised that this presupposition rests only on two pieces of evidence—the one positive, the other negative—neither of which can be regarded as conclusive. The church possesses, and has possessed from time immemorial, a Norman font. But a single block of marble carved to a Norman design, of the origin of which nothing whatever is known, is a slight foundation on which to rest the existence of an entire Norman church. The negative evidence has been shown in the excursus to be equally open to question. That evidence can be summarised in the form of a syllogism. No church in Bromley is mentioned in Domesday : therefore no church existed at that time. A church is known to have existed within forty years of Domesday : This church must have come into existence within that period of forty years, and was therefore a Norman structure. But examples drawn from every part of the country prove that the silence of Domesday is very far from being evidence against the existence of a church. When we consider that Norman builders built for all time, it is at least unlikely that they would have fashioned a structure so flimsy as to need rebuilding in the course of two or three hundred years.

BROMLEY PARISH CHURCH, 1795.

BROMLEY PARISH CHURCH, 1802.

From drawings found inserted in a copy of Lyson's " Environs of London " at the Guildhall Library.
Reproduced by the courtesy of the Library Authorities.

" The fact is," writes Mr. B. F. Davis, " we are not certain, we know nothing, about a Norman building, we do not even need to suppose that a Norman-built church existed.   It is improbable that the monks of St. Andrew left Bromley without a church in Saxon times, and this Saxon church, assuming its existence, may have been sufficient for the needs of the parish as late as the fourteenth century."

All that can be said with certainty is that, some time between 1250 and 1400, there was constructed a Gothic church, consisting of a chancel, nave, and south aisle, with an entrance porch on the south side, and a confessional within the building, and that this church continued to exist, without substantial alteration, until the closing years of the eighteenth century.   Three interesting relics of the medieval church still survive—an arched recess now situated in the chancel and used as a Credence Table, the massive oak door of the south porch, with its original lock and key, and the old sacristy doorway, now placed at the belfry door leading up to the tower.

Examining these in order, the recess consists of a Gothic cinquefoil arch, supported on pillars, with rather stiff foliated capitals, and ornamented with floriated cusps surmounted by a trefoil ornamentation ending in a finial.   It is attributed to early thirteenth-century workmanship, and was originally affixed to the north wall of the chancel, but at some period it was removed to the south aisle, and suffered serious mutilation in consequence. In order to fit it to its new position two-thirds of the trefoil top, including the finial, were cut off, and serious damage was done, either then or subsequently, to the cusps.   Careful and delicate restoration by Sir T. G. Jackson has given back to the recess its original form, the line of junction between the old work and the new being clearly indicated.

The old door of the south porch has been described by Hone in his *Table Book* as " a good specimen of the fast-decaying fine doors of our old churches."   Its decorated woodwork indicates, in Dr. Beeby's opinion, a fourteenth-century origin, for it was not until that time that ornamented wood panelling came into use.

The sacristy doorway, enriched by good mouldings, is contemporary with the fourteenth-century tower, and is probably the oldest doorway now existing in the church.

The medieval church was completed by the erection of the tower, which is a good specimen of the workmanship of the period, and still survives.   Though built for a church smaller than, and very different from, the present edifice, it still, by its position and design, is satisfying to the æsthetic sense of the beholder.   It is distinguished by diagonal buttresses and three string courses around its four sides, the uppermost of these being decorated with grotesques and gargoyles, such as are to be seen in the small quadrangle of Magdalen College, Oxford.   In the first stage of the tower is a large west window, and unusually good square-headed belfry windows which may have been inserted in the late Tudor period, though possibly of an earlier date. The tower, as a whole, does not seem to afford any adequate reason for assigning, as Rev. A. G. Hellicar does, so late a date for its construction as the fifteenth century. It is more probable, as suggested above, that it formed the completion of the new church begun somewhere in the thirteenth century and finished in the fourteenth. The embattled top was hideously disfigured at some unknown date by the addition of a cupola, surmounted by a weathercock, which would seem to have been designed in a vandalistic age such as the eighteenth century for no other purpose than to throw the whole structure out of harmony and proportion.

THE ARCHED RECESS
From a drawing in the British Museum, dated 1836

This cupola was removed in 1830, and at the same time the existing turret was added. In 1777 the old clock, for the repair of which a sum of £2 10s. was expended in 1719, was replaced by a new one at a cost of £150. Within the tower a commodious belfry contains the bells, of which a full account is contained in the section of this history which deals with the interior of the church.

The only structural change of which there is a record until the eighteenth century was the introduction of a window over the western door. This window dates from the sixteenth century, but little of the original stonework now survives. It was restored and the original tracery repointed in 1884.

In the eighteenth century began the period of reconstruction. The need for additional accommodation as population increased became pressing, and it was determined to meet it by the construction of galleries. In 1739 a gallery was erected for the accommodation of the widows in the College. In 1764 and in 1778 two western galleries were constructed in complete disregard of the architectural symmetry of the church. The original arches and piers were wantonly sacrificed, where necessary, for the construction of these galleries, but none the less the accommodation continued to be insufficient. In 1792 it was determined to add a north aisle to the church, with extensive catacombs beneath it, the then Bishop of Rochester, Bishop Thomas, contributing £500 towards the cost. In this period of wholesale reconstruction the original Gothic windows were transformed into rounded arches. The fine eastern window was reduced to a shadow of its former self, its tracery destroyed, and the greater part of it walled up. It was possibly about this time, though the precise date has not been ascertained, that the old chancel was destroyed, the east end of the church being squared, as appears in our illustration.   In 1800 the edifice was still further disfigured by the introduction of high-backed pews and " a three-decker " ;   more galleries were erected ;   pews were constructed above the ancient sacristy ; and a large pew " for the labouring poor " filled up the space previously occupied by " the fire engine," which was turned out-of-doors.

All these expedients, however, only resulted in a growing conviction in the minds of the parishioners that nothing but a complete renovation and reconstruction of the church as a whole would meet the necessities of the case.   In 1829 this work was in full progress, and the condition of ruin and desolation which followed is described under signature of ' Viator Antiquarius,' a contributor to the *Gentleman's Magazine*, under date September 13th :

" Passing through the town of Bromley in Kent, the other day, I found the old Church there nearly pulled down, nothing remaining but the well-built Gothic Tower, and portions of the side walls.   The gates of the Church were fortified by a palisade, so that it was impossible for an antiquary to enter and satisfy himself as to what might be the probable result to ancient vestiges in the Church of such desecrating and destructive appearances."

The general result of these extensive operations, which were completed in 1830, was that the north aisle was extended at both ends, a turret was added to the tower, and the old sacristy was thrown into the body of the church.   The interior was fitted with white oblong pews, with a high pulpit on the one side, and a reading-desk, with clerk's desk below, upon the other. The old Gothic arched recess was transferred to the south aisle ;   the Corinthian altar-piece, which had for long outraged all sense of architectural fitness, was removed, and a reredos with ornamental pinnacles, and a semicircular enclosure, was placed around the communion table.

The whole effect must have been hideous in the extreme, but Rev. A. G. Hellicar, in his *Notes on Bromley Church*, takes comfort from the fact that, at any rate, something of the old church was still allowed to survive, whereas, had nothing been done, probably the whole church would have been destroyed at a later date to make room for a new one adapted to the requirements of the parish.   Moreover, one disfiguring feature of the old tower disappeared—the ' cockney cupola ' surmounted by a weather vane, which had aroused the special wrath of ' Viator.'   By its abolition, and the construction of a turret, the general appearance of the tower was undoubtedly improved.

The total cost of the 1829 restoration was £4,367, which was raised partly by public subscription and partly by borrowing upon the security

ARTHUR GRESLEY HELLICAR, M.A.

Vicar of Bromley 1865–1904.

of the church rate. It is worthy of note that the original estimate, before the work began, was £760 10*s*. But a part, at any rate, of the enhanced cost was due to a change of plan. Stone was substituted for iron and wood in the construction of the pillars and arches, and an additional £150, over and above the original estimate, was spent in reconstructing the rounded windows to the shape which they now present. This cost, however, according to Dr. Beeby, was defrayed by a special private subscription.

During the period of over forty years between 1830 and 1873 a few improvements were introduced, but the main structure remained unaltered. Gas, as an illuminant, was fitted in 1842. In 1843 the churchyard was extended by the acquisition of a piece of ground, on the west side of the church, which had been a part of the rectorial property of the Bishop of Rochester. The present lych-gate was constructed in 1855 at a cost of £70 met by a church rate. The following year, 1856, the organ, originally installed in 1825, was reconstructed, and on September 14th–18th, 1857, the east window was filled with stained glass by Willement, the scene depicted being the Ascension, flanked by the figures of St. Peter and St. Paul. In 1866 the churchyard was still further extended by the purchase for £200 of a piece of land known as the ' Bell Garden,' which in some way unknown had been, from time immemorial, the property of the incumbent of the living. The purchase-money, raised by a voluntary rate, was invested, and subsequently employed towards the building of the present vicarage. Enclosing this extension of the churchyard a new wall of flint with brick coping, in keeping with the old wall of the churchyard, was built, the cost of it being provided by the munificence of Miss Ilott.

Meantime in the course of forty years the population was rapidly increasing, and the need for further accommodation in the church became again pressing. In the year 1865 the Rev. Arthur Gresley Hellicar succeeded to the benefice, and, under him, and largely as a consequence of the impulse applied by him, Bromley Church eventually became what it is to-day. The history of the changes effected under Mr. Hellicar's auspices in 1873 and 1884 is a history of much parochial excitement, and of opposition slowly but successfully overcome. It has been told, in full detail, by Mr. Hellicar himself. The thing, in his opinion, which was most essentially needed was a chancel, for, by such an addition, the church would be brought into harmony with what he calls " the improved tone of church feeling " since 1830, and also the need for more accommodation would be satisfied.

The proposal for a chancel, however, seems to have suggested to the minds of some of the parishioners visions of a surpliced choir and other innovations savouring of advanced and possibly anti-Protestant churchmanship, and it was obvious from the first that any changes would be strongly opposed. Strengthened, however, by the concurrence and advice of the churchwardens, Mr. J. M. Holworthy and Mr. W. W. Baxter, Mr. Hellicar called a parish meeting on July 18th, 1871, which resulted in the formation of an Executive Committee, and the appointment of Secretaries and Treasurers. On August 1st an architect, Mr. Thomas Vaughan, of Messrs. George & Vaughan, was commissioned to draw up plans, a subscription list was opened, and Mr. Vaughan's plans for alterations and the construction of a chancel were accepted by the Executive Committee. The consent of the Vestry was obtained on October 26th, 1871, a resolution to that effect by the churchwardens being carried by twenty-seven votes to twelve, and a tender for £2,100 was accepted. In the summer of 1872 a bazaar, held in Sundridge Park and attended by the Emperor Napoleon III, realised a net profit of £625, and all difficulties appeared to have been surmounted.

It was, however, at this point that the opposition became really formidable and organised. The alarm was raised that graves in the churchyard were to be interfered with—that thus the proposed changes involved the desecration of tombs. At a meeting at the Town Hall it was resolved to oppose the grant of the necessary faculty on the ground that a Vestry vote of twenty-seven to twelve did not provide sufficient warrant for the scheme. The promoters, being at the time without adequate funds, and in face of so serious a body of opposition, felt compelled to accept a compromise which involved the withdrawal of the main proposal.

In October 1872 Mr. Hellicar announced from the pulpit that the scheme for building a chancel was withdrawn. Whereupon some subscribers withdrew their contributions because the chancel scheme was abandoned, others because it was still proposed to proceed with other alterations; but the Executive Committee, fully resolved to do something, signed a contract with Mr. J. C. Arnaud, the builder. The church was closed from February to May 1873, and various alterations, costing about £2,000, were effected and generally regarded as improvements. The church was entirely reseated with open seats, the galleries were refronted, the tower arch was opened out so as to provide a new means of exit; the old font was provided with a new base, and brought out into a more prominent position. A new reredos, pulpit, and reading desk were installed, and better systems of heating and lighting were introduced. " But," says Mr. Hellicar, " the bald flatness of the east end was, I think, even more conspicuous than before, and the reading-desk was really more uncomfortable than the old high desk had been. It was impossible to rest content with such a state of things."

In the meantime at St. John's Church (a chapel-of-ease to the parish church) a surpliced choir had been introduced. Gradually it was recognised that a chancel with suitable arrangements for a choir was not necessarily a concession to Popery, and the gift of a fine organ by Sir Edward H. Scott in 1874 made the question of a chancel in which to install it still more pressing. In June 1882 a memorial was addressed to Mr. Hellicar requesting him to take steps to secure the erection of a chancel, and thus the last major alterations to Bromley Church were inaugurated. A Committee was formed, officers appointed, and a Bromley Parish Church Improvement Fund was set on foot, headed by a subscription of £500 from Sir Edward H. Scott, and one of £100 from Mr. D. P. Loe.

This time all went smoothly. Mr. T. G. Jackson (afterwards Sir Thomas Jackson, R.A.) was appointed architect, and his plans were passed. The tender of Mr. H. Balding for £2,640 was accepted, and on October 10th, 1883, the work was begun. It was finished and was consecrated by Archbishop Benson on December 16th, 1884.

Mr. Hellicar has described the general character of the finished work as follows. The additions consist—

" of a chancel, chancel aisle on the south ; and with vestries, and organ-chamber above, on the north. The chancel opens into the nave by a large arch, the inner order of which is carried on panelled brackets of pleasant and original design.

" In the south wall of the sacrarium are sedilia of rich and delicate design, and in the north wall is refixed the thirteenth-century arched recess, now used as a Credence Table. The chancel is paved with black and white unpolished marble, and, in the centre, hangs a large brass candelabrum.

" All the ancient monuments, necessarily removed from the east wall of the nave, were refixed in the new chancel ; some of the ancient tombstones were re-arranged, and the stucco removed from the south wall of the nave."

The east window, which now replaced the work of Willement, is of seven lights, richly traced. The centre light, a memorial of Mr. J. Bourne, represents the Crucifixion, with the figures of Faith, Hope, and Charity above. On the side-lights the Adoration of the Magi and Shepherds is depicted on the north, the Resurrection on the south. Below are angels bearing the emblems of the Passion. Above the side-lights are shields bearing the arms of the Sovereign, the Archbishop, the Patron, and the then Vicar. The figures of St. Peter and St. Paul flank the main design on either side, the remaining spaces in the tracery being filled with the emblems of the four evangelists, and sacred monograms. The window was executed by Messrs. Powell & Sons, who also designed the three windows in the chancel aisle erected as memorials—the window to the east commemorating Mr. J. N. Tweedy, those to the south, Mr. C. Harker. They represent the Transfiguration—the Virgin and Simeon—and Christ as " The Light of the World " and as " the Good Shepherd." Another window, erected later, on the south side of the chancel, represents Faith, Hope, and Charity in memory of Mr. J. Richardson. It is executed by Messrs. Powell from the designs of Mr. Woolridge.

The screen separating the chancel from the chancel-aisle is finely carved in oak. The oak pulpit, too, is decorated with curious lattice-work carving of the character found in Dalmatian churches.

BROMLEY PARISH CHURCH, FROM N.E.

Showing the Chancel, designed by Sir T. G. Jackson, R.A., erected 1883.

Mr. Jackson's work of building the new chancel was crowned in 1892 by the introduction of the existing reredos, a fine piece of sculpture representing the Last Supper. It is of white alabaster, executed by Messrs. Farmer & Brindley from Mr. Jackson's designs, a part of the colouring being from Mr. Jackson's own hand. The execution of the figures is by Guillemin.

Here the history of the structure of Bromley Church ends for the time. After its many vicissitudes it stands to-day, conspicuous upon its hill, as embodying much of the spirit of the past, while serving with fitness and dignity the needs of the present.

INTERLOR OF BROMLEY PARISH CHURCH, 1860.

From a photograph, by H. T. Melville, lent by Miss Nellie Dann.

[117]

SECTION II. THE INTERIOR

IN the preceding section it has been necessary to make some reference to a few relics of ancient times which still survive in Bromley Church, for those relics were incorporated into, or closely associated with, the ancient structure. The purpose of this section is to survey the interior of the church, and to consider the various memorials of the past which it still contains. Such a survey will involve some further remarks upon the old font, the arched recess, now used as a Credence Table in the chancel, and the old door of the south porch. Then we shall pass to the brasses, inscriptions, and various monuments which constitute so marked a feature of the structure. From them to the tower and the bells ; with some account of the peals which have made Bromley bell-ringers famous from times long ago, the section closing with the inventory of pre-Reformation church property, a document which seems to imply a degree of richness and importance attaching to Bromley Church in medieval times in striking contrast to the conditions existing at a later date.

THE FONT

The font, which, as has already been said, dates back to Norman times, is a square block of Bethersden marble, with the tracery of four plain arches still visible on each of its four sides. At the last restoration of the church in 1884 the stone was handsomely set in position upon a substantial central pedestal flanked by four small pillars of veined Greek marble supporting the font. The whole structure now occupies in the church that position of dignity and prominence which is fitting to a relic which continuously, for more than seven centuries, has served the single purpose of receiving within the bosom of the Church more than twenty generations of the Bromley people. It is, however, perhaps legitimate to wish that the setting of so ancient a stone were more in harmony with its own period and its impressive severity.

THE FONT

From a drawing in the British Museum, dated April 1831

The cover, though quite modern, is altogether appropriate. It is a solid flat square of carved oak, the gift of Mr. D. G. Simpson in 1924, the

117

wood-carving being the work of his daughter, Miss Agnes Simpson.   In
the centre the ring by which the cover is lifted is worked into a cross of
wrought iron, by Mr. David Chisholm, F.R.I.B.A., and the whole is surmounted by an inscription, of which the lettering is admirably cut, suggestive
of the uses of the font itself.

THE ARCHED RECESS

The arched recess, to which attention has already been drawn in the
preceding section, needs no description, as its appearance can be seen in the
illustration which accompanies that text.   It is a relic of the second church
which, at a time that can only be loosely fixed, superseded the original
building.   The architectural design points to a thirteenth-century
origin.

The question which still awaits a final solution is that of the purpose for
which the arch was constructed.   In the absence, so far, of any decisive
pronouncement, it is only possible to state and examine the various theories
which antiquaries have suggested as to its origin.

    i. That it was a shrine, so fashioned as to contain a heart, the whole
       constituting, according to Weever's *Monumental Inscriptions*, 1631,
       a cenotaph monument containing " the portraiture in stone of
       Richard de Wendover, sometime parson of the parish, and
       afterwards Bishop of Rochester."
    ii. That it was an " Easter Sepulchre."
    iii. That it was erected with no other purpose than to serve as a
       Credence Table.

Taking each of these theories in turn :

    i. It will be observed that in the centre of the sustaining wall which forms
the background of the arch there is a circle, carved in the stone, surrounding
what was once an oblong aperture of about four by five inches.   This
aperture, it is suggested by Mr. M. R. James in his *Churches of Kent*, was
possibly a shrine in which a heart, enclosed in a case, was deposited.   Admit-
ting this possibility, there is no evidence that the heart in question was that
of de Wendover, nor are there any existing indications of such " portraiture
in stone " as Weever asserts to have existed.   Moreover, it is upon record
that de Wendover was buried in Westminster Abbey, though this fact is not
conclusive against his memory having been perpetuated by a memorial in the
church from the ministry of which he had been raised to the dignity of a
Bishop.

    ii. The original position of the recess was beneath a small window in the
north wall of the chancel.   This significant fact has led to the supposition

that the structure was originally designed to be an ' Easter Supulchre,' or the shrine in which, in pre-Reformation times, the burial and resurrection of Christ were dramatically represented at the Easter season. Mr. J. G. Waller, F.S.A., has thus described the ceremonies associated with an Easter Sepulchre :

" Although this ancient rite approached very nearly to the mystery or miracle play, yet I think we may state as a distinction between them that whilst one was a popular drama on a religious subject, the other was a religious rite treated dramatically. A construction was made on the north side near the altar to simulate the sepulchre . . . on Good Friday, at the hour of Vespers, a crucifix, usually, doubtless, that from above the high altar, accompanied by the consecrated Host, was taken by the priest, with ceremonious reverence, and placed in the sepulchre prepared. A watch was appointed to be by it by day and night until Easter Day, when, previous to the Mass, the clergy proceeded to the sepulchre, and removed the Crucifix and Host, and bore them back to the altar. . . . Added to this, varying in many places, there was an impersonation of the Angels, the three Maries, the soldiers, etc., and a dialogue took place between them, derived in a great measure from Scripture, or founded upon it. In point of fact, it was representing the sacred narrative, to render it popularly intelligible, on principles similar to those which dictated the symbolic character of ecclesiastical art." (*Surrey Archæological Collections*, Vol. VII, pp. 69, 70.)

' Viator Antiquarius,' in a letter to the *Gentleman's Magazine* of 1829, expresses the view, rather dogmatically, that the Bromley recess is an Easter Sepulchre. His letter, as a whole, creates the impression that, whoever he was, he thoroughly understood what he was talking about. But his opinion has by no means gained universal acceptance, and many antiquaries hold strongly to the tomb theory.

iii. Dr. Beeby says :

" One other purpose has been suggested for the arched recess, which is, that it was intended for, and used as a Credence Table. This is possible, as Credence Tables always were, and still are, placed in the Chancel, near the Communion Table, which, till 1830, was the position of the arch in question."

And to that position in the new chancel it has now been restored.

THE DOOR

The old oak door, now carefully preserved in the church, is the original door of the south porch of the medieval church. It is carved in the manner of the Decorated period.   The ornamentation in quatrefoil above the pillars has suffered by the ravages of time, but the design is still distinct. The massive lock is of wood, 2 feet 6 inches in length, 7½ inches deep, and 5 inches thick, with a bolt 1 inch in height, and 1½ inches in thickness.   This bolt shoots out 2 inches on the application of a very heavy key, 9 inches long.   This key is now attached to the door by a chain, having been preserved by Mr. W. W. Baxter, for many years churchwarden, and handed over to the church in 1900, by his son, Mr. W. Baxter.   The old sacristy doorway, now leading to the belfry, has been referred to in the previous chapter.

BRASSES AND INSCRIPTIONS

In the Public Library of Bromley there is a tabulated catalogue of the *Monumental Inscriptions in the Church and Churchyard of Bromley, Co. Kent*, compiled by Richard Holworthy.   This catalogue, which gives inscriptions in full, with details of coats-of-arms where such exist, contains no less than eighty-eight entries of monuments within the church, of which all but a few still survive.   But, none the less, we have to deplore the disappearance of some records of antiquity which were covered up, lost, or perished in the various restorations of the late eighteenth and early nineteenth centuries. That period of artistic vandalism was as much distinguished by utter contempt for the records of the past as is the present age for its veneration of them. Within a space of about sixty years, from 1770 to 1830, several monuments which are recorded by Thorpe in his *Registrum Roffense* as existing in 1769 disappeared altogether, and Rev. A. G. Hellicar thinks that there must have been at one time in Bromley Church memorials to Bishops of Rochester and others, of which no trace is now to be found.   Of those which have been lost one of the earliest is a brass inscribed to the memory of a Rector of Bromley in 1360.   The text, erroneously given by Dunkin, following Weever, ran in all probability as follows :

" Icy gist Mestre Water de Hethe
 Qi fut Persone de Bromleghe.   1360."

(Here lies Walter de Hethe who was Parson of Bromley, 1360.)

Dunkin's statement that this " Walter de Henche," as he styles him, became Bishop of Rochester rests on no foundation.

Of existing brasses the most ancient now surviving is that commemorating Isabella Lacer.   This brass, which was discovered in 1829, is now inserted in the north wall of the chancel, and contains an inscription in abbreviated black-letter.   For the benefit of readers not familiar with

FOURTEENTH-CENTURY DOOR, IN THE SOUTH
PORCH.

From a photograph by Geo. C. Druce, Esq.

THE LACER BRASS

medieval truncation, in the following transcript the Latin word in full is given immediately beneath its abbreviation :

Hic jacet Isabella	qůdã		uͬ	Ricī	Lacer	nup		Major	Londĩn
	quondam		uxor	Ricardi		nuper			Londini
que	obiit°	qͬto	kl	Augt'i°	å°	do°	M°CCC°LXI°		cui'
quae		quarto	Kalendarum	Augusti	anno	Domini			cujus
aïe	ppiciĕt	deuſ°	aͫ.						
animae	propicietur		Amen.						

" Here lies Isabella, once the wife of Richard Lacer, at one time Mayor of London, who died on July 29th, A.D. 1361, to whose soul may God be propitious. Amen."

In a letter to the then Vicar of Bromley—the Rev. Donald Tait, now Archdeacon of Rochester—dated December 15th, 1912, Mr. Holworthy states that he has been making some researches into the history of the Lacer family, and has found a pedigree of three generations of the ancestors of Richard Lacer. Mr. Holworthy asserts that both Richard Lacer and his wife Isabella died of plague in 1361, and both were buried at Bromley. In this case it is curious that a commemorative brass to the wife should have made no mention of the death of the husband. It may be, however, that the existing brass is only part of an original in memory of both. Some particulars relative to Richard Lacer and his term of office as Lord Mayor of London were compiled by Mr. D. Benham and published by Mr. E. Strong, printer, of Bromley, in 1861. In addition to estates held at Deptford, Rotherhithe, and Peckham, we learn that Richard Lacer held the property of Blackbrook, and so became closely associated with the parish of Bromley.

The most perfect of the brasses, still preserved, is that commemorating, on a slab seven feet by four feet, Richard Thornhill and his family. The figure of Richard Thornhill is finely executed in half-size. He is represented as wearing a short frill, long cloak with extra long sleeves, and a closely cropped beard and a moustache. His two wives stand on either side of him, the figure on his left being that of a lady about two inches shorter than her husband. She is dressed in the stiff, perpendicular fashion of the Elizabethan age, head-dress flattened at the top, a full ruff, her dress closely fitting to the body with a front ornamented by an intricately interlaced pattern, a skirt full and hanging solidly. She stands with her hands together in an attitude of prayer. The figure of the other wife upon his right has been mutilated, only the lower part remaining, but from what is left it may be inferred that the two women were represented in much the same manner. The five children of the first wife are represented on a brass below, the three children of the second wife balancing the composition upon the other side. Above the figure of Thornhill is a plaque on which is inscribed :

"I do most assuredly believe that my Redeemer liveth."

Still higher up are his arms, and at the top of the stone a brass rebus, a thorn tree standing on a hillock. Above the figure of the second wife are her arms dimidiated with those of her husband. Above the first wife similar arms existed, but the stone containing them has been broken away. Below the central figures is the inscription :

"Here lyeth buried the bodye of Richard Thornhill late of Bromlye in the Countye of Kent, Esq : who deceased the XVth day of Februarye 1600, who first married Margaret Mills and had issue by her two sonnes and three daughters : and afterwards marryed Elizabeth Watson, and had issue by her two sonnes and one daughter."

This brass, which in the main is in fine preservation, was discovered at the time when the church was reseated in 1872, buried beneath the pews at the eastern end, to which position it had been ignominiously relegated during the alterations of 1830. It now lies in front of the lectern at the foot of the chancel steps, and a movable mat has been placed over it. The brass is of special interest by reason of its late date, for few figured brasses are to be found later than 1550. The elaboration of the arms is evidently in accordance with the instructions given by Thornhill in his will :

"What workmanship may be done to my gravestone I would have it done with the advise of Mr. Smith Heralde and to be layde at the discretion of my Executors by the licence of the Lord Bishop."

No other brasses bearing figures are preserved in the church, but there are several which contain inscriptions upon the floor of the nave : one commemorating the fact that :

"Hereunder lyeth buried the bodye of Mr. John King, of London, Draper, and free of the Companye of Cloth workers, who departed this

I DO MOST ASSVREDLY BELIEVE
THAT MY REDEMER LIVETH

HERE LYETH·BVRIED THE BODIE OF RICHARD THORNHILL LATE
OF BROMLYE IN THE COVNTYE OF KENT ESQ WHO DECEASED
THE XV DAY OF FEBRVARYE 1600 WHO FIRST MARRIED MAR-
GARET MILLS AND HAD ISSVE BY HER TWO SONNES AND THREE
DAVGHTERS·AND AFTERWARDS MARRYED ELIZABETH WATSON
·· AND HAD·ISSVE·BY HER TWO SONNES AND ONE DAVGHTER·

THE THORNHILL BRASSES IN THE PARISH CHURCH, BROMLEY, KENT.

worlde the fifte of September Anno Doni, 1603, aetatis sui [*sic*] LI." " He had to wife Susan Woodwarde by whom he lefte issue then livinge Henry, James, John, and Elizabeth."

and another immediately in front of the pulpit to the memory of Dr. John Yonge, Bishop of Rochester, Master of Pembroke Hall, Cambridge, and elevated to the see of Rochester in 1578. In the Parochial Register the burial of Bishop Yonge is entered under date May 14th, 1605 :

" his sonne, Mr. John Yonge, being the cheefe mourner."

and it is thought probable that a leaden coffin found under the Sacrarium in 1872 was the Bishop's coffin. The inscription on the brass, in elegant Latin, declares that it is :

" Memoriæ sacrum Joanni Yonge Episcopo Roffensi Sacræ Theologiæ Doctori Londini nato Cantabrigiæ bonis literis innutrito non minus varia doctrina et prudentia quam vitæ sanctimonia claro. Qui cum Domino diu vigilasset senex in Domino pie placideq obdormivit die x Aprilis MDCV cum annos XXVII sedisset Episcopus et LXXI vixisset."

(Sacred to the memory of John Yonge, Bishop of Rochester, Doctor of Divinity, born in London, nourished in good literature at Cambridge, and no less distinguished for varied learning and prudence than by sanctity of life. Having kept long vigil for the Lord, he, an old man, fell asleep in the Lord piously and placidly on the 10th day of April 1605, having sat as Bishop for 27 years, and having lived 71.)

As a complete description of all the monuments in Bromley Parish Church is contained in Mr. Holworthy's work previously mentioned, it is only necessary to mention here a selection of those which seem to be of chief interest and importance.

On the *west wall of the north aisle* is a tablet announcing that below is the vault of the Norman family, of Bromley Common ; and a tablet showing that John Thomas, D.C.L., Bishop of Rochester, gave in 1792 a sum of £500 towards erecting this part (i.e. north aisle) of the church.

On the *east wall of the north aisle*, inside the faculty pew, is the memorial to Coles W. J. Child, Esquire, Lord of the Manor, Deputy Lieutenant and Magistrate for the County of Kent, who died January 16th, 1873. On the brass are the arms of the family with their motto, " Imitari quam Invideri." Mr. Coles Child, father of the present baronet, devoted some of his time to collecting materials for a history of Bromley, of which full use has been made in this volume.

On the wall of the *chancel*, to the left, is a brass commemorating the consecration of the chancel on December 16th, 1884, by the Archbishop of

Canterbury, also an inscription on a stone : " I. H. deceased February 26th, 1652."

Above on the *north wall of the sanctuary* are the memorials of the Bagshaws —first an inscription to the memory of Abigail, wife of Harington Bagshaw, with the pathetic record of the premature death of three daughters, Mary, Francisca, and Prudence—

" Quæ omnes Fato heu ! nimis festino e Terris raptæ Animas Deo reddiderunt."

and then the simple entry " H. B." inscribed upon the stone by his son, with the record of the facts that Harington Bagshaw was vicar of the parish, Rector of Woolwich, and for about forty years Chaplain of Warner's College. He died May 29th, 1739, aged sixty-nine.

Close by is the memorial to Thomas Bagshaw, son of Abigail and Harington, who, after a short interval, succeeded his father as Chaplain of the College, an office which he held for nearly fifty-four years. He died November 20th, 1787.

Thomas Bagshaw was almost an exact contemporary with Dr. Johnson, whom he knew, and to whose famous Dictionary he supplied additions. Johnson, in acknowledging Bagshaw's assistance, handsomely recognises its value :

"If many readers had been as judicious, as diligent, and as communicative as yourself my work had been better."

Boswell asserts that Bagshaw resigned the living of Bromley some time before his death.

Here also is a memorial to Dr. Henry Smith, for forty-two years minister of this parish, who died July 22nd, 1818. Forty-two years from 1818 carries us back to 1776, and the time of Thomas Bagshaw's incumbency. Dr. Smith, therefore, was probably curate under Thomas Bagshaw before succeeding to the living.

On the *south wall of the chancel* the following memorials are seen :

(*a*) To Zachary Pearce, Bishop of Rochester, whose benefactions to Bromley College are noted in another chapter, and to his wife Mary. Mrs. Pearce died in October 1773, aged seventy years, and the Bishop in June 1774, aged eighty-four years.

A coat-of-arms contains a leopard and " in chief 3 bees volant, proper; impaling, erm, 3 mountain cats passant in pale, proper."

The inscription, after setting forth the various ecclesiastical offices held by the Bishop before succeeding to the see of Rochester, states that he died " in a comfortable hope of (what was the chief aim of all his Labours upon Earth) the being promoted to a happier Place in Heaven." Pearce being a noted pluralist, the word ' promoted ' has an ironic significance.

MONUMENT TO ZACHARY PEARCE, BISHOP OF
ROCHESTER,

On the south wall of the Chancel.

MONUMENT TO THE WIFE OF HARINGTON
BAGSHAW, VICAR OF BROMLEY 1698–1759.

On the north wall of the Chancel.

(*b*) The Memorial, erected by his parishioners and congregation, to Mr. Hellicar :

" To the glory of God and in loving remembrance of Arthur Gresley Hellicar, M.A., who spent 43 years here as a faithful Minister of the Church, first as Curate, and afterwards for 39 years as Vicar of the Parish until his death at the age of 69 on the 6th Sept. 1904."

Thus is fitly celebrated the memory of the man to whom, more than to any other, the present church owes its existence ; a man who, under a somewhat shy and aloof exterior, contained a driving force, a singleness of devotion to high ends, a fund of quiet humour, and a total absence of self-seeking, which endeared him to his many friends who still survive, and which mark him as an example for those who come after him.

On this south side of the chancel will be found, on the arch behind the reading-desk, a memorial to John Maunsell, 1625, dying " about the age of 50 years," with the curious inscription :

" SHORT WAS HISLIFEYETDYESHENEVER
DEATH WAS HISDUEYETLIVESHEEVER."

where it will be seen that the craftsman was determined to get the letters in somehow, doing so at the expense of any separation between most of the words.

The chancel aisle, or " Chapel of the Resurrection," as it is now named, was entirely furnished, including the reredos and pavement, by Mr. and Mrs. F. Schooling, and dedicated, in 1918, to the memory of their two sons Eric Charles and Cecil Herbert, who were killed in the Great War, as recorded on a handsome brass and marble tablet.

Otherwise the chapel is distinguished by memorials to several members of the Tweedy family, the first in order of time being that to Colonel George Tweedy, of Bromley House and Simpson's Place, who died at the age of eighty in 1860, and to his wife Violet, who died in 1865, aged seventy-seven years ; another to John Newman Tweedy, of Widmore House, Bromley, 1888 ; a third commemorating Lieutenant Robert P. Tweedy, of the Black Watch, who died in India in 1911.

Other memorials in this chapel are to John Richardson, of Ravensfell and Bromley House, 1889 ; to Thomas Chase, of Bromley Common, 1754; and Sarah his wife, 1760. Here also in a very dark and insignificant position is the bronze tablet containing the names of eighty-four men who " died the noblest death a man may die. Fighting for God and Right, and Liberty, and such a death is immortality " in the Great War, 1914–18.

The south windows here are inserted to the memory of Charles R. Harker, who died in 1885.

On the west wall of the chapel are memorials to Robert Boyd, J.P., of Plaistow Lodge, 1863, and his wife Mary Catherine, 1881, and three sons, the youngest of whom was killed in action in the Indian Mutiny, 1857; to Mary (1817) and Edward Dawson King (1815), children of Walker King, Bishop of Rochester.

In the *south aisle* the following monuments are seen : To Anna Louisa, eldest daughter of Charles Pott, of Freelands, 1882 ; the interesting memorial to Mr. James Scott, 1848, the famous surgeon, also his wife Mary, 1842 ; and to John Gifford, J.P., the biographer of Pitt and secretary of the Pitt Club.

Other memorials in this aisle are to Godfrey Meynell, of Shawfield Lodge, Widmore, 1834, and Godfrey Godfrey Meynell his son, 1844.

In the *nave*—immediately south of the font—is the gravestone covering the remains of Dr. Johnson's wife. The inscription is from the hand of Johnson himself, but in the cutting of it an error in date was made, Mrs. Johnson's death being entered in the Registers as having occurred in 1752, the date on the stone being 1753. Johnson's conjugal devotion to a wife whose attractions were visible only to himself finds expression in his epitaph :

> " Hic conduntur reliquiæ
> ELISABETHÆ
> Antiqua Jarvisiorum gente,
> Peatlingæ, apud Leicestrienses ortæ ;
> Formosæ, cultæ, ingeniosæ, piæ,
> Uxoris, primis nuptiis, HENRICI PORTER,
> Secundis, SAMUELIS JOHNSON :
> Qui multum amatam diuque defletam
> Hoc lapide contexit,
> Obiit Londini, Mense Mart,
> A.D. MDCCLIII."

The lady thus described as beautiful, cultured, ingenious, and pious, was honestly believed by Johnson to possess all these qualities. His devotion to his " Tetty " is proverbial, but perhaps her most pathetic epitaph is that inscribed on a slip of paper inserted in a box in which Johnson kept her wedding ring—"Eheu ! Elix. Johnson . . . Mortua, Eheu ! " (Alas ! Eliz. Johnson, Dead, Alas !)

But on others she produced quite another impression :

" Garrick," says Boswell, " described her to me as very fat, with a bosom of more than ordinary protuberance, with swelled cheeks of a florid red, produced by thick painting, and increased by the liberal use of cordials, flaring and fantastic in her dress, and affected, both in her speech and general behaviour."

The maxim that ' truth will out,' even in an affidavit and an epitaph, scarcely finds confirmation in Johnson's epitaph upon his wife.

In the floor of the nave are some brasses : one, fixed to a gravestone, tells us that beneath lie the remains of Jane Bodenham, the wife of Henry Bodenham, of Folston, Wiltshire, who died on November 12th, 1625, at the age of twenty-one, having borne to her husband three children, a daughter and two sons.

Her premature decease when still but a girl, prompted the curious and rather baffling epitaph engraved on the brass.

> " Me, Nuptus, Natus, frater, materve, paterve,
> Orbam non plorent orbis, ad astra feror :
> Se, Nuptus, Natus, frater, materq, paterq,
> Orbibus astrorum defleat Orbus ad huc.
> Dum Nuptu, Natos, fratrem, matremq, patremq,
> Quero ; beat sociam, nata, beata, matrem."

The pun upon *orbus*, an adjective meaning *bereft, deprived of*, and *orbis*, a circle, often used of *the world*, is twice repeated, and has no equivalent in English. The meaning seems to be :

" Let not husband, son, brother, father, or mother weep for me though deprived of the light of day. I am borne to the stars. Rather let them weep that so far they are bereft of the starry worlds. While I am looking for husband, sons, brother, and parents, the daughter in bliss blesses the mother at her side."

The mother in this case being the Virgin Mother in heaven.

Immediately in front of the pulpit is the brass to the memory of Dr. John Yonge, and under the litany desk is a large slate slab to William Passenger, J.P., of Plaistow, Bromley, a Commissioner of His Majesty's Victualling, 1727.

At the foot of the *stairs leading to the north gallery* is one of the most quaint and interesting memorials in the church, that to the centenarian Elizabeth Monk. The tablet is notable, alike for the character of the person whom it celebrates and for the style and contents of the inscription, composed by Dr. Hawkesworth, whose own monument, twenty years later, was to find a position in this gallery. The whole epitaph, long as it is, deserves transcription in full :

" Near this place lies the body of|Elizabeth Monk,|who departed this Life on the 27th day of August 1753,|aged 101.| She was the widow of John Monk, late of this Parish, Blacksmith,|her second husband,|to whom she had been a Wife near 50 years ;|by whom she had no Children,|and of the issue of the first Marriage none lived to the second.| But Virtue|would not suffer her to be childless.| An Infant to whom and to whose Father and Mother she had been nurse|(such is the uncertainty of temporal Prosperity)| became dependent upon Strangers for the Necessaries of Life ;|To him she afforded the Protection of a Mother. | The parental Charity was returned with filial Affection, | and she was supported in the feebleness of Age | by him whom she had cherished in the Helplessness of Infancy. |

"*Let it be remembered* | That there is no station in which Industry will not obtain | Power to be Liberal ; | nor any Character on which Liberality will not | confer Honour. |

" She had been long prepared by a simple and unaffected Piety | for that awful Moment which however delayed | is universally sure. |

" How few are allowed an equal Time of Probation ! | How many by their Lives appear to presume upon more ! | To preserve the Memory of this Person, | but yet more to perpetuate the Lesson of her Life, | This stone was erected by voluntary Contributions."

It will be admitted that the balanced and sententious periods of eighteenth-century literary style most admirably fulfil the purpose expressed.

The most conspicuous monument in this gallery is that to Dr. John Hawkesworth, the author of the eulogy of Elizabeth Monk. He died in 1773 at the age of fifty-eight. He was for several years a resident in Bromley, occupying the large house a little north of the Bell Hotel, which has since been pulled down. He was a man of some distinction in literature, and one time a friend of Dr. Johnson, editor and principal author of *The Adventurer*, and for some years editor of the *Gentleman's Magazine*.

The inscription on his monument, after reciting his age and the date of his death, proceeds to quote a long passage from *The Adventurer*.

On the same slab is an inscription to the memory of Mr. Benjamin Brown of this parish, 1777, the whole monument being inscribed " by their sorrowing Relict and sister, M. H.," being Hawkesworth's wife Mary, and sister to Benjamin Brown.

The window at the west end of the nave is divided into two parts. The upper portion (by Powell) is a memorial by the parishioners to the Rev. Arthur Gresley Hellicar, for thirty-nine years Vicar. The centre light exhibits the ascending Saviour with outstretched hands in blessing, flanked on the left by the appearance to St. Peter after the Resurrection, and, on the right, St. Paul's vision on his way to Damascus.

The lower portion is made up of parts of the old east window (by Willement) from which also came the figures of SS. Peter and Paul in the window at the west end of the north aisle.

In the *south gallery* :

An interesting monument (by Nollekens) commemorates the death of Thomas Chase, of Bromley Common. He was born in Lisbon, 1729, and was one of the survivors of the ever-memorable earthquake which befell that city on November 1st, 1755, when he was buried beneath the ruins of the house where he first saw the light. After a most wonderful escape, he, by degrees, recovered from a very deplorable condition, and lived till November 20th, 1788.

A coffin-plate of Thomas Chase was handed to the sexton, Mr. Charles Harris, in the presence of Mr. W. Baxter, by the gardener of Church House a year or two ago. He stated that it had been in a potting-shed there for thirty years ; it has now been cleaned and flattened by Mr. H. G. Dunn.

A large part of the wall of this gallery is devoted to monuments in memory of members of the Scott family of Sundridge Park, including Sir Claude Scott, Bart., who built the present mansion in 1796, and who died in 1830 ; Sir Edward Henry Scott, Bart., who was the donor of the organ in the church, and who died in 1883 ; and his son Henry Farquhar Scott, killed in the South African War, 1901. Other monuments are to the memory of Walter Boyd and his wife, of Plaistow Lodge ; Charles Pott and his wife, of Freelands ; Henry Hibbert, of Bromley Common ; Dr. John Scott, F.R.C.S., only son of Mr. James Scott, and his widow Mrs. Susannah Scott, who died at Church House, much lamented, in 1863.

TOWER

On the tower walls there hangs a miscellaneous collection of boards memorialising the donors of certain charities, of church furniture, and the like, and also the records of notable bell-ringing performances. The peculiar glory of the tower is its bells, and its commodious belfry in which eight bells now hang. In all probability bells have hung there since its first construction.

The inventory of church goods drawn up in 1553 notes :

" Item, iiii greate Belles, seeted in the steple, one Sants bell, and iii lettle sacrying belles and one hand bell."

Of these bells one was known as " the great bell," and special bequests were made for its upkeep. Thus in 1481 Randolf Bothe, gent, bequeathed Vs. (five shillings) " to the use of the said church for the grete belle." John Godewyn, in 1507, left XLs. " for the reparacion of ye Grete bell," and in 1524 Henry Moger left 6s. 8d. " to the grete bell of Bromley Church." In 1504 John Scott, of Chislehurst, bequeathed 6s. 8d. " to the bells of Bromley," and about this time the bells seem to have been removed for repairs, for, in 1512, Thomas Erliche left 12d. " to the bringing home of the bells." The " Sants bell " was the Saunce, or Sanctus bell, rung at the recital of the Paternoster, the " sacrying belles " being those rung at the elevation of the Host. The bells therefore used in the office of the Mass were in addition to and quite distinct from " the iiii greate Belles " in the steeple.

No further record of the Bromley bells is available until 1773, when a complete set of new bells was installed in the tower, the work of Thomas

Janaway (of Chelsea). Each bell is signed " T. Janaway fecit 1773," and
five of them are further inscribed. On No. 1 the inscription is " Prosperity
to the parish of Bromley." No. 2, " Musica est Mentis Medicina."

No. 3, " He, and he only, aims aright,
Who Joins Industry with Delight."
No. 4, " When from the Earth our notes rebound
The hills and valleys ecco round."
and on No. 7, " The Ringers' Art our Grateful Notes prolong,
Apollo Listens and Approves the Song."

On the eighth bell are the names of the churchwardens in 1773,
Joseph Shirley and John Mann.

In addition to these Janaway cast a Sanctus bell in 1777 which is under a
lead-covered table on the tower summit, and strikes the hours.

The old bells were apparently removed from Bromley to Chelsea, and
were used in the making of the new ones. In the churchwardens' accounts,
1773, 1774 (preserved in the Public Library), there will be found the following
entries :

" The Churchwardens of Bromley—Dr.
To the Executors of Jn° Martin.

		£	s.	d.
1773	For carrying the Bells to Chelsea with two Teams .	2	10	0
Jan. 12th	For one Team to fetch four of the Bells from Do. to Bromley	1	5	0
		£3	15	0

Rec^d June 8th, 1774, the contents of this Bill,
p.p. J. Martin."

" The Churchwardens of Bromly—to Moses Turner.

		£	s.	d.
1773	For beer to the men to help to unload the Bells an to			
May 21	get them into the Church	0	6	0
	For beer to the Bell-hangers	0	5	0
	For a saucepan for oile		7	7
	For Ringing the King's Bir^tday		5	0
		£1	3	7

Received the contents—Moses Turner."

It was in order fitly to celebrate the occasion, and to secure for the
bell-ringers the utmost degree of efficiency, that there was founded on
May 29th, 1773, " the Society of Bromley Youths." It is now, what it

always has been, an exclusive corporation, membership being confined to those experienced or interested in the art of campanology, and the records of the society show that, whatever a man's trade, he might be a potential bell-ringer, for in that record we find members designated as peruke-makers, coopers, cordwainers, shipwrights, watermen, breeches-makers, sawyers, and husbandmen.

On the first occasion when the bells were rung after being recast, the society apparently felt itself too young and inexperienced to face so great an occasion, and the inaugurating peal was rung by two London companies of campanologists, evidently without any conspicuous success, for, as a consequence of their failure to accomplish satisfactorily the task they had undertaken, James Barham, a noted Kent ringer from Leeds, near Maidstone, undertook to bring a team of " Kent youths " who would be equal to the task. In that team was included William Cook, of Bromley—the only Bromley man at that time versed in the art, and they rang a peal of " Oxford Treble Bobs," involving 5,088 changes, in three hours and seven minutes.

The first peal undertaken exclusively by the Society of Bromley Youths was rung on September 14th, 1774, when a peal of " Bob Majors " (5,040 changes) was given in three hours and eleven minutes.

The names of the team which manned the ropes on this occasion are worthy of permanent record :

> No. 1 Bell—John Cowderoy,
> „ 2 „ John Chapman, Jr.,
> „ 3 „ Thomas Day,
> „ 4 „ John Heath,
> „ 5 „ Henry Sale,
> „ 6 „ Thomas Kelly,
> „ 7 „ William Chapman,
> „ 8 „ William Cook, who acted as leader.

Many notable performances were accomplished in the early days of the Society. Thus, in 1775 (February 14th), William Cook conducted a ring of 10,080 changes in six hours and thirteen minutes ; in 1778, under the leadership of William Chapman, the longest ring on record was rung, 12,672 changes in seven hours and forty-eight minutes.

To record all the notable occasions in the history of the Society would occupy an undue amount of space in this chapter, but the muffled peal of Grandsire Triples rung in commemoration of their old leader William Chapman is worthy of special note.

Hone, in his *Table Book* (Vol. II, p. 527) records : " I stept into ' the Sun '—R. Tape—at Bromley, to make inquiry of the landlord respecting a stage to London ; and over the parlour mantelpiece, carefully glazed, in gilt frame, beneath the flourishing surmounting scroll, there appeared the following inscription *in letters of gold* :

" ' Rang at St. Peters Bromley.

" ' On the 15th January 1817, by the Society of Bromley Youths, a complete Peal of *Grandsire Triples*, which is 5,040 changes, with the *Bells Muffled*, in commemoration of Wm. Chapman deceased, being a ringer in the Parish of Bromley 43 years, and rang upwards of 60 peals. This Dumb Peal was completed in 3 hours and 6 minutes. . . . Being the first Dumb Peal of this Kind ever rang in this Kingdom, and conducted by J. Allen.' "

The scroll which Hone saw and copied now hangs in the belfry of Bromley Church, and was painted by C. T. Giles, aged twelve years.

Space does not permit the record of more modern exploits of the Bromley bell-ringers, except to say that the traditions of their ancestors have been worthily maintained up to the present day. The muffled peal of Grandsire Triples rung to commemorate their late Vicar, Mr. Hellicar, on September 10th, 1904, is still remembered, and doubtless equalled, if it did not exceed, in solemnity and precision the achievement of J. Allen and his companions in 1817.

When writing of the bells, reference has been made to " the Inventory of Church Goods " compiled in 1553. This Inventory, which has never yet been quite correctly recorded in print, is judged to be of such importance that it is given in full as an appendix. The document was carefully copied, and photographed, from the original record by the late Mr. Ernest G. Atkinson, F.S.A., of the Record Office.

The attention of readers is particularly directed to this Inventory because of the number of rich vessels and vestments which are there recorded as being the property of Bromley Church. They seem to imply a dignity, importance, not to say a splendour attaching to that church in the Middle Ages, which at the time of the Reformation was almost wholly eclipsed. The impression is confirmed by a record in Wharton's *Anglia Sacra*, which states that :

" in the year 1327, after the Coronation of King Edward . . . the Bishop of Rochester was extremely beset by the Prelates and other great men of the Kingdom for the Collation to the Church at Bromley,"

so much so that the Bishop, Hamo de Hethe—

" withdrew from Parliament to Trottescliffe and sojourned there the whole of Lent."

It is curious to think of the competition for the Rectory of Bromley producing such consequences and exercising the united energies of " the Prelates and

other great men of the Kingdom."
The researches of Mr. Davis in
the Rochester Registers render it
doubtful, however, whether the
Bromley rectory was the real
ground of the disturbance.

The Inventory shows, in possession of the church, silver
vessels, chalices, and other plate,
of a total weight of ninety ounces;
copes and other vestments of
"Bawdekyn" and Bruges; front
Cloths of velvet and cloth-of-gold;
and one *Paraphrasis of Erasmus*,
which proves that the injunction
of Edward VI was obeyed in
Bromley—

"that one great Bible, and one
book of the Paraphrases of Erasmus
on the Gospels, both in English,
should be set up in every church
that the people might read therein."

The date of the Inventory is of
itself ominous of the fate which
befell probably the greater part of
the property which it records.   In

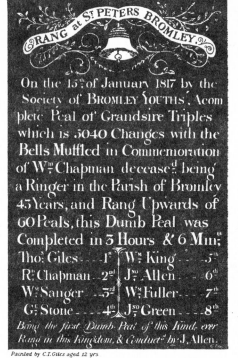

RANG at St PETERS BROMLEY.

On the 15th of January 1817 by the
Society of BROMLEY YOUTHS, A com
plete Peal of Grandsire Triples
which is 5040 Changes with the
Bells Muffled in Commemoration
of Wm Chapman deceased being
a Ringer in the Parish of Bromley
45 Years, and Rang Upwards of
60 Peals, this Dumb Peal was
Completed in 3 Hours & 6 Min;

Thos Giles	1st	Wm King	5th
Rd Chapman	2nd	Jno Allen	6th
Wm Sanger	3rd	Wm Fuller	7th
Gd Stone	4th	Jno Green	8th

*Being the first Dumb Peal of this Kind, ever
Rang in this Kingdom, & Conducted by J. Allen.*

Painted by C.T. Giles aged 12 yrs

RECORD PEAL

1553 the fervour of the Protestant Reformation was at the full, and the
intention of the Government, in causing these inventories to be drawn up,
was to remove from the churches everything which savoured of "Popish
Superstition."   In some cases, and the concluding paragraph of the Inventory
shows that Bromley was one of them, the Churchwardens were allowed to
sell some of the church ornaments, the proceeds being applied to the work
of repairs, but it is to be feared that most of the property entered upon the
Inventory was either destroyed or appropriated to the Crown.   How much
of it, if any, survived for use in the future cannot now be determined,
but in the seventeenth and early eighteenth centuries various gifts seem to
imply that previously the church had been stripped of practically everything
belonging to it.

In 1638 a citizen of London, Richard Hollingsworth, presented a large
silver chalice and paten; in 1705 Bishop Sprat gave "a cushion" and cloth
of black velvet and gold tabby, and ten years later his widow gave a silver
gilt chalice and cover.   Even these vessels were not destined to survive,

for in 1791 the church was entered by burglars, and the plate chest was robbed of everything that was portable, as recorded on pages 39 and 40.

The existing plate, therefore, is all comparatively modern. It consists of :

(*a*) A silver-gilt cup, with its paten-cover upon it, 10¾ inches high, the bowl having a diameter of 3⅞ inches, its total weight being 1 lb. 6¾ ozs. It was given by Mr. George Norman, a few months after the robbery, and bears the inscription :

" Ecclesia de Bromley (Com Cantii) furibus spoliata, hoc poculum Cænæ Salvatoris nostri celebratione utendum, donavit Georgius Norman, ejusdem Parochiæ Generosus, Junii mense A.D. MDCCXCI."
(The church of Bromley in the County of Kent having been despoiled by thieves, this cup, to be used for the celebration of the Supper of the Saviour, was given by George Norman, gentleman of the same parish, June 1791.)

(*b*) A silver cup with paten-cover, weighing in all 1 lb. 10¾ ozs., bears the inscription :

" *Bromley, Kent*, 1807, *Henry Smith, D.D.*, Minister, *Robert Smith, Sen*^r ! *Christ*^r *Fisher*, Churchwardens."

It was presumably purchased out of church funds. On the cover is engraved the sacred monogram, I.H.S., with cross and nails.
(*c*) Silver-gilt paten, engraved with the monogram and inscribed as " The gift of Robert Makepeace for the use of the Communion Table in Bromley Church, 1803."
(*d*) A silver-gilt paten, similar in almost every particular to the above, but 2¾ ozs. heavier.
(*e*) A silver flagon, gilt inside, 12 inches high, and weighing 3 lb. 11¼ ozs. It bears the inscription :

" James Edward Newell, M.A., gave this Flagon to the Church of Bromley, March 10th, 1854."

(*f*) A silver-gilt spoon or strainer, inscribed " Bromley Parish."
(*g*) A gilt brass alms-dish, 15⅞ inches in diameter, weighing 2 lb. 5½ ozs. It is inscribed :

" Presented to the Parish Church of Bromley, Kent, by Evelyn Arthur, Mabel Katrine, and Sydenham Malthus Hellicar, May 1873."
" It is more blessed to give than to receive."

The dish is the gift of children of a former Vicar.

More recent gifts include a silver-gilt chalice and paten, presented anonymously as a thank-offering in 1909.

CHURCHYARD

Of the gravestones in the churchyard there are at least four which date farther back than the eighteenth century. On one of those on the south side the inscription, which is partly obliterated, runs thus :

" Omne quod e et Mortis."

" Here lyeth intered the body of John S. . . . of Bromley, Gent . . . who died the 16th day of March Anno. Dom, 1635. . . . Mary his wife, by whom he had 3 sons John, Edward and . . . and one daughter . . ."

> " Within this tomb interr'd doth lye
> A Relique of Mortalitye
> The Holy Soul that did inherit
> This house of clay, is now a spirit
> To heaven gone, and there it is
> Possessed of Eternall bliss."

The present sexton, Mr. G. Harris, says that Mr. J. R. Pocock, a former sexton, drew his attention to the fact that this was the oldest grave, showing him a date, then plain, 1510 or 1518, on the top slab.

Another, attached to the south wall of the church, is to

" Martine French of this parish with 4 of his wives and 2 daughters. He departed this life ye 12th of January Anno 1661 aged 61, and his last wife departed ye 13th of ye same moneth leaveing behind him one sonne Martine, and 3 daughters Jane, Sarah, and Mary."

Close by the latter is the tomb of Richard Gratwicke, Gent., of this parish, 1674, and his wife Mary, 1682, and their daughter and granddaughter. The tomb exhibits what must have been elaborate carving when new. On its west face are the Gratwicke Arms, " 3 hurts each charged with a fret. Crest : An ostrich's head, in the beak a horse shoe." There is also the usual helmet and mantling.

Just to the north of the south-east door is a tomb to Elizabeth, wife of Daniel Giles, and daughter to John Herlackenden of this parish, 1668.

There are several headstones dated in the early part of the eighteenth century, and a few others are notable for some element of public interest or quaintness in the epitaph ; for instance :

It is only to be supposed that " William Ledger, late of this parish, who died 24th January 1823," was himself the author of the epitaph carved upon his headstone. Its sentiments are such that Mr. Hellicar was much exercised as to how such an obituary was sanctioned by the Vicar. In lines of uncertain scansion it calls for Divine Judgment on those who had wronged him—the robber in question being, according to a pencilled note in my copy of Mr. Hellicar's *Notes*, the then landlord of the White Hart Hotel. The inscription is as follows :

> " He who now lies beneath this sod
> Was ever mindful of his God :
> For years he was prepared to die
> And leave this world of misery.
> Though robbed on earth by pretended friends,
> Injustice done him for their selfish ends,
> He's now beyond their power and sphere,
> As thieves and robbers cannot enter there.
> But let those wicked beings know
> The time will come for them to go,
> To give account for crimes both great and small,
> Before the Lord, the righteous Judge of all,
> And there receive their final doom
> From whence they never more can come."

The headstone to Ann Ward, 1823, was :

" erected by her sorrowing friends, J. & A. C. Dunkin, That when the nettle shall skirt its base, the moss shall obliterate the inscription, and the Hillock sink level with the surrounding sod, Their children may recognise the spot where rests the remains of their affectionate and sincere benefactress."

This inscription may be presumed to be the work of John Dunkin himself, and upon the same stone is recorded the fact that

" in the adjoining grave reposes the body of John Dunkin of Bicester in the County of Oxford, who died suddenly November 12th 1823 in the 84th year of his age,"

but this is the Bromley historian's father, he himself being buried in Dartford Cemetery, 1846.

In a contribution to the *Morning Post*, November 29th, 1912, Mr. E. B. Osborn gave a selection of many quaint and characteristic epitaphs which had come under his notice. One of these is the inscription which he cites as being cut upon a gravestone of a sailor in the churchyard of St. Peter and St. Paul, Bromley :

> " Blow, Borrious [Boreas], Blow,
> Let Neptune's Billows Rore,
> Here lies a sayler, landed safe on shore.
> Thou Neptune's waves have torst him to and fro
> By God's decree he lies ancored here below,
> Here he lies amist the fleet
> Waiting orders Admirral Christ to meet."

In addition to the memorials within the church and in the churchyard there are subterranean vaults or catacombs under the north aisle which serve as the last resting-place of many Bromley worthies. The catacombs are entered from outside the church at the west end of the north aisle. They were excavated and cleared in 1792, and consist of a central passage flanked on each side by a number of oblong vaults in which are leaden coffins. On the north side there are nine such vaults, and on the south side three. The vault of Walter Boyd of Plaistow Lodge contains eight or nine coffins (1831); that of George James Hamilton four (1797). Among those whose coffins are ranged on the north side are Thomas Raikes, John Wells, Robert Booth, and George Norman. On the south side is the coffin of Claude Scott.

At the extreme east end there was an extension leading under the present approach to the chancel. This portion is now inaccessible, having been bricked up presumably when the chancel was built. There is a tradition that here were deposited the remains of some Bishops of Rochester, and past Rectors of Bromley Church, but in default of further investigation this must remain merely a tradition.

SECTION III. BEQUESTS, INCUMBENTS, AND MISCELLANEOUS

SCANTY as are the records of medieval Bromley, nevertheless what we have of them enable us, with the aid of a little historic imagination, to frame a mental picture in some respects in striking contrast to that presented by the Bromley of to-day. We are free to imagine a church, externally of considerable beauty, for it was the product of a fine period of ecclesiastical architecture, adorned within with many shrines sacred to the Virgin and to the saints, and possessing much rich furniture and splendid plate. We may suppose that the Rectory of Bromley was a very desirable benefice, if it is indeed a fact that in the fourteenth century the succession to it was a source of keen competition among the greatest in the land. We see Rectors of Bromley bearding Bishops in the very heart of their diocesan palace, and one of them, John de Frendsburie, going so far as to excommunicate the Bishop of Rochester in Rochester itself. We can conjure up a vision of Bromley Rectors exercising the rights of manorial lords in their rectorial courts, exacting quaint penances, and ruling all and sundry with the heavy hand of ecclesiastical authority. For such a picture as this there is the warrant of existing documents, and from them much more may be surmised. It is therefore the purpose of this concluding section of the chapter on the Parish Church to justify our imaginary picture by proofs drawn from the documents in question, and to add a few miscellaneous notes on certain matters, the treatment of which did not conveniently fit into the preceding sections.

It is clear that from very early times the absence of a north aisle was felt by some people to be a blemish upon the structure which ought to be rectified. Thus, in 1467, a certain Richard Smyth, alias Richard Bochier, left by will to the church the sum of 13s. 4d., and " if the parishioners have begun the new aisle of the Church within four years after my death, I bequeath to the said building 6s. 8d." Similarly a few years later, in 1479, Bernard Cavill, of Cheselhurst, left " to the works of the Church of Brome-leygh 6s. 8d." But exactly what " the works " were that were in progress is unknown ; possibly the reference is to the new aisle.

Some other curious bequests may be suitably cited at this point, for though not referring to new construction, they throw a light upon the interior of the church and the manners of the time.

The earliest record of a bequest to Bromley Church is the will of Abel de Sancto Martino, its Rector in 1295. He leaves all his property to be sold by his executors, " saving five marks sterling annually for the maintenance of a chantrey in the Parish Church of ' Bramlye ' for the good of his soul, and the souls of Alianora his sister and others."

In 1484 Margaret Lemans willed " that my beste gyrdyll [best girdle] be gewyn to oure Lady of Pity in the Church of Bromelegh, and a basyn to make a Candylesticke with."

In 1498 "Sir Wm Quynton, parish priest of Bromley" bequeathed " XIIJ*s*. IIIJ*d*. to by a processionall to ye use of ye seyde Church."

Two considerable sums of money are left for the purpose of buying a chalice. Thus, in 1499, Alis Shott bequeathed 26*s*. 8*d*. " To the buying of a chales to the use of the same church." Alis Shott also left two sums of 13*s*. 4*d*. " to the mendyng of Pad Lane—to the mendyng of hikks Lane." And in 1528 Richard Sharpe, Rector of Bromley, left the very large sum of £6 for a " chales or a vestyment," and " all my goods at Bromley to my successor for my dilapidacions, desiring hym to be content therew^h, for I have spent largely there in reparacions, and nothing at my entry. To Crists Colleg in Cambrig to bye 2 masers " (maple-wood drinking-cups or bowls).

Legacies in connection with the clock were left in 1533 and 1551. This clock of the sixteenth century must not be confused with the present clock in the tower, dating only from 1777. The old clock was apparently a dial clock, dependent on the sun, installed about 1551, for Elizabeth Watson, " wedowe," leaves 8*d*. " to the makyn of the clocke," and two years later John Halpenny, " bacar " (baker) leaves 20*d*. " to him that kepeth the clocke, towards his waigs [wages] for one year."

The music of the church was not overlooked. In 1494 Robert Shote left 3*s*. 4*d*. " to the organs in Bromley Church, and 20*s*. for 3 surplesse [surplices] for to be made to the said Church."

Stephen Kyte, in the next year, 1495, bequeathed £5 for " a sufficient antiphonar as any is now in the church," 'antiphonar' being a service book containing whatever was sung in the choir.

A curious legacy in 1515 leaves to the church " a tuell to be forth-cumyng at Eastre when Our Blessed Lorde is mynistred unto the parish " ; ' tuell ' apparently signifying table-cloth, or altar-cloth. It is a mere sugges-tion, quite without authority, that this may have reference to the ceremonies connected with the Easter Sepulchre.

In 1556 David Curson, priest, left 20*s*. " to the Church of Bromley where I now dwell towards the buying of a vestment." Curson was chap-lain to a private family, that of Robert Knight, and had no official connection with the Parish Church.

Among bequests frequently repeated in the wills of this period was one " for an honest prest to singe in the church of Bromley for halfe a yer after my decesse—5 marks." Another testator who died without heirs directed that the proceeds of his estate should go " to finde a prest in the church of Bromley as long as it will last, except part of it to the reparacion of the church of Bromley, 40*s*., and 40*s*. to mende fowle wayes in the same parish that most nede it."

The priests here named would be chantry priests from one of the many brotherhoods, who presumably lived in the town till their obligations were fulfilled, but otherwise had no connection with it.

It will be observed that the above entries refer for the most part either to the fabric of the church or to its furniture. The entries which follow are specific bequests towards the maintenance of lights on the high altar or before the images of saints contained in the various shrines in the church.

The actual terms of the various bequests will most forcibly indicate the multiplicity of these shrines, and the views entertained of the relative efficacy of their intercession. But before any saint comes the High Altar. Thus in 1456:

" To the High Altar, 7*d.*; to the light of the Blessed Marie, 6*d.*; to the light of the Holy Cross, 6*d.*; to the light of St. James, 6*d.*; to the light of St. Nicholas, 4*d.*; to St. Katrine, 4*d.*"

In 1467:

" To the High Altar, 12*d.*; to the light of the Holy Cross, 6*d.*; to the other lights in the same church, 6*d.*; to the fabric of the church, 13*s.* 4*d.* "

In 1471:

" To the High Altar for tithes forgotten, 6*d.*; to the light of the Holy Cross, 6*d.*; to the light of the Blessed Marie in the chauncel there, 4*d.*; to the light of St. James, 4*d.*; to the light of St. Nicolas, 4*d.*"

In 1503:

" To the High Altar, 6*d.*; to the light of St. Peter, 6*d.*; to the light of St. Paul, 6*d.*; to our Lady light, 6*d.*; to St. Nicholas light, 6*d.*; to St. James' lighte, 6*d.*; to the light of our Lady of Pity, 6*d.*; to St. Christopher light, 6*d.*; to the light of St. Loye [Eligius], 6*d.*"

In 1507:

" To the High Altar, 3*s.* 4*d.*; to the reparacion of the great bell in the said churche, 40*s.*; to the gilding of the tabernacle of Our Lady of Pitye, 26*s.* 8*d.*"

In 1520 Henry Kighley leaves " a taper of 4*d.* to our lady in the chaunsel," while William Both, in 1525, leaves 20*s.* for " a bassyn [basin] and 5 tapers of virgyn wex to be sett afore oure lady in the lytell chauncell."

A favourite shrine was that of Our Lady of Pity. Thus : " To Our Lady of Pity. Henry Payne 1455." " To O^r Lady of Pity a taper price 2*d.* Thos Matthew, 1500." " To O^r Lady in the chapel a taper. John Colman, 1500." " A taper to our lady in o^r lady Chaunsell. Andrew Littlegrome, 1513."

Robert Shote, who provided for the organs and 3 surplices, left 12*d.* " to the light of Saynt Loye." John Colman " 2 tapers of wax of 2*d.* a pece to the light of Petir and Powle." Thomas Matthew " a taper of a peny to Seynt Looye." Similar legacies are left for lights before St. Katherine, St. Nicholas, St. James, St. Christopher, St. Sebastian, St. Thomas, St. Michael " Archangel," St. John Evangelist, St. John Baptist, and St. Eligius. A taper of 2*d.* is left by Andrew Littlegrome " to the trynite " (Holy Trinity) " to stand on the hight aulter," and " to the aulter before the trinite a taper of 3*d.*" by Henry Kighley ; while in 1503 Robert Juler wills that his son John shall buy a lamp for 10*s.* " to hang afore the Rode in the Church of Bromley." The mere enumeration of these legacies gives an idea of the great number of images of saints which stood in the church, and suggests that where there were images of saints there might also have been in some cases shrines to contain them.

A noteworthy entry in old wills is the desire frequently expressed that the testator may be buried under, or as near as possible to, " the Yew Tree." An avenue of such trees led apparently to the west entrance, and one in particular at the east end of the church seems to have been there from time immemorial.

In 1544 Thomas Hubberd wills that " my body to be buried in the churchyard of Bromley under the Yew tree."

In 1588 Richard Hassall, who built the well-known inn the Rose and Crown, willed " to be buried in the churchyard of Bromley as neare to the Yewe Tree upon the eastside as conveniently may be done—to the poore people of the said Parisshe at the day of my buriall fower dozen of bread."

In 1543 James Thorpe wishes to be buried " on the hill toppe before the Church porche in the churchyard of Bromley."

And in 1588 William Jueller selects " under the wall of the vestry " as the place for his grave.

Passing to the incumbents of Bromley Church, it will be remembered that Bromley was a manor of the bishopric of Rochester, and that the church and its officers were, therefore, feudally as well as ecclesiastically, subordinate to the Bishop. The power of appointment to the living rested with the Bishop, who was himself very frequently in residence in the palace near by, for Bromley Palace was a favourite residence of Bishops of Rochester from the beginning until the sale of the property in 1845. None the less the living of Bromley was, apparently from the first, a rectory, i.e. the incumbents were Rectors, invested with certain rectorial rights which, in some cases, were practically manorial rights. The glebe land was their freehold, and the tenants under the Rector were subject to the jurisdiction of his rectorial court, a state of things which sometimes led to conflicts between the rival jurisdictions of Bishop and parson, the unfortunate tenants being compelled to pay dues to both. Records of the proceedings of the rectorial courts are only available for 1453, 1454, and 1455, but from them the general character of those proceedings sufficiently appears. Thus we read :

"Inquisition taken by the fealty of the suitors aforesaid who say upon their oath of fealty that Richard Dyse, William Abell, William Say, William Barnard, Richard Wolsy, and the heirs of Ralph Bothe are Freeholders of the Lord, and suitors of this Court. And now they do not perform suit at this Court. Therefore each of them is amerced according to the fines imposed by the Court, upon the head of each of them, to wit each of them at two pence."

"And the Bailiff is ordered to distrain them to perform their suit at the next Court."

Other examples will be found in Chapter II.

There are several cases before these rectorial courts of tenants who have alienated their land, or some part of it, to sub-tenants. They are ordered to pay a relief to the overlord, to wit, a fourth part of the rent received. A full list of the cases brought before the rectorial courts of 1453–5 would occupy much space, and would constitute a mere repetition, under other names, of the specimens already cited. But one further entry in the Court Roll of 1454 is important as establishing the right of the rectorial lord to recover by escheat the land of a tenant who died without heirs. A certain Roger Overton and Katherine his wife had purchased a messuage and garden to be held in perpetuity subject to a rent to the overlord, but both Roger and Katherine having died without heirs,

"the aforesaid messuage with garden adjoining deverted to William Freston, clerk-Parson of the Church of Bromleyh by escheat as in right of the Church and Lordship aforesaid."

Summarising the proceedings of these courts as a whole, Mr. Coles Child says :

"In these rolls we have evidence that at a very early period an allotment of land had been made for the support of the Church, and that in this case . . . a Manor had been created. Not only do we find the Rectors of Bromley holding their Courts, and levying quit rents and heriots in precisely the same manner as the Superior Lord, but actually recovering by Escheat the land of a tenant who died without heirs."

The Rectors of Bromley continued to hold this position of seigneurial and semi-independent importance for several centuries. But at the first whisper of the Reformation it had to be surrendered. In 1537 the King, Henry VIII,

"by his special grace and mere notion, also for forty pounds," transferred to the Bishop of Rochester the full rectorial rights vested in the living of Bromley,

" all and singular, glebes, tithes, oblations, obventions, fruits, and emoluments, and other advantages whatsoever appertaining in any way to the aforesaid Church and Rectory,"

subject, however, to the provision by the Bishop of a reasonable sum of money for

" the poor parishioners of the aforesaid Church in each ensuing year for ever."

The King moreover enjoined that perpetual Vicars should be ordained, appointed, and sufficiently endowed by the Bishop out of the rectorial revenues.   In this way the incumbents of the living of Bromley were converted from Rectors into Vicars or Curates, without glebe, tithes, or domicile, and with salaries which soon became quite inadequate to their position.   For the financial obligation imposed upon the Bishop to provide a sufficient endowment for the Vicar seems in practice to have resulted in the Bishop appropriating the whole of the revenues of the rectory, and paying to the Perpetual Vicar a sum in cash supposed to represent one-third of the total sum.   Fluctuations in the value of money brought it about that this fixed cash payment became in time what Dr. Beeby calls a " contemptibly small " fraction of the receipts from the rectory, which, in the main, went to swell the endowment of the bishopric, itself only scantily provided from other sources.   It is only within comparatively recent times that any considerable improvement has been made in the stipend of Bromley Vicars. Bishop Murray of Rochester added something to it ; in 1868, under the impulse of Mr. Hellicar, £1,000 was raised by contributions from the parishioners towards the construction of the present vicarage, which once more provided them with a domicile.

From the time when the transfer was first made it seems to have been the custom of the Bishops to grant leases of the tithes, glebeland, and the Church House which used to be the domicile of the Rector.   Thus Bishop Warner as from February 10th, 1639, granted leases for twenty-one years to George Buckeridge of Lewisham at the reserved rent of £60 per annum and forty quarters of oats.

In 1646 John Younge was lessee.   In 1706 the leases were in the possession of William Emmett.   Through his granddaughter they came into the possession of John Innocent.   Mr. Innocent's daughter, Eleonora, married Mr. James Norman, whose son, Mr. George Norman, became lessee in 1811.   He was induced by Bishop Walker King, of Rochester, in 1828 to part, at a low price, with the lease of the great tithes, glebe, and Church House, which, says Mr. Philip Norman, the Bishop kept " for himself and his family, producing a very considerable income for many years."   Since

1868 the great tithes and other endowments of the rectory have passed into the hands of the Ecclesiastical Commissioners.

Lists of the Rectors and Vicars of Bromley Church have been supplied by Dr. Beeby, Rev. A. G. Hellicar, and Mr. Geo. Clinch. None of them are complete, and Mr. Hellicar deplored the fact that no antiquary had so far taken in hand the task of compiling a complete and authentic record. It is not claimed for the list, given as an appendix to this book, that it is absolute or final, but it fills up many gaps in the other lists, and is, it is believed, as complete as, with present knowledge, it is possible to make it.

The main authority for the authenticity of the record for the last three centuries is the Parochial Registers, where entries are frequently endorsed by the signature of the incumbent. The Parochial Registers of Bromley Church, however, do much more than attest the existence of successive Vicars. They throw some interesting side-lights upon the life of the town, and provide some statistical information as to its population.

The original purpose of Parish Registers was that they might record the births, deaths, and marriages within the parish. Such Registers were first ordered to be kept under Henry VIII (1538), and a further order of Elizabeth enjoined that a Register Book should be provided in each parish. This was in 1558, and accordingly the first Parish Register of Bromley dates from that year. The book bears upon its cover, as a title, " The Register of Bromley in Kent, begun Anno Domini 1558, was all new bound wth addicons of new leaves, Anno Domini 1652."

Within, as a heading, there is entered :

> " Baptisms, 29th Nov. 1558—13 Jan. 1715."
> " Burials, 13th Nov. 1578—27 July 1678."
> " Marriages, 24th Jan. 1575—31st Jan. 1734."

Mr. Hellicar has left, in MS., an analysis of baptisms up to Charles II, and it is his analysis which provides evidence as to population (this MS. note, by the way, is in correction of the printed statement made in his History) :

> " There are," he says, "eleven leaves of the Register filled with Baptisms in Queen Elizabeth's reign, over 850 in all, as there is an average of 39 on each side of a leaf. The Baptisms in James I's reign fill 8 leaves (making 624) : those of Charles I 7 leaves (546) ; those of the Commonwealth 7 : and those of Charles II, 12 (936)."

These figures work out over a period of 127 years at a total of 3,502, or rather more than 27 baptisms per annum.

An entry on the fly-leaf marks the revolutionary period of the Commonwealth. With the abolition of episcopacy as a form of church government, Bishop Warner was turned out of his see, and the manorial rights of the Bishop's manor of Bromley were sold, March 1st, 1647, to Augustine Skinner for £5,665 11*s.* 11*d.* The forces of the Government had to be enlisted to secure possession for Skinner, and several documents are still extant which show something like organised resistance against his occupation of the episcopal palace. He was, however, eventually installed as Lord of the Manor, and he and his family held possession until the Restoration, when the Bishops were reinstated in their sees, palaces, and endowments. The entry on the fly-leaf of the Register testifies that it is to be remembered :

" that Mr. Henry Arnold of Bromleigh, Clerke, being elected at a Vestry to be Parish Minister of Bromleigh aforesaid, was approved by Mee William Skynner, one of the Justices of the Peace of this County, and took his Oath before me for the due Execution of the sayd office on the Eleventh day of October in the yeare of our Lord 1653. So I testify, William Skynner."

Materials are not available to determine what precisely was the position of Arnold at this time. Though episcopacy was abolished, the Church of England, as such, was in abeyance, and in London Presbyterianism was triumphant, yet the appellation " Clerke" (clericus) in the above document seems to imply that Arnold was one of those clergy of the English Church still permitted by " The Triers" to hold a benefice on the ground that nothing could be urged against his doctrine or his morals. The tolerant policy of Cromwell to all but Romanists may very well have admitted an arrangement of that kind at Bromley. Arnold retained the living after the Restoration until 1662, when he was ejected with some two thousand other Puritan clergy, on refusing to accept the Act of Uniformity.

The name of the first person entered in the Register is of some interest. It is that of Thomas Gammon, under the heading of " Christeninges, Anno Primo Elizabethæ, the 29th of November. Anno Dom. 1558."

The existing Registers, which are now carefully preserved, are voluminous, and, in Mr. Hellicar's opinion, of very much general interest. He selected, for the purposes of his History, the records which he thought to be of most value, and these, together with a few additional ones, are appended.

The Great Plague of London claimed its victims at Bromley in 1665 and 1666.

" Buried, 1665.

Aug. 14th.	Old Thomas Hunt	
„ 5th.	Mary the Wiffe of Thomas Haloway	
„ 22nd.	A strange Woman at the Windmill	
„ 26th.	A daughter of the Strange Woman	of the plague.
	A child of John Coatses [1]	
	Widdow Cooper [1]	
Oct. 11th.	Robert Banks	
Nov. 3rd.	John, the sonn of Robert Banks	

[1] These names scarcely decipherable.

Buried 1666.

Mar. 11th.	Old Whittinghame Fowler	
	Mary and Margerit, daughters of John Bradbarie	of the plague.
May the 12th, 1666.	Elizabeth Watts	
May the 28th.	Edmond Watts	of the plague.
June the 25th, 1666.	William Watts	

THE FOLLOWING ENTRIES ARE OF INTEREST

May 14th, 1605. The reverend father John Byshop of Rochester had his funeral solemnised, his sonne Mr. John Younge being chiefe mourner.

May 31, 1631. The Rt. Rev. Father in God, John Buckeridge, the Ld-Bishop of Ely, some time Bishop of Rochester —buried.

1725, Sept. 12. James Gheys from Emsted, killed by a coach.

1795, Aug. 31. William Burton, killed by Ld Lewisham's Chariot.

1796, July 2. Elizabeth Mann, murdered at Ch. Long's Esq., Bromley Hill.

1797, Aug. 4. William Apted, aet 28, killed in boxing.

1797, Nov. 26. John Reynolds, aet 85. This man was servant to James Norman Esq., of Bromley Common, and afterwards to his son G. N. Esq. He was by birth an American. He left that country for murdering a Custom House Officer in Long Island; he had been in the family for years, and was allowed his weekly wages to the day of his death; he was well known by the name of Old John.

1798, May 1st. Thomas Godley, aet 28. Thomas Godley was killed by Tunbridge Wells waggon, on Friday, 27th April, on Bromley Common.

May 26th. James Bayling, aet 23. James Bayling was Brewer's man to Mr. Tape and was killed a little beyond the 11th milestone on Bromley Common, by the dray running over his head.

1810, June 18. Samuel Morum, aet 41, B. Com. [Bromley Common] Sam. Morum, Ratcatcher and Horse Breaker, tumbled out of a cart near Chislehurst Bridge and broke his neck. H.S. [Dr. Henry Smith]."

The confirmation of the election of Bishop Horsley as Bishop of Rochester is recorded in 1792, presumably because the confirmation occurred in Bromley Church. On the fly-leaf of one of the Registers an entry runs :

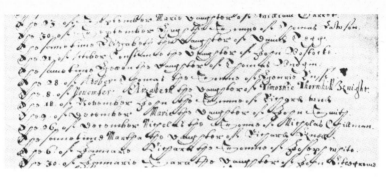

BAPTISMS, 1661.

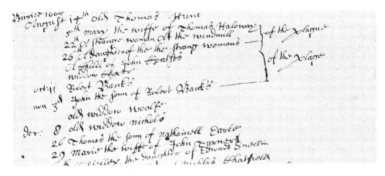

BURIALS, PLAGUE YEAR, 1665.

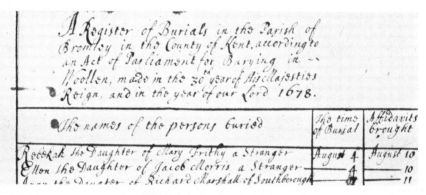

BURIALS IN WOOLLEN, 1678.

FACSIMILE EXTRACTS FROM THE PARISH REGISTERS.

" A register of those who have had certificates under the Hands and Seals of the Minister and Churchwardens of the Parish of Bromley in the County of Kent, of their not having been touched by His Majesty for the King's Evill."

By an Order in Council, January 9th, 1683, everyone who went to Court to be touched by the Sovereign must produce a certificate that he had not been touched before.   The practice of touching for the ' King's Evil ' (scrofula) ceased with the reign of Anne.   Dr. Johnson was among the last of the persons so touched.

The following are a few additional entries not given by Mr. Hellicar :

" *Christenings.*

1733.   Mr. Peter Kelk gave a black cloth pall trimmed with white sarcenet. The Poor are to use it gratis.   All others are to pay two shillings for its use to Wᵐ Dunn the Parish clerk and his successors.   He is to keep an account of the money, and on Christmas Day it is to be given to the poor, not receiving alms, in the Porch of the Parish Church.   W. Dunn to receive ten shillings yearly for keeping the Pall clean and the accounts, etc.

1734.   Thomas Cox of this parish of Bromley, gardener, did aid and assist in taking one William Albon in this parish who was convicted of Felony and Burglary, whereby the said T. Cox obtained a certificate exempting him from serving any office in the said parish. He, the said Cox, hath sold and assigned the said certificate with all the benefits unto Thomas Cummins in this said Parish, Vic-tualer, so that he thereby becomes excused of the same.

1735.   Four hundred pounds borrowed of John Lawson of Bromley at 5 % towards building the workhouse, on a bond given by the Church-wardens and Overseers.

1739.   The Widows of the College petition for seats in the Parish Church ' which they do constantly attend on every Lord's Day.'   The Vestry agree to erect a Gallary on the south side of the Ch. contᵍ in length from the Bishop's seat Eastward 20 foot, in breadth six foot.

1747.   The seats allotted to charity children were fitted up for families wanting seats, the charity children being removed to the north side of the Church, near the West door.   The cost of the work not to exceed £5."

This mention of the " charity children " at once suggests the Bromley Charity School, and various other charitable foundations established in the town, and recorded on the Benefaction Boards which are displayed on the interior walls of the church tower.   But these may be more conveniently treated in a chapter dealing with the Institutions of Bromley.

It only remains to record a few of the ancient customs which used to prevail in connection with Bromley Church. One of these was the custom, noted in one of the quoted entries in the Register, of distributing alms to the poor in the church porch every Christmas Day. Another was the ringing of the ' Pancake ' Bell on Shrove Tuesday, a custom continued to the present day, " without," says Dr. Beeby, " any apparent reason ; though tradition affirms that formerly the ringer of this bell was considered to be entitled to receive one pancake from each house in the town ; and no doubt anciently the bell was tolled for the purpose of calling people, in order that they might confess before Lent."

In the matter of a burial umbrella Bromley seems to have been in advance of most churches. William Hone tells us in his *Table Book* that, when visiting the church, he was struck by the sight of a

" large umbrella of old construction, which I brought out and set up in the churchyard : with its wooden handle fixed into a moveable shaft, shod with an iron point at the bottom, and stuck into the ground. It stood seven feet high ; the awning is of green oiled canvass, such as common umbrellas were made of 40 years ago, and is stretched on ribs of cane. It opens to a diameter of five feet, and forms a decent and capacious covering for the Minister while engaged in a burial service at the grave. It is in every respect a more fitting exhibition than the watch-box sort of vehicle devised for the same purpose, and in some cases trundled from grave to grave, wherein the Minister and Clerk stand, like the ordinary of Newgate, and a dying malefactor at the new drop in the Old Bailey."

Hone doubtless expresses the point of view of the minister. The clerk may have preferred the watch-box.

In bringing this lengthy chapter, on the Parish Church, to a conclusion, I know not whether to apologise to the reader for its length, or for the fact that, long as it is, so many more details might have been added. Such details, however, would merely have been amplifications of the particular question under discussion, and already each of those questions has been illustrated at some length. If the complaint should be that, as it is, the chapter is too long, I can only reply that the life of the town of Bromley has, from the earliest times, centred around its parish church, and therefore that, in any history of Bromley, the parish church should occupy a foremost position. Beneath the shadow of its venerated tower generation after generation of Bromley people, for over five hundred years, have lived and loved, have sorrowed, and have died. It has been the heart of the body politic of the town. It embodies much of its past history, and, irrespective of sectarian differences, it must ever be to every true son of Bromley a venerated and cherished monument of Bromley's antiquity and development.

NOTE

For a period of sixty years, from 1845 to 1905, the connection of Bromley with the diocese of Rochester was severed, the whole of that diocese, with a few exceptions, being transferred to Canterbury. The circumstances in which this transference came about are given in the *History of the Diocese of Rochester,* which appeared in 1927.

The growth of London had made its diocese quite unmanageable. It was, therefore, arranged in 1845 that the Bishop of Rochester should take the oversight of Essex and Hertfordshire, pending the creation of the see of St. Albans, while Canterbury assumed charge of the whole of the old Rochester diocese with the exception of those deaneries—Rochester, Cliffe, Cobham, and Gravesend—which were in the immediate vicinity of the Cathedral City.

When the diocese of St. Albans was created in 1877 it was expected that the see of Rochester would resume its ancient jurisdiction, but the matter was postponed until, in 1905, the new diocese of Southwark was called into being. Then Rochester reverted to its original area, save for Greenwich and Woolwich, and Bromley was once more included, after an absence of sixty years, in the diocese with which, until 1845, it had been continuously connected since the days of King Ethelbert, and possibly even earlier.

ST. MARY'S CHURCH, PLAISTOW, KENT.
One of the windows presented by Mr. Murray S. Richardson.
From a photograph by Mr. S. B. Webber.

Chapter VIII

CHURCHES OTHER THAN THE PARISH CHURCH

FOR more than seven centuries after its first foundation, the parish church of Bromley sufficiently satisfied all the ecclesiastical requirements of the town. As the town grew, so the parish church was altered and enlarged, and no suggestion that any other church was needed seems to have been heard till the beginning of the nineteenth century. By that time a considerable population had established itself in the district around Bromley Common, and a proposition appears to have been put forward that a chapel-of-ease, as an off-shoot from the parish church, should be erected there. No steps, however, to carry any such proposition into effect were taken for another thirty years, things remaining as they were.

It was in, or about, 1832 that a serious and combined effort was made to provide the necessary funds for building a church on Bromley Common which should be separate from, and independent of, the parish church. Colonel Long of Bromley Hill and his family contributed generously towards this project, and they were strongly supported by Bishop Murray of Rochester. In 1839 the Church of Holy Trinity, Bromley Common, was completed, though without its tower, at a cost of £2,648, the want of a tower being supplied three years later at an additional cost of £500. In more recent times the church has been very largely indebted to the benefactions of the Norman family, and both within and without everywhere it bears traces of their devotion and liberality. Within, the chancel apse was added in 1884 by the family as a memorial to their father, Mr. George Warde Norman ; the stained-glass window in the south transept preserves the memory, at the hands of his children, of Mr. H(enry) Norman ; the church was reseated, and provided with a suitable heating apparatus by the late Mr. Charles Loyd Norman ; the pulpit and the small window in the north transept were gifts from other members of the Norman family. Outside, a large portion of the churchyard was the gift of Mr. George Warde Norman, its surrounding wall being constructed at the expense of his son, Mr. C. L. Norman.

Originally it seems to have been assumed that the right of presentation to the benefice was in the hands of the Bishop, and the first incumbent was appointed by the Bishop of Rochester. The nomination proved unfortunate, the first Vicar being compelled to resign within a year or two of his appointment. In the meantime the question had arisen as to whether the power of appointment really did belong to the Bishop or to the Vicar of Bromley, and, in circumstances of which I have no record, it was ultimately determined that the Vicar, and not the Bishop, was the legal patron of Holy Trinity. Accordingly the then Vicar of Bromley, Mr. Newell, exercised his right, in 1843, in favour of the Rev. Arthur Rawson, and upon the resignation of Mr. Rawson, after a tenure of thirty-nine years, Mr. Hellicar presented the living to the Rev. F. W. Haines in 1882.   The living is now, however, in the hands of the Bishop of Worcester.

The Rev. Clement René Sharpe added, by his own exertions, a new vestry in 1905, and a village hall, opened in 1906, has proved of great value to the work of the parish.

An Order in Council of 1843 assigned a definite district to the parish of Holy Trinity, but some portion of this original parish has now been absorbed into that of St. Luke's.

In the meantime the claims of the northern portion of the town were becoming insistent, and about the year 1860 a scheme was set on foot to provide a church which should meet the wants of that district.   Thus, largely through the liberal contributions of the Rev. H. C. Adams, Chaplain of the College, and his family, there came into existence the Church of St. Mary, Plaistow, the nave being consecrated by Archbishop Longley in 1863. Since then the church has been enlarged by the additions of a chancel (1881), a south transept (1893), a north transept, accompanied by considerable extension of the vestries (1900).   A tower, however, is still lacking.

Within, St. Mary owes much to the munificence of benefactors.   The glass, by Mr. Curtiss, of Ward & Hughes, is good, consisting of an east window erected by Lady Scott in memory of her husband, Sir Edward H. Scott, a great benefactor to the church ; two chancel windows commemorate two infant daughters of Major Clement Satterthwaite, who, for over forty years, was constant in his devotion towards the church ; the seven windows in the nave are in memory of Mr. Emmett, and six, also in the nave, given by Mr. Murray Richardson, commemorate various members of his family. To Mr. Murray Richardson also the church owes its reredos and the decorations of the chancel.

The mural decoration of the nave was the gift of Mr. W. H. Bosanquet, and the fine brass lectern that of Mr. E. H. Bayley.   The chancel gates and rail, given by communicants, were dedicated in 1913.

There are within the church brasses to commemorate Hannah Graham, mother of the first Vicar ; F. Lewis Thomas, organist for thirty-seven years ; Gustav Loly, Headmaster of Quernmore School, and Chairman of the Education Committee ; Clement and Ellen Sarah Satterthwaite, "who worked for their church from 1864 to 1906" ; and the Rev. W. Hodgson, Vicar from 1873 to 1898.

A large church hall, erected in Farwig Lane (1904), at a cost of £5,000, testifies to the growing importance of the parish in population and parochial activity.

The patronage of St. Mary is now in the hands of the Bishop of Rochester.

About the same period which marks the erection of St. Mary, Plaistow, an entirely new centre of residential life and activity was springing into being towards the east and south-east of Bromley and Widmore.   Up to the year

1861 Bickley Park was what its name implies, a park surrounding a substantial residence, the property of Mr. Wm. Dent. In that year the property was sold to Mr. George Wythes, who immediately embarked on extensive schemes of development. These schemes included the erection of a church which should be in every way suitable to such a district, and by the arrangement of the sale a large sum of money was set apart for this purpose. The building of a church, dedicated to St. George, was begun in 1863. This church was opened for services, under licence from the Archbishop, in 1864, and was finally consecrated by Archbishop Longley on July 19th, 1865. Meantime arrangements were in progress for assigning to the church a parochial district which should be independent of the mother church of Bromley, but, as these arrangements took long to complete, the first minister of St. George's Church was one of the curates of Bromley Parish Church, the Rev. Walter Field. The Rev. J. P. Alcock was then in charge for a short time, though not apparently legally appointed, and it was not until 1867 that a perpetual curate was formally instituted in the person of the Rev. E. J. Selwyn. Six years later Mr. Selwyn exchanged livings with the Rev. E. H. Plumptre, who, in 1882, was translated from Bickley to the Deanery of Wells, being succeeded at Bickley by the Rev. G. W. Weldon. Unofficially the Vicars of St. George's have taken over the care of the Widmore portion of Bromley parish, an arrangement which necessitated the erection of National Schools, and of a supplementary mission church in Nightingale Lane.

The Church of St. George itself was an imposing structure, crowned by a tower and spire 175 feet high. This spire, however, being built of Caen stone, which is highly perishable, was found to be in a dangerous state within forty years of its erection, and in 1905–6 was at great cost rebuilt of more durable material to the design of Sir E. Newton, a native of the parish.

Within, the church consists of a nave, 100 feet by 30 feet, with five bays, north and south aisles, north and south transepts, and a chancel, 42 feet by 23 feet, with apsidal end.

The original organ by Hill was enlarged in 1910 at a cost of £1,500, and has thus been rendered worthy of all the other internal appointments of the church, and of the services conducted within it. The whole structure, whether judged from the point of view of architecture or from that of its fittings and decoration, constitutes a notable addition to the churches of Kent.

Notwithstanding the successive improvements and extensions of the parish church which have been recorded in the last chapter, the rapid growth of the town from 1850 onwards and the development of the area known as New Bromley were continually forcing the question of further church accommodation to the front. In 1870 that question, in spite of the quite recent construction of St. Mary, Plaistow, became urgent, and various schemes were put forward which were the occasion of lively controversy.

Some were for the further extension of the parish church ; some were for building an altogether new church in the area where it was required, others were for doing nothing. It is unnecessary to revive the somewhat heated correspondence in the local press, and what Mr. Hellicar calls " the war of pamphlets " to which these various opinions gave rise. Ultimately Archbishop Tait was called in to adjudicate, and he decided that if the Vicar of Bromley could supply the existing needs by means of a chapel-of-ease, he had the right to do so. A scheme on this basis was immediately adopted, and a site secured by lease in Park Road. A sum of £750 was raised without difficulty, and the Vicar and churchwardens set themselves to the task of securing a ready-built church. It so happened that the town of Ryde in the Isle of Wight had for sale a large iron church which had been used while the existing parish church of that town was under construction. Accordingly the Vicar, accompanied by his churchwardens, Messrs. Holworthy and Baxter, made an expedition to Ryde, and then and there effected a purchase for £450. At an additional cost of £224 the building was transferred to Bromley and erected upon the chosen site. The church was opened on Ascension Day, 1872, with the Rev. C. R. L. Engström as curate-in-charge. It was from the first regarded as only a makeshift—though the old iron church served its purpose very well—and constant efforts were made both to procure a freehold site and also the means to erect a permanent church. These efforts were so far successful that by July 1879 sufficient funds had been collected to enable the building to be begun, the foundation-stone being then laid by Dr. Parry, the Bishop of Dover.

In May 1880 the church was completed and consecrated by Archbishop Tait under the name of the Church of St. John the Evangelist. It was built from the designs of Mr. G. Truefitt by Mr. T. Crossley of Bromley at a cost of £5,400, inclusive of the site, as a chapel-of-ease to the parish church. This arrangement, however, was of very short duration. Before the end of the year the separate parish of St. John's was carved out of Bromley parish, with its own distinct functions and institutions.

From the first initiation of the scheme St. John's owed much to the activities and assistance of Sir Edward Scott, and since its completion there have been added, chiefly as the result of his munificence, some stained glass in the windows of the apse, oak choir stalls, a pulpit, and an organ. An oak screen, the gift of the parishioners, was added in 1914.

Meanwhile the development of the southern area of the town was proceeding apace, the Church of Holy Trinity being by this time quite inadequate to its ecclesiastical needs. Proposals for the erection of an additional church were in the air as early as 1872, but nothing was done till nine years later when Mr. S. Cawston, afterwards of Bromley Hill, purchased a piece of freehold land at the corner of Addison Road. On this site he erected at his own expense, save for a donation of £100 from Mr. G. W. Norman, an iron church, to which he appointed a curate-in-charge, and guaranteed the major portion of the stipend. All this, however, was merely preliminary to the erection of a permanent church on the site available when the iron church was removed.

Mr. Cawston, however, was a man of strong evangelical tendencies, and, in view of the pronounced individual part he had played in the proceedings so far, and of the fact that he had in so large a measure financed them, he was desirous of perpetuating the distinctively evangelical atmosphere in which the enterprise was moving. To this end arrangements were made to invest the perpetual right of patronage in a body of Trustees drawn from ' The Church Patronage Society,' a society which existed to advance evangelical views, and a Trust Deed to this effect was duly executed.

An arrangement of this kind, however, was by no means to the taste of a considerable number of those who had promised to subscribe to the expense, and, as Mr. Cawston himself objected to certain floral decorations which were introduced into the iron church on Christmas Day, 1883, he not only withdrew his promised subscription to the new church, but closed down the iron church as well. A situation apparently fatal to any further progress had arisen. For three and a half years some adjoining school premises provided accommodation for such services as had hitherto been held in the iron church.

But, at the moment when the original committee was on the point of being dissolved, it was determined to make a fresh and even more vigorous effort. Largely as a consequence of the untiring exertions of Mr. A. P. Jackson, an entirely new committee was got together, which proceeded to invite subscriptions and to negotiate for plans and a site. A letter received from the Archbishop's office with the endorsement of the Ecclesiastical Commissioners assured the committee that they were free to make their own arrangements in regard to the question of patronage, and a promising scheme seemed to be favourably launched. At this juncture the Church Patronage Society intervened with a notification that the society was preparing to exercise its right of appointment to the benefice whenever the new church should be constructed. This was a bolt from the blue, and for a time put a stop to any further activity until the legal question as to the right of patronage should be decided. Ultimately an agreement was reached by which the patronage was vested in three trustees on the understanding that they would transfer their functions in due course to the Archbishop of Canterbury.

The next difficulty to be overcome was that of the site, a difficulty which was successfully surmounted in November 1885, when the site on which the church now stands was secured. At last, on July 31st, 1886, the foundation-stone of the new Church of St. Luke's, Bromley Common, was duly laid by the Archbishop of Canterbury ; a little less than a year later the church, or rather such portion of it as was completed, was consecrated by the Bishop of Dover, and on April 10th, 1890, the complete building, excluding the upper portion of the tower, was consecrated by the Archbishop.   The total cost was about £8,500, the whole of which was provided before the date of the final consecration.

Twenty years later St. Luke's attained its present form.   Almost from the creation of the committee of 1884 Mr. J. W. Wheeler-Bennett had taken an active part in furthering the efforts of those who were intent that a church should be built.   In 1910 this gentleman crowned all his previous services by a munificent gift.   He completed the tower, added the spire, and rounded off these additions by installing in the tower eight bells and the clock.

Within, there is some good glass by Powell.   The four mosaic panels in the niches of the font were the gift of the Chatterton family in 1905.   The organ by Messrs. Lewis of Brixton was secured in 1888, very largely by the personal exertions of Mr. A. P. Jackson, whose brochure, *St. Luke's—a History*, has provided most of the materials for the foregoing narrative.   The facts seem almost to justify the opinion which Mr. Jackson obviously entertained, that, but for him, the difficulties in connection with the construction of St. Luke's could never have been surmounted.

The list of churches serving the interests of the Church of England is not even yet exhausted.   To meet the growing needs of a population rapidly gathering in the neighbourhood of the South Station, St. Mark's was built in 1897 to the design of Mr. Evelyn A. Hellicar as a chapel-of-ease to the parish church.   St. Mark's owes much to the munificence of private individuals, its tower being completed in 1903, largely by the energy and liberality of Mr. Thomas C. Dewey ; in 1911 a south chapel was added as a memorial to the Rev. L. J. Elwin by his widow and relatives; an east window, depicting ' The Resurrection,' was the gift of their daughter, in memory of David and Elizabeth Wishart, and Mr. E. Soames contributed the clock. The alabaster font was the gift of Mr. F. Lucas ; the lectern that of Mr. and Mrs. T. C. Dewey.

Christchurch, in Highland Road, built in the Early English style, was opened in 1887.

It is only within quite recent times that the Roman Catholics of Bromley have established a distinctive church of their own.   Before December 1886 the only church within convenient reach of Roman Catholics in Bromley was St. Mary's, Chislehurst, served by the Rt. Rev. Monsignore Goddard, but in this year the ' Religious of the Holy Trinity ' (founded 1198) took a house called ' Willow Bank,' at No. 8 London Road, Bromley, where services were held in a temporary chapel, served from Chislehurst.   In 1888 the above religious ' Order ' purchased the old Bromley Estate and mansion known as ' Freelands,' for £13,000, with the result that the London Road establishment was transferred to a temporary iron church, built close to the mansion, dedicated to St. Joseph.   The first Rector was the Rev. J. O'Meara.   In 1911, on a portion of the estate in Plaistow Lane, close to Upper Park Road, a new church, dedicated to St. Joseph, was built.

This is of plain Romanesque design, consisting of a nave, shallow north and south aisles, the base of a tower, and two side-chapels ; a gallery over the west end being provided for the Community of the Holy Trinity Convent housed at Freelands, which house has, since its purchase, been doubled in size.

Adjoining the church a presbytery has been built, and an elementary day school.

There is a branch church of St. Swithuns in Fashoda Road, Bromley Common.

We now pass to the numerous Nonconformist churches or chapels which have sprung up in the town during the last hundred and fifty years.

The history of Nonconformity in Bromley in any organised and permanent form seems to date from somewhere around 1770, when the influence of Wesley's great evangelical movement had already penetrated to Bromley. For on December 2nd, 1772, Wesley himself came to Bromley and preached at a house at Widmore even then in use by members of his organisation. In his *Journal* is the following entry :

" I preached, at the new preaching house, in the parish of Bromley. In speaking severally to the members of the Society I was surprised at the openness and artlessness of the people. Such I should never have expected to find within ten miles of London."

The reference to " the members of the Society " clearly proves that already there existed in Bromley an organised body of adherents to Wesley's general principles, though this fact by no means necessarily implies any definite breach with the Church of England, Wesley continuing to his dying day to designate himself as a member and minister of that Church, from which he had neither separated himself, nor wished that others should separate.

This visit, followed as it was by a supply of local preachers who were followers of Wesley, caused the community so to increase in numbers that in 1776 they erected a small chapel between Nos. 12 and 13 on the Chislehurst Road at Widmore Green. This seated about sixty persons, the services at first being held only in the afternoon. It continued to exist for its original purpose for over a century, served by such devoted men as Thomas How, James How, William Gomer, James Brown, and Thomas Gallon, but the erection, in 1884–5, of a new chapel in Tylney Road at last made it superfluous and it was surrendered in 1888, and now serves the office of a garage. On its front gable, however, is still the foundation-tablet worded : " Wesleyan Chapel, 1776. Restored 1847."

By the end of the first quarter of the nineteenth century the growth of Wesleyanism in Bromley had rendered necessary the construction of a chapel in the centre of the town. A suitable site was found off the Upper High Street, about thirty yards back between Nos. 66 and 67, and on it was erected

Zion Chapel, with a schoolroom beneath it, the whole structure being conspicuous for the want of all ornament or adventitious architectural attraction. An unfortunate split in the congregation resulted in the withdrawal of half the members, who thus found it necessary to construct a chapel for themselves, and so, in 1842, a second Zion Chapel came into existence at Farwig. The original chapel in Upper High Street has now given place to a handsome Gothic structure, situated in Lower High Street, from the designs of Mr. W. W. Pocock. Its foundation-stone was laid by Sir Francis Lycett in October 1875. The chapel was opened for public worship in November 1876. The interior of the chapel shows a simple arrangement of nave, chancel, and two aisles, contained under a single oak vaulted roof. An east window of five lights contains, in three of them, the figures of Faith, Hope, and Charity ; the remaining two lights being merely tinted. Some good glass is to be seen in some of the ten windows in the aisles, notably the memorial window to Mr. John Gibbs, of which the subject is ' The Light of the World.' Tablets and memorial brasses intervene between the windows to commemorate William Powell, Eleanor Ellis, John Gibbs, James How, and H. Ellis, the windows themselves being memorials to various devoted members of the congregation.

In 1925 the chapel was entirely renovated and beautified as a Jubilee gift. The chancel was finely panelled in oak as a memorial to William Marsh and John and Charlotte Gibbs. The marble font is to the memory of Louisa Hinchliffe, the oak reading-desk to that of Edward B. Rawlings, and the oak pulpit to that of J. H. Hall.

Complete and commodious school premises to the north-east of the chapel subserve the various extraneous activities of the congregation, being well adapted not only for the purposes of education but also for public meetings, gymnastic classes, and other miscellaneous uses. These were opened in 1893, having been erected at a cost of upwards of £3,000.

Bromley is now the centre of a Methodist circuit which includes Beckenham, Widmore, Keston, Clock-House, and Farnborough. The manse is situated at the rear of the chapel in Holwood Road.

In the long list of triennial ministers are to be found the names of Dr. I. S. Simon, afterwards President of the Wesleyan Conference of 1907. Two other Presidents have been at some time attached to the Bromley Circuit, Dr. Frederick Greeves and the Rev. Marshall Hartley.

Wesley's visit to Bromley, referred to earlier, immediately followed a tour in South Wales, whither he had gone in the summer of 1772 to visit the new seminary established at Trevecca House, near Talgarth, by the celebrated Selina, Dowager Countess of Huntingdon. This lady, who was the patroness of George Whitefield, her chaplain, had warmly embraced the most extreme tenets of Calvinistic Methodism, and had formed what was termed ' a connexion ' for the purpose of organising and propagating her theological views. This ' connexion ' included any who were generally sympathetic

WESLEYAN CHAPEL, UPPER HIGH STREET, 1863.

towards Lady Huntingdon's principles, regardless of denominational label, for Wesleyans, Whitefieldians, Baptists, and some ministers of the Church of England enrolled themselves under the banner of the Huntingdon Connexion. The noble birth, the high social position, and the aristocratic associations of this lady gave a tone of fashionable propriety to the new evangelicalism. Lady Huntingdon attracted to her drawing-room meetings men and women of the highest rank and consideration, to listen to sermons from Whitefield or Romaine. Lords Chesterfield and Bolingbroke paid grave compliments to the eloquence of the preachers. Bath, Cheltenham, and Tunbridge Wells followed London in enthusiasm for the new movement. At length there came the turn of Bromley to fall under its influence.

It was either in 1788, or shortly before, that a few London ministers began the practice of walking from Bishopsgate to Bromley on Sundays in order to teach the children, and to preach the Gospel to whoever would listen to them. Of these some, such as Aldridge, Harper, and Thomas Wills, were definitely associated with Lady Huntingdon, and her Connexion —some were Baptists, some were clergymen of the English Church. Meeting first in a house in Isard's yard, they soon found it necessary to contemplate the erection of a permanent building, and on September 26th, 1788, the foundation-stone of Bethel Chapel was laid in what was afterwards known as Centenary Place, the chapel itself being completed at a cost of £200, and opened on November 26th of the same year.

No departure, however, from the teaching of the Church of England was originally intended. The service book used from the beginning was the Prayer Book ; and Jacob's *Psalmody* or Rowland Hill's *Collection* provided the hymns. In the course of a few years, however, the congregation tended to assume an independent character, and, in 1796, on the formation of the London Itinerant Society, Bethel Chapel was placed under its care and supervision. A Mr. Browning, one of Whitefield's coadjutors at the Tabernacle in Tottenham Court Road, and himself a member, if not a minister, of the Church of England, was entrusted with the general superintendence of the Bethel Chapel and pulpit. Having formed a matrimonial connection with the lady who originally supplied tea to the visiting ministers, Mr. Browning established himself as a resident in Bromley, and continued so to reside until his death in 1827. His successor was Mr. William Holland, a member of the London Itinerant Society, and appointed by it, though neither a minister nor member of the Church of England, but a Baptist.

By this time, however, the original chapel had become too small to accommodate all those who were desirous of attending it. It was therefore determined to build a larger one. A subscription list was opened with such satisfactory results that a site was selected in close proximity to the old chapel, and the work of clearing the ground for the foundations of the new building was on the point of beginning.

But just at this time Mr. John Bromley, an auctioneer and land surveyor of Commercial Road, London, who had been an agent of the Itinerant Society for many years, came to live in Bromley and at once attached himself to the Bethel Chapel community, with whose tenets he was in complete accord. Being, of course, made acquainted with the project in hand, he asked to see the lease. Mr. Bromley's inspection of the lease led him to the opinion that the land in question was not the property of Mr. Isard, the lessor, but of the Bishop of Rochester as Lord of the Manor, an opinion which ultimately proved to be correct. It was therefore necessary to begin all over again and secure a suitable site. Mr. Bromley himself solved the problem by purchasing a plot from the sale of Mr. Cator's land in Widmore Lane. A portion of this land he offered to the Trustees on a lease of 99 years at £10 per annum with the right of purchase within ten years. Mr. Bromley fixed the purchase price at £160, as against £200 suggested by the Trustees, and showed himself in every way anxious to assist the cause. He himself laid the foundation-stone of the new building in June 1835, and on a tablet outside the building the name 'Bromley Chapel' was inscribed.

Before the completion of the building, however, fresh difficulties arose owing to differences of opinion between Mr. Bromley, the Itinerant Society, and the Bromley Committee, as to the exact theological doctrine for which Bromley Chapel stood. In Mr. Bromley's opinion the chapel was being erected not for Independents, or for any other specific denomination, but in order to give substance in Bromley to Lady Huntingdon's Connexion, which, as has been seen, was supported by individuals belonging to many and varying schools of thought. In the Trust Deed Mr. Bromley insisted upon the insertion of fifteen Doctrinal Articles, acceptable to the Huntingdon Connexion, and recognised by the Church of England. These articles therefore became a condition of the Trust, and at the same time a subject of violent controversy and disagreement. The question was submitted by the Itinerant Society to the Congregational Board of Ministers, in direct opposition to the views of Mr. Bromley, who denied that the Congregationalists had any status in the matter. Feeling ran high. An anonymous partisan came forward with an offer of £1,000 on loan at 4 per cent. if the fifteen Articles were excluded from the Trust Deed. Mr. Bromley threatened to cancel the Trust Deed altogether and to withdraw from the undertaking if the Articles were excluded. Eventually the dispute was composed in a manner favourable to Mr. Bromley, who paid arrears due to the builders, advanced considerable sums on mortgage, presented the land on which the chapel stood, together with a right of way to it, in freehold for ever, and himself for a time, in conjunction with others, ministered within the building. These casual ministrations were, however, in the course of a year or two supplanted by a permanent residential pastorate. In April 1837 George Verrall became Pastor of Bromley Chapel, and it was he apparently who, in the course of a ministry extending over twenty-two years, gave to it that distinctively Congregational character which it has since maintained.

CONGREGATIONAL CHAPEL, WIDMORE LANE.
Built 1835 ; pulled down 1880.

BAPTIST CHAPEL, PARK ROAD.
Built 1864.

Verrall resigned in 1859 and was succeeded in turn by E. Bolton, D. F. Longwill, and R. Tuck, who resigned in October 1880.

By this year the activities of the chapel had outgrown its dimensions. It was therefore determined to build an entirely new one on the existing site, and for two years the work of demolition and reconstruction was in progress. In 1881 the foundation-stone of the new building was laid by Mr. Samuel Morley, M.P., and by the end of that year the work was completed at a cost little short of £15,000. It provided seats for 650 people, but in a few years even this accommodation was found to be insufficient. In 1886 the chapel was enlarged by 350 additional sittings at a cost of over £4,500, and two years later a further sum of £1,400 was provided for enlarging the schoolroom. The chapel was again enlarged in 1894, providing about 200 more sittings. A handsome war memorial was erected in the entrance lobby in 1920, and in the same year a minister's house was presented.

This new chapel was built from the designs of John Sulman, A.R.I.B.A. Facing north and south it consists of a nave, two aisles, and transepts ; the latter and the north end of the nave being surmounted by galleries. The organ is by Brindley & Foster. The pulpit, in marble and stone, was erected in memory of the first permanent pastor, George Verrall, by his sons. Various brasses upon the walls commemorate past ministers, deacons, and benefactors.

On the completion of the new chapel in 1882, the Rev. Robert Henry Lovell was appointed pastor, a man still remembered for his eloquence and power as a preacher, for the unaffected simplicity of his life, and for his influence as a man. It was he who laid the foundations of the future strength and prosperity of the church. Practically all its growth took place during the thirteen years of his ministry, and it was in those years that the two enlargements already referred to became necessary. Two mission chapels, one at West Wickham and one at Shortlands, were opened in 1888 and 1891 respectively, largely as a consequence of Mr. Lovell's influence and activity. In the year 1880 the membership of the church was 132. In 1894, the year of Lovell's death, it was 452. In the same period the number of scholars in the Sunday school rose from 260 to 603. These are eloquent figures. Lovell came to the church when it was small, and few in numbers ; he left it greatly enlarged, prosperous and strong, as it has been maintained throughout subsequent ministries. Mr. Lovell died in 1894, and was followed by the Rev. Thomas Nicholson. In 1904 there was a vacancy in the ministry for a year or so. In 1906 an invitation was extended to the Rev. W. Justin Evans to accept the pastorate. In him the Congregationalists of Bromley secured one of the great outstanding personalities in their denomination, a cheery, courageous, and businesslike man, Chairman of the London Congregational Union in 1906. He often filled the pulpit of C. H. Spurgeon's Metropolitan Tabernacle, and was a man of mark in the Religious Tract Society. In Bromley he enjoyed a wide popularity during the term of his ministry. After his retirement in 1911 he still continued to reside in the town, maintaining, till his death in 1924, his active interest in, and constant work for, the causes to which his life had been devoted.

No building specially designed to meet the requirements of Baptists, as such, appears to have existed in Bromley till 1864, though Baptists were included among those itinerant preachers who, as has been seen, first laid the foundations of Nonconformity in the town in or about 1788. In 1863 Archibald Geike Brown, one of C. H. Spurgeon's band of devoted young men, came to Bromley and conducted services in the Baptist interest, in the White Hart Assembly Rooms. His character, eloquence, and organising ability soon gathered round him an enthusiastic following. A permanent and regularised place of meeting became a necessity, and thus, in 1864, the foundation-stone of the Baptist Chapel at the corner of Park and Tweedy Roads was laid by C. H. Spurgeon. The opening sermon was also preached, a year later, by Spurgeon. The chapel was renovated in 1877. In 1890 an organ was installed which was enlarged by an extra manual and additional stops in 1896. In 1905 the ample school premises at the back of the chapel were built at a cost of £2,000.

Archibald G. Brown himself continued his ministrations in the newly erected chapel until 1867, when he left Bromley for wider fields of activity. For twenty-five years he laboured in Stepney, distinguished equally by his missionary zeal and his spirit of practical philanthropy. He became President of the London Baptists' Association in 1877. It was he who was invited to speak the funeral oration over C. H. Spurgeon in Norwood Cemetery in 1892, and, on the resignation of Thomas Spurgeon, Brown was appointed to the pulpit of the Metropolitan Tabernacle which Charles Spurgeon himself had so long adorned.

Altogether a notable figure in the history of Christian endeavour, Archibald Brown, who came to Bromley a mere stripling of eighteen, and who left it before he was twenty-five, has left behind him there both a reputation and a record of achievement which will not readily be forgotten.

There is also a Baptist Church in Gravel Road, Bromley Common, opened in 1870, but which for many years was undenominational, a church not being formed till 1892.

The Primitive Methodists of Bromley owe their existence as an organised community to a Mr. and Mrs. John R. Homewood, who, about 1869, migrated from Woolwich where they had been members of a Primitive Methodist church. Not finding any similar body to which they could attach themselves, they, in conjunction with the Rev. John Phillips, their minister at Woolwich, hired a room at the back of 48 Stanley Road—the room is now a stable—and were joined a year or two later by Mr. William J. Wickens of West Wickham. A little community was thus gradually established under the ministrations of the Rev. Jesse Ashworth of the Croydon circuit, who had travelled extensively in Palestine. Troubles, however, in the course of time arose with the landlord, a Mr. Goswell Johnson, himself a man of very pronounced views with which it may be supposed the little community in some way found itself in conflict. It was excluded for a time from its premises, and, with small prospect of renewing the lease, it was found necessary to take immediate steps to secure a permanent building as its own property. Notwithstanding the fact that there were no available funds, nor any wealthy members, nor any large or influential body of supporters, the project advanced, and, largely through the energies of the Rev. Elijah Jackson, a sufficient sum was ultimately collected to justify a beginning. The foundation-stone of a new chapel was duly laid in Bloomfield Road, Bromley Common, and the building opened for services in March 1877. By the beginning of the present century, however, the chapel had proved too small for its congregation. It was therefore determined to erect a new building upon the unused portion of the site, and to relegate the existing chapel to the uses of a schoolroom. The principal foundation-stone of the existing structure was laid in April 1907 by Alderman R. W. James, Mayor of Bromley ; the architects being Messrs. Mould & Porritt, and the builders Messrs. J. Podger & Sons. The total cost amounted to over £5,000.

In 1899 Bromley became established as part of a new circuit, with Penge and Orpington, and in 1907 the superintendent minister—the Rev. John T. Taylor—removed from Penge to Bromley in order to be in the centre of the circuit. Mr. Taylor was succeeded in turn by the Revs. W. Curry, E. Lucas, Harvey Roe, and J. Marcus Brown, the present minister, who came to Bromley in 1920.

The Presbyterian Church, though late in coming, finds itself worthily represented in Bromley. It was not till 1895 that the existing church was erected, but when once the project was started it was carried through in a thoroughly effective way. The group of buildings, at the junction of Upper Park and Freelands Roads, comprise not only the church, but a commodious lecture hall, easily adapted for the purposes of a Sunday school, a session room, classrooms, kitchen, deacons' room and offices all suitably equipped, the whole being admirably planned, and adding in the mass an architectural attraction to that part of the town.

The church, surmounted by a spire 118 feet high, is cruciform in shape, its transepts, however, being very shallow, and consists of a nave and two aisles, the east end being raised by two steps above the level of the main building. Over the transepts are galleries, as also over the lobby at the west end. The windows, filled only with tinted glass, present no feature of special interest, but the plain unpolished oak panelling of the east end, the choir stalls and pulpit of the same wood give distinction to the interior. The font is of highly polished Carrara marble set upon coloured marble pilasters, all of these adornments, panelling, choir stalls, pulpit, and font, being gifts to commemorate friends and benefactors. Among the benefactors the name of Mr. Robert Whyte, Jr., stands out conspicuously—a man remarkable for loftiness of character, integrity of purpose, and disinterested public spirit. He still remains in the memory of the writer as one whose mere appearance inspired confidence and respect. In the sphere of social service great things were expected of him, and in that sphere no expectations, however high, were disappointed. A marble tablet, affixed to the wall of the north aisle, commemorates his virtues, and the services rendered by him to the church of which, for thirteen years, he was an elder.

Other memorials in the form of brasses and marble tablets recall the memory of departed friends and benefactors, one in particular being worthy of special note. It is a brass, commemorating the ministry and devoted services of Dr. Charles Moinet, the first minister of the Presbyterian Church in Bromley, whose reputation extended far beyond the limits of any given locality, for, in 1899, he was chosen as Moderator of the Synod of the Presbyterian Church of England.

In addition to the various churches and chapels of which some story has been given, it may be mentioned that the Strict Baptists had for many years an iron building in College Slip; the Plymouth Brethren have a gospel hall in Freelands Grove; the Salvation Army first established barracks in Bromley in 1886; and, in comparatively recent times, the Christian Scientists have attracted a considerable following, and have lately converted their temporary accommodation in Widmore Road into one of those structures which now distinguish so many towns in this country and in America.

It is appropriate here to mention the Bromley Common Iron Room Mission, instituted and carried on by Mr. Matthew Henry Hodder for nearly forty years. Coming to Bromley about 1861, he resided at Bromley Common. Finding that district lacked opportunity for religious worship, he at once endeavoured to supply the need by services in the open air and in a tent. In 1873 he had an Iron Room erected in Great Elms Road. From that date he continuously carried on, with the aid of friends, undenominational services until 1910, when advancing years compelled him to transfer the responsibility to others. Every object for the betterment both physical and spiritual of those among whom he lived had his sympathy and support. He was a member of the Cottage Hospital Committee, and was associated with the Charitable Society from its inauguration in 1885 until his death in 1911, serving it as Treasurer for twenty-three years. Outside Bromley, the Y.M.C.A., of which he was a founder and for fifty years a staunch supporter, the Ragged Schools, for which he worked for more than sixty years, are but two of the many good causes to which he devoted his services. His funeral furnished a significant illustration of the impression a really good life makes upon those who come in contact with it. The barriers of sect were thrown down. Churchmen and Nonconformists united in showing affectionate and sincere respect to one who for fifty years had lived among them a life of unselfish devotion to the welfare of others.

Chapter IX

BROMLEY COLLEGE

AMONG the institutions of Bromley there is one which takes a very prominent, if not the foremost place, and that one is Bromley College, or, as it was originally called, Bishop Warner's Hospital. It is notable alike for its antiquity, the original foundation dating back for more than 250 years, for the beauty of its structure and surroundings, and even more for the fact that it has continuously fulfilled, and still fulfils, the original purpose of its founder. There, in cloistered seclusion, but in close contact with the busy world of the High Street and the London Road, live forty widows of diocesan clergymen, each separately housed, and in part maintained, through the munificence of Bishop Warner and subsequent benefactors of the institution.

Dr. John Warner, Bishop of Rochester, died in the twenty-ninth year of his bishopric, at the age of eighty-seven, on October 21st, 1666.[1] A few weeks before his death he made a will by which he instructed his executors to provide out of his personal estate

" a Hospital or Almeshouse for twentie poore widowes of orthodox and loyall clergiemen, to be seated as near as conveniently may to the Cathedrall Church of Rochester."

By the terms of the will a preference was to be given to widows of clergy in the diocese of Rochester, but, failing a sufficient number of these, the hospital was to be available to clerical widows from any diocese. The will also stipulated that the office of chaplain should be held only by a member of Magdalen College, Oxford, the Bishop being himself a Magdalen man, and at one time Fellow of that College. The sum assigned to this purpose was £8,500.

In order to carry out this generous and charitable design his executors (Sir Orlando Bridgeman, Lord Chief Justice ; Sir Philip Warwick, Knt., Dr. Thomas Pierce, President of Magdalen, and Dr. John Lee, Archdeacon of Rochester) were directed to provide a suitable building, and, in addition to this capital sum, the testator further charged his private manor of Swayton, Lincolnshire, to the amount of £450 per annum, to supply a pension of £20 a year to each of the twenty widows, and a salary of £50 a year to the Chaplain.

It was not possible, owing to the cramped and confined conditions prevailing in the city of Rochester, to find a suitable site there, and therefore it was determined to erect the building at Bromley, where for so many centuries the Bishops of Rochester had possessed a palace, in which Warner himself had died.

---

[1] The College commemorates Warner's death on October 14th ; Archdeacon Tait's investigations have established the 21st as the correct date.

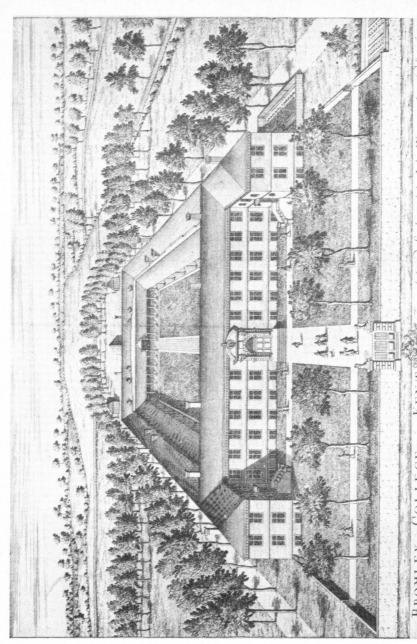

BROMLEY COLLEGE in KENT Founded and Endowed by John Warner late B[p] of Rochester for twenty Clergymens Widows and a Chaplaine AD 1672.

This Plate is Humbly Inscrib'd to Lee Warner Esq[r] of Walsingham in the County of Norfolk 1730.

Thomas Badeslade delin.   Joh: Harris sculp.

By a deed in the possession of the Lee-Warner family, John Baynes, of London, Gent., conveys the land on which the College was erected to Sir Orlando Bridgeman and others. It is dated June 4th, 1669. The " Buttings and Boundings," or, in other words, the boundaries of the property, are precisely defined therein.

A special Act of Parliament, passed in 1670, authorised the executors to build anywhere within the diocese, at their discretion, and as the Bishop's will made no adequate provision for repairs, the executors, with the consent of the heir-at-law, raised an additional £5 per annum from the manor of Swayton, supplemented by a donation of £100 apiece from each of the executors, by which a fee-farm rent of £10 per annum was purchased, thus inaugurating the system of voluntary contributions which, from time to time, has been practised ever since.

It is probable that the actual structure was begun immediately after the passage of the 1670 Act ; the actual date of its completion is not known. There is a tradition, not supported, however, by any documentary authority, that some part of the materials, especially the stone columns in the original cloister, were brought to Bromley from the ruins of the great Fire of London (1666).

The original building consisted of one large quadrangle, with cloisters, which remains to-day almost as it was originally built. Two projecting wings in front serve as the houses of the chaplain and the treasurer. The chaplain's house still fulfils its original purpose, but that of the treasurer has been long ago surrendered for the benefit of the College, and is let at a yearly rental as a private residence.

The building is approached through a handsome wrought-iron gate, bearing the date 1666, supported by stone gate-posts surmounted by mitres. The style of the design, however, suggests to expert authorities that the gate is of the Early Georgian period, about 1720, to which the date of the founder's will has been affixed.

The entrance to the quadrangle itself is through a stone archway, over which are placed the arms of the founder impaled with those of his see, surmounted by a mitre, under which is the inscription :

" DEO ET ECCLESIAE.
THIS COLLEGE FOR TWENTY POORE
WIDOWES (OF ORTHODOXE AND LOYALL
CLERGYMEN) AND A CHAPLIN WAS
GIVEN BY JOHN WARNER LATE L^D
BISHOP OF ROCHESTER,
1666."

The archway leads into the cloisters, and abutting on the cloisters are the original twenty houses occupied by the beneficiaries of the bequest. They

BROMLEY COLLEGE.

The first quadrangle.

BROMLEY COLLEGE.

The main entrance.

are not exactly uniform, some being rather larger than others, but for the most part they consist of a hall, a sitting-room on the ground floor, a basement kitchen, and two bedrooms on the first floor.   Some of the occupants have constructed comfortable attics in the original roof space, thus enabling a daughter, or daughters, to live with their mother.

On the east side of the original quadrangle was a small chapel.   With the extension of the institution, however, this chapel was found to be insufficient and inconvenient, and was replaced by another which is described in its place in this chapter.   The faculty for the demolition of the old chapel was granted by the Archbishop, and the new one was consecrated by Thomas Sprat, Bishop of Rochester, on October 30th, 1701.

The total cost of the entire foundation, including presumably the charges on the Bishop's Lincolnshire manor, could scarcely have been less than £10,000.

The institution had not been long in existence before complaints were made by some of the widows that their pensions were not regularly distributed, and they claimed that such pensions with arrears ought to be paid to them by the existing holder of the Bishop's manor of Swayton, Mr. Lee-Warner. These complaints led to a lawsuit, the Grace Featley case, which was carried to the House of Lords, and of which it is now possible to give some account.   In September 1925 an old chest was discovered in the College, which contained a mass of papers, most of them in a state of decomposition. Among these papers was the original Trust Deed, books of receipts from widows for their pensions, the agreement with John Baynes to buy the land, and a vellum deed and many legal papers connected with the Grace Featley case.

It appears that the owner of Swayton Manor, Mr. Lee-Warner, had either refused to pay the widows' pensions chargeable on the estate, or had fallen into serious arrears in payment.   As a result the widows had incurred debts with the tradesmen of the town, who at last threatened to resort to legal action.   Whereupon Mrs. Grace Featley assumed the rôle of the widows' champion, and appealed to the Bishop of Rochester.   But being herself subjected to pressure by one of her creditors, she secured in some way the services and support of a lawyer, William North, who threatened proceedings on behalf of the widows generally against Lee-Warner.   Whereupon Lee-Warner came to Bromley, broke into Mrs. Featley's house, threw her effects into the quadrangle, and installed a Mrs. Oliver in her place.

North now took the case into Court, with the ultimate result, after an appeal, that Lee-Warner was compelled to reinstate Mrs. Featley, and to pay all arrears due to the widows.   North also brought the matter before the Archbishop of Canterbury, who appointed a commission of inquiry.

The inquisition, taken under this " Commission of Charitable Uses," March 28th, 1693, found that the terms of the Bishop's will had, by this time, been duly executed with the exception that some arrears of pensions were still due. But the commissioners arrived at the conclusion that any flaws in administration were owing to the fact that no properly constituted trustees had been appointed for the inspection and administration of the charity. Consequently they enacted that the Archbishop of Canterbury, the Bishop of London, the Bishop of Rochester, the Judge of the Prerogative Court of Canterbury, the Chancellor to the Bishop of Rochester, the Dean of St. Paul's, and the Archdeacon of Rochester should be, in virtue of their office, trustees of the College, together with Sir Stephen Lennard, Sir John Shawe, and Sir John Morden, Barts.; Abraham Harrison and Philip Boddenham, Esqs., with full powers to make such orders and rules for the well government of the said College, and the due execution of the trust as to them should seem most meet and convenient.

The holders of the various ecclesiastical offices above mentioned, as far as they still exist, continue to be the trustees of the College, together with other gentlemen elected by them, to the total number of eleven, no appointment having been made to replace the Judge of the Prerogative Court when that office was abolished. For very many years a member of the Lee-Warner family has served as a non-official trustee.

In 1735 a strong appeal for funds was issued in the form of a two-leaved folio tract entitled *The State of Bromley College in Kent*, in which the writer urged that the money available for keeping the fabric in proper repair was altogether insufficient ; that incumbents of the diocese of Rochester, and indeed incumbents generally, seemed to have little realisation of the value of such an institution to themselves and their families. If only sufficient funds were forthcoming, the building might not only be put into proper repair, but extended so as to make provision for a larger number. The more generously benefactions were contributed from all dioceses, the greater the claims of all clerical widows to the benefits of the charity.

It was long, however, before a response of any importance was made to this appeal, and the College continued in a poor way. Some relief was afforded by an Act of Parliament, 1757, exempting the institution from the payment of taxes, but it was not till 1770 that the Rev. W. Hetherington of North Cray gave £2,000 for the benefit of widows, a bequest followed four years later by another £5,000 given by Dr. Zachary Pearce, Bishop of Rochester, for augmenting the yearly pensions of the widows and the stipend of the chaplain. In 1782 Mr. William Pearce, brother of the Bishop, left a contingent reversion of £12,000 to be applied to the extension of the institution, and in 1788 Mrs. Helen Bettenson of Chislehurst left £10,000 for the same purpose.

As a consequence of these bequests a new quadrangle was begun for the accommodation of twenty more widows, and was completed in 1805. The new quadrangle is built on the same general plan as the original one, though rather wider. The two together form a connected and harmonious whole, breathing the very atmosphere of peace, contemplation, and retirement, and the visitor is scarcely conscious that more than one hundred years divide one part of the structure from the other.

In the course of the nineteenth century benefactions, testamentary and otherwise, were received by the College on such a considerable scale that it is only possible to make individual reference to the most important, the total sums thus contributed between 1821 and 1893 being about £30,000. Among these a donation by Miss Jane Brooke of Norwich in 1821 is worthy of special notice, for it was given to provide a water supply for the institution ; it has also provided a punning inscription, of which all traces have now disappeared :

> " While round these College walls this water goes
> Forget we not the Brooke from whence it flows."

In 1824 a Mrs. Rose, at one time a pensioner in the College, who came into a fortune, left to it by will a sum of £8,000.

About the same time, 1823, Dr. Walker King, Bishop of Rochester, left £3,000 in the 3 per cents. to provide a pension of £30 a year each to three non-resident widows.

Other benefactions in the same period have made it possible to increase the widows' pensions from the original £20 prescribed by Bishop Warner's will to £38 in the case of all resident widows, except the five oldest who receive £44, this particular increase being the result of a benefaction from the Rev. J. E. Newell, a Vicar of Bromley. The present purchasing power of money, however, is so much less than it was that the increased pensions by no means represent their value at the original figure. No one can live to-day, even rent-free, on £44 per annum, much less on £38. It has been necessary to make it a condition that every applicant for admission shall have some small private income. This, with the pension, free accommodation and free medical attendance, makes life at any rate possible, if not luxurious, for the pensioners.[1]

But by far the most important benefactions of the nineteenth century were those of Mrs. Sheppard for the building and endowment of Sheppard College, and the sums contributed personally or collected by Mr. Joseph M. Holworthy of Bromley, and the Rev. J. E. Newell, for the purpose, originally of repairing, subsequently of completely rebuilding, the College chapel.

In 1840 Mrs. Sheppard, widow of Dr. Thomas Sheppard, Fellow of Magdalen College, and sister of the famous president of that College, Dr. M. J. Routh, left a sum of £7,650 for the purpose of establishing what

---

[1] At the time of writing (1927), the payment of pensions of £38 has been discontinued in the case of those newly elected. Widows now elected are dependent on their private resources. The increased cost of rates and repairs have necessitated this step. Pensions will be resumed when the financial position improves. It is since this note was penned that an anonymous contribution of £30,000 has completely restored the financial fortunes of the College.

may be called a hostel in the grounds of the College for the daughters of widows, who, during the tenure of their mothers, had resided with them in the institution. The position of some of these ladies was a sad and pathetic one. On the death of their mothers, with whom perhaps they had resided for many years, they found themselves cast upon the world, without either the opportunities or the qualifications to make a living for themselves. It was to meet cases of this kind that Mrs. Sheppard resolved to build and endow, as an annexe to the College, and within the College grounds, an institution for pensioners' daughters. The original gift was supplemented two years later by a further gift of £2,000 and in the following year, 1843, an additional sum of £2,000 was provided by Mrs. Sheppard in order to supply financial assistance in the form of out-pensions.

The hostel which thus came into existence in 1840 is known as Sheppard College, and consists of a block of five houses in the north-east corner of the grounds, fronted by a lawn conspicuous for its cedar trees and a profusion of flowering shrubs. The College accommodates five maiden ladies, daughters of clergymen, who had previously resided with their mothers in the College proper. Each of them receives, in addition to a residence, £44 per annum and free medical attendance. Moreover, the two out-pensions of £30 provided by Mrs. Sheppard have been increased to five by the action of Archdeacon Tait of Rochester, and Dr. Joshua, as trustees for Mrs. Finnie, who, in 1907, left her fortune to these gentlemen to be used for charitable purposes at their discretion, and further increased to seven by a bequest from Rev. H. A. Soames in 1921.

Two inscriptions, one in Latin over the centre house of the building, and one in English, celebrate the munificence of the founder, and express its purpose. The latter inscription also commemorates the fact that the first stone of the building was laid by Dr. George Murray, then Bishop of Rochester, and resident in Bromley Palace, on October 1st, 1840, His Grace the Archbishop of Canterbury, William Howley, being at that time a trustee ; John Wells, Esq., being treasurer and trustee, and Thomas Scott, B.D., the chaplain.

Among the daughters of residents in Bromley College, two may perhaps be signalised as of special interest : Miss Hildyard, who was one of the earliest teachers of Queen Victoria, by whom Miss Hildyard was presented with a residence in St. Katherine's Hospital, Regent's Park ; and Miss Mary Anne Gayton, who was the first to teach Mr. W. E. Gladstone his letters. This lady died in the enjoyment of the hospitality of Sheppard College in 1881, after a residence there extending over twenty-three years.

Of the first and original chapel of the College nothing is known. It was replaced, as has been seen, in 1701. This new chapel,[1] constructed in

---

[1] Sir John Morden was the first treasurer of Bromley College, and it is significant that when building his college at Blackheath he employed Sir Christopher Wren as his architect. Was Sir Christopher the architect of Bromley College ?

the style of Sir Christopher Wren's existing chapel at Morden College, Blackheath, fitted appropriately into the general structure, and was suitable to the primary needs of a small institution. Its dimensions, however, were only 39 feet by 18, and its windows afforded very little light. When, in 1805, the College was doubled in size, the old chapel no longer supplied the necessary accommodation, and the need for a larger building became pressing. It was not, however, till 1863 that any active steps were taken to supply this need. In this year the then chaplain, the Rev. H. C. Adams, author of *The Cherry Stones,* and other stories which had a considerable vogue in Victorian days, collected a sum of over £1,800, which was supplemented by the proceeds of a bazaar in the College grounds. With the money thus accumulated the new chapel was built, from designs by Waring and Blake in the Early Decorated style. Though only two feet broader than the original building, the new chapel is nearly twenty feet longer (56 feet by 20 feet, and 33 feet in height), and provides stalls for all the pensioners of the College, with additional seats in front of them for daughters, visitors, and staff.

On entering the chapel the attention is immediately drawn to four blind windows, two on the north and two on the south sides, filled up with various illuminated coats-of-arms, among them those of Bishop Warner, of Magdalen and University Colleges, Oxford, and of Bishop Murray. The space thus occupied was presumably intended to accommodate the four tablets which hung in the original chapel, inscribed with the names of the various benefactors of the College from its foundation. These tablets, however, have entirely disappeared, though the record of their contents happily survives. From the point of view of decorative value it is probable that the chapel has gained rather than lost by their disappearance.

The eight windows of the chapel which do in fact serve the purpose of windows are executed in stained glass by O'Connor of Birmingham, and represent scenes of female life drawn from the Bible. All are in triplets, with the exception of the west window, which has four lights. The central window at the east end depicts the appearance of Christ to the women, flanked on either side by the Crucifixion, and the visit of the women to the empty tomb. The west window, a memorial to Bishop Murray, shows St. John leading away Mary from the scene of the Crucifixion, St. Stephen ministering to the widows, St. Peter raising Dorcas to life, and the story of Lois and Eunice. The arrangement and contents of the lateral windows are as follows, reading from west to east :

	Sarah and the angel.	Eve and the serpent.
	Rahab and the spies.	Moses and Pharaoh's daughter.
South side Nave.	Ruth and Naomi.	Deborah triumphant.
	Rizpah watching the dead.	Hannah praying.
	Elisha and the widow's cruse.	Solomon and the Queen of Sheba.
	Esther and Ahasuerus.	The son of the Shunammite widow.

North side Nave.

South side Apse.	Anna, the prophetess, and Simeon. The widow of Nain. The widow's mite.	The Nativity. Christ with Mary and Martha. The washing of Jesus' feet by the woman which was a sinner.	North side Apse.

On the chapel walls hang two portraits, the one of Bishop Warner, the other of Bishop Zachary Pearce. The portrait of the founder, by an unknown artist, supplied the place of an altar-piece in the original chapel. At the time of the construction of the new chapel the picture was removed to the chaplain's lodge, where it remained until the chaplaincy of the Rev. Willoughby Parr, who has restored it to its appropriate place.

The portrait itself, which is life-size, has been described by Mr. Philip Norman as " a rather pathetic picture," representing Warner at an advanced age, wearing a thin white moustache and an imperial, kneeling on a crimson cushion with gold tassels. His careworn, melancholy face perhaps reflects the experiences and sufferings of long ago, when, in the days of the Civil Wars and the Commonwealth, Warner was a wanderer and an exile, sadly contemplating the unquiet times which had deprived him of his office, had humbled episcopacy to the dust, and had brought Church and Monarchy to a common ruin.

Two other portraits of Bishop Warner, somewhat similar in character, are in existence, the one at Walsingham Abbey, the seat of the Lee-Warners ; the other in the President's Lodge at Magdalen College, Oxford.

The other portrait which hangs in the chapel of Bromley College is that of Bishop Zachary Pearce, a half-length by Edward Penny, 1768.

Past benefactors to the College are still further commemorated by two mural tablets, one in honour of Mr. J. M. Holworthy, to whose efforts the chapel, in so large a degree, owes its existence, and one to the Rev. James White, one of the executors of General Gordon, and chaplain of the College from 1891 to 1915.

None of the sacred vessels belonging to the chapel are of any great antiquity. A chalice, dated 1784, was given by Anne Oare. A paten, dated 1797, was given by Anne Fawkes. There is an alms-dish of the same date, and a flagon of about 1857.

The list of chaplains contains some noteworthy names. Among them the name of Bagshaw is conspicuous. The Rev. Harington Bagshaw became chaplain in 1696, and held the office, together with that of Vicar of Bromley, till his resignation in 1734. He was succeeded by his son, the Rev. Thomas Bagshaw, who, on the death of his father in 1739, became also Vicar of Bromley. He held the chaplaincy till his death in 1787. Thus, for only nine years short of a century, a Bagshaw ruled the College, and doubtless enjoyed the happiness which is derived from creating no history, for no record of any achievement of importance by the Bagshaws has come down to us, except that Thomas left £200 to increase the chaplain's stipend.

JOHN WARNER (1581–1666), LORD BISHOP OF ROCHESTER 1637–1666,
FOUNDER OF BROMLEY COLLEGE.

From the oil painting in the College Chapel.

The rule of the Rev. Thomas Scott, who added to his ecclesiastical functions the duties and the dignities of a Justice of the Peace, is notable for something in the nature of a mutiny on the part of the ladies. A complaint was lodged with Mr. Lee-Warner against the arbitrary and meddlesome regulations of the chaplain, under which the pensioners were required to be within the College by 10 p.m., on pain of being locked out, and were also made liable to the forfeiture of their pension on such days as they did not attend chapel. It would be interesting to know what was the final result of this spirited resistance by the widows, but our materials only allow of an inference that a satisfactory arrangement or compromise was arrived at, for Scott continued to be chaplain for seventeen years after the incident, and it may be assumed, for want of records to the contrary, that peace and harmony prevailed.

The chaplaincy of the Rev. James Landon (1846–55) was marked by the erection of the existing turret and clock, a structural addition which was immediately followed by an era of extensions and alterations. The tenure of the Rev. H. C. Adams, extending over the thirteen years from 1855 to 1868, is notable for the erection of the porter's lodge in 1860, for the repair of the old quadrangle, including the strengthening of the old chapel wall, and, in 1863, as has been seen, for the building of the existing chapel. The works, both of fiction and devotion, of Henry Cadwallader Adams have probably by now sunk into complete oblivion, but I can still recollect *The Cherry Stones* as being a part of the literary pabulum of my childish days, and the name of Adams, in those far-off times, was quite a household word.

The memory of the Rev. James White, who was chaplain from 1891 to 1915, is still cherished with affection and respect by many of the older inhabitants of the town. Among many other useful services may be included the excellent article on the history of the College which he contributed to the *Home Counties Magazine* in 1899.

From 1915 to 1925 the holder of the office of chaplain was the Rev. Willoughby Parr, distinguished alike by the urbanity of his manners, the range of his culture, and the dignity, efficiency, and spirit of friendly comradeship with which he administered his trust. He himself, however, is inclined to rest his claims to fame mainly on the fact that he is the brother of Admiral Parr, for ever famous for his achievements in Arctic exploration.

Since this chapter was written the Rev. Willoughby Parr has resigned office, and Canon Arthur S. Hichens, the brother of the well-known novelist, was appointed his successor.

Before his resignation Mr. Parr effected an important change in the conditions under which the chaplaincy was held.

The stipulation of Bishop Warner's will was that the chaplain of the College should have been at Magdalen College, Oxford. After much discussion and correspondence, it was agreed that if, after a certain fixed period, which might run to five months, no Magdalen man could be found who was considered by the trustees to be suitable to undertake the duties of the office, the trustees should be allowed to nominate and elect to the chaplaincy, for that term only, a man from another house at their discretion. The plan was accepted by the Charity Commissioners, and made part of the constitution. The preference given by the founder to Magdalen men is maintained, though it is not now absolute, but conditional on Magdalen being able to find, within reasonable time, a man fitted for the work.

Any account of this old foundation would be ungratefully incomplete without some reference to the services rendered to it by the family of Norman. The office of treasurer has been held by five representatives of that family in the course of a century-and-a-half, and the existing representative of a name which Bromley will always hold in honour can look back with satisfaction on the fact that his great-great-grandfather, his great-grandfather, his grandfather, and father have, from the year 1776, as treasurers, rendered memorable service to the beneficent foundation of Bishop Warner of Rochester.

ZACHARY PEARCE (1690–1774), LORD BISHOP OF
ROCHESTER 1756–1774.

From the collection of engravings at the National Portrait Gallery

Chapter X

PLAISTOW AND FARWIG

THE old historians of Bromley—Dunkin, Freeman, and Wilson— have little to say about Plaistow and Farwig. Indeed of Farwig there was nothing for either Wilson (1797) or Dunkin (1815) to say, for the district subsequently known as Farwig did not exist under that name until nearly a decade after Dunkin wrote. Freeman, writing in 1832, asserts that

" The whole of the buildings at this place have been erected within the last nine years, before which time not even a cottage was to be seen."

The whole expanse of country lying immediately to the north of the town was known as Plaistow, where a few estates and substantial residences, approachable by circuitous lanes and bypaths, varied the otherwise unbroken range of a purely pastoral landscape.

The name Plaistow is said to signify a playground, and has been traced back to Anglo-Saxon *plega*, play, game, and *stow*, place, though it is also asserted in an article on Bromley place-names in the *District Times* of September 1921, that a Mr. Samuel Plaistow owned much property in Plaistow in 1765. Of this gentleman, however, no record has reached me, and the name, as attached to the particular district, is of far older date than 1765.

Antiquarian research has not succeeded, so far, in tracing the land tenures in this locality farther back than the early sixteenth century, but it is known that in A.D. 1500 an estate with house attached was in the hands of a family named Ryder, " of Battersey and Bromley," the estate, which was situated in what was then known as Milk Street, passing before 1589 into the hands of the King family, which retained possession till 1754. The property then was sold to a Mr. Jones Raymond, ultimately coming into the hands of the Scotts of Sundridge Park.

A portion of the land was, in early days, the property of the influential Knight family, who parted with that part of it on which Springhill now stands to Arnold King. The land on which Plaistow Hall was subsequently erected is thought by Mr. B. F. Davis to have been in the possession of the Shott family in the sixteenth century, though other authorities think it more probable that this piece also belonged to the Kings.

There were in all four principal demesnes in the Plaistow district— Plaistow Lodge, Plaistow Hall, Springhill, and Milk Street, and the early history of Plaistow is the history of these estates.

Of these by far the largest was PLAISTOW LODGE, the grounds of which, 126 acres in extent, stretched northward from the present London Lane, and

PLAISTOW LODGE.

Erected by Peter Thellusson, Esq, 1780.

contained all the land to the west of Burnt Ash Lane.   The property did not apparently become a single estate until well into the eighteenth century, the owners in 1675—the earliest date to which the tenures have been traced— being three members of a family named French.   Passing through several hands, either by inheritance or purchase, in 1777 the whole property was bought by Peter Thellusson, a gentleman who had accumulated an enormous fortune, estimated at £800,000, of which he spent £40,000 in erecting the present mansion known as Plaistow Lodge.   The sudden rise in the rateable value of the estate, from £84 in 1777 and succeeding years to £175 in November 1796, was evidently the consequence of the construction of Plaistow Lodge.

Peter Thellusson is chiefly remarkable for his extraordinary will dated April 2nd, 1796, which was drawn in such terms that an Act of Parliament was passed in 1800 prohibiting any such will in the future.[1]   A sum of £4,500 per annum, and a further capital sum of £600,000, was to be placed in the hands of trustees, who were directed to allow the whole to accumulate, by investments in land, until the grandson of his existing grandson (then an infant) should reach the age of twenty-one, when the whole property was to be at his disposal.   Failing such issue the Thellusson estate was, after the lapse of three generations, to be sold, and the proceeds to be applied, under direction of Parliament, towards the liquidation of the National Debt.   As the family survived in direct male descent the clauses of the will relative to the National Debt did not come into operation, but the other clauses gave rise in 1856 to a hotly contested lawsuit, the expenses of which were so enormous that the property ultimately emerged from it no greater in value than it was when the will was made.

After the death of Peter Thellusson early in 1797, his widow, Anne, remained in possession until 1804, when, presumably upon her death, the ownership passed to Peter Isaac Thellusson, son of the original Peter. In 1806 he became the first Baron Rendlesham in the Irish peerage, and in all probability retired from the south to the Thellusson estates in Yorkshire. At any rate in 1810 Plaistow Lodge was leased by the Thellusson trustees to a Mr. Thomas Maltby, and two years later the whole estate was purchased from the trustees by the Hon. Hugh Lindsay of the family of Crawford and Balcarres.   In 1822 Mr. Lindsay in turn sold it to Walter Boyd, or rather to a group of grateful clients who presented it to Mr. Boyd, as a token of their gratitude and esteem, at a cost of £17,000.

This remarkable man, whose life is traced in the *Dictionary of National Biography*, was a banker and financier of great repute who was born in or about 1754.   He had large interests in Paris, where he was residing at the outbreak of the French Revolution.   There he remained, refusing to seek refuge at home for ten years, safeguarding as far as possible the interests of

---

[1] By " the Thellusson Act " accumulations are limited to the grandchildren of the testator.

PETER THELLUSSON (1737–1797).

From an oil painting belonging to Lord Rendlesham.

his clients, of his creditors, and of his bank. It was in acknowledgment of these services that Plaistow Lodge was presented to him at the conclusion of the Napoleonic wars. During those wars he had acted as contractor for Government loans to the extent of some thirty or forty millions.

" He was " (says an obituary notice in the *Edinburgh Evening Courant* of October 5th, 1837), " the intimate and warm friend of William Pitt, and their published correspondence shows how much that minister was indebted for many of his brightest financial schemes to the genius of Mr. Boyd. Through the interest of the Empress Josephine, who was the schoolfellow and friend of Mrs. Boyd, his extensive banking establishment and property in Paris were not only protected during a most sanguinary struggle, but restored to him untouched when the reign of terror was over. Sir Walter Scott often expressed a wish to write his singular and chequered life. He was for many years Member of Parliament for Lymington, and other places, and his deep knowledge of all matters connected with finance rendered his opinion on those matters always valuable."

During his residence at Plaistow Lodge the place was well kept up, and it is said that fifty persons slept under its roof every night. Open house to tradesmen and others was practically the rule in the servants' quarters, and it was no uncommon thing to hear three or four fiddles going in the servants' hall of an evening.

On Walter Boyd's death in 1837 the estate passed to his son, Robert Boyd, who held it till his death in 1863. The remains of both the Boyds, Walter and Robert, were deposited in the Boyd vault in the catacombs beneath the parish church of Bromley, those sombre and ghostly recesses of the very existence of which most of the people of Bromley are probably quite ignorant.

From 1869 to 1873 the estate was held by Mr. J. Mackenzie, who sold it in the latter year to the Hon. Arthur Kinnaird. In 1878, on the death of his brother, ninth baron, he succeeded to the barony, residing at Plaistow Lodge till his death in 1887. He was succeeded in turn by his eldest son, Arthur Fitzgerald Kinnaird, who thus became the eleventh baron.

Lord Kinnaird, in a different way, was no less remarkable a man than Walter Boyd. He was conspicuous equally as an athlete and an extreme Low Churchman, and his beneficence as a philanthropist was only equalled by his prowess on the football field. An Eton and Trinity, Cambridge, man, he held the office of Lord High Commissioner for Scotland from 1907 to 1909. He was President of the Y.M.C.A. ; President of the Football Association from 1890 ; Founder of the Old Etonians Football Club, and the holder of nine medals commemorating his appearance in nine finals for the Association Cup.

In 1896 Lord Kinnaird ceased to reside at Plaistow Lodge. He resolved to break up the estate and to develop it as a residential centre. The house itself, with a sufficiency of surrounding land, was leased by my old friend and colleague, Mr. Gustav Loly, who transferred to this palatial and commodious situation the boys' school known as ' Quernmore,' originally established by Mr. John Gibson in Holwood Road.

Already, many years before the Plaistow Lodge estate was broken up by its present intersection of roads lined with private residences, the spread of Bromley towards the north had given rise to a desire that a church should be erected to serve the needs of an increasing population. Accordingly in 1863 the nave of the Church of St. Mary, Plaistow, was consecrated, and gradually assumed its present form. As its history is fully traced in another chapter of this book, it is unnecessary here to do more than indicate its place in the development of Plaistow as a residential centre.

Before closing the history of Plaistow Lodge, some reference must be made to the presentation to the town by the Kinnaird Park Estate Syndicate of a pair of iron gates which had stood for some years as the entrance gates to the demesne. They now guard the entrance to Queen's Garden. The gates were purchased in 1876 by the then Lord Kinnaird from a dealer in Sloane Street, and they were represented to the purchaser as having formed part of the original enclosure round the western end of St. Paul's Churchyard. On the occasion of their presentation to the town it was confidently asserted that the gates were designed by Sir Christopher Wren, or under his direction ; that they were examples of the old Sussex ironwork fashioned at Lamberhurst in Kent, of which material the railings round St. Paul's were undoubtedly made. The same gentleman, however, who made these statements to the Bromley District Council on November 9th, 1900, subsequently wrote a letter to the *District Times* of July 5th, 1901, in which he detailed the further investigations which he had made into the origin of the gates. A very careful comparison between the existing old railings round St. Paul's and the Kinnaird gates revealed such differences as to make it evident that the gates at any rate could not have formed part of the external railing. Nor did they in any way resemble any of the existing ironwork in the interior. Accordingly Mr. W. R. Mallett, the gentleman in question, withdrew his original assertions in the following terms :

" If, through inadvertence, I have misled the public in assuming that these gates formed part of the external railing (of St. Paul's) removed in 1873, I express my deep regret, and trust that my efforts to arrive at the real facts of the case may be accepted in mitigation of the error."

A note, supplied by Mr. Philip Norman, seems rather to clench the matter :

" It is quite certain that the gates were not part of the old ironwork of St. Paul's Cathedral, as they are not in the style of the period of its manufacture."

In the face of such a pronouncement, and of Mr. Mallett's assiduous labours to ascertain the facts, the connection between the Queen's Garden gates and St. Paul's Cathedral must, it is feared, be regarded as a legend.

A curious discovery, opening up a wide field for the imagination, was made in the autumn of 1900, when operations were in progress for the widening of London Lane. A portion of the road fell in opposite the house occupied by Mr. F. W. Atkins—the house, by the way, to which Charles Freeman, Bromley's historian, retired, and in which he died. On investigation a passage way leading towards Plaistow Lodge was discovered under the roadway. In one part of this subterranean tunnel there was found hanging from the wall a gold-laced coat which fell to pieces on being handled, and also a considerable quantity of old wine, some of which was " consumed on the premises," and some, it is said, was sold to the landlord of the Beech Tree Hotel. The passage would have given access to Mr. Atkins's house, had it not been bricked up at that end.

What was the original purpose of this subterranean tunnel ? How did the gold-laced coat, which crumbled at the touch, get there ? How came it about that a store of wine, still saleable, lay there neglected and forgotten ? Prosaic answers to these questions are doubtless possible, but upon the slender foundation of the available facts we are free, if we choose, to build a fabric of romance, and to associate in our minds the matter-of-fact Plaistow of to-day with the secret and mysterious exits and entrances of medieval times.

PLAISTOW HALL, now demolished, was a substantial red-brick building situated opposite where Cambridge Road now meets Plaistow Lane. On its site a house appears to have stood long before the erection of the hall, the property in the sixteenth century being either a part of the Shott estate, or of that of the King family. The tenures have been successively traced through a Henry Mills, who sold to Andrew Broome in 1597 ; in 1605 the estate was sold by Andrew Broome to Henry Walton, and from the Walton family it passed in due course to Peter Burrell who built Plaistow Hall about 1700. Peter Burrell sold to Richard Swift, and from the latter the property was acquired by William Passinger. Ultimately it passed into the hands of the Scott family of Sundridge, who had as tenants of Plaistow Hall one of the Boyds, and later a Mr. Kincaid, from whom the remainder of the lease was taken over by Mr. William Sewell Shuttleworth, who, at its expiration, renewed it for twenty-one years. Mr. Shuttleworth died in 1863, and his widow remained in occupation until 1882.

Mr. Shuttleworth was a great figure in Plaistow. His memory, as a philanthropist and friend of the poor, still survives :

> " Friend of the poor, beloved of friends, and dear
> To all who knew thy worth, and felt how near
> Thy kind heart beat to poor man's wants and ways
> And how, with open hand, thou cheer'st their days."

Such was his fitting obituary contributed to the *Bromley Record* in 1863. His Christmas present to the poor in 1858 was three bullocks, with a corresponding supply of bread and soup. His eldest son, Wm. S. Yorke Shuttleworth, performed the extraordinary feat of riding a bicycle from Russia to Calais, in order to disprove the opinion " that a religious zealot must be a muff."

From 1885 to 1900 Plaistow Hall was the home of Mr. Henry Hicks, whose son, William Hicks, was a somewhat conspicuous figure in the Bromley of my day. He varied an assiduous devotion to his business as a solicitor in London with an equally assiduous devotion to the cause of " Protestantism " as against the High Churchman. " I am a Prot," he once said to me, and for the moment I was at a loss to recognise the particular sect to which he thus proclaimed his attachment. He gave the impression of a man who meant to get on in the world, and Sir William Joynson-Hicks, Bart., M.P., and Home Secretary, has justified the promise of his youth.

From ancient times there seem to have been a house and farm on the site of SPRINGHILL. It was a part of the possessions round Bromley of the Knight family, from whom it was bought by Arnold King early in the seventeenth century. It remained in the hands of successive members of the King family throughout that century, or the greater part of it. A Robert King sold to a Mr. Walsingham King, who in turn sold to Roger Peck in 1712. The deed cementing this sale describes the house as a very ancient one. This ancient house in due course disappeared, to be replaced by the present structure, but the precise date of the present house and the name of the man who caused it to be built are alike unknown, but if in 1857 it was in fact, as it was reputed to be, about a hundred and fifty years old, that would carry back its origin either to Walsingham King or Peck. About the middle of the last century the property was divided, roads being made to enable the fields to be turned into a building estate. The house itself with its surrounding gardens was bought by Mr. Edwards, who lived there for some years, but in 1857 Mr. Edwards sold it to Major Clement Satterthwaite of the Stock Exchange, who resided at Springhill for over thirty years. It was to him that the house was represented as being about a hundred and fifty years old.

Thus was formed that close connection between the family of Satterthwaite and the town of Bromley which has lasted for nearly three-quarters of a century, and which still, happily, continues. None of the old residents who were at any time contemporary with Major Clement Satterthwaite are likely to have forgotten his familiar and dignified figure as he made his way on Sundays to his seat in St. Mary's Church, for which, from its first inception to its completion, he was so indefatigable a worker, and in which he was so devoted a worshipper. Nor will his services to the Volunteer movement of the district be readily forgotten. Indeed he and Mrs. Satterthwaite were foremost in all good works for the benefit of their country, and of the locality in which they resided. Not the least of their good works was the fact that they were the parents of Colonel Edward Satterthwaite, who still splendidly maintains the family tradition. It is not within the scheme of this history to celebrate inhabitants of Bromley who are still living, but in the case of one who has been Mayor of the Borough, who, as Secretary to the Stock Exchange, has occupied for many years a position of great importance in the world of finance, who has commanded both the Volunteer and Territorial Infantry in the county, and whose services at the War Office, in connection with the Territorial Force, were, during the Great War, of national value—in the case of such a one some slight, though far from exhaustive, tribute to an honoured name may perhaps be permitted.

In Major Clement Satterthwaite's time the house itself was enlarged, the changes in the Springhill property, mentioned on the previous page, were made, Cambridge Road, and the roads adjacent to it, came into existence, and were speedily bordered by houses. In 1888 the ownership of Springhill passed to Mr. John Gordon, and later to Mr. William Bowley, 1895–6, and to Miss Bowley, 1896–9. After a vacancy of two years, Springhill was acquired by the Kent County Council as a school for Domestic Economy.

Of the house property in MILK STREET little is now known. As early as 1500, if not earlier, a large house a little to the east of Marshall's farm was in the hands of the Ryders " of Battersey and Bromley." In the course of the sixteenth century it became a part of the property owned by the King family, passing on the death of John King into the hands of his widow, who by another marriage became Mrs. Susan Walton. Successive generations of Waltons held the property until 1754, when it was sold to Mr. Jones Raymond, passing in due course into the estate of the Scotts at Sundridge. It is now known as Hall's Farm.

Pousty's Hill, or Hilly Fields, was known as Mount Misery. It is the only circular viewpoint in the borough, and may possibly, it is thought, have been a British settlement in ancient days. Fragments of pottery have been unearthed there which have been tentatively estimated as pieces of British Burial Urns. The site is now chiefly notable for the enormous reservoir, constructed since the war, designed to contain 5,000,000 gallons of water supplied by the Shortlands Pumping Station.

The district known for the last hundred years as FARWIG was originally a part of the Plaistow Lodge estate, but was separated from it, by sale, in the days of the Thellusson occupation, the principal purchaser being Mr. Johann Farwig, a member of the great metal-working firm established in Newington Causeway. The property thus acquired extended to what is now the Beech Tree Hotel on the London Road, and included the area around Farwig Lane and a part of College Road. It consisted exclusively of meadows and cornfields interspersed by trees and hedges, and even as late as 1860 the view from the town end of College Road presented little else but a purely rural landscape.

In the hands of Mr. Farwig a portion of the estate, between 1825 and 1832, was laid out in a row of small houses, with forecourts flanked by battlemented towers, which were built mainly for the accommodation of artisans, and the name of Farwig Place, and the general name of Farwig, are derived from the gentleman who was the first to develop it as a building site. Two public-houses, the Farwig Arms at the north corner and the Royal Oak at the south, were constructed in due course to serve the requirements of an industrial population, chiefly engaged in the service of the first Bromley Gas Company, whose office was established in Farwig Lane. The western extremity of Farwig, previous to the existence of the Beech Tree Hotel, was a nursery garden in the possession of Mr. Godfrey Stidolph, whose fine half-timbered house was a notable feature as you approached the town. In front of it was a handsome purple beech tree, which, however, would not for itself command mention here. Its interest lies in the curious story, tradition, fact—one knows not what to call it—associated with it. The story goes that Sir Joseph Paxton, when laying out the Crystal Palace Grounds, was attracted by this beech tree, and managed to convey it bodily to its new home at Sydenham. To a certain degree the tradition is supported by Mr. George H. Bascombe of Chislehurst, who states in a book called *The Arborist* (a copy of which is in Mr. W. Baxter's possession) that—

" My machinery was used by Mr. P—— of Kent to move bodily trees 40 feet high."

If " Mr. P—— of Kent " disguises the name of Paxton, this is an evidence favourable to the tradition. On the other hand, a very old resident in Shortlands, Mr. Ford, has stated that the tree was cut down and disposed of to a sawyer in Bromley named Rose. Whatever be the truth of the matter, the Beech Tree Hotel gains its name from this tree.

The development of Plaistow, as we know it to-day—a labyrinth of houses in a thickly populated district—began as early as 1867 when parts of Crescent and Cambridge Roads were laid out. Up to that time it still retained its purely rural character, an old Farwig smithy and the office of the gas-works being, apart from the artisans' cottages already mentioned, the only centres of industrial activity. In No. 6 Crescent Road the distinguished geographer, scientist, and revolutionary, Kropotkin, Prince Peter Alexeievitch of Russia, found a refuge after the turmoils of his stormy career. Stepniak, in his *Underground Russia*, has recorded the imprisonment of the Prince in the fortress of SS. Peter and Paul and his romantic escape, which was aided by the playing of a viola as a signal. In recognition of this assistance Kropotkin named his house " Viola."

Of Farwig it only remains to record the activities of the Farwig Wesleyan Mission, which first established itself, in 1881, in a cottage at No. 12 Mooreland Road. In 1883 the Mission had sufficiently extended to justify the construction of a distinct and permanent establishment which took the form of an iron building constructed on the site on which St. Mary's Hall now stands.

Here, with constant extensions, the Mission carried on its work for twenty years. The range of that work was indeed, and is, extensive, including, besides Sunday services, a Band of Hope, social meetings for the young, gospel temperance meetings, and popular meetings for adults. Notwithstanding enlargements, which were at last represented by a large hall accommodating six hundred people, and schoolrooms and classrooms for three hundred scholars, the premises were still too small for the full development of all the purposes of the Mission. Largely under the impulse given by the enthusiasm of Mr. W. J. Gibbs, from the first the Secretary and Honorary Superintendent of the Mission, a project took shape in April 1905 in the form of the Central Hall on London Road, erected by Messrs. Minter of Putney at a cost of £15,500, where all the old activities of the Mission are still in vigorous operation, together with many others made possible by the existence of such ample premises.

All that is now needed to do justice to the fine orchestra, which has always been a feature of the Mission, is an organ.

SUNDRIDGE

TO the north-east of the town, midway between Bromley and Chislehurst, lies the Sundridge estate—Sundridge Park—surrounding, until quite recent times, a single mansion, of which the architectural features admirably blended with the quiet beauty of its environment. A public footpath across the park considerably curtailed the distance by road between the two points, and no more charming walk was to be found in the neighbourhood than from Bromley to Chislehurst by way of Sundridge Park. At one point the mansion lay in full view below, but, imposing as it is, no one, viewing this fine example of comparatively modern architecture, could guess that the origins of this estate are lost in the mists of antiquity and that the Manor of Sundridge is almost coeval with that of Bromley itself.

The name Sundridge has in the course of ages undergone so many vicissitudes that its derivation and meaning must necessarily be a matter of speculation and controversy. If, as is conjectured, the name is a contraction of Sunderidge, it may be that it denotes the dividing ridge or watershed of the two streams, Ravensbourne and Kyd Brook. It is asserted that the name appears as indicating a distinct locality, and under a spelling which makes it capable of identification, in an Anglo-Saxon Charter of A.D. 987, but it does not emerge as an historic entity until more than a century later—some time after the Domesday Survey.

In that Survey there is no mention of any holder of land in Bromley, or its immediate vicinity, other than the Bishop of Rochester, and from this it may be assumed that the episcopal manor was at that time intact.

Within a comparatively short period of time after Domesday, the Bishops appear to have begun to alienate some portions of their manorial lands, on the principle of sub-infeudation, for, in less than a century, as many as twenty-seven persons are cited in *Textus Roffensis* as holding land of the Bishop under the terms of Knight's Service. Some of these alienated lands became themselves subordinate manors, and of these Sundridge was probably one.

Unfortunately for the historian there is another Sundridge in the neighbourhood of Sevenoaks, and, as a consequence, it is extremely difficult to distinguish, in the old records, the one from the other. Not only so— there was near Rochester a place called Bromhey, easily capable of being confused with Bromley. Thus the minute and careful investigations instituted by Mr. Coles Child into old documents preserved at the Record Office, by which he established the existence of a certain Galfrid, and of a Walter de Braibroc as tenants of the Manor of Sundridge, appear to have no relation to Sundridge near Bromley. Hasted himself has fallen into the trap, and has quite excusably confused, in his narrative, a John Blunt of Sundridge by Sevenoaks with a John Blunt of London and Bromley. Where there is so much uncertainty it will be wiser to confine this narrative

SUNDRIDGE BEFORE 1792.

SUNDRIDGE AFTER 1792.

within the limits of unquestioned fact, and, excluding the problematical Galfrid and de Braibroc, to come directly to the Blunt family, which was certainly at one time possessed of the Manor of Sundridge near Bromley.

In days before the Norman Conquest the family of Blund, or Blound, held the lordship of Guisnes in France. Three sons of one of these lords came over to England in the train of William the Conqueror. Two of them, Sir Robert and Sir William Blound, remained here after the Conquest, settling respectively in Suffolk and in Lincolnshire, and from them the various families of Blount or Blunt in this country are derived.

In the reign of Henry III a cadet of this family, Peter le Blund, became Constable of the Tower (39th Henry III, 1254), and Hasted seems to imply that at an earlier date this Peter was already in possession of the Manor of Sundridge. The first documentary evidence, however, which we have of the ownership of the Blund family is from the *Pedes Finium* preserved in the Record Office. From this document it appears that a certain Henry of Gloucester and Margaret his wife put in a claim against John le Blunt, draper of London, to the possession of " the Manor of Sundresshe near Brumlegh," which claim was arbitrated in the King's Court at York in the 30th of Edward I (1301) with the following result—that " the aforesaid Henry and Margaret his wife acknowledge the aforesaid Manor with the appurtenances to be the right of the said John." They therefore abandon all claims to it for themselves and for their heirs. In consideration of this acknowledgment, John le Blunt " gave to the same Henry and Margaret the sum of Twenty pounds sterling."

The next document relating to the Blunts of Sundridge, preserved in the *Book of Aids*, refers to the year 1346, the 20th of Edward III. In that year, on the occasion of conferring knighthood upon the King's eldest son—it was the year of Crecy and the initiation of the Black Prince into the arts of war—a requisition up to 40s. on every Knight's fee was made by order of the King. A transcript of the accounts of the collectors was made many years later by Cyriac Petit in the 35th of Henry VIII, and therein under title " Hundred of Bromleigh & Bekenham " there appears the entry—" Of Edward de Blound, for one quarter of one fee, which John de Blound held in Bromleigh of the Bishop of Rochester—Xs."

A few years after the death of Edward de Blound, Sundridge appears as the property of Robert Fourneaux, " citizen and fishmonger of London," and it passed by the marriage of his widow to Andrew Pykeman, also a citizen of London and member of the same city company. Pykeman died in 1391 leaving the property to his daughter, whose husband, John Sibile, thus became the owner. She died in 1401 and his property was left in the hands of his three sons, Thomas being the one who lived at Sundridge, where he died in 1421. A short time later Sundridge is found to be the property of Ralph Booth, whose father had married a daughter of John Sibile and thus by descent from him it passed into the hands of the Booth family.

From this point it will be sufficient to follow Hasted.

" A descendant of this family," he says, " William Booth, was found by Inquisition taken in the first year of Henry VII (1485) to die possessed of the Manor of Sundrigg, held of the Bishop of Rochester, by Knight's Service, and by service of making suit at the court of the Palace ; and that Robert Booth, was his son and heir, who was, with one hundred other gentlemen of this county of Kent made Knights of the Bath in the 17th of Henry VII (1501). In whose descendants Sundridge continued till Sith Booth Esq., dying without male issue, one of his daughters and co-heirs carried it in marriage to Thomas Bettenham of Shurland in Pluckley, Esq., whose great-grandson, Stephen Bettenham of Bromley, Gent., gave it in marriage with his daughter Anne, to Robert Pynsent, third son of John Pynsent, of Chudleigh in Devonshire, and Prothonotary of the Court of Common Pleas. . . . He died here in 1679 without issue, and was buried in the Chancel of the Parish Church. He was succeeded in the possession of this seat by Thomas Washer of Lincoln's Inn, Esq., formerly of Lyneham in Devonshire, on whose death in 1720 it came to his son John Washer of Lincoln's Inn, who dying in 1749 without male issue, his only daughter and heir carried it in marriage to William Wilson Esq., Sheriff of this County in 1766. He died possessed of it in 1776, leaving three sons and two daughters, of whom the eldest, William, alienated it to Edward George Lind Esq., who is the present owner of this seat and manor and now resides at it. From the family before mentioned, and its situation among the woods, this seat acquired the name of ' Washers in the Woods,' by which I believe it is generally known among the common people at present."

This transaction, the sale to Mr. Lind, took place in 1792. Four years later this gentleman sold the estate to Mr. Claude Scott of Chislehurst.

The new owner immediately carried into effect a scheme which seems to have been contemplated by his predecessor. A Mr. H. Repton had pre-pared for Mr. Lind a book of suggestions, with numerous sketches, for the general improvement of the property. One of the proposals evidently was that the old house should be pulled down, and a modern mansion erected in a more suitable position. This plan carried with it extensive alterations in the grounds, among them the incorporation of a considerable extent of arable land and pasture into the park and pleasure-grounds surrounding the house. Mr. Claude Scott, afterwards Sir C. Scott, Bart., resolved to adopt Mr. Repton's advice, and employed him, together with Mr. Nash and Mr. Wyatt, as architects for the new structure. Thus came into existence, about a century and a quarter ago, Sundridge as we know it. It is notable for its fine proportions, for its Corinthian columns and its three porticoes, with a dome crowning the centre one. Its position also sets it off to the fullest advantage. The old Bromley-Chislehurst footpath was closed in 1823, and a new and more convenient one was substituted. The estate remained until comparatively recently a principal residence of the Scott family.

Circumstances, however, with which we have no concern led the late Sir Edward Scott to sell some portion of Sundridge Park as building land. A large part of it now constitutes the excellent golf links of the Sundridge Park Golf Club, and the mansion itself has now been put to the uses of an hotel.

Thus the history of Sundridge ends in an anti-climax. It begins, some eight centuries ago, as a diocesan manor ; it ends in an hotel.

"WIGMORE. This hamlet is about one mile east of Bromley."

This is the opening sentence of Dunkin's section on Widmore, and from it the present-day resident of Bromley may learn two facts of which possibly he was ignorant—that the locality in Dunkin's time (1815) was known as *Wigmore*, and that it was not then attached to Bromley as an integral part of it, but was a separate hamlet lying some little distance away, containing, as Dunkin goes on to say, " 30 houses some of which are very handsome." Dunkin, however, includes Bickley in his brief notice of Widmore.

If we knew the circumstances in which the name was originally given we should be able to decide between Widmore and Wigmore. As it is, the derivation is a matter of speculation, seeing that, according to Mr. George Clinch, the name is given, in ancient maps and documents, as Windemere, Wymere, Wyndemere, and Wigmore. Readers of old documents—those indeed who have read our account of Sundridge—will know that consistency in spelling was not a conspicuous virtue in ancient days. But if Mr. Clinch's conjecture is correct that the name is derived from Anglo-Saxon *Wig*, meaning war, and Moor, or waste ground, some military associations must be attached to its origin. If, on the other hand, the theory that the place simply signifies wide–moor is correct, then probably the present name of Widmore is the name which it originally bore. It is so spelled in the earliest references to it found in the Parish Registers, which date back to the last half of the sixteenth century. In less than a century from that time, however, the name Wigmore became commonly accepted, and it remained Wigmore until comparatively recent times.

The first authentic record which we have of this hamlet, apart from the will of a Christofa Allanson " of Wigmore, Kent," 1626, is in connection with a lawsuit between the Bishop of Rochester as plaintiff and a Mr. King as defendant about a pond at Wigmore. The depositions on behalf of the defendant and the interrogatories and depositions submitted on behalf of the plaintiff are still extant among the Exchequer Depositions. From these we learn that the suit was brought by the Bishop in the 13th of Charles I (1637) and that at that time the locality was uniformly written Wigmore. As to the suit itself, unfortunately, the record has not survived—at any rate, it has not come to hand—and research has only succeeded in unearthing one short order which gives no particulars, but simply adjourns the hearing of the action. It may be that the case was settled out of court.

As far as I am able to ascertain from the depositions and interrogatories there was a threefold issue in the case. Was this pond a part of the manorial property of the Bishop ? Had Mr. King any proprietary rights over it ? Was it common property over which neither the Bishop nor Mr. King had

WIDMORE.
Built about 1630; destroyed by fire 1857.
From a pencil drawing lent by Cosmo Bevan, Esq.

FREELANDS.
Built early in the eighteenth century.

proprietary rights?   The last contention is put forward strongly by " John Wooden of Bromley, aged seventy-four years," who, in his deposition " taken at the ' Bell ' in Bromley, 17 & 18 July, 1637," declares that he has known the pond called Wigmore Pond for sixty years and more—" the said pond, as far as he remembers, has always been a common watering place for the parishioners' cattle."   By the time the suit was brought, however, the pond seems to have disappeared, for Robert Bowle of Chislehurst, aged sixty, deposes that " there is no water now in the pond called Wigmore pond."   This elaborate lawsuit for rights over a non-existent pond seems to show that the litigious spirit has not materially altered in the course of centuries.

Interrogatory No. 4 on behalf of the plaintiff asked whether there was a " Cucking stool set in the said pond, and at whose charge was it built ? " The answer of John Wooden was that

" About fifty years since there was a cucking stool, towards the high way, and about the same time ' a single wench ducked there,' "

and Robert Bowle supplements this information by stating that the cucking stool was set up at the charge of the Bishop—at that time Bishop Young.

Such is our first introduction to Widmore or Wigmore.   But, though three centuries have since passed away, an historic imagination still allows us to picture a secluded hamlet, with its scanty, self-contained, and self-conscious inhabitants, keenly exercised about a road-side pond, hilariously excited over the ducking of some scolding wench in its muddy waters, and eagerly canvassing in the village inn the respective claims of the contending litigants.

The village inn is not a freak of imagination.   The Bird in Hand seems to have been one of the earliest houses built in Widmore—and where an inn existed its customers and their converse pass out of surmise into the region of established facts.

At this time, however (*circa* 1650), " Wigmore " consisted mainly, if not entirely, of one considerable mansion with the property attached to it.   It is described in a marriage settlement as " the Manor, or Mansion House and Capital Messuage of Wigmore."   On the property were a barn, outbuildings, and a few cottages for the rustic inhabitants.   The whole estate comprised between eighty and ninety acres, and though designated as a manor, it does not appear to have been a manor in the strict sense of that term.

By means of existing title-deeds the ownership of Wigmore can be traced back to about 1650, when we find a Mrs. Mary Walker, a widow, in possession.   This lady, in her will, dated August 13th, 1686, bequeathed the estate to her cousin, Elizabeth Vokins, with remainder to her two daughters. In 1697 one of these daughters, Elizabeth, married Thomas West, her property in Wigmore being brought into settlement.   From this document we learn the exact extent of the estate, and the place-names attached to the various sections of it, such as " the Upper House—used for a stable " ; " Waterfield Orchard," called " The Nursery, " Heathfields," " Jenning's Heath " " Pickle Croft," " Little Close," or " Cross-a-Hand," etc.

Of the three children of Thomas and Elizabeth West the only son, Robert, died unmarried. His two sisters, Elizabeth and Mary, married two brothers, Samuel and John Hyde respectively, and to Elizabeth and Samuel Hyde the property in due course descended. On the death of Elizabeth Hyde without issue, the bulk of the property passed by her will to her nephew, General West Hyde of the 1st Regiment of Foot Guards, who, by his will dated March 4th, 1774, entailed his property upon the male issue of his brother John, and in default of such issue, to the second, third, and successive sons of his sister Althea, wife of the Rev. Francis Wollaston. Under the terms of this will the estate in due course descended to George Hyde Wollaston, second son of Althea, and he, in 1809, sold it to Mr. John Wells.

The Wells family remained in possession for nearly half a century, until 1853. In that year the house and part of the property was bought by Henry John Telford and his three sisters, Sarah, Mary Ann, and Susan. The Telford family, though hailing from Yorkshire, carried on business in London as sherry shippers, in partnership with John Ruskin's father. They had already become attached to the locality, having been tenants for many years of Mr. John Wells. They were men of some distinction in the world of culture, and their houses were visited by, among others, Lord Macaulay, David Cox, John Ruskin, and Fanny Kemble.

In 1873, on the death of the last-surviving sister, Mary Ann, the property descended under her will to her cousins, the Misses Marian and Louisa Ellis, these ladies being the daughters of Thomas Flower Ellis, " the one friend," says Sir George Trevelyan, " who had a share in the familiar confidence which Macaulay otherwise reserved for his nearest relatives."

On the death of Miss Louisa Ellis, in 1898, the property descended to her nephews and niece, the children of her brother, Arthur Danvers Ellis.

The old Elizabethan house at Widmore, known as the " Old Cottage," was no doubt the original manor house, but about 1630 another and larger house was built which stood where the lodge to Widmore Court now stands. This house survived till 1857, when it was completely destroyed by fire. One of the Miss Telfords accidentally set alight some bed hangings which surrounded a four-post bed. There were no proper means of extinguishing a fire in those days, and no adequate water-supply. A pond in the neighbourhood was, it is said, drained dry in the attempt to check the conflagration. The present building, Widmore Court, which stands farther back from the road, was built by the Miss Telfords to replace the old mansion thus unfortunately destroyed.

The " Old Cottage " still survives. Its quaint gateway bears the initials " A.B.," thought to be the initials of the builder, and the date 1599.

THE OLD COTTAGE, WIDMORE, IN 1714.

From a block lent by Mr. Philip Norman, F.S.A.

An old engraving of this gateway, dated 1714, shows a board attached to the arch with the notification " John Curtis, licensed to let Post Horses." This has caused the mistaken notion that the place became an inn, the fact being, according to Mr. G. W. Norman, that, on the death of his master, whom he had long served as coachman, Curtis, either by will or gift, came into possession of his employer's horses, and was prepared to let them out on hire. A member of the Curtis family was still living in the " Old Cottage " a century later, in 1813.

When the estate came into the hands of the Telfords the Cottage was used as a residence by some of the ladies of the family. In 1861 they decided to relay the floors. On the removal of the old flooring a number of curious and interesting objects were disclosed to view—two silver sixpences of Queen Elizabeth, coins of almost every subsequent reign, and a copper token of the White Hart, Bromley, dated 1660, in perfect condition. Besides these, several Roman Catholic, Latin, and English books were discovered concealed in the floors or wainscoting. Inside one of the books a set of verses was found inscribed which might have come from the pen of the Vicar of Bray. They are ingeniously contrived so as to convey either a Roman Catholic or Protestant sentiment according as they are read vertically or horizontally :

" I hold as faith	What England's Church allowes
What Rome's Church saith	My conscience disallowes
Wheare the King's heade	The Church can have noe blame
The flocks misleade	That houldes the Pope supreme
Where the altares drest	The Sacrifice is scarce divine
The people are blest	With table bread and wine
He is but an asse	Who the Communion flies
That shunnes the masse	Is catholique and wise."

At the time when Henry John Telford acquired Widmore House with a part of the property attaching to it, his brother Charles bought the remaining part, and built upon it the house known as Widmore Lodge. On Charles Telford's death Mr. George Simon purchased the estate, which, on his death, passed into the occupation of the Tweedy family, whose close associations with Bromley are recorded elsewhere.

The cottage at Widmore known as " Well Cottage " is like the " Old Cottage," credited with an Elizabethan origin. There is a tradition that the beams in the roof came from the timbers of one of the ships engaged in the Great Armada fight of 1588, the tradition probably originating from the shape of the beams, which is consistent with the theory that they were once part of a ship.

In another chapter an account is given of the formation of a little society of Methodists who were the first begetters of the Nonconformist movement in the Bromley area. It was at Widmore that the first meeting house and chapel of this Society was established, and it was to Widmore that John

Wesley himself came to preach on one, and possibly more than one, occasion.

What is now the Widmore Road was, until about the middle of the last century, designated only as a lane, a lonely road bordered on the south by the palace estate, and on the north by the property owned by Mr. John Wells. Up to 1845, in the interval between Bromley and Widmore, houses were few and far between; the rural aspect of the country was unbroken. In 1845 Mr. Wells's property was sold in building lots, with the result that roads were made, houses sprang up, and New Bromley and the parish of St. John's gradually came into existence.

A little to the north of Widmore Lane, near the spot where Orchard, Homefield, and Upper Park Roads converge, there stands the old red-brick mansion known as " Freelands."

This name appears to have been derived from a field or fields called " free lands " belonging to a family of husbandmen named Juler, who, as existing wills indicate, had been living in the immediate neighbourhood for a great many years from the middle of the fifteenth century or even earlier.

In 1543 the property was still in the hands of this family, being then held by John Juler, husbandman. He had sons—John (i), Richard, John (ii), and a daughter Joan. At his death in that year the lands passed to his son John (i),[1] who, dying in 1560, bequeathed them to his son William.[2] William Juler had a daughter Mary, who, in 1583, was married to Thomas Ffrench. Her father died in 1588, and by his will bequeathed the property to his son-in-law Thos. Ffrench,[3] who thereupon took possession of " free lands," using the rents and profits therefrom.

Upon this occurring John Juler (ii) set up a claim to the property, supplicating the Lord Chancellor, Sir Christopher Hatton, to direct that Thomas and Mary Ffrench should appear before him to answer John's (ii) complaint.[4]

The supplication was granted and Thos. and Mary Ffrench duly appeared to answer the complaint. John (ii), however, was not successful. He did not win his case, for it could be shown that John Juler (ii) was not given any title to " Freland " by his father in 1543 and that William Juler, to whom the property had rightfully descended, had bequeathed it to his son-in-law, Thos. Ffrench. From that time onward until the end of the seventeenth century, upwards of one hundred years, Freelands remained in the hands of the Ffrenches. To the memory of one of them, Martine Ffrench, there is a stone tablet, dated 1661, fixed to the south wall of the parish church, describing him as " of this parish," the probability being that he lived in the house the foundations of which were laid bare when alterations were carried out in 1888 after the transfer of the estate to the Religious of the Holy Trinity. This Martine Ffrench left the property to his son Martine, who subsequently sold the estate to Wm. Foster of Northants. In 1708 it

---

[1] Roch. Wills 10, f. 33.
[2] Ibid. 12, f. 324.
[3] Ibid. 17, f. 306.
[4] Chancery proceedings C 2, 426.

CHARLES POTT, OF FREELANDS (1823–1864).

was bought by John Hulls and remained in the possession of that family for upwards of seventy years. It was probably at the commencement of their ownership that the house as it was known throughout the greater part of the eighteenth and nineteenth centuries was built.

In the course of the eighteenth century various tenants held it on lease, the owners, as already stated, for the greater part of the century being the Hulls family. Early in the century it was in the occupation of John Whalley, merchant. This fact is attested by Lysons and also by a gravestone in the south aisle of Bromley Church to the memory of—

" Mariabella, wife of John Whalley (merchant) who dyed in childbed ye 5 of May 1701 at Freeland House in ye parish of Bromly."

Another of these tenants was " Robert Nettleton, Esq., Governor of the Russia Company, a person of consequence in his day." This gentleman was a close friend of Mr. James Norman. He was one of the witnesses who signed the register on the marriage of James Norman to Eleonora Innocent on January 8th, 1761.

Mr. Nettleton was succeeded at Freelands by one of the Wells family, who in turn was succeeded by Thomas Raikes, a friend of Wilberforce and Pitt, and Governor of the Bank of England. In this capacity he was called upon to deal with the great financial crisis of 1797 caused by the disturbed state of Europe and the fears of a French invasion.

A tablet in Bromley Church with a Latin inscription perpetuates the memory of Thomas Raikes. The property eventually passed, in or about 1770, from the Hulls to the family of Assheton, but continued to be held on lease. Mr. Charles Browne was there, says Dunkin, in 1810, but shortly afterwards (1815) we find Mrs. Moore in occupation, the widow of John Moore, Archbishop of Canterbury. In 1818 Freelands was bought by Sir Samuel Scott, as a part of the Sundridge estate, but was occupied by Mr. Charles Pott, as tenant of Sir Samuel, during his lifetime and that of his wife. Miss E. O. Parr, who has special knowledge of this particular district, is the granddaughter of Mr. Charles Pott, and it is to her that we are chiefly indebted for the facts contained in this section of our History.

On the death of Mrs. Pott in 1876 Freelands was vacant until Mr. Edward Packe, Sir Edward H. Scott's agent and brother-in-law, occupied it from 1885 until 1888, when the freehold was bought by the Religious of the Holy Trinity, in whose possession it still remains.

When adapting the house to the purposes of a convent drastic changes were found to be necessary. The basement of the old mansion was entirely gutted, and all evidence of its age destroyed. In this part was found what was held to have been a tiny chapel, with the marks where a small altar had stood, and a four-centred arch of wood spanning the altar space. This was in such a state of decay that it was impossible to preserve it.

An underground passage was discovered under the kitchen floor about 5 feet 6 inches high and extending in a curved line for some 35 feet and leading to a small rectangular chamber about 3 feet 6 inches square. No coins, or other relics of antiquity, were discovered, either there or elsewhere, but a particularly fine lead cistern was recognised as of value, and was sold to the Victoria and Albert Museum. It is adorned with several crests, the chief one being a stag's head with collar of oak-leaves between the Pillars of H Hercules. It also bears the initials I R and the date 1713. These initials have been identified as those of John Hulls and Rebecca his wife, who were the owners of the property from about 1708 to 1721.

In old days, before the invasion of the district by the builders, the direct way to Bromley from Freelands, and indeed from Chislehurst and Sundridge, was by a path which crossed Plaistow Lane at a step-stile against the Freelands fence. The path then followed the line of the present Park Road to the palace gates, crossing five fields on the way. Mr. Pott conferred a lasting blessing upon the pedestrian in 1845 by substituting gates where stiles had previously been, a blessing celebrated by Dr. Thomas Scott, at that time chaplain to the College, in lines which at any rate scan, and express clearly what the poet has to say :

> " And thanks to him who now at Freelands dwells,
> His praise the pleased pedestrian justly tells :
> For passing to his house no stiles dismay,
> Nothing impedes the walker on his way."

Quite at the east end of Widmore Lane is the property known as " Beechfield," which was originally a farm, dating from 1637 and possibly earlier. Through old title-deeds the passage of this piece of land can be traced through successive hands from 1713, and these documents have established its position as being closely adjacent to the famous pond, which seems in the course of years to have become a pond once more. In 1713 Richard Smith sold the property to William Round of Shoreham, Kent, from whom it descended to his only child, Jane, the wife of John Day, who in 1767 sold it to Mr. William Child. This gentleman was a surgeon living in Bromley, who carried on a medical practice in partnership with Mr. William Roberts. Child left the Beechfield property to his partner, Roberts, who transferred his residence from the Bromley market-place to the house which he now built upon his newly acquired estate, which house he christened Beechfield after the two trees, a green and copper beech, which he planted about it. Roberts in turn, after the death of William Child, had taken a partner, Mr. Thomas Ilott, and to him Beechfield was bequeathed in remainder after the death of Mrs. Roberts. Thus it was that arose the long and honourable association existing between Bromley and the family of

LEAD WATER-TANK, DATED 1713 AND WITH INITIALS $^H_{I\ R}$.

Formerly at Freelands; now at the Victoria and Albert Museum, South Kensington.

LEAD WATER-TANK, DATED 1721 AND WITH INITIALS J.W.

At the Rookery, Bromley Common.

WIDMORE FARM

Ilott, an association which has never been broken, and which only deepens in strength and affection with each new generation of that family.

On the death of Mrs. Roberts Beechfield passed in due course into the hands of Thomas Ilott's son James W., who, after letting it for some years on lease to a Mr. J. Dalton, added largely to it, and made it his own residence until his death in 1897. A portion of the property was voluntarily surrendered by Mr. James W. Ilott to the Bromley Local Board in order to allow of a much-needed widening of the road, and the cutting away of a steep and dangerous corner. Some alterations in the grounds during Mr. Dalton's tenancy brought to light many coins and other Roman remains which are now in the possession of the town and are preserved in the Municipal Buildings. The old sundial on the terrace at Beechfield is thought to have been transferred there from Dr. Hawkesworth's house.

At the bottom of Widmore Hill on the opposite side to Beechfield used to stand a picturesque cottage, with a saw-pit, inhabited by a wheelwright named Harber. The pair of red cottages just above in Plaistow Lane still stand, but the old Widmore Farm disappeared many years ago. This was a very pretty old house with gables and large chimney-stacks standing at right angles to the road, and the loss of it is much to be deplored.

The little dip between the two hills at Widmore has changed much in appearance in recent years. At the bottom where is now a small triangular garden two neat white cottages used to stand enclosed in their gardens. The first cottage, built upon what was then a piece of waste land, was erected for himself by a Manx carpenter who accompanied Dr. Murray, Bishop of Sodor and Man, when he was translated to the see of Rochester in 1827. Subsequently two iron houses were set up which were regarded as very wonderful structures, for they mark one of the first attempts to build in iron, but their discomforts soon became obvious. They were over-cold in winter and over-hot in summer, and consequently were displaced in favour of the white cottages, which, in turn, were displaced by the construction of Sundridge Avenue (1887).

Some thirty years previously Widmore was being rapidly developed by the construction of a new road upon the extreme verge of the palace property —Tylney Road—and around it there gathered that region of small houses now included under the name of Widmore.

A little to the eastward of Tylney Road and on the north side of Widmore Lane was a small property of about twelve acres with a house upon it called Shawfield Lodge. The house was built in 1785 for two brothers, John and Andrew Harrison ; it was built on three sides of a square courtyard, the flanking wings containing separate kitchens and stables for each of the brothers. Freeman mentions another " mansion " close by Shawfield Lodge, but no trace of this building now exists.

In 1832 the property was bought by Mr. Godfrey Meynell of Bradley Hall, Derbyshire, who had been living at Shawfield Lodge since 1822. He died in 1834 and was buried at Bromley, a tablet to his memory and that of his wife and only son (died 1844) being placed in the south aisle of the church. The property passed into the possession of Godfrey John Meynell Meynell, the only grandson of Godfrey Meynell. In 1852 it was let on lease to David James Noad. This lease was subsequently transferred to George Fenning, who made some alterations and additions to the house and left in 1866. The next tenant was Mr. Morgan Yeatman.

During the twenty-five years that Mr. and Mrs. Yeatman and their family lived at Shawfield Lodge they identified themselves with much of the social and philanthropic work of the neighbourhood, more especially the parochial organisations of the recently formed parish of St. George's, Bickley, which soon included Widmore, and in so doing they gathered a large circle of friends about them. Mr. Yeatman died in 1889, his widow and family remaining at Shawfield Lodge till 1891, when they removed to Eltham. The house was empty for three years, and in 1894 Mr. Meynell sold the estate to Mr. John Jarvis Rodgers, a London solicitor, for £6,000. He at once proceeded to develop it, constructing the road now known as Shawfield Park. The house, with its garden, was sold to Mr. Gilbert Wood, F.R.G.S., an architect, founder and proprietor of *The Architect*, a journal devoted to the interests of architecture and building, who lived there till 1904, the remainder of the estate being divided into small plots.

In December 1897 J. J. Rodgers and his wife both died, when the property was sold and the proceeds divided among their children.

BICKLEY HALL.

Erected in 1780 by John Wells, Esq.

TO the east of Widmore lies Bickley, now one of the most opulent centres of population in the parish of Bromley. Its rise and development, however, are comparatively recent, and, indeed, it can only boast a name within the last 150 years. There existed in ancient days a small hamlet known as Cross-in-hand, towards the north-east corner of the present Bickley Park, containing one substantial residence, afterwards known as " Farrants " from the name of its owner, but otherwise the whole area now known as Bickley was uncultivated common covered with gorse, furze, and heather, and useful only as a sporting estate and a cover for foxes.

Near the site of the present Bickley Hall a hunting lodge was maintained about the middle of the eighteenth century by the owner of the property, " Thomas Jukes, Esq., who," says Dunkin, " kept a remarkable fine pack of Foxhounds which were hunted under the famous Potter."

In 1759 the whole estate was bought by Mr. John Wells, and by successive additions to their property the Wells family became the most important landowners in the parish, Widmore, as we have seen, being purchased in 1809, and further purchases of land to the north of the palace grounds extended the Wells's estate almost to the town.

The Wells family had carried on business at Deptford as shipbuilders through many generations. There can be little doubt that it is to one of this family that Pepys refers in his *Diary*, under date Ap. i. 1664 :

" This day Mrs. Turner did lend me as a rarity a manuscript of one Mr. Wells, writ long ago, teaching the method of building a ship, which pleases me mightily."

The entry seems to imply a long-established connection between Mr. Wells and the shipbuilding industry. The business proved extremely lucrative, as the purchases of landed estate in Bromley, Widmore, Bickley, and Southborough clearly indicate.[1]

Under the Wells régime modern Bickley begins to appear. In 1780 the mansion, now generally called Bickley Hall, was built for himself as a residence by John Wells, on the site of the old hunting lodge known as Highway Bush. Much of the surrounding wastes of furze and briar were cleared and added to the pleasure grounds. The winding lanes which intersected the property began to be replaced by thoroughfares, as, for example, the Chislehurst Road constructed by Mr. John Wells in 1825.

The original purchaser, who was also apparently the originator of the name Bickley, died a bachelor and intestate in 1794. He was succeeded by

---

[1] Several editions of *Pepys's Diary* have the name " Wallis " instead of " Wells " in this passage. The Pepys Librarian at Magdalene College, Cambridge, has kindly verified the reference. In the original the name is " Wells."

his brother, William Wells.   On his death in 1805 the estate descended to his eldest son Thomas, who sold it to his brother John, High Sheriff of the County in 1812, and for some time M.P. for Maidstone.   By him the property known as "Farrants" was acquired, the old house was pulled down and its grounds were thrown into Bickley Park.   The cedars which formed a conspicuous ornament for the old "Farrants" still survive in the garden of a house adjoining.

John Wells, having made a large fortune from his shipbuilding business, retired from active work in order to devote himself to the adornment and development of his Bickley estate.   He was a patron of the arts, and formed for his mansion a fine collection of pictures.   But he was destined to experience in hard measure the vicissitudes of fortune.   Anxious to provide a career for his second son, he became connected, as a sleeping partner, with the firm of Whitmore & Company, bankers of Maidstone.   This firm failed in 1841, with such liabilities for John Wells that the estate either had to be sold or passed into the hands of a receiver.

The arrangement, whatever it was, enabled at least some members of the Wells family to retain a portion of the estate, including Southborough Lodge and a fairly large acreage of the land surrounding it.   As this house was the residence of John Joseph Wells, son of John Wells, until his death in 1858, it is possible that the father had made over this property to his son before the financial crisis occurred.   At any rate John Wells, after the crash, had a refuge in Southborough Lodge to which he could go, and it is a current story that he walked out of Bickley Hall with his Bible in one hand, his gun in the other, these being his only remaining possessions, and became an inmate of his son's house at Southborough.   Mrs. John Joseph Wells remained in occupation until her death, which occurred nearly forty years after that of her husband.

It was then, in 1894 or 1895, that the final dispersal of the Wells's property was effected.   The greater part of it was bought by a Land and Building Company which proceeded to develop it, and in due course, from 1897 onwards, the new roads, such as Park Hill, Waldegrave, Blenheim, Burford and others, which now branch out from the southern end of Southborough Road, came into existence.

Bickley Hall itself, soon after John Wells left it, was taken on lease by Mr. Edlmann, and a letter from Mrs. Chalmers, Mr. Edlmann's daughter, seems to make it clear that the estate was not immediately sold, but was placed in the hands of the creditors.

"We came to Bickley," she writes, "in 1844 . . . renting it from a man named Noakes, who was, I think, a sort of manager for the creditors of the Wells Estate."

The Edlmann family remained at Bickley Hall for eight years, when, in

JOHN WELLS.
From an engraving lent by Miss D. F. Gedge.

1852, it was sold over their heads, and to their great annoyance, to Mr. William Dent.

" It was sold," Mrs. Chalmers writes, " over my father's head for an extra £500 which he wd. willingly have given, as he wished to remain, and thought he had bought the place, when he suddenly discovered it had been privately sold to Mr. Dent."

Mr. Dent, who now became the owner of Bickley, had been a Director of the East India Company. He does not appear to have set much store by his new domain, for in 1861 he sold the estate to a wealthy contractor, Mr. George Wythes, who, while retaining the mansion as a residence for himself, immediately proceeded to develop his purchase to the utmost economic advantage. It was his principle to have upon his property only large and commodious houses enclosed in fairly extensive grounds, from two to five acres in extent, and that characteristic of Bickley in some measure continues to survive.

New roads were opened up in every direction—much of the Park was cut up for building land, and by 1864 the locality had become so popular that Mr. Wythes built, at a cost of £12,000, St. George's Church, the full story of which appears in another chapter.

The residence itself has now passed into the hands of Messrs. A. J. & B. S. Farnfield, and is a flourishing Preparatory School for Boys.

There still remains in the garden of the original mansion a curious memento of the connection of the first proprietors with ships and shipping. An arch over a pathway is formed of the huge jawbone of a whale, and Miss E. O. Parr has recalled that the road now known as Pines Road was originally " Jawbone Lane," and moreover that the posts marking the footpaths over Chislehurst Common and along Chislehurst Hill are, or were, of bone, and not of wood or stone.

Mr. Wythes, in developing his estate, was not unmindful of the recreations of the residents. A portion of the Park was allotted to the purposes of cricket, and the splendid ground of the Bickley Park Cricket Club, and the prowess of successive generations of members, worthily maintain the reputation of our county as one of the chief centres of the national game.

Included in the Wells property of Bickley lay the hamlet of Southborough, a name which is found in old maps and ancient charters as South-Barrow, Sowborough, Side Borough, and Sugebeorge. It contained in 1832, when Freeman published his *History of Bromley*, about sixteen houses, among them the

"pleasant seats of Abraham Welland Esq., and the late Governor Cameron," and others.

There is a tradition that George III used frequently to visit Governor Cameron at Southborough, with whom he was on terms of special intimacy. But the tradition which specially distinguishes Southborough is to the effect that it contained a property which was once a barony of a feudal lord whose tenure entitled him not only to exercise jurisdiction in his baronial court, but also to pronounce a capital sentence.

" At a farm now in the occupation of Mr. Alexander," writes Dunkin, " some of the aged inhabitants assert that, in the memory of their fathers, stood a gate house, the windows of which were strongly grated with iron bars, and had formerly been used as a prison. They further say that, at a more distant period, there stood a Courthouse near the opposite farm, and executions occasionally took place on a spot not far distant."

It was this tradition which attracted our local historian Thomas Wilson to visit the place towards the close of the eighteenth century, but he was clearly dissatisfied with the evidence forthcoming.

" Could collect nothing authentic : therefore gave up the search,"

and Dunkin, a few years later, regards the whole story as fabulous.

" There are no records," he says, " which countenance any such tradition, and the circumstance of this hamlet constituting a part of the Manor belonging to the Bishop of Rochester generates a strong suspicion that the whole is fabulous, or at least exaggerated by the mistakes of the ignorant rustics."

This old and now exploded tradition is associated with an old house and farmstead at Southborough known as " Turpington," which has stood for many centuries near the junction of Crown Lane, Turpington Lane, and Southborough Lane. Close by it until about a century ago was a water-splash where the nameless tributary of the Ravensbourne crosses the road, a wooden footbridge being provided for the use of pedestrians.

The farm-house itself is one of the oldest houses remaining in Bromley. The evidence which an examination of its structure affords leads to the conclusion that part of it dates from the fifteenth century or earlier. Originally it was smaller than at present, and was evidently very similar to the old house known as " Sparke's Cottage " on Mason's Hill. It consisted of a main building with a wing at its western end having an overhanging upper story with a gable. Apparently in Tudor times the then owner enlarged it by building the gabled wing at its eastern end. The interior still contains the timbers on which the sloping roof of the original building rested.

TURPINGTON, SOUTHBOROUGH.

THE CROOKED BILLET, SOUTHBOROUGH.

The name " Turpington " appears to be derived from a family with the cognomen " Tubbenden," a family which was living in the Cray Valley as early as the thirteenth century.   At Orpington a farm and a lane retain to the present day the name of Tubbendens.   A member of this family came to live in Bromley about 1355, and he and two subsequent generations bearing the name of Richard de Tubbenden lived at Southborough.   The last member of the family, named Alice, died in 1440.   It is not impossible that these were the builders of the original house, and their name in various corrupt forms has remained attached to it.

The next reference we have to this property is that in 1532 it was in the possession of Thomas Knight, citizen and brewer of Westminster. He was one of those wealthy Londoners who were at this time purchasing country estates within easy distance of the Metropolis.   He was the owner of many acres in and around Bromley, and was himself the owner and occupant of the large house on the north side of the High Street called the " Grete House," of which more is said in another part of this book. On his death, in 1544, he left his Southborough property to his son Edmund, another son, Robert, receiving the house in the High Street.

Edmund Knight lived and died at Orpington, the house at South-borough being leased to a local yeoman.   Edmund Knight left the property to his wife for life and after her death to one of his brother Robert's sons.

We have no definite information that any of the Knight family actually lived at this house, but it is not unreasonable to suppose that some members of it did, and that they were responsible for the enlargement already referred to which took place at about this date.   In support of this is the fact that this addition bears the initials " M. K." still remaining on the original plaster, evidently placed there to commemorate its erection and associate it with some name.   At this period there was no other family in Bromley with a name commencing with K, and in that family there were two persons named Mary.   These circumstances appear to warrant the supposition that these initials commemorate one of these Mary Knights.

Robert Knight died in 1558, and in the next few years his family sold their interest in the Bromley property.   Arnold King of Foxgrove Manor, Beckenham, bought the larger part of it, " Tuppington " being among his purchases.

At his death in 1611 the property came to his son John, who died in 1621.   His widow seems to have lived at Southborough ; their son Robert certainly did, and was succeeded by his son Robert.

Like many another the family appears to have fallen in fortune, for in a deed now preserved at the Public Library we find that in September 1666 Robert King :

" For and in consideration of certain dettes and dutyes "

arranges with

" Sir Edmund Bowyer of Camberwell, Surry, Knight to compound and discharge for him out of the issues and profits of the Land hereafter demised and for and in consideration of the rent herein reserved and for divers other good causes and considerations."

He then demises to him his " capital messuage called Turpington in the Parish of Bromley with its barns, stables, outhouses, yards, orchards gardens, lands, and closes commonly occupied and enjoyed together with the said messuage all lying together by or near the said messuage and in the parish of Bromley lately in the tenure and occupation of Robert King or his assigns or some of them, To have and to hold to the said Sir Edmund Bowyer for ninety-nine years paying to the said Robert King the sum of £5 yearly at Michaelmas."

The land associated with the house varied from time to time, but, generally speaking, it included all the land stretching from it across both Turpington and Crown Lanes as far west as the common, by which it was then bounded, with detached pieces on the farther side near " the Hooke."

Within six years, in April 1672, Sir Edmund Bowyer surrendered up the land and tenements, together with all right, title, and interest in the same, back to Robert King, who at once appears to have mort-gaged the property to Lydia Hall. Ultimately, in 1681, by arrangement with Robert King's children, it was sold to Henry Nurse to pay off the mortgage.

Henry Nurse died in 1705, leaving in his will " Turpington Farm " to his son. This family held it till 1748, when William Tyser bought it from them. William Tyser was not a Bromley man. He and his descendants let out the property on lease for successive periods of twenty-one years. The people who are of greater interest to us are those who lived in the house and farmed the land. For two or three generations these leaseholders were a well-known family of yeomen named Westbrook, whose tombstones can still be seen in the Bromley parish churchyard north of the church. They were succeeded by Thomas Newnham, a resident gentleman of Southborough, and he in turn by William Alexander, the butcher who is mentioned elsewhere.

The property was afterwards owned for a short time by Mr. George Warde Norman, and was subsequently added to the large purchases made by John Wells in this neighbourhood.

Following the final dispersal of the Wells's property, Turpington, in 1897, came into the hands of Lord Cobham and Mr. Richard Creed, F.R.I.B.A., jointly. On the death of Mr. Creed in 1913 Lord Cobham became sole owner, and he, in 1920, sold the property to Mr. Victor Heal, also an architect, and a close friend of Mr. Creed. Under the appreciative and fostering care of these two gentlemen this ancient house has been preserved to us.　Most of the accretions with which former occupants had covered and hidden features of its original construction have been removed, and the house restored as near as may be to what it was in Tudor days.

In addition to Turpington there is in Southborough another estate known from time immemorial as Blackbrook.　There appears to have been a family deriving its name from the place living in this part of the parish from about 1250 to 1400.　The names of several members of this family, William de Blakbroke, Symon de Blakbroke, are found during this period in the Lay Subsidies and other documents.

In the first quarter of the fourteenth century the Blackbrook estate, or a part of it, was in the possession of William le Latimer, for in the post-mortem inquisition on his holdings, 1327, he is stated to have held in addition to the property in Bromley, derived from William de Bliburgh :

" a tenement called Blakebroke, and one messuage with a garden containing one acre of land, and it is worth per annum 4*d.*, and six acres of arable land worth per acre 3*d.*"

As is shown in the section on " Simpson's," William le Latimer exchanged his Bromley property, including Blackbrook, with Conan FitzHenry, Knight, for the Manor of Liverton in Yorkshire.　By Conan these estates were sold to Richard Lacer, and they passed in due course to the families of Simpson and Style.

A part of the estate, however, still continued in the hands of the original Blackbrook family, a William de Blakebroke being rated for his land at 14*d.* at the time when Richard Lacer was paying 8*s.* as a tax on the Blackbrook land acquired by him.

Very little, except the names of various tenants, Shotts, Bedells, Masters, and others, has come down to us in connection with this place during the sixteenth and succeeding centuries.　Like most of the property in the neighbourhood it was eventually acquired by John Wells and added to his Bickley estate.

The house was for a long time the residence of Rev. J. E. Newell, the Vicar or Curate of Bromley, who held the living from 1826 to 1865.　In 1873 it was occupied for a few months by George Eliot and her husband, George H. Lewes.　In one of her letters, dated September 4th, 1873, she writes :

" Went to Blackbrook, near Bickley.　We are really enjoying the country and have more than our share of everything . . .　We have fine bracing air to walk in—air which I take in as a sort of nectar.　We like the bits of scenery round us better and better as we get them by heart in our walks and drives. . . .　We had become very fond of the neighbourhood.　The walks and drives around us were delightfully varied ; commons,

14

BLACKBROOK, SOUTHBOROUGH, 182c.

COTTAGES NEAR BLACKBROOK.

From a water-colour sketch by Miss A. Pott, 1854.   Pulled down 1899.

wooded lanes, wide pastures, and we felt regretfully that we were hardly likely to find again a country house so secluded in a well-inhabited region."

Alterations and additions had been made to the house during the course of its existence, but part of the ancient fabric remained until 1897.

On Sunday, February 7th, in that year, a few days after Sir Christopher R. Lighton had entered into occupation, an outbreak of fire consumed the whole of the old part of the buildings.

Close by the house up to quite recent times there still survived some picturesque timbered buildings which used to be occupied either by those who farmed the land, or as cottages by the labourers who worked upon it.

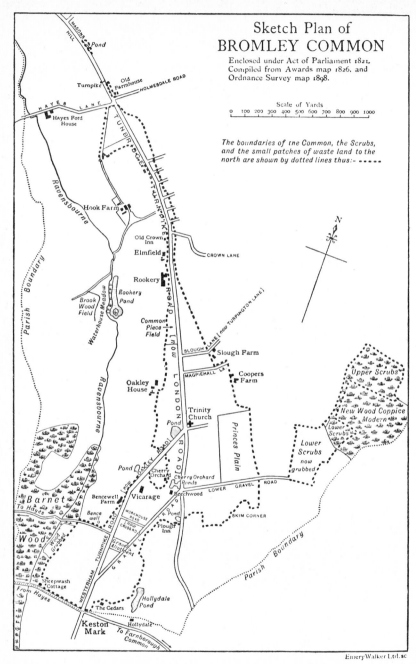

Sketch Plan of
BROMLEY COMMON

Enclosed under Act of Parliament 1821
Compiled from Awards map 1826, and
Ordnance Survey map 1898.

Scale of Yards

The boundaries of the Common, the Scrubs,
and the small patches of waste land to the
north are shown by dotted lines thus:-

Prepared by Mr. Philip Norman, F.S.A.

Emery Walker Ltd. sc

THE extensive district lying to the south of the town from the top of Mason's Hill to Keston Mark is popularly styled Bromley Common, and comprises at the present time one ward of the borough. We must, however, in any history of the common, clearly differentiate between this loose general name of Bromley Common and what was in truth the original common, or common lands, the boundaries of which by no means coincide with the existing ward.

To do this it may be well to begin by defining what a common, in the legal sense of the term, really is, and so dispel the popular notion that common land is land held by the community in common—that is, that it has no owner, but is the possession of the public who enjoy sole rights over it.

Legally, common land, though accessible to the public, is not common to all, in the sense of all men having proprietary rights over it. The soil belongs to one person, the Lord of the Manor, while certain persons have the right to take certain profits from it, such as the right of pasture, of cutting bushes, gorse, or heather, sometimes of lopping, of cutting turf or peat for fuel, of digging sand, loam, or gravel. Such persons are known as commoners, and the above rights are strictly confined to those entitled to exercise them, either as being freeholders, or copyholders of the manor, or to such as, having been copyholders, have become enfranchised. The actual Bromley Common was owned by the Bishops of Rochester as Lords of the Manor, but under conditions that the " commoners " should freely enjoy their privileges. Moreover some portions of the common were known as " Half-year lands," or Lammas lands, which were the exclusive property of the Lord of the Manor from April 5th to October 10th in each year, and then for the remainder of the year were thrown open to the tenants of the manor to make what they could of them in the time at their disposal.

The common lands of Bromley which came within the definitions just given amounted only to about three hundred acres in all, and they extended, very irregularly, along each side of the existing main road leading to Tonbridge and Hastings.

The common began at the top of Mason's Hill just about where Napier Road now joins the main thoroughfare, and there, upon the south-western side, stood the toll-gate, which remained in evidence till November 1865, when it was removed to find a home for some years in a building yard in the neighbourhood of the Plough Inn. Immediately facing the toll-gate on the north-east side was a farm-house which is said to constitute the subject of a rough sketch by David Cox, now in the Birmingham Art Gallery. At this point the width of the common was little more than the width of the road. Immediately beyond Brick Kiln Lane, or the modern Homesdale Road, the common broadened out on each side of the turnpike, and con-

tained on the south-west a triangular area of about twenty acres known as
the "Shooting Common." The name is probably derived from the practice
of archery—long enjoined by law—which was carried on here, a derivation
which becomes the more probable from the fact that two fields in the neighbourhood were known as "Long Shots" and "Short Shots," possibly from
the length of the targets erected here. But it must not be forgotten that a
family named Shott, or Shot, or Shotte, were large landowners in the
district, and it is possible that "Long Shots" and "Short Shots" have
reference to this family rather than to archery practice.

At about the point where St. Luke's Church now stands, the common
again narrowed to little more than the width of the road, and extended as
merely a narrow strip as far as the site of the Rookery. There it widened
out on both sides, extending, on the east, in a line roughly diagonal to the
existing main road, to Slough Farm, Cooper's Farm, and so to the limit of
Prince's Plain. A little beyond this limit the boundary turned sharply to
the west, and in a zigzag line, touching Skim Corner, it bisected the main
road at the Plough Inn, and thence, with devious turnings inclining westward, to its extreme limit at Keston Mark. The Hayes–Farnborough Road
now for some distance became the southern boundary, the line turning
sharply to the north at Sheepwash Cottage towards Barnet Wood. This
wood now formed the boundary as far as Bencewell House, when a sharp
rectangular turn brought it almost up to the present Westerham Road.
Turning to the north, past Bencewell Farm, Oakley Road became the
boundary for some little distance, when, doubling back upon itself to form
an oval, the land known as Cherry Orchard, though not the ponds, lay just
outside the common land. This curious "island," as it has been called,
completely dislocating the natural course of the boundary line, doubtless
indicates some successful encroachment upon the common lands of which
no record has come to hand. Resuming its normal course after this interval,
the line passes to the east of Oakley House, and curving gradually towards
the north-east, with the Rookery and Elmfield upon its borders, it narrows
to scarcely more than the width of the main road except where it forms one
side of the triangle of Shooting Common.

Such were the limits of the real Bromley Common, to which, however,
there must be added an isolated patch, lying away from Prince's Plain on the
east, known as the Upper and Lower Scrubs, a curiously shaped detached
area, which seems on the map to be altogether out of relation to the common
proper.

An examination, such as that just conducted, of the exact boundaries
of the common discloses a fact which, though obvious on a moment's
consideration, may yet come as a surprise—the fact that not one of the
estates, mansions, houses, or farms most naturally associated in the mind
with Bromley Common falls actually within the precincts of the common
itself. Elmfield, the Rookery, Oakley, the Cedars, Hook Farm, and all

the rest, lie just outside the boundary, though a part of the land now attached to some of them was once common land. This fact, however, is in the nature of things, for private ownership and common land are contradictory terms. For an individual to own land in freehold within a common is incompatible with those common rights which certain individuals enjoy over common land. Such holdings, however, as are mentioned above lie within the parish of Bromley, and therefore fall within the scope of this history. I propose therefore first to give such history as is available of the common itself—of the common proper as I have called it—and then give some record of the properties immediately contiguous to it.

For centuries Bromley Common was a waste, grown over with gorse, heather, fern, and broom, through which various tracks, rather than roads, led the traveller towards Hayes or Southborough or Tunbridge Wells. Even as late as the middle of the eighteenth century the main coach road from London to Tunbridge Wells was, when it crossed the common, little more than a track, for when Mr. James Norman came to the neighbourhood in 1755 he had posts put up and painted white in order to mark it out. Freeman remarks that this road was " not only dreary, but afforded every facility for the commission of robberies," and footpads and highwaymen took every advantage of conditions so favourable to their profession. John Evelyn in his *Diary*, under date June 11th, 1652, records that he was robbed on Bromley Common, his assailants concealing themselves, until the crucial moment arrived, behind the trunk of a huge tree known as " Procession Oak."

" Having been robbed by two cut-throats near Bromley, I rode on to London, and got 500 tickets printed. The robber, refusing to plead, was pressed to death."

On the eastern side of the road between the Rookery and Oakley two pollard elms used to stand, known as the Large and Small Beggars Bush, and behind these trees, or in a thicket immediately below them, tradition tells us that highwaymen used to lurk and await their victims. As late as 1798 a highwayman was hanged upon the common for robbing His Majesty's Mail. Indeed, until comparatively recent times a journey from Bromley to Keston Mark was at once adventurous and picturesque. In the marshy land, known now as Prince's Plain, snipe and other game were plentiful, and for many generations the echoes which subsequently resounded from a well-hit cricket ball were awakened by the sportsman's gun.

The first material change in ancestral conditions came in 1764, when a portion of the common lands in Bromley Parish were enclosed by Act of Parliament, but unfortunately no map accompanying the Act is to be found, and in the Act itself no specification is given of the lands actually enclosed. The exact land thus enclosed in 1764 is therefore a matter of guess-work, but it is beyond question that it was a portion of the common proper. This Act, which extinguished " the right of common in, over and upon certain commonable lands and grounds within the Manor and Parish of Bromley," made over such lands and grounds, in sole proprietorship, to the Lord of the Manor—the Bishop of Rochester—or rather to Mr. William Scott, who represented the Bishop as lessee—on payment of a yearly sum of £40 to the churchwardens and overseers of the poor

" in full compensation of all manner of right of common, or common of pasture, of the freeholders and inhabitants of the parish, and all other persons claiming right of common."

At the same time the permanent rights of the holder of the see as Lord of the Manor were expressly reserved.

The Enclosure Act of 1764 was followed about sixty years later (1821) by an Act of Parliament enclosing the whole of the old common. Such Enclosure Acts were largely due to the wasteful character of the methods of cultivation practised on the common lands, and to a sense of the necessity, in a country mainly dependent upon itself for its food supplies, of making every part of it produce to the full extent of its capacity.

Thus Dunkin in 1815, speaking of the common, deplores the fact that " so large a tract of land is unproductive," and Freeman, after the enclosure, rejoices that so extensive a space of unproductive land should now be put to its proper uses. The sense for open spaces and for wild natural beauty is of very recent growth, and encroachments upon public rights, which to-day would be resented as acts of vandalism, were not only accepted without demur, but regarded as benefactions in the general interests of the community. This statement, however, is not to be taken to imply that no opposition to enclosures from any quarter was forthcoming. Mr. George Norman had been for many years a resolute opponent of the enclosure of Bromley Common, and " at length," says Mr. Philip Norman, " yielded with reluctance when he found that further opposition would be of no avail."

The Act, dated April 6th, 1821, is a lengthy document of over eight thousand words, and in it the area to be enclosed is specified as

" about 300 acres of commons and waste land—and a certain tract of commonable or half-year land called the Scrubs, containing by estimation fifty acres or thereabouts."

The Act, in fact, absorbed into itself the whole of Bromley Common.

A Commissioner, Mr. Richard Peyton, was appointed to carry out the provisions of the Act, to make awards in compensation to those dispossessed of their common rights,

" to stop up and discontinue, divert and turn, and set out and appoint any public roads, ways, or paths " anywhere within the parish—not only within the limits of the common—and generally

" to do his duty without favour or affection, prejudice or partiality, to any person or persons whomsoever."

The Commissioner's Awards were engrossed upon a map, which is now preserved in the parish church. Five years elapsed between the passing of the Act of Parliament and the completion and signature of the terms of the awards, and thus the new order of things on Bromley Common dates from March 21st, 1826. Under this new order it is found that the Bishop of Rochester, as Lord of the Manor, was the chief beneficiary under the Act. The Bishop was to receive in compensation for the surrender of his manorial rights over the " Common, commonable, and waste lands," so much of such lands as should be equal to one-seventeenth part of their value—

" after deducting thereout the public roads, drains, water courses, and land sold for the purpose of paying the expenses of carrying this Act into execution."

A further deduction of ten acres was made for land to be set aside for the construction of a workhouse, with garden attached, which garden should either be cultivated by the inmates of the workhouse or let by the Vestry, the proceeds being applied as part of the poor rate. The project of a workhouse, however, was not carried into effect, for the subsequent formation of the Bromley Workhouse Union rendered any such scheme superfluous. The vicarage and garden of Trinity Church, the house known as Beechwood, and certain cottages which formerly stood opposite Bencewell Farm-house, contain the greater part of the ten acres originally set aside as workhouse land.

To the Bishop was also awarded that part of the common called the Scrubs, but on condition that he was to compensate from lands allotted to him those who were dispossessed of their common rights. After all the special requirements of the Act had been met, the remainder of the land was to be allotted to the Bishop as Rector of the parish in right of his glebe, and to others who at the time of the division should be entitled to common right.

Apart from the Bishop, no one seems to have originally enjoyed common rights to any considerable extent. The awards, by way of allotment of land to such as held such rights, were numerous, but the amounts allotted were small in quantity. It was by subsequent purchase rather than as compensation that the common land now in possession of, for example, the Norman family was secured. But among those to whom allotments were made by way of compensation mention may be made of Sir Thomas Baring, the trustees of Bromley College, William Isard, John

Lascoe, Edward Latter, George Norman, and the parish of St. Mary Aldermary in London. Altogether 239 allotments of land were made, their extent, excluding the Scrubs, being 316 acres, 3 roods, and 2 poles. To others grants in money, in lieu of land, were made, the amounts varying from £42 5s. to £3 7s. 6d. Among the recipients of such money grants were George Grote, the father of the historian of Greece, and Samuel Baxter.

By the provisions of the Act of Parliament the enclosed common was to be laid out in new roads, ditches, fences, and drains, involving the expenditure of considerable sums of money. To meet these expenses many pieces of the old common were sold, either by public auction or private contract, the proceeds being paid into Messrs. Grote, Prescott & Co., the bankers appointed by the Act. Those landowners who had frontages abutting on the common were allowed to purchase the land adjoining them, and to effect exchanges by mutual consent. Many such landowners took advantage of this permission, and so, by purchase, acquired the greater part of the common land they held. In the case of the Norman family, almost all their property on the old common lands was obtained either at the time by purchase or exchange, or by subsequent purchase. In this way that family has become possessed of Oakley, the Scrubs, Prince's Plain, Elmfield, the frontage of Cooper's Farm, the Cherry Orchard, and the Gravel Road Meadows. In fact the whole business of enclosure seems to have been carried through without spoliation, hardship, or complaint, and the public of that time was little affected by the loss to the community of an open expanse of ground distinguished alike by its natural beauty and its traditions.

The effects of enclosure were immediately seen in the diversion of some existing tracks or roads, in the formation of new roads, and in the construction of ditches, drains, and fences in preparation for the development of the old common as a residential area. Gradually the operations of the builder and the amenities of the situation attracted a residential population with requirements, both material and spiritual, which needed satisfaction. These latter needs were met in 1839 by the erection of Holy Trinity Church at the junction of the Hastings and Westerham Roads, and, as the population increased, by the foundation of St. Luke's Church in 1886, at the corner of the main and Southlands Roads. A full account of these churches will be found in the chapter of this book dealing with the subsidiary churches of the parish. By gradual but successive processes of development the district has assumed the forms which are familiar to-day, and Bromley Common has become but the shadow, or symbol, of a name which for many centuries had accurately described it.

Now therefore we pass from the actual common to its environs, where the chief source of interest lies in the various habitations which bordered on the common land, and which by their close proximity are often identified with it. Dunkin, writing in 1815 about Bromley Common, specifically states that "there are 25 houses on this Common," by which he presumably means houses upon its borders, for, as we have seen, private ownership is not compatible with common land. Let us start from the entrance to the common at the toll-gate beyond Mason's Hill, and follow the boundary line to the east of the main Hastings Road.

The first building to attract our attention is the old farm-house, already mentioned as providing a subject for the pencil of David Cox. The most notable fact recorded about it is that the site on which the farm-house stood was at one time advertised for sale, and, with ingenuous impartiality, was commended to purchasers as being equally "suitable for a church or a tavern." In the early part of the nineteenth century the land was farmed by a Mr. Thomas Smith, and later on, beyond 1862, by Mr. Reuben Mansfield. For rather more than a mile beyond this farm there were no houses immediately fronting the common boundary, but some little distance away lay Turpington House and farm, the picturesque house and grounds remaining to the present day. It was here that horse races used to be run in the eighteenth century. A programme has survived of a fixture in August 1734, which, in language not very intelligible to me, announces, as the principal prize, a purse of twenty-five guineas for

"any horse, mare, or gelding that never won above that value at any time in purse or place, fourteen hands to carry nine stone, all under or over to carry weight for inches. To pay a guinea and a half entrance, or three at the post."

These races "on Bromley Common" were said to have been patronised by Frederick Prince of Wales, but the appellation of Prince's Plain to part of the common is probably due, as will be seen later, not to this Prince, but to another.

Hereabouts also, close to Blackbrook, and east and west of it, were two old and picturesque hostelries, known respectively as the Chequers, and the Crooked Billet. Both have been reconstructed or entirely rebuilt, but both still stand upon their ancient sites, and bear their ancient signs—that of the Chequers being a black-and-white draught-board, which originally indicated that the game of draughts could be played within. Immediately beyond what was known as Slough Lane, now Turpington Lane, there lay Slough Farm, almost touching the boundary, and a little farther on, beyond Magpie Hall Lane, Cooper's Farm, now the Club House of the Bromley and Bickley Golf Club. The links of this Club were originally the Bromley Race-course, not to be confused with the eighteenth century races just recorded. The Bromley Race-course at Cooper's Farm was established by William Pawley of the White Hart in 1864, and an account of it appears in the chapter on Sport.

Beyond Cooper's Farm lies that part of the old common known as Prince's Plain. Originally marshland overgrown with scrub, it offered, by its wide extent of level surface, a golden vista to the cricketer. In 1812 the area was cleared and turned into a cricket ground, on which many famous matches (to be further referred to in the chapter on Sport) were played.

Rounding the boundary bend we come to Skim Corner, where some cottages of considerable antiquity, judging by the nature of the bricks and internal timbers, still stand, flanked on the other side of the track by a house which, in its present state, shows at least five periods of addition. Now it is a curious nondescript, with the old original wattle and daub still constituting the chief feature of the building. Still following the boundary for a quarter of a mile we reach the high road, and the famous Plough Inn, with its pond within the boundary, abutting on the road, while the inn itself stands just outside.

How far back in antiquity the Plough extends is not recorded, but, situated as it is at the southern extremity of the common on the main coach road between London and Hastings, it may be assumed that a hostelry of some sort has occupied the position from time immemorial. The Plough first appears as such a hostelry in the Parish Registers for 1733. Modern restoration has unfortunately obliterated the most essential features of the old inn, but from contemporary engravings we can still visualise the quaint and picturesque structure, fronted by three large elm trees with the inn sign upstanding across the road, and its enormous wooden horse-trough, a prince of its kind.

Some acres of land were attached to the inn, and from its hospitable doors the guests looked out over a green meadow which extended to the western boundary of the common. The Plough was the headquarters of the Prince's Plain Cricket Club. There the club was initiated, and there, on match days, the players used to dine in a long wooden shed at the back, provided by the members for the purpose. The Plough pond, fed by a stream which ultimately finds its way to the Ravensbourne, was so contiguous to the inn as to be a trap for anyone a little unsteady in his gait.

Leaving the Plough and still following the boundary, we skirt the road known still as Gravel Road. The name comes from a special award, made under the Enclosure Act, of two acres of land set aside to provide gravel for the making of the new roads in the enclosed land. After fulfilling this purpose for many years, this allotment was converted to its present uses as a recreation ground.

Almost at the extreme end of the southern limit of the common stood the house known as the Cedars : a little beyond it, at the junction of the main road with the road leading to Hayes and Farnborough, we reach Keston Mark, and the old inn with the sign of the red cross.

The term " Mark " as applied to Keston, still fulfils its ancient function

THE OLD PLOUGH INN

of indicating a barrier, or boundary, between two communities. In modern times Keston Mark indicates the boundary between Bromley and Keston parishes, and has an innocent and friendly significance. In primitive times when men lived in tribes, each tribe, jealously hostile to its neighbours, protected its own isolation and independence by a boundary, or mark, of virgin forest which was crossed only at the peril of the intruder.

" In this primitive love of separation," says Mr. Grant Allen in his *Anglo-Saxon Britain,* " we have the germ of that local independence and that isolated private life which is one of the most marked characteristics of modern Englishmen."

To-day, Keston Mark stands rather as a symbol of hospitality and good-fellowship, for hard by its picturesque hostelry the Red Cross invites all comers, and obliterates all enmities with a welcome and good-cheer.

Having reached the extreme limit both of the old common and of the parish, we retrace our course towards the town by the outskirts of the western boundary. Bencewell House is the first habitation of old standing to attract attention, with Bencewell Farm a little beyond it, almost abutting on the main road. In the considerable oval cutting into the old common stands Cherry Orchard, a house and grounds where, in their season, an abundance of tempting cherries used to belie by their bitterness the expectations of adventurous youth. This neighbourhood abounds

KESTON MARK
From an old engraving

in ponds, and there is a tradition that one of these ponds gave away the secret of an illicit still operating in Cherry Orchard House. The refuse from the still was emptied into the pond with such intoxicating effect upon the ducks that suspicions were aroused, and the nefarious traffic was revealed.

Passing from Cherry Orchard, in less than half a mile Oakley House is reached, now one of the residences of the Norman family. The Oakley estate has been identified by Mr. B. F. Davis with the property frequently mentioned in deeds under the name of "Goodwyns." In the seventeenth century it was in the possession of the King family, for in 1701 Walsingham King sold it to Matthew Walraven of Pickhurst Manor. After passing through various hands it became the property of Captain, afterwards Admiral, Sir William Cornwallis, popularly known as "Billy Blue." By the Admiral, Oakley was sold in 1787 to Mr. Major Rohde, by whom it was sold to Mr. George Norman in 1825. Thus the two properties of Oakley and the Rookery were joined into one.

Mr. Philip Norman has himself contributed an account of the Rookery estate :

"This house," he writes, "with the adjoining grounds, contains portions of several former properties. Apparently the earliest document relating to them is a title-deed of June 7th, 1660, wherein mention is made of a ' capital messuage or tenement ' the exact situation of which is not

THE ROOKERY, BROMLEY COMMON.
Before alteration in 1890.

ELMFIELD, BROMLEY COMMON.
Erected early in the eighteenth century.

defined. It had, however, some of the Rookery land connected with it—e.g. two pieces of meadow ground called 'Great Mead' and 'Russia (i.e. rushy) Mead,' both now forming part of the great meadow at the back."

In 1700 this house was bought by Anthony Ball from Sir Jeffrey Jefferys. A deed of 1722 supplies the information that a capital messuage, or mansion house, had been built by him, and had been some time in his possession. In another deed it is said that the mansion already existed in 1716, when it was mortgaged by Ball for £2,500, and the question arises when it had been rebuilt. From the deeds at the Rookery one learns that there were purchases of Bromley Common property in 1700, 1703, 1707, and 1710. No statement appears as to the date of the rebuilding, but there is a large increase in the rating between December 1706 and June 1707. According to information at present available the year of Ball's rebuilding must remain therefore uncertain, but its style alone convinces one that it cannot be later than the time of Queen Anne. This mansion was the still existing part of the Rookery (not known by that name in these early deeds).

Anthony Ball the elder died in October 1718, and the estate came to his only son, Anthony, who, in the rate books of 1719, is described as occupier and owner. In a deed of 1720 he and his wife Elizabeth are mentioned in connection with it, and that year, or early in 1721, they sold the house and land to John Webster and John Cock " for the sole benefit of " (the former) " and his heirs and assigns for ever." The lead cistern in the garden of the Rookery, of which we give an illustration, has on it Webster's initials and the date 1721, and on the painted staircase ceiling, which is most likely coeval with Ball's house, appear the arms of Webster, namely, a cross between four mullets. Conveyance of the estate does not appear to have been formally ratified until May 1st and 2nd, 1722, as shown in a deed which is at the Rookery. John Webster died on November 26th, 1724, having made his will a few days before. In this he bequeathed all his property to his mother, Sarah, for the benefit of his and his wife Judith's children. In December 1734 Sarah Webster made a will leaving all her estate to William Guy, a salter of Wapping, in trust for the benefit of John, Thomas, Robert, Sarah, and Elizabeth, the children of her late son John Webster, and " Judith, their mother, now wife of William Guy."

In a deed dated March 1743, John, Thomas, and Sarah, the surviving children of John Webster, appear as joint owners of the Rookery, and we are told that it is " now and for some time past in the tenure of occupation of William Guy."

On January 23rd and 24th, 1744, the estate was bought by Thomas Chase the elder, who died in 1754. He left his Bromley Common estate to his son Thomas. This latter was the Thomas Chase who narrowly escaped with his life from the great earthquake in Lisbon in 1755. Both these Chases are commemorated in Bromley Parish Church, the monument to the younger recording his experience at Lisbon. James Norman (my great-grandfather) had occupied the Rookery as a tenant of Thomas Chase from about 1755.[1] According to a deed still in existence, he bought it on February 8th, 1765, with the land then attached to it, which only amounted to little over thirty-seven acres. He it was who materially added to the house by building two wings in the Adam style.

" From the end of the century downwards each generation at the Rookery has seen some changes. In 1858 George Warde Norman, grandson of the original purchaser, made additions to the south end of the house, and under the ownership of his son Charles Loyd Norman, the house was further enlarged and quite transformed under the plans of the well-known architect Norman Shaw, R.A."

A little further north, adjoining the Rookery grounds, are the house and estate known as Elmfield, which was at one time, in all probability, the property of Anthony Ball. By 1727 it certainly was in the hands of one of that family, for it was sold in that year by an Anthony Ball, presumably the son of the original Anthony of the Rookery. In 1754 Elmfield was bought by Thomas Chase, of Lisbon earthquake fame, who thus owned all the land comprising Elmfield and the Rookery. After selling the latter, Chase still retained Elmfield and forty-one surrounding acres, and himself lived there till his death in 1788. When the Chase ownership of the property came to an end is not known, but the occupant in 1815 was a Mr. Martin. It passed into the hands of the Makepeace family, and in 1822 Mr. Robert Makepeace was the owner.

Then for a good many years the house was occupied by Miss F. Shepherd, who conducted a very successful girls' school on the premises. On Miss Shepherd's retirement, about the middle of the century, Elmfield was occupied by Mr. and Mrs. Elias, one of whose sons, Ney Elias, became a distinguished explorer and diplomatist, his travels in unexplored parts of Asia gaining for him the Founder's Medal of the Geographical Society.

In 1858 Mr. Charles Barry was in occupation of Elmfield, but in 1862 the house and grounds attached to it were purchased from J. Makepeace by Mr. George Warde Norman, and in the hands of that family it still remains.

Incorporated into the garden of Elmfield there is now a piece of ground which in old days was attached to the Crown Inn, whose premises abutted on the western side of the high road. This ancient hostelry was originally known as the Pye House, and is so styled in a map of 1765. " The Pye House, the sign of the Crown." The name ' Pye ' was no doubt associated with the Upper and Lower Pye fields at the back, though that is no explanation of the name as given to the fields. The inn may be said to have corre-

---

[1] His eldest son, James, who died aged nineteen, was born at Wimbledon in 1754, but his second son, George, was born at the Rookery in 1757.

THE OLD CROWN INN

sponded at one end of the common with the Plough at the other. There were the same homely and familiar features—the picturesqueness of the buildings, the water-trough, hay-trough, pond ; the fine trees which shaded their frontages, the swinging signs in wrought iron, and the atmosphere of invitation which pervaded them both. In the rate books of 1832–5 Mary Quint is rated at £12 for the Crown ; then William and Henry Cooper, rated respectively at £10 15*s*. Ultimately E. Ilsley became the last proprietor of the old Crown. About the year 1866 the house was pulled down and a new inn built immediately opposite on the eastern side of the road. Some Bromley memories still extend as far back as Edwin Fownes, first landlord of the new Crown, a man whose character suggested his familiar name of " Cheer'o Fownes " (it would doubtless have been " Cheerio " if he had lived a little longer). A celebrated coachman on a four-in-hand, an owner of greyhounds and a patron of coursing, a breeder of black-and-tan terriers, and a genial or terrifying host according to the character and conduct of his customers, Edwin Fownes was a fine specimen of a vanishing type, and by his personality transferred to the new Crown something of the prestige of the Crown which was no more.

    A short distance from the Crown the old road, diverted by the Enclosure Act, led past Hook Farm, and joined the existing main road at the corner of Hayes Lane. A part of it formed one side of the triangular space called Shooting Common. And thus we reach the toll-gate, the point from which this itinerary of the common started.

Hook Farm, lying away to the west of the main road, is of great antiquity. Its record has been traced back to Edward III's time, 1334, when " Henry atte Hook " figures in deeds of that period. Towards the close of the fifteenth century Hook was in the possession of a family named indiscriminately Bedle and Bedyl. Thomas Bedyll, yeoman, who was buried in Bromley churchyard, left in 1492 a sum of forty shillings—a large sum in those days—on condition that

" yt be spente in mending of ye hie weye in Bromley Common."

A Thomas Bedle in 1509 leaves by will his house called " Hooke " to his wife, Mary, until his son Thomas reaches the age of twenty-four. In 1521 " Thos. Bedill," probably the son in question, is found to be in financial difficulties in regard to "the hoke," and says in his will that "counsell is to be taken " on the matter. These difficulties appear to have been fatal to the tenure of the Bedle family, for Hook, after much litigation over mortgages on the property, passed into the hands of Robert Knight in 1540. His son Oliver sold it in 1566 to Simon Lowe of Bromley, and in the possession of that family it remained until purchased by James Norman.

This chapter on Bromley Common must not end without a more particular reference to that family which has been bound up in the story of Bromley Common and of Bromley town for the last 170 years. In the foregoing narrative I have shown something of the various stages by which the family of Norman has acquired the various properties which it holds on or adjacent to the old common. But a mere record of property held and acquired leaves out of account that further record which so far transcends any other—the record of continuous beneficence, of unremitting public service, of the pride and pleasure which each successive generation of the family has taken in everything which has tended to the welfare of the town.

The family connection with Bromley began in 1755 when James Norman rented the Rookery and subsequently bought it. His earlier life therefore does not concern us, but it may be mentioned that he was ' out ' in the '45, carrying a musket in opposition to the Young Pretender. His son and successor, George Norman, was prominent in the world of business as a timber merchant with large interests in Norway. His connection with the College, as Treasurer, and with the formation of the Bromley Volunteers in 1798, is shown fully in other chapters of this history. On his death in 1830 he was succeeded at the Rookery by his son, George Warde Norman, whose wide culture and eminent services to the nation as a financier have secured him a place in the *Dictionary of National Biography*. One of his earliest recollections was the occasion when he was taken by his father to call on Pitt at Holwood.

On leaving Eton he joined his father in business, paying frequent visits to Norway, where he formed lifelong associations with many prominent

GEORGE WARDE NORMAN (1793–1882), ÆTAT 79.
From an oil painting by G. F. Watts, R.A.

Norwegians, and acquired a command over the Norwegian language and literature. In 1821 he became a Director of the Bank of England, and doubtless it was due to the many important duties now imposed upon him that he sold his business in 1830, and devoted his energies and talents to national finance. He became a leading authority on banking and currency, and was thus constantly in association with the Government of the day. As a Liberal, a free-trader, and an economist, he made from time to time contributions to economic science, one of which at least—his treatise on " prevalent errors with respect to Currency and Banking "—produced definite effects in important changes in the currency.

In the domain of general literature he was himself distinguished by his wide range and extensive knowledge, but perhaps his greatest service to literature and scholarship was that of persuading his early friend, George Grote, to write his *History of Greece.*

In Bromley itself George Warde Norman was indefatigable in the services of all kinds which he rendered to the town and its neighbourhood. For nearly forty years he was Vice-Chairman of the Bromley Union, set up in consequence of the Poor Law Amendment Bill in 1834, and became so much identified with the work of the Poor Law Guardians that the new workhouse was commonly spoken of as ' George Norman's House.'

For thirty-seven years he was President of the Bromley Literary Institute ; for thirty years President of the West Kent Agricultural Association ; President for many years of the Bromley Cricket Club—cricket being a game which commanded his devotion up to within a week of his death —and in the ecclesiastical sphere the Church of Holy Trinity, Bromley Common, practically owes its existence to his initiative and generosity. In short, there was scarcely any sphere of life which he did not touch, and none that he touched which he did not adorn. He died within a few days of his eighty-ninth year, leaving not only a distinguished name, but enduring marks almost everywhere in Bromley of his keen interest in and practical service to anything which concerned its moral, physical, and spiritual welfare.

So long and beneficent a life could scarcely fail to establish a tradition which has been worthily maintained by those who have followed him. His eldest son, Charles Loyd Norman, who succeeded to the Rookery, succeeded also to many of those offices which his father had held, among others to the treasurership of the College, a position which may almost be called hereditary in the family. His health, however, always somewhat delicate, was a bar to too strenuous exertion. Compelled at last to seek refuge from the English winter in the Riviera, he died at San Remo in 1889.

The second son of George Warde Norman is happily still with us. Mr. Philip Norman has gained distinction by his antiquarian researches into old London. For twenty years he was Treasurer of the Society of Antiquaries, and has served the office of its President.

In Bromley itself he will ever be remembered, as long as its history is read, for the arduous labours which he has devoted to collecting the materials from which that history may be written.

For many years past one man has stood out as pre-eminently fitted to write such a history. Unfortunately Mr. Philip Norman has not been able to see his way to undertake that actual task, which has been assigned to a far inferior hand, but he has been persuaded to allow one chapter of this book to stand in his name, and I must here frankly acknowledge that, without the aid of the materials collected by him, it would have been impossible for the book to be written.

The family is at present represented by Mr. Archibald Cameron Norman, the Chairman of the Bromley Bench of Magistrates, an alderman of the Kent County Council, and Treasurer of Bromley College.

A record of all the services done to the town by the Norman family is not called for here; an acknowledgment of those services will suffice. But it must be the hope of everyone in Bromley that a family association which has had a continuous existence for 170 years may remain unbroken in the succession of years to come.

SIMPSON'S PLACE

DWELLERS in the comfortable, if unromantic, villas of Ravensbourne, Ringer's, and Ethelbert Roads probably live their lives and sleep their just sleep in blissful ignorance that romance is all about them ; that their modern houses now mark the site where once stood, after the Bishop's palace, the mansion and estate of most account in the town of Bromley. They are not troubled at nights by visions

" of the lady dressed in white with a lighted torch in her hand, accompanied by a gentleman in dark clothes with a high-crowned broad-brimmed hat which flapped over the sides of his face,"

for they are unaware that such apparitions were wont, according to tradition, to haunt the courts and galleries of Simpson's Place. Its crenellated walls, its encircling moat, its massive chimney which was the architectural wonder of its day, have all passed into the limbo of forgotten things, and in their stead the modern villa reigns supreme.

And yet, within the memory of those who are still living, Simpson's Moat was a pleasant place enough. Where Ethelbert, Ringer's, and Ravensbourne Roads now are was a wild piece of spinney with blackberries, violets, and ferns growing in their season, interspersed by rough paths flanked by the moat.

"To me," writes Mr. William Baxter, "this spot has great associations, as it was one of the playgrounds of myself and my companions. At that time it was approached by a pretty lane, Ringer's Lane, leading out from the High Road about where Ringer's Road now is. It was uninhabited ; only a moated ruin in the midst of a wild tangle of blackberry bushes. Kestrels used to build in Simpson's estate, and I gave a case of them, shot there, to the Council some few years back."

To trace the rise, development, and decline of Simpson's is the purpose of this chapter.

It is believed by those who are responsible for the materials from which this volume is composed that it is now possible to present, for the first time, the true story of the tenure of this property in medieval times. This story differs so materially from everything which has hitherto appeared in print, it so completely shatters facts and traditions accumulated by antiquaries in the past, that some preliminary remarks as to the nature of the hitherto accepted version and its origin seem to be required. It would indeed be disrespectful to antiquaries such as Philipot and Hasted completely to ignore them, and to proceed to state what is believed to be the truth without first examining what it is that they have said.

SIMPSON'S PLACE, BROMLEY, FROM S.E., *CIRCA* 1828.

Drawn from Nature by Henry Warren.

The first narrative account of what he supposed to be Simpson's Place was given by John Philipot, Somerset Herald, in his *Villare Cantianum*, published in 1659. In this work he ranks Simpson's Place in Bromley as second only in importance to the manor of the Bishops of Rochester.

" Simpson's," he writes, " is the second seat of account, though in ages of a later inscription it contracted that name, yet anciently it was the demesne of *Bankewell*, a family of signal repute in this track. *John de Bankewell* held a Charter of Free Warren to his lands in *Bromley*, in which this was involved, in the thirty-first of *Edward the First*, and Thomas de Bankewell dyed feifed of it in the thirty-fifth year of *Edward the Third*, and when this family was shrunk at this place into a finall extinction ; the next who were eminent in possession of it were the *Clarks*, and one William Clark that flourished here in the reign of *Henry the Fifth*, that he might not be obnoxious to the Statute of Kernellation, obtained licence to erect a strong little pile of Lime and Stone, with an embattell'd wall encircled with a deep moat, which is supplied and nourished with a living spring ; but this man's posterity did not long enjoy it, for about the latter end of *Henry the Sixth John Simpson* dwelt here by right of purchase, & he, having much improved the ancient Fabrick, settled his Name upon it, & indeed that is all that's left to evidence they were owners of it, for in an Age or two after this it was conveyed to Mr. *John Stiles*, of *Beckenham*, Esquire, from whom descends Sir *Humphrey Stiles*, Knight & Baronet."

Here is the first record of the tenure of the De Bankewells—(or De Benquels, or Banquells, as subsequent historians call them)—of William Clark who crenellated the mansion in the time of Henry V, and of John Simpson as the first of that name to own the place.

Hasted, who was writing his *History of Kent* between 1770 and 1800 (his first volume appeared in 1778) follows Philipot, but adds, either on the strength of a tradition or as a piece of embroidery, that " Nicolas Sympson, the King's Barber, descendant of Robert, alienated Sympsons."

This passage is apparently the written foundation on which the belief has been built up that Henry VIII's barber was at one time owner of Simpson's, and lived in Bromley. In the Hall of the Barber-Surgeons' Company in London there hangs a famous picture by Hans Holbein in which the King, and the King's barber, Nicolas Simpson, figure prominently. It was originally intended that a photograph of this picture should appear in this volume, but unfortunately Nicolas Simpson, the King's barber, must disappear from the list of Bromley's worthies.

Subsequent historians have for the most part simply repeated what they found in previous records, though Lysons made some attempt to verify the statements made. In his *Environs*, published in 1796, he expressly states that he could find no document to support Philipot's assertion as to a licence to William Clark to crenellate his house at Bromley. This is not surprising seeing that no such person as William Clark ever existed in this connection, and the only licence to embattle a house in Bromley was granted in Edward II's reign, at least sixty years before Henry V was born.

And yet, although no family of De Bankewelle, or De Banquel, ever held Simpson's, although no such person as William Clark ever existed in association with it, and although, as a consequence, no licence to crenellate his mansion could at any time have been granted to him, nevertheless the mistakes of Philipot and his copiers are capable of a simple explanation. (The origins and authority for the barber-surgeon story rest entirely on tradition.)

There *was* a family of De Banquels which held property in Lewisham, Bromley, Modyngham, Eltham, and Chislehurst, as we learn from an Agreement made in the thirty-fifth year of Edward I (1306). It is to this document that Lysons, Hasted, Wilson, Dunkin, Freeman, and Strong refer in their respective histories. But this property did not include Simpson's. Apart from the fact that the " Bakwell " or Bankewelle, or de Banquel lands *in Bromley* are defined in an Inquisition of the thirty-fifth Edward III as

" certain tenements in Bromley and Shrofholt held in gavilkind of the Bishopric of Rochester,"

now identified as quite a small holding lying on the slopes of Pousty's Hill adjoining Shrofholt, and some fields afterwards included in Kinnaird Park, we now know who was the actual holder of Simpson's at the time when the de Banquels were supposed to be in possession. The de Banquels are not fiction, but their property has been confused with that of another.

A licence to crenellate the mansion at Simpson's *was* actually granted, though not by Henry V, but by Edward II, and it was granted to the known owner of that property, who was " a clerk "—a clerk in Chancery, and possibly also a priest. Hence arose the figure of the hypothetical " William Clark." There is no desire here to disparage the admirable work done by the antiquaries and historians of the past. It is only for the purposes of this particular book that close and critical research has disclosed the true facts of the case. And indeed this chapter was actually written and ready for the Press, on the lines of the old narratives, when Mr. Bernard F. Davis, conscious of some specific errors in Hasted's account, " had a mind to get to the bottom of this story," and searched out the references.

It was, however, felt that Mr. Davis's researches could scarcely be accepted without expert confirmation of his results. In due course an authoritative statement was secured that Mr. Davis's reading of the original documents, and his conclusions therefrom, were correct. The papers dealing with this matter are now in the care of the Bromley Public Library

Committee, together with all the raw materials from which this book has been compiled. Those papers, if consulted, would be sufficient, I think, to prove that the story now to be told is the true one, and that Mr. Davis, though only professing to be an amateur in deciphering medieval documents, has indeed " got to the bottom " of the mystery.

The earliest document relating to the property afterwards known as Simpson's Place is contained in the Patent Rolls of 1310. It is a permit to William of Bliburgh—" our clerk "—

" to strengthen and crenelate with a wall of stone and lime his house at Bromle Kent, & to hold that house to him and his heirs for ever."

An inquisition held after de Bliburgh's death in 1312 to determine his holdings recites that :

" William de Bliburgh did not hold any lands or tenements in the County of Kent in chief of the Lord King, but he held in the town of Bromlegh of the Bishop of Rochester a certain messuage with a garden containing two acres of land, one and a half acres of wood, three acres and three roods of meadow, twenty six acres of arable land, and three acres of alder ; by service of rendering yearly to the said Bishop 5*s.* and suit of Court for all services, and they say that the Messuage, garden, wood, meadow, land, and alder are worth yearly 18*s.*"

The question which at once arises is this—What is the evidence that the aforesaid property held by William of Bliburgh included the estate known as Simpson's ? The evidence is found in the fact that it is possible to trace, practically without a break, the passage of this property, through successive hands, to Robert Simpson, and in the further fact that, apart from the Bishop's palace, no other crenellated and moated house than that of de Bliburgh is known to have existed in Bromley, and that such a crenellated and moated house came eventually into the possession of Robert Simpson.

We may therefore with tolerable certainty place William de Bliburgh as the first known owner of Simpson's Place.

William de Bliburgh was for many years a servant of Edward I, and was a clerk in Chancery, and possibly also a priest. His name occurs frequently in the early records, and towards the end of the reign he held the position of Chancellor to the King's son. On the accession of Edward II in 1307, de Bliburgh retired from public life, probably to his mansion and estate at Bromley, and three years later " William de Bliburgh, our clerk " received his licence to crenellate. Thus, in some odd fashion, arose the fiction of " William Clark," and a licence granted to him by Henry V.

On the death of William de Bliburgh he was succeeded by his niece Agnes, wife of Richard de Doulee, and daughter of Emma " sister of the said William." But in the course of a few years the property, either by purchase or some other means, came into the hands of William le Latimer, for from an inquisition held in 1327 on the holdings of William le Latimer we learn that he was the owner of " that same tenement that in former times William de Bliburgh was." Details of the property are given which correspond with similar details in the Inquisition of 1312, and it is also stated that William le Latimer held

" a certain water-mill which is worth 20*s.* per annum," a messuage and several acres of land at ' Blakebroke ' (Blackbrook) and
" three acres of pasture in the marsh in Bromlegh of the Prior of Christchurch, Canterbury, by service of 4*d.* per an., and it is worth per an. 12*d.*"

It is worth noting here that William de Bliburgh, according to the 1312 inquisition, held land of the Prior of Christchurch, Canterbury, a fact which still further identifies the de Bliburgh property with that held later by William le Latimer.

The Latimers, however, did not, as a family, belong to Kent or to the south of England. Their property lay mainly in the north and midlands. When therefore an opportunity occurred to exchange the Bromley estate for a manor in Yorkshire that opportunity was taken. William le Latimer transferred " his right in (within) the Manor of Bromlegh and Blakebroke " to Conan, son of FitzHenry, a knight, in consideration of receiving from Conan the Manor of Liverton in Yorkshire. Conan in turn sold his Bromley property to Richard Lacer, and Juliana, his wife, and Thomas le Latimer, son of William, confirmed the Lacers in possession of their newly purchased lands.

The Latimers therefore and Conan FitzHenry are of little importance in the history of Bromley. They are only transitory figures in the records of the town. They are, however, important as links in the chain which connect the de Bliburgh estate with that of Robert Simpson.

Richard Lacer, on the other hand, while forming another link in this chain, stands out prominently in the medieval life of Bromley. He was a prosperous mercer in the City of London, an alderman, and in 1345 Lord Mayor of London, and he also represented the City in Parliament. In or about 1339 he bought the Latimer estate in Bromley, and used the mansion as his country house; on his retirement from public life in 1359 he made Bromley his permanent residence. He founded a chantry in Bromley Church, and in that church he and his second wife Isabella were buried. They both died, probably of the plague which was prevalent in that year, in the same week of July 1361. The brass which commemorates his wife

Isabella, examined in detail in our section on the church, is probably only a part of a much larger brass inscribed in memory of both husband and wife.

There are several items of local interest in Richard Lacer's will, made just prior to his death, the manuscript copy of which is extant in the Registers of the Bishops of Rochester.

After enjoining that his body shall be buried " in the Church of the Holy Apostles, Peter and Paul, of Bromlegh, before the cross," he bequeaths to the High Altar of the said church the sum of 10*d*.

To the clerk or priest celebrating in the said church at the time of " my obit," 12*d*.

To the expenses of his funeral " 100*s*. or more if necessary," at the discretion of his executors—a sum at least equivalent to £60 to-day.

At the time of his burial 40*s*. was to be distributed to the poor.

To his wife Isabella he leaves all his household goods, live stock, and movables " in my Manor of Bromley in which I dwell," with special reference to his " vasa " of silver and wooden mazers : also his house in Eldefish Street in the parish of St. Peter's, London.

The rents of two of his shops in London are charged with the yearly sum of ten marks for the sustentation of a Chantry Priest, celebrating in the parish church of Bromley for his soul and the souls of his wives and sons—" the aforesaid 10 marks to be paid twice a year at the feast of St. Michael the Archangel, and the feast of Easter in equal portions ; which same Chantry I wish to be kept by Sir John de Hulle priest . . . and after his decease or resignation I wish the Chantry to be at the disposal and appointment of my heirs "—and for the use of the priest celebrating in the Chantry he bequeaths to Bromley Church one vestment with all fittings, one chalice, two missals, and one " *preiosoyon deo* " (if the words are correctly deciphered), which seems to mean a breviary or something of the kind.

His executors were John atte Hulle, Rector of Hese (Hayes), the Sir John de Hulle mentioned above, Walter, Rector of Bromley (Walter de Hethe), and John Hardringham.

The bulk of Richard Lacer's landed property was left to his son Richard, whose claims, however, were at once contested by the representatives of his half-sisters, the children of Richard Lacer's first marriage. As these ladies form an important link in the chain of succession between the de Bliburghs and the Simpsons, a brief genealogical note is required at this point.

Richard Lacer, by his first wife, Juliana, had four children : Thomas, an Augustinian monk, to whom his father bequeathed a sum of ten shillings ; John, who predeceased his father in 1359 ; Alice, who married first William le Brun, and, secondly, Robert de Marny ; and Katherine, who became the wife of John atte Pole. By Isabella, his second wife, he had one son, Richard, the heir to his estates, and a minor.

The terms of Richard Lacer's will were no sooner known than—

" Thereupon came William Brun, Alice his wife, and Katherine, wife of John atte Pole, and put in their claim upon the aforesaid testament, and tenements therein devised."

(The authority for this quotation is Sharpe, in his *Hustings Wills*.)

The premature death of young Richard, however, in 1363, left his half-sisters as their father's heirs-at-law, with the result that the whole estate was partitioned between them, a part of the property in Kent falling to the share of Alice, who became the wife, after her first husband's death, of Sir Robert Marny. The issue of this marriage was a son, William Marny, and two deeds preserved respectively in the Hustings Rolls and in the Harleian collections show that in 1389 and 1391 both the ladies, Alice and Katherine, transferred their property to Sir Robert Marny and his son William.

The complications arising from the fact that both Alice and Katherine had previously vested their property in the hands of trustees for the benefit of the Church are outside the scope of this narrative. It is sufficient for the purpose to note the possession of the whole Lacer property by the Marny family, and that family, either personally or through trustees, retained possession during the early years of the fifteenth century.

In 1407 William Marny, Knight, in conjunction with several other persons who were evidently in the position of trustees, deliver over to another body of trustees, among whom were William Askham, William Crowmere, and John Weston, and Thomas Aleyn, all the Kentish property which had come by inheritance from Richard Lacer to his daughter Alice. In 1411 a similar delivery of all the Kentish property inherited by Richard Lacer's daughter Katherine was made to the same trustees : Askham, Crowmere, and Weston.

Up to this point, 1411, the chain of succession to the Simpson's property has been traced without a break or flaw. The ground is perfectly certain as to the identity of property between William de Bliburgh and the daughters of Richard Lacer.

It is at this point that the difficulty of further identification arises. For between 1411 and 1433, no documents are to be found, and the required documentary links in the chain of succession are missing. This fact, however, is no proof that such documents never existed. The Harleian collections are admittedly mutilated and imperfect. Many of the deeds which would be expected to form part of any carefully preserved set of evidences are missing. In all probability all the requisite deeds to prove what is wanted must once have existed in this collection. What is certain is that in 1433 a body of trustees, none of whom figure in the lists of trustees to Alice and Katherine Lacer,

" demise enfeoff and confirm to Mercy, wife of Nicolas Carew, (and her Trustees,) all those lands and tenements, rents, services, etc., which they have in the towns of Bromley, Beckenham, Lewisham, Chislehurst and Hayes to the use of Thomas Alleyn, Mercer of London,"

and also certain land in the parish of Orpington.

Was this property thus conveyed to Mercy Carew the same property as that held by the daughters of Richard Lacer ?

The name of Thomas Alleyn, the last surviving trustee under the deed of 1407, may indicate a connection, but the fact that this property conveyed to Mercy Carew ultimately passed into the possession of Robert Simpson —the chain of succession between them is complete—the fact that Robert Simpson's mansion was the only moated and crenellated house in Bromley known to exist, and the fact that the only licence to crenellate a mansion in Bromley was granted to William de Bliburgh, all contribute to establish something approaching a certainty that it was the original Bliburgh estate which passed, through the hands of Richard Lacer, his daughters, and their trustees, into the hands of Robert Simpson.

From Close Roll, No. 289, we learn that Mercy Carew and her trustees sold the property to John Stanlove (or Stanlowe), and Margaret his wife, and from Margaret's trustees, after the death of her husband, the property was bought by Robert Simpson. An inquisition on the holdings of Robert Simpson, in 1471, is conclusive as to the identity of the estate held by him and that held by Mercy Carew, and transmitted to him through Margaret Stanlove.

The inquisition just referred to also states that Robert Simpson died on August 8th, 1471, and that his heir was Robert Simpson, his son, at that date aged two years and five months. Robert, the father, was a rich London merchant, a member of the Drapers' Company, and a pious donor to the Church of St. Benet Fynk in the City, under the shadow of which church he himself resided in Fynk Lane. He also left twenty marks to the parish church of Bromley.

His Bromley estate was held in trust for his son Robert until he became of age, and in due course Robert succeeded his father, not only as owner of Simpson's Place, but also as prominent citizen of London.

In 1503, however, he disposed of all his holdings in Bromley and the district to a body of trustees acting for some person unknown, but two months later a new and single owner appears in the person of John Style, mercer of London, who had already purchased Langley Park, Beckenham.

His title, however, was disputed by the aforesaid body of trustees, and a protracted lawsuit, extending for some years beyond John Style's lifetime, ended in favour of his widow, Elizabeth, and their son Humphrey.

From this point onwards the history of Simpson's harmonises in all essential points with that given by past historians of Bromley.

It is with regret that we discard the traditional figure of Nicolas Simpson, barber-surgeon to King Henry VIII. But the inexorable logic of dates and documents allows of no other course. The Simpson family ceased to hold the property six years before Henry VIII's accession, and there is in any case simply no room for him in the chain of succession which recent research has so carefully and laboriously traced. The actual Nicolas Simpson, barber-surgeon, appears to have belonged to quite another family of Simpsons, and to have resided at Chigwell in Essex, where he died in 1552.

Although it would have been easy to support the foregoing narrative with still fuller references to old deeds and records, the story has already been protracted—it is to be feared at tedious length—far beyond the limits originally assigned to it. But it is felt that where our account of Simpson's departs so entirely from that of all previous historians, from Philipot downwards, it is essential that such a departure should manifest its justification to every reader by ample documentary proof. The full transcript of such records as have been utilised here in an abridged form will be found, as has been said, among the materials for this History deposited at the Public Library.

The association formed in 1503 between Bromley and the Style family was destined to be of long duration. Simpson's remained in the hands of the main or collateral branches of that family for over two hundred years.

None of its members, throughout that long period of time, seems to have played any prominent part in the affairs of the town, or to have imprinted any distinctive mark upon its history. The fact that the chief seat of the family was Langley Park may have withdrawn its main interest from the Simpson's estate. All that can be recorded here is the succession of the property from one member to another.

The original purchaser, John Style, was succeeded by his son, Sir Humphrey Style, who died in 1552. Then, by direct descent, through Edmund, son of Humphrey, and through William, son of Edmund, the estate passed into the hands of a second Sir Humphrey (son of William), a knight, and baronet, and cup-bearer to King Charles I. This Sir Humphrey died without issue in 1659, the succession passing to his brother William. His son, yet a third Humphrey Style, succeeded, who left as his heir a daughter, Elizabeth, wife of Sir John Elwill, Bart. This lady caused to be affixed at the east end of the south aisle of Bromley Church an unsightly tablet—still to be seen at the back of some pews at the top of the stairs leading from the tower into the south gallery—commemorating the ascendancy of the Style family in Bromley. Beneath their coat-of-arms is an inscription, announcing that:

" The pews beneath are Appropriated to the Sole Use of the family of the Styles's, Ancient Owners of Simpson Place in this Parish; now in the Possession of ye Lady Elwill of Langley, Anno 1727."

In or about 1732 Sir Edmund Elwill, brother and successor to Sir John, sold Simpson's Place to Hugh Raymond of Great Saling, Essex, who settled it on his only son, Jones Raymond, in tail general, with remainder to his daughter Amy, wife of Peter Burrell, and to her heirs male. In accordance with this provision the property passed to her in 1768, and, on her death, to her grandson, Sir Peter Burrell, Knight and Baronet, who was created Lord Gwydir in 1796.

On Lord Gwydir's death in 1820 his property was sold by auction, and that part of it which included Simpson's was bought by Robert Veitch, who established his gardener in the old mansion. By this time it was ruinous and in a few years became uninhabitable. The land around it and on which it stood passed into the possession of Violet Veitch, and so, through her marriage to Lieut.-Colonel George Tweedy of the East India Company's service, into the hands of her husband in 1833.

The requirements of the Mid-Kent Railway Company necessitated the sale of some part of the property in 1859, and on the death of Colonel Tweedy in the following year all the sentimental interest in the estate seems to have died out. In the course of a few years it was secured by the British Land Company, which sold a portion of it to Mr. John Richardson to round off his purchase of Bromley House, but regarded the remainder merely as building land suitable for development. The old moated farm-buildings were swept away in 1868–9, roads were constructed, and in due course the modern villas in Ringer's, Ethelbert, and Ravensbourne Roads obliterated all traces of the moated grange, which had stood through all the changes of nearly six hundred years.

It was apparently during the tenure of the Style family, in the seventeenth and eighteenth centuries, that the practice of sub-letting the house and grounds immediately surrounding it to tenants began. For fifty years it was the residence of Jeremiah Ringer, whose death, at the age of ninety-seven, is entered in the Parish Registers of Chelsfield on December 19th, 1789. His son, another Jeremiah, died in the following year and was buried at Bromley. Hence *Ringer's* Road, a name which commemorates a worthy and respected inhabitant of Bromley, overseer in 1766, but whose principal achievement seems to have been the filling up of the old moat on two of its sides.

Previous to the tenancy of Jeremiah Ringer the Registers record the christening in 1674 of " James, son of Joseph Embry, of Simpson's Place " ; the burial, in 1678, of " Elizabeth Redder of Simpson's Place " ; and many entries follow between 1702 and 1718 of the burials of various members of the Tandy family, who occupied the house and farmed the adjoining land.

On the death of Jeremiah Ringer in 1789 Lord Gwydir (then Sir Peter Burrell) granted a lease for seventy-two years of Simpson's Place to Samuel Rickards, who farmed the land for some years, ultimately disposing of the remainder of the lease, in 1802, to Colonel Samuel Jackson. The old

Simpson's Moat. Bromley, Kent. View from the East.

W·H·T·
1869.

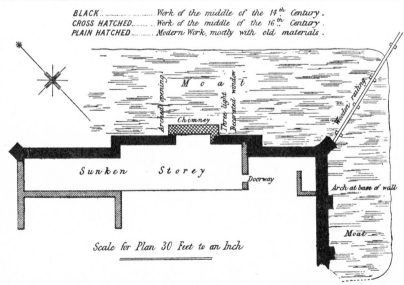

BLACK..................... Work of the middle of the 14th Century.
CROSS HATCHED............ Work of the middle of the 16th Century.
PLAIN HATCHED........... Modern Work, mostly with old materials.

Moat

Chimney

Three light Decorated window

Arched opening

Wooden railing

Sunken Storey

Doorway

Arch at base of wall

Moat

Scale for Plan 30 Feet to an Inch

RUINS OF SIMPSON'S PLACE, 1869, WITH PLAN

237

moated farm by this time had fallen probably into such a state of disrepair as to be of practically no value, and it was last used, as has been seen, as a gardener's cottage, by Robert Veitch of Bromley House, in 1816.

Having traced the history of Simpson's Place from the point of view of ownership, it only remains to give a description of the architectural features of the house and its surroundings. This can best be done by quoting descriptions already given by those who had opportunities of personally examining the ruins before they were demolished to make room for the requirements of modern life.

" The original structure," says Mr. W. Tregellas, " appears to have been a quadrangular fortified building, surrounded by a moat, 25 to 30 ft. wide on all sides. The walls were strong and lofty, supported by very substantial buttresses at the sides and angles, and built of flint and rubble masonry, the facings of dressed stone. A huge and very handsome red-brick chimney built in the time of Henry VIII adorned the centre of the N.E. side of the building."

Dunkin, in his *Outlines of the History and Antiquities of Bromley*, gives the impressions produced on him by a careful personal examination :

" It appears," he says, " that the deep moat extended close to the walls of the ancient castellated building on the north, east, and south sides, and that the angles were secured by a strong buttress projecting into the moat. The whole extent of the foundation of the eastern wall, together with the two buttresses which still remained perfect, were found by admeasurement (to be) about 34 yards in length ; and the breadth of the building, as far as could be conjectured from its ivy-mantled walls on the south, about 14 or 15 yards. These foundations are built of large flints intermixed with stone and cemented with strong lime mortar. It is probable that the building was square, and entered by a drawbridge on the northern side ; and from the circumstance of the wall not extending to the verge of the moat it is probable that it had a small terrace on the east. The apartments inhabited by the lord of the domain probably either lined the outer wall, and were lighted from a small court in the centre, or consisted of an isolated building within the walls, as was generally the case in castellated mansions, and perhaps the best plan that could be adopted for the purposes of defence.

" The present building is formed of brick and timber, and appears to have been erected in more settled times on a part of the foundation of the ancient structure, probably on its decay, and about the sixteenth century. The interior indicates it as designed for the residence of a gentleman of that period. The fireplace of the hall, doorways, etc., still remain, though much disfigured by the alterations occasioned by its conversion into a farmhouse, in which state it has remained for many years. The moat on the western and northern sides has been filled up by the present inhabitant, Mr. Jeremiah Ringer, who has occupied the house for more than 50 years."

As Ringer died in 1789, it must have been about that date that Dunkin made the investigations which he here details. It is to Dunkin also that we owe the ghost story referred to at the beginning of this section, together with other stories of mysterious noises heard in and about the house, as of furniture falling down and being broken to pieces.

Dunkin, as one of Bromley's early historians, is entitled to the respect and gratitude of all succeeding generations of his fellow-townsmen, and it is with genuine compunction and regret that we have been compelled to discard his early history of Simpson's Place.

BROMLEY HILL

THE early historians of Bromley—Wilson, Dunkin, Freeman—do not include in their pages any detailed reference to Bromley Hill.

This omission may have been partly due to the fact, recorded by Mr. George Clinch, that until the closing years of the eighteenth century

"the domain had nothing to distinguish it from the ordinary class of suburban villas."

But the more salient fact, that the house stood outside the boundaries of the parish, is sufficient in itself to account for the general silence.

But though Bromley Hill House itself is in the Borough of Lewisham, two of its lodges, more than half of the estate, and the whole of it sentimentally, lie within the Borough of Bromley. To exclude it, therefore, from this History on purely technical grounds would, it is felt, be regarded as an omission as serious as unnecessary.

The once compact and beautiful estate known as Bromley Hill Place was bounded on the east by the main Hastings Road, on the north by the property of the Cator family, on the west practically by the Ravensbourne, and on the south by Beckenham Lane.

Until a few years ago little seems to have been known about it previous to the advent of the Long family to Lewisham towards the end of the eighteenth century, but the examination of some old deeds in the possession of the executors of the Cawston estates has recently thrown some light upon the earlier history of the property. Of these deeds two in particular are important :

    i. A marriage settlement dated January 1684, and
    ii. An abstract of title of the Rt. Hon. Charles Long, dated 1801.

The marriage settlement of 1684 details an arrangement between Sir Robert Knightly of Ashtead, Surrey, and Sir John Chapman, Knt., Alderman of the City of London, in regard to the marriage of Sir Robert's son, Robert, to Anne, eldest daughter of Sir John. The latter agrees to purchase from the former for £3,000 on the day of the marriage, and for the use of his daughter Anne, various properties owned by Sir Robert in Surrey, Yorkshire, and Bromley, Kent. Sir Robert, on his part, contracts to give his son a marriage gift of jewels, plate, and goods to the value of £1,000.

A detailed inventory of the Bromley property thus purchased seems to establish the fact that it included the estate which came to be known as Bromley Hill Place.

Thus the first owner of whom we have record was Sir Robert Knightly, who made it over, for a consideration, to Anne, his son's wife. A son of their marriage, John Knightly, succeeded and remained in possession till his death in 1762.

The Knightlys, however, though owners, were never occupiers of the estate. It was let on lease to various tenants, and continued to be so held until the last quarter of the eighteenth century.

On the death of John Knightly without living issue, the property passed by the terms of his will to his cousin Aquila Wyke. But he died intestate in 1772, and consequently Charles Browne and Anne his wife, respectively nephew and niece of Aquila Wyke, became co-heirs at law to John Knightly. They at once leased the estate for a period of sixty-one years to a certain George Paterson at a rent of £300 per annum.

It now becomes exceedingly difficult to know what happened, for the records of the parish of Lewisham were destroyed by fire between 1776 and the close of the century, and consequently accurate information is not available. It would appear that the Brownes, who lived on very bad terms with one another, determined to sell the estate outright, for we find it in the hands of Aquila Dacombe, of William Slade, who made the house his residence, and of George Glenny, who also resided there, and actually effected a mortgage upon it. But none the less, when, in 1796, Mr. Charles Long proposed to purchase the property, his negotiations were carried on neither with Glenny nor Slade, but with Aquila Dacombe, and it was for him to show a valid title to the same. Dacombe found a difficulty in doing this, doubtless owing to the destruction of the necessary papers by fire. At length, after what seems to have been a protracted suit in Chancery, the title of Aquila Dacombe was pronounced good in 1799, the claims, whatever they may have been, of George Glenny were satisfied, and Charles Long entered into undisputed possession in 1801.

Of the Long family Mr. George Clinch assures us that they had been settled in the neighbourhood of Tavistock, Devon, as far back as Queen Elizabeth's time. In the middle of the eighteenth century one of the family, Captain Charles Long, is found at Lewisham, where he is rated in the parish books of 1747 at £18. His mother was Jane, daughter of Sir William Beeston, and therefore a brother of Charles was given the name of Beeston. This Beeston Long, "a very eminent West India Merchant" (Clinch), married Susannah, daughter and heiress of Abraham Cropp, of Richmond, Surrey. Their third son was Charles Long, who purchased Bromley Hill in 1801.

Charles Long, born in 1761, was entered at Emmanuel College, Cambridge, in 1778. In 1789 he entered Parliament as member for Rye, and from this date onward his parliamentary career, either in the Commons or the Lords, was unbroken. As a politician, as the friend of William Pitt the younger, and as the holder in his day of various important offices, a column and a half in the *Dictionary of National Biography* has been assigned to him, and for his public record as " a respectable official and a successful placeman,"

readers are referred to that volume.   We are only indirectly concerned with
that side of his career in so far as it was his close intimacy with Pitt which
mainly influenced him to purchase Bromley Hill, where Pitt, at Holwood,
Keston, would be a near neighbour.   It is in his private capacity that he
enters into the history of Bromley as the maker of Bromley Hill Place.

To the embellishment of his house and of his estate he, in conjunction
with his gifted wife Amelia, daughter of Sir Abraham Hume of Wormleybury,
Herts, devoted those gifts of artistic taste and judgment which were his real
and chief distinction, with the result that a mansion came into existence under
his hands fitted to enshrine the treasures of art collected within it, and the
grounds surrounding it were converted into a miracle of landscape design.

His reputation as a connoisseur extended, however, far beyond the
limits of his own domain.   This " Vitruvius of the present age," as he was
once styled in Parliament, was a trustee of the British Museum and of the
National Gallery, Chairman of the Commission for the Inspection of National
Monuments, Deputy President of the British Institution, a Fellow of the
Royal Society and of the Society of Arts, and the friend and adviser of both
George III and George IV in decorating several of the royal palaces.   These
various activities, coupled with his official duties, left him but scant leisure
for the adornment of his own estate, but when in 1826, at the request of
Canning, he relinquished his office as Paymaster-General, and became
Baron Farnborough of Bromley Hill, he was free to devote uninterrupted
energies to the gratification of his artistic tastes in his own house.

A description of Bromley Hill Place by George Cumberland was published in 1811, and re-published and brought up-to-date in 1816.   From
Cumberland's brochure Strong derived his material for the account of the
estate which appears in his *History of Bromley* published in 1858.   The
description which follows is also derived very largely from Cumberland,
supplemented from knowledge of the further developments and improvements made between 1816 and 1838, the date of Lord Farnborough's death.

Cumberland says nothing of the original house, which was either pulled
down or incorporated, either wholly or in part, into a stately mansion.

" All that there was here to work on," he says, " was a fine rising knoll,
a few acres of wood on a little hill, three or four low meadows, a winding
brook which skirted them, and a small head of pure water.   How that knoll,
that wood, and those meadows have been treated "

was to form the subject of his descriptive sketch.

To approach the mansion from the main London Road two entrance
lodges were constructed, both of which are still in existence, one at the foot
of Bromley Hill, where now Ashgrove Road begins, the other at the top of
the hill.   Two fine carriage sweeps led from the lodges to the house, and yet
another carriage drive gave an exit on to Beckenham Lane.   The lodge to

CHARLES LONG, BARON FARNBOROUGH, AND LADY FARNBOROUGH.
Resident at Bromley Hill 1801–1838.

this drive was not constructed when Cumberland wrote. It was designed by Lady Farnborough and still stands, bearing the date 1825. The mansion itself was built in the Italian style,

" well broken into masses by varied angles. The entrance, which has no porch, opens into a covered and glazed corridor containing bronzes, busts, candelabra, and china vases."

From this corridor a handsome flight of steps led to a vestibule supported by fluted columns, its distinctive ornament being a fine statue of Flora by Westmacott. The principal living-rooms, dining-room, breakfast-room, library, and drawing-room, were entered from the vestibule. The drawing-room was finely proportioned and ended in a semicircular recess supported by two Scagliola Ionic pillars. This recess formed a sort of shrine for one of Canova's latest masterpieces. Three French windows opened out into a spacious conservatory trellised and fragrant with orange trees and various exotics. From the conservatory access could be gained to the library, which itself was flanked outside by a flower garden and enclosed terrace with its sundial and Watteau bench, its low balustrade surmounted by vases of flowers, and shaded at both ends by some well-grown pinasters.

" From this ancient terrace," says Cumberland, " the view commands at times St. Paul's Church (Cathedral), its dome and turret towers appearing as if banded with white ; and beyond extend the Hampstead and Highgate Hills, forming a broad line of background ; but that which renders the scene more remarkably interesting is that you see nothing of London except its spires, and the great church seems to rise like a vision from the edge of a wooded hill. Shooter's Hill, Blackheath, and best of all, Sydenham Common, makes a noble distance owing to its long lines and purple tints of heath."

Adjacent to the terrace was a spacious saloon with a fine roof, suitable for concerts and general entertainments.

From the terrace a rock garden sloped down towards the spacious lawns and wooded ground beyond, composed of large masses of fossilised rocks over which cheddar pinks, saxifrages, and rock roses spread themselves at will. But first, before the beauties of the gardens, some of the artistic treasures within the house call for comment.

Lord Farnborough's principle as a collector was quality rather than quantity, hence his pictures, though not very numerous, were the best obtainable examples of the best masters. Of the English School, Reynolds and Gainsborough were represented, the former by the 'Infant Samuel,' now in the National Gallery. Van Dyke's ' White Horse,' a choice landscape by Rubens, and a Teniers, all masterpieces, were the principal examples of the School of the Netherlands. A Canaletto, a Poussin, and a Mola figured conspicuously in the collection.

Lady Farnborough herself was an artist of no mean capacity. Her landscapes found a regular place on the walls of the Royal Academy, and to the enthusiastic vision of Cumberland she was the equal of any living artist. Her landscapes were

" incomparable—have never been rivalled even when put into competition with practical professors, and placed side by side with their happiest efforts."

His only regret is that none of these incomparable masterpieces were actually displayed in any of the rooms at Bromley Hill open to his inspection.

Whatever may have been Lady Farnborough's talents as a painter, there is no doubt that to her taste, judgment, and skill as a landscape gardener many of the most pleasing features of the grounds were due.

In fashioning a design there were certain natural advantages on which to work—the slope of the ground, its perforation by innumerable springs, and the river winding at the foot of the slope. Everything lent itself to the formation of a water garden, and a water pleasaunce of considerable extent. The slope itself was mainly devoted to fine and carefully tended lawns, broken by occasional oaks, acacias, firs, and birch, and by shrubberies of Portugal laurel and nut trees. On the lawn upon an open space stood a pedestal, 12 feet high, crowned by a beaker-formed vase of freestone reminiscent of fifteenth-century workmanship. Then came the water gardens, or spring-shores as they were sometimes called. These consisted of winding water-ways fed by the many springs, here and there artfully widened into pools, a little island perhaps in the centre, crossed and recrossed by rustic bridges or by stepping-stones. Wherever there was a vista of water and winding path some little rustic temple or rustic seat afforded a place for rest or contemplation. There was one specially pretty sexagonal temple-seat of rustic work paved with portions of tree-trunks driven into the ground and sawn off flat.

Another similar temple enclosed a basin in the centre of its floor continuously fed by the principal spring upon the estate. A parapet of fossiliferous stone around the basin, surmounted by a rustic railing, acted as a protecting barrier, the parapet being open at one point in the form of a lip to conduct the overflow in a meandering course to the River Ravensbourne a little way below.

The slope of the ground allowed of these various waterways being here and there fashioned into cascades, of which one was 6 feet in height and 10 feet in width, the whole pleasaunce being full of murmuring sounds of falling waters. It was the haunt of trout in the streams, of kingfishers flashing above them, of stately osmundas and other ferns, of nightingales, dabchicks, moorhens, even of bitterns in the winter time, and of herons in search of eels. In one pool a Botany Bay swan ruled supreme; another pool

IN THE GROUNDS, BROMLEY HILL.

was a carp-stew; pheasants rose from the undergrowth upon approach. Everywhere there was variety and the beauty of pleased surprise.

The social and political distinction of Lord and Lady Farnborough, and the fame of their estate, brought to Bromley, from time to time, many distinguished visitors. Two kings were among them and a queen. George IV, who had numbered Lord Farnborough among his friends from the days of the Regency, and later William IV and Queen Adelaide honoured Bromley Hill by their presence. On the latter occasion the sovereigns were escorted by the Chislehurst Yeomanry, and by a detachment of the police force just newly established by Sir Robert Peel. The novel sight of the 'Bobby Peelers' in their tall chimney-pot hats proved a temptation too strong for one Bromley youth, Joe Burgess, who, in after days, when a respected bootmaker and townsman, used to relate how he knocked off the hat of one member of the force, and yet succeeded in making a successful escape across the fields.

William Pitt was a frequent guest, and one of the river walks was christened "Pitt's Walk." The Duchesse de Dino, niece of Talleyrand, relates in her *Memoirs* that she, in company with the Countess of Sutherland and Countess Batthyani, spent a morning at Bromley Hill.

"A delightful habitation which is remarkable alike for its fine situation, its beautiful woods, flowers, and water, and the perfect taste and care with which it is managed. We were quite delighted with everything, and sorry to go back to the smoke and politics of London."

But the amenities of the place were not reserved exclusively for Lord Farnborough's distinguished friends. Every Thursday from May to November the grounds were thrown open to any presentable people who cared to visit them, and Bromley could feel that Bromley Hill Place was almost a part of itself. In the streets, too, Lord Farnborough's coach and four blacks vied with Sir John Lubbock's four bays for the admiration of the public, and many other well-appointed equipages, together with the stage coaches constantly passing, gave to the town an air of gaiety and movement more attractive perhaps than any which the rush of modern traffic can supply.

In June 1796 a tragic event occurred on the Bromley Hill estate. A gardener, John Clarke, murdered Elizabeth Mann, a dairy-maid also employed there. In accordance with a not unusual practice, the murderer, upon his condemnation, was executed on Bromley Hill, near to the actual scene of the crime. His victim was buried at Bromley, and soon afterwards a catch-penny eight-paged pamphlet detailing the circumstances of the murder was published.

Lady Farnborough, having no children of her own, took a particular interest in one or two of the children connected with the estate. One of them, the daughter of James Linn, the steward, was Lady Farnborough's god-daughter and bore her name Amelia. Through her Mr. William Baxter became the owner of some portraits of the Long family, and of some of Lady Farnborough's sketches, which he has presented to the Public Library.

On the death of Lord Farnborough in 1838, exactly a year after that of his wife, his property was divided between his three nephews, sons of his younger brother Samuel who married Lady Jane Maitland. Bromley Hill fell to the share of Samuel Long, Lieutenant-Colonel in the Grenadier Guards, who was born in 1799. For over forty years, until his death in 1881, Colonel Long was a conspicuous figure in the life of Bromley. Active in the performance of his duties in local affairs, he was also a keen sportsman and a genial host. His shooting parties over his own and the adjoining estates were a regular feature of the winter season.

He was four times married :

1. to Louisa Emily Stanley, daughter of the 13th Earl of Derby ;
2. to Sydney, daughter of Arthur Atherley ;
3. to Emily, daughter of Charles Mucros of Killarney, and
4. to the Hon. Eleanor Stanley, a maid of honour to Queen Victoria.

These frequent marriages gave rise to amused comment among his friends, and one story connected with them seems too good to be apocryphal. It runs that Colonel Long, before his last marriage, remarked to Lord Sydney that he would be unable to attend Quarter Sessions on Thursday because he was going to be married.

" Thursday ! " replied Lord Sydney, " I thought you were always married on a Tuesday."

Colonel Long died on August 31st, 1881, leaving three daughters by his third marriage, but no son. Consequently the estate was sold, and passed into the hands of Mr. Samuel Cawston. By him it was speedily ' developed ' for building purposes, and now a network of roads and villas has replaced the gardens, the wooded glades, and the spring-shores of the past.

The mansion itself, during the Great War, served as a hospital, and since then it has been converted into a private hotel.

Chapter XI

LOCAL GOVERNMENT

THE forms of Local Government in the country being ordained and regulated by Parliament, the history of Bromley in this particular follows the general course of the history of the nation. The successive steps in the administration of an urban area from the earliest times are the Manorial Courts, the Vestries, Local Boards, Urban District Councils, and lastly, as in the case of Bromley, incorporation as a chartered Borough under a Mayor and Town Council. In this chapter I propose to trace these successive steps in relation to the history of the town.

The Manorial system, which operated throughout the Middle Ages, and which only began to be superseded in the sixteenth century, afforded but a meagre opportunity to the people of the manor to make their voice heard in the management of their affairs. Court Leets or Court Baronies were set up and assembled as occasion might demand, but they were presided over and controlled by officials appointed by the overlord, or by the overlord in person, the tenants of the manor being present—as far as they were present —as spectators rather than as actors in the administration of the Manorial Court. The business of these courts was to dispense justice within the manor, to determine the rights of the tenants as to what they might do and might not, and to collect all fees and dues payable to the overlord. The part played by the tenants themselves was to assemble and obey the injunctions laid upon them.

Bromley, as a manor of the Bishops of Rochester, was subject for many centuries to this form of procedure, though at a very early date, as has been seen in the record of church history, the Rectors of Bromley set up their own Rectorial Courts, and sometimes the Rector and the Bishop came into collision in regard to their several and respective jurisdictions.

Towards the close of the first quarter of the seventeenth century, about 1623, Parliament ceased to confer jurisdiction upon the Manorial Courts, and the right of the Vestry, or Parish Meeting, to direct and control the fortunes of the parishioners was successfully asserted against the manorial overlords. These Parish Meetings for the regulation of affairs, both secular and ecclesiastical, within the parish, date back to pre-Reformation times. Thus the parish of St. Martin-in-the-Fields, Westminster, possesses the records of such meetings as far back as 1525. The vestry books of the parish of Steeple Ashton, Wilts, date back to 1542, though the actual name ' Vestry ' does not appear in the records until 1569 in the case of Steeple Ashton, and 1576 in that of St. Martin's. But both the powers and popularity of the Vestries were evidently increasing to a point when some Parliamentary control became necessary. In 1663 an Act of Charles II for the Regulation of Vestries for the first time introduces the name itself into the Statute Book, and marks the point in our national history when the jurisdiction of Vestries finally supersedes that of the old Manorial Courts.

It is impossible to say at what date the Bromley Vestry assumed control over the local government of the town. Our only guide is the Minute Books themselves, which, as far as they have been preserved, begin in 1703. From that date onward these books have been kept in a fairly complete state, and they are now securely housed in the safe of the parish church. Bromley, indeed, is peculiarly fortunate in the possession of its old records, for it possesses, but for two gaps, the complete series of Parish Rate Books from 1673, and also the Church Rate Books, though in a very incomplete state, from 1706. The Parish Rate Books up to 1870 have now been transferred to the Public Library. The Church Rate Books are in the custody of the church.

Until quite recent times a curious indifference existed as to the preservation and safe keeping of old local records. In the case of Bromley, for example, some of the Parish Rate Books lay for generations neglected and indeed forgotten in the attics of certain business premises in the town. Other old documents relating to the Board of Guardians, to the support and administration of the Charity Schools, and to the church, were regarded as of so little importance that they were marked out for destruction. All of these, and many others, have been discovered, examined, rescued from oblivion, and placed in permanent security by the research and enterprise of Mr. W. Baxter. In many directions his labours on behalf of the town have been indefatigable, but, among his many services, none can surpass in value and importance the task which he has so laboriously and successfully completed—the task of disinterring from the débris of forgotten things, and depositing in safe and permanent quarters, a mass of ancient records which, but for him, might have mouldered away or been destroyed. Every citizen of Bromley is now in a position to examine for himself, if he cares to do so, either in the church vestry, or in the Public Library, or in the proper quarter, a large part of the original material out of which a history of his town must necessarily be composed, and every citizen is under a personal debt to the man who has made this possible.

The word 'Vestry,' as applied to Parish Meetings—from the *Vestiarium*, or robing-room of the officials of the church—might seem to imply that the business of such meetings was purely ecclesiastical in character. This was not, however, the case, for the Vestries met for a two-fold purpose— (*a*) to regulate all matters connected with the church ; (*b*) to administer the general business of the town. The transactions were entered in the Vestry Minute Book and signed by the incumbent of the parish, as the *ex-officio* chairman of the Vestry, by the two churchwardens, the two overseers of the parish, and, finally, after an audit, by two Justices of the Peace. The right to attend the meetings extended to every parishioner who paid poor rate, irrespective of his religious denomination, and it was open to any parishioner in attendance, if dissatisfied with any decision, to demand a poll of the parish upon the question at issue.

The duties of the Vestry were, in relation to the church, to appoint churchwardens, the parish clerk, the sexton, and other minor officials, and from the proceeds of a church rate to maintain the fabric, and to make such enlargements as might be necessary. In relation to secular business, to appoint the Vestry clerk, the overseers, the highway surveyors, the high and the petty constables, and other officials such as the beadle, the ale-conners, the leather-sealers, the swine-ringer, and to levy and to regulate the expenditure of the parish rate.

The functions of the church officials are sufficiently indicated by their names, which still retain their old-time meaning : those of the secular officials, while in some cases indicating duties with which we are familiar, in others signify the execution of tasks which no longer tax the energies of a special functionary for their performance. The genius of Dickens has preserved for ever the memory of the erstwhile parish beadle, but the dog-whipper, the leather-sealer, the ale-conner, the swine-ringer, the pinder, and the burley-man are functionaries with whom we are no longer familiar. All, however, appear in the Bromley records, and all were at various times to be found exercising their several functions in the town.

The duties of the dog-whipper were to supervise the conduct of dogs brought to church ; of the leather-sealer to attest the standard quality of leather exposed for sale ; of the ale-conner to test the quality of the ale, and to guarantee the accuracy of the ale measures ; of the swine-ringer to impound any swine found wandering in the streets ; of the pinder to keep the pound ; of the burley-man to appear as the god-out-of-the-machine to settle petty disputes, and, as his name implies, his physique had to be correspondent to his office. In addition, the night-watchmen, as in the days of Dogberry and Verges, were employed to perambulate the town, announcing, from time to time, the hour, the state of the weather, and that all was well. In Bromley, however, sentry-boxes were provided for the night-watchmen—and it is reported of these officials that they found their boxes very favourable for slumber, subject, however, to occasional violent disturbances at the hands of practical jokers. All of the above officers were appointed by the parish Vestry, and were the paid servants of that body.

In the higher grades of the service the Vestry clerk held a position somewhat analogous to that of a town clerk in a modern town, his business being to take the minutes of the meetings, and to act as the executive officer of the parish meeting. The first recorded Vestry clerk of Bromley was John Salmon, appointed in 1673. The name of Dunn occurs very frequently in the lists ; early in the nineteenth century the head of the firm known later as that of Latter & Willett became Vestry clerk, and the office has remained continuously in the Latter family from that day to the present time.

The overseers, of whom there were two, were responsible for the collection of the poor rate, for keeping and posting the lists of voters, and the general finance of the parish came to some extent under their control.

The highway surveyors were empowered to levy a rate for the maintenance and repair of the highways, the rate being payable either in cash or in personal service. Such of their account books as are extant can be seen in the Public Library.

The duties of the constables were similar in character to those now performed by the police.

Having enumerated the various officials appointed under the Vestry, and the general nature of their functions, a few particulars extracted from the old Vestry Minute Books will still further illustrate the methods of local government which obtained until the supersession of the Vestry by a Local Board in 1867. Transactions to be recorded will conveniently group themselves under two heads :

(*a*) those concerned with the regulation of ecclesiastical matters,

(*b*) those dealing with the administration of the town.

In 1739 the trustees of Bromley College, on the petition of the widows, approached the Vestry with a view to the erection of a gallery in the church, twenty feet by six feet, for the accommodation of the widows when at church. They complained that, so far, no convenient sittings were allotted to them. This request was granted.

In 1752 an eightpenny rate was imposed by the Vestry for repairs to the church. In 1756 it was resolved to construct a further gallery over the vestry room, at a cost of £30 7*s*.

In June 1777 it was resolved, apparently without a previous estimate, that a new clock and chimes be provided for the church, and that Mr. Charles Penton and Mr. Thwaites be commissioned to carry out the work. The cost, however, proved to be so formidable that it was subsequently resolved to forego the chimes.

In September 1778 yet another gallery was added to the church at a cost of £32 10*s*.

In December 1791 the Vestry granted permission to the Bishop to enclose a piece of the common, not exceeding two acres, in return for the promised liberality of the Bishop in the matter of enlarging the church. The Vestry itself voted £400 to this purpose.

In February 1817 a special Vestry was summoned to appoint a parish clerk in the place of John Dunn deceased. This appointment created an unusual amount of interest and excitement, for the Vicar, Dr. Henry Smith, asserted against the Vestry his exclusive right to make that appointment. The special meeting was largely attended, sixty-two parishioners being present, of whom John Dunkin, Bromley's historian, was one. It was resolved, with one dissentient, that " the right of appointing a Parish Clerk is vested in the inhabitants of the Parish in Vestry assembled," and accordingly Edward Dunn was unanimously elected.

The Vicar, however, protested and instituted proceedings in Doctors' Commons, which eventually developed into a case for the High Court. In March 1818 the question was argued before Baron Graham at the Maidstone Assizes, a decision being then given against the parishioners and in favour of the Vicar. Dr. Smith thereupon set aside the nominee of the Vestry and appointed William Bateley instead.

Three months later, however, the Vestry secured some small consolation for its discomfiture by carrying its own candidate for the position of sexton, and subsequently by awkward questions thrown into the enemy camp as to the number of trees the Vicar was entitled to cut down and appropriate to his own use. The Vicar's plea that·he was too ill to attend to business caused this matter to be adjourned until he could attend. The plea, however, was a genuine one. The Vicar was ill, and in fact died without returning any answer to the Vestry's questions, and, with the death of Dr. Smith, all interest in the tree question seems to have evaporated.

Regulations affecting the bell-ringers appear in the Minute Books under dates 1823 and 1838. In the first case the ringers petitioned that their remuneration should be paid to them quarterly in cash instead of in refreshments supplied at a public-house; in the second case ringers were prohibited from ringing, as they had previously done, on the anniversaries of the Stuart Restoration of 1660, of the Coronation of Queen Anne, and of Gunpowder Plot.

Sufficient entries have now been recorded to show the general character of the ecclesiastical business transacted by the Vestry. We now pass to its secular activities, which display the Parish Meeting as the administrator of the general affairs of the town, and as the guardian of the rights of the parishioners.

A principal civil function of the Vestry was the care of the poor, and the maintenance of a suitable establishment, or workhouse, for the destitute. There is some indication of something resembling a workhouse being established as early as 1631 when Bishop Buckeridge of Rochester gave the sum of £20 for the use of the poor in the parish of Bromley. This sum, with some small additions to it, was expended in the purchase of a house for the free use of paupers, and further sums from time to time were bequeathed to the service of the poor. But no proper provision, under civic authority, for the housing of the destitute was made till 1731, when the Vestry determined to borrow £400 for the purpose of erecting an official workhouse. The house was built nearly opposite to Farwig Lane upon a wayside strip bordering the London Road (see plan on page 437). Though paid for by the Vestry, the Bishop, as Lord of the Manor, claimed that it had been erected on manorial land and consequently that the Vestry were tenants of the manor and not freeholders. In the following year, 1732, the churchwardens and overseers took a lease of the land from the Bishop for twenty-one years at a rental of three shillings and fourpence per annum. These particulars are important in view of what happened some thirty years later, and it may be well at once to complete the story irrespective of strict chronological sequence.

After the expiration of the first lease a period of thirteen years followed, during which the parishioners held the land on which the workhouse stood without any lease at all. This position was regularised in 1766 when a fresh lease for twenty-one years was taken out from Bishop Zachary Pearce at an annual rental of five shillings and fourpence.

But in the interval between the framing of this lease and its expiration a battle royal was taking place between the Bishop and the public authorities on the question of the Bishop's rates. The Bishops, though assessed to the highway rate, had never, it appears, been assessed to poor rate, and in 1784 a strong agitation on the part of the parishioners and the magistrates was started with a view to compelling the Bishops to pay poor rate. Accordingly, by a process from the magistrates, the Bishop's palace and grounds were duly rated, but whether or not any rates were paid is not recorded. An opportunity was, however, afforded in 1788 to the Bishop to retaliate upon this imposition. The lease of the workhouse had just expired, and Bishop Thomas refused to renew it except upon his own terms. The terms were that the Vestry should pay to the Bishop such a rent as he demanded on pain of ejectment. The result was that a new lease was drawn up for twenty-one years from Lady Day, 1789, the rent payable to the Bishop being £10 per annum. This was approximately the sum due from the Bishop as poor rate, and on the back of the new lease there was endorsed a memorandum stating that, on the Bishop's part, no rent would be required so long as no rate was demanded from the Bishop's Bromley estate. By this compromise both sides saved their faces for the time being. The Bishop's estate was still rated, but no rate was collected, and no rent for the workhouse was paid by the Vestry.

Some twenty years later, however, a new assessment increased the rateable value of the Bishop's estate from £60, at which it had previously stood, to £200, the amount of rate thus payable per annum becoming £40 instead of £10. The existing Bishop, Dr. Walter King, gave no definite refusal to this increased demand, but contended that an increased rent for his workhouse should accompany an increased poor rate upon his premises, at the same time offering to submit the whole case to counsel's opinion. As a result, Serjeant Shepherd, of Serjeants' Inn, was called upon to decide two questions :

(1) Is the Bishop entitled to insist upon a Rack Rent for the Workhouse premises ?

(2) If the Parish rejects the Bishop's terms, is he entitled to execute a writ of ejectment from the said Workhouse ?

The answer in both cases was emphatically in favour of the Bishop, and the Vestry was strongly recommended to accept a proposal from Dr. King that some impartial third party should be called upon to decide what rent the Vestry should pay. The Vestry acted upon this advice, and an agreement arrived at in June 1813 between Mr. John Forster on the one part as arbitrator, and Mr. Newnham representing the Vestry, brought about a satisfactory accommodation, the Vestry agreeing to pay for the workhouse a rack rent of £20 per annum, the Bishop consenting to pay the full poor rate demanded as from April 1810. As the rate for three years amounted to £132 7s. 6d., and the rent for the same period to £60, the amount payable, and actually paid, by the Bishop amounted to £72 7s. 6d.

The narration of this virulent and protracted quarrel covers a period of many years, and has taken us rather far afield from the Minute Books of the Vestry. We now return to them, and, in regard to workhouse questions, with a better understanding of the importance which evidently attached to what might seem to be comparatively trivial matters connected with that institution.

For example, in 1781, the question of the appointment of a master of the workhouse aroused public feeling to a high pitch. Evidently this matter was in some unexplained way mixed up with the great contention then in progress. Whereas ordinarily the Vestry meeting was a somewhat sedate and formal affair, attendance being limited to a few prominent churchpeople and local dignitaries, whenever the public mind was stirred by some burning question a tumultuous assembly, indiscriminately composed of men of all parties, grades, and denominations, would gather in the Vestry in order to show the parson and the local ' bigwigs ' that the people were not to be trifled with. Thus, at the particular meeting in question, no less than sixty-five parishioners were present to decide whether Mr. John Furlough or somebody else should be master of the workhouse.

In 1783 there was another gathering of the clans to protest against a previous decision of the Vestry in regard to the farming out of the workhouse inmates. The protesters carried the day, and the order permitting such an arrangement was rescinded by a popular vote.

In 1822 an apparently innocent proposal that an assistant overseer be appointed, who should act in the double capacity of rate collector and master of the workhouse, aroused a storm of opposition. The proposal was decisively defeated by fifty-one votes against thirty-five, and a motion that " this Vestry adjourn sine die " was carried by a majority of twenty-nine. The Vestry Minute Books indeed provide throughout ample evidence that in the arts of popular agitation the Parish Meeting had little to learn even from a modern Local Board or Town Council.

Reverting now to the more sober and humdrum activities of the Vestry, we have an entry, under date June 1735, notifying that a Mr. Kelk, nominated to serve the various offices of churchwarden, overseer, constable, and borsholder (or petty constable), was excused from serving in any of these capacities by virtue of the payment of a fine of twelve guineas. A previous entry, 1734, discloses the fact that certificates of exemption from service in public offices were by some means obtainable, and that quite a lucrative trade was carried on by the holders of such certificates, who assigned them, presumably for a cash consideration, to other people

In 1761 Dr. Hawkesworth claimed exemption from service as overseer on the ground that he was a Doctor of Laws, and on this plea he was exempted by the Justices of the Peace. None the less the Vestry insisted that he was liable to serve, duly nominated him, and notwithstanding the doctor's truculent protests, and some delay, he was compelled to serve his term of office in 1763.

In regard to finance, the Vestry was dependent upon the rates levied and collected by its authority, but where a considerable capital sum was required, such as £400 for the building of the workhouse (1735), or a similar sum for repairs to the church (1791), the money was either borrowed from private individuals who were ready to invest upon the security of the Vestry, or was raised by a policy of insurance upon the life of some prominent citizen. Thus, in 1791, the money required for repairs to the church was raised upon the life of Mr. George Warde Norman at a premium of $7\frac{1}{2}$ per cent.

As the guardian of public rights the Vestry has left behind it a fine and almost consistent record of fidelity to the interests of the people, and determination to maintain them. It seems to have been weak on only one occasion, when, in 1763, it accepted a sum of £40 from William Scott, the lessee under the Bishop of the Lammas lands of the parish, to extinguish the rights of the parishioners over those lands. It is true that those rights covered only one-half of each year, and for the half-year did not amount to very much, but the sum accepted very inadequately represented their value. With this one exception every encroachment, or proposed encroachment, upon public rights was strenuously resisted.

In 1779 the Vestry resisted the claim of the Bishop to enclose land on Bromley Common. In 1801 it was resolved that a pathway stretching along the top of Martins Hill, which had recently been closed, should be " restored and opened for the public use as heretofore." In 1816 the Vestry again vehemently asserted public rights over various footpaths which had been closed or appropriated for private use. In 1845 when the Gravel Pit at Page Heath was locked against the parish the Vestry decided that " the rights of the Parish must be firmly maintained." In a word, there is no instance throughout the record, except perhaps in one doubtful case, which shows the Vestry deficient in courage and determination in asserting against all attempted encroachments its own rights and those of the general community which it represented.

The miscellaneous activities of the Vestry throw some light upon the social conditions of the times, and serve to illustrate the wide differences in manners between then and now. Thus, in 1756, the highway surveyors and the High Constable were instructed to prosecute any who threw any water or " newsance " into the street ; any who suffered their drains to empty themselves into the street ; or who allowed their "hoggs " to wander at large. These measures only resulted in a partial success, for some years later (1768) the trouble with pigs became so acute that, as recorded in Chapter XV, two special officials, John Adams and Samuel Drury, were appointed to deal with it.

In 1747 the workhouse was cleared of its normal inmates in order to serve as a hospital for soldiers, an entry which serves to remind us of the war then raging on the question of the Austrian succession, and of the part played by this country in the contest with Frederick the Great of Prussia.

In March 1784 an application was made to the Vestry by William Obee, whose son had been bitten by a mad dog. The Vestry was asked to contribute to the expenses involved in taking the patient to Gravesend in order that he might be " dipped in salt water." A donation of half-a-guinea was given.

In December 1820 a sum of £20 was expended in repairing, strengthening, and cleansing " The Cage," but none the less, in 1824, a prisoner effected his escape therefrom by burrowing underneath it.

In 1831 an epidemic of cholera forced upon the attention of the Vestry the condition of the streets, which were still defiled by pools of foul water and heaps of decomposing refuse indiscriminately scattered abroad. Severe measures were taken against offenders, but they were felt to be insufficient to meet such a crisis as had arisen. It was therefore resolved to establish a Board of Health—a great step in advance, and an approximation to modern methods—and to this Board all matters connected with sanitation and the purification of streets and houses were delegated by the Vestry.

This reform was followed in 1836 by a petition to Parliament for an Enabling Act to establish and regulate an effective system of lighting, paving, and policing the town ; more effective provisions were called for to protect life and property against fire ; in short, the rapid development of the town in the first half of the nineteenth century produced a demand that the Vestry should confine its activities exclusively to ecclesiastical affairs, and that the general administration and control of the town should be in the hands of an authority specially appointed for the purpose—in other words, that Bromley should adopt the provisions of the Local Government Act of 1858 and elect a Local Board to supersede the secular functions of the Vestry. On February 21st, 1867, a meeting of parishioners was held at the Town Hall for the purpose of " considering " the Local Government Act of 1858. It was resolved, with only five dissentients, to take advantage of the Act, and to establish a Local Board for Bromley to consist of twelve elected members.

The first election to the Local Board took place in May 1867, there being thirty-four candidates for the twelve places. Mr. C. F. Devas headed the poll with 651 votes, and at the first meeting of the Board, held in the vestry room of the parish church, was elected Chairman; Mr. Robinson Latter was appointed Clerk to the Board, and Mr. Charles Newman, Collector.

The system of local government thus established lasted for nearly thirty years, until it was superseded by the Local Government Act of 1894. The history of this period is a tumultuous one, for, from the first, it seemed to be impossible for the Board to do anything right. Where it did not act it was accused of apathy, and where it did act it was accused, in equal shares, of folly and incompetence. It was a period when Bromley was beginning to realise itself as an important centre of population; when a vigorous public opinion was being formed; when shrewd and acute critics abounded, and when the exhilaration which is derived from being always " agin the government " had all the charm of novelty. For all this, it was the great period of Bromley's expansion, and the Local Board, upon its decease, could look back upon its career with satisfaction and complacency. It could point to the fact that a town of less than 10,000 inhabitants at the time when the Board first came into existence had become, under its administration, a town with about 30,000 inhabitants; that, during its period of office, the 1,900 houses of which Bromley was composed in 1867 had increased to about 6,000 by 1894, and, with that disregard for the operation of natural forces which often characterises an executive body, it might attribute this development to its own virtues and superhuman exertions. And, indeed, a survey of its administration does show some remarkable achievements. The purchase of Martin's Hill in 1878, the acquisition of the Queen's Mead in 1887, the ample provision made in the matter of cemeteries, the Local Board being also the Burial Board, afford lasting evidence of initiative displayed and activities usefully employed.

But from the first it failed to secure either the confidence or affection of the public. Even when the opposition became the government, the public soon found reasons for organising a fresh opposition, and the proposals of such a champion of the people as Mr. C. W. Gedney in October 1883 to take over the market were as hotly and uproariously opposed as the sale of public rights to Mr. C. F. Devas for a sum deemed wholly inadequate.

The Board on its election in 1867 was without a home, and all the machinery of administration had to be constructed *ab initio*. The first thing to do was to obtain suitable premises to serve both as a Council Chamber and as offices for the Board's officials. A piece of ground was secured between East and West Streets, and a suitable building, now the offices of Messrs.

Baxter, Payne & Lepper, was duly erected. In the interim the Board meetings were held in an iron room in the Cage Field.

The first important question to engage attention was that of the sewerage of the town and its disposition. In due course the Board elaborated a scheme, under the Public Health Acts of 1848 and 1858, which included the construction of a sewage farm at Holloway Farm, Chinbrook, the plan proposed involving a charge upon the town of £50,000. The scheme was bitterly opposed, not on the ground of the expense, but because the proposed expenditure would be practically wasted in carrying out a plan which, in a few years, would prove quite inadequate to the needs of the town. In February 1869 a " Ratepayers' Protection Society " was formed at a meeting held in Market Square, of which Mr. G. F. Chambers was appointed Chairman, with Mr. W. T. Ayling as Secretary, the purpose of the Association being not merely to frustrate the sewerage scheme, but generally to keep a watchful eye upon the Board's proceedings. The Minute Book of the Society is now in the Public Library, and contains some lively reading. The battle between the Society and the Board raged furiously for more than three years, and produced, among other things, a curious publication under the title of *Bromley Bells*, which ran to six numbers. Of these, one (No. 6) is to be seen in the Public Library. The brochure was effective in giving currency to much ingenious satire at the expense of the Local Board under the title of " The Rise and Fall of the Commune of Bromville." All the principal antagonists on both sides are introduced under pseudonyms which everybody could recognise at the time, though now they need elucidation. Thus, to name a few, Mr. Devas, Chairman of the Board, becomes " Magistras "; Mr. Robinson Latter, the Clerk, is " Lexanlarge "; Mr. J. W. Ilott is " Quackenboss "; Mr. Coles Child is " Giganticus "; Mr. G. F. Chambers is " Camerius," and Dr. H. S. Hughes is " Bolus."

The ultimate result of this contest was the complete defeat of the Board's scheme and the triumph of the Ratepayers' Association. This body adopted the plan of running its own candidates at the first available election, and this policy was so successful that not only did several of the Association's men secure election, but Mr. Chambers, the Chairman of the Association, secured appointment as Chairman of the Local Board itself. A Government inquiry resulted in a refusal by Government to sanction the proposed scheme, which was finally dropped in favour of another, which had been witnessed in operation at Ealing. The Ratepayers' Society, having accomplished its purpose, was dissolved, 10s. 6d. in debt, on April 9th, 1872.

None the less the scheme adopted seems to have been ineffective to solve the sewerage problem, for in the next year a largely signed memorial from the inhabitants of Lower High Street complained bitterly to the Board of the state of the drainage in that quarter of the town. The fact was that the very rapid increase in population and houses outran the existing administrative machinery. What was needed was a system of expert supervision under responsible officials to safeguard the interests of public health against the wiles of the jerry-builder and the ignorance and indifference of the householder.

The appointment of a Medical Officer of Health, Dr. C. O. Baylis, in 1875, and of an Inspector of Nuisances, Mr. Hugh S. Cregeen, in the following year, is to the credit of the Local Board, and with these appointments, and with the establishment of a Rural Sanitary Authority, and the West Kent Main Sewerage Board in 1878, the drainage problem seems to have been finally solved. The Board " which drains our pockets, not the Town " had at last succeeded even in its secondary effort.

Apart from this protracted and burning question of drains, much solid progress and many useful improvements marked the period when the Local Board was in control. Under its auspices, and by the initiative of Major Clement Satterthwaite, a new and commodious Drill Hall was erected in East Street in 1872, its opening being celebrated by a grand concert at which Mr. Arthur Sullivan acted as accompanist.

In 1878 the Science and Art School was opened—one of the many services, to be recorded fully elsewhere, rendered to the town by Mr. T. Davis—and at the opening conversazione the first three telephones ever constructed were exhibited to an astonished public. Fourteen years later this school became the property of the town, by gift from Sir E. H. Scott.

In 1883 the widening of what was known as Uridge's Corner was effected at a cost of about £2,500.

A School Attendance Committee was appointed by the Board, and the main responsibility for the education of the town rested upon its shoulders until 1889, when the control of education passed into the hands of a School Board.

But, in spite of much useful activity, the Local Board was a constant scene of bickerings within, and the constant object of criticism and recrimination outside. One of its most vigorous critics was General H. P. Babbage, himself a member of the Board, who, in 1881, resigned his position as a protest against what he considered to be its apathy and incompetence. The elections of that year were lively affairs. The issue was in effect a vote of confidence in the existing Board. Feeling ran high. Accusations of intimidation at the polls were freely bandied about, and the result was the defeat of the Chairman, Mr. R. F. Sandon, and the election of Mr. C. W. Gedney at the head of the poll, and also of General Babbage, who had resigned only again to present himself as a candidate and to secure a popular verdict upon his line of action. The infusion of new blood into the Board only served still further to accentuate internal animosities. The conservative element still predominated, and the voice of the critics was louder and more specific than before.

The General, in a letter, declared that the Board's method of keeping accounts was faulty, and that, in allowing no less than £4,500 in rates to remain uncollected, they had shown themselves as remiss as they were incompetent. The feeling in the ranks of the opposition found expression in some lines inserted in the *Bromley Record*:

> " Tell me not in mournful number
> That our Local Board is dead.
> Oh ! dear no !—they only slumber :
> Wake them not, they're best in bed."

The difficulties of the Local Board, however, were not so much inherent in the composition of the Board as in the fact that in the closing years of the century the administrative functions of such a body had increased more rapidly than the power granted for their exercise. The national Government had already recognised this fact by the Local Government Act of 1888, which established County Councils throughout England and Wales. This was followed, in 1894, by the Local Government Act, which extended the general principles of the former Act to Urban and Rural Districts and to small parishes. Under the Act of 1894 the Local Boards were swept away and replaced by Urban District Councils, and it was under such a body that Bromley was administered from that date until its incorporation as a Borough in 1903.

For the purposes of administration and elections the parish was divided into five wards, designated Town, Bickley, Bromley Common, Plaistow, and Sundridge. Each ward returned three members with the exception of Town, to which four seats were allotted, and it is notable that only three members of the defunct Local Board held seats in the first Urban District Council. Mr. W. H. Bosanquet was the first Chairman, with Mr. J. Wheeler-Bennett as Vice-Chairman. The services of the principal permanent officials of the old Board were retained, Mr. F. H. Norman as Clerk to the Council, and Mr. Stanley Hawkings as Surveyor.

Under the Act which transformed the Local Board into an Urban District Council that Council had the right to exercise powers far in excess of those held by the former body. It became the authority, under various adoptive Acts—if it chose to adopt them—to regulate libraries, baths, and wash-houses, artisans' dwellings, gymnasiums and museums, and public parks. The Bromley Council was content to claim authority only in regard to public parks and libraries, and hence it differed rather more in name than in powers from its predecessor.

In 1892 the Public Libraries Act was adopted, the nucleus of a public library was formed, and housed in 1894 at the building which is now the Science and Art School in Tweedy Road.

During the ten years of administration a good deal of solid and useful work was done ; indeed, it is scarcely too much to say that it was in that period that Bromley assumed practically the form which it bears to-day.

In the construction of new roads, in the widening of existing roads, and in the rounding off of awkward corners, the Urban District Council was specially active, and it was fortunate in enlisting the co-operation of land-owners, such as Mr. Coles Child, Major Satterthwaite, Mr. Eley Soames, and others, in securing on favourable terms the land required for the second of these purposes.

A proposal to enlarge and improve the Market Square by demolishing the houses in Middle Row was, however, rejected, and perhaps wisely, for whatever advantages such a policy would produce, the time had not then come, and perhaps will never come, when public opinion will sanction, at an enormous cost, the disappearance of some of the oldest and most characteristic features of the town. The removal of the old bridle posts and projecting steps at the entrance to the College was doubtless rendered necessary by the increasing traffic on the High Road, but it is not without regret that we have to record the displacement of such ancient memorials of the past.

It is to the resolute opposition of the Urban District Council that Bromley is indebted for the fact that its streets are not encumbered by a suburban tramway system, and that it is not bisected by some form of light railway. The latter proposal, for a light railway through Bromley to Farnborough, was brought before the Council and rejected in 1898, while, in the spring of the following year, the South-Eastern Metropolitan Tramways Company made its first effort to extend its operations through Bromley. The Council at once expressed its disapproval of the scheme, but, in January 1900, the Tramways Company had managed to secure such a measure of support that at a special meeting of the Council, called to consider the question, the votes for and against tramways were equal. It therefore fell to one man, the Chairman, to decide by his casting vote the fate of the town in this matter. That vote, given by Mr. T. Davis, was given in favour of opposing the scheme. It is somewhat surprising that among the townspeople themselves only a languid interest seems to have been aroused by this question. When petitions, either for or against tramways, were organised less than seven hundred persons took the trouble to sign, and of these 347 were for opposing the scheme and 324 for supporting it.

Early in 1903 a further effort was made by the Tramways Company to gain over the Council to its side, and a scheme was actually formulated. But in the meantime public opinion had been strongly organised in opposition. So powerful an antagonism had manifested itself in the town, that the Council, already half-committed, found itself in a difficulty. This was surmounted by inserting into the agreement terms which were obviously impossible. A document was drawn up, signed and sealed, by which the District Council gave its required sanction on condition that the Company would provide £160,000 for widening the streets, and would deposit £10,000 in gold in the bank. These conditions proved fatal to the plan, and the menace of the tramways was thus finally removed.

FRANK GRIFFITH (1862–1917).
First Mayor of Bromley, 1903–4.

Among the useful improvements which mark this period we may note the re-numbering of the town in 1900 ; the introduction of incandescent gas into the street lamps ; the erection of a number of fire-alarm posts in the district, as well as alarm bells in the houses of the firemen ; the intro-duction of a refuse destructor and depot ; and further extensions in sewers and cemeteries. These thoroughly practical and valuable measures were, it must be remembered, supplemented by those æsthetic and cultural achieve-ments recorded elsewhere, the conversion of the White Hart Field into a recreation ground, the construction of the Public Library, and the opening to the public of the Neelgherries Gardens.

In the domain of education one of the first duties of the Council was the election of a committee to advance the interests of technical education in the town, as for this department the Council was directly responsible. Elementary education was delegated to the School Board, which remained in control of that branch until the Education Act of 1902 came into opera-tion, completely revolutionising the system of educational administration throughout the country. Under this Act it devolved upon the Council to elect an Education Committee, and to this body, set up in June 1903, the control of the Council's schools was entrusted.

By this time the population of Bromley had increased to over 30,000, and the town had acquired a dignity and importance which seemed to entitle it to a Charter of Incorporation as a Borough. Such a proposal had indeed been made many years before by Mr. G. H. Payne (1888), and had then been supported by the great majority of the District Council, but it was not received with any marked enthusiasm outside, and the matter was dropped. Several attempts were made to revive it, notably by Mr. G. W. F. Loftus and by Mr. Daniel Grinsted, but without any result, until, in 1901, on New Year's Eve, Mr. Frank Griffith suggested that a public meeting of the inhabitants be called in order to obtain an authoritative vote on the question. The meeting was duly called and held in the Drill Hall, on February 26th, 1902, and was attended by an immense number of the townspeople. The resolution presented ran as follows :

" That a petition be presented to H.M. The King praying him to grant a Charter of Incorporation to Bromley in Kent."

On being put to the vote the resolution was carried by an overwhelming majority, the opposition numbering only about fifteen. An Incorporation Committee was immediately formed with Mr. F. Griffith as Chairman, Mr. R. W. James, Vice-Chairman, Mr. Ernest Watts, Hon. Sec., and Mr. F. Medhurst as Hon. Treasurer.

The Petition, engrossed on vellum, was signed by 3,575 persons out of a possible number of 4,500. The business was put through with really remarkable celerity. The reception of the Petition was followed by a

Government Inquiry under Mr. Commissioner Cresswell in July. The Report of the Commissioner proving favourable to the project, a Draft Charter was drawn up and deposited at the Office of the Privy Council in February 1903, and the Charter itself, with the Great Seal attached, was handed to the Incorporation Committee's solicitor, Mr. E. T. Lea, on August 25th. Eighteen months almost to the day was the time which elapsed between the public meeting which inaugurated the scheme and the reception of the Charter as the crown of success.

The ceremonials and celebrations attendant upon the reception were observed on September 2nd. In the Draft Charter submitted to the Privy Council the names of the chief officials appointed to serve for the purposes of that Charter had been inserted—the name of Mr. T. C. Dewey as Charter Mayor, that of Mr. E. Packe as Deputy Charter Mayor, that of Mr. F. H. Norman as Charter Town Clerk, and that of Mr. E. T. Lea as his deputy. Upon these gentlemen, therefore, there fell the principal share in commemorating the occasion. On the morning of the appointed day a deputation appointed by the Incorporation Committee proceeded to London, where the Charter was handed to Mr. E. T. Lea. The deputation immediately returned to Bromley in a special saloon carriage, bearing the Charter with them enclosed in a silver casket. On arriving at the South Station at 11.46, the deputation was received by the Charter Mayor, the Town Clerk, and a notable assembly of distinguished guests and townspeople. A procession was formed headed by a detachment of the Bromley Volunteers with their band, in the centre marched the Bromley Town Band, and in the last carriage there rode the Charter Mayor, Mr. Norman, Mr. Lea, and Mr. Frank Griffith, Chairman of the Incorporation Committee. The procession reached its destination at the foot of Martin's Hill, where a large platform had been erected with an open face towards the hill. It was thus possible for almost unlimited numbers to view the proceedings, and even to hear some part of them. Thus, after prayer by the Vicar of Bromley, the Rev. A. G. Hellicar, and a statement by the Charter Mayor, Mr. F. H. Norman read the text of the Charter in a voice so clear that it could be universally heard, the proceedings ending with the National Anthem. The troops presented arms, the Union Jack was unfurled on the hill, and a discharge of maroons, the cheers of the assembled multitude, and the triumphant clash of the church bells provided that mingled element of noise which such events demand.

Such occasions equally demand the element of food and speech-making. Ample opportunities were provided for both at a banquet held in the Drill Hall, where a distinguished company, which included Lord Avebury, various Mayors from Kentish Boroughs, the Sheriff of London, Sir George Truscott, did full justice both in action and in speech to the hospitality and public spirit of the Charter Mayor, who had insisted upon bearing the whole cost of the day's rejoicings. Sports on the Queen's Mead in the

SIR THOMAS C. DEWEY, BART. (1840–1926).

Charter Mayor, 1903.

From the oil painting by Arthur Hacker, R.A.

afternoon and a Carnival Procession in the evening brought a memorable day to a close.

The day of celebrations was succeeded by an interval of two months, during which the town was preparing itself for the inauguration of the new system of local government upon a footing of practical business. On November 2nd the elections for the new Town Council were duly held in the six wards into which, by the Charter of Incorporation, the Borough was divided—viz. Plaistow Ward ; Martin's Hill Ward ; Town Ward ; Sundridge Ward ; Bickley Ward ; Bromley Common Ward. There were 34 candidates for the 18 seats (among them 10 members of the Urban District Council, 7 of whom were elected), those who were successful being Messrs. W. J. Gibbs, T. D. Graty, W. R. Mallett, F. Hudson, R. Taylor, G. Weeks, Jun., P. Harper, C. E. Ingall, A. E. Price, T. Davis, F. Griffith, W. Powell, W. J. Homewood, T. C. McIntyre, M. H. Newton, G. Lawrence, E. G. Peill, and J. Rogers.

On November 9th the first meeting of the Council was convened under the presidency of the Charter Mayor. Its principal business was to elect a Mayor and six Aldermen. The honour of being chosen as first Mayor of the Incorporated Borough of Bromley fell to Councillor Frank Griffith, to whose untiring exertions the incorporation of the Borough was so largely due. Five of the six Aldermen were elected from the existing Councillors, viz. Messrs. Davis, Lawrence, Mallett, McIntyre, and Price, the sixth being Mr. R. W. James, who had been a prominent member of the Urban District Council. He was in addition appointed by the Mayor to act as Deputy Mayor.[1] The Council being thus constituted, the Charter Mayor presented to the Mayor, on behalf of the town, a Mace as a symbol of authority. This handsome ornament was designed by Ambrose Lee, Bluemantle Poursuivant of Arms, in the style of the late Italian Renaissance. On the butt of the handle the Arms of the donor are worked in colour enamel, the stem is wreathed with the broom which gives the town its name, the whole being surmounted by a crown, with the Borough Arms in the space beneath it.

The presentation of the Mace was followed by that of the Mayoral Chain, the gift of Mr. Frank Griffith. The centre link contains the Royal Arms, two other links show the White Horse of Kent and the initial letter B ; the links on each side of the Royal Arms are engraved with the donor's monogram entwined with broom, and the remaining links were left clear to receive the crests or monograms of succeeding Mayors. The Badge attached to the chain was the gift of Mr. Paul Henwood.

The Mayor then took the chair and the business of appointments

---

[1] This election rendered by-elections necessary in five of the wards of the Borough to replace those Councillors who had been elected to aldermanic rank. The result of this was that Messrs. R. Whyte, Jun., G. Haywood, A. Lindsay Bell, Arthur A. Worley, and A. Sparks were elected members of the Town Council.

proceeded. The existing officers of the Urban District Council were appointed to their present positions and Mr. David Aiers was appointed Sergeant-at-Mace. A resolution that a portrait of the Charter Mayor should be executed for the decoration of the Council Chamber was carried, and a further resolution that a formal application be made to the Earl Marshal to grant a warrant for the use of Armorial Bearings was received with enthusiasm.

The Arms of Bromley, of which an illustration is given, consist of a shield with four quarterings, each quarter symbolising either the town, the district, the diocese, or the county. The broom stands for Bromley ; the sun for the ancient Manor of Sundridge ; the escallop shell for the diocese of Rochester, the white horse stands for the County of Kent. The wavy fesse intervening between the quarters shows three ravens, in honour of the Ravensbourne ; the motto : " Dum cresco, spero " (While I grow, I hope) signifies that there is still no limit to the aspirations of Bromley. The helm is merely a conventional piece of heraldic decoration, except for the two branches of broom encircling an escallop shell which constitutes the town's crest.

This explanation may enable any reader of the original Warrant to comprehend its meaning when it declares the Arms of Bromley to be " Quarterly Gules and Azure on a fesse wavy argent three Ravens proper between in the first quarter two branches of broom slipped of the third in the second a Sun in splendour in the third an Escallop shell or and in the fourth a horse forçene also Argent. And for the *Crest* on a wreath of the colours upon two bars wavy Azure and Argent an Escallop shell as in the Arms between two branches of Broom proper."

In the course of this chapter many changes have been recorded in the forms of local government. It only remains to mention that for a period of nearly forty years the tenure of the two chief executive officers of the governing body remained unchanged.

Mr. Stanley Hawkings was appointed Surveyor to the Local Board on September 6th, 1892. He was re-appointed by the Town Council on November 9th, 1903, no longer as Surveyor only, but as the holder of the more responsible office of Borough Engineer. This office he retained till 1928, when, under the provisions of the Superannuation Act, his retirement became necessary. Everywhere in Bromley are to be seen the evidences of the initiative, enterprise, and taste he expended in the service of the Borough throughout that period.

Mr. Frederic Henry Norman has devoted a lifetime to the service of the town.

He came to Bromley in 1890. At that time Mr. Robert Gordon Mullen held the offices of Clerk to the Bromley Local Board, Clerk to the Board of Guardians and to several other local bodies in the district.

Mr. Norman obtained the post of Assistant to Mr. Mullen to take charge of the Local Board department.   On Mr. Mullen's retirement from the office of Clerk to the Local Board in 1893 Mr. Norman was appointed to the vacant position.   With the coming of the Urban District Council he was appointed Clerk to that body, and in 1903 became Town Clerk to the newly incorporated Borough.   The executive duties entailed by the transition of Bromley from one form of local government to that which succeeded it have in large measure fallen upon him.   For thirty-five years he has filled, and still fills (1928), the responsible office of Chief Adviser to the governing body of the town, deservedly earning increased appreciation of his loyal and valuable services with each successive year.

THE BOROUGH ARMS

Chapter XII

EDUCATION IN BROMLEY—SCHOOLS

IT is a startling fact that a country which to-day is spending many millions a year on education was less than a hundred years ago contributing no money out of public funds for that purpose. The first grant from Government for purposes of national education was made in 1834, the amount of the grant being £20,000. There were many who were of opinion that even such a grant was superfluous, and a dangerous departure from the true functions of government.

" The ends of civil government," wrote Macaulay in 1839, " are to protect our persons and property—to compel us to satisfy our wants, not by rapine but by industry—to compel us to decide our differences not by the strong hand but by arbitration.

" If," he goes on to say, " the functions of government be universal, why should not rulers take away the child from the mother, select the nurse, *regulate the school*, overlook the playground, fix the hours of labour and recreation ? "

And evidently he thought such propositions to be too monstrous to require either consideration or refutation. To-day, even the most conservative of Governments would consider most of these matters as falling naturally within the sphere of its activities.

In the many centuries preceding the Victorian epoch the education of the children was regarded as purely a question for the individual, or else as a matter which concerned the Church. That some form of education might serve as a supplement to the policeman was recognised from the earliest times.

" Let every Monastery," says the Capitulary of Alcuin of York (A.D. 787), " and every Abbey have its school, where boys may be taught the Psalms, the system of musical notation, singing, arithmetic and grammar."

The principal end in view here was the efficiency of the choir, but the interest of the general community in education was ultimately based chiefly upon the belief that a thorough grounding in the principles inculcated by the Church Catechism would prove a valuable safeguard to the existing structure of Society. It was certainly in accordance with ideas of this kind that the first school was established in Bromley.

Reference has already been made in the historical section of this book to the foundation in 1716 of a Charity School in Bromley. The purposes for which it was founded are succinctly set down in the preamble to the list of original subscribers, dated November 11th, 1716.

11th Novembr 1716.

Whereas Prophaneness & Immorality are in a great measure owing to a gross Ignorance of the Christian Religion, especially among the poorer Sort of People: And Nothing is more likely to promote the Practice of Christianity & Vertue, than an early, & pious Education of Youth. We whose Names are under-written, do hereby Agree to pay Yearly, at four quarterly payments, during pleasure, the several Sums of Money, over against our Names respectively subscribed, for the setting up of a Charity-School, in the Parish of Bromley, in the County of Kent; for Teaching poor Children to Read & Write; and for Instructing them in the Knowledge & Practice of the Christian Religion, as professed, & taught in the Church of England, & such other things, as are useful, and suitable to their Condition & Capacity. For these Purposes

	£	s	d
I Francis Bishop of Roch: subscribe Ten pounds p ann	10		
if we want forty pounds it is to be supplyed by ye inhabitants, or if not a fifth part of what shall be subscribed			
I Thomas Blomer subscribe forty shillings — Withdrawn		2	
I Harington Bagshaw subscribe forty shillings p An		2	
I Thomas Washer subscribe forty shillings p An		2	
I Lancelot Polson subscribed three pounds p ann	3		
I Willm Emmett subscribe three pounds p Annu	3		
Ri. Graham Forty Shillings per ann		2	
I Elizabeth Hangood subscribe forty shillings p An — Dead		2	
I Anthony Hall subscribe forty shillings p annu		2	
Dw. Wall Ten shillings p An — Withdrawn		10	
I H. Bagshaw subscribe more for a Friend one pound	1		
I Anthony Johnson subscribe one pound p Annu			
I — Innocent subscribe one pound — Withdrawn Christmas			
I Willm Waldron subscribe Ten shillings p Annu — Withdrawn		10	
I Saml Oxenbridge subscribe Ten shillings p Ann — Withdrawn Christmas 17½		10	
I John Witney subscribe Ten shillings p annum — Dead		10	
I John Cobb ten shillings p An — Withdrawn Christmas 17½		10	
I Charles Boyce ten shillings p An — Withdrawn Christmas 17½		10	
I Daniel French subscribe one pound p an — Withdrawn Xtide 1717	1		
I John Harvell ten shillings p an — Withdrawn Lady day 1718		10	
I John Lawson subscribe one pound p annum — Withdrawn	1		
I William Fisher subscribe four shillings per an			

LIST OF SUBSCRIBERS TO BROMLEY CHARITY SCHOOL, NOVEMBER 1716.
Photographed from the original in the Public Library.

" Whereas Prophaneness Immorality are in a great measure owing to a gross Ignorance of the Christian Religion, especially among the poorer sort of people, and Nothing is more likely to promote the Practice of Christianity & Vertue than an early & pious Education of Youth, We, whose Names are under-written agree to pay, ... (during pleasure,) " an annual subscription for setting up a Charity School, where the children may be taught to read & write, be instructed in the principles of Christianity as interpreted by the Church of England, " & in such other things as are useful and suitable to their condition and capacity."

This preamble approached, as near as the times of its composition permitted, to the modern ideal of education as primarily designed to form and establish character.

The list of subscribers was headed by Francis Atterbury, Bishop of Rochester, with a contribution of £10 per annum conditional on the other subscriptions reaching a total sum of £40. Failing this, the Bishop agreed to subscribe a fifth part of whatever sum was raised. A sufficient amount was ultimately promised to justify the promoters in proceeding with the project, and thus, in due course, the Bromley Charity School became an accomplished fact.

It is a gratifying reflection that Bromley came quite early into the national movement for establishing such schools in the country. An interesting testimony to the existence of that movement may be found in a paper by Richard Steele in the *Spectator* (No. 294) in which he remarks that :

" The Charity Schools which have been erected of late years are the greatest instances of public spirit the Age has produced."

The date of this paper is February 6th, 1712, nearly five years earlier than the foundation of the Bromley Charity School, and the specific mention by Steele of a period of fourteen years, during which less than £5,000 had been contributed for such a purpose, leads to the conclusion that about twenty years elapsed after the first initiation of the movement before Bromley came into it.

It is fortunate that ample original material still survives for writing the history of the Bromley Charity School. The vellum sheet on which, in 1716, the preamble was inscribed, together with the signatures of the first subscribers, is now, by the gift of Mr. W. Baxter, preserved in the Public Library.

On July 5th, 1921, Mr. Baxter, rummaging in a toolshed in the parish churchyard, discovered in a tin box a white-vellum bound volume, in fair condition, containing particulars and accounts, for more than a century, regarding the administration of the school. Loose within the covers was found a list of the charity sermons preached on behalf of the school between 1739 and 1826 ; and three reports of the National Schools Committee, dated respectively 1854–5, 1858–9, 1859–60.

About the same time Mr. Baxter also discovered in the attics of Messrs. Latter and Willett's offices a book in green vellum which was evidently reserved for registering all particulars concerning the various wills under which benefactions were made to the Charity School. These documents are lodged in the safe of the Parish Church, and are now presumably secure.

The original Charity School was established in order to provide free education and clothing for ten boys and ten girls, being children of necessitous parents, selected from time to time by the subscribers in general meeting. Notice of such meetings was to be given in the Parish Church on the Sundays preceding them, and on February 11th, 1717, the first meeting of subscribers was held. The purpose of this meeting was to draw up certain orders, nine in number, for the better support and government of the school, and certain further orders, eleven in number, to be observed by the master, mistress, and scholars. These latter orders prescribe the hours of teaching, in summer from 7 to 11 in the morning, and from 1 to 5 in the afternoon; in winter, from 8 to 11 a.m., and from 1 to 4. They prescribe the precise subjects to be taught and the special dress the children were to wear daily:

" Whereby they shall be known to their benefactors : for the boys—yellow stockings, knee breeches and bob-tailed jacket of dark blue ; a black or blue cap with yellow tassel, and laced shoes ; for the girls—a gown and petticoat of ' blue Long Ells,' a coif and band of fine ghenting, a leather bodice or stomacher, and a white, blue or chequered apron."

The total outfit of each boy represented a cash cost of 15s. 10d. ; of each girl 16s. 1d. For purposes of comparison between modern prices and those of a century ago, it may be of interest to extract the details which made up these respective costs :

" Cloathing of Boy.	s.	d.
1⅛ yds. grey Yorks Broad cloth 1½ yd. wide for coat	3	0
Making coat, pewter buttons, etc.	1	0
Waistcoat of same cloth lined	3	6
Breeches of cloth or leather, lined	2	6
Knitt cap with tuft of any colour	0	10
One Band 2d. 1 shirt 1/6	1	8
1 Pr. woollen stockings, 8d. 1 pr. shoes 2/0	2	8
1 Pr. Buckles, 1d. 1 pr. knitt or washleather gloves 7d. . . .	0	8
Totall	15	10 "

" Cloathing of Girl :	s.	d.
3½ yds. Blue long ells—for gown and petticoat	5	3
Making same—string, body lining etc.	1	0
A coif and band of fine Ghenting	1	0
A shift 1/6, White, blue, or chequered apron 1/0 . . .	2	6
Leather Bodice and Stomacher	2	6
1 Pr. Woollen Stockings, 8d. 1 Pr. Shoes 1/10 . . .	2	6
1 Pr. Pattens, 8d. Buckles 1d. Knitt or washleather gloves, 7d. .	1	4
Totall	16	1 "

Particulars are unfortunately lacking as to what happened when a change of the " 1 shirt, 1 shift, and 1 Pr. woollen stockings " became necessary. The children were to be brought to church twice every Lord's Day, and also on Holy Days and weekly prayer days, " the master and mistress to sit with them."

The orders then determine the salary to be paid to the master and mistress. It was presumed that they would be husband and wife, and a sum of £20 was fixed as their annual stipend, together with " 2 chardron of coal annually," the cost of which was reckoned at £3.

Thus the total annual expense of clothing the children and providing instructors was estimated at about £39. The total subscriptions promised amounted to a little more than £53, leaving a balance of £14 for books, incidental expenses, and reserve fund.

The meeting then proceeded to elect as trustees Mr. William Emmett and the Rev. Lancelot Tolson, and as master and mistress Mr. John Soane and Anne, his wife.

Having settled all preliminaries, the way was clear for making a start. A month later, on March 11th, 1717, the second meeting of subscribers was held, when ten boys and ten girls were duly selected as the first charity scholars, of whom it is reported that one boy, " Wm Morris, aged 10," ran away, and one girl, " Sarah Doodney, aged 8," was turned out. The rest have no history, save that " Jno Woodman, 9 years was apprenticed."

The school thus established in the spring of 1717 was conducted in a building situated in what was then known as "the Gravel Pits," a depression at the foot of Mason's Hill, now absorbed into the premises of the Southern Railway Company. Launched upon a wave of philanthropic enthusiasm, for a few years the new institution flourished amain. In 1718 a credit balance of over £60 in the hands of the trustees seemed to justify an extension of the original plan, and four additional boys and six additional girls increased the numbers on the foundation from twenty to thirty. A legacy of £200 " for ever " from the Rev. George Wilson of Chislehurst and a further legacy of £100 from the Rev. Lancelot Tolson were put to capital account, and the interest upon this capital, together with subscriptions, provided for some years an income adequate to the school's requirements.

Gradually, however, enthusiasm began to subside, subscribers died, and new subscribers were not forthcoming. A balance of £42 in 1723 shrank to £38 in 1724. For the next five years each successive year shows a diminishing balance, and by 1728 the Charity School, if it had not actually expired of inanition, was certainly in the last stages of exhaustion. Yet there was in the town a genuine desire to maintain the institution, and, moreover, the legacies standing to its credit practically forbade its complete extinction. Accordingly, in the autumn of 1729, a vigorous effort was made to obtain new subscribers, with the result that, by reducing the number of the foundationers to the original figure of twenty, the school was set upon its feet again and entered upon a decade of comparative prosperity. Of the actual scholars there is but a scanty record. Achievements to their credit are not recorded, but of Elizabeth Woodney we learn that she was expelled " because her mother would not keep her cleare of vormint," a like fate overtook John Tew for playing Truant, while Easter Turner was struck off the register because it was discovered that her father was not necessitous.

By 1735 the number of scholars had been increased from twenty to thirty-eight, and a balance of £18 is shown to the credit of the trustees at Michaelmas, 1736. In the following year the balance stood still higher (£20 3s. 9d.), but two years later, owing to causes not recorded, the school was once more on the verge of bankruptcy. The crisis was averted in some small degree by a timely legacy of £100 from Mrs. Emmett, and by again reducing the numbers, but mainly by the institution of a Charity Sermon, to be preached for the benefit of the school in the Parish Church in the autumn of each year. The first recorded Charity Sermon was preached by Dr. Bateman, on September 16th, 1739, the offertory amounting to £14 0s. 6d., and from that date to 1857 we have a complete record of the preachers, and of the amounts subscribed, this record being printed in full in Strong's *History of Bromley*. An analysis of the record, from the point of view of sermons preached, shows that from 1739 to the year 1800 there was only one break in their continuity, viz. in 1792. But in the first decade of the nineteenth century there is no record of a Charity Sermon except in the years 1802, 1803. The reasons which account for this intermission can only be surmised, but are possibly to be found in the disturbed state of the country during the Napoleonic wars. In 1811 the sermons were renewed, and, save for six breaks, were continued annually until they ceased finally in 1857.

When the record is analysed from the point of view of contributions received it is found to throw some light upon the development of the town during a period of about a hundred and twenty years. It has already been seen in a previous chapter that, until the end of the eighteenth century, Bromley remained, if not actually stationary, yet very much the same, as regards population and material prosperity, as it had been at the beginning of the seventeenth century. From the sixty sermons preached, from 1739 to 1799 inclusive, an average contribution per annum from the congregation amounted to £23 14s. The average contribution from 1800 to 1857 was £57 12s., or nearly two-and-a-half times the former sum. From 1821 onwards, for some thirteen or fourteen years, the trustees of the Charity School could count confidently upon an income of at least £70 accruing from this single source, and men of the first eminence in the Church were frequently secured as preachers. On three occasions an Archbishop of Canterbury gave his services ; on nine occasions the preacher was the Bishop of the diocese, while deans, doctors, and archdeacons were of frequent appearance.

The Charity Sermon was not merely a scholastic appeal: it was a civic institution, a red-letter day in the humdrum life of the town, and doubtless of as much moral benefit to the parish as of financial benefit to the school.

From the time of the institution of the Charity Sermon the Bromley School sailed in fairly smooth financial water, and maintained, though it only very slightly increased, its original design. The number of twenty scholars was raised to thirty in 1760, but was reduced to twenty-four twenty years later, and at no time during the first hundred years of its existence did the school provide for many more than thirty at any one time. But, limited as were its activities, none the less the work accomplished was considerable, as may be seen very clearly, if not quite accurately, set forth in the following " Abstract of Accounts from 1716 to 1796," compiled by whoever was the keeper in 1796 of the old vellum volume rescued by Mr. Baxter. It summarises the history of eighty years :

" RECEIVED.		£	s.	d.	EXPENDED.		£	s.	d.
Subscriptions	. .	1,670	12	0	Cloathing .	. .	1,781	4	6
Sermons	. .	1,728	11	4	Teaching .	. .	2,513	12	8
Legacies	. .	499	17	0	Books, etc. .	. .	314	5	1
Interest on Capital .	.	1,625	4	7	Cost of Stock	. .	854	15	1
		£5,524	4	11	[*sic*] £5,465	1	4 "		
					(correct total	. .	£5,463	17	4)

showing a balance on total working of £59 3s. 7d., or, more correctly, of £60 7s. 7d.

There follows in the Abstract the list of legacies received :

		£	s.
1728 (should be 1718)	Rev. George Wilson .	£200	0
	Lancelot Tolson .	100	0
1736	Thomas Moore . .	50	0
1745 (should be 1738)	Ellen Emmett . .	100	0
1770	Mr. Wilcox . .	22	10
1771	Mr. Hamilton . .	7	7
1793	Mr. Thorn . .	20	0
		£499	17

This sum of £499 17s. was supplemented a year or two later by a legacy of £100 from Mr. Robert Booth.

The actual number of children educated in the Charity School during this period of eighty years is not recorded, but can hardly have exceeded three hundred and sixty-five.

The cost per annum of each child is estimated in the Abstract as being £1 5s. 2d. up to 1741, rising to as much as £3 19s. 11d. in 1758 and onwards.

It is obvious that such educational results as have been noted above, however creditable from certain points of view, do not indicate any very general enthusiasm for the cause of education. But the growth and development of Bromley in the course of the nineteenth century happily synchronise with an ever-growing national recognition of the importance and value of education to a well-ordered State. In the early years of the new century, when this country and all Europe were distracted by wars, it was scarcely to be expected that anything would be done in such parochial matters as Charity Schools. There is indeed, as we have seen, reason to suppose that such effort as had been common in the past was now suspended except in so far as was necessary to keep the Bromley School in being. But in 1814, the year of Napoleon's abdication, the wave of educational enthusiasm, which had been slowly and silently gathering in the country, touched Bromley. It was determined to enlarge, upon a great scale, the facilities for the instruction of the children of the poorer class, and to convert the Charity School into a National School on what was known as the "Madras model" inaugurated by Andrew Bell.

Andrew Bell, a Scotchman, had been for some years Superintendent of the Madras Male Orphan Asylum in India. In this Institution he had developed a monitorial system of discipline and self-government, with so much success that he became a personage in the educational world. In 1811 Bell came to England and assisted in the foundation of "the National Society for promoting the education of the Poor" which was to operate in the exclusive interest of the Church of England. The need for some such organisation is sufficiently indicated by the fact that in the course of time the Society was instrumental in founding 12,000 National Schools. Of these Bromley National School was one. It came into being in 1814, and absorbed into itself the old Charity School and its site in the Gravel Pits. New buildings capable of accommodating two hundred and fifty children, a large playground in which lime-trees were a conspicuous feature, and a cottage for the schoolmaster replaced the ancient structure, and, in a short time, one hundred boys and eighty girls were being educated under the supervision of Mr. and Mrs. Campling.

In a *Short History of the Charity School* (still existing in manuscript) the Rev. J. E. Newell supplies some useful details as to the disposition of the original endowments.

"When," he writes, "in 1814 the schools on the National plan were established in Bromley, the children heretofore educated in the Charity Schools were transferred to them, and the Charity School Fund, being relieved from the expense of their education, it was thought proper to expend the whole of the interest, viz. £42 per annum, in clothing 30 poor children (15 boys and 15 girls)."

The annual income, he tells us, amounted to an average of about £157, raised by subscriptions, sale of needlework, and, he might have added, by the annual Charity Sermon. Of this income £80 was expended in the salary of the master, £50 in the salary of the mistress, £10 in fuel, and the balance covered repairs, insurance, books, stationery, etc. It is certainly a fact which may rouse the envy of the taxpayer of to-day that little more than a hundred years ago two hundred children could be educated at a cost of less than £160, or less than 16s. per head ! We can only hope that now, when the cost per child is about fifty times that amount, the quality of the education received has increased fifty-fold.

The new buildings for the school set up in 1814, though doubtless considered not only adequate but palatial at the time, were not constructed to endure. The material of which they were composed was woodwork purchased at second-hand, and it was necessary to accommodate the size of the schoolrooms not to the number of scholars but to the amount of the woodwork purchased. Thus a schoolroom 33½ feet by 29½ feet in dimensions had to serve the requirements of one hundred boys, and a second room, 29½ feet by 27 feet, provided cover for eighty girls. It is not surprising that in the course of forty years the National School House should have fallen into a grave state of dilapidation, so much so that the conscience of the town seems to have been awakened to a sense of something approaching a scandal.

At a large parish meeting called on February 11th, 1854, to consider the question, the opinion was freely expressed, and prevailed, that any attempts to repair the existing building would be a waste of effort, and also that the Gravel Pits site was not in fact any longer suitable to the purposes of a school. It was determined to set on foot a public subscription, and to seek for a suitable site where adequate schools might be erected.

The difficulty in connection with a site was solved by the action of the Bishop of Rochester, Dr. Murray, who gave, with the consent of the Rev. James King, who held a rectorial lease on the property, an acre of land in a field (afterwards known as School Field) lying to the eastward of Bromley College. The response to a public appeal for funds was met by contributions amounting to over £1,100. A committee was immediately formed, plans were submitted by Mr. St. Aubyn, and his estimate for a school which would accommodate four hundred and fifty children, boys girls, and infants, was ultimately reduced to £2,200. Tenders were made by several builders, the lowest tender, £1,883, by Mr. Harris of Croydon being accepted. The work was promptly put in hand, and was eventually completed at an inclusive cost of about £2,700, that sum being derived from the public subscriptions, from the sale of the old site and buildings, and from £1,100 contributed by the committee of the Council of Education. The new school was completed, and opened for use, on July 6th, 1855, and presented to the eye a sightly, indeed an imposing appearance. A succession of gables, the central one crowned by a bell turret, produced a pleasing æsthetic effect, and a substantial residence at each end for the master and mistress contributed both to the adornment and to the convenience of the structure as a whole.

The recreations of the children were amply provided for by a spacious playground at the back of the school, and in the course of a few years the erection of swings, horizontal bars, giant strides, and other gymnastic appliances supplied the elements of a physical training which to-day is regarded as one of the essentials of a true education, but which, fifty years ago, was very commonly ignored.

From the first inception of the new school it conclusively proved its value. In the course of a few years each department, Boys, Girls, and Infants, was full to overflowing, notwithstanding the fact that supplementary schools were established in 1865 both at Farwig and at Plaistow. In the Infant Department especially more accommodation was necessary, for, with the construction of the new buildings, a previously existing infant school was incorporated into the National School. This infant school had been established at Plaistow in 1847, and was conducted in an iron building situated at the back of what is now St. Mary's Church. It was supported by voluntary contributions, and was under the charge of a committee of ladies, who, on an income never exceeding £60 a year, were able to provide the rudiments of education for over three hundred and seventy children. In 1855 the number of infants in this Plaistow school exceeded one hundred, and their transference to the new National School made heavy demands upon its space. In 1869 the Bromley National School was so overcrowded that it was judged to be inadequate to the requirements of the parish. A Scheme of Extension was proposed. Subscriptions were invited and received to the extent of £150, and the enlargement and general sanitary improvement of the buildings were satisfactorily accomplished by Messrs. Payne & Balding in 1870 and 1871.

This was the precise period when Mr. Forster's Education Act of 1870 established the system of School Boards for the administration of education in the country. By the Act these Boards were not to come into operation unless the voluntary system had clearly shown itself to be inefficient, and it was, not unnaturally, one of the primary objects of church school managers to keep their schools clear of a School Board.

The Bromley National School was in no immediate danger. Its premises had just been brought up-to-date, and though the rapid growth of the town implied a corresponding demand for educational facilities, it was hoped that by further extensions, by the establishment of additional schools at Mason's Hill and Bromley Common, and by the enlargement of existing schools in the surrounding districts, the threat of a School Board could be successfully met. But by the Act of 1870 a Government Board of Education had been brought into existence with rights of inspection over all schools, whether ' provided ' or ' unprovided.' In 1886 the Education Department reported to the school managers that there was a grave deficiency in the supply of accommodation for education in Bromley. In the following year it was reported that the existing schools were insufficient, to the extent of six hundred and ten children, to provide for the needs of the town. All attempts to deal with the situation locally were met with hopeless failure, notably an effort initiated by Mr. T. Davis to establish a " British School " on non-sectarian lines. In 1887 the Education Department was informed that Bromley was taking steps to form a School Board.

A manifesto directed against the Nonconformists at this very moment did not improve the situation. All teachers and monitors were notified that they were expected to attend only Church of England Sunday Schools, if they attended any, and not Nonconformist Sunday Schools. Feeling ran high in the town. On May 5th, 1888, the elections to the first Bromley School Board were held, and thus the control of the National Schools, which had so long been entirely in the hands of the Church, passed to some extent into the hands of the elected representatives of the people.

The *Bromley Record* for April 1888 gives a list of the candidates for the nine seats, viz. :

Church Party .	.	Rev. A. G. Hellicar.
,, ,, .	.	Rev. R. I. Woodhouse.
,, ,. .	.	Mr. T. Davis.
,, ,, .	.	Mr. W. H. Bosanquet.
,, ,, .	.	Mr. G. Weeks, Sen.
,, ,, .	.	Mr. J. Batten.
Nonconformist	.	Mr. A. Gurney Smith.
,,	.	Mr. G. Pamphilon.
,,	.	Mr. J. Watson.
Wesleyan	.	Mr. J. H. Hall.
Independent .	.	Mr. C. W. Gedney.
,,	.	Mr. E. L. S. Horsburgh.

Later Miss M. L. Heppel and the Rev. Urwick Cooke entered the field, and Mr. E. L. S. Horsburgh and Mr. A. Gurney Smith withdrew and did not go to the poll. The results of the first election to the School Board were that the following were elected :

Mr. C. W. Gedney .	.	.	.	2,576
Mr. J. H. Hall	.	.	.	2,222
Miss M. L. Heppel .	.	.	.	2,189
Mr. J. Batten	.	.	.	1,817
Rev. A. G. Hellicar .	.	.	.	1,789
Mr. W. H. Bosanquet	.	.	.	1,607
Rev. R. I. Woodhouse	.	.	.	1,575
Mr. T. Davis .	.	.	.	1,341
Mr. G. Weeks (Sen.)	.	.	.	1,223

Mr. T. Davis was elected its first Chairman.

With the election of a School Board the distinctive history of the old Charity School, and of the National Schools of Bromley, may be said to end.

In 1902 Mr. Balfour's Education Act swept away the old School Boards, and placed the control of education in the hands of Education Committees composed of members of the municipal governing body, and of persons co-opted by them. Since that Act was passed, and possibly to some extent as a consequence of it, enormous advances both in elementary and secondary education have been made in this country. In the elementary schools of to-day it is scarcely possible to recognise the schools of a generation ago. In respect of school buildings, sanitary arrangements, the curriculum of the schools, the calibre and competence of the teaching staff, and the methods of instruction, there is no comparison to be made between education as we see it in operation and education as it was in the days of the School Boards.

I speak from some experience when I say that to visit any one of our elementary schools to-day, and to observe the daily practice of education therein, is to awaken to high and inspiring hopes for the future of the country. Accompanying this vast improvement in our elementary system we have the equally enormous advance in secondary education.

All over the country County Schools, as they are termed, have sprung up, and are affording so sound an education to our boys and girls that these schools have become a menace to our old-established Grammar Schools and even our Public Schools are not unaffected by them. Or rather instead of a menace, I should say a source of emulation, for none of our Grammar Schools can now afford to be anything else than as efficient as, if not more efficient than, our County Schools.

Bromley affords no exception to the general rule. The County School for Girls established in 1905, and that for Boys established five years later, have proved an unqualified success under the initial guidance of Miss C. M. Waters, B.A., and Mr. Reginald Airy, M.A.

These schools of course, and the elementary schools, are run by the public, for the benefit of the public, and at the public expense. We now pass to schools which are conducted by Educational Trusts or by private enterprise, and therefore outside the control of any public authority.

Of these the High School for Girls occupies a prominent position. Established in 1883 by the Girls' Public Day-School Trust, Limited, it entered from the first upon a prosperous career, largely as a consequence of the character and energy of its first headmistress, Miss M. L. Heppel, B.A. The position which Miss Heppel held in the educational world of Bromley was unique. Her striking personality commanded alike admiration, respect, and affection, and her influence extended far beyond the boundaries of the school over which she presided. She was elected a member of the first School Board in 1888. Either as a member of the Board or of the Education Committee she served the cause of education in Bromley for a continuous period of some forty years, for even after her retirement from the High School in 1908 she continued her public services to the town. As one who was privileged to know her well in days now long ago it is a pleasure to be able in these pages to pay a personal tribute to a fine, lofty, though unassuming character. Under her successors the High School continues to maintain the stamp and character impressed upon it by Miss Heppel.

Turning now from schools of a public or semi-public character to those conducted by private enterprise. I have before me a list of such schools containing about five-and-twenty entries. Of these ventures some were unimportant by reason of their very limited scope, and some were short-lived, but a few of them call for record as having contributed, or as still contributing, something distinctive and valuable to the life of the town. The record will begin nearly two centuries ago, when, about 1730, a boarding-school for boys was established in the High Street, on land adjoining the present premises of Messrs. G. Weeks & Sons. It flourished for over a century under the name of Rawes' Academy. The situation of Bromley, the purity and health-giving properties of its air, its proximity to London, and the vogue of Mr. James Scott, surgeon, were all factors which made for success in a scholastic venture, and Rawes' Academy soon achieved a distinguished position. At the height of its prosperity one hundred and fifty boys were receiving their education at the school.

By whom it was originally founded and the date when it fell into the hands of the Rawes family are not recorded, but in 1787-8 Messrs. Booth & Rawes are assessed in the Rate Books at £100, and in 1789 Richard Rawes was churchwarden. In the Census of 1801 the establishment of Richard Rawes contained 124 males and 9 females, from which we may infer that the number of boys then at the school was well over one hundred. On the death of Richard Rawes in 1814, at the age of seventy-two, the school passed into the hands of his son, Robert Booth Rawes, and either by him, or by members of the family, William and Joseph Rawes, or by all of them together, the institution continued to flourish until its sudden and un-explained extinction about 1850. There is a local tradition that Robert Booth Rawes was the original of Mr. Pickwick, and it is possibly not without significance, as associating Bromley with the immortal *Pickwick Papers*, that a family of stage-coachmen of the name of Weller is frequently mentioned in the records of the town.

In 1845 the school issued a monthly magazine, under the title *The Bromley Magazine*, of which one issue, No. 7, for October, may be seen in the Public Library.

" I have the Magazine," writes Mr. Philip Norman, " in one octavo volume. It is dedicated to Thomas Scott, Chaplain of Bromley College. It is not without merit, though unfortunately it contains very little topographical information except a list of wild plants found in the neighbour-hood of Bromley."

With the publication of the issue in December 1845 the magazine seems to have been discontinued.   It was apparently an expiring effort, for the school was closed soon after that date.

Mr. Norman records that he visited the site of Rawes' Academy in company with Mr. William Waring, the squire of Chelsfield, who had him-self been educated there.   Mr. Waring's recollection was that the boys suffered great hardships and discomfort, but probably not greater than was customary in those days.   The school in all likelihood was as well managed as others of its class in the earlier half of the nineteenth century ; otherwise it would scarcely have maintained its reputation for so many years.

Among the assistant masters at Rawes' School in the years immediately preceding its collapse was Thomas Morley, who saw his own opportunity in the loss of his position.   He determined to start a school upon his own account, and first at 68 High Street, and later at 74 High Street, the " Brom-ley Academy," or " Morley's Academy," continued the tradition of Rawes' School.   Among men of the older generation living in Bromley to-day there are several who, from personal experience, could write an adequate history of Morley's Academy, for Mr. George Weeks and some of his brothers, the late Mr. George Clinch, the antiquary, and three members of the Crowhurst family, Frank Wells and his illustrious brother the famous novelist, Mr. H. G. Wells, were among its pupils.   Ineffectual efforts have been made to induce Mr. H. G. Wells, perhaps the most distinguished of all Bromley's sons (for he was born at 47 High Street), to contribute some of his reminiscences of Bromley to this volume, but all that has been obtained from him is the assurance that his old schoolmaster, Thomas Morley, does not figure in any of his novels.

The boys at Morley's Academy, on account of the spirit and pugnacity which distinguished some of them, were known as " Morley's Bull Dogs," a name we should hardly associate with Mr. George Weeks, unless there was a period when he suffered such a violent " sea change " as effected a complete transformation of his character.

Mr. Morley himself was a man who, apart from a really considerable reputation as a teacher, played a conspicuous part in the life of the town, as, for many years a member of the Local Board, as a prime mover in the foundation of the Ratepayers' Association, and as a trustee of Lascoe's Charity, he closely identified himself both with the general interests of the town and its administration.

The picturesque brick house, known as " Ravenscroft," on the west side of Mason's Hill, in the possession of the Soames family, was for very many years a school maintained by someone named Jones, but whether Mr. or Mrs. Jones is not recorded.   In or about the years 1770–87 we find the house in the possession of John Compson, and being used by him as a school. Mr. George Norman, the first of that name born at the Rookery, was one of Compson's pupils. Later, 1790, an Edward Compson seems to have taken into partnership John Pieters, for they are rated jointly at £54 in the Rate Book for 1790–3, and in the following year " Pieters & Co." are rated at that figure. The school in 1798 fell entirely into the hands of John Pieters, and upon his death in 1812 it was conducted by members of the family ; then, in 1829, by the Rev. John Turnbull ; then, from 1836 to 1845, by James Craden. At some subsequent date, unknown, Ravenscroft ceased to be a school, and passed in 1856 into the tenancy of Mr. Eley Soames for use as his private residence. In his family it still remains. Its history, apart from its scholastic associations, is given in the chapter on Mason's Hill.

Notwithstanding the established position and continuous prosperity of Rawes' School and " Ravenscroft " there evidently was ample room in Bromley in the first half of the nineteenth century for other schools which could be run with profit and success.

Standing high in public estimation was a school conducted by Mr. Booth Hibbert, and subsequently by his son and others which certainly was in existence as early as 1797, and which had a flourishing career for about fifty years. It was established in an old-fashioned red-brick house, subsequently known as Redwood House, on the east side of Lower High Street. The school, on falling into the hands of the Rev. Samuel Crook, was removed farther south to Ravensfell, where Mr. Gerard Norman was one of the pupils.

In a house hard by, on the same side of the road, the Rev. John Baker carried on a school. Among his boys was George Sparkes, who, many years afterwards, on his retirement from the Madras Civil Service, bought the premises in which his schooldays had been spent. He christened the house " Neelgherries." It is from his widow that Bromley has acquired the Neelgherries property on which stands the Public Library.

About the middle of the nineteenth century we note a curious tendency for all existing schools to disappear, however long and flourishing their previous careers may have been. By 1880 there existed a real need for the establishment of a high-class school in the town, and the advent of Mr. John Gibson supplied that want by the foundation of Quernmore House School.

Mr. Gibson was a distinguished scholar of Trinity College, Cambridge, where he took high honours as eleventh classic in 1874. Coming to Bromley for the purpose of founding a school, he first took a house on Bromley Common, but very soon removed to Holwood Road, where two houses, Quernmore and Grasmere, with the considerable space then intervening between them conveniently served the dual purposes which Mr. Gibson had in view. For Quernmore was not originally exclusively a school for boys. The establishment combined the functions of a school with those of an army " Crammer," and from twenty to thirty young men, desirous of passing their examinations into the army, civil service, the universities, or the legal profession, constituted for a considerable time what was perhaps the more important side of the business.   In 1881 the writer of this History joined Mr. Gibson, first as an assistant master, and subsequently as his partner, the supervision of the house known as " Grasmere " being his special charge.   In 1891 the claims of his own University of Oxford called him away from Bromley.   But on the strength of his ten years' residence there he has been invited, thirty years later, to act as Bromley's historian, and in that capacity he is only too sensible that a residence of ten years affords but a very slender equipment for the adequate discharge of such a task.

Both departments of Quernmore continued to flourish to such an extent that it soon became necessary largely to increase the resident staff.   We were joined by two Oxford friends of mine, Mr. H. C. Bond and Mr. C. S. Hand, and in due course, by the influence of Mr. E. Solbé, Mr. Gustav Loly was added to the staff as an all-round man with a special knowledge of modern languages.

In the grounds we erected a commodious billiard-room for the recreation of the pupils, and laid down a hard tennis court for general use.   Among the boys in the school were twins, Wilfred and Herbert Baddeley, who from their childhood showed exceptional ability in the game of lawn tennis, and who were destined to be world champions.

When, for various reasons, the older members of the Quernmore staff separated themselves from the enterprise, Mr. Loly became Mr. Gibson's partner, and in due course they determined to separate the two departments, each partner becoming responsible for one, and one only.   Mr. Gibson with the adult pupils removed to Norwood, and carried on that side of the business there ; Mr. Loly took control of the school.

By 1896 Quernmore School had outgrown its accommodation in Holwood Road.   By that time the development of the Kinnaird estates at Plaistow as a residential area was in full operation, and Lord Kinnaird had ceased to reside at Plaistow Lodge.   Mr. Loly seized the opportunity thus offered to secure a lease of the mansion and extensive grounds immediately surrounding it, and transferred Quernmore School bodily to the convenient, not to say palatial, quarters which it has occupied since 1896.

Mr. Loly soon devoted himself actively to the public work of the town.   He became a member, and subsequently Chairman, of the School Board, and for two years Chairman of the Education Committee.   Under his hands Quernmore School developed rapidly in numbers, in efficiency, and in prestige.   His sudden and lamented death in November 1913 deprived the town of an enthusiastic and energetic public servant, and inflicted upon the school, of which he was in so large a degree the inspiration, an irreparable loss.

But the foundations of Quernmore were too solidly laid by Mr. Loly to be shattered even by such a calamity as his untimely death. Quernmore, under worthy successors, still continues to flourish and doubtless will long continue to maintain the traditions of its past.

A Preparatory School for Boys was founded in 1876 by the Rev. Edmund Fowle. In 1877 it was found necessary to move this school to quarters specially built for the purpose at Page Heath, Bickley. In 1887 this school, known as Amesbury House, was taken over by Messrs. E. H. Moore and E. A. Thompson, whose administration was attended with such success that in 1902 the whole establishment was transferred to Bickley Hall. The accidental death of Mr. Moore, who was drowned while bathing in 1903, placed Amesbury House School in the hands of Mr. E. Cotgreve Brown, and under his auspices the school maintained its long-established reputation. The present proprietors are Messrs. A. J. and B. S. Farnfield.

In addition to schools already mentioned, there were others, in the course of the nineteenth century, which existed for a time with varying success. Nothing survives of these but their names, or the names of their proprietors. There is no history of them which calls for record.

The popularity of Bromley as a centre for schools was by no means confined to the education of boys. From comparatively early times girls' schools, some of them of fashion and national repute, have existed in Bromley, one of the earliest being domiciled at Elmfield, Bromley Common, under the control of Miss Fanny Shepherd. In the first half of the nineteenth century Miss Shepherd was a notable personage in the world of girls' education. She was a particular friend of the Norman family, who, at the Rookery, were her next-door neighbours, and her connection extended to the high aristocracy of the land. Among her pupils was Miss Dalbiac, who married the sixth Duke of Roxburgh.

The extensive grounds attached to Elmfield added space and dignity to the amenities of the school, but the modern passion for athletic games had not yet developed. It was the age of " prunes, prisms, and deportment," and the only recorded recreation of the Elmfield young ladies was the practice of archery in an adjacent meadow, an exercise peculiarly adapted to exhibit the graceful lines of the female figure.

In the town itself Mrs. Hawkesworth, the wife of the celebrated doctor, conducted a school for girls in the ancient house on the east side of the Upper High Street; Eleonora Innocent, the second wife of James Norman, being one of her pupils. Early in the nineteenth century a Mrs. Durand was running a school for girls in the Church House, where she was succeeded by Mrs. Chalklin. Dunkin mentions three girls' schools as flourishing in his time (1815), Mrs. Brown's, Mrs. James's, and Mrs. Chalklin's, but their existence was not a lengthy one if Freeman's statement is correct that in 1832

" the boarding-school now in the possession of Mrs. Blaxland is the only one of celebrity for young ladies."

Of later schools those conducted by Miss Colbourne, 1836; the Misses Lamb, 1858; Miss Wheeler, 1864; Mrs. Cowtan, 1866; Miss Sturt, 1867; and Mrs. Fertel, 1870, serve to remind us of a persistent faith in Bromley as a field for educational ventures.

In a different category Mrs. Knott's mixed school for small children in South Street calls for mention, because under her care H. G. Wells received the first rudiments of his education.

In the days before technical schools came into existence—days when the opportunities for evening students to study any branch of art or science were very limited—institutions began to spring up all over the country known as science and art schools, where, under the auspices of South Kensington, pupils who had pursued a systematic course of study could gain a useful recognition of proficiency in the form of a South Kensington certificate. The value of such schools both as pioneers of our modern systems and as educational centres can scarcely be exaggerated, and many still living in Bromley can testify to the benefit derived therefrom. For Bromley was not behind-hand in establishing such an institution. In October 1873 classes in various departments of science and art were started in one of the elementary schoolrooms at Mason's Hill, the need for them being clearly shown by the fact that ninety students were attracted at the outset. The first secretaries, Mr. T. C. Dewey and Mr. Gurney Smith, were able to boast of thirty certificates gained in the first year of the venture, and these were presented to the successful students by Sir John Lubbock at a conversazione in the Town Hall in October 1874. This initial success seemed to justify an appeal in 1877 to the public for subscriptions with which to erect a permanent and suitable building to be known as the Bromley Science and Art School. The subscription list was headed by Mr. E. H. Scott with a contribution of £1,000, and the appeal generally was well supported by the public, and by such special efforts as a conversazione, a gathering which was not merely of local but of national importance in that the first telephones ever publicly seen in operation in this country were then exhibited by Mr. William James, the father of Alderman R. W. James, on January 15th and 16th, 1878.

A few weeks later the foundation-stone of the Science and Art School was laid by Mrs. E. H. Scott with much ceremony and many speeches. One speech in particular by one of the original students attracted special attention. The speaker was a young man destined in after years to make his mark upon the history of the town as Councillor, Alderman, Mayor, and citizen— Mr. George Weeks, Chairman of the committee responsible for the publication of this History.

The building which was ultimately erected was designed by Mr. John Sulman, and built by Mr. J. C. Arnaud at a cost of about £3,000. Its laboratory, and various class-rooms, for the study of art and science were well adapted to the primary needs of such an institution, and by November

1878 all was ready for the opening ceremonies, which partly consisted of a banquet in the Drill Hall at which Earl Sydney presided.

But in a very few years the activities of the school increased and developed to such a degree that its income was quite inadequate to its requirements. Recourse was had to the expedient of bazaars, and in two successive years, 1881 and 1882, this method of raising money was successfully adopted, the bazaar of 1882 being opened by H.R.H. the Duchess of Teck, mother of our present Queen. From this date, for a period of ten years, the school pursued its increasingly useful course as a public institution supported by private effort.

In 1886 the addition of a good chemical laboratory and a painting room added immensely to its educational value, the cost of this extension being defrayed by voluntary contributions, a grant from South Kensington, and by the liberality of Sir E. H. and Lady Scott, who had been bountiful friends to the school from the first.

But in 1892 the Bromley School of Science and Art was presented to the Local Board, and under this authority and that of the Urban District Council, which succeeded it, the school became a part of the municipal responsibilities of the town.

Having accepted an appointment in 1887 on the staff of the London Society for the Extension of University Teaching, it seemed to me highly desirable that a University Extension Centre should be formed in Bromley. A preliminary meeting of various people interested in the movement resulted in the formation of a committee, on which the Rev. A. G. Hellicar served as Chairman, Sir Gainsford Bruce, Q.C., as Treasurer, and Mr. H. C. Bond as Secretary. The first course of Extension Lectures given in Bromley was delivered by Mr. H. E. Malden, Secretary to the Royal Historical Society, on " English History in Shakespeare," and among early lecturers, Professor H. G. Seeley, F.R.S., on geology ; Dr. Samuel Rawson Gardiner, the eminent historian ; and Professor Churton Collins were conspicuous. The Extension Centre then established survives to the present day, and the convenience afforded by the fine lecture-room in the Public Library has long ago solved the original problem of finding a suitable hall for its requirements. It is to be hoped that a movement which has proved of incalculable value, over a period of forty years, to not a few of the inhabitants of the town, will in due course reach its jubilee, and then find itself only strengthened and invigorated to pursue its work as a valuable aid to adult education.

Perhaps this chapter, dealing as it does with education, is the most fitting place in which specially to commemorate a man whose many and varied activities could almost equally appropriately be recorded in several chapters of this History.

Mr. Thomas Davis, born in 1836, came to Bromley in 1862. Five years later he built a house for himself in Widmore Road, and lived in it till his death in 1917. From the first he took a warm interest in educational affairs,

ALDERMAN THOMAS DAVIS, J.P. (1836–1917).

Mayor of Bromley 1904–5, 1909–10, 1910–11.

From a photograph lent by Miss Davis.

and it was he who, in association with Mr. T. C. Dewey, was chiefly instrumental in starting the evening classes which in due course developed into the School of Science and Art. Of the classes and the school Mr. Davis became Honorary Secretary, and remained in that position until, at his instigation, the management was taken over by the Local Board. Under the Board he at once became Chairman of the committee who had charge of the school, and may be said to have remained so until his death, for at that time he was Chairman of the Higher Education Committee, into whose control the School of Science of Art had passed. There is no doubt that the welfare and prosperity of that institution owe more to Thomas Davis than to any other individual. His interest was not, however, restricted to that School. He was one of the few who recognised the need which existed for improved schools of another type, and it was largely due to him that the High School for Girls was established in 1883.

Later, during the agitations consequent upon the proposal or threat to set up a School Board, Mr. Davis, in conjunction with his friend and neighbour, Mr. James Scrutton, endeavoured to reconcile conflicting interests by the establishment of a " British School," which the various parties into which educational opinion was divided might unite in supporting. The project fell to the ground, and the advocates of a School Board prevailed. Of the first School Board, elected in 1888, Thomas Davis was chosen its first Chairman, a position which he held until defeated in the election of 1891. With the coming of the Education Act of 1902, Mr. Davis was elected to the Education Committee brought into being by that Act, and succeeded to the chairmanship in 1905. In this capacity he not only resumed his active association with elementary education, but was prominent in the formation of two secondary schools, one for boys in Hayes Lane and one for girls in Nightingale Lane. In these schools he maintained his interest to the last.

But education was only one side of Mr. Davis's activities. For nineteen years he was a member of the Local Board, and when that body was succeeded by the Urban District Council he was among the members elected to serve upon it. Four times he filled the chair, the first occasion being the Jubilee Year, 1897.

While a member of the Council he was instrumental in securing the adoption of the Public Libraries Act, and it was in a very great measure, if not entirely, due to him that Mr. Andrew Carnegie made his generous gift to the town, and himself came down to take part in the opening ceremonies of the new Library in May 1906.

One of his last duties as a member of the District Council was to sign, as the first citizen, the petition to H.M. King Edward asking for the grant of a Charter of Incorporation.

The charter being granted, Mr. Davis was elected on the Town Council, and was one of the first six Aldermen of the Borough. There is indeed little doubt that he could have become its first Mayor had he not himself entertained the opinion that the services of Mr. Frank Griffith as Chairman of the Incorporation Committee had been such as to entitle him, before any other, to that position. Mr. Davis, however, had not long to wait. He became Mayor in 1904, and again in 1910 and 1911.

In addition to his public work for the secular interests of the town he was an enthusiastic churchman. For twenty years he was Secretary to the Ruridecanal Conference, was teacher and superintendent for many years at the Parish Church Sunday school, and assistant in the choir and at the lectern to the Vicar of St. John's.

Thomas Davis was a man of considerable force of character, a leader among his fellows by example and precept. Without question he was one of Bromley's great men, to whom the Borough is indebted for the large share he took in securing the provision of many of the advantages which it enjoys to-day.

An excellent portrait of him by Wilfred de Glehn hangs in the Council Chamber at the Municipal Buildings.

Chapter XIII

INSTITUTIONS AND SOCIETIES

AN account of the various institutions and societies which have existed or which still exist in Bromley involves a rather wide survey over a varied field of activity. For in the course of a century, organisations in almost every department of life have come into being, which, for the sake of convenience and clarity, may be classified under sectional headings. The headings which suggest themselves as being most suitable to the purpose are:

    (*a*) Educational and Social,
    (*b*) Medical,
    (*c*) Philanthropic,
    (*d*) Social and Economic,
    (*e*) Musical,

and it is under this arrangement that I propose to group the various entries in the long list of societies which has been supplied to me.

(*a*) EDUCATIONAL AND SOCIAL.

Foremost both in importance and in date of origin stands *The Bromley Literary Institute* founded in 1845.

A century ago opportunities and facilities for obtaining a knowledge of books, and of the current news in the newspapers, were strictly limited to the individual, who had to supply his own requirements, and adapt those requirements to the depth of his purse. Public libraries, reference libraries, reading-rooms, were unknown outside the universities and a few large towns, and a lending library, where it existed, probably contained little more than what may be called the offscourings of literature, and survivals of extinct divinity. Of public halls and lecture-rooms which could be used for the purposes of popular education and entertainment there were none, except in so far as a local inn could supply occasional accommodation for a town meeting. The general dullness and stagnation of life only two or three generations back constitute a very startling contrast with the conditions of variety, excitement, and somewhat feverish sensationalism which characterise the present age.

It is less than a century ago that the country at large began to stir under new impulses which were in part intellectual and in part social, and out of these impulses was generated the idea of literary institutes. They were to provide accommodation for their members in rooms where the current literature of the day was collected together for perusal on the premises, and the formation of a library of books was to enable members to obtain access to a far wider range of literature than their own private purses could supply. The assembly of members under the same roof made for social intercourse, and where the institution could boast of a good-sized room, capable of seating a numerous company, it was possible to organise entertainments, lectures, conversaziones, and so forth, all contributing to the intellectual and social life of the locality.

The originators of such institutions are unknown, but it was not long after their first inauguration in the country that Bromley fell into line with the movement, and the Bromley Literary Institute was founded. On October 24th, 1845, a meeting was called to consider the formation of such a society. Among the names of those attending this meeting we find such familiar ones as Ilott, Latter, Baxter, Acton, Eaton, Nettlefold, Ray, Sparkes, Tweedy.

It was unanimously resolved to carry the scheme into effect, and two rooms were secured at 129 High Street at a rental of £16 a year. Mr. G. W. Norman was elected President, a position which he retained for thirty-eight years. Mr. Robert Booth Latter accepted the Treasurership, and Messrs. J. Loveday and S. P. Acton became joint Honorary Secretaries. As Librarian and Custodian Mr. Jabez Wood was appointed under a provisional arrangement which it was hoped might result in a permanent engagement.

The subscription for membership was fixed at ten shillings per annum, and at the first general meeting of members, held on the last day of 1845, it was reported that the Society consisted of one hundred and twenty-four members, and that a sum of £125 was in hand to meet financial requirements.

One of the primary objects of the institution was to build up a library. It has been said that there are three methods of forming a library—by purchase, by gift, and by acquisition. The latter method applies rather to libraries acquired by individuals than to those accumulated by institutions. It seems clear that the balance in hand was devoted very largely to the method of purchase, for, though many gifts of books were made, large numbers were bought. At the first annual meeting of the Society, in January 1847, it was announced that the library then contained over eleven hundred volumes, and that the balance in hand was £6 13s. 8d.

Another great object of the institution was to provide entertainments for the members. Obviously two rooms in the High Street were quite inadequate to this design, but the difficulty was overcome by the public spirit of Mr. Wm. Pawley, the landlord of the White Hart Hotel, who offered the use of his Assembly Room for lectures, readings, musical entertainments, and so forth. An attempt was made to develop the musical talents of the members by forming within the membership a " Vocal Association." This proved to be so vocal, not to say vociferous, that the landlord of the premises at 129 High Street threatened to eject the institution, bag and baggage, on account of the noise, and the nuisance created thereby. Nothing further is heard of the "Vocal Association," which, apparently, succumbed to the landlord's protest.

For some eighteen years the accommodation in the High Street proved to be sufficient for the requirements of the institution, which numbered during that period an average membership of about a hundred and seventy. In 1862, however, under the secretaryships of Messrs. W. W. Baxter and J. Nettlefold, a large increase in members with an ever-increasing library called for a change to more commodious quarters. In 1864 the Society migrated to temporary premises in White Hart Slip, but this was only preparatory to securing adequate and permanent accommodation in the newly built Town Hall. Here, in the rooms now occupied by the Prudential Assurance Company, the institution flourished for over twenty years, migrating at last, in 1887, to the premises in Widmore Road which it still continues to occupy.

The institution was established to provide the conveniences of a library and reading-room for those who wished in quiet and in comfort to secure access to standard literature, and to the current newspapers and periodicals of the day. Occasional lectures by prominent local persons served at once a social and an educational purpose, which no other organisation than a Literary Institute existed to supply. But such institutions have met the fate which commonly befalls pioneers. They have beaten out the path for others to walk at ease. The adoption of the Public Libraries Act, and the consequent construction of a Free Public Library with all the opportunities and amenities which it affords, the introduction of the University Extension system of lectures, and of the popular lectures under the auspices of the Gilchrist Trust, have together tended to usurp the place which literary institutes once filled, and Bromley's institution has suffered with the rest.

In 1892 the Public Libraries Act was adopted by the town, and in December of 1894 the Bromley Public Library was established in an annexe of the Science and Art Buildings in Tweedy Road, where it remained until the construction of the existing Carnegie Library in 1903. The effect of these changes upon the Literary Institute was immediate and continuous. A membership which in 1894 amounted to two hundred and seventy-five had sunk to one hundred in 1903, and has scarcely exceeded that number since that date. But it still remains a quiet haven of rest and comfort to those who do not care for the promiscuity of a public library, and its collection of books, more than seven thousand in number, is in itself a title to continued existence and support from the residents in the town.

Among the activities of the Literary Institute in bygone days there is one which calls for special reference, for it contributed in a marked degree to the pleasurable anticipations and amusement of the Bromley populace, and to the satiric powers of some of her leading citizens. This was the annual Christmas entertainment, which, while affording opportunities for festivities of a general and seasonable character, was made the occasion for a topical recital in which any notable occurrences of the past year were embodied in a set of humorous and satirical verses. The deeds, or misdeeds, of the local governing authorities frequently lent themselves to the purposes of the poet, who, if he possessed a happy turn for wit and versification, could minister effectively to that keen enjoyment which the governed always experience in the castigation and criticism of their governors.

Among the authors of these annual skits the names should be preserved of Mr. Nettlefold (1860), H. Deane (1863), (1865), Dillon Croker (1868), and R. V. Harman (1884).

Extracts from these Prologues are used occasionally, in their appropriate context, in various chapters of this book. Their general style may be illustrated by a few examples.

> " These Yankee notions too our tradesmen mimic,
>   And one which specially we must deplore—
> With some it seems to be an epidemic
>   To deal in everything, and run a store !
> For instance—Pay a visit to your Draper,
>   And ask for gloves, or dress for Fancy Ball,
> He'll try to sell you pens and ink and paper,
>   And other things you don't require at all."

The Town Hall and John Hall, the Bromley philanthropist, are associated in 1884, in the following passage :

> " Which is the *Great* Town *Hall* ?   You should remember,
>   That is if you the local papers con,
> Because they advertise him each December
>   And, well we know, his Christian name is John.
> He is the greatest Hall the Town possesses,
>   And kind philanthropy, we may be sure,
> Will well support him, while his Maker blesses
>   His welcome mission to the humble poor."

One is tempted to linger over these effusions which roused so much enthusiasm in their day ; but the topical and personal allusions of forty or fifty years ago would be practically unintelligible to the present age.

Among the institutions of the town the *Bromley and County Club* holds, and has held since its inception, an important and indispensable place. When I first came to Bromley in 1881 nothing of the kind existed, all opportunities for social intercourse being limited to a man's individual domestic circle of friends and acquaintances, or to the societies, or political or sports clubs, to which he happened to belong.

The idea of forming a purely Social Club, entirely unconnected with political opinions, originated in 1889, and found ready support. The members were provided with temporary accommodation in rooms placed at their disposal by the proprietor of the White Hart Hotel, but in the same year suitable premises were secured in the newly constructed Grand Hall building, where the Club still retains its quarters. A handsome and commodious reading-room on the ground floor has above it an equally commodious room which contains two billiard tables. A dining-room, card-room, two bedrooms and offices supply members with most of that which they can reasonably require, and, under the able secretaryship of Mr. J. H. Lepper, whose services in that capacity have been continuous since the start, the Club rapidly reached, and has consistently maintained, its position as one of the most comfortable and most sociable provincial clubs.

The Naturalists' Society was founded in October 1888 as the result apparently of a simultaneous inspiration which seized the Rev. H. Soames of Ravenscroft and Mr. William Baxter of the Broadway. As the result of a meeting held at Ravenscroft Schoolroom, attended by A. E. Collings, F. Lewis, H. H. Mellon, G. H. Payne, and others, it was decided to form a Society. Eventually Mr. Justice Gainsford Bruce became President, Mr. Soames Chairman, with Mr. Baxter as Hon. Secretary. For the convenience of Mr. Soames, who was incapacitated by lameness, the meetings of the members were to be held at Ravenscroft.

A Conversazione and Exhibition held in 1889 in the Parish Room was so successful that, in the following year, it was found necessary to engage the Town Hall, and subsequently the Drill Hall, for the purposes of the Society. The general interest in what the Society was doing was notable, but the membership remained small until it was realised that many would not join if the meetings continued to be held in a private house. The situation was a delicate one, for any change of venue almost necessarily excluded the presence of the Chairman. Mr. Soames's patriotism, however, triumphed over his personal predilections. The use of rooms was secured at the Literary Institute; the Society flourished, and much good work was done. On the departure of Mr. Baxter from Bromley in 1890, Mr. H. H. Mellon became the Secretary, and held the office for thirteen years.

Apart from Exhibitions, the reading of scientific papers and their discussion, the Society printed some records and also formed a valuable collection of scientific books, cabinets of specimens, etc. When the end came, as it not unnaturally did, in October 1914, the question arose as to the disposition of the Society's property. A proposition to hand it over to the Public Library was not acceptable. The cabinets were eventually divided up among the members, and the books were entrusted to certain named persons to be held by them in trust for any members of the Society who might desire to have access to them in the future.

(b) MEDICAL INSTITUTIONS

Of all institutions, hospitals perhaps have the best claim to the epithet 'philanthropic.' Nevertheless, and because of their importance, I am including them in this chapter under the distinct heading of Medical, in order to distinguish them clearly from those charitable organisations of a different character which will be treated in the next section.

There are two hospitals in Bromley—the *Cottage Hospital*, now titled the Bromley and District Hospital, and the *Phillips Memorial Homœopathic Hospital*. Of these, the Cottage Hospital was the first to be established.

Up to 1869 no institution of the kind existed in the town. In that year a committee was formed to consider the establishment of a hospital in Bromley, with the result that two small cottages were acquired in Pieter's Lane (now Cromwell Avenue). Mr. Eldon Watts consented to act as Honorary Secretary, and Drs. W. T. Beeby and H. Willey accepted the position of Honorary Medical Officers.

It was at once evident that a sorely felt local need was at last being recognised, though not adequately supplied. Applications for treatment were far in excess of the accommodation. As the scheme from the first commanded very influential support, it was possible in 1875 entirely to demolish the existing cottages, and on the site to erect a new building more adequate in every way to immediate and future needs.

On the completion of the work Mr. T. C. Dewey assumed the office of Honorary Secretary, and Dr. H. J. Ilott took the place of Dr. Willey on the visiting staff.

From 1875 onward the external history of the hospital is little more than the story of continuous demands upon its resources, and continuous enlargement, made necessary by the rapidly increasing population. In 1886 extensions were carried out which provided accommodation for twenty beds : ten years later a new wing, attached at a cost of £2,000, enabled the number of beds to be increased to thirty. In 1896 Mr. and Mrs. Wheeler-Bennett erected a children's ward for eight cots, in memory of their son, and three years later Mr. Wheeler-Bennett gave £4,000 for its endowment.

In 1900–1 further developments required the expenditure of £1,500 ; in 1910 two new wards were added at a cost of £10,000, the number of beds being thus increased to forty-two, and in 1911 the enlarged and modernised hospital was formally opened by Constance Dowager Countess of Derby.

Increases in the medical staff proceeded *pari passu* with extensions of the structure. In 1901 five local doctors and a dental surgeon accepted positions as medical officers to the hospital. Three London consulting surgeons and a consulting obstetric physician were enlisted in the service in case of emergencies. In 1905 two London consulting physicians were added to the honorary staff, and the number of local doctors upon the staff was increased to six.

The names of all those who have thus rendered devoted service to the hospital and the town are too numerous to be included in a general history of Bromley. The roll of doctors, dentists, matrons, secretaries, and

1869

1875

1910

BROMLEY COTTAGE HOSPITAL

299

treasurers is long and honourable. There is, however, one name which is identified with the Cottage Hospital almost from its inception—that of Sir Thomas Dewey, who as Mr. T. C. Dewey was its Honorary Secretary from 1875 to 1880, and its Honorary Treasurer from 1908 to 1924. Throughout fifty years of a very strenuous life Sir Thomas's interest in the institution never flagged, and for more than twenty of those years he served it in an official capacity.

The *Phillips Memorial Hospital* takes its origin from a homœopathic dispensary which was opened in Bromley in 1865.

This was opened under the charge of Dr. Alfred Orlando Jones, M.D., M.C., M.R.C.S.E., L.R.C.P., who, however, in 1876, surrendered it to Dr. Robert Edward Phillips, B.A., M.D., C.M.

Dr. Phillips was the son of a Harley Street physician, and had received the advantage of a sound education. He took his bachelor's degree from Clare College, Cambridge, and acquired his medical degrees at Edinburgh University. It was immediately after obtaining his M.D., in 1876, that he established himself in Bromley as successor to Dr. Jones. He built for himself Burlington House, 118 Widmore Road, in which he lived until his death, and by his genial manners and wide sympathy he gained the esteem and affection of all classes in the community.

It was, therefore, only natural that upon his death in 1888 a general desire should have been expressed to erect some fitting memorial to his memory, and as it was known that he himself had contemplated the building of a small hospital as an adjunct to his dispensary, no proposal seemed more fitting than to carry out his project. His successor, Dr. E. M. Madden, M.D., threw himself heartily into the plan, and in October 1888 a foundation meeting was held which resulted in the opening of the first Phillips Memorial Hospital in August 1889. This was situated at the junction of Park Road with Widmore Road.

The demand for homœopathic treatment led Dr. Madden to associate with his practice Dr. H. Wynne Thomas, and the pressure upon the Memorial Hospital became greater than it could bear.

Moreover, the houses which composed it were damp and unhealthy, and it was felt that if anything effective was to be done, a new building on an entirely new site would alone meet the case.

On the committee of the hospital was Mr. W. Willett—the man subsequently and for ever famous as the author of the Daylight Saving Act. It was he who most strongly opposed the plan of rebuilding on the old site, and it was he again who was instrumental in securing from Mr. Coles Child, who was just about to present the White Hart Field to the town, a suitable site within that enclosure.

Thus, on June 9th, 1900, the existing Phillips Memorial Hospital came into being, still further extensions being added in 1907 through the beneficence of Mrs. Dobbing, who desired to perpetuate the memory of her husband.

(c) PHILANTHROPIC CHARITIES, AND SOCIETIES

Apart from hospitals, three charitable organisations existed in Bromley, the Philanthropic Society, established in 1841; John Lascoe's Charity, founded in 1854; and the Bromley Charitable Society, formed in 1885.

The formation of the *Philanthropic Society* is closely associated with the name of John Hall, and was one of the innumerable methods which he used for alleviating the lot of his poor and suffering fellow-creatures. To this work John Hall devoted both his life and substance, even to the extent of his own impoverishment. The fine portrait of him which hangs in the Public Library should serve to keep alive the memory of perhaps the noblest of Bromley's sons, who, in a long life extending over almost the whole of the nineteenth century, was animated by that large and generous spirit of humanity and sympathy which has won for him the name by which he will be ever remembered—" the Bromley Philanthropist."

The Society was established on January 6th, 1841, at the Duke's Head in the market-place, with the title of " The Philanthropic Friendly Society." Members of the Society paid an entrance fee of 1*s*., and met every Wednesday evening in the winter, and every alternate Wednesday in the summer. The aim of the Society was to give temporary relief to the necessitous residents in the parish, under a strict guarantee that each case relieved was really a deserving one. This was effected by the rules of the Society, which laid it down that every member had the right to propose, at the meetings, that such-and-such a case was worthy of relief, but only after a full personal investigation of the merits of the case proposed. The proposition was then considered by the members present, and, if agreed to, relief was given either in food or coals according to the requirements of the applicant.

In 1855 the funds of the Society were materially increased by a legacy of £400 from John Lascoe, which was invested in the hands of trustees. A further legacy of £50 accrued from the estate of Mr. Samuel Poole Acton in 1885.

The Society still continues to carry on its beneficent work on the lines of its original foundation. In recent times the name of Mr. Alfred Wright was prominently associated with it, Mr. Wright acting as its Treasurer for sixteen years.

Lascoe's Charity.—The Lascoe family established itself in Bromley early in the seventeenth century, carrying on at 39 High Street the business of saddlers. The last representatives of the family were Thomas and John Lascoe and a sister, Elizabeth. Living next door to them, at No. 40, was Mr. W. Baxter, chemist, who was not only a neighbour but an intimate friend. The Lascoes had accumulated a little fortune, and having no relatives they consulted Mr. Baxter as to an appropriate way of disposing of it. He suggested that, as they had made the money as tradesmen in the town, they might leave it in trust for the benefit of tradesmen who had fallen on evil days, a proposal which commended itself to the brothers.

Upon John's death in 1850 the Charity bearing his name was set on foot and came into being in 1854. By his will a sum of £2,880 in Consols was bequeathed in trust for the formation of a " Decayed Tradesmen's Charity Fund,"

" The dividends whereof are to be paid and applied by 4 Trustees, inhabitants of Bromley, according to certain Rules approved by the Charity Commissioners."

The capital itself was to stand in the names of the official Trustees of Charitable Funds, under the Charitable Trusts Act of 1853. Copies of the rules of the Trust and of its accounts were to be from time to time deposited in the Parish Chest.

The original trustees, " being inhabitants of Bromley," were R. Latter, S. P. Acton, R. J. Payne, and John Innous, and on the lists are the names of W. W. Baxter, John Nash, Christopher Eaton, Edward Isard, George Weeks, Edward Dunn, and G. Shillcock.

On the death of Elizabeth Lascoe in 1853 a further sum was added to the Trust. She bequeathed £194 11s. 11d. in Consols on condition that the dividends arising from her specific legacy were to be divided between four widows of master tradesmen of Bromley, to be selected by the trustees. This bequest was largely increased in 1885 by a legacy of £800 to the Trust from Mr. Samuel Poole Acton, and thus the Elizabeth Lascoe bequest has been able to supplement in a really useful and effective manner the charitable designs of her brothers.

The terms of both these charities are to be seen inscribed on panels in the tower of the Parish Church.

Of the Lascoe family it may here be recorded that a William Lascoe was High Constable from 1782 to 1788, having held the office of "borsholder," or petty constable, in 1781 and 1782. John Lascoe, the founder of the Charity, volunteered for the Defence of the Realm in Trafalgar year (1805), and successively filled the offices of churchwarden, High Constable, and overseer.

The Bromley Charitable Society.—This Society, founded in 1885, was established for the purpose of organising charitable relief throughout the town.

A general committee of seventy residents was subdivided into district committees whose business it was to be cognisant of the needs of the respective districts. For this purpose the town was divided into six districts— the Town, Plaistow, New Bromley, Widmore, Mason's Hill, and Bromley Common.

The public support received, and the quality of the work done, show that the system, by which overlapping and waste were avoided, was thoroughly sound and beneficial. Though the Society itself ceased to exist in or about 1914, its extinction was only due to the fact that the organisation of the Mayor's Fund rendered it no longer necessary. Since the war it has been revived under the name of the Bromley Benevolent Association.

(d) ECONOMIC AND SOCIAL-ECONOMIC ORGANISATIONS

The term ' economic organisation ' is used in order to cover such an institution as the *Bromley Savings Bank*, the primary purpose of which was economic rather than social or philanthropic. The term ' social-economic ' is used to imply such organisations as came into existence in order, partly, to further material and economic interests, and, partly, to serve the purposes of social intercourse. In the latter category I place such institutions as working peoples' clubs, friendly societies, Y.M.C.A., and any similar societies.

Of purely economic institutions the earliest to arise was the Bromley Savings Bank, founded in 1816 in order to serve the needs of the seventeen parishes comprising the division of Bromley, and of any persons resident in the county of Kent, or in any neighbouring parish in the county of Surrey.

It was founded by Benjamin Harenc, Jnr., of Foot's Cray, who placed the bank under the control of a President, Vice-President, and any number of trustees not exceeding twenty, and a Managing Committee. The hours of business, which was transacted at the bank's premises, 75 High Street, were fixed from 12 noon till 2 p.m. on Mondays, separate periods of these hours being allotted to the reception of deposits (from 12 till 1.30), and for the payments to depositors (1.30 to 2). The rate of interest paid to depositors was originally £3 6s. 8d., subsequently reduced to £2 18s. 6d.

That the bank served a very real public need is shown by its continued and prosperous existence for a period of nearly fifty years. In 1863 such banks were rendered unnecessary by the passing of the Post Office Savings Bank Act, which created a Savings Bank out of almost every Post Office. Consequently on December 31st, 1863, the Bromley Savings Bank automatically closed, its undischarged accounts passing into the hands of the Post Office authorities.

The history of the bank is one of uninterrupted usefulness and prosperity, save for a crisis in 1856 when its actuary levanted with nearly £1,000 of the bank's money. By means, however, of voluntary contributions, promptly supplied by the inhabitants of the town and neighbourhood, the deficiency was made good, and no loss was sustained by depositors. The mere fact that so large a sum was so quickly forthcoming is evidence of the general esteem in which the institution was held. For some years the Organising Secretary of the bank was Mr. George Dennen, who, on its extinction, entered the service of the then London & County Bank, and in due course became the manager of its branch in Bromley.

Four of the ledgers of the old Savings Bank are now in the possession of the Town Council by virtue of a gift from Mr. Alfred Wright.

Passing now to social-economic institutions, the first place in point of date, and perhaps of interest, falls to *the Female Friendly Society*, founded over a hundred years ago, in 1821. It anticipated in quite a remarkable degree those measures of industrial insurance which have been comparatively recently placed upon the Statute Book.

The original articles and tables of the Society—published in 1821 by J. Dunkin—are before me as I write. After a somewhat long preface the aims of the Society are set forth in a series of articles. The two first articles are worth quotation in full :

" This Society has for its object to enable women of the poorer classes of the community, by the payment of small sums while in health and strength, to assure to themselves needful comforts in sickness, and honourable support in age.

" To the attention of the poor it is therefore earnestly recommended, as a means by which they may be enabled, in hours of sorrow and infirmity, to claim as a right those necessaries and comforts which, without it, they must painfully, perhaps unsuccessfully, solicit as alms."

There follows a series of actuarial tables showing the amount, according to age, to be contributed weekly to entitle the contributor :

(*a*) to a weekly allowance in sickness ;
(*b*) to an annuity of £10 after the age of fifty-five ;
(*c*) to an annuity of £25.

The Society was open for membership to all women of good character between the ages of fifteen and fifty, provided they were neither " infirm, blind, or subject to fits."

The administration of the Society was placed in the hands of four trustees (the original trustees being Stewart Erskine, William Roberts, Major Rohde, and John Wells), and a committee of eight ladies, the Treasurer and Secretary being also, originally, ladies, and they, by article 2, pledge themselves that they voluntarily undertake the office " from benevolent motives, and without view to profit or advantage."

The finance of the Society rested upon entrance fees (2*s.* for an unmarried woman, 4*s.* for a married one), quarterly contributions, and benevolent subscriptions and donations, and from these resources the Society was able to flourish for many years. It was indeed an insurance society, conducted on the general principles of insurance, but irrespective of any idea of private profit.

Extracts from its actuarial tables will best show the nature and extent of the benefits derived. Thus—a quarterly payment of 3s. 3d. by a member under twenty-one on admission entitled that member, up to the age of sixty-five, to a weekly allowance in sickness of 6s. a week while bedridden, 3s. during convalescence, and 10s. on the birth of each child, and to a weekly payment of 3s. a week between the ages of sixty-five and seventy ; of 6s. after the age of seventy.

Similarly a payment of 10s. 2d. quarterly by a member aged 25 on admission carried an annuity of £10 after the age of 55.

A payment by such a member of £1 5s. 5d. quarterly entitled her to an annuity at 55 of £25.

It is a curious fact that though the Society was still in existence in 1858, but not in 1868, no information is forthcoming as to the causes or date of its extinction.

(e) MUSICAL SOCIETIES

The record of musical societies may be initiated by a reference to *The Musical Nunnery*, which was formed in 1787 in order to advance the musical education of twelve young ladies. The only notice I have of it reads very much like an advertisement by an enterprising entrepreneur, for it states that Signor Tenducci established the Nunnery to train twelve ladies in the theory and practical knowledge of vocal and instrumental music—for opera, stage, or otherwise. The Nunnery was perhaps rather a school than a society, but even so, its early date gives it a significance in the musical history of Bromley.

It was not, however, until a much later date that definite societies began to be formed to educate the musical taste of the Bromley public. The first serious effort in that direction resulted in 1860 in the organisation of singing classes, which were held, under the direction of Mr. West, at Miss Mumford's schoolroom in Market Square.

This was followed by a Choral Union, which met at Harman's in the High Street and dates from 1863. Ten years later *The Bromley Vocal Association* came into being, and met at the Drill Hall, its principal object being to give good concerts once or twice a year, or to render an oratorio. The performances of *Judas Maccabeus* in the autumn of 1874 and of *The Ancient Mariner* in 1876 were among its principal achievements.

From 1869 to 1874 Mr. Walter Latter, R.A.M., organist of the Parish Church, conducted a Choral Society which was extremely popular, and gave a series of annual concerts.

With the advent in 1880 to Bromley of Mr. F. Lewis Thomas, organist to St. Mary's, Plaistow, a great impetus was given to the musical activities of Bromley. Mr. Thomas was a man as remarkable for his social as for his musical qualities. He quickly made himself felt as the soul of musical activities in the town. *The Plaistow Choral Society* was at once inaugurated by him, and shortly afterwards the *Bromley Orchestral Society*, the two societies being ultimately merged, in 1888, in the *Bromley Musical Society*, which was dissolved in 1914. The names of Edward and Bertram Latter must also be associated with that of Mr. Thomas in their whole-hearted devotion to the cause of music, the former being for some time Secretary of the Musical Society, which could muster at its concert ninety voices and an orchestra of forty, the latter being always ready to aid in any musical endeavour, he himself contributing much to the enjoyment of the public by his very admirable baritone voice. Of both Lewis Thomas and Bertram Latter I speak in terms of pleasant memory and sad regret.

Of the *Bromley Amateur Philharmonic Society*, started in 1886, I have no details ; while the *Bromley Choral Society*, founded in 1905, under the presidency of Sir Thomas C. Dewey, is so comparatively recent as to be outside the period allotted to this history. It still continues, under the baton of Mr. Frederic Fertel, through its excellent concerts, to be of great service to the town.

Chapter XIV

PART I. SPORT

THE general term 'Sport' includes a variety of activities differing materially in their character and aims. They may be roughly classified under two heads : Sport and Games, the distinction lying in the fact that 'sport' may be taken to connote the association of animal life in some form with the recreative impulses of man, whereas the term 'games' implies in every case that man is matched against man, the animal element being entirely excluded. In such a sport as cock-fighting, for example, animal is pitted against animal, and, though man has played his part in training the birds for their encounter, in the actual contest man plays no part. In horse racing, though there it is a case of animal matched against animal, man, in that he is in a large measure the controller of the racing horses, counts for much in the result. In hunting, shooting, fishing, and the like, man directly opposes his prowess and intelligence against the instinct and survival powers of the creature he pursues. In every case the association of man and animal is the distinctive element in the sport.

In games, on the contrary, it is man against man in a competitive trial of skill, and from the fact that games are more easily capable of purely local organisation than sport, the history of sport in Bromley will be chiefly a record of the doings of the Bromley clubs which have been formed for the pursuit of various forms of games, though other forms of sport will first claim our attention.

Hunting

In primitive days, so remote as to be beyond the reach of records, we may yet picture the deer browsing on the common, and wolves lurking in the neighbouring forest in constant conflict with the few human inhabitants. From very early times a systematic warfare against wild and dangerous animals was waged by the episcopal lords of Rochester from their palace in Bromley. Walter de Merton, Bishop from 1274 to 1277, has been styled, justly or unjustly, " the mightiest hunter before the Lord," and in course of time the larger beasts of the chase disappeared from the neighbourhood. Foxes, which still survived, were regarded as vermin, rewards being paid for their destruction. The preserving of foxes for the purposes of hunting does not seem to date farther back than about A.D. 1700.

The first recorded pack of foxhounds operating in the Bromley area is the " Old Surrey," whose range extended to the outskirts of London itself. The kennels indeed at one time were said to have been situated in Bermondsey. The Old Surrey country was very extensive, a meet at Peckham Rye being followed by a meet at the Fox Inn on Hayes Common. Bromley itself was only incidentally connected with the pack, though a few Bromley

men were members of the Hunt.   Of these Mr. William Mortimer, originally
a Lewisham man, Master or Joint Master about 1850, was a conspicuous
figure as he rode forth, in the full uniform of the Hunt, through Bromley
streets from his house, " The Valley," in Glass Mill Lane.   Associated with
him in the management was Harry Nicholl from Lewisham, and other local
members were : W. D. Starling, of Beckenham Lane, Charles F. Devas, of
Bromley Lodge, and Mr. W. Hine Haycock, of Blackheath, Honorary
Secretary from 1852 to 1874, who, under the pseudonym of " Scrutator," was
sometimes the historian of an " Old Surrey " run.

" All these worthies," writes Mr. Philip Norman, " have long joined the
majority, but there are still a few living who knew them and cherish their
memories."

Famous among Bromley sportsmen and muscular Christians was the
Rev. Henry Smith, D.D., who became Vicar of Bromley in 1785.   His
qualifications for the sacred office strike a modern mind as anomalous,
for his reputation as a Doctor of Divinity was enhanced by the further
reputation of being able, in company with his Parish Clerk, to consume
more alcohol, without showing signs of intoxication, than any other two
men in the parish.   Dr. Smith, in association with a few farmers of the
neighbourhood, of whom Tom Soane of Milk Street was the leading
spirit, started a pack of harriers, each member being responsible for
providing three or four hounds.   The Vicar's hounds are said to have
been kept in a stable at the College.   Various hand-gates in the grounds
behind " The Rookery " were originally put up to accommodate Dr.
Smith, who dearly loved a horse, and was a fine horseman, his connection
with horses being strengthened by his marriage to the daughter of James
Wilson, proprietor of the Bell Inn.   An unlucky contretemps, however,
brought his career with the harriers to an end, for one day his Bishop
(Horsley) happening to see the Doctor make a wonderful leap into the
high road, and urge the pack in full cry, was not appreciative, and forbade
a continuance of such unclerical exploits.

In comparatively recent years a pack of harriers was privately
maintained by Mr. Henry Lubbock, whose hounds used to meet at cockcrow
in order to permit Mr. Lubbock to put in a decent appearance in Lombard
Street in the course of the morning.   At these early meets Mr. Tom
Nickalls, then a resident at Bromley Common, and afterwards Master of
the Surrey Stag Hounds, brother of Sir Patteson and Conrad Nickalls,
was sometimes to be seen—a famous family rendered more famous by the
prowess of Guy and Vivian Nickalls (sons of Tom) upon the river, and of
Sir Patteson's sons upon the polo field.

When Mr. Lubbock's harriers became amalgamated with Russell's
—a quasi-public pack—they ceased to hunt in the Bromley neighbourhood,
and no local pack has replaced them.

Horse Racing

The history of Bromley as itself a racing centre, officially recognised as such, is brief, extending only from 1864 to 1875. But from time to time, over a period of two hundred years, Bromley Common seems to have been the scene of horse races. An advertisement in the *County Journal* for July 27th, 1734, announces a three days' meeting " on Bromley Common in Kent, the 26th, 27th and 28th of August next." Purses of twenty-five, fifteen, and ten guineas were to be run for on the respective days under prescribed conditions :

" All the horses that run for the above said Purses are to be kept in the Parish of Bromley aforesaid seven days before running, and to be entered at Mr. John Maclatcheys at the Queen's Head in Bromley six days before running, or to pay double entrance fee at the post."

From this it may be inferred that the Common was regarded as a suitable place for such races, and that they were occasionally held there.

But no regular and recognised race-course was constructed there till 1864, when Mr. William Pawley of the White Hart, in association with Messrs. Bridden and Verrall of Croydon, laid down a course on the Common, and held authorised race meetings four times a year. These meetings, which were officially styled " The Bromley Races and Steeplechases," were two-day meetings in February, April, October, and December. The steeplechase course, three miles, was a severe one, and casualties were not uncommon, but no objection was laid against the meetings on this score. Objection came from the sober and orderly opinion of the town itself against the disorderly and disreputable crowds which the races attracted. That a meeting passed off in 1865 without requiring any interference on the part of the magistrates was specially recorded with pleasure by the *Bromley Record*. With each succeeding year the scandals associated with the race meetings seem to have become more pronounced, and when, in 1874, a serious fire caused the death of a night-watchman on duty, the race-course fell definitely into disrepute and was shortly afterwards closed down.

In 1892 the ground was appropriated to the uses of the game of golf, and became the course of the Bromley and Bickley Golf Club.

Fishing

To-day a section in *Bromley's History* devoted to fishing can only run in the terms of that section in the *History of Iceland* devoted to snakes. There is no fishing in Bromley.

But this is only true of comparatively recent times. It is a melancholy reflection that within living memory trout were caught in the Ravensbourne, the last recorded catch within the parish—of a two-pounder—being made below the fall in Glass Mill Lane by Joseph Wells, famous in the cricket field, famous as the father of H. G. Wells, and famous as the captor of the last Ravensbourne trout.

In the neighbourhood of Southend, however, trout continued to be plentiful until quite recent times. The Rev. W. Cator, Rector of Beckenham from 1873 to 1885, used to stock the river running through the Cator estate with young trout, and not a few fell to the rod of the inmates of Flower House, the residence of Major Forster at Southend. Our late member of Parliament, Mr. H. W. Forster, now Lord Forster, doubtless has reminiscences of successful days in these waters, but from an account given by Mr. Paul Taylor of *Fishing near Bromley*—a handbook published in 1902—the Southend trout were as artful as they were shy.

In the Bromley section of the river the extinction of the fish is said to have been due to the construction of the Gas Works. An underground tank for storing ammonia used occasionally to overflow. The contents gradually intermingled with the waters of the Ravensbourne with fatal results ; an attempt to safeguard the fishing by an action at law against the Gas Company ended in a judgment for the Company. But apart from this the constant encroachment of bricks and mortar upon the sources of the stream has had its inevitable effect, and the Ravensbourne, like the Fleet, and Wallbrook before it, has been reduced to such exiguous limits that fishing is no longer practicable.

GAME-SHOOTING

For the same cause the game which used to be plentiful on and about Bromley Common has now practically disappeared. Mr. Philip Norman relates that in the days of his grandfather, about 1770, partridges, hares, rabbits, woodcock, snipe abounded on Bromley Common, and an occasional pheasant would sometimes fall to the sportsman's gun. These have for the most part, but not entirely, disappeared, except the woodcock, the number of which, curiously enough, has not appreciably lessened.

" The woodcock," says Mr. Norman, " return to their old haunts as long as they find food enough, regardless of the proximity of villas, gas-lamps and motor omnibuses."

Even more curious is the changed attitude of the country gentleman of to-day towards shooting as a sport as compared with that of his forefathers a hundred and fifty years ago. To shoot game with a gun was not then considered a suitable diversion for a gentleman. It was the office of the gamekeeper to supply the kitchen with game, the business of the gentleman was to eat it. Gradually this conception yielded to the fascination of the sport, and, irrespective of game laws and property rights, for a sportsman of recognised social position the whole country was in a manner open.

Mr. Tom Hankey, the banker at Southborough, who had no land of his own, and Mr. Philip Norman's grandfather, " who had not much," were accustomed to shoot together and to go almost where they pleased. Other people, without the claim of belonging to the neighbourhood, acted in the same way. Sportsmen came from London and shot over the whole country until they were stopped, and to stop them was considered a somewhat ungracious act. The officers of the Army in camp or quarters used to be great marauders, and stringent regulations were issued from time to time by the Horse Guards to check their filibustering propensities. Even the Princess of Wales, when living at Blackheath, employed a game-keeper to shoot for her benefit promiscuously, though what he shot on or at was equally somebody else's property.

No regulations enforcing a close time for game appear to have existed until about the middle of the eighteenth century, and it was not until three-quarters of a century more, under Lord Grey's administration, that the game laws placed the sport more or less upon its present footing.

In comparatively recent times Sir Edward H. Scott both bred and preserved pheasants at Sundridge, where he was often honoured by the presence of King Edward VII, then Prince of Wales, as his guest.

PART II. GAMES AND PASTIMES

PASSING now from those forms of sport which imply either the destruction of animal life or the participation of animals in them, we have now to record the history of games as practised in Bromley. " Paullo majora canamus "—let us now sing a nobler strain—for Bromley as a town has a record in competitive recreations of which it may well be proud. It can boast of being second—if indeed it was second—only to Hambledon, Hants, in the annals of the great game of cricket. There was a time, some thirty years ago, when the Bromley Hockey Team contained four internationals, while the Bromley Lawn Tennis Club supplied, in W. Baddeley, the world's champion on three occasions, and in W. and H. Baddeley, the world's champion double players for three successive years.

These, of course, are star achievements, but even without them Bromley can give a good account of itself in the field of competitive games.

ARCHERY

But centuries before cricket, hockey, or lawn tennis was even heard of there existed almost universally throughout the civilised world a form of sport which was in its day much more than a sport in that it was a prime element in national defence.

Apart from any extant evidence we are justified in the belief that the men of Bromley, from very early times, were constant in the practice of archery. Indeed as late as Henry VIII every able-bodied man was under legal compulsion to shoot with the bow and arrow on Sundays and on holidays. It is significant that the name of " Shooting Common " has applied from time immemorial to that part of Bromley Common which extends immediately southwards from Hayes Lane and Homesdale Road, a part of this area being at one time distinguished by the names of " Long Shots " and " Short Shots." The inference may be drawn that it was here that, in medieval times, the practice of archery was carried on, though these names may possibly have been derived from the then owners of the land, the great family of Shot, or Shotte. As in course of time the bow and arrow yielded, as weapons of defence, to fire-arms, archery declined into a pastime, but a pastime developing so much grace in its execution, and demanding so much skill in acquiring any proficiency, that it is to be hoped that this fine exercise will never entirely die out. Bromley for many years has been to the fore in the endeavour to keep it alive. The West Kent Archery Club, established in 1863, has had its home in Widmore almost from its initiation, and has attracted to its membership some of the finest archers in the country. Among these the name of Mr. C. E. Nesham, many times the winner of the Grand National Championship,

OLD COTTAGES OPPOSITE THE FORMER ARCHERY GROUND,
WIDMORE.

Pulled down 1891.

From a painting by Yeend King, R.A.

is conspicuous, as is that of Mr. W. Inderwick, who was G.N. Champion in 1921–23 and is at this moment a member of the Club.

But limits of space forbid anything more than this cursory reference to archery as a sport, for our main concern must necessarily be with those games in which a ball of some kind is the most distinctive element. From the days of Atalanta to the days of Jack Hobbs and Bobby Jones it is a ball which has played the most conspicuous part in the diversions of mankind.

Though of all ball games now played Bowls perhaps may claim precedence by right of seniority, this ancient pastime has been only so recently rejuvenated in Bromley that it must necessarily yield to Cricket in the arrangement of this chapter.

CRICKET

Bromley, as a cricket centre, has been very closely identified with the origins and early history of the game.

In its present form Cricket is not, like Bowls, of remote antiquity. Though there is mention of it as early as the sixteenth century, no reference to it in a newspaper has so far been traced before 1700.

By 1735 Bromley begins to figure prominently in the game.

In the *Grub Street Journal* of July 31st of that year, the following announcement appeared :

" Yesterday at the Cricket Match on Bromley Common between the Prince of Wales and the Earl of Middlesex for £1,000 the Londoners got 72 first hands, the Kentish men 95. London side went in again and got only 9 above the Kent, which were got the second innings without one person being out by the Kentish men who won the match."

The Prince in question whose team suffered defeat at the hands of the " Kentish gamesters," led by the Earl of Middlesex, was Frederick, Prince of Wales, father of George III, who was not only a great patron of the game but died of it, if it be true that his death was due to the effects of a blow from a cricket ball. Thus Bromley Common may be called the cradle of Kent County Cricket, and it continued, for more than a generation, to be one of the principal Kentish grounds.

A few years later, in 1742, the game had gained a sufficient hold on the town of Bromley to supply a team of purely local players. Two matches were played in that year on the Artillery ground near Bunhill Fields—at that time the headquarters of cricket in the metropolis—between eleven gentlemen of Bromley and eleven of London.

In the following year, 1743, Bromley Common was again the scene of an historic match between the Kentish eleven of Lord John Sackville and Lord Montfort's eleven drawn from London, Middlesex, and Surrey. The stakes were " for 300 guineas, some say £500 a side," and among the spectators were the Prince of Wales, Lord Waldegrave, and Lord Baltimore. These were the particulars which really interested the public. Of the actual game we are told nothing, and of the result only that Kent " gave it up." This expression is either an euphemism for " Kent lost," or else it conceals a course of action on the part of Kent which is best left in oblivion.

In the same year the combined forces of Bromley and Chislehurst contended against London " at Bromley," when the local side " won with great difficulty."

In 1745 Bromley met London in three matches, the first being won by Bromley on May 24th on a ground behind the Bell Inn. The second, for £100, was won by London by " eleven knotches " according to one account, " by 10 runs " according to another. The third was played on June 17th, on the Artillery ground, when it is sad to relate that

" The Londoners won with only three hands out."

In the same year the " noblemen and gentlemen of the London Club " arranged a match between two elevens picked out of " the most famous places in England." The winning team was drawn from Bromley, Sevenoaks, and Addington, the losers from London, Chislehurst, Horsmonden, and Slindon. It is significant that Bromley and Chislehurst should be cited as among " the most famous " cricket centres in England.

On July 11th, 1745, Bromley Common was again the scene of the first of two historic encounters between a Kent eleven and all England. Each was for stakes of a thousand guineas, and at Bromley the Kent eleven was successful in a single day. The second match, played on Smith's ground in Chiswell Street a few days later, was won by England by 119 runs.

Bromley's chief local rival at this period appears to have been Addington. It is recorded in 1746 that Addington beat Bromley " with great difficulty " at Bromley.

In that year, and again in the succeeding year, Bromley Common was the scene of a match between the county of Kent and " all the world," or, in other words, all England, the return games being also played on the Common. In 1748 a single-wicket match between " Long Robin " Mills, a boot-maker of Bromley, and T. Faulkner of London, is recorded. This was one of a set of three to be played on Bromley Common, at Addington, and on the Artillery ground, and on his own ground Long Robin was decisively beaten. At Addington he avenged this defeat, but no record has come down to us of the result of the rubber game. As a native of Bromley, and as one of the best cricketers of his day, Long Robin's name deserves to be remembered.

The part of Bromley Common upon which these matches were played is believed to be that known as Shooting Common in the neighbourhood of the old Brick-Kiln Lane—now Homesdale Road. Mr. George Warde

Norman records that he himself had often played there, and there is no mention of the game being ever played anywhere else upon the Common until the establishment of the Prince's Plain Cricket Club in 1812.

From 1747 Bromley Common ceased to be the venue for important county matches, though the game continued to be played there apparently without interruption. The local team flourished and there are records of their prowess in 1749, 1756, and 1766.

With these exceptions there follows a gap of about half a century in the history of Bromley cricket.

When the record of Bromley cricket begins again, in the early nineteenth century, it is found in a vigorous and flourishing condition. In 1801 and 1802 the combined forces of Bromley and Beckenham played four matches against Woolwich for five hundred guineas a match, and all of them were drawn. Of these one was played somewhere in Bromley. In 1806 an eleven of Bromley played an eleven of Middlesex on the original Lord's Cricket Ground in Marylebone (now Dorset Square) for five hundred guineas a side, and on the first innings Bromley led by thirteen runs. The names of Budd and Pontifex—cricket giants of old days—figure on the Middlesex side, while for Bromley the chief scorers were William and Robert Ayling, of whom the former played for Kent, for Players against Gentlemen, and for England. In his day William Ayling was one of the greatest of English cricketers. Particulars about him in other capacities are given in the chapter entitled " Itinerary of the Town."

Another famous Bromley cricketer of the time was W. Lambert, who was the author of a little handbook entitled *Instructions and Rules for Playing the Noble Game of Cricket.*

A somewhat curious match was played in 1808 between six players of Dartford and six of Bromley. Notwithstanding the limited number of players the game extended over three days, Bromley eventually winning by one wicket. It is said that two of the best batsmen in the country appeared for the respective sides, W. Beldham for Bromley, and the Rev. Lord Frederick Beauclerk for Dartford.

The costume of the latter is described as follows :

" Lord Frederick Beauclerk in his neat nankeen breeches, and silk stockings, with another pair drawn tight over the insteps ; a scarlet sash round the waist, and a white beaver hat which he would dash on the ground if things did not go to his liking."

In 1812 a number of influential people from the neighbourhood of Bromley proposed to establish a new cricket club, which was duly inaugurated by a dinner held at the Plough Inn on Bromley Common. The site selected for the Club's ground was that part of the Common, lying rather less than a quarter of a mile east of the present Trinity Church, known as Prince's

Plain. The Club assumed the name of its site—the Prince's Plain Cricket Club. Whether the Club christened the spot, or whether the name preceded the formation of the Club, is a matter of conjecture. Either of two derivations may be accepted—the one, that horse races patronised by Frederick Prince of Wales used to be run there ; the other, that when the name to be given to the ground was under discussion among members of the Club the Prince Regent, afterwards George IV, happened to drive past on his way to Tunbridge Wells, and so provided a happy inspiration.

The level of the ground lent itself fairly naturally to the purposes in view, and the Club flourished from the start. The members were chiefly drawn from the locality, but outsiders distinguished in the world of cricket were admitted, prominent among them being Lord Frederick Beauclerk, Mr. William Ward, whose achievements as a batsman still live in the memory, and Mr. Benjamin Aislabie, secretary for many years of the M.C.C.

The first Secretary of the Prince's Plain Club was George Warde Norman, then a youth of nineteen, who was equally efficient at the wicket or in his secretarial chair. His programme of fixtures included matches with the M.C.C., East Kent, Sevenoaks, and the principal clubs of the surrounding district, and at least three paid professionals were engaged as groundsmen and coaches, or, as the name then went, as " scouts."

The two Aylings, Robert and William, were attached to the Club in this capacity, and also a mounted policeman named Mynn, who lived in a cottage hard by. It was not, however, then a custom for the professionals to play in matches, the line of demarcation between professional and amateur being much more marked a century ago than it is to-day.

The members of the Club met for practice every Monday during the season, when sides were chosen and a formal match was played, but as dinner at 3 o'clock in the afternoon was not the least important part of the proceedings, the hours of actual play must have been somewhat limited. Dinner in those days was a serious business, and it is not likely that much strenuous play succeeded it. Originally a tent served as a dining-room, but this soon gave way to a long wooden room specially erected at the back of the Plough for the convenience of the diners.

When, by the Enclosure Act of 1821, the ground at Prince's Plain was no longer available, the Club removed to Chislehurst and assumed the name of the West Kent Cricket Club, and under that name it has continued to flourish to this day. In 1897 was published *The Annals of the West Kent Cricket Club*, wherein are duly recorded some of the exploits of the old Prince's Plain Club in their matches with the M.C.C.

In the meantime the town of Bromley seems to have maintained its own cricket club and its old reputation. There is a record of a match between Bromley and Mitcham on Mitcham Common, in 1818, when Bromley won by 121 runs ; while in 1825 Bromley and the neighbouring parishes met the redoubtable West Kent club at Chislehurst and defeated it in the face of an opposition which could boast of several county cricketers on its side.

Among the townsmen playing for Bromley about this period there are some names which bring the game within the range of living memories : James Painter Davis, landlord of the Rising Sun, and subsequently of the Bell ; Joseph Nash, the leading Bromley linen draper ; W. Lambert, the tallow-chandler ; Thomas Battersbee, C. Chitty, and W. Wybrow. Davis seems to have acted as captain ; Chitty was renowned for the speed of his underhand deliveries ; Wybrow occasionally played for M.C.C. The match against West Kent became for some years an annual fixture, and was regarded by the Bromley men as the most important match of the season. On one occasion, in 1828, the ranks of the enemy were raided to secure a valuable recruit to the Bromley team. This was Mr. William Ward, described as the " W. G. Grace " of his time, who, though a member of the West Kent Club, played for Bromley ; his powerful assistance was, however, insufficient—to quote a contemporary humorist—to " ward " off defeat.

In 1833 first appears in the records of Bromley cricket the name of Sutton. This must have been William Sutton who kept the White Hart Inn at Mitcham for many years, eventually succeeding Davis as landlord of the Bell at Bromley. Owing to an injury to the hip, Sutton always had a man to run for him, and in the field his position was that of wicket-keeper. He retained to a ripe old age the traditions of a past generation. His high hat, swallow-tailed coat, black choker, and an endless store of anecdotes of Felix, Mynn, and other famous cricketers with whom he had been on intimate terms, give him a conspicuous position among the old-time worthies of Bromley.

In 1831 the *Weekly Dispatch* announced that a match for twenty-two sovereigns would be played between Bromley and Dartford " on the new ground." It is conjectured, but by no means certain, that here we have the first reference to the White Hart Field as the venue of Bromley cricket, a conjecture which is strengthened by the appearance, about this time, of Mr. William Pawley, landlord of the White Hart, in the Bromley eleven.

Mr. Pawley was a notable figure in the life of Bromley in his day. He was a man of striking personality and of varied activities. The annual flower shows in the White Hart gardens, promoted by him, are even now within the memory of some who are still living. The race meetings on Bromley Common, close to his own residence at Cooper's Farm, were largely originated by him. His memory both in Bromley and throughout the county was perpetuated by his nephew, Mr. Tom E. Pawley, whose loss we are even now deploring, and whose services as manager of the Kent County Cricket Club, and of the M.C.C. team which visited Australia in 1911, it would be difficult to over-estimate. It was this team which brought back " the Ashes."

In 1840 and the two following years the match, Kent *v.* All England, was again played at Bromley. The scene of the first of these matches was a ground near Widmore Lane, the other two matches were played on the White Hart Field, doubtless under the inspiration of William Pawley. In 1841 Kent won by an innings, but lost the other two games. The high-sounding title of these matches, however, is not to be taken too seriously. Though some fine cricketers took part in them, the sides were scarcely representative, and the matches were rather of the nature of exhibition games than a genuine test of the country against the county.

In 1844 and 1845 Mr. Pawley engaged John Lillywhite—son of the famous William—as groundsman for the White Hart Field. Famous as he himself became as a cricketer, John Lillywhite's immortality rests upon an exploit performed in his capacity as umpire. He no-balled Willsher in the Surrey *v.* All England match at the Oval (August 25th, 26th, 27th, 1862) because *the bowler delivered the ball with his hand above his shoulder.* In other words, Willsher was inaugurating the epoch of overhand bowling. Any form of bowling other than under or round hand had up to this time been illegal. The decision of Lillywhite led to a reconsideration by the authorities of the whole question of bowling, with the result that, in 1864, any form of bowling was legalised, provided that the ball be not thrown or jerked.

An historic match, of which a pictorial record hangs in the pavilion at Lord's, was played on the White Hart Field on September 29th, 30th, 1846, between the two men, both of Kent, who were regarded as the finest cricketers of their day: Alfred Mynn and N. "Felix," whose real name was Wanostocht. It was a single-wicket match, nominally for the championship of England.

The paragraphs which follow in inverted commas are by Mr. Philip Norman:

" Felix, who kept a school at Blackheath, was by far the more scientific as a batsman, but he was seriously handicapped, being an indifferent bowler, while Mynn's bowling was terrifically fast, so that it was difficult to hit it in front of the wicket. Two ' fields ' were allowed for each. Felix stayed in altogether considerably more than two hours, but in his two innings he only got one run off the bat, his score being made up to 12 by wides and a no-ball. Mynn got four in his first innings. He began his second innings within a quarter of an hour of ' time,' but soon knocked off the nine runs required to win the match.

" The last effort in the way of high-class cricket on the White Hart ground was a match, July 10th and 11th, 1847, between the Gentlemen of Kent and the Gentlemen of Surrey, which was unfinished, Kent leading on the first innings. Felix played for Surrey because, though residing in Kent and largely identified with Kentish cricket, he was born in the former county.

" Mr. Robert Pott, of Bromley, was playing on the Kent side.

ALFRED MYNN.   NICHOLAS FELIX.

From the picture in the Pavilion at Lord's Cricket Ground.

" The Bromley Cricket Club almost died out in the forties of last century, the decade in which the Bishop of Rochester ceased to reside at Bromley, and various schools were given up. Our great surgeon, James Scott, had left the town some years before. These events had an adverse effect on the prosperity of the town ; tradesmen failed, and between 1841 and 1852 the population actually diminished.

" In 1856 the Club was revived by Joseph Wells and Richard Stubberfield. The former was born in 1828, and for some years kept a china shop at No. 47 High Street, Bromley. He was one of the professionals of the West Kent Cricket Club from 1857 to 1869 inclusive, and during the next three seasons was with the Bickley Park Club. He was a fast round-hand (not overhead) bowler, with slinging delivery, and in 1862 and 1863 played for the county, which was then rather at a low ebb. On June 26th, 1862, in a match for Kent against Sussex, he bowled four wickets in four successive balls, this apparently being the earliest performance of the feat in first-class cricket. Mr. Wells, who retained his cheerfulness and interest in cricket till the last, died at Liss, Hampshire, October 1910, in his eighty-second year.

" In spite of the revival mentioned above, it does not appear that in 1860 the Club was flourishing, for in May of that year a correspondent signing himself ' One of the Old Ones ' writes to the *Bromley Record* asking why

" ' When so many of our fellow townsmen confess themselves eager for amusement, we have so few enthusiastic enough to seek it by forming an eleven in the standard old English game ? '

The letter is headed ' A Cry from the Cricket Field.' The ' Old One ' seems to have missed the fact that matches had quite recently been played with fair success against such opponents as Banstead, Bexley Heath, Farningham, and the City of London. Doubtless there were others of which no scores have been kept.

" Soon afterwards, namely September 1st, 1860, in a match between Bromley and Beckenham, Wells and Mr. C. B. Griffith, bowling for our Club, got their opponents out for 39 and 40. In 1861 the latter became joint secretary with Mr. Belwood.

" About that time, and for some years afterwards, Griffith used often to act as captain of the Bromley team. He had been in the Winchester school eleven of 1858, and besides batting fairly was above the average as a fast bowler.

" There were three Griffiths, sons of one of the widows resident in Bromley College, of whom C. B. was the eldest and most distinguished on the cricket field. Both of his brothers, however, sometimes played for Bromley, and rendered useful service with bat and ball.

" If the ' Old One ' who, in 1860, talked so gloomily about Bromley cricket, was still to the front in 1861, he may almost have been made young again by the remarkable performance of the Bromley eleven on July 30th of that year. In a match against Hayes, on the ground of the latter club, they dismissed their opponents, who were two short in the first innings, without allowing them to get a single run off the bat.

" The Bromley bowlers who did the mischief were Tom Sherman and William Blundell, brother of the fishmonger and himself afterwards a fish-monger at Beckenham. The latter was left-handed, with what was then an exceptionally high delivery. He bowled very well for a man with only a local reputation. Sherman, the Surrey professional from Mitcham, who about this time played occasionally for Bromley through the influence of Mr. Sutton, is described in Lillywhite's *Scores and Biographies* as ' one of the fastest bowlers that ever was seen.' The ground at Hayes, like most common ground, was apt to be fiery, the ball sometimes getting up in a very awkward manner, which accounts for the fact that Blundell made no fewer than five catches in the slips.

" The other Bromley cricketers who played in this match may be briefly referred to. Richard Stubberfield, a police-constable, has already been mentioned as having, with Joseph Wells, given a fresh start to Bromley cricket. He loved the game and continued playing for many years. As a batsman he was of the stone-walling variety. Robert Doe's trade was that of shoemaker, but his heart was always in cricket. In fact he was half a professional, his bowling and batting being useful, and he excelled at point. His father about that time usually umpired. Edward Solbé became after-wards Conservative Agent in Bromley. James Mowat could hardly have been much of a help to the Bromley side, being probably better at golf or curling than at cricket. He was a Scotch tailor whose shop was opposite Baxter's the chemist. Charles Ellis was a butcher, James Carpenter an upholsterer, Augustus Farwig did not come from the hamlet so called, but lived in one of the small houses near the turnpike. Of Titmarsh nothing is known, not even his Christian name. I have left to the last Mr. Douglas Payne, the builder, one of the most prominent members of the eleven. He and his brothers, H. and J. Payne, were great supporters of Bromley cricket.

" In 1862 the Bromley eleven were beaten by Hayes, and played with varying success against Meopham, Mitcham, and Westerham. In 1863 there was a similar list of matches. That year a very good cricketer settled here, namely Mr. James Watts, not long ago taken from us at a ripe old age. He had played a few times for the county, and sometimes helped the Bromley club, besides belonging to other clubs in the neighbourhood."

The subsequent history of Bromley cricket is a record of vicissitudes —of occasional eclipse varied by energetic and temporary resuscitations. On two occasions when the game seemed to have sunk into a decline the *Bromley Record* raised a trumpet call for its revival. The " cry from the cricket field " coming from " one of the old ones " resounded with the

BROMLEY CRICKET CLUB, 1867.

Standing (left to right) : W. H. Cooper, W. W. Baxter, Col. J. Walmisley, G. Weeks, Sen., W. H. McKewan, R. Roscorla, Charles Hoare, J. Carpenter (scorer), S. Stephenson, H. Stephenson, G. Doe (umpire).

Seated (left to right) : A. Bone, Walter Walmisley, R. Stubberfield, W. P. Neal, A. E. Willett, " Bob " Doe.

question, " Where is the B.C.C. ? " with the result that new blood was introduced into the committee, and a fresh impetus given to the game.

Material for a really good eleven was still available in the persons of Charles Hoare of Kelsey Park, the brothers Goodhart of Langley Park, the Stephensons and the McKewans of Bickley. The Walmisley family by itself was almost a match for any team which could be put into the field against it, and Colonel John Walmisley is still remembered for his vivid blazer, his brown pads, and a fearless daring in the field which led to the remark that Colonel Walmisley could stop a cannon ball.

The brothers Griffith, the brothers Douglas, A. E. Willett, and Richard Stubberfield were far from being extinct volcanoes, and with so much talent to call upon the B.C.C. took on a new lease of life. In 1866 a new flag-pole set up at the entrance of the White Hart Field displayed the White Horse of Kent—" a rampagious looking animal with a liberal allowance of tail," to quote the *Bromley Record*—against a setting of brilliant red, and fluttered as a symbol of the revival of Bromley cricket.

Any detailed account of matches played is difficult from the fact that the score sheets have either not been preserved or not supplied to the writer. Only a few isolated performances have descended to posterity. One such performance was that of Mr. Robinson Latter, who in a match *v.* Dartford in July 1866 hit a ball right out of the White Hart Field. The methods of Mr. J. A. Mowat in dealing with the slow deliveries of Sydenham Albion prompted the somewhat obvious witticism that he could only " mow at " them. A match played at Woolwich *v.* the Officers of the Royal Artillery in August 1867 is notable for the " cannon-ball " catch made by Colonel Walmisley :

" What is the use," it was said by Woolwich supporters, " of playing against these Bromley men ? They would stop a cannon ball."

Matches *v.* " The Gryphons " and " I. Zingari " testify to the quality of Bromley cricket in the sixties. It was a time when the ancient traditions of Bromley were justified in her children.

At the same time the old White Hart Field was frequently the arena where rival groups of tradesmen fought out their battles with ball and willow. Records are extant of a Plumbers' eleven ; of an eleven of Fishmongers who challenged the Butchers ; of the Fishmongers reinforced by the Poulterers plucking victory from the Butchers. In this match a ten-guinea cup for the highest score was won by Mr. Blundell, a " Fishmonger." Comic matches such as B.C.C. *v.* Thirteen Clowns were an occasional attraction, and the rising generation was encouraged, by the arrangement of matches for boys, to aspire to higher flights in a more mature future. Late in the season of 1873 the Walmisley family confronted a Bromley eleven captained by the redoubtable Mr. Blundell. At the last moment the " Walmisleys " were reinforced by the advent from the West Indies of

George Walmisley—a dark horse, who turned out to be a " demon " bowler, whose deliveries seemed likely to be so physically destructive to the opposing side that they prudently sacrificed their wickets in order to preserve their lives.　The Walmisleys won by five wickets.

It was, however, in the seventies that the glory of the White Hart Field as the venue of distinctively Bromley cricket began finally to wane. The formation of the Bickley Park Cricket Club transferred to that beautiful ground much of the prestige which had hitherto attached to Bromley itself. The surroundings, the privacy, the expanse, and the perfection of the pitch naturally attracted the established or rising talent of the neighbourhood. The best cricket in West Kent became identified with the Bickley Park Club, which could boast of one of the finest grounds in the county, and of an eleven in which county players not infrequently figured.

Thus the very best type of club cricket has not ceased to centre—as it had centred for over two hundred years—around Bromley.　It has been transferred, and with its transference to Bickley Park the distinction so long attaching to the town as the cradle and home of cricket has in a large measure departed.　Moreover, in the early eighties the White Hart Field was no longer capable of accommodating all those who desired to play the game.　Clubs independent of the B.C.C. began to be formed with grounds of their own in the neighbourhood of the town.　The Plaistow Cricket Club, for example, which had an excellent ground, at first immediately adjacent to Plaistow Church and afterwards near the North Station, offered attractions superior to those of the White Hart Field, and became the recognised centre of the game for Bromley.

The Plaistow ground was also the cricket field for Quernmore House School.　Among its pupils in the early eighties a small boy of the name of Frank Solbé gave considerable promise for the future.　It was one of the duties of the present writer as a master at the school to superintend the cricket of the Quernmore boys, and he very early foresaw that in the sphere of cricket Solbé was likely to prove the worthy son of a worthy father.　In due course Solbé became a member of the Bickley Park Cricket Club, and gained such distinction there that he was given a trial in the Kent County eleven, and for some years Bromley had the distinguished honour of being occasionally represented in one of the finest county teams in the country by a born and bred Bromley man.　His son has also represented the county, and another Bromley man, W. L. Knowles, has enjoyed a similar distinction.

But meantime, and as a consequence of the changes just indicated, the White Hart Field fell more and more into disuse except as a playground for the boys of the town, and in 1897 the field itself was presented to the Corporation by the Lord of the Manor, and was converted into that picturesque and pleasant garden which commemorates the Diamond Jubilee of Queen Victoria.

FOOTBALL

The enormous popularity of football to-day is in striking contrast to the almost complete indifference of the general public towards both forms of the game some forty years ago. It was a game associated in the public mind with the great public schools and the universities, and readers of "Tom Brown" and other authorities were led to understand that kicking a ball about a field aroused inexplicable enthusiasm among undergraduates, masters, and boys alike. But outside these privileged centres no form of football exercised any general attraction. The great newspapers ignored it, and even the local press seldom contained more than cursory and intermittent notices, with the result, in the particular case of Bromley football, that it has been difficult to secure authentic records or information, earlier than 1892, on which to base a survey of the development of the game in the Bromley area.

Long before that date, however, there was one name, subsequently to be closely associated with Bromley, which stood out as the most conspicuous name in the ranks of British footballers—that of the Hon. A. F. Kinnaird, afterwards eleventh Baron Kinnaird of Plaistow Lodge.

From his early days at Eton he showed a keen enthusiasm and a remarkable aptitude for football as played under Association rules. At Trinity, Cambridge, he was captain of the College Association Football Club, and in 1866 was chosen to play for London in a memorable match against Sheffield, and contributed more than any other to the success of his side. As a member of the "Old Etonians," of the "Corinthians," and as an international (he played in 1873 for Scotland, in the first international match between Scotland and England)—he gained the reputation of being one of the finest players of his day, and on the formation of the Football Association, he became in due course its President. It is only, however, by virtue of his occasional residence at Plaistow Lodge that he can be associated directly with Bromley football. There is no record of his taking any personal part in any of the games played there, and, indeed, it is doubtful if, either in Bromley or the neighbourhood, any club playing under Association rules existed in his day.

The earliest reference to Bromley football which careful search and full inquiry have been able to discover is an announcement in the *Bromley Record* which appeared in the first week of October 1870. It stated that an effort was being made to form a football club in the town, and that a meeting would be held at the Bell on the evening of October 4th to devise the best means of effecting that object. In a November number the same paper announced that the football club seemed to be fairly started, that practice games would be played on Saturdays on the White Hart Field, and that intending members should apply to W. Sutton, Jnr., the honorary secretary.

No reference is made to the kind of football which was to be played, but it may be inferred that the Association type of game was the one selected. For it is probable that the movement in Bromley was a reflex of a general movement in the country in favour of football, and towards its organisation and co-ordination. From the public schools the game had gradually advanced into the world outside, largely through the medium of " Old Boys " clubs, such as the Old Etonians, the Corinthians, and many others, and to such an extent had these, and other clubs, multiplied that in 1863 it was felt to be desirable to affiliate as many of them as possible with a central controlling body. Thus there came into existence The Football Association, which, gathering strength with advancing years, was able in 1871 to establish a competition within the Association for a challenge trophy, or cup, which, though of no great value in itself, might stimulate a healthy rivalry between members' clubs, and improve the general standard of play.

From these small beginnings there has developed that condition of ' Cup ' frenzy under which the country labours during the early months of each year.

The Football Association was, in 1871, under the control of a committee of ten members. Of these, at that date, two were connected with Bromley, M. P. Betts and A. F. Kinnaird. M. P. Betts was a Bickley man, and a prominent member of the Bickley Park Cricket Club, and of " The Wanderers " Football Club. In the records of the game his name will be found under the pseudonym of " A. H. Chequer," and under that name he shot the winning goal in the final tie of the first English Cup Competition played in 1872. He remained a prominent figure in the football world and in the Association after he had himself ceased to play, for in 1883 he and A. F. Kinnaird were both appointed by the Association members of a special committee to investigate the evils of pseudo-professionalism which were beginning to invade the game.

These touches of biography, however, have led away from the point which it is sought to establish—that by the early seventies an organised movement for popularising the game was in progress, and that it may be inferred that the proposal to form a club in Bromley was, at any rate in part, an outcome of that movement.

But in part it arose, as did the Hockey Club, from the very natural desire of the members of the Bromley Cricket Club to organise some game which they could play during the winter months, and as a boom in football was in progress, that seemed to be the game which answered the requirements. The first members who enrolled themselves in the club formed in 1870 were all of them prominent members of the Cricket Club. But apart from the selection of club colours and the purchase of a supply of jerseys, " distinctive by their ugliness," the duties of Mr. Sutton as Honorary Secretary do not seem to have been onerous. He is still happily available to assist the compiler of this history, and he has rendered all the assistance in his power ; but he is unable to recollect that any matches were played, and with his temporary departure from the town the Club seems to have collapsed. Whether it actually ceased to exist, or whether it maintained an unregarded existence, it is equally the fact that no further record of football in Bromley appears in the local press until 1881.

Early in January of that year the readers of the *Record* were informed that the Bromley Football Club had played its first match of the season on Boxing Day against Queen's House, when Bromley suffered defeat by two goals against two tries.

The game obviously must have been played under Rugby rules, but whether the Bromley Club of 1880 was a newly established club or the old one redivivus does not appear.

In 1882, at a meeting held in July at the Bell, the Penge Football Club and the Bromley Football Club decided to amalgamate under the name of the " Kent Rovers," who, in the first month of the season, distinguished themselves by a succession of creditable victories. Their home ground was in Bromley.

But in the meantime another club had come into existence, composed to some extent of Bromley men, under the name of the " West Kent Football Club," its home ground being at Chislehurst. This Club played under Rugby rules, and in its early days, 1875-8, Colonel Edward Satterthwaite pretty regularly assisted it.

By 1882 the West Kent Club was arranging fixtures with some of the strongest Rugby sides in the country—Clapham Rovers, Harlequins, London Scottish, and Blackheath. This is an evidence of its status and consideration in the football world ; but, as the years went on, the Club proved no match for such antagonists, who had so much larger a recruiting area.

The records of both Clubs—the Kent Rovers and the West Kent Football Club—for 1883-5 are so fragmentary that there is nothing of interest to record, and after 1885 all information ceases until 1889. In December of that year the acting Honorary Secretary of the Kent Rovers, Mr. George Hopton, was presented on his retirement with a testimonial at a smoking concert under the chairmanship of Mr. G. W. F. Loftus. In his acknowledgment, Mr. Hopton felt proud to be able to say that now the Club was numbered among the best of the second-class clubs.

The lack of information over a period of years may, and probably does, imply a lack of activity on the part of the clubs, and such a lack would be accounted for, in the case of the Kent Rovers, by difficulties in obtaining a playing field. In a review of the first months of the season, 1889, the *Record*, in January 1890, stated that :

" Football has continued to flourish, though at one time it seemed that the Bromley Club would be without a ground, in consequence of the Cricket

Club having established a Hockey Club, and requisitioned their ground for that purpose."

The establishment of yet another football club at Plaistow, with an excellent ground immediately adjacent to the church, seemed to offer a solution of the difficulty by the simple process of amalgamation. The negotiations, however, fell through, a ground for the Bromley Club being eventually found at the back of Crescent Road on a field where Holligrave and Babbacombe Roads now exist.

Meanwhile the Kent Rovers had been experimenting with the Association game, and apparently found it to their liking. They seem to have played it with success throughout the season 1889, and a reorganisation of the Club followed. In September 1890 the Bromley Assistants Cricket Club approached the Football Club with the result that a combined meeting was held at the Rose and Crown under the presidency of Mr. J. King. A resolution was carried that a football club, to be known as the " Bromley Assistants Football Club," should be formed, under Association rules, and the old Rugby organisation became a thing of the past.

In the course of a year or two the word ' Assistants ' dropped out, and the Club became the " Bromley Football Club." Its history, as an exponent of the Association game, may be said to date from 1892.

From the first its record was one of continuous achievement. The change in the character of the game, the amalgamation with the Assistants, the growing popularity of the game throughout the country, were all of them doubtless contributory causes to a career of notable success. In the season of 1893–4, out of forty matches played thirty-one were won and only four lost, the most conspicuous achievements being the capture of the Kent Junior Cup, won at Faversham on March 17th, 1894, and the " Oliver–Isaacs " shield, being the trophy of the First Division of the South London League. Of the latter competition Mr. E. A. C. Thompson, Sport Contributor to the *Star* newspaper, has kindly given the following particulars :

" I was the founder of the South London League, and really the ' Father ' of the Football League movement in London, for the South London League was the first to be formed. Bromley, one of the original entrants, was a fine amateur club, as good a club, I think, as any existing to-day in amateur football. The shield originated thus : Mr. Lewis Isaacs, M.P. for Walworth, and Mr. F. Oliver, largely interested in the Tottenham Hotspur Club, jointly gave a sum to purchase a shield, and I determined to call it the ' Oliver–Isaacs ' shield. It is still competed for by the Southern Suburban League."

In May the Bromley team was called upon twice to visit London : on May 4th when at the Cannon Street Hotel the medals given by the Kent

County Football Association to the winners of the Kent Junior Cup were presented by Mr. M. C. Prall, and again when at the Champion Hotel, Aldersgate, the " Oliver–Isaacs " shield was handed to the Club President by Mr. C. E. Tritton, M.P. Mr. Oliver himself was present, and several of the leading men in the football world, to do honour to a team which, in the words of the Chairman, " had made a record . . . whose career had proved an unbroken triumph."

At the annual meeting of the Club in August 1894 the Treasurer's report showed a highly satisfactory balance, notwithstanding the fact that £15 out of the funds had been contributed to local charities.

The successful team was composed as under :

Goal . . C. Bayman.
Backs . . B. Gedney, J. Jeary.
Half-backs . W. L. Hopton, J. Hutton, R. C. Fawcett.
Forwards . A. Borer, A. Bunbury, R. Simister, E. J. Gedney, F. H. Gedney.

It is curious that, after a season crowned with such notable successes, the record of the Club for the next season should be an absolute blank. There is nothing to be gathered either from the Minutes or from the local press about the doings of 1895. That the Club continued in being and cherished still higher ambitions is clear from the fact that in 1896 it was decided to withdraw from the South London League in favour of a more exalted organisation, the London League. This resolution brought Bromley into competition with all the clubs in the London area which were affiliated to that League.

Allotted a place in the Second Division, the Bromley Football Club was immediately successful, 1896–7, in carrying off the championship trophy of their division, and was thereupon promoted into the First Division.

In the following season they were defeated in the contest for the London Cup, at an early stage of the competition, by the Old Etonians, and Bromley could get no higher than the sixth place in the London League tables, a result which reflected a condition of demoralisation which, for reasons not explained, afflicted the Club for some years. Finance fell into confusion and deficit, and a debt of £84, disclosed at a special General Meeting held in the summer of 1900, indicated a state of affairs little short of collapse. It was there and then determined to make a vigorous effort to revive the past glories of the Club. A new Secretary, Mr. L. Beeston, was appointed, a new set of officers installed in office, a new code of rules was drafted, and what practically amounted to a new start was made, under the presidency of Sir Samuel Scott, Mr. R. Gordon Mullen having felt compelled in 1901 to retire from the office of President in consequence of ill-health.

Under this new régime the Club appears to have speedily regained its position, for, at the General Meeting of 1903, the President was able to congratulate the members on the fact that all old debts had been liquidated, and that a balance of £20 was in the hands of the Treasurer.

From this time forward until the outbreak of the war the record of the Bromley Football Club is one of continuous and ever-increasing success. In the season of 1904 Bromley reached the final round in the South London Charity Cup, the final itself resulting in a draw of one goal each with Townley Park. The tenure of the Cup was therefore shared between them, each Club holding it for six months. Finance flourished to such an extent that twenty-five guineas out of the funds were allotted to local charities, ten guineas each to the Cottage Hospital and the Charitable Society, and five guineas to the Philips Memorial Hospital. The acquisition of a suitable ground—(further reference will be made to this)—doubtless contributed towards the growing popularity of the Club. In some seasons it was possible to run as many as three teams, and it would almost seem that Bromley only had to compete to win. The list of successes can most conveniently be shown in the form of a catalogue.

1905– 6   Kent Senior Cup, Bromley Football Club in the Final.
1906– 7   Kent Amateur Cup, Spartan League Trophy, both won.
1908– 9   Champions of Isthmian League, London Senior Cup won in
1909–10   1910.
1910–11   Defeated the Crystal Palace Club—a professional organisation.

" The first occasion," stated the reporter of the *Daily Telegraph*, " on which a professional club had been defeated by Amateurs since the days of the Corinthians."

In April of this year, 1911, success culminated in the capture of the Amateur Cup of England—the most coveted of all football trophies.

The closing story of this notable triumph must be related in some detail. On March 25th Bromley defeated the Coldstream Guards by three goals to nil. This victory brought Bromley into the final against Bishop Auckland, a famous North Country club which in this particular competition had won great renown. Four times it had reached the final, and twice had won the Cup. The form shown in previous matches was so convincing that, to its partisans, a victory to Bishop Auckland seemed assured.

The match was played on April 8th at Herne Hill before four thousand spectators, when Bromley proved the winners by one goal to nil. The excitement of the encounter unfortunately proved too much for one of the Bromley players, who was turned off the field by the referee, but notwithstanding this loss, the remaining ten men proved equal to the occasion.

Winners of the Kent Junior Cup, 1894.

G. W. Hopton, W. L. Hopton, J. Hutton, B. Gedney, C. Bayman, J. Jeary, R. C. Fawsitt, — Elliott (trainer).
A. Bunbury, A. Borer, R. Simister, F. Gedney, E. J. Gedney.

Winners of the Amateur Cup of England, 1911, and Members of the Club.

Back row (*left to right*) : T. Prentice, P. Smith, D. McWhirter, A. T. Peacock, H. Carter, S. Whitehead,
T. Mockford, F. H. Wood, C. J. Juniper, W. H. Willson.
Middle row : H. L. Beeston, J. W. Cox, P. C. R. Legh, L. Beeston (Hon. Sec.), H. W. Noall, S. F. Edwards,
A. H. Button, G. W. Hopton, W. L. Hopton.
Front row : R. W. Dilley, R. Noble, A. M. Kennard, C B. Landrey, S. G. Grayer.

BROMLEY FOOTBALL CLUB.

The Bromley team was made up as follows :

Goal . . F. H. Wood.
Backs . . A. T. Peacock, C. Watson.
Half-backs . D. McWhirter, H. W. Noall (Captain), P. Smith.
Forwards . R. W. Dilley, R. Noble, A. M. Kennard, C. B. Landrey, and S. G. Grayer.

In 1908 the President of the Club, the ex-Mayor, Colonel F. Griffith, who succeeded Sir S. Scott in 1904, was elected President of the Kent County Football Association—a recognition of the place which Bromley had even then taken in county football.

In addition to its seasonal engagements the Club from time to time sent a team abroad during the Easter holidays, the Channel Islands being visited in 1904, and Brussels and Paris in subsequent years.

In connection with the remarkable successes just recorded there are two names which call for special mention, those of Mr. Lewis Beeston and Mr. H. W. Noall. The former, as Honorary Secretary, and the latter as Captain, worked together throughout these years enthusiastically and harmoniously to promote the welfare of the Club, and it was to them in a great measure that its achievements were due.

With the outbreak of war in 1914 the activities of the Club were suspended for a period of four years.

It has been said above that the acquisition of a suitable ground was probably responsible in no small degree for the renaissance of the Club in 1904. Throughout its existence up to that date the Club had been in a constant state of migration. Starting on the White Hart Field, it had been driven from there to the Cricket Ground in Widmore Road ; thence to the Plaistow Cricket Club field, and thence to a piece of land, acquired on lease, at the back of Crescent Road. The rapid development of this portion of the town made the Club's tenure exceedingly precarious, and yet no other playing field seemed available. The Bromley Town Cricket Club being in a similar plight, the two organisations joined forces, and in January 1904 put the case before the Mayor, Colonel F. Griffith; Deputy Mayor Alderman R. W. James, and Mr. T. C. Dewey.

These gentlemen recognised that a real need existed for a permanent ground on which sports of various kinds could be played. Mr. A. C. Norman was approached, with the result that Mr. Norman consented to let a large area of land in Hayes Lane upon a long lease. Thus there came into existence the Bromley Sports Ground, on which the Town Cricket Club, the Football Club, the Lawn Tennis Club, and the Bromley Town Bowling Club have found a permanent home, the whole being under the control of a representative committee composed of members of the various clubs. The transaction was so speedily carried into effect that the Football Club was installed in its new quarters in time for the season 1904–5.

The achievements of the Bromley Football Club since the war have been in keeping with its previous history, but these fall outside the scope of this chapter.

The Bromley Football Club by no means exhausts the town's enthusiasm for the game.

By 1897 a "Bromley and District League" had come into existence, and proved a strong local attraction. Among the members, distinctively Bromley clubs figured largely—the Bromley A's, Bromley St. Luke's, Bromley Swifts, Bromley Albion, and Bromley Excelsior.

At the beginning of the present century the early-closing movement led, in 1903, to the formation of the "Bromley Wednesday Football League," an association of clubs in Bromley and the neighbourhood which joined in competition for a Cup presented by Mrs. Adams of the Swan and Mitre. A condition of the gift was that all proceeds from the matches should be contributed to local charities.

The "Wednesday League," suspended during the war, still retains its popularity, and by its instrumentality quite considerable sums have been added to the resources of local hospitals.

LAWN TENNIS

Well within the memory of the present writer a ball game was introduced by Major Wingfield into this country under the name of "Sphairistike." Players armed with racquets faced each other on each side of a net, and struck a resilient ball to and fro. The object of each opposing player was so to strike the ball over the net as to prevent his opponent from returning it or to force him to play it outside the limits of the game.

"Sphairistike" was an adaptation and simplification of the ancient "Jeu de Paume" or Tennis, the origin of which extends far back into the mists of time. But that was a game which could only be played under cover in a court specially built for the purpose, and was thus essentially a pastime for the few. "Sphairistike" brought the players into the open air. The game rapidly developed; its original name was forgotten; it became Lawn Tennis, and has long ago achieved the position of the most popular and world-wide game that the genius of man has invented.

The first lawn tennis club to be formed in Bromley—the "Bromley Lawn Tennis Club"—was founded in 1880. Its ground lay just to the south of Holwood Road, being bounded on one side by Love Lane. The first Secretary was Mr. J. H. Lepper, who was the very life and inspiration of the Club—himself quite a formidable player, as the present writer not infrequently discovered to his cost. But the ground was not very suitable, and moreover was, from the first, marked out for the builder. After a year or two an admirable ground was acquired beyond the South Station

WILFRID BADDELEY.

HERBERT BADDELEY.

Lawn Tennis Champions 1891, 1892, 1894, 1895, 1896.

From photographs lent by Mrs. Coxwell.

at the foot of South Hill Park, and it was on that ground that the Bromley Lawn Tennis Club established its reputation as certainly the strongest club in the county of Kent, with very considerable claims, for several years, to be considered the strongest club in the world.

For, concurrently with the growth of the Club, there was growing up an astonishing pair of twins, Wilfred and Herbert Baddeley, in whom a genius for lawn tennis was implanted by nature. Encouraged by a wise father, and with a good grass court in their own garden, they began to develop almost from infancy their remarkable aptitude for the game. As pupils at Quernmore School they had the advantage of a hard court which was laid down between the two houses, Quernmore and Grasmere, in Holwood Road, and it was the business of the writer not only to direct their scholastic education, but also to supervise their games. At the age of eleven either of the boys could give a hard game to one who rather fancied himself as no mean player, and by the time they were old enough to join the Tennis Club they were practically invincible. In doubles they had that perfect understanding which, in the game of lawn tennis, has so often marked twin combinations. In singles Herbert Baddeley was superior to any other member of the Club, except his brother. They made it a rule not to play against one another in serious matches, but there was no question of the superiority of Wilfred as a single player. Indeed, for accuracy, judgment, anticipation, and neatness of stroke it is a question if any player has ever surpassed Wilfred Baddeley. The only deficiency in his game came from his slightness of build, and some consequent loss of power—a deficiency which he almost overcame by artfulness. The opinion of the writer has received notable confirmation in Commander Hillyard's *Forty Years of First Class Lawn Tennis*.

" W. Baddeley," he writes, " was another fine all-round player. He had no weak point anywhere. His game, however, just lacked that little extra sting and power which the superman must possess. For accuracy and judgment he has seldom been equalled, never surpassed, certainly not in the first named attribute. One might go through a whole season without seeing W. Baddeley miss a ' sitter.' I can't say this of any other player I have ever known. His quickness on his feet was also remarkable. Very small and very light, had he possessed more physical power and weight, it is quite possible he might have been the greatest player the world has ever seen."

On three occasions Wilfred Baddeley won the world's championship at Wimbledon—in 1891, when he beat Ernest Renshaw in a preliminary tie, and J. Pim in the final. He retained the championship in 1892, and was champion once more in 1895, and on three consecutive occasions in 1894, 1895, and 1896 he and his brother won the world's championship doubles.

The first club of which they became members was the Hope Park Lawn Tennis Club, and about 1886 they also joined the Bromley Lawn

Tennis Club. In the club matches, played as three pairs, against all the strongest clubs round London, the Baddeley twins played as our first pair, and, in my recollection, they were never beaten. We could count absolutely on three matches to the good before a contest started, and five matches in all were sufficient for a win. No club at that time, whether it were the London Athletic Club, or Gipsy Hill, Beckenham, or any other, could hope to win against Bromley, unless perchance, by some accident, the invincible twins were not playing.

And even then Bromley was hard to beat, for at this time the Club could boast of players who, though lesser stars, were yet stars of great brilliance. Foremost among these was H. S. Barlow, a tall, wiry, tried athlete in many departments of sport, and a lawn tennis player of that class which placed him as runner-up in the world's championship at Wimbledon, Barlow losing the championship when within a single stroke of game by missing a ' sitter.' Barlow, in company with E. W. Lewis, held the doubles championship of the world in 1892.

Stuart Baddeley, a cousin of the famous twins, was another fine player, and close student of the game. He laboured under the disadvantage of his name, and of inevitable comparisons, but as a club player he was far above the average, and with a competent partner he could be depended on to win for the Club more matches than he lost. He was champion of Kent in 1895, and winner of his club championship on six occasions.

At the same time D. E. Payn of Bickley was a member of the Club, a man who subsequently aspired to Wimbledon, and who came out of that ordeal with considerable credit. He was a regular player for the Bromley first team, which, with the very sound assistance of J. H. Lepper and another tolerable player or two, was locally invincible while the Baddeleys flourished, and during that period Bromley would, in the writer's opinion, have beaten any other club in the world.

In 1890 Mr. Lepper resigned the secretaryship of the Club in order to assume the position of Chairman. He was succeeded as Secretary by the present writer, Mr. E. L. S. Horsburgh, who was a member of the Club almost from the first. He held office, however, for but a brief period, being called away from Bromley to other spheres of activity in 1891.

Information concerning the Club since that date is scanty. It continues to flourish, though no longer in its old quarters. In 1910 it was compelled to leave South Hill Park and to find and lay out a new ground in Sandford Road. In 1924 this ground was purchased by the Club, and at the present time it supplies its members with seven grass courts and three *en tout cas* hard courts. Fixtures during the season with other clubs maintain the team spirit which, from the first, has been a conspicuous feature of the Bromley Lawn Tennis Club.

In 1886 the Bromley Park Lawn Tennis Club was founded, with Lord Kinnaird as President and Mr. H. H. Pain as Honorary Secretary. It ceased to exist in 1895, but was reconstituted as the Glen Lawn Tennis Club, with a very picturesque ground off the Highland Road.

The Hope Park Lawn Tennis Club, founded in the early eighties, was a semi-private, but also a most sociable and delightful institution. The Baddeley twins, as boys, were members of this club, which enjoys the distinction of having contributed to their training and skill.

The Sundridge Park Lawn Tennis Club was founded in 1908, its ground being situated in Garden Road, adjoining the Sundridge Park Golf Club. It has twelve grass courts, and a membership of one hundred and eighty full-playing members.

It is during the period since the war that the Club has made such strides, and is now established as one of the leading lawn tennis clubs in Kent. The Club has won a number of county inter-club competitions, and since the war twelve members of the Club have represented Kent in inter-county championship matches.

HOCKEY

In the *Bromley Record* of October 1889 the following announcement appeared :

" In connection with the Bromley Cricket Club a few members have arranged to play Hockey during the coming season on their ground in Widmore Lane. The first meeting was held on Saturday, 28th September."

In these bald, prosaic terms was heralded the birth of perhaps, in its day, the most famous hockey club in the country.

It arose directly out of the financial embarrassments of the Bromley Cricket Club consequent upon its migration from the old historic pitch on White Hart Field to a private ground of its own in Widmore Lane. Faced with the necessity of maintaining the ground throughout the year for the purposes of a sport which was only practicable for some four or five months in the summer, the committee began to cast about to find some means of making the ground remunerative during the autumn and winter. Could not a Lacrosse Club be formed ? Or could the ground be rented to a Football Club ? The latter expedient was adopted, but it was soon found that Rugby football enthusiasts could be a source of considerable annoyance to residents in the vicinity of the ground, and also that the game itself was likely to prove destructive of the turf for the purposes of cricket. Accordingly the arrangement with the Football Club was broken off, and the first proposal, namely that a club should be formed for the purpose of playing some winter game other than football, was brought forward by Messrs. Henry Green and William L. Crossley, who thus became the fathers of the Bromley Hockey Club. For their proposal was agreed to, and, finally, hockey was the game decided on.

When, however, some forty players turned out for the first practice match, several initial difficulties had to be surmounted. What was hockey? How was it played? With what sort of an implement was it played? On these elementary but important points the members of the newly formed Bromley Hockey Club were sublimely ignorant. Nothing daunted, the forty enthusiasts formed themselves into two sides of twenty each, and began hitting the ball about the field with any sort of sticks with which they happened to be provided. One player conceived the happy idea of inserting lead into the handle of a stout oak walking-stick, and felt much aggrieved when this formidable weapon was pronounced illegitimate. But in this rough-and-tumble, unsophisticated crowd there were great players in the making, and when, in the course of a season or two, the members became acquainted with standardised implements and authenticated rules, the Bromley Hockey Club could boast of a first and second team, could arrange a small list of fixtures, and, as a junior club, could venture to enter into competition with other clubs for the Kent Junior Cup. This trophy Bromley succeeded in winning in 1892, and automatically ascended into a higher sphere as a senior club. From this moment the Club advanced, both in success and in prestige, from strength to strength. In 1898 Bromley won the distinction of being champion club of the South of England, with a record of 22 matches played, of which 16 were won, 6 drawn, and none lost, only 23 goals being scored against them out of a total of 126.

Such success was undoubtedly due to efficient team work, and also to the careful training of recruits. What can almost be called a " Hockey Nursery " was formed by Mr. H. C. Bond out of the boys at his preparatory school. A constant succession of carefully trained players was thus available, season after season, and if one stalwart fell out, another, almost if not quite equally good, was ready to take his place.

But though team work and training played their part—and a most important one—in the successes attained, the individual prowess of particular players was perhaps even more important. It so happened that in the heyday of the Club's achievement it could command the services of some of the most brilliant players in the country. No historian of the Bromley Hockey Club can ignore the names of the brothers P. R. and E. A. Earnshaw, the one as steady on the back as the other was transcendent in the forward line—of the brothers Solbé, Frank and Phil, the reputation of the latter being scarcely eclipsed by that of his more famous brother, and of E. G. S. Hose. All of these, with the exception of Phil Solbé, were English Internationals, and in the International match against Ireland in 1899 the three goals which won the match were all scored by Bromley men. But behind these men in the Bromley Club team there were others who were only just their inferiors. It is surely a record that the Kent County authorities, when selecting the county team to play against Surrey, should have chosen

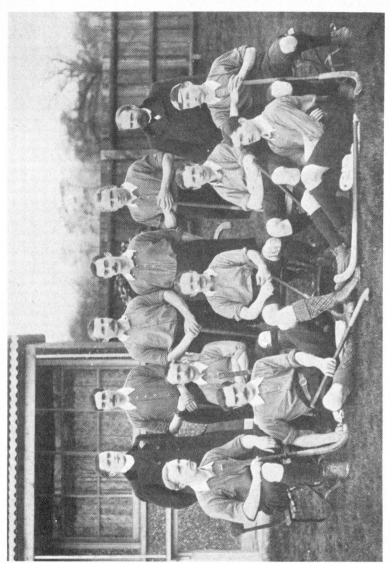

M. Baker,   T. W. Heaysman,   F. Earnshaw,   R. H. Smith,   C. Earnshaw,   H. Green,
P. Earnshaw,   W. G. Beach,   H. Lovell,   F. Solbe,   E. Hose,
F. Clark,   M. Smith.

BROMLEY HOCKEY CLUB TEAM, 1895-6.

From a photograph lent by E. Hose.

ten Bromley Club men to represent the county, the eleventh man being chosen by Surrey to play against them !

There is one other name which cannot be omitted from this record, that of Howard Lovell, who captained the Bromley team through the five most eventful years of its history. When he assumed the position the Club was comparatively unknown ; when, owing to injuries, he retired, it was famous throughout the hockey world. To Lovell's tact, judgment, and untiring energies a large share in Bromley's great achievement is due.

With the beginning of a new century the Bromley Hockey Club entered upon a new epoch in its existence, and it is satisfactory to know that the Club is still not only in being, but flourishing, and carrying forward the great tradition inherited from its past.

GOLF

Though golf is one of the oldest of games, and though the Blackheath Golf Club—so adjacent to Bromley—dates from the reign of James I, a profound ignorance of the game, its merits, difficulties, fascinations, and exasperations, may be said to have prevailed generally throughout the country until about the last decade of the last century. Golf was regarded as an idiosyncrasy of the Scottish people, whose passion for endeavouring to hit " a very small ball into a very small hole with implements singularly ill-adapted to the purpose " was only one problem the more presented by the Scottish character. But the extension of Blackheath enthusiasm to the dunes and wastes of Westward Ho, Sandwich, and Hoylake, the founding of the Royal Isle of Wight Golf Club in 1882, and of other clubs, about the same period in various parts of the country, awakened the consciousness that such a game existed, and that there were people, not otherwise insane, who found pleasure and satisfaction in playing it.

The first course in Bromley was the private course in Sundridge Park laid out by Sir Samuel Scott, which since 1908 has been used by the Elmstead Golf Club.

In 1891 a sufficient number of enthusiasts were to be found in the town and neighbourhood to justify the idea of founding a golf club. Moreover the old Bromley race-course on the common had now ceased to be used for its original purpose. A stretch of ground not altogether unsuitable for the game was thus available. Consequently it was decided to call a meeting of those in any way interested in the proposal, and this meeting was held in October 1891 in the vicarage of St. Luke's, Bromley Common, under the presidency of Rev. R. I. Woodhouse, the Vicar.

It was then and there decided to form a golf club and to lay out a nine-hole course on those portions of the common known as Cooper's Farm and Norfolk's land.

Thus came into existence the Bromley and Bickley Golf Club, the oldest club course, Blackheath and the Beckenham Club at Woodside excepted, in the neighbourhood.

The original Club House of the Bromley and Bickley Golf Club was a small shed, covered with corrugated iron sheeting, and situated in the neighbourhood of the present fourth green. In due time, however, the demand for less cramped and more luxurious conditions became irresistible. The shed was abandoned, and the quarters of the Club were established in the old house attached to Cooper's Farm. At the same time more land was acquired, enabling the original nine-hole course to be extended to a full course of eighteen holes.

Among the original members of the Club two stand out conspicuously —Mr. A. C. Norman, first President, and Mr. J. W. Wheeler-Bennett. Mr. Norman was succeeded in the presidency by Sir Everard Hambro, and later by Lord Avebury.

The name of Hambro is practically synonymous with golf, and the exploits of that family in the game are known to every golfer. Prominent among the members of the Bromley and Bickley Golf Club was Mr. Angus Hambro, whose pre-eminence for some years would have been unchallenged save for Mr. Stuart Wyatt, who proved a foeman worthy of Mr. Hambro's steel. These two players, while they lived in the neighbourhood, were the most formidable competitors in the various club competitions.

The course itself has undergone successive improvements as the popularity of the game has developed. By the courtesy of the Secretary I have been privileged to walk over the ground, and I was much impressed by the fine texture of the greens which I examined, and by the admirable manner in which so flat an area of ground has been induced to provide so many sporting and interesting holes. No inland golf course, in the opinion of a golfer of forty years' standing, can vie with a genuine golf links—a golf *course* and golf *links* are two different and scarcely comparable things— but as an inland course the Bromley and Bickley golf course has much to commend it, apart from its excellent greens which would be a credit to any course.

This result has been achieved by the art of various well-known golf architects. In 1910 Mr. H. S. Colt, the architect of Rye, carried out a new scheme of bunkers, and altered some of the greens ; in 1913 the seventh hole and green were reorganised by Mr. F. G. Waterer, and since the war the skill and experience of Mr. F. G. Hawtree and of Mr. Simpson have effected still further improvements in several of the holes.

The course is laid out so that there is no crossing, and the turf through- out shows a remarkable power of recovery from both excessive rain and excessive drought.

The professional record for the course is sixty-nine, held by Frank Ball, and the amateur record is jointly held up to the present time by two brothers,

Messrs. T. C. and A. G. Bower, who are to-day the recognised champions of the Club.

Sundridge Park Golf Club.—The history of the Sundridge Park Golf Club begins almost at the period when this History of Bromley is designed to end. But as the two histories do in fact overlap for a brief space of time, it is legitimate to introduce here a brief account of so excellent a course, and so flourishing a club.

The idea that portions of Sundridge Park were admirably adapted for the purposes of a golf course originated in the minds of a number of the sportsmen who were accustomed to shoot with Sir Samuel Scott over his estate, and for their benefit a private course was laid out. The idea developed in 1901, when the Sundridge Park Club was formed, and an eighteen-hole golf course was laid out by Willie Park, Jnr. His design was carried into execution by John Randall, who also laid out an additional nine holes, the work being completed and the course being fit for play by the early summer of 1902. A commodious and comfortable Club House was being erected simultaneously with the laying out of the course, and this was completed by the early spring of 1903, the architects being Messrs. Swan and Norman of London.

Accordingly the opening ceremony of the Sundridge Park Golf Club was performed by the Rt. Hon. A. J. Balfour on April 25th of that year under the presidency of Sir Samuel Scott, M.P., Mr. H. W. Forster, M.P., being Vice-President, and Mr. W. Hardy the first Captain.

The course itself, as regards a considerable part of it, lies in the angle formed by the main railway line to Ashford and the branch line from Grove Park to Bromley.

The Club, which numbers over five hundred members (men 350, women 160), has turned out some notable players, and of these Mr. J. B. Beck stands out as the most conspicuous. He is an International; and in 1925 he won the Gold Vase after a tie with Sir E. W. Holderness.

Other principal clubs are the West Kent Golf Club and the Shortlands Golf Club, originally a ladies' course.

BOWLS

Though it is computed that the bowling clubs of Great Britain contain at the present time more than a million members, it is only in comparatively recent years that the ancient game of bowls has taken on its new lease of active and vigorous life. Well known to Shakespeare, and played—as the legend runs—by Francis Drake and the captains who fought the Armada, the game was confined for centuries to a select body of devotees, its appeal to the general public being but slight. The Bromley Bowling Club therefore, formed in 1889, can boast of quite a respectable antiquity, and can also, as will be seen, be proud of some players who can worthily hold their own in any company.

On April 18th, 1889, a meeting was held, at the instance of a few enthusiasts, at the Bell Hotel, when it was decided to form a bowling club. Mr. Edward Packe of Sundridge accepted the office of President, and Messrs. Colin Campbell and J. Melling were elected as Honorary Treasurer and Secretary respectively.   As many as forty members were soon enrolled, and a site for a green was leased to the Club by Mr. Packe at the back of Lady Scott's Schools in Plaistow Lane.   The Club has been fortunate from the first in securing for its quarters so suitable and beautiful a situation.

It was at first resolved to limit membership to fifty, but in a short time the growing popularity of the Club necessitated an increase of the numbers to eighty.   The original rough wooden pavilion, erected for the accommodation of members, gave way to a new pavilion, and later the use of the school buildings was acquired and these were converted into a Club House.   For some years apparently the social attractions offered and the beauty of the surroundings somewhat eclipsed the primary purpose for which the Club was formed.

Mr. Packe was succeeded in the presidency by Sir Samuel Scott, and Mr. Melling by Mr. John King, whose geniality and enthusiasm were of infinite service to the Club.   Upon Mr. King's death in 1907, Mr. Hy. Jas. Green was elected Secretary, an office which he still holds, to the great advantage of all concerned.

In recent years important changes in organisation have taken place, the Club having been incorporated into a limited company in 1923.   The company succeeded in securing from Sir Samuel Scott the freehold of the ground for £2,200, and then built its new pavilion.

The green itself, which is a fine one, was laid down many years ago. It is constructed of Cumberland turf, and is of such a quality that the most noted clubs are glad of an opportunity to visit it.   In 1912 the Australian bowlers were entertained by the Bromley Bowling Club.

The Club is affiliated to the Kent County and to the English Bowling Associations, and indeed in the formation of those associations the Bromley Bowling Club played a prominent part.

Apart from matches with other clubs the fixture list includes several important competitions open to members only, such as the Championship Cup, the Lindley-Jones Challenge Cup, the Loftus Woods, the Edward Packe prize.

In these competitions for club prizes several members have won distinction, notably Colin Campbell, who was Chairman of the meeting in 1889 at which the Club was formed.   He was the winner of the Club Championship in 1891, again in 1901, and yet again in 1907—a notable achievement !

Mr. F. Medhurst had two successive wins in 1902 and 1903, and, being still a member, he may still show that the lapse of a quarter of a century has not impaired his skill.

Mr. J. Grindley with three victories to his credit, in 1914, 1915, and 1918, has a brilliant record to maintain.

But successes in club competitions, important as they are from the point of view of the Club, are of comparatively small value in placing a man in the general bowling world. It would be strange, however, if such a club as the Bromley Bowling Club had not produced players of the first rank, and such players it has produced in Mr. H. J. Green, its Secretary, in Mr. A. P. Poingdestre, and, in the writer's opinion, in Mr. W. W. Gomer.

Mr. Green, Club Champion in 1913, won the Kent County Association Championship in 1911, skipped the winning rink in the London and Southern Counties Association Tournament in 1916 (another Bromley man, Mr. H. Edger, being a member of his rink), skipped the Bromley team which won the Chatham Cup in 1911 and 1913, and with his rink won the Open Rink Competition at Hastings in 1916.

In the organisation of the game in the county Mr. Green has taken a leading part, especially in the formation of the Kent County Association, which dates from 1911.

But greatest of all Bromley bowlers is Mr. Poingdestre. Club Champion in 1924, and Kent County Champion in 1919. Runner-up for the same championship in 1926 and 1927, he crowned his career—until he becomes the actual champion—in 1926, when he reached the final in the English Bowling Association Championship, the highest honour obtainable in the bowling world.

The present writer has had the opportunity of witnessing in other fields than in Bromley the fine spirit of sportsmanship and the equally fine play of Mr. W. W. Gomer. His recent play in the Hastings tournament of 1927 has been in itself sufficient to demonstrate his ability in the open field of bowls. If he has just missed the highest honours it is only because he has competed in the lists with the most dexterous exponents of the game, and in any tournament in which Mr. Gomer is taking part his opponents recognise in him a most dangerous antagonist.

The Bromley Town Bowling Club came into existence as a consequence of the formation of the Bromley Town Cricket Club in 1901. In the following year a Bowling section was formed within the Cricket Club, the titles, Cricket and Bowling, being amalgamated.

As a result of the negotiations with Mr. A. C. Norman for securing a permanent sports ground for the town—(the details of this negotiation are given in the Football section of this chapter)—the Club secured in 1904 a suitable green in Hayes Lane, and a Bowls Pavilion was erected, to be replaced in 1924, upon the immediate prospect of a renewal of the lease for another term of years, by the present structure. The contribution of £100 from Sir Thomas C. Dewey, to signalise the coming of age of the Town's Charter, freed the Club of all debt upon its new Club House.

The Club has a membership of eighty-two playing members, and its long list of fixtures and club competitions is sufficient indication of the vitality of the Club, and of its value to the bowling community in the town.

The Club has come into existence and has flourished outside the period assigned as a limit to this history. This cursory notice aims at nothing else than to indicate the development of the game in Bromley.

CYCLING

It has been the lot of the present writer to have ridden in his day practically every form of bicycle which has ever been in common use. This experience is of value in writing the history of cycling in Bromley, for the first essential in the historian is that he should know something of the evolution of the modern bicycle. Omitting the hobby-horses propelled by the feet operating from the ground, which go back to remote antiquity, the machine, as I first knew it some sixty years ago, went by the name of a " velocipede," or, more colloquially, a " bone-shaker "—the latter name sufficiently indicating its principal characteristic. Whatever joy was derived from riding this machine was due not to its smooth and rapid progress over the ground, but to satisfaction in having gained such a sufficient mastery over it as to be able to progress at all. The driving power was derived from cranks fixed to the axle of the front wheel, and in the original " bone-shakers," if my memory is not at fault, the two wheels were of very much the same size, the front wheel being rather the larger. But this pattern soon gave way to what is now known as the " high bicycle," that is, a machine with an enormous front wheel and an exceedingly small back wheel. My own bicycle, I remember, had a front wheel sixty inches in diameter with a back wheel about the size of a soup plate, and two steps were required in order to reach the saddle. This was the type of machine which was in common use for road and track when the Bromley Cycling Club was established in 1877.

The earliest reference to cycling in Bromley goes back to 1869, when the word ' bicycle ' was scarcely known, the thing itself being called a " dandy-horse," or " velocipede." In the *Bromley Record* of June in that year, under the heading " Bicycle Mania " (the name was known but was not in common use) the following notice appears :

" A highly amusing performance took place opposite the Bell Hotel on Saturday evening, the 22nd of May. A meeting had been announced to which all young gentlemen with any pretension to smartness were invited, to make preliminary arrangements to form a Velocipede Club. Some dandy-horses (to call them by their old name) were in attendance, but proved as unmanageable as unbroken colts, throwing off their riders as soon as they got on, thus creating an amount of fun worth going a mile or two to see. . . . In our opinion the pleasure of riding on a velocipede must be about on a par with that of the Irishman in a sedan chair with the bottom out. But as a certain amount of skill is required in the management, emulation may supply sufficient inducement to make them popular among young gentlemen who have time on their hands. The exercise required to propel them may be beneficial, and, if so, may be a further excuse for their use. Their utility otherwise appears doubtful."

In such terms of semi-humorous contempt the *Record* heralded a movement soon destined to become one of the most popular of pastimes, one of the most convenient methods of locomotion, and one of the great industries of the country.

In the same issue appeared an advertisement of the French Velocipede Company showing a rider mounted upon a machine, and announcing that Mr. Walter M. Walmisley, Wilton House, Palace Grove, Bromley, had been appointed an agent of the company, and that machines could be secured from him at a price of £10, or "payment can be made by instalments if preferred."

Two years later, in July 1871, an advertisement in the *Record* announced that a "Phantom Velocipede Club" had been established for the purpose of supplying each member with a "Phantom" bicycle on payment of a subscription to the Club of ten shillings or one pound a month. A sketch of the machine and its rider was again appended, and a comparison of the two advertisements shows some advance in construction. Though the method of propulsion remains the same, the later machine shows the embryo of a diamond frame.

No further mention of velocipedes or bicycles is to be found either in local newspapers or elsewhere during the next six years, but in that time the machine was rapidly making way with the public, and was improving in design and construction. A trade in bicycles, both distributive and productive, had arisen. A local manufactory had been established in the town under the charge of Mr. W. Bourdon, and in May 1877, probably on the initiative of Mr. Bourdon, the Bromley Cycling Club was founded, with W. Bourdon as Honorary Secretary, mainly, it would appear, for the purpose of organising road races. The Club soon numbered twenty-one members, and of these four turned out on September 11th, 1877, to contest a six-mile race for the Championship of the Club. (They were J. F. Arnaud, A. Brown, J. Doyle, and W. Bourdon.) The course was from the Tiger's Head, Mason's Hill, to Downe Church, and thus was mainly up hill. The day proved most unfavourable. A strong head wind and pouring rain were fatal to the chances of two of the competitors, who were blown off their machines. The winner was W. Bourdon, who completed the distance, without dismounting, in twenty-eight minutes.

An advertisement in 1878 announced that the Club's season would be inaugurated on April 9th by a run to Brighton, but no particulars of this run are available, nor of a plucky ride in 1881 by the Captain, H. Line, and the Secretary, W. Bourdon, from Bromley to John o' Groats, a distance of 805 miles.

In 1887 the Club celebrated its tenth birthday by a concert in aid of its funds, and by this time had secured the interest and support of the Lord of the Manor, Mr. Coles Child, who presided on the occasion, and also presented a Challenge Shield to be held by the winner of the Club Championship. About this time Mr. Coles Child accepted the position of President of the Club, and showed considerable interest in it.

The Club competitions, and indeed the main activities of the Club, were still confined to road racing. New names begin to appear in the lists of winners, notably that of C. L. Newland, who for the next ten years practically monopolised the honours of the Club, and achieved a national reputation as one of the finest riders in the country.

But by 1890 road racing had begun to attract the attention of the police, as being dangerous to the public, and it seemed by no means unlikely that competitors in road races would be made liable to a police summons. The situation, if it occurred, would be awkward for Mr. Coles Child, the Chairman of the Bench of Magistrates, if it were explained to the Bench that the racers were competing for a trophy presented by the Chairman. As a result of a conversation with Mr. W. L. Crossley, Chairman of the Club's Committee, it was resolved to substitute track racing for road racing, and in August 1890 the first of a series of races was held on the Bromley Cricket Ground, though road racing was not entirely abandoned until a somewhat later date. In 1891 C. L. Newland was credited with the $7\frac{1}{2}$ mile championship " on a hilly road," accomplishing the distance in twenty-six minutes, five seconds, and in the same year the same young rider, upon the track of the London County Cycling Club at Herne Hill lowered the 100-miles world record by no less than ten minutes, his time being 5 hours, 30 minutes, $12\frac{2}{5}$ seconds, the whole distance being ridden without dismounting. On this occasion he not only beat the 100-mile record, but all previous records from his sixty-fourth mile onwards. This fine achievement, though not mentioned in the Badminton Book on Cycling, was properly recognised by the N.C.U.

In 1892, at the annual General Meeting of the Club, the Chairman was able to announce that the Bromley Cyclists Club ranked as the third oldest in the kingdom, and held, at that date, thirty-seven records.

In 1894 Messrs. C. L. Newland and F. O. Monkhouse presented a Challenge Cup to the Club entitled " The Vivid Cup," so named after their Cycle Works. This was competed for annually in a 100-mile race. The winner for several years in succession being C. L. Newland, one of the donors, the Cup passed to the man who came in second. In the first year the holder was W. Ware, in 1895 J. E. Ingles, in 1896 S. A. Marples, and in 1897 J. Steer.

In 1898 the 100-mile race was eliminated in favour of a 50-mile distance in the hope that the change would attract a larger attendance of the public. It was evident that a race lasting over four hours was apt to become tedious to all who were not actually taking part in it. The new 50-mile race C. L. Newland won, on its initiation, in 1 hour, 56 minutes, 47⅕ seconds on the track at Catford. The race is notable for the fact that Newland, after covering fifteen miles, was thrown owing to an accident to his pacers, and lost two laps upon the other competitors. In spite of this tremendous handicap, and a rather shattering spill, he none the less came in a winner with about nine minutes to spare, but the cup of course went to the second man, L. G. Jezzi.

By this time the Club was beginning to feel the pinch of circumstances. Track racing requires a properly prepared track, and there was no such track in Bromley. The necessity of transferring to Catford was prejudicial to local interest and local support, and the advent of the motor cycle tended to oust enthusiasm for more sober methods of progression. It was felt that the career of the Bromley Club as a racing institution was over, and that its activities must be given a new direction. It was therefore decided, in 1901, that the Club should concentrate upon its " social aspects," two final race meetings being held to dispose of the various cups which the Club had acquired. These meetings were held on the track at the Crystal Palace; and were something of a scandal inasmuch as the entries numbered but three, for the three cups to be won, and the competition degenerated into a crawl.

In 1902 the official name of the Club was enlarged to " The Bromley Cycle and Motor Club " in the hope that motor cyclists might be attracted to it. Every effort was made, under the secretaryship of Mr. J. E. Carter, to stimulate interest and to infuse new life by country runs, paper chases, and events of that character. But the Report issued on the thirtieth birthday of the Club, in 1907, could only deplore reduced membership and waning enthusiasm, as after dragging on a precarious existence for a few years more the Club became extinct in 1912.

This section cannot be closed without recording the fact that Captain Malcolm Campbell, who established the world's motor speed record of 206 miles an hour on Daytona Beach, Florida, in February 1928, is a Chislehurst and Bromley man, his parents at one time residing at "Bonchester," Chislehurst, and he himself having lived in Bromley from 1905. About the year 1909 he was responsible for the Wanderers Motor Cycle Club, which he originally formed in conjunction with certain of his friends. The Club was limited in membership to thirty and ran some very sporting competitions, including hill climbs, reliability trials, etc. It was upon Bromley's roads that he learned to drive his first machine.

PART III. ADDENDUM

THERE are a few activities, only indirectly associated with the idea of sport, though possessing some affinities with it, which must necessarily find a place in this History. Exactly in what category, or chapter, to place them has proved a problem which I have solved by appending to this chapter an addendum which contains some necessary references to the practice of Gymnastics in Bromley, Ploughing Matches, and Beating the Parish Bounds. All of these have a definitely serious and practical intent from which, however, a sporting element is not entirely excluded.

GYMNASTICS

If it be one of the primary aims of gymnastics to cultivate the *corpus sanum* and the *mens sana*, then, and to that extent, the aims of gymnastics may be said to coincide with those of sport. Gymnastics indeed are the concomitants and forerunners of many forms of sport in so far as they seek to train and develop all the potentialities of the human body, and to make it fit for any form of athletic exertion. Sport is an end in itself ; gymnastics are a means to the attainment of that end, and no boxer, mountain-climber, runner, big-game shooter—in short no sportsman—would regard himself as properly trained for pursuing his special sport unless by gymnastics in some form or other he had previously disciplined his body to its highest point of efficiency. The body thus disciplined is the proper home for the *mens sana*. The one perhaps does not necessarily imply the other, but it is at least much more probable that the sane and healthy mind will be found resident in the trained and disciplined body.

The Bromley Gymnastic Club therefore calls for recognition in this chapter, as having done perhaps more than any other local institution to develop not only physical fitness, but character in the boys and girls, the men and women of the town.

The first serious attempt to form a gymnastic club in Bromley was made in 1873, the members meeting for exercises in the Drill Hall. A class for boys was formed and among the boys who joined this class was William Baxter, at that time a small boy of twelve years. This small boy has proved the true father of gymnastics in Bromley. His association with the movement has lasted from 1873 to the present day, and by virtue of his national and international reputation in the world of gymnastics he was able to invest his own local club with a special prestige and importance.

The experiment of 1873 was not crowned with permanent success. After a more or less precarious existence of six years the Club died away, and a second attempt in 1880 met with even less success. In 1892 a third effort resulted in the formation of a club which existed for six years.

The new enterprise was initiated and conducted by Messrs. Montagu Ilott (Honorary Treasurer), H. E. Bryer (Honorary Secretary), G. C. Harrison (Captain), and Mr. M. L. P. Crozier, who succeeded Mr. Bryer as Secretary. Among the members were W. L. Crossley, A. H. Hewett, L. Lepper, D. Payne, and H. T. Weeks.

On the collapse of this third venture in 1898, Mr. Baxter, having secured the support of Mr. T. C. Dewey, called a meeting at the Bell on October 2nd, 1900, when it was unanimously decided to again form a club with W. Baxter as Captain and Honorary Secretary.

Thus came into existence the Bromley Gymnastic Club, which celebrated its coming of age in 1921.

Mr. Baxter himself would be the first to admit that it was to the cordial support and co-operation of others that his success in founding the Club was due. Foremost among these was Mr. T. C. Dewey, a tower of strength financially and otherwise, Mr. W. R. Gunton, who provided the first home for the Club in the Victoria Hall, High Street, Mr. M. L. P. Crozier, Treasurer, Messrs. H. Marment and B. Gale, Vice-Captains, and W. Logan, Instructor, whose services until his departure for Hong Kong in 1904 proved invaluable.

The first year of the Club's existence was full of activity. A class for boys was formed and in the following year a class for ladies, both with conspicuous results in the future.

A few brief notes indicating its progress and achievement follow :

1902. First gymnastic display in the Grand Hall. Illuminated address and Founder's gold medal presented to Mr. W. Baxter.

1903. Silver challenge shield presented by the ladies of Bromley, also a cup for competition in the boys' class, presented by Mr. Marment. Resignation of Mr. Baxter as Captain, and election of Mr. R. Ayling to that office.

1904. Negotiations for building a gymnasium, the Victoria Hall proving inadequate. Gymnastic Hall, 70 feet by 30 feet, constructed at the back of College Slip. Funds were raised by subscription, and by guaranteed overdraft at the London & County Bank, Mr. Alfred Wright, manager of the bank, becoming Treasurer of the Club.

Inauguration of the new hall by a grand concert and dance, October 4th, 1904.

1905–6. A juvenile class established which proved very effective. Silver plaque presented by Mr. Baxter for the winner in an examination on theory. Resignation of Mr. Baxter as Honorary Secretary and appointment of Mr. W. A. Crossley.

1907–8. Mr. Baxter appointed Steward for the Olympic Games in London.

1908–9.   Gymnastic 'Fest' at Frankfort.   The Bromley Gymnastic Club represented by three ladies, Misses G. L. Ayling, M. M. Baxter, and N. Arnaud, and Mr. Baxter.

National gymnastic display at the Crystal Palace.   Bromley ladies win the tug-of-war.

1910–11.   Miss G. Ayling wins the bronze medal in the Women's Championship of the Metropolitan and Southern Counties Amateur Gymnastic Association.

Mr. H. W. Evans, a member of the Bromley Gymnastic Club, third in the Open Marathon Race from Windsor to Stamford Hill.

1911 and subsequent years.   Financial troubles; appointment of Mr. F. Essex Webb as Honorary Secretary, 1913.   Financial problem solved.

1913.   Great gymnastic 'Fest' at Leipzig, attended from Bromley by Messrs. H. H. Dunn and W. Baxter.

1914–18.   The war.   Club still maintained in being by efforts of the ladies' section.

1919–20.   Mr. W. Whittaker, then Captain of the Bromley Gymnastic Club, wins the individual championship of the Metropolitan and Southern Counties Association.

1920–21.   Roll of Honour unveiled in the gymnasium.   Fifty-five names, five killed.

1921.   Coming of age of the Bromley Gymnastic Club.   Debt on gymnasium finally extinguished, owing mainly to the exertions of Mr. F. Essex Webb.

1923.   Thirty members attend the French Federal Gymnastic Fête at Rouen. Successes of all classes, men, women, and girls, in team drill championships of the Metropolitan and Southern Counties Amateur Gymnastic Association.

1924–8.   The Club has continued to carry on its work with efficiency and success.

These notes are but a bare record of a noteworthy career.   They are, however, sufficient to explain why it is that each successive Mayor of Bromley, since the foundation of the Club, has found occasion to commend the Bromley Gymnastic Club for the useful work which it has done, and is doing, for the Borough.

"This commendation," writes Mr Baxter, "we are still striving to merit."

PLOUGHING MATCHES

The history of ploughing matches in the Bromley district is closely associated with the agricultural history of the country.   They were a local part of a national movement in which West Kent, and the Bromley neighbourhood in particular, figured conspicuously.   They imperatively call for recognition in any history of Bromley.

Only very indirectly can they be associated with sport.   They were competitive contests for prizes, but they were not games ; they were not races ; they were in no sense *play* to those who took part in them ; they can scarcely be called recreation, and as a result of them a piece of valuable and accurate work was accomplished.   They provided what is colloquially called " a day out " for competitors and spectators alike, and they partake therefore of that hybrid form of exertion which, while not play, is not entirely work.

Throughout the nineteenth century these matches played an important part in the life of Bromley and its immediate neighbourhood.

They originated out of the severe conditions of agricultural distress which existed in the years which followed the cessation of the Napoleonic wars.   In and about 1820 various Agricultural Associations came into existence for the purpose of alleviating the prevailing distress and improving the conditions of agriculture, among them the West Kent Agricultural Association, having its centre in the town of Bromley and the support of the landowners and farmers in the various parishes surrounding that town.

The primary aim of these associations was to promote a petition to Parliament for the relief of agriculture.   But in addition, definite and more practical plans were devised having the same object in view, among which ploughing matches were inaugurated in order to improve the standard of skill in this branch of agricultural work.

These contests were divided into various classes with money prizes for each.

Class   I.   Two horses and no driver.
„   II.   Three or four horses and a driver.
„   III.   For Turnrise ploughs with three or four horses and a driver.
„   IV.   For youths not exceeding nineteen years of age.
„   V.   The Champion class.
„   VI.   Champion Turnrise class.

Each team was required to plough a given equal area, about half an acre, and the prize was allotted to the one which, within a given time-limit, succeeded in showing the most perfect furrows in the area ploughed.

The prizes varied from three guineas to ten shillings and sixpence, with an additional few shillings for a driver.   It was usual, also, to present a sum of five shillings to each competitor as an encouragement to enter.

Prizes were also allotted to farm servants according to the length of time they had worked on one estate or for one employer.   " Prizes for ' servitude ' " is the term employed in many of the extant accounts, and they varied in amount from two guineas to one.   Nor do " servitude " prizes exhaust the list.   Farm labourers who had brought up the largest families without receiving parish relief were frequently rewarded, and some figures both for servitude and family awards are worth recording.   In 1822 service prizes were given for 24 and 34 years of service ; in 1870, 29 years and 44 years ; in 1875, 33 years and 41. Family prizes were won with totals of eleven, twelve, and fourteen children.

The number of competitors varied ; there were usually more than thirty ploughs and sometimes over forty. The first match promoted by the Association took place at Kidbrook Farm, Blackheath, in 1820. This was followed by annual contests until 1876. The places selected differed each year ; among them were Hayesford, Hither Green, Holwood Park, Hook Farm, Kent House, Pousty's Hill, Southend, Sundridge Park, West Wickham, and Widmore. A notable feature in the record is that up to as late as 1860, they were frequently held on farms to the north of Bromley, indicating the wide expanse of farm land and open country which then lay between Bromley and London, in contrast with the conditions which prevail to-day.

A notable incident in the match at Bromley " on Captain Satterthwaite's land," 1870, was the first appearance of a steam plough. This was the property of Mr. Edward Wilson, proprietor of the *Melbourne Argus*, who had recently come to live at Hayes Place. The ponderous character of the engine employed, and the lack of stability in the roads at that time, are indicated by the fact that the machine, when passing through Bromley on its way from the manufacturers, caused such a vibration that the plate-glass windows of one of the shops in the town were shattered as it passed. On its arrival on the ground the combined clatter and smoke emanating from it so frightened the horses that its operations had to be suspended until the horse-ploughing was over. The general verdict upon its ultimate performance was that it had done its work better than had been expected.

In true English fashion the proceedings ended in a dinner, attended by members of the Association, their friends, and distinguished persons specially invited.

They were important functions, and were under the presidency of some notable public personage or some established local magnate. In the list we find the names of Sir Edmund Filmer, M.P. (1843), Sir John Lubbock (1859), Lord Cranworth (1861), Mr. E. H. Scott (1870), Viscount Sydney (1871), with the President, Mr. G. W. Norman, always available in case of need.

In 1873 Mr. G. W. Norman resigned the office of President. A tenure of office existing continuously for over thirty years could not be broken without a severe shock to the organisation over which he had so long and so ably presided, and moreover the times were rapidly changing. Steam ploughs were replacing the old familiar horse-drawn instruments of agriculture. Arable land was yielding to grass, and much old-established farmland was being converted into building sites. In 1877 the end came. In October of that year the *Bromley Record* announced with regret that " the West Kent Agricultural Association, which has been in existence for fifty-seven years, has suspended operations for want of funds. The Committee, in acknowledging the services of Messrs. R. and P. Owen, father and son, who had acted as Hon. Treasurer and Hon. Secretary respectively for many years, intend to invite them to a complimentary dinner at the Bell."

This funeral feast was held on October 10th. The Secretary, in explaining the causes of the collapse, was able to show that financial difficulties had been practically overcome. The true reason lay in the fact that land for the purposes of these matches was no longer obtainable, and that agricultural conditions in the district had so entirely changed that it really appeared that the Association had served its purpose, and should therefore come to an end.

BEATING THE BOUNDS

The practice of Beating the Bounds goes back to remote ages, and is perhaps a survival of the solemnities which, among the Romans, celebrated the worship of Terminus, the God of Boundaries. In a very early stage of civilisation each tribe, or association of families, is found to have established itself within its own proper territorial limits, and to have zealously safeguarded from external encroachment the area which it had appropriated as its own. " Thou shalt not remove thy neighbour's landmark" is a specific injunction imposed by the Mosaic law, reinforced by curses on anyone who should disregard it (Deuteronomy xxvii. 17). The " territorial integrity " guaranteed to members of the League of Nations is only a modern expression of the Mosaic principle.

A convenient method of keeping inviolate the territorial rights of the parish was that of " beating the bounds," or, in other words, of officially surveying from time to time the boundary line enclosing the parish, and forcibly removing any encroachment which might be found to have been made upon it. The ceremony implied the preservation of public right against external neighbours and against private individuals within the parish who, by ploughing up footpaths, stopping rights-of-way, or by any other means, might be attempting to deprive the community of its established prerogatives.

No records of the practice, as observed in Bromley, are to be found earlier than 1772, but the proceedings of that year are a sufficient indication that an old custom was then revived ; not a new one initiated.

In the Minute Book of the Parish Vestry Meetings there occurs the following entry under date April 21st, 1772 :

" Whereas the Bounds of this Parish are known by few people at present by reason of the long distance of time since the last procession, and it is thought that some of the neighbouring Parishes have incroached upon this Parish—Resolved that the Churchwardens and Inhabitants of this Parish do walk the Bounds thereof on Holy Thursday next."

This Minute was signed by seventeen persons.   Among their signatures are to be found the names of Robert Booth, Henry Staples, John Dunn, Jeremiah Ringer, and Thomas Proudlove.

It is to be presumed that this resolution was duly carried into effect, but the Minute Books are silent upon this point, nor do they contain any reference to any form of Report to the Vestry on the procession or its results. Such an omission, however, was not unusual, for it seems to have been regarded as sufficient for the Vestry to pass a resolution, the due execution of that resolution being subsequently taken for granted.

In 1782 and 1792 similar resolutions were carried at the Easter Vestry meetings, and thus there was an evident intention to carry out the procedure every ten years, an intention, however, which was either impeded, forgotten, or overlooked, for neither in 1802 nor in 1812 is there any record of beating the bounds.

In 1816, however, at a Monthly Vestry held on September 29th, it was stated that :

" Divers incroachments have been made in this Parish, and Footpaths stopped up since the Bounds of the Parish were last gone round by the Inhabitants—Ordered—that the Rev. Dr. Smith, William Alexander, Martin Smith, John Burgess, John Costin and Edward Costin be and they are hereby appointed a Committee to view and ascertain the extent of such incroachments and Paths being stopped, and report the same to the next Court Leet and Court Baron to be holden for this Manor, and also to the next Vestry."

Accordingly, after due notice was given, a special Vestry meeting was held in the church on November 12th, the Vicar, churchwardens, overseers, and twenty-five other persons being present, when a resolution was passed unanimously :

" that the Bounds of this Parish sh^d be gone round by the Inhabitants on the next Ascension Day,"

and a Committee of thirteen was appointed to make an independent perambulation in order to ascertain and report upon the facts.

The " perambulation," as it is called, of the parish was made by the Committee on November 27th, which on the same day drew up its Report. This document affords ample evidence of the great value of such periodical investigations.   It shows that serious encroachments upon public rights had been made by the owners of Sundridge Park ; also at Bromley Common, where—

" it had been dug up, and carried away in a most shameful manner,"

the culprit here being Mr. Cooper ; encroachments at Keston Mark and at Mason's Hill are complained of, and the condition of stiles and footpaths leading from the church to Beckenham Lane, of those in the neighbourhood of Simpson's Place and of Plaistow Lane, is in turn the subject of severe condemnation.

That this Report was something more than a mere pious opinion, and that it had an effect, is proved by the fact that Mr. Cooper of Bromley Common, the Hon. Hugh Lindsay, and others, were at pains, either personally or through representatives, to justify or excuse their conduct, and the Vestry Clerk was instructed to send extracts from the above Report—

" to Sam¹ Scott Esq., Robert Makepeace, and Stewart Erskine Esq and Mr. Robᵗ M. Smith so far as the same relates to the matters complained of against them respectively."

Notwithstanding this official perambulation by a specially appointed Committee, the bounds were duly beaten in customary procession on Holy Thursday 1817, but at this point the sources of information run dry, and the custom of beating the bounds fell into abeyance for a period of forty-two years.

(I think it may be of interest, and possibly of real value, to insert here, even at the risk of a somewhat long digression, a list of the actual encroachments upon the rights of the parish of which this Report complains. I therefore quote the salient extracts from the Minutes of the Vestry Meeting to which the Report was presented. There will thus be on record, in this History, the precise claims, put forward more than a century ago, to public right in various parts of the parish, and the reader will be able to judge how far those claims coincide with the actual conditions of to-day.

Encroachments—at Sundridge :
The ancient footway and bridleway leading through Sundridge Park from Plaistow to Elmstead—diverted, not by order of the Justices ; but another, equally good, substituted.

But access to the said path, hitherto freely enjoyed, now only obtainable through " the carriage gates which were this day locked."

Foot passengers debarred from " passing that way " by the gatekeeper, acting on the instructions of Mr. and Mrs. Scott.

Inside the Lodge gates a board was found " with ' No Footpath or Carriage Road ' written thereon."

Gates across the paths and highways at Milk Street leading to Tandy's Farm and Marvels.

About a quarter of an acre added to one of Mr. Scott's fields.

A footpath from Hyde's wood through Scott's wood stopped.

But, as a set-off, " In Plaistow Lane Mr. Scott's fence set back, widening the road for 200 yards much to the benefit of the public."

At Kickley's Farm :
Two ancient footways barred by spiked gates, and notices of " No Thoroughfare through this yard."

At Bromley Common :
Encroachments on several pieces of the common.
Erection of a post and chain fence, and the planting of fir trees near Mr. Cooper's house.
The common " dug up at divers places, and carried away in a most shameful manner," the sheep-washing pond thus being spoiled for its purpose.

At or near Keston Mark :
" Mr. Moissard has taken considerable quantity of sward, and packed the same at the edge of the lawn in front of his house, which is an enclosure from the Common, and dug a very deep ditch which is dangerous for cattle."

At Mason's Hill :
Encroachments from the waste, adding to the ground of Robert Makepeace, and also ground carried away at Shooting Common.
And miscellaneous complaints as to the condition of stiles in various parts of the parish.)

Subsequent to 1817, it was not until 1859 that the old custom of beating the bounds was revived. At a Vestry Meeting held on March 26th of that year it was resolved :

" That the Parish officers be authorised and requested to perambulate during the present year the boundaries of the Parish, and to take all such steps as may be necessary (by application to the Poor Law Board or otherwise) to legalise an expenditure not exceeding £40 for that purpose."

No further entries relative to this business appear in the Vestry Minutes, nor is any information afforded as to the costs involved, or as to the persons to whom costs were paid. It is therefore to the *Bromley Record* of May 2nd, 1859 that we must turn for an account of the actual proceedings, which were in fact conducted with all due ceremony in accordance with the Vestry's resolution. The day chosen for the " procession " was Wednesday, April 20th—the Wednesday immediately preceding Easter Day, and on that day a posse of the principal inhabitants, accompanied by the churchwardens, overseers, vestry clerks, surveyor, and reinforced by a strong contingent of " lads,"

" started from Shortlands Station at 9 a.m. They returned to the same spot at 7.30 p.m., having accomplished a round of about 18 miles. The officers of the adjacent Parishes met the Bromley gentlemen at various points to compare maps etc., and everything appears to have passed off pleasantly in that respect as well as in every other. Although 42 years have elapsed since a similar duty in this parish was performed, the old-time custom of ' bumping ' was not forgotten. The day was fine, and full of incident not likely to be soon forgotten by the juvenile portion of the party. Having completed their task, they all adjourned to a welcome repast provided in the best style by Mr. Sutton at the Bell Hotel."

Possibly the last paragraph of this report provides the solution of the problem of costs incurred in the execution of these parochial duties.

The last occasion on which the bounds were beaten was in 1890, after an interval of thirty-one years, Messrs. W. J. Ardern and G. King being the overseers and Mr. George Stone assistant overseer. It is especially memorable in that the procession was joined, at Shortlands, by Mr. J. B. Walter, who had " walked the bounds " in 1817, and again in 1859. This gentleman was at the time eighty-five years of age, and therefore, in 1817, he was one of the " lads " who, armed with their white sticks, appear to have been from time immemorial an indispensable adjunct to the proceedings.

The company consisted of about a hundred persons, including some scores of boys from the Bromley and Plaistow Schools, in charge of their respective masters, Messrs. J. Churchill and L. R. Laumann. The expedition was equipped with ladders to surmount walls and hedges, a sledge-hammer to remove obstructions, and an axe to blaze the trees standing on the boundary line.

The full report given in the *District Times* of May 23rd is chiefly concerned with the victims of the " bumping " rite which was duly and somewhat indiscriminately observed. Among the sufferers were a passing "parson" and a "cook" who were reluctantly transformed from mere spectators into actors in the drama.

But serious business was not neglected. In the neighbourhood of Grove Park the overseers of the parish of Lee met the beaters and agreed upon their respective boundaries ; or, rather, as the construction of the railway had obliterated the boundary marks, a meeting of the respective overseers was arranged to determine the line of demarcation. As a token of good feeling the Chislehurst overseer, Mr. H. J. Willis, was "bumped" upon his own limit. At the junction with the parish of Hayes the overseers of that parish were conspicuous by the courteous assistance which they rendered to the expedition, and in due course the round was completed, about 9 p.m., the proceedings ending by " bumping " the police constable who had been assiduous in his attendance from the start.

The really serious business of the day was, however, yet to be transacted. The whole company adjourned in due course to the Bell, where under the genial presidency of Mr. R. G. Mullen a plethora of food and speeches brought the day to an appropriate conclusion. One remark by Mr. Mullen calls for attention to-day. He congratulated the beaters on

"BEATING THE BOUNDS" OF

William J. Ardern and George King, Overseers.

BROMLEY PARISH, MAY 21ST, 1890.

George Stone, Assistant Overseer.

1. P. C. Stewart.
3. — Vousden.
6. John Perry.
10. William King, son of No. 43 ; brother of No. 32.
11. J. Saunders.
12. A. H. Potter.
13. Neville Flux, Bandmaster R.E.; son of No. 35.
14. Will Gedney, brother of C. W. Gedney.
15. Fred Hunt.
16. Leonard Heaysman, son of No. 48.
17. Harry Lansbury.
20. Sidney Heaysman.
21. Tom Jayes, son of No. 44.
22. Amos Borer.
26. F. Lowrence.
27. Jos. Ayling, son of No. 49.
28. Tim Borer, son of No. 22.
29. Wm. Hopton, brother of No. 34.
30. J. Churchill, Headmaster, National School.
31. E. Mitchell, son of W. Mitchell.
32. J. King, son of No. 43.
33. Robt. Girling.
34. George Hopton, brother of No. 29.
35. R. Flux, Host of Duke's Head.
36. Robt. Cooper, Corn Chandler, Market Place.

38. — Widgery.
39. Reg. Lewis, son of Louis Lewis.
40. J. Bond.
41. Dick Fawsitt.
42. Martin J. Dickins.
43. George King, Overseer.
44. H. Jayes, Host of Rose and Crown.
45. George Stone, Assistant Overseer.
46. Henry Heaysman.
47. Chas. Knight, Knight's Farm.
48. Thos. Heaysman, Drum Major, 18th Kent R.V.
49. Wm. T. Ayling.
50. Regd. James.
51. C. F. W. Gedney, son of C. W. Gedney.
52. Robinson Latter, Solicitor, Clerk to Justices.
53. Harry Gooding.
54. Henry Redfern.
55. — Ayling, son of No. 100.
56. George H. Payne, Junr., son of No. 60.
57. G. Bartlett.
58. Jas. Birch Walter.
59. — Williamson.
60. George H. Payne, Member of Local Board.
61. Wm. Alex. Grubb.
64. — Scott.

65. Thos. Ranson.
67. W. J. Ardern, Junr., son of No. 77.
69. H. A. Amos.
71. Geo. Amos, son of George Amos.
72. William Gomer.
73. Ed. Latter, son and successor to No. 52.
75. Sidney Pearce.
76. Albert Sales.
77. Wm. J. Ardern, Overseer.
79. Jas. R. Pocock, Sexton.
81. Wm. Wood, son of A. Wood.
82. G. Smith.
83. A. Ruegg, son of H. Ruegg.
86. — Arnold.
87. G. O. Eastwood, Police Inspector.
88. — Blanks.
89. — English.
90. G. F. Barwell.
92. — Hunt, son of W. Hunt.
93. Louise Laumann, Headmaster, Plaistow School.
95. Hy. Fryer.
96. Jno. Arnold.
98. F. G. Green.
100. Edwin Ayling.
102. Alex. Ayling.
104. J. Amos, brother of No. 71.
105. — Burgess.

" having accomplished their task as well as, if not better than, their fathers accomplished it thirty-one years ago. He sincerely trusted they might live to beat the bounds again thirty-one years hence."

Having traced the history of this ancient ceremony from the earliest recorded times it only remains to add a word as to procedure.

From the extant records it would appear that tradition assigned " Holy Thursday," or Ascension Day, as the proper day on which the function should be performed. " Holy Thursday " is specifically mentioned in the resolutions of 1772 and 1782, while " May 17th "—the day prescribed in 1792—was Ascension Day in that year. In 1816, on the proposition of Dr. Henry Smith, it was resolved that " the bounds should be gone on the next Ascension Day "—i.e. on Ascension Day, 1817—though in the meantime a specially appointed Committee had made a " perambulation " on November 27th for the purpose of formulating a Report. Though there is no record on the Vestry Minutes that the resolution adopted in 1816 was actually carried into effect, we know that it was, and that on Ascension Day 1817 an organised " procession " supplemented the " perambulation " of the previous November. The long intervals between 1817 and 1859 and between 1859 and 1890 seem to have obliterated the memory of the ancient tradition, the ceremony being observed in 1859 on a Wednesday (April 20th) and in 1890 again on a Wednesday (May 21st). Where old survivals, straight from remote antiquity, are still preserved, it seems only fitting that they should be preserved in their integrity, and that the date, as well as the ceremonial rites, should be strictly adhered to.

Of the ceremonial rites themselves the actual " beating " of the bounds was by no means a mere metaphorical expression. Hence the white sticks with which the company was armed as being essential ingredients in the performance. These were the weapons most frequently in use, though the ladders, axes, hammers, etc., played their part wherever obstruction was encountered. The particular rite, however, which most appealed to all except the victims of it was that of " bumping "—a practice derived from the remote past. The boundaries of the parish were marked at intervals either by posts, specially erected and known as " parish posts," or by some particular tree or stone, or other feature of the landscape which served the purpose. When any one of these " posts " was reached tradition demanded that somebody—either a member of the party or an outsider—should be " bumped " upon it. The selected individual was poised between two captors, one at the shoulders and one at the legs, and swung with a " one, two, three " against the post, thus apparently establishing it as the faithful guardian of the boundary until the next occasion. There were naturally variations in the point of view, some regarding the bumping as an honour to be courted, others as an unwarrantable indignity to be resented. Instances are recorded of " stout resistance " on the part of the latter, but however stubborn the resistance it had eventually to yield to superior force. On arrival at the end of the day at the original starting-point a series of indiscriminate bumpings preluded the ample repast, and accompanying " bumpers " which brought the proceedings to a close.

At the Public Library there is a photograph of the party which last " beat the bounds " in 1890, which is reproduced here.

Chapter XV

PART I. LONDON ROAD TO MARKET-PLACE

IT must be difficult for those who have come to live in Bromley since the close of the nineteenth century to realise adequately how very rural in appearance, and character, it had remained right up to and rather beyond the middle of that century.

For many years, possibly for centuries, there seems to have been but little change.

Compared with the present sixty-five miles of roadway there were then but four miles of main road and ten miles of subsidiary lanes, veritable lanes, narrow and winding, without footpaths, bordered on both sides, in many places, and for long distances, by tall trees, whose interlacing branches completely overshadowed them.

Of the four thousand six hundred and ninety-six acres of land comprising the Borough, nineteen-twentieths of them were then still used either for agriculture or as parks to embellish the mansions of some eight or ten landowners.

A number of flourishing farms [1] were scattered over the area, some of which have entirely disappeared. In others the farm-house is still left, and is now used as a private dwelling, while in a few cases farming is still carried on, the substantial outbuildings indicating how important the industry had formerly been.

Fields on every side came right up to and touched the backyards and gardens of the houses in the High Street and the Market-place, and hop-gardens were within a few hundred yards of both. One of these was at the foot of Martin's Hill, between it and the Ravensbourne, and a group of such gardens was on the Palace Estate midway between the town and Bickley. The conical roofs of their oast-houses, and wooden ventilators of their drying kilns, were a marked feature as one walked across the " Paddock," the name by which the stretch of meadowland in front of the Palace was then known.

These gardens were notable for their frequent success in sending the first pocket of hops of the season into the London market.

---

[1] *Names of Farms.*—Hall's in Milk Street, Sundridge Hall in Burnt Ash Lane, Sundridge Park in Plaistow Lane, Blackbrook in Southborough, Oakley, and Hook on Bromley Common, Bencewell in Oakley Road, Hayesford in Hayes Lane, all of which are still with us ; but the following farms have gone : the Palace in what were the Palace Grounds, Spring-hill in College Road, Widmore on Widmore Hill, Eaton's in Tylney Road, and the following farms are now private residences : Bickley Hall, Hawthorn Road ; Turpington in Southborough ; New, off Westmoreland Road, S. Hill ; Cóoper's in Magpie Hall Lane, now a golf clubhouse.

BROMLEY PALACE FARM, OFF WIDMORE ROAD, PULLED DOWN 1927

In the middle of the last century there were about fifty shops in the High Street and Market-place, most of them small, and many very small, and without what is styled a shop front. To-day in the same area there are over two hundred, many of them large establishments.

With the advent of the railway in 1858 an era of change set in, which rapidly led to the cutting up of estates, and the planning of roads in every direction.

This chapter is an attempt to present a picture of Bromley as it was before the change took place, and at the same time to give a brief account of some of those who had lived there who do not find a place in other parts of this volume.

It is, however, necessary to put drastic limitations to the material actually available for this chapter. The recovery of the Rate Books from 1673 onwards, with only one gap of twenty-nine years, enables the historian of Bromley, if space were no object, to record the names not only of the owners, but also of the tenants, of each house in the town for practically two hundred and fifty years. To do this, within any reasonable compass, would be as impossible as it would be tedious. It is not therefore proposed to go back beyond the eighteenth century, except in special cases where some name is of peculiar interest or importance.

Coming towards Bromley from London the boundary stones of Lewisham and Bromley were seen on the right-hand bank a little below the top of Bromley Hill. There the first things which met the visitors' gaze were : the old ninth milestone from London Bridge ; and, on each side of the road, an entrance Lodge and gates giving access to two estates.

The estate on the left or eastern side was a house and park—Plaistow Lodge, now Quernmore School—bounded on the south side by London

Lane, or, as it was then called, Boyd's Lane, from the name of the occupier, narrow and winding and bordered by fine elm trees.

In the area south of Boyd's Lane, bounded by London Road, Farwig Lane, and what is now College Road, was a collection of fields, orchard and nursery ground, widening as the town was approached. In that area, with the exception of some cottages in Farwig Lane, and the farm at Springhill, lately demolished, there were but three houses — Hawthorn Cottage, which is still at the corner of Hope Park, Godfrey Stidolph's house, a picturesque half-timbered dwelling situated where the Beech Tree Inn now is, and the old cottage in London Lane close to its junction with College

WINDMILL FORMERLY ON LONDON ROAD
From a drawing by David Cox owned by Mrs. Boys Behrens.

Road. Over this area the whir of a covey of partridges might be heard as they rose from the stubble, and pheasants were at times disturbed from their nests in one of the orchards ; hares were a common sight. Godfrey Stidolph's picturesque house and nursery ground occupied the S.W. corner of this area, and in front of the house stood a fine purple beech which gave its name to the Beech Tree Inn that has replaced it. The alleged transportation of this tree to the Crystal Palace is examined in the Plaistow section of this book.

The only houses along the western side of London Road were two small houses for persons employed on Colonel Long's estate, a row of sunken cottages known as Tranquil Place, built in the old parish gravel pit, where flints were formerly obtained for road-making, building, and the fashioning of flint locks for guns. There were also the Laurel Inn, the row of houses adjoining it called Salubrious Range, and the white gabled house that lately stood where motor works are now. Occupying a site just north of these last-mentioned premises from 1731 till 1845 stood Bromley Workhouse.

A windmill, mentioned in the will of Edmund Style of Langley, dated 1614, as having then lately been erected by him, formerly occupied a prominent and rather awkward position near the high road ; probably somewhere near to the corner of Park End. A noteworthy achievement in connection with this Mill is recounted in the *Annual Register* for 1768, (Vol. XI, p. 164), where the moving of it bodily some 400 yards by means of "capsterns" is described. It is shown on Rocque's map published in 1744–5 and on some old plans.

In a copy of Dunkin's *History of Bromley* at the Public Library with original sketches made in 1825 by T. Crofton Croker there is an excellent sepia drawing of this windmill.

The mill disappeared in 1845.

Sir Edmund Style's will, mentioned above, also states that the mill was let by him for £3 per annum. In May 1821 the Right Hon. Charles Long let the windmill, messuage and tenement, and five acres of land to John Humphrey for £62 per annum, an indication of the growth in value of property between the seventeenth and nineteenth centuries.

A little way down Farwig Lane, formerly the main carriage-way into the town from Plaistow, there might be seen on the left one of the picturesque blacksmith's forges for which the district was notable, this one being for many years in the hands of Mr. King. On the right were the offices of Bromley's first gas works; in fact, the porticoed entrance is still there. The works stood behind, and partly covered, the ground now occupied by houses in Longfield, in the cellar of the last of which can be seen part of the wall of one of the gasometer foundations.

Adjoining these old gas works, and reaching to the boundary wall of the College grounds towards the south, and to what is now College Road towards the east, was a large cornfield called College Field. This was traversed by two footpaths which crossed the field diagonally from corner to corner, joining on its eastern margin another path which has now become College Road.

At "Lauriston," a modern house built in the London Road immediately opposite this field, lived from 1883 to 1896 Sir Joseph Wilson Swan, who invented the electric lamp in which an incandescent filament was the source of illumination. This invention was but one of many contributions to science made by him.

Bromley College presented the same appearance that it does to-day, except that the fine chestnut trees, which embellish that side of the roadway, are now more fully grown, and that in front of its entrance gate stood two stone hitching-posts with curled wrought-iron hooks on the top of them to which equestrian visitors, who were much more numerous in those days, could hitch their horses. These were removed in 1899, being an obstruction to the footway, but are now erected along the edge of the roadway leading into the College from the lodge.

At this point opposite the College main gateway the High Street begins.

Here was a group of houses, two of which were set back behind iron railings enclosing small forecourts.

THE CORNER OF HIGH STREET AND BECKENHAM LANE.
Pulled down 1925.

In one of these lived Joseph Churcher, a man of parts, a member of one of the old families of Bromley which have contributed service to the town in several capacities, the name appearing continually from the latter half of the eighteenth century. Thus John Churcher in 1807 was appointed High Constable for five years in succession, a very unusual procedure.

The houses at the corner of Beckenham Lane formed a characteristic and picturesque bit of old Bromley. The varied wares of the tradesmen displayed on open stallboards abutting on the pavement, a group of wooden cottages, erected in 1811 by Abraham Nettlefold, overhung in the springtime by clusters of wisteria blossom, all contributed to create a scene which, viewed at sunset, remains as a treasured memory to those who are still left to recall it.

The illustration here given will help, those who knew it not, to realise something of its charm.

This corner was associated for upwards of ninety years with the family of Browning, and hence was known as "Browning's Corner." Their business was of a varied character : bacon and ham-curing, sausage-making, green-grocery in all its branches, the vegetables being mostly grown upon their own land in Plaistow, were its principal activities. Charles H. Browning was conspicuous among his family for his stalwart Nonconformity, which led him constantly to refuse to pay church rates, and to laugh at all threats of distraint. He died comparatively recently, in 1896, his wife surviving him till 1924. She contributed some of her reminiscences to the *District Times* of May 14th, 1920.

At the Public Library there are two old plans of all the land north of Beckenham Lane and west of London Road ; one, dated 1720, by John Holmes, surveyor, and another dated 1794 by James Taylor, of Chancery Lane, London. In that of 1720 the corner piece of land is given as belonging to the late Richard Swift. North of this piece and extending up to the present site of Park End is the Pest House Field of 11½ acres, and in its extreme south-east corner is shown the Pest House itself.

This Pest House is mentioned from time to time in the Rate Books. Thus in 1722 : " ½ yrs. rent of the Pest House £3 John Drury," and again in 1723, " for the Pest House £6." During the Plague of London, 1665, the bodies were carted out to be shot pell-mell into vast pits prepared for them in the surrounding country. It is accepted that the country to the south and south-east was much chosen for this purpose owing to the Thanet sand deposits, and it is a local tradition that in this Pest House Field one of these pits was dug. Bodies that were labelled with name, address, etc., were first deposited in the lazarettes known as pest houses. This ensured their entry in the nearest Parish Register. There are such entries in the registers of the Parish Church.

To the west of the Pest House Field, down Beckenham Lane, was

Pitt's Field of nine acres situated opposite what is now called " Pixfield," possibly a corruption of " Pitt's Field."

On the farther side of Beckenham Lane facing the High Street stood, as now, the Swan and Mitre, a low-roofed inn, standing well back from the road to afford room for the country carriers' carts and wagons that might at all times of the day, and especially in the late evening, be found there baiting their horses on their journeys to and from the London markets. This house certainly dates at least from the middle of the eighteenth century. Of its landlords William Fownes (1848) was conspicuous as a crack whip in the old coaching days. Joseph Harradine, who became the landlord in 1855, found there a large number of crutches left by patients who had been cured by Bromley's noted surgeon, Mr. James Scott, and also a list of twenty-four landlords previous to 1839. It is unfortunate that this list, which would have helped to establish the antiquity of the inn, has been lost.

Dealing generally with the upper part of the High Street from the Swan to the drinking fountain, opposite the Bell Hotel, the whole of the buildings on the right-hand (W.) side were pulled down in 1901–2, with the exception of the house which is now Collings Brothers' shop.

Of the houses on the left-hand (E.) side, less than half of the original structures remain, and most of those have been materially altered Until the end of the seventeenth century the whole of this area as far as the Bell Inn was mainly park land, in which was situated the " Grete House " connected with the important families of Knight and Thornhill.

With the disappearance of the Great House its place was taken by the houses which constituted the east side of the High Street. Many of these were of wood, few of them more than two stories in height, some having attics in the roof lit by projecting dormer windows.

The shops were mostly very small, many having semicircular bow windows of small square panes, the one least altered being now occupied by F. Lowrence, shipping agent.

At the doorways of many of the houses on each side of the street there were steps projecting on to the footway, and a few had forecourts with pollarded lime trees in front of them, giving a shady and picturesque aspect to the Upper High Street in striking contrast to its present appearance.

The illustrations (facing page 368) of this part of the High Street, one dated 1835, and another 1865, afford a very fair idea of its appearance at these dates.

Reverting to the west side and starting from the Swan, the first house beyond the inn was a wooden one, with stables, standing back from the road, approached through the gateway now forming part of Messrs. Gunton's premises. Here lived Thomas Baxter, who first established in Bromley the business of auctioneers and estate agents now known as Baxter, Payne & Lepper. His father had carried on a business of the kind at Eltham in the latter part of the eighteenth century, and his eldest brother, Samuel, con-

THE SWAN INN.

From a water-colour drawing by J. T. Wilson, 1869, lent by Mr. P. Norman, F.S.A.

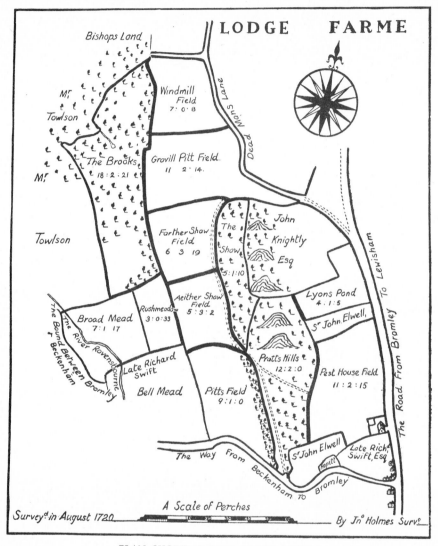

PLAN SHOWING PEST HOUSE FIELD

ducted a similar business in the early part of the nineteenth century at Chislehurst. Thomas, however, realising the better prospects which Bromley offered, transferred both enterprises to the town. He died in 1858.

The business then devolved upon his nephew George Bodle Baxter, who later took into partnership his elder brother Samuel, and their nephew

Frederick Payne. Later both the Baxters retired, and, with the advent of J. H. Lepper in 1876, the firm assumed its present title of Messrs. Baxter, Payne & Lepper.

Next to this was a large white-timbered house of three stories with many green-shuttered windows and a handsome pillared doorway of the Queen Anne type, with a small forecourt in front. This was the home of the Misses Lamb's school for girls which had some fame in its day.

Beyond this was the house now forming Messrs. Collings Brothers' shop. From our illustration of this part of the High Street it will be noticed that this is the only brick-built house among those which are visible. Being the house of a builder it was perhaps constructed as an advertisement of his capabilities, for these premises were the residence of the principal builders in Bromley for over 220 years, being occupied for over 140 of these years by the family of Staples.

The chief member of this family was Henry Staples, who was buried in a vault under the north aisle of the Parish Church in 1803. He is repeatedly mentioned in the Rate Books and also in Wilson's *History of Bromley*, 1797. He was High Constable in 1768 and overseer in 1765, and was evidently a man of substance, judging by the property he owned. His father, or perhaps grandfather, John Staples, was overseer in 1723, and before him (1695) there were Henry Staples, senior, and Henry, junior. In 1673 a John Staples appears in a list of those rated under the hearth-tax, in 1662 another Henry is recorded, and also George, Thomas, and Charles, who resided somewhere on Bromley Common.

The Staples family were succeeded in High Street by the Muffets, William who died in 1817, and Charles who died in 1883. Both were the leading builders in Bromley, and for some period the only ones, albeit in later times there arose a formidable competitor in the person of Richard Barrett.

Charles Muffet was a man of some importance, a prominent member of the Ratepayers' Protection Society of 1872, Chairman of the Local Board 1872–1876, and the builder of the present chapel in Bromley College.

The next range of buildings consisted of six wooden houses, their construction being well shown in our picture. They were tenanted by various tradesmen. The first was the shop of William Gomer, a dairyman, who still adhered to the custom of wearing a grey swallow-tailed coat, knee-breeches, worsted stockings, and buckled shoes. Another was that of John Innous the tailor, an original Trustee of Lascoe's Charity, 1859.

Next to these were two brick houses set back behind iron railings enclosing small forecourts with short flights of stone steps leading up to their front doors. The first of these was the home of the Bromley Savings Bank, established on March 25th, 1816, for the use of the inhabitants of Bromley and the surrounding seventeen parishes, of which an account is given elsewhere.

THE UPPER HIGH STREET, 1835.

THE UPPER HIGH STREET, 1865.

Subsequently it became the business premises of the photographer and music seller, R. V. Harman of West Wickham. He was indeed a man of many parts—an enthusiastic Volunteer, a prominent member as Colour-Sergeant of the 18th Kent Rifle Volunteers, and later Major of the 2nd Tower Hamlets Rifle Corps. On his retirement he was the oldest efficient Volunteer in the service.

For six years he served as Deputy Superintendent of the voluntary fire brigade, and also as a special constable at the time of the Fenian disturbances in 1868.

To these activities he added a lively faculty for assisting and promoting the entertainment of the Bromley public by composing and reciting some of the Prologues which formed an essential feature of the annual Christmas Entertainments organised by the Literary Institute.

The adjoining brick house was Thomas Morley's " Bromley Academy," carried on in union with the College of Preceptors, of the Council of which body Mr. Morley was a member. The " three R's " were soundly taught.

" Writing in both plain and ornamental style, Arithmetic logically, and History with special reference to ancient Egypt."

Such is the tenor of Mr. Morley's advertisement. He had formerly been an usher at Rawes' famous Bromley School, which appears to have closed about 1849, for in that year Mr. Morley took the opportunity to open his academy at No. 67 High Street. In 1855 he removed to No. 74. He earned a well-deserved reputation in that he turned out many boys who have since served their town and other places in various useful capacities. The scholar of Morley's Academy who has attained the greatest fame is the author H. G. Wells, who received some of his early training here. On Mr. Morley's retirement he was presented with a testimonial from his old pupils, who were to be found scattered in all parts of the world. The function took place at a dinner given at the Bell Hotel on February 22nd, 1881, when an address on vellum and a silver ink-stand were presented as a gift from eighty-two of the old boys, about half of whom were present, one of them, Mr. W. R. Mallett, presiding.

After these two more substantial houses noted above came another series of wooden houses extending as far as a stone flagged passage-way, which led up past some cottage gardens, gay with flowers, to the old Wesleyan chapel. In the first of these small houses lived a man named Hall, who was one of the last of the post-boys plying between Bromley and Sevenoaks.

On the right-hand corner of this paved way lived John Hall, of whom a notice, supplementary to that given elsewhere, seems fitting here. He was a tallow-chandler and candle-maker by trade, one of his specialities being the small coloured candles used to decorate Christmas trees, which had then but recently been introduced into English homes. His chief title to be remembered, however, was his great benevolence. Although but a poor man, no case of genuine distress appealed to him in vain. He would suffer himself in order to give relief, and thus became known as the Bromley philanthropist. For nearly forty years he was treasurer to the Bromley Philanthropic Society. He also acted as almoner to several of the more wealthy inhabitants. During the period of severe distress in the winter of 1878–9 he issued an appeal, and collected personally over £400 for the relief of those in need. This charitable work always had the first claim upon his time and services, to the detriment of his personal affairs. In 1881, when upwards of eighty years of age and past work, 258 of his fellow-townsmen, in recognition of the good that he had done, presented him with an annuity for himself and his wife, which he enjoyed till his death in 1891.

On the opposite corner lived a carpenter named James Peerless, the adjacent building becoming in due course the premises where Mr. John Howard originally started the business which has since developed into Howard's Stores.

Below this were the last pieces of greenery that adorned this part of the High Street—a row of lime trees and some shrubs, which remained until the widening of 1902, standing in front of Rawes' School. The school-house itself afterwards became the business premises of George Sweeting, a plumber. He took an active part in the town's affairs, as did his nephew, George H. Payne, who succeeded him. The latter served on the Local Board, the Urban District Council, and various other boards. He was a guardian for seventeen years, and, when he died, only one other of Bromley's public men could point to a greater length of service to the town. He, like R. V. Harman, was an enthusiastic Volunteer, joining the 18th Kent Rifle Volunteers in 1864, and retiring, after sixteen years' service, with the rank of quartermaster-sergeant. He afterwards obtained a commission in the 2nd Tower Hamlets Rifle Corps and retired as captain in 1896.

The adjoining house, substantially built of red brick with iron railings enclosing a forecourt, occupied the site of the present premises of Messrs. George Weeks and Sons. For about a century and a half it was the home of a succession of doctors and surgeons, of whom the earliest on record secured an unenviable notoriety.

This was William Vade, an apothecary, who is quoted in Burns's *History of Fleet Marriages*, 1834, as—

" An example of the lamentable consequences ensuing from the facility which Fleet marriages afforded to the artful and designing of effecting their objects."

A certain Sir John Leigh, widower of Addington, called in Vade to attend him for mortification of the toe. The treatment was so successful

JOHN HALL, PHILANTHROPIST.
(1800–1891.)

JAMES SCOTT, SURGEON.
(1770–1848.)

that the apothecary gained not only Sir John's warm gratitude, but a complete ascendancy over his patient.   Luring him to London under some false pretence, Vade, having reduced his victim to a state of hopeless intoxication, secured the services of a Fleet parson, who at midnight married Sir John, aged seventy, to Vade's daughter Elizabeth, aged seventeen.   Subsequently the old man was induced to make a will in his wife's favour, which, for practical purposes, meant a will in favour of Vade.   On the score of undue influence this will was contested in Chancery, the case being ultimately carried to the House of Lords, where it was confirmed.   The record of this marriage is to be found in the " Fleet Registers," under date May 16th, 1733.

Vade was succeeded in due course by Dr. Bradshaw, but the man who brought the house into celebrity was Mr. James Scott, who came to Bromley in 1792 as *locum tenens* to Dr. Bradshaw, and ultimately as his partner.   On Bradshaw's death Mr. Scott carried on the practice alone, and established a reputation which extended far beyond the limits of Bromley, and beyond the limits of his own day and generation.

In a history of Bromley, therefore, a somewhat extended notice of James Scott is imperatively called for, not merely by virtue of his own eminence, but because of the marked effect which his extensive practice produced upon the development of the town.

James Scott was born at Royston in Hertfordshire in 1770.   Being left an orphan at an early age, and ill-provided for, he was thrown almost from boyhood upon his own resources, and was thus called upon to rely for future success upon his own energies and exertions.   He became apprenticed to a Royston surgeon, and, in due course, a student at the London Hospital.   There his zeal and ability soon secured for him the confidence and esteem of his superiors, notably of Sir William Blizard, on whose recommendation he was selected to act as *locum tenens* for Mr. Bradshaw of Bromley while the latter was incapacitated by an attack of fever.   In this capacity Scott acquitted himself so well that Mr. Bradshaw urged him, on the completion of his studies, to join him at Bromley as a partner.   This proposal was accepted, and, on the retirement of Bradshaw, Scott succeeded to the practice.

From the first he had shown a strong interest in surgery, and had made a speciality of the treatment of diseased joints and ulcerated hips.   Rumours of hopeless cases successfully treated by him must evidently have spread abroad, for, after a few years, a practice worth originally about £300 a year increased to £1,500, an increase which could not have been the result of a purely local connection.   In order to free himself from the routine of general practice he took into partnership a Mr. Robert T. Taynton, who was already established in Bromley, thus leaving Scott free to devote himself to special cases.

The success which attended him was phenomenal.   For several years, we are told, his practice showed a profit of at least £10,000 a year, his patients being drawn to him from all ranks of society and from all quarters of the kingdom.   A full examination and explanation of the technical and novel methods which he applied are proper subjects for a medical treatise, but not for this History.   It must suffice to say here that Scott's manipulative treatment, "Scott's dressing," his originality in seizing hold upon the principle of mechanical support, and applying it to various forms of chronic disease, gave him in the medical world an unique position, which was enhanced by his personality, by his unremitting personal attention, and by a cheery optimism which, by some magnetic power, he was able to transmit to his patients.   The fame of the doctor gave rise to the composition of various doggerel poems—we quote the concluding verses of an eulogy of Scott by one of his patients—Sir Thos. Elmsley Croft, Bt. :

> " My friend ! if your ague
> Should e'er again plague you,
> Alternate, with fits cold and hot :
> Should your pain be diurnal
> Or in- or ex-ternal
> You have nothing to do, but see Scott.
>
> " So when you are ill,
> Lacking potion or pill,
> To Bromley repair—famèd spot ;
> At the Bell put up, pray
> Just step over the way,
> And be cured by miraculous Scott."

We, however, are concerned with Scott as a Bromley man.   His influence upon the town, though undesigned, was enormous.   Patients flocked to him from all parts of the country to such an extent that special " Scott's Coaches " were run from London to bring them to him.   Many were not satisfied with an occasional visit, but came to reside in the town in order to be under Scott's charge.   The existing accommodation proving insufficient, new houses were erected for those who wished to live constantly under his care.

On his retirement in 1829 he lived at Clay Hill, Shortlands, until his death on December 3rd, 1848.

He was succeeded by Dr. Edward Augustus Williams of Leominster, who started practice in Bromley in October 1830.

Next to these doctor's premises stood, from, at all events, as early as 1673, one of the grocers' shops in the town.   It remains a grocer's shop to this day.   For about a hundred and fifty years the business was carried on here by different members of the Ashworth family, the last, Leonard Ashworth, being in business from 1790 to 1828, serving as churchwarden in 1813.

About 1859 Frederick Bean added the adjoining premises, making out

THE OLD POST OFFICE AND BEAN'S SHOP, 1855

of them a fine old-fashioned shop with three bow windows, many of the square panes of which were of bottle-glass.

In 1882 Mr. John Howard took over the business and altered the shop. He relates that the walls of Mr. Bean's " sanctum," papered in white, were covered with texts from floor to ceiling, it being the habit of Mr. Bean to add a text daily, thus securing an effect which, when completed, was probably unique. In 1886 the whole premises were rebuilt as we see them to-day.

Adjoining the last-mentioned premises was an entrance gateway to a large yard, in front of which was a dwelling-house, facing the street, now known as Pamphilon's. This property extends right through to the two wooden cottages in Church Road (which date from the middle of the eighteenth century), and originally comprised two other sets of buildings in the yard, namely, a builder's workshop of two stories under the middle of which was an archway leading out into Church Road, and a cottage on the north side of the yard.

In the middle of the eighteenth century, about 1752, these premises were owned by Joseph Sale, a builder, and remained in the possession of the Sale family till the end of the century, when Hugh Hair appears to have become the owner.

According to Wilson, in his *History of Bromley*, Hugh Hair was, in 1796, a linen-draper in Market-place, but he seems to have diverted his attention from the yardstick to wine and spirit barrels, for at a later date he figures as a wine merchant. He also was the postmaster. He died in 1802, at the early age of thirty-five, leaving his business to his widow, Anne Hair, who carried it on until 1811, when it was purchased by John Acton, who shortly afterwards married her.

He, too, became postmaster. They had two sons, both delicate, namely : John, a surgeon who died after a health voyage to Australia, and the other, Samuel Poole Acton, one of the conspicuous worthies of Bromley in his day. His father, John, dying in 1839, he succeeded to the business and to the office of postmaster, which latter appointment he held till 1857, when Mr. J. B. Shillcock took his place and transferred the Post Office to his chemist's shop across the road.

Mr. Samuel Poole Acton was a man who exercised quite an extraordinary influence in the town. In spite of his somewhat retiring nature his advice and help were sought by all sections of the community, and no enterprise seemed assured of success unless it had secured at least the support of his name.

He was a director of the Gas Company, on the committee of the Cottage Hospital, an overseer, and for a short time a member of the Local Board, a position from which he retired as being uncongenial to his nature. He was also one of the first trustees of Lascoe's Charity. But the institution which aroused his greatest interest, and through which he did so much for the elevation and entertainment of the people of Bromley, was the Literary Institute, of which he was one of the founders in 1845, and for many years its Honorary Secretary. No one who did not live here from 1850 to 1870 can realise what a boon this institution was to the town, or how largely its success was due to the inspiring influence of Samuel Poole Acton.

In 1859 he retired from business and went to live at Lynton House, Widmore Road, where he remained until his death in 1885. He left by will £800 to Lascoe's Charity, £100 each to the Literary Institute and the Cottage Hospital, and £50 to the Philanthropic Society.

His successor in the wine business was a Mr. Frederick J. Smith, who altered the appearance of the old building in 1860 by putting in a shop-front at its south end. He was a man of musical ability, and, during the three years he was in Bromley, took a very active part in promoting the formation of the band attached to the 18th Kent Rifle Volunteers, of which he was himself a member.

After F. J. Smith, the business was taken in 1865 by Mr. George Pamphilon. In 1876 he rebuilt the whole of the front premises as we see them to-day. Mr. George Pamphilon, who had devoted much of his energy to the work of the Congregational Church, died in December 1890, and was succeeded by his son Mr. George F. Pamphilon, who combined with his qualities as a man of business much artistic ability, being a good musician and a skilful painter. He died at an early age in 1911.

At the corner of Church Road stood the fine old Georgian House, recently demolished to make way for the new premises of the National

JOHN DUNKIN.   SAMUEL P. ACTON.
THOS. MORLEY.   JOHN NASH.

Provincial Bank. It was connected with two of Bromley's noted professional firms, namely : Latter's, the solicitors, and Ilott's, the surgeons.

From about 1774 to 1802 Enoch Holding, a solicitor, and founder of the firm of Latter & Willett, lived here.

The picture of the Parish Church in Wilson's *History of Bromley*, 1797, is dedicated to him with respect and gratitude by Thomas Wilson.

He died October 13th, 1802, aged sixty-three, his widow remaining here till about 1807.

The business passed into the hands of Edward Latter, who had been clerk to Holding, and as Mr. Latter was already domiciled at Pixfield, the house was not required as a residence. Accordingly in 1809 Mr. Thomas Ilott, surgeon, took up his residence here. He died in 1849.

He was succeeded by his son, Mr. James W. Ilott, who in due course removed to Beechfield, Widmore, when Dr. Walter Thomas Beeby, his partner, took these premises. Mr. James W. Ilott served on the Local Board, and generally interested himself in the town's affairs.

Dr. Beeby wrote a *History of Bromley Church* (1872) which has materially assisted in the compilation of the chapter on the church in this volume. He also contributed occasional papers to the Kent Archæological Society. Later Dr. Beeby went to live at Park House, Beckenham Lane, when Dr. Herbert James Ilott took up his residence in this old corner house.

Though taking no very active part in public life, Dr. H. J. Ilott will long be remembered as one of Bromley's most devoted sons. His practice practically absorbed his life. He was certainly one of the ablest surgeons that Bromley ever had, by no means confining his energies to his own large practice, but applying, in a real spirit of self-sacrifice, his skill and services to the work of the Cottage Hospital. He retired, after fifty years' practice, in March 1926, and took up his residence at Midhurst, with the knowledge that he had earned the gratitude and respect of the people of Bromley.

This family of doctors has held a very high reputation during the hundred and twenty years they have continuously practised here. The connection is not yet broken; on the contrary, it is being most worthily maintained by Dr. Herbert's son, Dr. Cyril Ilott.

Through the researches of Mr. Bernard F. Davis, the whole property just treated as " Pamphilon's " and " the Georgian House " is found to date as far back as 1325. A deed preserved in the Harleian Collections in the British Museum, dated the nineteenth year of Edward II, runs as follows :

" I Wm. Cissor have given, granted, and by these presents confirm to Hawysie, who was the wife of Nicholas Cissor, late my father, my house, with a farm, which extends in length twenty feet and in width nineteen feet, and lies in length towards the East to my house, and towards the West to the house of Richard Mandy, and lies in width between the tenement of

Rich. Mandy on the North, and the way which leads towards the Church of Bromley Kent ; to have and to hold to the said Hawysie and her heirs. . . .

Witnesses.—Thos. Pistor, Richard Mandy, Alexander Fernywu (Forneaux), Wm. Pleg, Roger Musard, Adam Abell (by his attorneys), Roger Andrewe, John Cocke."

These names are all of Bromley residents. They occur in Lay Subsidy lists of a year or two later. Fourneaux was the father of William and John Fourneaux, who held Sundridge Manor. Roger Musard is the father of William of the White Hart ; Nicholas Cissor means Nick the tailor.

A second deed records a further transaction :

" Given at Bromle on the Thursday next after St. Michael the Archangel 21 Edw. III. 1347.

I Hawysie who was the wife of Wm. de Langeleye of the town of Bromley, in my widowhood—have given and granted to Matilda and Cristin my daughters, and Alice the daughter of Alexander Symond, to their heirs and assigns, all that my house with the farm, &c., which same house the said Wm. my husband and I the said Hawysie, had by the gift and feoffment of Wm. Cissor, by his deed then made ; and which extends in length between the King's highway on the East, and my house adjoining on the West, and in width between the tenement of the heirs of Rich. Mandy on the North, and the way which leads to the Ch. of Bromley Kent on the South . . . to have and to hold to the said Matilda and Cristin and Alice and their heirs for ever.

Witnesses.—John Furneaux, Wm. the Clerk, Will Cordywainer and Andrewe le Webbe."

Alexander Fourneaux having died, his son John appears as one of the principal townsmen. William de Wyklewood was still Rector, and may have been the " William the clerk " who witnessed the deed. William the Cordwainer (a bootmaker and leather-seller) and Andrew the weaver appear in the subsidy rolls as ratepayers ; also Alexander Symond.

The specific definitions of the property given in these deeds leave no doubt that they apply to the land on which Pamphilon's and the old Georgian House subsequently stood.

Facing up the High Street there were originally a group of red-brick houses called "Church Row," all, with the exception of the corner one, being private residences, ivy-covered, with forecourts planted with shrubs and enclosed by open wooden fences on a dwarf wall. They were much sought after by professional people, lawyers, doctors, musicians, and others ; thus, in 1850, one was used by Messrs. R. B. & R. Latter as their offices. There the magistrates would sit occasionally, the prisoners waiting for trial being ranged along the railings outside. One rather notorious J.P. deeply incensed the people by actually questioning the prisoners before entering to judge them, and everyone was glad when later, through a pompous indiscretion, he was asked to resign. Another of the houses was occupied by Joseph Smith, organist to the Parish Church from 1825 to 1854.

The corner house already mentioned was a seventeenth-century building, interesting from the fact that for two hundred and fifty years it was continuously in the occupation of butchers. In front, on the edge of the footpath, were several wooden hitching-posts to which the butcher boys tethered their ponies, also a substantial mounting-block wherefrom they clambered more easily with their heavily loaded baskets on to the ponies' backs.

The house presented this aspect till 1889, when the old premises were pulled down, and a modern butcher's shop erected on the site, the right-angled corner being rounded off by the sacrifice on the part of the owners of a strip of land on each façade for that purpose.

In 1673 one John Giles was a butcher here, rated at £4; and members of this family continued to occupy it for nearly a century.

In 1757 we come to another family, who for more than a century carried on business here as butchers, namely, the Alexanders; their Christian names, Nicholas, John, James, and William, repeatedly recur.

They frequently served the parish in the offices of overseer and church-warden. They evidently had a considerable business, for the Rate Books show that in 1828–33 John and William Alexander were rated for seventy acres of grazing land, apart from farm buildings, etc.

This William was one of four tradesmen that kept hunters and rode to hounds " in the pink "; the others being Thomas Baxter, auctioneer, already mentioned, Thomas Ray, corndealer, and George Battersbee, copper-smith, Ray and Battersbee also keeping packs of beagles, the latter's kennels being behind the " Compasses " in Widmore Lane.

In 1859 William Alexander died, his widow seemingly carrying on the business for a year or two, when she evidently sold it, in 1861, to the first of our third family of butchers, namely : James George Covell, in whose family the business remained until quite recent times. In 1923 the shop was added to the premises of the Midland Bank.

At this point we turn and retrace our steps to the College, to note the principal features of interest on the East side of the Upper High Street.

On the south side of the College is " College Slip," being a little passage, or accommodation way, originally into fields, but to-day into College Road and North Street. On the left this is bounded by the old College wall, which is shaded by fine chestnut trees, and at the end there is a little private wicket giving entrance to the College grounds. Adjacent to this is a very picturesque old cottage standing at the south end of a large nursery, for many years occupied by a succession of nurserymen, named Stidolph and Pocock.

This nursery ground was originally purchased in 1830 by the Trustees of the College to preserve it from building speculators. It was formerly graced by a fine old mulberry tree planted by William Stidolph's grandfather.

Facing this ground stand the National Schools, transferred from Mason's Hill. A field belonging to Mr. Christopher Eaton the butcher occupied the south side of the Slip, where circuses were wont to establish themselves from time to time, but which is now covered with a terrace of houses and the Gymnastic Hall.

At the corner of the Slip and High Street was a handsome walnut tree standing within the stable yard of a substantial house, originally notable for its timbered front, until spoiled by being covered with plaster. This house stood a little back from the street, behind a row of lime trees, a wooden fence separating its forecourt from the footway. Until its demolition in 1896 this house was successively in the occupation of Miss Lamb, of scholastic fame, of Dr. Morgan, and of Mr. Henry Selby.

Beyond this there were some small wooden houses and shops ; the Star and Garter Inn, then a much less pretentious place than it is to-day ; some more small shops, and then, sloping away from the road, the business premises of Christopher Eaton the butcher.

In the recess where the Palais de Luxe Cinema now stands were the premises of a succession of builders, of whom the most notable were Mr. W. L. Mallett, father of Alderman W. R. Mallett, and Messrs. Payne & Balding, to whom the construction of many buildings in the town, among them the Drill Hall, was entrusted.

There is considerable interest attached to the next house, for it was the home of two of Bromley's historians, and still remains not greatly altered from its original appearance, at least as regards its five upper windows, roof, and dormers.

It was here that Thomas Wilson carried on the business of a printer and bookseller from 1792 to 1799. His *History of Bromley* was published in 1797. Four hundred and thirty copies of this History were subscribed for. Amongst other interesting matter it contained a list of the principal inhabitants, and it is worthy of note that many of the names of tradesmen and others persisted until the middle of the nineteenth century, and some even to the present day. The names of Norman of Bromley Common, Churcher, Dunn, Isard, are with us still, while such names as Alexander, Bath, Battersbee, Barrell, Borer, Brown, Draper, Eaton, Lascoe, Stidolph, and Storer, all to be found in Wilson, have scarcely yet passed out of recollection.

Wilson was succeeded in 1799 by William Starkey Heard, and in 1812 by John Dunkin, who, in 1815, published his *Outlines of the History and Antiquities of Bromley in Kent*, possibly inspired with the intention of producing something more worthy than that of his predecessor. In our picture it will be seen that he also ran a circulating library and dealt in patent medicines, powders, etc. His History is a small volume of considerable value, especially having regard to the opportunities for research at that time.

John Dunkin was born at Bicester, Oxfordshire, in May 1782, and in or about 1812 came to and settled in Bromley; while he carried on a business for a livelihood, his real interests lay in antiquarian research, which resulted in 1815 in his *History of Bromley*. He followed this up in 1816 by a *History of Bicester*, and after his migration to Dartford in 1837 he wrote an elaborate History of that town also. On his death there in 1846 he was buried in Dartford cemetery, his memory

JOHN DUNKIN'S SHOP

being preserved by a brass in Dartford Parish Church whereon he is described as "a good citizen and most industrious antiquary."

Dunkin's own private working copy of his *History of Bromley* has somehow found its way into the Public Library at Woolwich. It is unfortunate that so interesting a volume does not belong to the town with which it is concerned.

In 1840 the premises were converted into a grocer's shop and came into the hands of George Wells. The introduction of a double-fronted shop front by his successor Thomas Wells, in 1864, necessarily destroyed the character of the lower portion of the house, but, as already mentioned, the upper portion remains substantially unchanged.

Next to it stands to-day a small bow-windowed shop which has altered very little, now occupied by F. Lowrence, a shipping agent.

By the side of this is a passage leading into Hooker's Place, at one time a picturesque group of small houses, some half timbered, surrounding a small square. That these are of considerable age was made evident in 1922, when some fine seventeenth-century timbers were exposed in the demolition of some of them. The place derives its name from the original owner, Mrs. Hooker, who bought the land from Mrs. Hawkesworth of the "Grete House." From Hooker's Place to the corner of Walter's Yard the old houses have, for the most part, been pulled down or altered out of recognition. In the premises at the corner of Walter's Yard, for over a century dating from 1797, the business of whitesmiths and bellhangers was carried on, the occupants during the greater part of the time being John Walter (1806–42) and his son, James Birch Walter (1842–70). They earned a deservedly high reputation extending over a wide area. They took an active share in the affairs of the town. John Walter was churchwarden during the great alterations to the church in 1829–30. His son was for several years a member of the Local Board, and served also the offices of overseer and churchwarden, and as a trustee of Lascoe's Charity.

This passage, known now as Walter's Yard, but formerly as Sanger's Yard from a blacksmith of that name, a part owner of premises behind Walter's, gave access to what was formerly a part of the estate attached to the Knight-Thornhill, or " Grete House," referred to in an earlier part of this chapter, and elsewhere.

Here, until some forty or fifty years ago, was an orchard, the memory of which is perpetuated by Orchard Place, with its group of cottages.

The old barn belonging to the Knight-Thornhill mansion, which occupied a position near by, was demolished in 1853, the splendid oak timbers taken from it and other outbuildings being an evidence of their antiquity.

A portion of Walter's Yard, lying close to the old barn just referred to, was known as " Prison Yard," from the fact that a temporary building had been erected there as a lock-up for French prisoners when being marched through the country in the war times of 1797–1815. There, too, in the early nineteenth century (1820) John Brand, formerly in the service of William Baxter, had "as many as 150 kegs of spirits hidden in his house in the orchard." (Extract from a diary or notebook of Samuel Baxter of Chislehurst.)

This was Bromley's chief smuggling depot ; the contraband being brought there, and to the Chislehurst caves, from Lewes in Sussex, and places on the Kent coast, by bridle and field paths to avoid the horse patrols and excisemen on the roads. No doubt many a resident got his liquor at the expense of the Government in the good old days of long ago.

In 1745 a gang of twelve to fourteen such smugglers was surprised on March 12th at Green-Street-Green by three custom-house officers, with unfortunate result for the officers, who were wounded and then robbed (*Gentleman's Magazine*, 1745, p. 160). Bromley, like so many other parts of England, had its exciting times in " doing " the customs.

On the corner of this passage, opposite to Walter's shop, was Burgess the bootmaker's. First William, then Joseph Burgess, his cousin. The reputation they had gained by their very excellent craftsmanship carried their business far beyond the limits of the town. Joseph Burgess was a member of the first volunteer Fire Brigade and of the 18th Kent Rifle Volunteers.

Next to Burgess's was the most important shop in this the undoubted shopping centre of the town. From 1792 to 1805 Robert Atkins carried on the business of linen-draper, followed in 1806 by the brothers Joseph and Benjamin Nash, silk mercers. Joseph died in 1847, when Benjamin, after a time alone, was joined by John Nash. Benjamin retired, and John was in 1850 joined by Henry Clarke Lukey, who was accidentally killed by the fall of a girder near Aldgate when that portion of the Metropolitan Railway was being constructed in 1866. He was a much-respected man, a good Rifle Volunteer, and was the first to be buried in the eastern portion of the parish churchyard in the presence of a great gathering of townsmen.

To this business of Nash's was added a species of banking, very greatly to the convenience of the residents, for London was the nearest place where banking facilities could be obtained, and the nearest railway station for London was Greenwich. A magnificent business had been built up, and it was no uncommon sight to see a long row of handsome equipages, with fine horses, liveried coachmen and footmen, lining the High Street in waiting for their employers.

The élite would be ushered into a secluded part of the shop where various fabrics were submitted for their inspection in a most courtly manner, sherry and biscuits being brought for the customer's refreshment. Mr. Philip Norman relates how he was taken as a child into the shop parlour at the back, and was there served with dainties, while through the window he saw with wondering eyes the operation of brewing being carried on in a courtyard.

" I have since been told," he adds, " that Nash's home-brewed beer was excellent, and was given away freely to those who appreciated its merits."

Subsequent proprietors were T. J. Nightingale, then H. J. Lukey (son of H. C. Lukey), and his partner Henry Edger, after which the premises were taken by the International Tea Company.

Next to Nash's were two more shops, to enter which it was necessary to mount three steps. The first of these was for some fifty or sixty years a barber's, occupied in succession by William Woodham and Richard Hodges. The latter was something of a character popularly known as " Barbarossa." He was a portly man and his rotundity was made specially noticeable by a great display of white apron.

He showed some talent as an amateur artist, making sketches of some of the old buildings of the town, none of which, however, appear to have survived.

While he plied his trade on the first floor of the premises his wife on the ground floor carried on a stationery, toy, and Berlin wool shop.

The second shop was for nearly fifty years a pastry cook's.

In 1845, however, Joseph Bradley Shillcock transferred his business as chemist from the middle row to this site, and the family has continued to conduct that business there to the present date.   It is one of the few old-established personal businesses still existing in the town.

Mr. J. B. Shillcock figured largely in the life of Bromley.   In 1857 he was appointed postmaster, a position he held till 1876.   He held, in addition to other offices, that of Honorary Secretary to the Literary Institute from 1848 to 1859, and that of churchwarden, which he retained until his death in 1884.

Passing Shillcock's we come to a recess, in which is an entrance to a yard, flanked by two shops.

Between these were the gates leading to what was probably, apart from the Bishop's palace, the finest mansion in Bromley, namely, the "Grete House."   From the character of the brickwork and the style and size of these two buildings it has been surmised that they originally served as lodges to the Great House.   Two stone balls that surmounted the gate piers are now fixed above one of the shops.

In the first shop, which in 1840 was a private residence, lived Dr. Ray, and subsequently, for a time, Messrs. J. & E. Dunn carried on business there as upholsterers.

The other has been for over a hundred and twenty-five years a corn-dealer's.   In 1805 Thomas Ray, brother of the doctor, occupied the premises.   Then came William Kelsey (1864), who had a mill at Southend; then William Stubbs (1874–9), finally Daniel Grinsted.

The last-named was for many years a very prominent citizen.   He was a member of the Local Board and of the Urban District Council, being chairman of the Council in 1896.   He was a promoter of the Charter of Incorporation.   To these public offices he joined those of director of the Electric Light and Power Company, Limited, and other companies; church-warden for thirteen years (1888–1901), manager of the National Schools, and a Freemason holding Provincial rank.

We now reach the Royal Bell Hotel; royal because of its appointment as posting house to Queen Victoria.

References to this famous hostelry and the part it has played in the activities of the town will be found here and there throughout this volume.

Here an endeavour will be made to supply something concerning its individual characteristics.

The long low building stretching from the corndealer's at its northern end to the baker's in the market-place at its southern, which was demolished in 1897–8 to make way for the present hotel, was certainly an ancient one, as may be gathered from the illustrations which are here given.

It will be noticed that in spite of accretions the general style of the architecture is similar to that of other ancient buildings which have existed in the town.   The bow windows, for instance, are reminiscent of the Rose and Crown, which is known to have been built prior to 1588 and the gables at the rear have had their counterpart in old buildings long since destroyed.

THE BELL HOTEL, 1870.
Pulled down 1897.

Towards the end of the eighteenth century the inn had attained to some notoriety due in all likelihood to the increase in posting and coaching consequent upon improvements in road-making. Later on, the widespread renown of James Scott, the eminent surgeon, whose house stood nearly opposite the Bell, certainly contributed to its fame and it is not unlikely that it was during this period that the Bell reached the zenith of its popularity and fortune.

Of the early occupants of the inn nothing notable seems to be known. Their names have come down to us, but little else. None of them appear to have filled any of the parochial offices. The occupants about whom most is known are those who were connected with it during what has already been suggested as the period of its greatest popularity.

These were James Wilson and his widow, and other members of that family, who were its landlords from 1773 till 1822, James Painter Davis and his daughter from 1823 till 1845, and William Sutton and his family from 1846 till the old house was pulled down in 1897.

The three men mentioned were all good sportsmen, the last two being keen followers of our national game, cricket.

In Wilson's time, as recounted by Mr. Philip Norman, a Beefsteak Club was formed in Bromley. It doubtless met at the Bell, and was patronised by the sporting element among the gentry of the town. Among its supporters and frequenters the hilarious Vicar of Bromley, Dr. Henry Smith, was certain to have been found. His sporting proclivities have been mentioned in a previous chapter and he was married to Wilson's daughter Sarah.

James Painter Davis was notable as a cricketer and appears to have acted as captain to teams that played in important matches during the early years of the nineteenth century. His daughter Mary Ann Davis took over the management of the hotel after her father's death in 1843, retaining it till 1845, when she accepted the appointment of housekeeper to the Lord Mayor of London at the Mansion House.

In 1846 came William Sutton, who retained the management until his death in 1894, one of his sons carrying it on for the next three years. In spite of lameness caused by an injury to his hip when a schoolboy, William Sutton was an ardent cricketer and was on friendly terms with most of the famous exponents of the game during his time. He was a well-known figure in Bromley, conspicuous by his adherence to a costume that was then somewhat behind the times—a black suit with swallow-tail coat, tall hat, and stock. He took a good deal of interest in the affairs of the town, promoted the establishment of the Bromley Gas Consumers Company, of which he was one of the original directors, retaining that position until his death.

There is little doubt that not a few of the plans and schemes relating to the progress and welfare of the town had their origin in the unofficial confabulations of those influential townsmen who were accustomed to assemble regularly in the Bell's cosy and comfortable smoke room.

In 1897, the property having been acquired by Messrs. Reid the brewers, the present imposing and many-storied building was erected, one of the new features being a handsome ballroom. The first occupants of the new building were Messrs. James & With, who carried it on successfully for something like twenty years.

THE MARKET HOUSE AND TOWN PUMP (*CIRCA* 1860).

PART II. THE MARKET-PLACE

THE main Hastings Road, down the Upper High Street through the town, formerly bent to the left at the Bell Hotel, and then almost immediately to the right directly into the Market-place, along the western side of which it proceeded towards the Lower High Street.

The road which now passes in front of the premises of Messrs. Medhurst was not made until after 1830. The accompanying illustration shows that the aspect of the Square, as it has been called in later years, was very different from that which it now presents.

As you entered it from London, the town pump stood prominently before you on the left, and, instead of the red-bricked Town Hall, a quaint wooden Market House, erected at an unknown date, occupied the centre. This had a red-tiled roof surmounted by a small cupola with a *fleur-de-lis* finial. Around it, projecting from the level of the first floor, was a sloping roof supported by oak posts and trusses, under which tradesmen were allowed to shelter their carts, etc.

On the north side of the building there was only one small window, on the south side none. On the east was a stairway built out, rather spoiling the appearance of the main structure on that side. On each side of this was a shuttered window. Three similar windows appeared on the west side, under a gable; in fact this west side must be regarded as the front of the building.

On the first floor of this old Market House was a room which seated some two hundred persons. Here were held some of the entertainments and lectures occasionally provided for the townsfolk; also the Court of Requests Commissioners met here, every other Thursday, to hear cases: " Long Bob " Sutton was their bailiff. There is a copy of the fees and fines levied at such court in the library.

The Market House was demolished in 1863. The foundation-stone of the new Town Hall was laid on November 7th, 1863, by Sir Coles Child when an infant.

There were several trees about the Square which added very much to its picturesqueness; thus a large elm tree stood in the road at its north-east corner, which, after it was felled, lay for a year or two alongside the Market House. A row of limes stood in front of the Duke's Head, and another tree in front of the Rose and Crown. At the south-east corner were more lime trees standing in the forecourt of a house, while over the wall of a garden, where Messrs. Latter and Willett's offices now stand, the blossom of the pear and plum trees made a pleasant picture.

The three principal events that took place here regularly were: the weekly market, the fairs, and the Parliamentary elections.

The weekly markets remain with us, changed doubtless in some respects,

BROMLEY MARKET-PLACE, CIRCA 1850

but in the main probably not very dissimilar from those which preceded them.   The fairs have ceased to be, as has already been narrated, but a brief account of their characteristics is possibly desirable.

The Market House itself was smaller than the present Town Hall, consequently there was more open space around it.   Here the fair was held twice a year in February and August.   On these occasions the place was crowded with booths of various kinds, Wombwell's Menagerie, Richardson's Show, where tragedy, comedy, and farce succeeded each other in a short half-hour.   Tight-rope walking on a rope stretched from Messrs. Isard's premises to a scaffold pole set up on the other side of the way.   Roundabouts, the motive power which moved them being a score or two of the boys of the neighbourhood pushing it round, capstan fashion, for the reward of a free ride ; exhibitions of living skeletons, fat women, real Kaffirs, and other marvels.

All kinds of things were on sale at the stalls, gaudy and glittering ornaments, sweetmeats and cakes, one of the most famous and favoured of the latter being ginger-bread supplied by a local " Ginger-bread Baker," Storer by name.   Quantities of this, fashioned into a variety of shapes, crowns, lions, unicorns, etc., richly gilded, ornamented the shelves at the back of this stall.   In addition to this amusement fair was a cattle and horse fair.   Pens for pigs and sheep being set up opposite the Bell and in Church Road, horses, ponies, and cattle standing, tethered to the fence of the Cage field, upon a strip of greensward which bordered the north side of Widmore

Lane from the market-place to the end of the existing shops. It was the custom to show off the paces of the horses and ponies by galloping them up and down the roadway from this point to the Bell. The yells of the drivers, the cries and shrieks of jostled onlookers, the strident shouts of the showmen made an intolerable din, welcomed as a proper accompaniment to the joys of the fair.

Of the Parliamentary elections an account has been given in Chapter V; it is therefore unnecessary to do more than mention them here.

Beginning at the northern side, as far as Isard's Yard, the buildings are, in the main, still much as they were over a century ago.

In 1768, No. 1, the shop now known as Maunder's, was in the occupation of Thomas Proudlove, who is rated for a shop, but whatever trade he carried on, his main business seems to have been that of an estate agent or surveyor, for his name appears as the draughtsman of many old plans of places in or about the town. He was also evidently a man of some standing, for he was churchwarden in 1765 and Vestry Clerk 1773-4. In 1773 Robert Bentley, a baker, lived here. He was Vestry Clerk in 1792, and had two sons, William, a tailor, and Matthew, the writing-master of the town, who seems to have lived here from 1790 to 1802. If Matthew lived with his father, this house must have been a baker's for over a hundred and fifty years; the next successive occupants, all being bakers, were Mrs. Elizabeth Stone (1803), James Welch (1827), James White (1839-49), James Mitchell (1849), Coutts & Company (1869), and, in the early seventies, William Maunder, in whose family it has remained.

Of these occupants the most remarkable was James White. He was a man of exceptional ability, taking a very active share in all local affairs, and filling most of the parochial offices. His probity, his sagacity, and wisdom were recognised by all who had to do with him in his various vocations. The sense of the loss that was sustained by the town at his death in November 1876 at the age of sixty-seven was evidenced by the very large number of people, from far and near, and from every section of the community, who attended his funeral, the Rev. A. G. Hellicar, the Vicar, paying a tribute to his worth from the pulpit on the following Sunday.

In 1828 No. 3 was occupied by William Beckley, bookseller, and printer of Freeman's *History of Bromley* and *The Bromley Magazine*, issued by Rawes' pupils. He was Parish Clerk for many years.

Subsequently the house was occupied by James A. Mowat, a boot-maker, popularly called " The King of Delhi," from the exhibition, in his shop window, of a pair of Wellington boots, richly worked in Indian fashion in gold on red morocco, labelled " as worn by the King of Delhi." Beside them was a diminutive pair made for General Tom Thumb, a noted dwarf.

No. 4 was originally two tenements, in one of which, from 1792 to 1836, lived James Churcher, shoemaker, and James How, watchmaker, both members of very old Bromley families. In the other lived Chas. Wayte from 1827 to 1836. Then these two tenements were taken down and the premises rebuilt and occupied for upwards of forty years (1836–80) as the offices of Messrs. Latter, solicitors.

Their chief clerk at this time was Mr. Charles Freeman, commonly dubbed " Dandy," a man of some parts, writer of a *History of Bromley*, published in 1832 by William Beckley.

For nearly a century, from 1768, No. 5 had a succession of occupants of whom there is nothing calling for record. In 1861 Mr. Samuel Bush came to Bromley and here started business as a stationer and bookseller. Possessing a good bass voice he joined the Glee Union, which met in the old Market House, and was a popular soloist at their concerts. He was also, for over forty years, a valuable member of the Parish Church choir.

The most striking of all the buildings surrounding the Market-place is undoubtedly the range of red-bricked houses including what are .now Nos. 6, 7, and 8.

This group in the early part of the eighteenth century was an inn, styled in 1717 the Queen's Head, but in 1743, the Bull.[1] It must have been a house of importance judging by its imposing portico, which still remains, and also by its Assembly Room on the first floor, which extended the full length of the buildings. In a room on the ground floor there are some thirty-six oil paintings on the panelling which almost entirely encloses the apartment. These are thought to be some two hundred years old, the subjects represented being landscapes, seascapes, baskets of flowers, castles, ships ; and no artist's name has been discovered. By the courtesy of Mr. W. F. Skilton I was allowed to inspect these compositions. They impressed me as being most interesting and curious, and worthy of an expert examination.

In another part a portion of the old main staircase still exists. There is an indication of an archway between what is now Skilton's and Isard's.

In 1717 the whole property seems to have been in the possession of a young graduate of Trinity College, Cambridge, named Russ, who apparently had received many accommodations in money from some persons on this security, for, on coming of age, he disposes of it all to them, and John Isard's name appears.

In 1765 this property, and nearly all the north side of the Square, belonged to William Stich, who also owned Alexander's the Butcher's. In 1773 it was divided into two tenements, the inn, for some reason, having been given up.

---

[1] Mr. George Clinch in his *Antiquarian Jottings* states that the house was subsequently known as the King and Queen. Mr. Edward Isard has on more than one occasion given access to all his deeds, but no confirmation of Mr. Clinch's statement is to be derived either from them or from the Rate Books.

In the Vestry Minute Books there is an entry—" Several gentlemen to meet at the Queen's Head on Friday come sennit [week] at 3 of the clock in the afternoon to audit the accounts for 1720."

The first house, or No. 6, was then occupied till 1780 by Thomas Groombridge, the owners being William Stich's heirs till 1779, when the whole property was bought by Richard Fitchett. Henry Groombridge was at No. 6 till 1790, but in 1791 it was bought by John Isard, a butcher, who had been living on the east side of the Square, in whose hands, and those of his family, the business remained for about fifty years, when, in 1855, it was taken by Thomas Heaysman, who had come to Bromley in 1844 and commenced business as a butcher at No. 26 High Street, and it remained in that family till 1905. In that year the business was acquired by the present occupier, W. F. Skilton.

No. 7, after many changes in its occupants, came into the hands, in 1807, of William Isard, a tallow-chandler who seems to have become the actual owner by 1833, and from that date the house has remained without interruption in the possession of that family, a family which continuously has enjoyed the respect and esteem of the whole community.

Bromley townsmen are not sorry that the business has lost some of its earlier characteristics, for the tallow melting and soap boiling subjected those whose olfactory nerves were not entirely deadened to recurring and highly disagreeable shocks.

The following wailing rhyme appeared in the *Bromley Record* for February 1883 :

> " Oh ! smells of grease, Oh ! smells of grease,
> Pervading Market Square.
> Oh, will you never, never cease
> To poison Bromley's air ? "

Of serious fires in Bromley some few have occurred in the Market-place, and two or three of them on Messrs. Isard's premises.

In the evening of July 1st, 1828, during the absence of John Hall, the foreman tallow-chandler, at Northampton, on his first holiday for eight years, a serious fire broke out, and although, owing to the direction of the wind, the front was saved, the factory, stables, cottages, in fact everything behind, were destroyed. On returning from his holiday John Hall said :

" I haven't taken a holiday for eight years, and now, when my back's turned, this must needs occur."

Another fire occurred here in the early morning of December 22nd, 1882, due to the ignition of some turpentine in the cellar beneath the shop, and was notable for the bravery shown by Fireman Dan Vass, who, attached to a life-line, descended with the hose from the cellar flap in the pavement into the basement and put out the fire, that had involved the whole of the shop floor, he being drawn up afterwards in a semi-conscious state from the dense turpentine fumes. This fire, like many others, was fought by volunteers—the volunteer Fire Brigade under the command of Conrad Nickalls.

A third fire occurred in July 1921, when what might have resulted in a serious conflagration was averted by the promptitude and up-to-date modern appliances of the professional Fire Brigade.

No. 8 was occupied for nearly a century by a succession of bakers and pastry cooks, among them, from 1837, being Benjamin Beezley.

Beezley was clerk for many years at the Congregational Chapel. His shop was once raided during the Bread Riots in the forties.

After this there were various occupants, but in 1854 Miss Mumford set up a business there in toys, Berlin wool, etc., and also kept a school assisted by her sister, a brother meanwhile carrying on as a baker in the rear of the premises. Then, in 1869, came John James from Croydon as baker, confectioner, and refreshment caterer. He was an ardent Wesleyan local preacher, walking out every week to serve the outlying villages.

He died at 9 Palace Road on November 26th, 1896, aged seventy-five.

The rooms above this shop, besides being used for a school, were used for meetings of small societies. Thus the Bromley branch of the Y.M.C.A. started here in June 1858; the Literary and Discussion Society, in which Mr. Henry Amos took the lead, in 1870; The Ratepayers' Protection Society, Secretary W. T. Ayling, founded in 1869. Subsequently the premises were incorporated into Messrs. Isard's establishment.

Next to No. 8 came Isard's Yard, which, up to about 1850, was known as Marshall's Yard from the fact that all the land and tenements on the east side of it belonged to Mrs. Mary Marshall. The yard at this date was a passage-way leading to a labyrinth of alley-ways, paved courts, and tradesmen's yards which covered the area at the rear of the buildings at this corner of the Market-place and upon part of which the present Post Office has been erected.

The group of buildings from Isard's Yard to the corner of the Market-place contained nothing but small houses and shops, with perhaps the exception of the corner house. In 1862 the entire row was pulled down and more dignified shops erected.

No. 10 was originally two shops, the first of which was that of the first pawnbroker in Bromley, William Humfrey, who startled the town with his florid advertisements in the *Bromley Directory*, one of which ran thus:

> " W. Humfrey the right man
>   In the right place (deny it who can).
>   Who is he ?   What is he ?
>   Why, uncle to all, Relative to none,
>   The Pawn Broker,
>   Money lender (but no bill discounter),
>   His hands always in his pockets
>   Ready to relieve the needy.
>
> Halloa boys ! Fire the guns ! Make the Bells ring !
>   Here's W. Humfrey as happy as a King."

HENRY CHECKLEY.

Town Crier.

Beadle.

The other was for a time Messrs. Baxter, Payne & Lepper's offices.

The corner shop was occupied by William Callow, a haberdasher, in 1797 ; but in 1798 by George Cooper, an army clothier. In 1814 he took into partnership a Mr. Marshall, whom his son, John Cooper, joined about 1825 ; Marshall retired in 1827, and John Cooper, set up as a tailor, bought the property, and laid the foundation of a prosperous business, which, in 1845, he transferred to 137 High Street. He was " a man before his time," a Chartist, with go-ahead radical tendencies, served as overseer in 1839, was very active in getting gas introduced into the town, and was the first tradesman to have it laid on to his business premises.

After a period of occupation by Barnabas Blake, the premises became the Prince of Wales public-house. In 1880 Mr. H. Waterer, later Messrs. Waterer & Dickins, took them for offices as auctioneers and estate agents, and here the Conservative Club was housed on the first floor.

Round this corner was a group of cottages, four of them brick-built, but one a tumble-down dwelling facetiously called " Rat's Castle " by its occupier Henry Checkley, a recognised character in the town.

A notice board over his door announced that he was a boot and shoe maker and mender, and that he had a pony-chaise and bath-chair for hire. But these vocations did not monopolise all his time, for he was also a bill-sticker, and the last of Bromley's town criers, a duty he carried out very well, with the familiar formula of : " Oyez ! Oyez ! Oyez ! This is to give notice . . . Lost ! between . . . etc." and ending up with " Gawd save the Queen ! "

He was also Bromley's last Beadle, and on Sunday mornings stood at the lych gate of the Parish Church dressed in long braided frock-coat with gilt buttons, white choker and gold-braided hat, carrying a tall staff of office surmounted by a gilded crown.

He claimed to be descended from the Churchills. He was the son of a clergyman and his widowed mother lived for a time in Bromley College. He was educated at Mr. Baker's school where the Public Library now stands. Occasionally his good breeding would show itself, but a life of intemperance brought him to poverty and ruin.

During one of his drinking bouts he was found by two of Mr. W. W. Baxter's assistants, who deprived him of his staff and carefully hid it away. Time went on without its hiding-place being discovered and the matter was forgotten. Many years afterwards the present Mr. W. Baxter happening to mention the subject to one of the assistants, the whole story came out, the staff was recovered, cleaned, and repaired, and handed over to the Town Council.

Henry Checkley died about 1896 and is buried at Reading.

The whole of these buildings, with two shops that faced towards the Market-place, and the houses covering the area now occupied by the Post Office, were demolished in 1913 in order to widen the access to the Square from Widmore Road and improve the approaches to West and East Streets, the first widening at this corner having taken place in 1883 on the opposite side, as will almost immediately be told.

On the *eastern side* of the Market-place the premises on the north-east corner seem to have been a grocer's from at least 1797 and perhaps before. However, in 1811 James Knowles carried on his grocery business there until his death in 1842, and was evidently a prominent man in the town, for he was Town Constable in 1813, overseer 1816, Surveyor of Highways 1819–22, and churchwarden in 1824. The business remained in his family for over forty years. They were an influential family, contributing liberally to the various demands made upon their benevolence.

George Knowles, the last of the family to carry on the business, was succeeded by Joseph Radmall in 1855, who, in turn, was followed in 1859 by Isaac Uridge, who transferred his grocery business from No. 5 Market-place. Mr. Uridge was not a Bromley man, but came into the town from Lindfield, Sussex.

The house at this time consisted of a large triple-fronted shop, with two entrances, facing the Market-place, behind which was a shop-parlour, office, and large yard entered from Widmore Lane. Round the abrupt corner was the entrance to the private house, in front of which was a trim little garden enclosed by low palings. At the corner, on the edge of the pavement, was a tall stone post which still further constricted the already narrow entrance from Widmore Lane into the Market-place.

After Mr. I. Uridge's death in 1874 the business was continued by his widow till 1880 and then by her two sons H. and W. Uridge till September 1881, when it was transferred to their present premises in Widmore Road, the Market-place shop being closed in March 1882.

This removal was due to the fact that since 1866 the very narrow outlet here from the Square had been a source of anxiety to the authorities in view of the growing increase in traffic. An opportunity occurring at this time, the premises were acquired by arbitration for £2,502 10s., and pulled down; the sharp angle of the corner was cut off, and the space obtained added to the roadway in 1883. On putting up the diminished site to tender, it was bought by Mr. Herbert Collins, a draper, for £1,820, and the present lofty building was erected by H. Balding for him at a cost of £2,818. Before 1883 the width of the roadway at this point, from curb to curb, was 11½ feet, in 1883 it was extended to 24½ feet, and in 1913 to 35 feet.

From 1830–3 the next house (No. 14) was Thomas Parry's, the leather-seller, who afterwards removed to Lower High Street. He was followed by various occupants until 1865, when Edward Strong removed his well-known printing business here from the northern corner of the White Hart building where he was originally established in 1857. He died in 1875, but the business was carried on by his widow and sons, under the

ENTRANCE TO MARKET PLACE FROM WIDMORE LANE IN 1848.
From a pencil drawing by Miss Pott.

ENTRANCE TO MARKET PLACE FROM WIDMORE LANE IN 1880.

title " Edward Strong & Sons," and after her death in 1879 by her son Thomas Strong, who died in 1886. In 1902, under the style " Strong & Sons," the firm removed to its present position in East Street.

Edward Strong was a man of some force of character and enterprise, for we owe to him four publications, namely, the earliest local newspaper known as *The Record & Monthly Advertiser*, the first local *Directory*, a *History of Bromley*, and the first *Map of the Neighbourhood*.

The *Record*, published for the first time òn Tuesday, June 1st, 1858, was of demy 8vo size and consisted of eight pages and was sold at one penny. From the very first it gave the local railway and omnibus time tables. In 1859 it was increased to twelve pages, and in 1860 to sixteen pages. Its great usefulness was immediately recognised, its success far exceeding Mr. Strong's expectations.

In January 1866 it was enlarged to royal 8vo. It only ceased to exist in 1913. A glance through the copies of this periodical now preserved at the Public Library presents numbers of interesting pictures of the doings and sayings of days that are gone.

The first local *Directory* was published in 1866. It was enlarged and revised in 1869 and cost sixpence. It was periodically enlarged, the price increasing with each enlargement, until, in 1906, it was taken over by Kelly's, who retained the name of Strong till about 1908, when it was dropped and the Directory was merged in their own series of publications.

From 1867 a circular *Map of the Neighbourhood* on a scale of two inches to the mile, drawn from the Ordnance Survey and other sources by B. R. Davies, of 16 George Street, Euston Square, London, was issued with this Directory.

Finally, following in the footsteps of Wilson, Freeman, and Dunkin, we are indebted to this energetic townsman for the last *History of Bromley* prior to this one, a small octavo volume of 146 pages, published in 1858 at 3s.

Passing over the next houses (Nos. 15–19), the occupants of which were continually changing, we come to probably the most notable business house in Bromley, namely, Dunn's, the house-furnishers, upholsterers, and undertakers. No other can show a similar record of unbroken tenure in one and the same line of business. For more than two hundred years the family have to their credit that they have been active and successful in taking a not unimportant part in the business life of the place, and at the same time have borne their share in civic duties.

The connection of this family with the trade of Bromley may possibly be from 1710, because some years ago when the premises were being rebuilt a stone was found inscribed " J.D. . . . 1710," forming part of the old building, so that a John Dunn may have occupied these premises then and probably even earlier. The earliest definite record concerning them is that a William Dunn was Vestry Clerk in 1721, and there was another William who died in 1801. There were also *John* Dunns, 1735–1801, 1765–1817, and

1833–1878, and Edward Dunns, 1774–1830, 1803–1865, 1818–1909, this latter being the father of the present H. G. Dunn, both trustees of Lascoe's Charity. There was also a cousin, Edward, 1835–1906, for forty years a bell-ringer, and both a John and Edward who were firemen.

It is worthy of notice that they have throughout this long period been office-bearers of some kind in connection with the Parish Church, such as parish clerk, sexton, bell-ringer, or churchwarden. This last position the present head of the family now holds, having been appointed to the office in 1900 and re-elected by the Vestry without opposition each succeeding year.

A family with such a record naturally cherishes many memories connected with the town. The late Mr. Edward Dunn, who died in 1909 aged ninety, was a very familiar figure to the townspeople for the greater part of the last century. He could recall the time when the roads were lit by a few oil lamps only, and remembered his first journey to London in a four-horsed coach, when he was taken on to Ramsgate by steamboat and had a rough passage; also the visit of King William IV and Queen Adelaide, Duke of Wellington and others, to Lord and Lady Farnborough at Bromley Hill. He could give a vivid account of Lady Farnborough's funeral procession at Wormley, Herts, where it fell to him to lead the horse bearing her coronet, on January 15th, 1837.

As a youth of about twenty he took part in the local celebrations in connection with Queen Victoria's coronation, when the aged poor and the children were feasted in the grounds of Bromley Palace at tables ranged along the avenue, reaching from the entrance gates in Widmore Lane to the palace itself, and in the year 1901, at the age of eighty-two, he shared in the festivities that marked the coronation of her successor Edward VII.

Adjoining Dunn's there stood an interesting range of four shops, Nos. 21–24. The houses with their dormer windows and old roofs have only recently been demolished, Messrs. Dunn having bought them, and built new premises as an extension to those which they already held in the rear.

In the first of these houses was a family of coopers, a handicraft that is now almost extinct, but which formerly was a lucrative means of livelihood. William Brown was there in 1797, John from 1798 to 1825, and then Joseph from 1826 to 1869. Several now living remember seeing this old man through the open door of his workshop, for that is what it really was, clad in white apron and brown paper cap, busily keeping up the incessant tap, tap, tap of his peculiarly shaped hammers on the oak staves of the tubs, broken only by spoke-shave work, or the manipulation of a four-foot plane, set sole upwards in a slanting position to joint the staves. The handles of all the tools bore a rich brown polish from years of use, and these were seen either hanging on the walls or lying about on bench and floor, while the peculiar smell of the freshly worked oak pervaded the air. This old man was a very great talker and also very deaf, consequently what with his tapping and the shouting of

MARKET-PLACE, EAST SIDE, 1868

MARKET-PLACE, EAST SIDE, 1873

speakers to him, there was usually a tolerable amount of noise about his doorway.

Earlier in life he had filled the office of constable, and it is said that in connection with the murder of Mr. and Mrs. Bonar at Camden House, Chislehurst, in 1810, he walked from Bromley to Maidstone, a distance of over twenty miles, armed with a blunderbuss, presumably as the custodian of the prisoner.

In 1873 the premises passed to F. Fawsitt, a currier and leather seller, whose son occupied them until the demolition.

The shop adjoining Brown's was a shoemaker's ; occupied from 1837 to 1844 by Thomas Ayling. After serving for some years the purposes of a butcher's shop, it was, in 1855, again taken by a shoemaker—George Doe. He and his son " Bob " were noted persons in the cricket world. The former was for many years the deservedly respected umpire of the Bromley Cricket Club, and the latter a remarkably safe catch at point.

The next house, which had a gateway on its south side leading to a yard, possesses some amount of interest, for at some time it seems to have been an inn. From an accumulation of evidence, derived from deeds, the Church Registers, Court Baron, 1639, and Hearth Tax Returns (1662), etc., we seem warranted in placing the Cross Keys Inn here from 1662 to at least 1792. This becomes the more interesting because one of Bromley's tokens refers to this inn, which was in the occupation of Robert Kinge at least from 1662 till his death in 1668, when he is described in the Church Registers as " of the Cross Keys." A succession of occupants can be traced from 1714 up to the present date.

At this south-east corner of the Market-place was a secluded house with an ample forecourt containing three or four lime trees, and enclosed by wooden railings. In the 1801 Census it seemed to be the home of Edward Broad, the household consisting of four males, five females, and one servant. However, from 1822 to 1869 it was occupied by Miss Anne Broad, a very select dressmaker, many of the county families from the surrounding neighbourhood being her patrons.

After Miss Broad the most noteworthy occupant was Mr. Charles W. Gedney, whose many and varied activities are recounted in the appropriate chapters of this volume.

After he left this corner house to live in retirement, it became a shop, the forecourt and trees being done away with.

Along the south side of this corner house was " Jordan's Passage," leading to the footpaths across the White Hart Field. It was so named because where the police cottages and the Misses Hopton's house now stand, Peter Jordan, the greengrocer, had a yard in which was erected annually a huge bavin stack as large as a moderate-sized house, its purpose being to provide kindling for the winter fires of the local inhabitants.

We next come to the solitary building on the south side of the Market-

EDWARD STRONG AND HIS STAFF.

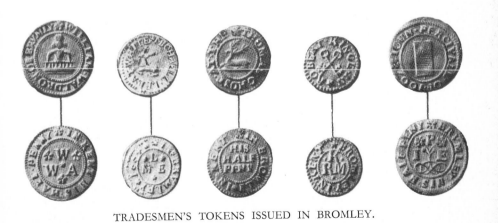

TRADESMEN'S TOKENS ISSUED IN BROMLEY.

place, a substantial three-storied house which was the residence of William Child, surgeon, from 1757 to about 1809, his partner, William Roberts, living apparently in the eastern part from 1793. In 1807 William Child seems to have retired, probably to Beechfield, Widmore, which he owned. He died February 16th, 1811, aged eighty-two. The association of this practice, and of Beechfield, with the Ilott family is traced fully in the Widmore section of this book.

About 1814 the most southern part of the big corner house seems to have been turned into a draper's shop and let to Barnabas Blake, who was Petty Constable in 1819. On the departure of Blake in 1844, the premises were taken in the following year by Mr. Robert Crowhurst.

It was in 1839 that Mr. Crowhurst came to Bromley from the village of Burwash in Sussex to a shop on the west side of the Square for the sale of the more homely necessaries of a draper's and clothier's stock. Increasing business, and a favourable opportunity, led him to secure the whole of these more commodious premises, where he developed a most successful business of quite a distinct character. He was one of those who recognised the solid advantages of a purely cash trade, as opposed to the prevailing system of credit. Nothing was put down, no books were kept, the nearest approach to any ledger or day book being a collar-box lid stabbed on to a nail behind the counter.

Another feature of the business was the decidedly countrified atmosphere that prevailed: smock frocks, hobnailed and " Cookham " boots, bandana handkerchiefs, fustian coats, corduroy breeches, were among the staple wares.

The founder of the business retired in 1884 to Sussex Lodge, Bromley Common, his three bachelor sons, Samuel, Joseph, and David, carrying on the old traditional methods until their retirement in 1902. In that year, for the purpose of widening the southern entrance into the Market-place, the Urban District Council acquired this and adjoining properties, as far as the White Hart Hotel, pulled down all these ancient buildings, and those we see to-day were erected in their stead. A portion of the land forming the garden of this corner house was purchased in 1880 by Messrs. Latter and Willett for the erection of their present offices and a Court House. This Court House served as a County and Petty Sessions Court until the erection of the existing Courts.

Prior to 1830 the row of buildings on the *western side of the Market-place* bounded the main coach road from London through the town. In May of that year an Act of Parliament was passed which authorised a straightening of the road, south from the Bell Hotel. By arrangements with the trustees of the New Cross Turnpike Roads Board, who had approached the Vestry on the subject on March 10th, 1831, the work, which, by the terms of the Act, had to be completed within five years, was actually finished in 1833.

This enterprise swept away the old Back Lane or Alley that existed behind all these houses, and, in doing so, got rid of a squalid portion of the town.

The " New Cut " or "New Road" thus constructed gave to this middle group of houses the unique characteristic of facing both ways. The circular-fronted building at the south end was added shortly after as a "finish" to this island block, and was utilised as the Police Station from 1841 until 1864, when the police went into premises at the south end of the new Town Hall. From a police station the house was transformed into the Forester Inn, though two other public-houses already existed in the same block.

Of these the old Rose and Crown, next door, and the adjoining green-grocer's shop, formed a most quaint and characteristic bit of old Bromley. The fine bow-window of the inn overhung the footway ; and the panes of its windows were brushed by the branches of a tree which stood in front of it ; projecting steps led up to its doorway. From the will of Richard Hassall (Rochester Wills No. 18) dated December 9th, 1588, we learn that this house was built a little prior to that date. It must therefore be among the oldest houses in Bromley.

He bequeathed

" to my dear Elizabeth Hassall my new house with appurtenances latelie erected in Bromley towne commonlie knowne or called by the name of the rose and the crowne, for life."

After her death he left it to his son and heir Percivall, to whom he also left

" my sword and dagger, all my bows and arrowes unbequeathed, a hal-berite, my coat trimmed with red velvet and fringed with red silke, a ring of gold, a dublette and hose of best sorte,"

and other odd things.

A tradition has long been current than Daniel Defoe stayed at this house, and it is of course possible that, during his journeyings about England as a secret agent, he may have come to Bromley early in the eighteenth century. But as it has been definitely ascertained that Defoe did stay in 1713 at a Rose and Crown, Back Lane, Halifax, Yorks, it is probable that this fact gave rise to the tradition.

In contrast to the inn, which had steps leading up to it, the quaint little shop next door had two steps leading down to it. Baskets of fruit and vegetables adorned the approach, and within was conducted the leading greengrocery business of the town.

In the early nineteenth century the greengrocer was named Ashby. He was followed in the same business by Richard Gabbitas, who, in 1824, sold to Peter Jordan, who married Miss Frances Isard. We have referred to his great bavin stack in what is now White Hart Slip. He also had stables

THE ROSE AND CROWN, MARKET PLACE.

From a water-colour drawing by J. T. Wilson, 1869, lent by Mr. Philip Norman, F.S.A.

there and a large kitchen garden, now the site of Stanhope Villas. He possessed in addition other plots, one of which, known as Jordan's Orchard, Mr. C. W. Gedney cultivated. Jordan died in January 1891 and is buried at St. Mary's, Plaistow.

In 1858 Mr. James Hopton, who had married Miss E. Fyfe, a niece of Mrs. Jordan's, succeeded to the business, and carried it on very successfully for many years.

Mr. Hopton took a very active part in the work of the volunteer Fire Brigade from its inception in 1868, becoming Captain in 1887; a position he held till 1900, when the weight of advancing years compelled him to resign. He died in 1908, aged 74.

In the next house William Day, described in Wilson's History as a breeches maker, carried on his business from 1772 till 1800. He seems to have actively associated himself with the town's affairs, being overseer, High Constable, and filling other offices.

In 1801 James Day, a licensed victualler and freeman of the Vintners' Company, occupied the premises, remaining till his death in 1816, his wife continuing till her retirement in 1827. It was probably during their occupancy that it became the Duke's Head, so named from the Duke of Cumberland of Culloden fame. It was a favourite resort of some of the tradesmen of the town which led to that which is the chief interest connected with the house, namely, that here came into existence that very useful institution the Bromley Philanthropic Society of which an account appears in another chapter.

Of the remaining buildings on this side of the Market-place little need be said. In an old house next to the Duke's Head in 1818 William Baxter opened business as a chemist after leaving James Scott, the surgeon. The house was rebuilt after New Cut was made. The rebuilt premises ran right through into New Cut and were taken as a toyshop by the Misses Mary Ann and Sarah Green. At that time such a shop was much wanted in the town.

From 1877, for a period of twenty years, the Post Office occupied this site until its removal to its present quarters in East Street.

The building now occupying the centre of the Market-place—the Town Hall—was erected in 1863-4 by the Lord of the Manor, Mr. Coles Child, from designs furnished by Mr. T. C. Sorbey of Bedford Row, London, at a cost approximating to £10,000, the foundation-stone being laid by Mr. Child's infant son on November 7th, 1863. No contractors were employed, the entire erection being carried out, under the direction of the architect, by workmen directly employed by Mr. Child. The basement of the building for several years formed part of the Market. The whole of the south side was used as the Police Station, a charge room, cells, and accommodation for two police officers being provided. The ground floor, raised a few feet above the level of the roadway, was occupied by

Messrs. Baxter & Payne, auctioneers, the London & County Bank, and the Bromley Literary Institute. Extending completely over this range of rooms was the hall itself, a handsome room, sixty feet long by thirty-two feet wide with a sloping timbered roof rising to a height of forty feet, reached by staircases at each end of the western side. The appearance of the building was enhanced by a lofty clock tower at its north-west corner.

When built the hall was a welcome addition to the amenities of the town. In it for many years all the entertainments in Bromley were given. It was also the scene of important meetings to discuss changes in local government, political questions, and other matters of consequence.

That part of the High Street known as the New Road or the New Cut, now almost entirely occupied on the west side by Messrs. Medhurst's drapery stores, presented in past days a few features and personalities of interest.

In 1839, a few years after its construction, Mr. J. B. Shillcock first established himself as a chemist in the newly erected premises at the northern end of the east side.

He was followed by W. H. Ingles, a saddle and harness maker, who, having been foreman to the Lascoe Brothers, seems to have succeeded to their business. Subsequently Mr. Ingles built a house and shop on the opposite side of the street and transferred his business to that position.

His former premises were occupied by a succession of grocers, one of whom, E. Martin, was, in his day, a noted eccentric. His patent inductive egg-laying box suggested, however, an ingenious if eccentric mind, for it was constructed in such a way that the egg disappeared into a receptacle out of sight immediately after it was laid. The idea was that the hen seeing no visible result of her efforts would promptly lay another, and would continue to do so indefinitely.

In adjacent premises the Literary Institute for a time housed its library, the house subsequently becoming the surgery of the well-known firm of Drs. Morgan, Hughes, & Willey.

On the western side the ground sloped steeply away towards the outbuildings belonging to the butcher's shop at the northern corner, and to a low fence with a stonemason's yard and a cottage or two at the bottom, the slope being a piece of grassy land which served as a playground for boys and a grazing ground for the butcher's sheep.

The development of this side of the New Road commenced with the building of a row of five shops at its southern end. Of these, the fourth one, No. 47, was taken by Thomas Churcher, a bootmaker, this being subsequently taken under the name of Atlas House by George Wells as a china, glass, and pottery emporium. This business was sold about 1858 by G. Wells to his cousin Joseph, who announced among his wares " Cricket Materials of every description."

In our chapter on cricket due note is given of the achievements of Joseph Wells upon the cricket field. It was there that his interests lay, and cricket was indeed his profession. He acted as professional for many years to the West Kent Cricket Club, and subsequently to Bickley Park. He left Bromley eventually in order to be near his son Frank, who was in business at Liss, near Petersfield, and there he died in October 1910 in his eighty-second year.

His great distinction lies in the fact that he was the father of H. G. Wells, who was born at No. 47 High Street, on September 21st, 1866, and whose childhood and youth were largely spent in the town. There he attended first Mrs. Knott's dame school at No. 8 South Street, afterwards Mr. Thomas Morley's Academy, 74 Upper High Street. At the age of thirteen he left the town, being bound as an apprentice (on trial) to Messrs. Rogers & Denyers, drapers, at Windsor. The experiment proving a failure, he was sent in December of 1879 for a brief period to Wookey (Somerset) Board School. In 1880 he was again apprenticed (on trial) to Mr. S. E. Cowap, chemist, at Church Street, Midhurst, but in June 1881 was bound apprentice to Mr. E. Hyde, draper, of Southsea. It was from here, after two years of uncongenial work, that he ran away to his mother, who was living at that time at Up Park near Hastings, Sussex, the family having then left Bromley.

The subsequent career of Mr. Wells and his remarkable achievement and success are a source of much pride to Bromley. These triumphs have not, however, had any direct association with the town, and do not require more than this brief notice.

The remaining houses in the row call for no special comment. The adjoining piece of land was left unbuilt upon for more than forty years after the New Road had been opened.

In 1879 Mr. Thomas Satchell, a builder, erected two shops, Nos. 49 and 50, upon it. These were promptly occupied by Mr. Fred Medhurst, and from that date onward as the successive adjoining premises became available they have been acquired by him until, as has already been stated, almost the entire western side is occupied by " Medhurst's Stores."

PART III. LOWER HIGH STREET TO MASON'S HILL

THE section of the town which extends along the Lower High Street from the Market-place to Mason's Hill originally presented characteristics exactly similar to those of the upper portion, namely, several private houses, some small shops, a few more important ones, and some inns. Forecourts and front gardens, with here and there a group of elm or lime trees, still preserved the general country appearance which was distinctive of the town as a whole.

On the eastern side, starting from Crowhurst's corner, was a quaint little barber's shop with its striped pole projecting over the footway. This was a very low wooden-fronted building with a dormer window in its tiled roof, which a tall person might almost reach with outstretched arm.

The entrance to it was down two somewhat deep steps to two doors in the centre of the frontage. On the left of these was a bow-fronted shop front extending half-way up towards the eaves, surmounted by a board announcing the name of the proprietor and that he was a hair-cutter and dresser, and a dealer in tobacco, cigars, etc. On the right was a smaller window of a parlour, to the right of which again was a shutter-box against the front wall.

The premises appear to have been a barber's shop for over a hundred and seventy years : thus in 1731 " John Jones," a barber, was rated as occupier at £6. In 1757 William Tibbett, barber, is rated at £8. He was succeeded in 1761 by Samuel Millen, who served as overseer in 1774, and was the barber to the workhouse. An old bill dated 1771 claims payment from " Messrs. Roggers and White Overseers " in terms as follows :

" To Sam Millen for shaving the menn at Workhouse—Items Thos. Dannel onst a weake, 44 times 7/4 ; John Grant onst a fortnight 3/8 ; Cutting Nat. Soans' hair 3 times 6*d*."

In 1788 John Pippitt, barber, occupied and owned the house. He was overseer in 1793 and churchwarden in 1800. On his death in 1808 his widow Martha carried on the business, and by her will, dated June 19th, 1834, she left to the church a charity of £5 to be distributed at Christmas in the form of bread and coal.

She was succeeded by Anthony Tye in 1836, who had risen from a " charity brat " to a position of consideration in the town. He died in 1850, and his wife, Mary, continued the business, with the assistance of an Irishman, John Doyle, whom she afterwards married. The name of Doyle is that usually associated with the house. Mrs. Doyle was famous for her home-brewed ginger beer, made in the copper, which she sold in considerable quantities around the country-side.

John Doyle died in 1864, and in 1869 his widow took as her third

DOYLE'S AND BATTERSBEE'S SHOPS

husband a man of rather superior attainments, who lived in Church Road—Mr. Charles Bayman—under whose name the business was carried on. They were one of the last to have an outside shutter-box, which mischievous boys found very convenient to hide in after shop hours. Mrs. Doyle-Bayman outlived her third husband, and died in 1897 in her eighty-second year.

Next to Doyle's was a red-bricked house and shop of three stories, quite imposing in character in those days. On each side of the central doorway, which was reached by ascending two large stone steps, were two projecting bow windows containing the usual small square panes. Below these were sloping wrought-iron bars, three or four inches apart, which enabled the passer-by to see what was going on in the workshop below, if attracted by the noise of the tinsmith's hammers, or by the pungent odour from the flux used in the process of tinning. Some of the windows of the floors above the shop had been blocked up, a relic of the window tax.

The occupants were members of an old Kentish family named Battersbee, who had succeeded one another for at least three generations. They were braziers, tin and coppersmiths, and did an extensive trade in the making of watering pots for the gardens of the mansions for many miles around, also in the re-tinning of copper utensils, then so universally used in the kitchens of the larger houses. Thus in 1788 the business was carried on by William Battersbee, followed in 1798 by his son George.   He seems to have been of a sportive turn of mind, for besides being a cricketer, he was one of the four tradesmen who rode to hounds " in the pink."   Evidently he did the thing well, for we find him rated in 1801 for stables and kennels at the back of the Compasses (£3 10*s*.), where he kept his two horses and small pack of beagles.

In his later days it was no uncommon thing to see, on summer evenings, the old gentleman of eighty, dressed in a grey tail coat with brass buttons, knee breeches, grey worsted stockings, and buckled shoes, seated on a chair on his doorstep enjoying his long churchwarden pipe.

He was in turn succeeded by his nephews George and Charles, the latter of whom died in 1865, his brother carrying on till his death in 1873. With them lived their sister Sally, who kept house for her uncle and them. She was a very amiable and pleasant old lady, with her ribboned cap and closely curled ringlets.   It was currently reported that she was the sole possessor of the first and only umbrella in the town, and it was distinctly the proper thing for her neighbours to borrow Miss Battersbee's umbrella.

Adjoining Battersbee's was a tailor's and livery maker's shop, whose windows were quite gay with the plush breeches, striped waistcoats, and braided coats worn by the men-servants of the gentry in the early part of the last century.

From 1779 to 1798 the premises were taken by a tallow-chandler, John Wood, who was succeeded by George Innous, Junior, tailor, and then by his brother John in 1832, who became the leading tailor of the town. In 1846 the business was bought by John Cooper of Market Square, who retired in 1857 to Lewisham, selling the business to James Mowat, who styled himself a trouser maker; Mowat was a Scotsman, with a very distinct accent, shared in a more marked degree by Mrs. Mowat, whose speech when they first came to the town was sometimes scarcely understood.

The premises next to this tailor's shop constituted the northern wing of the White Hart Hotel, which had for some years been let off separately, first in 1838 to William Shearman, a watch and clock maker, and then in about 1850 to George Taylor, printer and bookseller.

After him the premises were taken by Edward Strong, the printer and publisher, whose share in the story of the town has already been mentioned.   After this the White Hart retained the first floor for bedrooms, and let the ground floor only to Edward Gould, homœopathic chemist, and later to Mr. W. H. Corrie, whose assistant, Richard Skinner, eventually bought the business.   It became the recognised centre of homœopathy throughout a wide surrounding district.

Among the doctors connected with it there was Dr. Orlando Jones of Lightbrown-Cod-Liver-Oil fame, but the one who was universally esteemed was Dr. Robert Edward Phillips, to perpetuate whose memory the Homœopathic Hospital in the Queen's Garden was founded.

The houses on the western side of the street opposite to those just dealt with, namely, Nos. 43, 42, 41, and 40, were evidently of a more substantial character than those removed in 1832 to make way for the New Road and had been standing for from one to two hundred years or even more. On the demolition of No. 43, for the erection of Victoria Chambers, evidence of Elizabethan architecture was revealed, indicating that this house, the oldest of the group, possibly dated from the sixteenth century. Nos. 42 and 41 appear to have been built in 1694–5, and No. 40, which still remains, in 1712.

The Rate Books yield evidence of occupancy from 1694 onwards, but of the early occupants little is known beyond their names and avocations. Until about the middle of the nineteenth century No. 43 seems to have been a private house ; from 1843 for some seven years a greengrocer named John Ashby carried on business there. In 1852 Mr. George Weeks came to Bromley and started in business here as an ironmonger and whitesmith.

The business grew, and in 1865 he added to his premises the adjoining house, No. 42, which had, during the previous seven years, been used as offices by Mr. G. B. Baxter, the auctioneer and estate agent. The business continuing to grow, in 1877 Mr. Weeks availed himself of the opportunity that arose as a consequence of the death of Dr. E. A. Williams to acquire the much more commodious premises in the Upper High Street which had been in his occupation. Pulling down the old buildings, he erected those which now occupy the site, and transferred his business to that position, taking some of his sons into partnership.

The demands of his growing business and his unassuming character prevented Mr. Weeks from taking an important part in the public affairs of the town. He was a member of the first School Board, on which he sat for some years. He also contributed his share to the management of the Literary Institute, the Philanthropic Society, the Science and Art Schools, and various other societies which were from time to time set up for the welfare of the inhabitants of the town. He was one of the founders of the Bromley Bowling Club in 1889, and took an active share in its management until his death in 1908. His sons, as they grew to manhood, in their turn became interested in some of the various institutions of the town.

The story of No. 42 is similar and has been partly told in that of No. 43. On the removal of Mr. Weeks to the Upper High Street, Mr. S. Bush transferred his bookseller's business from the Market-place to No. 42. In 1884 printing was added to the business and in partnership with his son, Mr. H. C. Bush, he carried on until his death in 1922. In 1910 Messrs. Bush bought their premises together with No. 41, which they added to the business. In 1923 Mr. H. C. Bush sold to Messrs. Lyons & Co. and retired.

In like manner No. 41, after about a century of private occupation, became business premises, associated, as will now be narrated, with both Nos. 42 and 40.

In 1716 an important family of brandy dealers named May were in possession of No. 40 and remained there until 1797, the vaulted basement of the building doubtless rendering itself very suitable for their business.

In 1797 they appear to have transferred their business to Nos. 41 and 42, where it was carried on until 1808 under the style of May and Hollis.

The business seems to have been a lucrative one, for John May retired in 1781, going to live at Widmore Cottage (now the Grange), and became the owner of much property in Bromley and elsewhere. There is a somewhat elaborate tomb to his memory and that of other members of the family in the northern portion of the parish churchyard. For the next twenty years No. 40 was alternately shop, private house, and again shop; in this later stage it was the first shop of Messrs. Nash, the silk mercers, whence they removed to their well-known premises in the Upper High Street.

In 1820 William Baxter, chemist and druggist, transferred the business he had opened in the Market-place two years previously to No. 40, and here for eighty-seven years " Baxter's " enjoyed a deservedly high reputation. With the exception that the old bow-fronted shop windows were, after some few years, replaced by plate glass, and the two hitching posts, which originally stood on the kerb, were removed, the premises remained throughout much as they originally were.

William Baxter came to Bromley as " dresser " to Mr. James Scott, the eminent surgeon. He was a foundation member of the Pharmaceutical Society of Great Britain, one of the founders of the Bromley Literary Institute, and it was the advice he gave, at the solicitation of his old friends and neighbours. at No. 39, that led to the bequest of the Lascoe Charities.

He married a member of a noted Westminster family, Mary Walmisley, daughter of William Walmisley, clerk of the papers in the House of Lords, and sister to the celebrated musician, Thomas Forbes Walmisley. William Walmisley spent the last years of his life in Bromley and was buried in the parish churchyard.

Baxter's business throve. In 1836 he bought the premises and Nos. 41 and 42 adjoining, using part for the extension of his business, and part as a domicile for members of his family. He opened branch businesses at Dartford and Greenwich and his son added one at Beckenham. He died in September 1857, leaving a large family. The business was carried on by his son William Walmisley Baxter, who had been destined for the Church, but owing to the early death of his brother, Herbert W., he surrendered his intention of proceeding to St. John's College, Cambridge, and at his father's request entered the business. He retained his interest in classical studies, was a good Greek scholar and had a knowledge of Hebrew.

W. W. Baxter took a very active part in local affairs throughout his life; was Churchwarden of the Parish Church for twenty-one years, Manager of the National Schools, Trustee of the Philanthropic Society, and of Lascoe's

NOS. 40 TO 43 LOWER HIGH STREET, 1862.

SOUTHERN END OF LOWER HIGH STREET, 1865.

Charity, Honorary Secretary of the Literary Institute, and on the Committees of the Cottage Hospital, Science and Art Schools, and other bodies.

He died in April 1900, having retired from business in 1897, being succeeded by his only son William, who retired from business in 1907, selling the premises to Messrs. Lipton, Ltd.

The story of " Baxter's " would be incomplete without some reference to Mr. C. J. H. Saunders, who was an assistant there for more than twenty years during the middle of last century. He was universally known as " Tim." He was a *persona grata* to everybody, especially to the youth of his time, in whom he awakened and encouraged an appreciation of the beauties of nature and of art. It was at his instigation that a Round Robin was sent to the Science and Art Department, Kensington, asking for the establishment of classes in Bromley.

In addition to being an amateur artist he practised photography by the old wet-plate process, and some illustrations in this volume are from negatives of his taking.

His skill in making fireworks was in demand whenever functions called for displays of that character. He was an enthusiastic Volunteer, and for many years served in the 18th Kent as Quartermaster-Sergeant.

On the south side of No. 40 is a passage between it and No. 39; this latter house was owned by a family named Lascoe, who for nearly a hundred and fifty years (1706–1852) carried on here the business of saddlers and collar makers. They were possibly established in Bromley at an earlier date, as their name figures in the first Rate Books, those of 1673, as owners of several properties in the town, among them being the Rose and Crown, which belonged to them for more than fifty years. They evidently possessed a sense of duty and were patriotic, for in 1729 John Lascoe was churchwarden, in 1782 William Lascoe was borsholder or petty constable, and thence until 1787 High Constable. In 1805 another John Lascoe volunteered for the Defence of the Realm against Napoleon's projected invasion, served as High Constable in 1807, as churchwarden in 1809, besides filling the office of overseer. In the 1801 Census the family is entered as two males, one female, and two servants.

This worthy family, principally Johns and Thomases, is not likely to be forgotten, for one of its last representatives, John Lascoe, who died in 1850, bequeathed the sum of £2,880 in Consols :

" Upon trust, to pay and apply the dividends to arise from time to time unto, and equally amongst, yearly or oftener, four decayed Tradesmen Inhabitants of the town of Bromley,"

and his sister Elizabeth, a spinster who died in 1853, left

" £194 11s. 11d. consols, in trust to apply the annual interest or dividends to the use and benefit of poor widows of such a class of tradesmen of Bromley in decayed circumstances, as are intended to be assisted from the funds provided by the will of my late brother John."

The Lascoe Charity did not exhaust their benevolence, for John also left £400 to the Philanthropic Society.
There are several entries in the Rate Books about them, one dated 1714, e.g.:

"6 Bell-ropes supplied by John Lascoe 31s. 8d.," these being for the belfry at the Parish Church, for, in addition to being saddlers, they were rope makers and had a rope walk extending along the backs of the houses in the High Street as far as the Public Library.

No. 38 was also the property of the Lascoes, and was occupied from 1765 to 1780 by them, then from 1789 to 1811 by Jacob Hind the shoe-maker, who was followed by Mrs. Ann Bexhill, widow of Jarvis Bexhill the plumber. She was a woman with a forceful character, as may be judged from the inscription on her tombstone near the south-east door into the Parish Church.

It is related that just before her death in 1845, at the age of seventy-nine, she called one of her workmen to her bedside and gave instructions as to her burial, namely, that she was to have a lead coffin, the lead to weigh 7 lb. per square foot, bars of iron 2 inches square were to be placed across the grave to support the weight of her coffin; bars of 1 inch square were suggested as strong enough, but she insisted on the 2 inches, as "she did not want to come squash upon Jarvis." She warned the workman, who was William Bateman, that she would "haunt" him if her wishes were ignored.

In No. 37 Samuel Porter, having converted the private house into a shop, started a draper's business, adding to it No. 36. This business was afterwards taken over by George Maydon, then by his brother-in-law, John King, who retired and sold it to Rouch & Sons, who still successfully carry it on. Mr. King ("Cheery Jack") was a very popular man, taking high rank in Freemasonry, and was Honorary Secretary of the Bromley Bowling Club until his death in 1907.

Beyond S. Porter's was the Rising Sun with its painted sign creaking in the wind as it swung on its wrought-iron bracket, but, like all our inns, it has been entirely rebuilt (1899).

This was the headquarters of the Society of Bromley Youths, or Bell-ringers, where they held their monthly meetings and practised their hand-bell ringing, previous to visiting the principal houses in the town and neigh-bourhood at Christmastide, a custom which has now regrettably fallen into disuse. A framed memento of a record performance on the bells at the Parish Church used to hang over the mantelpiece of the club room at the Rising Sun, the possession of which was claimed by one of the landlords, but through the determined efforts of the then Vicar, the Rev. Donald Tait, it was transferred at last to the belfry of the church, where it now is.

It is to be regretted that the fine sign mentioned above is no longer seen. It depicted a sun rising above a pretty landscape of trees and water, and was of creditable execution.

A record of its landlords from 1706 exists. One of them was James Davis, 1792–1816, who was overseer in 1815. He was followed by his son James Painter Davis, afterwards landlord of the Bell. He was followed by Richard Tape, 1820–7, who had a brewhouse in another part of the town, and also established a skittle alley on his premises. His widow continued in possession till 1832, when first William Bateman, and then George Porter, who came from Lincoln, carried on the business. He supplied the ringers with liquid refreshment on the occasions of weddings and other ceremonies that require campanological accompaniment. He could be seen, as soon as the sound of the bells notified the conclusion of the ceremony, hurrying up the High Street with a two-gallon can of beer, a couple of pewter pots hanging on its spout, and a bottle of gin protruding from his coat pocket.

Adjoining the Rising Sun was an open blacksmith's forge. For more than a hundred and fifty years (1765–1919) a blacksmith's forge occupied this site, and for over ninety of those years (1774–1865) it was in the hands of a family named Bath, after which followed a succession of veterinary surgeons, until ultimately the premises were pulled down in 1919 to make room for Woolworth's Stores.

Beyond the forge and the house of the proprietor adjoining it was a long row of small low-roofed houses and shops originally extending down to where the Public Library now stands. Various changes have been made, but some slight indication of the old appearance of this part of the High Street may still be gained from the few older buildings that remain.

No. 32 was from 1773 to 1800 a cordwainer's, John Cowdrey, a noted bell-ringer; then followed, up to 1816, three Aylings in succession, viz. John, Robert, and William. From 1816 to 1855 it was the home of the notorious Robert Sutton (" Long Bob ") to whom reference has been made. Edward Hood succeeded him (1855–62), a very clever grinder of surgical instruments.

No. 31 had a large number of tenants from 1772 onwards, of whom there is nothing of interest to record.

The next house was one with a low pan-tiled roof with moss- and lichen-covered dormer, now occupied by Achille Serre. This, the most noted of the old ' tuck-shops ' in the town, was occupied from 1774 to 1876 by several members of the Storer family. William, described as a ginger-bread baker in Wilson's History, from 1774 to 1787, Elizabeth till 1794, Anne till 1800, William till 1831, and George till his death in 1872. They were all famous pastrycooks and confectioners, their specialities being buns, jumbles, and brandy-balls, the fine peppermint flavour of the last being due to the use only of English oil.

The best-known member of the family was the last, namely, George Storer. His ginger-bread was made up into fancy shapes which were richly gilded, and in special demand at the local fairs. Another marked feature of his business was Sunday baking. As the homes of many people at this date were not fitted with conveniences for such cooking as the Sunday dinner demanded, just about one o'clock on this day straggling processions of youths and maidens could be seen issuing from Storer's, carrying dishes containing a sucking pig, or bullock's heart, fruit pies and other pastries.

Mr. Storer was a very fat man, and therefore unable to move about readily, so, in order to serve his customers with ease, he had a seat so placed that he could, with a sort of toasting-fork, reach from any part of the shop the various comestibles demanded. At his death in 1872 some sensation was caused in the town, due to the fact that his coffin was so large that it could not be taken out of the house without removing the whole of the upper front window, and that over £2,000 was said to have been found under his bed.

A member of his wife's family carried on the business for many years under the name of Nash & Co., until about 1898, and at the present day a descendant, at No. 20, carries on the tradition of the family.

No. 29 was taken in 1850 by Thomas Parry, the leather seller who came from the Market-place.

No. 26 was a private house in 1805, but was in due course converted into a shop and became the business premises of a succession of butchers, Thomas Heaysman, Alfred Ellis, George Bligh, and Amos Borer. This house must once have been an inn called the Bull, for it is so styled in a deed dated July 15th, 1841, where its situation is exactly indicated.

No. 25 is especially associated with the well-known Bromley family of Ayling.

The first Ayling to come to Bromley appears to have been William Ayling, who was found to be here in 1802 (aged thirty-five). In 1804 Robert Ayling, a younger brother of William (aged twenty-four), is in Bromley owning the premises No. 25 High Street with William in occupation.

They were the sons of a Sussex farmer, but were both shoemakers by trade.

William seems to have come to Bromley in consequence of some trouble in connection with game, and soon after his arrival here he, in company with John Burgess, was engaged to kill game for the Bishop.

Both of them were excellent cricketers, William, while in Sussex, playing for the Players, All England, and Kent. He also, after he came here, played for Bromley against Middlesex on the old Lord's ground at Marylebone. Robert was famous as a fast underhand bowler.

The two brothers remained associated as shoemakers at No. 25 High

Street till 1811. Robert the younger appears in the Rate Books as owner of the premises and William the elder as occupier.

In 1811 William left No. 25. Apparently he was not very successful, for later he is found filling the office of Beadle, and later still occupying a small tenement and classed as poor in the Rate Book. He died in 1826.

Robert Ayling seems to have been more prosperous than William, from the first intimation we have of him in 1804, where he appears as owner of the shop and premises No. 25 High Street until his death in 1839. After William had ceased to occupy No. 25 in 1811 Robert carried on the business alone until 1822, when, having built himself a house, Sinclair Villa, on Mason's Hill, he retired into private life.

From 1822 till 1824 John Burgess (the father of the Joe Burgess who later on became the well-known bootmaker of Upper High Street) carried on the business, followed in 1825 by Francis Mullett, who remained in occupation till 1842, three years after the death of Robert Ayling.

Mullett was succeeded by Thomas Ayling, a son of William and nephew of Robert, who had since 1837 been carrying on a shoemaker's business in the Market-place, and here he remained until his death in 1884.

Thomas Ayling had four sons: William Thirkettle, Robert, Edwin, and Thomas Stephen, who were all brought up to the shoemaking trade.

William Thirkettle, the eldest son, disliking his trade, in 1854, at the age of twenty, enlisted in the Crimean Expeditionary Force and was on the staff of Mr. J. Beatty, engineer, engaged on constructing a tramway to convey big guns from Balaclava to Sevastopol. He was at Balaclava two days after the famous charge of the Light Brigade.

Later he went to Australia during one of the Ballarat gold rushes, but finding no " Welcome Nugget " he returned to England and in 1867 opened a business as an oil and colour merchant at 97–8 Upper High Street.

Robert went to New Zealand, and died there in 1899.

Edwin and Thomas Stephen joined their father in the business in 1869 and remained partners until their father's death in 1884. The partnership was then dissolved, Edwin going to Beckenham and starting in business there, while Thomas S. remained in Bromley, transferring the business to new premises on the Broadway. Here it continued to flourish, and, after his death in 1914, was carried on by his sons Richard and Bernard, both of whom became prominent officers in the Boy Scout movement.

After Thomas Ayling's death the buildings at No. 25 High Street were pulled down and new ones erected. From 1887 till 1894 these were occupied by his eldest son W. T. Ayling, who, in addition to his oil and colour business in the Upper High Street, carried on here the business of china, glass, and tobacco dealer.

Subsequent occupants were B. Pyrke, a grocer, 1896–8, followed by H. Aught, who brought the house back to the boot trade, which he carried on here for the first ten years of the present century.

Mr. W. T. Ayling was Honorary Secretary of the Ratepayers' Association started in 1869, with the object of " watching the affairs of the Parish and primarily to elect as Parish Officers, and on the Local Board such persons, members of the Association, or others, whom they may think eligible." The underlying purpose was to oppose a scheme for sewering the town, then being promoted by the Local Board. In this they were completely successful. The Minute Book of this Association is now at the Public Library.

Mr. W. T. Ayling served as overseer with Mr. William Maunder in 1886, and also on two or three assessment committees. His reliable memory made him a sound source of information, much of which has been drawn upon in compiling this book.

The next seven houses (Nos. 18–24) were originally all small houses, either private cottages or small shops. The Rate Books show the names of the successive occupants, which were many in number.

Numbers 22–3 were pulled down for the erection of the Grand Hall and County Club in 1889, built at the cost of Mr. Harris, of Covell & Harris. This building is from the designs of Mr. W. A. Williams, A.R.I.B.A. It originally included a swimming bath extending throughout the basement, but this had to be abandoned owing to constructional difficulties.

The other houses remain, but have been modernised by having shop fronts inserted and by internal alterations to make them suitable for business premises. A few names of their inhabitants have some interest for old Bromleians. One was a postman named Alfred Mitchell, who lived at No. 20 from 1858 to 1868 and his widow till 1874. His duty was to carry letters to and from Downe. No conveyance was provided, but folks knew how to walk in those days, postmen, lay preachers, and schoolboys being notable examples; several Bromley boys went to school at Keston, and Keston boys at Bromley, and devoted preachers thought nothing of walking from Greenwich or Croydon to Bromley.

Mitchell carried out his duties regularly in all weathers for at least ten years, during which time he must have covered over 43,000 miles. In the spirit of the times he was chaffed about the lovely country walks he enjoyed in the summer time, but Mitchell reminded them that even in the summer there was always twelve feet of " Snow " up at Downe, a family at Downe named Snow being remarkable for their height. This energetic postman also found time to dabble in wet-plate photography.

Another occupant was George Boorman, a pork-butcher and fly proprietor, who lived at No. 22 from 1845 to 1858, and at No. 23 from 1860 to 1888, when he died, aged eighty-two. He was generally considered one of the last of the old postilions, although his son John ("Buckie") also held that position until the day of postilions ended.

Still another was James R. Pocock, who, for his sterling qualities and quaint characteristics, was known to everyone. He was a gardener and bee-keeper, having special facility in handling these insects. He moved from here about 1892 to the little cottage in College Slip, renting the Nursery ground from the College trustees, in succession to W. Stidolph, whose family had occupied it for many years. He was sexton to the Parish Church for several years (1880–1905), giving up the post because he disagreed with chanting the Litany on the ground that one could not sing and at the same time call oneself a miserable sinner.

The last business place on this side of the High Street was for one hundred years more or less connected with coach-building. From 1765 to 1810 it was more particularly a wheelwright's, carried on successively by George Chapman, his widow, then William, and lastly Richard Chapman. From 1810 it became a high-class coach and carriage builder's. This was carried on by Stephen Osborne until 1828, by Osborne and Davis till 1858; the business was then taken by C. S. Middleton, who ceased to carry it on in 1864. John Brister then established himself here as a plumber and decorator, followed from 1869 to 1876 by Thomas Satchell.

Here ended the business premises of the town, the land to the south of it being now the site of the Public Library.

In 1688 the present site of the Public Library and grounds seems to have been destitute of any building upon it, for a Mr. Jeffery Amherst is rated for land only, stretching from the High Street down the slope to the River Ravensbourne. In 1773 John Booth is rated £5 for land, and £5 for some tenements, probably one or two adjacent small houses standing near the main road. However, in 1774 a large house seems to have been built, probably for the occupant, Mr. Dorrington, for the rating is suddenly raised to £40. In 1790 it seems to have been rented from Booth for the purposes of Messrs. Clendon & Company's School, which was carried on here until it was transferred to Church House in 1793.

After a brief interval the Rev. John Baker set up a school here, with George Sparkes as one of his pupils. Mr. Baker was for many years lecturer to the parish, and Vicar from 1818 to 1820, when he resigned. He died in Bromley in 1824, his widow continuing to live in the house until her death in 1845.

In 1848 George Sparkes, who had held a good position in the Madras Civil Service, returned from India and bought his old school, naming it " Neelgherries." On his arrival in Bromley from India he first lodged at Mr. James Carpenter's on the opposite side of the street (now Pyrke's) where Emily Carpenter, daughter of " Old Billy " Carpenter, Mr. Norman's gamekeeper at Crofton Woods, was servant. When he took up his residence at Neelgherries she became his housekeeper. Later, however, in order to retain her services during his declining years, he educated and married her.

He evidently added to the house, for its rateable value increased to £63. George Sparkes was somewhat of a recluse and invalid, devoting himself to botanical and other studies. He had already written a useful *Introduction to Chemistry*, a copy of which is in the Public Library.

He was very fond of natural history, and was very friendly with Mr. Baxter, and especially with his assistant " Tim " Saunders, to whom he repeatedly asserted that he should leave the house and grounds to the town for the purposes of a museum and pleasure garden. This purpose, however, he did not effect, for his very short will left everything to his wife, who, no doubt, was acquainted with his wishes.

He died January 30th, 1878. His splendid collection of coins was sold, after his death (February 1880), at auction in London for £3,375 18s. 6d., the highest bid being £110 for a Charles II Reddite crown, a veritable Queen Anne farthing fetching £3 8s. His widow, anxious to see more of the world than her quiet life and opportunities at Bromley had afforded, decided to make an extensive tour in Europe under the guidance of a courier named Denis John Dowling. This gentleman by his devoted services so commended himself to her that he became her second husband.

Unfortunately this marriage did not prove to be a success, so later she found it politic to provide her husband with an income on the condition that they lived apart.

At her death in March 1900, at the age of eighty-one, it was found that in her will (120 folios) she, mindful of her husband's wishes, had left her house and estate upon trust for the benefit of the inhabitants of Bromley :

" For the purpose of a public museum and park, or of a technical and industrial institution, or of any other kind of institution or establishment for the public benefit for which land might lawfully be held in trust for the inhabitants of Bromley."

She also left

" £1,000, plus the proceeds from the sale of furniture and jewellery, for an Emily Dowling Fund,"

to be devoted to the purposes of the proposed institution. The sum was £1,729 9s., which was invested in Consols and produces £46 14s. 8d. per annum.

Questions arose as to how Mrs. Dowling's intentions could be carried out, the trustees feeling that they were unable to deal with the matter as set out in the will. An application to the High Court of Justice resulted in an order adopting a scheme setting up an educational trust under which the property was to be conveyed to the Urban District Council of Bromley. This was carried out by an indenture dated April 7th, 1903.

At this time Mr. Andrew Carnegie offered the sum of £7,500 for the purpose of erecting a new Public Library, which was accepted and a library erected on a portion of the property. This was opened by Mr. Carnegie on

May 29th, 1906. In the meantime the matter came within the purview of the Board of Education, who held that the establishment of a library by itself did not come within the terms of the trust, and that it must be established in connection with some technical institution.

After protracted negotiations the Board of Education made a scheme, dated May 23rd, 1911, constituting an Educational Trust to be known as the " Emily Dowling Foundation," such scheme to be administered by nine Governors—six to be appointed by the Town Council of Bromley, and three by the Kent County Council. This scheme empowered the Governors to convey to the Town Council of Bromley, who had then succeeded the Urban District Council, the site on which the Public Library had been erected with certain additional land. The Board of Education also approved a lease from the Governors to the Town Council of the residue of the land at such a rent as would bring the total income of the foundation up to £100. The grounds thus leased have been very tastefully laid out and now form a charming public garden.

The scheme provides for the provision of exhibitions tenable by the student at any institution or classes for technical, professional, or industrial instruction approved by the Governors, to be awarded to persons of either sex resident in the Borough of Bromley.

The house called " Ravensfell," now embodied in the row of modern shops, named Ravensfell Parade, opposite the tenth milestone from London, was built in 1858 by Mr. John Richardson, owner of the estate, as his private residence. A house had formerly stood there, dating from the end of the seventeenth century. Its successive occupants can be traced through deeds and Rate Books from as early as 1673 until it was pulled down in 1858. Mr. Richardson died in 1889, and is buried at Holy Trinity Church, Bromley Common. There is a memorial to him with his arms emblazoned upon it, on the south side of the Chapel of the Resurrection in the parish church. The property remains in the family, the present owner being his son, Mr. W. Ridley Richardson.

From this point to the foot of the hill, where the railway now is, was one estate, namely " Simpson's," which is dealt with in a special chapter. It includes the mansion known as Bromley House, which is now used as offices by the Valuation Department of Inland Revenue and the Inspector of Taxes, and also the modern roads—Ethelbert, Ringers, and Ravensbourne, which were made by 1873.

Returning now to the upper part of the eastern side of the Lower High Street, the building that at once arouses attention and awakens expectation as to its story is the " White Hart."

The authentic history of this inn can be traced back to the early years of the sixteenth century, but there is reason to believe that it may really date from the latter part of the fourteenth.

The fact that the Hart in the sign wears a golden crown about its neck in the form of a collar is in itself an indication of this, for a hart so ' collared ' was the favourite badge of Richard II (1377–99). Writers upon our ancient inn signs are agreed that when this sign is found attached to an old inn it may reasonably be supposed that the inn has come down to us from the days of that monarch.

Passing now from supposition to actual fact, it is known that in the year 1509 the inn was owned by Robert Beckyngham, a native of Guildford, Surrey, and " Citizen and Grocer of St. Olaffs, Southwerke."

How long he had been the owner is not known, but in that year, 1509, Robert Beckyngham, in his will dated November 3rd, bequeathed, in certain circumstances, his property in Bromley, Kent, and in Newenton, Surrey, " to make a free schole at the towne of Guildeford," the overseers to this will being Thos. Polsted, John Lane, and others.

That the circumstances, mentioned in the will, arose is clear, for a certain George Austin, in 1596, in a " Monument for the Schole of Guldeford," quotes a deed of 1512 in which Polsted and others, the feoffees to the uses of Beckyngham's will, conveyed the lands, etc., at Bromley to Sir George Manners, Knt., Robert Wintershall, and others, " to keep and mayntayne a free grammar schole in the town of Guldeford, and that there should be a sufficiente Scholemaster there from thenceforth to kepe the schole." The Mayor of Guildford and others were to receive the rents of the property and to appoint the " Scholemaster."

In the *Victorian History of Surrey* there is the following entry for the year ending Lady Day, 1545, " Imprimis Received from the Inn in Bromley Kent called the Hart (le hart) and le litell house with a mede called Hartmede, 40*s*."

From a document dated October 23rd, 1605, we learn that the Mayor and five approved men of Guildford " granted and sould unto Andrewe Broome all that Messuage or Inne commonly called the Harte situate in Bromley Kent to have and to hold the same in fee farme for ever Yieldinge and payinge therefore yerely to the said burgesses of Guldeford £12 yerely to the use of the Scholemaster and Usher of the free grammar schole in Guldeford."

The connection thus set up at the beginning of the sixteenth century between the White Hart Inn of Bromley and the Grammar School of Guildford remains still in existence and is operating to-day.

The inn itself was sold in 1605 by the aforesaid Andrewe Broome to Henry Walton, and it remained in the possession of his descendants until 1671.

Two tenants who occupied the inn during the last few years of this period are of note, inasmuch as they issued two of the five Bromley tokens mentioned in Chapter III.[1] Their names are Michael Lee and Thomas Ghost.

---

[1] These tokens are illustrated at p. 396.

THE WHITE HART HOTEL, 1830.

Research among some Chancery proceedings at the Record Office has yielded interesting particulars concerning Michael Lee. He was the son of " Edmund Lee of Dorking Surrey Gentleman." He appears to have been an innkeeper, and to have come to Bromley in 1664. In that year he obtained a twenty-one years' lease of the White Hart premises from the heirs of one of the Waltons at a yearly rent of £46 and a fine of £50. He issued his tokens in the same year, possibly to signalise his arrival in the town. The following years 1665–6 were the years of the Great Plague of London. With a view to escaping the risk of infection Cornelius Cage, a vintner of London, sent his wife, some friends of his, and servants to stay at the White Hart. Lee was apparently in a poor financial position. He owed Cage £500 for wines supplied, and also owed £110 to a John Ellsworth. In order to secure his debt of £500, Cage obtained a mortgage of the lease which had been granted to Lee, and Lee having failed to make the necessary payments, he foreclosed and took possession of the property. Shortly after this Lee was arrested for debt and cast into the Fleet Prison, where he died intestate in 1668, John Ellsworth, who may have been responsible for his arrest, obtaining letters of administration of Lee's estate.

Finding Cage in possession of the White Hart, Ellsworth endeavoured to make him responsible for Lee's debt. Cage, however, denied liability and was able to show that, as Lee had failed to redeem the mortgage, he had taken the necessary steps to constitute himself the rightful owner of that property, and had already installed Thomas Ghost as the innkeeper— the second occupier of the White Hart to issue tokens.

Among the numerous documents in connection with this business is an inventory of the contents of the inn at this date. It is too long to be given in full, but some of the items may be mentioned : 12 tables, 9 beds (6 flat, 2 cased, and 1 old tester), 32 leather chairs, 4 needleworked chairs, suites of furniture in purple scarge, green, blue, and red perpetuana striped, seven spits and racks, andirons, iron dogges, bellowes, a large brass chaffing dish, bell metal skillet, brass pots and kettles, and a quantity of pewter articles the weight of which is given as 309 lb.

Thomas Ghost was followed in 1670 by William Watts, who is the earliest occupant to appear in the Bromley Rate Books. Succeeding Watts there were, during the next hundred and fifty years, a series of owners and occupiers of whom there is nothing notable to record.

From 1818 till 1827 the inn was in the hands of John Collins. Some horse-dealing transactions which he had with William Ledger led to the latter believing himself to have been swindled. To give vent and expression to his feelings Ledger employed the very odd device of recording them in an inscription upon his tombstone, given in Chapter VII, page 136.

Collins was succeeded in 1828 by William Pawley, a man of considerable energy and enterprise, a keen sportsman and a lover of horses, whose personality and influence commanded attention and respect throughout the many years be remained in Bromley. Up to this time the front of the inn had closely bordered the narrow highway. The development of the coach and post chaise traffic during the latter part of the eighteenth and the early part of the nineteenth centuries had made this position a source of inconvenience, the space in front of the building not affording sufficient room for these vehicles to draw up properly. With land to spare at the rear of the building (for their property extended to and covered what is now Lownds' Avenue) the owners, possibly on the prompting of Pawley or at least with his willing accord, pulled down the old building and erected a new one some twenty-eight feet farther back from the road with a curved wing at each end brought out to meet the adjoining premises, thus affording a " draw up " ample for any demand.

Not only was the front of the building thrown back from the roadway, but a spacious assembly room was built over the entrance to the great yard. This was an acquisition of some importance, supplying as it did a need from which the town had suffered for some time. For more than thirty years, that is until the erection of the Town Hall in 1863, every sort of public function was held here, meetings of the magistrates in Petty Sessions, the County Court, county and town balls, political and parochial meetings, concerts, lectures, and entertainments of all kinds. It was at the White Hart that the meetings were held which led to the setting up of the Association for the Defence of the Realm in 1792, of the Bromley Gas Consumers Company in 1853, the formation of the 18th Kent Rifle Volunteers in 1859, and here were the headquarters of the Volunteer Fire Brigade from 1868 until the Fire Station in West Street was built.

In 1858 William Pawley gave up the tenancy of the hotel—as the house may perhaps be fitly called after its alteration, and was succeeded by William Lownds, who remained in it till his death in 1888, carrying it on in an unostentatious but very efficient manner befitting his own somewhat determined though quiet and retiring character. For several years he served the town as a member of the Local Board, contributing to the deliberations and work of that body a fund of sound common sense and practical ability.

On William Lownds' death the tenancy of the hotel came into the hands of Maurice Lloyd, who had married Lownds' daughter, and Mr. and Mrs. Lloyd carried it on for several years.

During their occupancy of the premises a large part of the garden was taken away, the row of residential flats called Lownds' Avenue being erected on the site.

Various changes of tenancy and alterations in the structure have since taken place, but the portico, with the badge of King Richard II surmounting it, still remains.

The south wing of the White Hart was let off separately as a " Tap." Next to this was the house and yard of George Page, a builder, from 1788 to 1822, who was succeeded in 1832 by William Vokins; from 1844 to 1879 it was in the continuous occupation of William Bateman (" Putty ") the plumber. Two big gates led into a commodious yard. In front of the house was a small garden, confined by iron railings, and on each side of the path to the door a quantity of strongly scented musk growing about the roots of box trees. W. Bateman was overseer in 1858, with his neighbour J. Nettlefold.

Next to these premises came two small wooden tenements, eventually swept away by the premises of the Westminster Bank, which, as the London & County Bank, was established in Bromley in 1865.

Beyond this was Nettlefold's, excellent cabinet makers and upholsterers, auctioneers and valuers. The firm was founded in 1802 by Abram Nettlefold, to whom reference has already been made. He was succeeded by his son John.

John Nettlefold was certainly one of Bromley's ' characters.' He was an eccentric man, used ' I ' instead of ' J ' for his name over the shop-front. He always wore a tall hat and a stock, and accompanied his talk by a sort of snort, which became an altogether unintelligible splutter if his temper was tried or he in any way became excited.

When the change was made in the method of voting at Parliamentary elections from the open vote at the Hustings to the secret vote by ballot, Mr. Nettlefold invented a sort of cupboard containing a machine by which, on pulling a lever, the voter would not only vote in secret, but his vote would be counted at the same time.

Demonstrating its usefulness one day, he entered the cupboard, closed the door behind him, and proceeded to vote, but, on attempting to let himself out, his efforts to emerge were unavailing. His choler arose, and he vehemently declared some trick had been played upon him, and angrily demanded to be released; but this could only be done by breaking up part of the apparatus. Needless to say, his device was not adopted.

Beyond Nettlefold's was what afterwards became known as Redwood House, a handsome Georgian residence which certainly adorned this part of the town.

In 1697 the land was known as Needom's Field, rated to William Waldron at £3. He was another Bromley tradesman who issued tokens. His halfpenny, illustrated at page 396, shows that he was a tallow-chandler.

The handsome red-brick house as many of us knew it was evidently built in 1720, for it is referred to in a deed of that date as " the house now building." By that time the ownership had passed to William Emmett. It was taken by Mr. Thomas Washer in 1722, whose widow, Katherine, seems to have lived on there till 1736. Throughout, however, it remained in the ownership of William Emmett, who was quite an important person, one who could always be relied upon to help in advancing money when needed for public work, such as the building of the Workhouse, restoration of the church, etc. He was an architect, and prepared the plans for the Workhouse in 1731, which, although they can hardly be styled beautiful, yet fitted no doubt the requirements of the time.

He was the eldest son of Maurice and Elizabeth Emmett of St. Margaret's, Westminster, and was trustee of the Charity School. His wife, Ellenor, was the daughter of John Thornhill of Rossby, Lincs. She gave £100 to the Charity School and 40s. to be given to the poor yearly on St. Andrew's Day.

Elizabeth Emmett, the daughter of William Emmett, married Richard Innocent, to whom she brought this property inherited from her father. Their daughter, Eleonora, became the second wife of James Norman of the Rookery, Bromley Common, to whom she conveyed it in 1772. James Norman let it on a lease for fourteen years to Jeremiah Redwood at £40 per annum, from whom the house took its name. He died in 1776, Mrs. Redwood occupying it till 1780.

About 1786 Mr. and Mrs. James Norman sold Redwood House to Booth Hibbert, who established here one of the schools for which Bromley in the eighteenth century was famous. The dimensions of the property were then given as : north to south, 136 feet ; east to west, 183 feet. The house stood 22 feet back from the street, with a forecourt garden planted with lime trees and shrubs, bright in the springtime with crocuses, and separated from the footway by tall iron railings and a handsome wrought-iron gate.

Mr. Booth Hibbert died in 1818 and was buried at the Parish Church. The school was carried on by his son, the Rev. H. Booth Hibbert.

There not being sufficient space here for a playground for the boys, the field was secured on which the present Baptist Chapel, schools, and adjoining house stand, a pond, formed from springs where Park Road joins Widmore Road, being called Hibbert's Pond.

In the Census for 1801 the inmates were registered as 40 males and 7 females. On March 28th, 1828, the whole of the Hibbert property was sold by Mr. Hoggart at his Auction Mart, Old Broad Street, in seven lots which included all the land, about 183 feet deep, behind a frontage of 256 feet, Mr. John Vernell of London purchasing almost the whole of it. The Redwood House portion of it realised £2,060 in two lots, namely, £1,640 for Redwood House proper and £420 for the portion at its north-west corner, having 30 feet frontage to the street and 62 feet depth, in the occupation then of John Walker. Redwood House then consisted of nine bedrooms and four reception rooms, a large schoolroom with six bedrooms and boxroom over it, a bakehouse, stabling, garden, and playground. The whole of the seven lots realised only £3,405.

After H. Booth Hibbert the school was carried on by the Rev. William Butt, a relation of Mr. S. P. Acton, till 1839, when it was taken by the Rev. Thomas Nicholl. In 1844 the Rev. Samuel Crooke brought his school

REDWOOD HOUSE, HIGH STREET.

Built 1720; pulled down 1905.

here from the west side of High Street. In 1859 the house became the private residence of Miss Clarke, and in 1869 it was taken by Mr. John Leatherdale. Mr. and Mrs. Leatherdale were worthy, unassuming, and very charitable people, ever tireless in doing good by stealth and blushing to find it fame.

In 1874 Dr. Hugh Spencer Hughes removed here from Tweed Cottage lower down, and remained till he retired from practice in 1884. His cheery nature endeared him to everyone in the town, especially to children. From 1885–7 the house was occupied by James Fraser, F.R.C.V.S., as a Veterinary Infirmary. In 1888 Dr. David T. Playfair, Dr. Hughes's partner, took the house. He was a good botanist and Fellow of the Linnean Society. His herbarium is now in the possession of the Bromley Town Council. He died in 1903 esteemed by all. The next year Redwood House was demolished and shops erected on its site, and it is to be regretted that the fine wrought-iron gate and railings were not preserved.

The premises south of the above, namely No. 146, were, from 1818 to 1840, those of James Greenaway, his son Thomas, who died in 1844, succeeding him. They are described as bricklayers, which often meant small builders. In later years this was the familiar stationery and Berlin-wool depository of (Mrs.) Nash and (Miss) Milstead.

Then came, where Pyrke's furnishing warehouse now stands, what was, until about 1884, the last shop at this end of the town, for the Broadway was not made until a year or so later, and the few houses below this were private residences. This shop in the late eighteenth century was in the hands of James Tape and Son, who had brewhouses here and also at Mason's Hill. In 1809 it was the cabinet-making and upholstery business of Jabez Carpenter, Petty Constable in 1815, who was succeeded in 1846 by James Summers Carpenter.

The appearance of the place was very different from what we see to-day, for the house and shop lay well back from the road. In front was a somewhat sloping gravelly forecourt on which stood three large elm trees, which gave an umbrageous appearance to this end of the town.

James Carpenter (" Jimmy ") was an enthusiastic member of the Cricket Club, and when taking part in the games played in the White Hart Field presented an appearance that could not escape notice. He was a shortish man, thickset, and rotund, and played in dark trousers, white linen shirt, scarlet braces, and a silk top-hat, but when scoring he appeared in frock-coat and top-hat. He died in 1869.

After his death his widow remained in occupation till 1871, when Mr. George Pyrke, whose family still carry on the business, secured the premises. Mr. Pyrke was for many years a prominent member of the West Kent Yeomanry, where he was a great favourite. He was also a good Freemason, and was ever ready to assist in anything connected with local sport.

After Carpenter's there were two small houses occupied by professional men, solicitors and architects.   One of these (No. 149) was, about 1838–9, the first Police Station, removed in 1841 to the corner of the Middle Row, Market Square.

Here also was the builder's yard of Richard (" Dicky ") Barrett, who was one of the first to take advantage of the demand for new houses on Bromley Common, Widmore Lane, and other parts of the town.   He was followed by J. Cooper Arnaud, who had come into Bromley when Bickley was beginning to develop, and saw an opening for building activities. When first setting up for himself he had his yard down by the Old Malt House at Vale Place.   This business increased and became one of the chief builders' establishments in the town; his son, J. F. Arnaud, and his grandson, J. N. Arnaud, carrying it on till recent years.

Adjoining this was Verandah Cottage, a picturesque little house with a covered way, smothered with creepers, leading from the entrance gate to the front door.   The Marquis of Townsend lived here for a few years, and later George Edey the dentist.   It is now " Johnsons'," the dyers and cleaners.

Next to this was another pleasant-looking private house, called Tweed Cottage, with a raised terraced garden in front, enclosed by an ornamental balustrade of stucco.   Dr. H. S. Hughes lived here (1869), before moving to Redwood House, and here, too, for nearly fourteen years, lived Mr. Thomas C. Dewey, afterwards Sir Thomas C. Dewey, Bart.

Below this to the gravel pits was originally only one estate, namely the park of Bromley Lodge, which occupied the oblong portion of land bounded on the north by the White Hart Field, on the west by the High Street and the high road, on the east by Love Lane and the Palace grounds, and on the south by the Gravel Pits, or later the railway.

Its boundary below Tweed Cottage was for some distance oak park palings grey with age and lichens, followed by a high brick wall enclosing the kitchen and fruit gardens.   Then came the entrance gates, the first leading to the stables and offices, and the next to the white stone house itself (now the Constitutional Club), which stood on a grassy knoll with clumps of trees about it.

The mansion itself has been strangely neglected by previous historians of Bromley.   It was certainly one of the large residences of the neighbourhood, standing as it did in the centre of an estate of about twenty acres. Owing to the gap in our Rate Books there is no certainty who occupied this house before 1792, when Edward Burrow possessed it, rated at only £26 10s., which seems to indicate that if there was a house there, it must have been small, but the next year the rating is nearly three times as high (£77 10s.), which looks as if a good house had been built, probably part of the present house.   Mr. Burrow was there till 1799.   He was a Justice of the Peace, serving with George Grote, the father of the historian.   In

BROMLEY LODGE.

Built in late eighteenth century.

BROMLEY RAILWAY-STATION, 1860.

1803 it was bought by William Menish, when the rates levied upon it were increased to £120, so probably he added to the house. His widow lived on there till about 1814.

In 1815 it was purchased by Stuart Erskine, a lineal descendant of the Earls of Kellie, who died here in 1826 and is buried at the Parish Church; his widow Mary lived on here till 1837. After this it was taken by a Mr. Laine, but in 1843 came William Pott, the brother of Charles Pott, who was living at Freelands, who is rated at £198 for house, etc., and £28 for parkland. The Potts were vinegar makers of high repute in London.

He was succeeded in 1855 by Charles F. Devas, who was rated at £200 for house, £3 for Gravel Pits, and £26 for parkland. He was a Justice of the Peace, and a gentleman who interested himself very actively in the affairs of both the church and the town during the fifteen to sixteen years he lived here, and in 1870 he went to live at Pickhurst Manor, where he died in 1897.

He was among those who, in 1867, promoted the setting up of a Local Board under the Local Government Act of 1858. In the May election for the Board thus established he headed the poll and became its first chairman, which position he filled with distinction for three years. After he left the town this house was taken by Sir Eardley Wilmot, Bart, M.P., J.P., and very soon after it ceased to be a private residence. On the frontage land shops were erected, and the house became the home of the Conservative Club.

From the entrance gates, to the bottom of the hill or the railway, this demesne was bordered by a lofty bank crowned with bramble and other bushes, corresponding very much to the opposite side of the road, where it rose to a considerable height, as may be judged by the present position of Rosebank perched above the railway cutting. There was a well-beaten footpath adjoining the fences, or banks, on either side of the highway, and between these and the road itself there were grass-grown ditches and narrow strips upon which road scrapings were dumped in irregular heaps, both the ditches and the heaps forming traps for the stumbling steps of the unwary.

Before the railway came the ground sloped down to a low gravel escarpment known as the Gravel Pits. This was one of the four parish pits from which the surveyors of the highway had the right, under an Act of George III, to draw gravel for the repair of the roads, the others being at Southborough, London Road, and Pageheath. (When the Mid Kent Railway Company came they paid to the town £105 compensation for ground absorbed by them in making Bromley's first railway station.) This cutting back left a high cliff of gravel on the north side of the station from which the surveyors still continued to exercise their right to draw gravel, a proceeding resented by Mr. C. F. Devas, who, no doubt, began to wonder where and when this right was going to stop. This meant stormy meetings, with the result that at last the Local Board in August 1870 sold their rights to dig gravel, tð Mr. Devas, for £250.

Being left untouched, this cliff was soon riddled with sand-martins' nests, but after a few years this gravel escarpment was swept away to make room for existing buildings.

The first railway station, opened Monday, July 5th, 1858, was a rather primitive structure. On the north or ' down ' side there was a slope from the highway, railed off from the line, with footpath and roadway ; on the left of the latter being the gravel cliff already referred to. At the bottom there was a covered shed. On the south or ' up ' side of the line there were the stationmaster's house and booking-office, the signal levers being on the platform. Outside was a carriage drive with a larger space in front of the booking-office to allow room for carriages to turn. Beyond this was the goods yard, as now.

Until 1869, with the exception of Bromley Lodge, the last house in the town was Tweed Cottage. Important developments, begun about that date, led to the construction on the west side of the high road of Ethelbert Road, commemorating the charter by the Saxon King granting to his Minister Drythwald lands at Bromley ; Ringer's Road, recalling the last tenant of Simpson's Place ; and Ravensbourne Road, named after Bromley's river. These were completed by 1873.

By 1876 Elmfield and Holwood Roads had been constructed, the Wesleyan Chapel built, and some private houses erected. By 1884 shops had begun to be built in Aberdeen Buildings. By 1885 a beginning of the Broadway had been made. Finally by 1906–7 the Broadway was completed almost as we see it to-day.

Mason's Hill

THE district known as Mason's Hill—the origin of the name is uncertain—comprises that portion of the Borough which slopes up from the side of the present South Station towards Bromley Common.

Before the construction of the railway station the ground on and adjacent to which it stands was known as the Gravel Pits, the name still surviving in a row of twelve cottages running at right angles to the main road. With the gradual excavation of the gravel for purposes of road repair, houses have by degrees sprung up within the area, extending as far as Vale Place.

As early as 1716 the Charity School was established there, and there, but in a school house constructed a century later (1814), they remained, until removed in 1855 to their present quarters in College Road.

In addition to the school and some small wooden houses the site was occupied in the eighteenth century and on into the nineteenth by a brewery and malthouse associated with the names Tape, Davis, and Osmar. The name of John Tape appears on the list of Volunteers in 1798, and in Pigot's *Directory* of 1839, James Tape is found among the nobility, gentry, and clergy, while William and Thomas Davis are the brewers and maltsters. William Osmar, who appears to have followed the Messrs. Davis at the brewery, was the last of the brewers.

A small alehouse with the sign of the Two Brewers stood at the corner of the entrance-way to the brewery, of which it was an adjunct.

The brewing business was discontinued about the middle of last century, the premises being let or sold to various occupants. Part became a farrier's, part a cart and coach builder's, and part was occupied by Mr. J. C. Arnaud, the builder. The small alehouse was closed, the sign and the licence being transferred to much more commodious premises, with yard and stabling, erected on the opposite side of the main road a little nearer the town.

South of this new inn a narrow lane led to New Farm, and thence by a footpath to Pickhurst Green. Here, at a bend in the road on a triangular piece of roadside waste, stood the Pound or Greenyard. This was an enclosure of stout posts and rails about fifteen feet square in which animals found straying on the highway were detained until the owners had been discovered, and had paid the fine imposed for allowing the animals to be at large. That this was no uncommon occurrence may be gathered from the frequent references that are made to the Pound and its use in the old parish books.

An entry which gives some idea of the necessity for the Pound is to

MASON'S HILL.
From an etching by Miss Janet Simpson.

MASON'S HILL 1860

be found in the Minute of the Vestry Meeting held in September 1768, where it is ordered that :

" John Adams and Sam Drury do traverse the Town from College Gate to Pound Lane, one to carry a bell and ring it, twice every day opposite the College, by the Three Compasses, and opposite the White Hart warning those persons who allow swine, etc., to roam about."

With a change in conditions the Pound became unnecessary and was removed, the former narrow lane beside it being widened into the present approach to what is known as the South Hill district.

In 1871 close to the roadside near here the Mason's Hill Schools were erected. Owing to the conformation of the ground, which fell away steeply from the road, part of the schools was supported upon brick piers, the space beneath forming a sheltered playground in wet weather.

At this point the main road crosses a stream, a nameless tributary of the Ravensbourne, which takes its rise in Holwood Park. The bridge over it is so insignificant that few people using the road are aware of its existence. The ratepayers, however, have not been unconscious of it, for the stream, small though it usually is, has on more than one occasion been the cause of considerable expense. The Rate Books show that Tanners, or Tenners, bridge, as it was called, was in frequent need of repair. A four-penny rate was levied by the county officials for this purpose in 1765 and again in 1798. On a more recent occasion the stream, which skirted the south side of the Mason's Hill Schools, was a source of anxiety and expense to those responsible for them. At the time of the flood of April 1878 the buildings were in great jeopardy, for the bank around the supporting piers and foundations was washed away, and the buildings were only saved by driving piles to protect and keep them secure. In consequence of the increasing traffic the position of these schools became a source of danger to the scholars. They were therefore abandoned in 1910 and new schools erected to the design of C. H. B. Quinnell, F.R.I.B.A., on the other side of the stream, in the grounds of South Hill House.

From here, on the left-hand side, there was formerly a field stretching half-way up the hill. Beyond this to the top of the hill the pathway rose high above the road, into which pedestrians were prevented from falling by a wooden railing. Perched above this path, from which it was reached by a flight of steps, was Sinclair Villa, built in the early part of last century by Mr. Robert Ayling for his private residence. It was afterwards occupied by Mr. John Nash, the draper, Mr. John Sulman, the architect, and others.

Beyond this again was a group of small houses, a chandler's shop, an alehouse with the sign of the Three Horse Shoes, and a blacksmith's forge, this latter in 1840 being occupied by a farrier of some local reputation,

RAVENSCROFT, MASON'S HILL.
Erected 1660.

Nos. 61, 62, etc., UPPER HIGH STREET, 1902.

named Dunkley, the last occupant of the alehouse from 1867 to 1874 being Thomas Partridge. This alehouse gained for a time a sinister reputation from its association with a mysterious murder case in which Partridge was involved. In 1868 a woman's hat was drawn up out of a well situated in what was known as Sparke's Cottages on the opposite side of the road, followed by the recovery from the well of the body of a woman. The woman was identified as one who had lodged at the Three Horse Shoes. This led to the arrest of Partridge and another man, named Deadman, on a charge of murder. They were tried and acquitted at Maidstone Assizes.

On the opposite or right-hand side the hill is bordered by a lofty and steep bank. About midway along it is Cromwell Avenue. This was formerly a rough lane, known as Pieter's Lane, leading to a footpath through fields towards Hayes. It was in two cottages in this lane that the Cottage Hospital was first started.

On the north side at the top of the lane was a fine clump of pine trees commemorated in Pinewood Road. In front of these, on the brow of the hill, was built, towards the middle of last century, South Hill House (now the Masonic Hall). It was first occupied by Mrs. Devas (mother of C. F. Devas, J.P., the first Chairman of Bromley Local Board), followed by Mr. Thomas and Mr. William McAndrew, and later by Mr. T. Adams Phillips, who, in association with his neighbour, Mr. Eley Soames, interested himself in promoting the work of the Church in this part of the town. Their efforts resulted ultimately in the building of St. Mark's Church.

The last private occupant was Mr. William Willis. His name will always be famous as the inventor of the platinotype process of photography. During his residence in Bromley he served on the committee of the Cottage Hospital, and both that and the Phillips Memorial Hospital are indebted to him for the material assistance he gave in the installation of X-ray apparatus.

Mr. Willis's father lived for a time in Bromley. After attaining great distinction as a steel engraver, he devoted his leisure, upon retirement, to the production of pencil drawings of remarkable merit. He drew his subjects exclusively from the neighbourhood, and one of them is reproduced in this volume.

At the top of the hill, south of the Lane, stands Ravenscroft, one of the oldest and most picturesque houses in the Borough, and one which attracts the attention of every discriminating passer-by.

In style and appearance it confirms its date—1660—conspicuously displayed on its shapely gable. It is of brick, colour-washed. Additions to the original structure have been made both on the north and west sides.

There is reason to suppose that this was the site of the house referred to in the will of Anthony Calthrope, dated April 20th, 1594, in which he bequeaths to—

" Johane, my wife, my mansion house at Masons Hill Bromley which I lately bought of one Pope."

If this supposition is correct the story of this house is carried back to the days of Elizabeth, or even earlier, for, according to the researches of Mr. Bernard F. Davis, the Calthrope family were already established at Mason's Hill in A.D. 1500.

Anthony Calthrope, born in 1522, appears to have been a member of the Mercers Company of the City of London, to which he left a piece of plate value £10. He had a large family of seven sons and nine daughters and died July 19th, 1594. He was buried in Bromley Church, where a small brass executed in his memory is inserted in the floor of pew No. 30. His widow survived him for at least fourteen years, as her will, in which she directs that she is "to be buried in the chancell of the Parish Church of Bromley, as near the body of my late husband as may be," is dated 1605, and has a codicil dated 1608.

After her death the property passed by sale to Edmund Pershall, and from him to his son Robert, who, about 1630, left Bromley and went to the midlands.

From this date till 1707 the ownership and occupancy are uncertain. It is thought to have been the home, for some part of this time, of a member of the Bodenham family, probably Philip, son of the Henry Bodenham whose brass in memory of his wife, in the nave of the Parish Church, dated 1625, is referred to in Chapter VII.

For considerably more than a century after 1707 this house was the home of a school, enjoying a deservedly high reputation, a record of which will be found in the chapter on Education in Bromley.

In 1856 Mr. Eley Soames obtained a lease of the property, becoming the owner by purchase in 1875. For more than half a century Mr. Soames and his family resided here, pursuing throughout the whole of that time an unostentatious career of active benevolence; they were at all times generous benefactors of the poor.

The purchase of the site for St. Mark's Church was the joint act of Mr. Soames and Mr. T. C. Dewey, and the building of the church was made possible by their further generosity, while, for long years before, the maintenance of the temporary iron church and the assistant clergy connected with it were matters which had received Mr. Soames's especial interest and support. He not only gave liberally to religious and charitable objects, but to everything that concerned the public good of the town, Mr. Soames's last and most conspicuous gift being the strip of land required for the widening of Mason's Hill, a monument not only to his memory but to his public spirit.

Immediately adjacent to this house is the Tiger's Head Inn. It stands at the top of the hill, and, as seen in the chapter on Bromley Common, may be regarded as a connecting link between the common and the town. It has a history which goes back into the early eighteenth century, if not beyond it. From 1673 to 1697 the Rate Books only show a rate levied on the land, but in 1706 they record a house, stables, barn, orchard, and meadows " at the back called Tygor Grove," which may indicate that in the interval these buildings had been erected, or that a house, known as The Tiger, already existed there. The Parish Registers record the burial, in 1729, of " Richard Joans, ostler at the Tiger's Head, Mason's Hill," and various deeds preserved in the Public Library testify to its antiquity. Originally the house stood farther back from the road, a sort of wing projecting out towards the highway, with its main entrance facing the common. The present structure is the result of rebuilding towards the close of the last century.

It was formerly the custom to hold a fair in connection with this inn at Whitsuntide, the stalls and shows spreading down the hill and into the meadows at the rear, with the usual accompaniment of greasy-pole walking, peepshows, and other amusements characteristic of those times.

Beyond this inn on the same side of the road stood what was un-questionably the most picturesque group of buildings in Bromley. An oil painting of it is in existence upon which is written " built 1561." The authority for that statement is unknown. It is quite possible that the buildings may have dated even from the preceding century. At all events they were built at that period in the progress of domestic architecture when it was customary for the upper stories to overhang the lower, the ends of the beams supporting them being exposed, the trusses and other timbers of the construction also being visible. Its chief glory from the artist's point of view was probably its wide-spreading roof covered with tiles mellowed by age and weather to a beautiful tone of colour upon which grew lichens, mosses, and stonecrops in tints that varied from grey to green and from gold to crimson.

In 1673 it was an important farm-house called Stubarfield's or Stubberfield's Farm, but of its occupants generally little or nothing appears to have come down to us. By the middle of the nineteenth century it had become useless for farm purposes, and was divided into cottages, being then known as Sparke's or Clarke's Cottages, from the names of the occupants. Falling into further disrepair its dilapidated condition rendered it untenantable, and it was finally pulled down and destroyed in 1877.

On the opposite side of the main road was a group of buildings pleasant in character but in quite a different way, a cluster of small villas erected during the early part of last century. Their front gardens were gay with flowers, the two largest of them having good-sized lawns shaded by trees.

Beyond these villas, occupying the space now covered by the motor works at the corner of the Wendover Road, was a roadside pond, Mason's

Hill Pond, accessible from the highway at one end to enable horses to be watered and carmen to 'plim' their cart or wagon wheels when shrunken by hot weather. Part of this pond extended into the adjoining meadow, shut off from access by a wooden fence. Here it was overgrown with reeds and sedges, among which dwelt newts, croaking bull frogs, fish of various sorts, including carp and other interesting creatures.

Mr. George Jessop records that on one occasion, when the pond was cleaned out, the fish were so numerous that he was able to scoop them up with a bucket. The pond was filled up in 1897.

Beyond the pond, extending as far as the present Napier Road, was a broad strip of rough land, covered with brambles. A row of fine elm trees and a rough open fence separated it from the Palace Estate, which stretched as open fields and paddocks across the valley to Widmore. A similar strip, extending to Hayes Lane, not so wide or so rough, bordered by a deep ditch and with a similar row of elm trees, ran along the other side of the road with fields stretching away towards Hayes. These roadside strips had evidently formed part of Bromley Common. An attempt was made to move the boundary of the palace estate forward to the edge of the strip on that side of the road. This was successfully opposed on behalf of the townsfolk, the Lord of the Manor subsequently arranging a transfer and exchange satisfactory to both parties.

A short distance south of Napier Road was a yard leading to a cottage, flanked by a long range of open wooden sheds. This for many years was occupied by a family named Draper, a name which has been associated with Bromley for some centuries, people of that name having been owners of property, residents, or tradesmen in the town since the early part of the sixteenth century until the present day.

In Wilson's *History of Bromley*, 1797, a William Draper, wheelwright, is mentioned in his list of Bromley tradesmen. Mr. Philip Norman in his notes on Bromley says of this last:

" William Draper, Wheelwright, is the only person in the list whom I remember. When I was a little child his son was carrying on the trade at the Wheelwright's shop near the turnpike, and he, a blind old man living at the cottage behind, used to walk backwards and forwards along the straight path which led to the high road, feeling his way. Sometimes he would smoke a long clay pipe or 'churchwarden.' I talked to him more than once, for we knew the family well. I remember his telling me that he had served under my grandfather, who was Captain of the Bromley Volunteers, enrolled at the end of last century when there was risk of French invasion."

Close by, the toll gate crossed the highway with its toll house, a little wooden structure of one story, on the western side. Toll gates were first set up in 1663, but about the middle of the last century they were con-

SPARKES' COTTAGES, MASON'S HILL.
Pulled down 1877.

430]

sidered a hindrance and inconvenience to traffic, and steps were taken to bring about their removal. In 1865 an Act of Parliament was passed abolishing sixty-one of them on the south side of London, and the Bromley " Gate " was removed on November 1st of that year.

Beyond the gate at the corner of Brick Kiln Lane (as Homesdale Road was then called, its present name only dating from 1873) stood at one time a farm-house with barns, outbuildings, and duck pond. These gradually fell out of use, the last of the buildings being cleared away about 1870, and the land put up for sale. The land agents entrusted with the transaction, unconscious apparently of the irony of their suggestion, erected a large notice-board on the corner announcing :

" This eligible plot of freehold building land for sale, suitable for the erection of a Church or a Tavern."

The development of this portion of the Borough, which commenced about 1864 with the construction of Napier and Stanley Roads, was continued throughout the following years till 1900, when Wendover Road (named after Richard de Wendover, first Rector of Bromley and Bishop of Rochester) was planned and laid out.

Unfortunately this development (advantageous as it may have been in some respects) has involved the complete sacrifice of the charmingly rural aspect and character we have endeavoured to delineate, and which had been so conspicuous a feature of this entrance to the town. The only reminders of it are the elm trees which still grace the gardens of the houses on the western side of the highway.

WIDMORE ROAD AND NEW BROMLEY

Until comparatively recent times the only avenue of approach to the town from the eastward was by a road known from time immemorial as Widmore Lane, which ended at the Market-place. At the point of junction the lane narrowed to such an extent that at last the task of widening, the details of which have already been given, became imperative.

The aspect of Widmore Road to-day differs very materially from that which it presented sixty years ago. The first house on the right on emerging from the Square was the private residence of Isaac Uridge, flanked by two shops which still survive. In succession to them were four wooden cottages, demolished in 1872 to make way for two shops which were regarded on their completion as among the best in the town. The house which followed was the Three Compasses, an inn now rebuilt, which in old days exhibited over its little wooden porch its sign of three open compasses, now relegated to the wall above its corner door. A long trestle hay trough before the entrance, together with the field on the opposite side of the way, brought an atmosphere of the country very close to the town.

The old Tudoresque house adjoining the inn still remains and presents much the same appearance as of old. Occupied in 1822 by Mr. Charles Browne, it soon afterwards became the property of Mr. John Bromley, who bought it, and a good deal of adjacent land, from the executors of Mr. John Cator of Beckenham. For some years (1833–44) Mrs. Blaxland carried on a school there until the property was secured by Mr. Henry Clarke Lukey as his private residence. On his death his family continued to reside there until 1886, when the house was secured by the Congregational Church, and became what it is to-day, a part of the Morley Institute.

The present Congregational Chapel, built in 1881, occupies the site on which there stood not only the old chapel,[1] but also a substantial red-bricked house which was for some years the residence of Mr. Robinson Latter. The construction of the new chapel involved the demolition of this house, and other very considerable changes in the appearance of the road. The original chapel, constructed in 1835, stood some way back from the road, and was approached through an iron gate and railings by a paved way leading to the main entrance. Two bridle-posts, a mounting-stone, and a pair of fine trees broke the line of houses, and embodied the spirit of a vanishing age. All this had to go, and the frontage of the new chapel was brought much nearer to the roadway.

The three Georgian houses beyond the chapel still remain, their commodious interiors, their forecourts, and their pleasant gardens extending back as far as the White Hart Field, causing them to be much in request as private residences. At various times they have been the homes of John Nash, A. E. Willett, Samuel P. Acton, and a succession of doctors. Adjoining these was a house of later construction, for many years the residence of Major S. Talman. It is now the home of the Literary Institute.

Until 1869 the land between this house and the entrance lodge to Bromley Palace was a meadow forming part of the palace estate. It had an open fence and one could see across it to the row of limes beyond the southern boundary of the Queen's garden. At this date the meadow was purchased by Mr. John Garle, who built a handsome house for himself and his family, called Parkfield, and laid out the rest of the land as a garden. He remained a resident till 1876, when he was succeeded by Mrs. Hay, who, with her sons and daughters, then came to live here. This family from the commencement of their residence here have taken an active interest in various benevolent institutions. Mr. John Y. Hay has been for several years Honorary Secretary to Bromley Cottage Hospital, and Mr. W. R. G. Hay is associated with the Phillips Memorial Hospital and the Bromley National Schools.

After Mrs. Hay's death the house was pulled down, Queen's Road was constructed, and the existing buildings covering the whole site were erected.

---

[1] An illustration of the old chapel appears at p. 162.

West of the entrance to the Palace Grounds, and running at the back of the houses on the east side of Queen's Road, is a footpath. This path was a part of Bromley's "Love Lane." This portion of it at one time coincided with the private drive to the palace, an obviously inconvenient arrangement. Therefore, in 1866, Mr. Coles Child was allowed, with the consent of the Vestry, to divert it to its present position, on condition that it should be bordered by open railings with shrubs not more than four feet high, and that he should dedicate the path to the public. Consequent upon this arrangement a slight modification was made in the direction of the path leading across the White Hart Field.

Previous to 1870 East and West Streets did not exist, for the site they occupy was open field—the Cage Field. This open space, covering some seven and a half acres, was generally laid down in corn, and entered by large and small swing gates which stood about opposite the yard of the present Post Office. Two footpaths at once spread away from this entrance, one to the left for Farwig, coinciding with West Street and College Road of to-day, and one to the right for Plaistow and New Town, coinciding with East Street and Sherman Road of to-day.

Widmore Lane eastward from the two gates was flanked by a strip of waste land belonging to the Lord of the Manor, which at fair-time was given up to horses and cattle. Behind it was a low fence separating it from the Cage Field, and on it, a short distance from the Market-place, stood two small brick buildings adjoining each other.

One was the fire-engine shed erected in 1823, containing at one time the two engines prescribed by law to be kept; one of these the town possesses to-day in excellent condition. The other building was the Cage or lock-up, which, erected at the beginning of the nineteenth century and repaired in December 1821, gives its name to the field behind it.

The stocks and pillory were said to have stood by the side of this Cage, but there are those who assert that they were in the Market-place opposite the Duke's Head. Possibly, however, they were at one time removed from the Market-place and set down here where there was more room.

Between the Cage Field and what is now Tweedy Road stood the only residence on the north side of this part of Widmore Lane. This was Widmore House, a residence standing well back from the roadway, with which the front entrance was connected by a covered walk, the supports of which were entwined by a luxuriant growth of creepers. Attached to it were gardens, a pleasure ground, and meadows.

In the early years of the nineteenth century this little estate was the property of a Mr. William Shearman, whose name, though misspelt and mispronounced, is preserved to us in Sherman Road.

The property later passed into the hands of the well-known family of Tweedy, several members of which have been intimately connected with Bromley life, their name being perpetuated in Tweedy Road. Mrs. Tweedy, widow of J. Newman Tweedy, lived here from 1869 till 1900, and her son and daughters till 1904.

Such parts of the property as had not already been sold for the construction of Tweedy Road and other purposes was acquired by the Town Council in 1905, and upon it was erected the group of Municipal Buildings now standing. The house itself was, for a short time, allowed to remain and became the County Schools for Girls. In 1912, however, it was demolished and the site has been converted from an unsightly heap of débris into the pleasant little garden which the public now enjoy.

Where Tweedy Road now begins there used to be simply a large and small gate, leading into Shearman's Field, and to footpaths; one going in a north-west direction across to Longfield in the London Road, and another leading to Plaistow. The latter still partly exists. At this point Park Road branches away to the left, the portal, as it were, to what was formerly known as New Bromley.

Previous to the first half of the nineteenth century all the triangular portion of land lying between Park, Widmore, and Freelands Roads was pasture. The portion where Park and Widmore Roads meet contained at its apex a large pool of water. When it was required to build two houses on this corner, an attempt was made to choke the spring by filling up the pond, but ultimately an accommodation drain had to be laid across Widmore Lane into a surface drain in the palace grounds.

These two houses were first a school, and then became the first Homœopathic Hospital, but the basements and foundations were always damp, and it is only of late years, by dint of great expense, that the trouble has been remedied.

By about the middle of the nineteenth century houses had begun to appear all along this north side of Widmore Road, the first batch being some eight houses known as Rochester Place, and by 1869 there were thirteen more houses erected nearer the town and known as Palace Villas; also Denmark Road was made containing six houses. For a corresponding distance on the south side of the road were the palace grounds, outside the boundary fence of which was a row of noble elms which sprang up from the pathway. Later on the fence was moved by the Lord of the Manor to a position outside the trees, " to protect the public from falling over the roots," with the result that in recent years, when Widmore Road was widened along this stretch, this strip of land had to be bought from the Lord of the Manor, and another of the leafy entries to the town was destroyed by cutting down these noble trees.

Freelands Road had been made very early in the nineteenth century, and from here to the top of Widmore Hill fine trees flanked the way on both sides, some of which happily are left to us. Houses of a good type were constructed and were the residences of retired or professional gentlemen. Thus in the house next Freelands Road lived, for some years, Samuel

WIDMORE HOUSE, 1864.

FIELDS NORTH-EAST OF THE TOWN.
From a water-colour sketch by F. Walmisley, 1858.

Rawson Gardiner the historian ; in the next Mr. J. M. Holworthy, a much-respected man who was for many years churchwarden, and a devoted worker on behalf of Bromley College.

Where Homefield Road now is there stood a large stucco house, the residence till 1881 of the Rev. George Verrall, who was the first minister of the Congregational Chapel, where he devotedly served the congregation for twenty-two years (1837–59). Homefield Road was made in 1882, Wanstead Road on the south side was not made till 1884.

Just beyond Homefield Road there are four old cottages, and beyond them is a yard. These four cottages, the yard and Widmore Cottage (now Grange) form the subject of a large number of deeds, which have been perused by the courtesy of the present owner, Mr. T. Fry. There seems very little doubt that these cottages, together with the outbuildings of Widmore Cottage, once formed an inn, having the yard as its approach. The out-buildings contain an extensive old bottle rack and a large brewhouse, in which there used to be two huge vats.

The cottages also exhibit signs of the past. At the end nearest the town, where probably the postboys' ' tap ' was, the space between the ceiling and the floor above was found packed with sand, presumably to deaden any noise that might proceed from the post-boys' bar underneath.

All the rooms, too, on the first floor communicated with each other, a common arrangement in hostelries long ago. There was also found a pigeon-hole opening from the ' tap ' communicating with the other part of the inn, through which special drinks could be passed to a waiter for the ' quality ' in the inn-parlour. On a big tree that was cut down, which stood in front of the inn, was found a bridle-hook evidently inserted in the tree when young.

It was only for a brief period, however, that the premises were so used. In 1761 documents declare it to be the White Horse Inn with William Beezum as landlord, probably brother to John Beezum who had the Bell Inn in the town. In 1778 Thomas Graves was its landlord. Thus it continued till about 1795, when four cottages with separate tenants, described as " poor," appear in the Rate Books, so the inn, as such, had disappeared. From 1821 onwards the cottages have frequently changed hands.

Adjoining the cottages was a piece of land upon which in 1761 John Staples of Deptford appears to have built the house known as Widmore Cottage. It passed in 1781 into the hands of John May, the brandy merchant of 40 High Street, who made it his private residence. Subse-quently, about one hundred years later, it became the domicile of Mr. G. B. Baxter, and later still, of his brother Samuel, both of them originally partners in the firm of G. B. & S. Baxter, auctioneers.

Along the southern side of the road was the Bromley Palace estate, with its lodge and estate office. The portion of the land east of the lodge was the first to be developed by the erection of some large houses, in two of which lived two well-known doctors, Dr. H. Willey and Dr. R. E. Phillips, to whose memory the Homœopathic Hospital was erected.

The intervening space as far as the brow of the hill was soon covered by substantial residences, one of which, Birkenfeld, was built by Mr. Thomas Davis in 1867, and was his residence for about fifty years. His manifold services to the town have been recorded elsewhere in this volume.

BELT OF LAND LYING WEST OF THE MAIN ROAD THROUGH THE TOWN, SLOPING TOWARDS THE SHORTLANDS VALLEY FROM BROMLEY HILL TO MASON'S HILL

The geological drift map of Bromley shows that the Oldham or Blackheath Pebble Beds end along the crest of the slope into the valley of the River Ravensbourne, west of the main road traversing the town. Below this there are the Woolwich and Reading beds, which here evidently largely consist of clayey sand, more or less impervious to water. There is, moreover, from Bromley Hill to Glassmill Lane an outcrop of London Clay totally impervious to water, superimposed on the river gravels, so we are not surprised to find that a characteristic feature of this area is the large number of adventitious springs that issue from the hill-side.

Below the mansion at Bromley Hill there were several such springs that were cleverly made use of by Lord and Lady Farnborough in constructing their beautiful system of river walks, known as the " spring-shores."

Though many of these springs have now disappeared, owing to the increased demands by the Water Company, some still remain, appearing in the gardens of the houses in Madeira Avenue and in Highland and Farnaby Roads. At the bottom of Swan Hill, just below its junction with Blyth Road, there was always a strong spring, the water from which was conveyed into a trough that served horses. There is a special note inscribed on the flyleaf of the Rate Book for 1797 by John Sale, being an extract from the original agreement, as follows :

" Memorandum the 13th day of April 1797.

" Agreed with John Cator, George Grote, Robert Hoggartt Esqrs., THAT the Parishioners of Bromley shall have Liberty to go into a wood called —— Wood belonging to Jno Cator, and being situate near the town of Bromley Kent, and there make from a certain spring water within the wood, a Drain, to convey the water thence into a Resevoir made aside of the High Road leading from Bromley towards Beckenham, and at any time when necessary likewise to have Liberty to go into the said wood and repair the said Drain. And in consideration of which the Parish of Bromley do permit John Cator to inclose with a pale fence a piece of waste land and an ancient spring of water adjoining the said Resevoir and High Road.

Signed by Geo Grote, Robt. Hoggartt, Dr. Henry Smith, Henry Staples, Robt. Smith and John Sale."

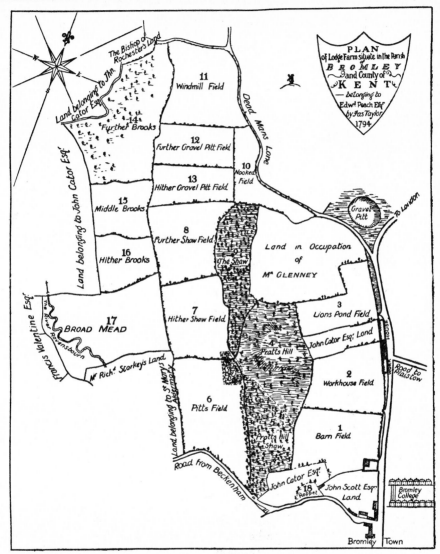

PLAN SHOWING POSITION OF OLD WORKHOUSE

It was at this time, no doubt, that the footpath, now represented by the one along the top of Martin's Hill and down Deadman's Steps, but which used to continue straight on through the woods towards the old windmill, was closed; for at a Vestry held April 12th, 1801, a resolution was passed that this

" path should be restored and opened for the benefit of the public as heretofore."

This, however, was not done, probably on account of the above agreement.

In a book of Surveyors' Accounts (1808–24) at the Public Library is an entry :

" May 6th, 1808, for an Iron Furnace Pot for Spring in Beckenham
    Lane, obtained from Carron Co. £9 18 0
    Carriage of same .   .   .   .   .   .   14 11 "

When Blyth Road was made and Beckenham Lane was first widened, this wayside water tank was done away with, but Mr. Robinson Latter arranged with the surveyor, Mr. H. S. Cregeen, to insert a pipe from the spring, under the road, into Pixfield, where other similar springs occur.

On Martin's Hill again there were two springs, one of which has been apparently choked, but the other is still connected with the garden of Mill Vale, and has to be maintained by the Town Council.

Proceeding down Beckenham Lane from the High Street, where Park House now stands, there seems to have been a farm, probably the Lodge Farm owned by Edward Peach, as shown on two old plans at the Library dated 1720 and 1794. In 1793–8 it was owned by a John Scott, and on the plans a house is shown, but in 1798 it was certainly the residence of Mr. Robert Waller and rated at £40. He served as overseer in 1802.

In 1822 it had passed to Thomas Waller, who probably much improved the house and grounds, for in 1844 he is rated at £120. Subsequently it came, about 1847, to his sister Miss Sarah Waller, who died there in 1869 much beloved by the people of Bromley. She left £100 to the Benevolent Society and the interest of £100 for the poor annually.

On the opposite side is the residence known as The Hill, which for many years was owned by Mr. William Dallison Starling, who bought the land in 1853 from the trustee of Robert Martin Smith, built the house about 1856–7, and lived there till he died in 1878, his widow remaining on for two or three years. He was a member of the Local Board from the first, but resigned on the collapse of the Board in 1870, over the sewerage question. Rather an arrogant and pompous man, he was not popular ; but Bromley owes him a debt of gratitude for his efforts in promoting the new railway to the North Station. In 1872 he attempted to enclose a strip of land from eight to nine feet wide in the London Road opposite the College Field, which was frustrated by the spirited action, recorded elsewhere, of Messrs. C. W. Gedney and Edward Tuck.

Following him the house was taken by Mr. and Mrs. D. P. Loe (1878–90), both very highly respected in Bromley, and generous supporters of all good causes.

In later years it was the home of Mr. Charles J. Tapp, and afterwards of his widow.

At the bottom of this estate is a portion of the ancient footpath, already referred to, rising sharply up on to Martin's Hill by what was known as Deadman's Steps, now as Martin's Slip. The origin for this first name is rather obscure, but on the older maps, farther north, winding down through Bromley Hill Estate from the London Road, was Deadman's Lane at the foot of which lived a Mr. Deadman, a keeper to Lord Farnborough, and Colonel Long, so the name may be derived from him.

The acre of woodland or spinney between the top of Deadman's Steps and Pixfield was originally glebe land. It was leased with other lands to Robert Booth Latter in 1848 for ninety-nine years, and afterwards, in 1874, the freehold was sold to R. B. Latter's executors and now forms part of Pixfield.

The sloping land on the west of Deadman's Steps was part of the purchase by Mr. Starling, mentioned before, and on it, some years afterwards, he built the two villas that still stand.

Then comes Pixfield, the home for a hundred and twenty years of the Latter family, whose members have throughout been closely connected with the life and government of the town, especially in the capacity of clerks to the magistrates, to the first Local Board, to the Guardians and Vestry, and registrars of the County Court, one of which offices is still held by the present representative of the family, Mr. Edward Latter, of the highly respected firm of Latter & Willett, solicitors. In addition to this, they have also been great supporters of the Volunteer and Territorial Forces, proving themselves devoted and efficient officers, and, as a family, they have added very much, at all times, to the musical activities in the town.

Pixfield was built by Robert Booth in or about 1774, and from that date to 1796 it was owned by Robert Booth, and after his death by his widow Rebecca until 1807. On her death she left it to Anne Latter, an old friend, wife of Edward Latter, who was appointed Vestry clerk in 1798. Thus began the residence of the Latter family at Pixfield. The close friendship between the Booth and Latter families is indicated by the fact that the eldest son of Edward and Anne was named Robert Booth Latter. This gentleman succeeded his father in 1831, and on his death in 1870 his brother, Robinson, removed here from Widmore Road.

This commodious old red-bricked house is surrounded by pleasant grounds with a good meadow sloping down into the valley. In the entrance hall are the twenty-two carved panels probably from the old " Grete House." These have been described in the historical section of this volume.

Nearly opposite Pixfield is the pretty lodge to Bromley Hill Place designed by Lady Farnborough, and erected in 1825 as an entrance to one of the drives. Formerly from here to the railway it was pasture land on both sides, through which flowed the River Ravensbourne. On the north side the land was of the nature of a swamp, covered by a growth of reeds and alders, known as Frogs' Island from the vociferous croaking of the bull frogs which inhabited it. In the early nineteenth century it was owned by Abram Nettlefold, who built upon it the first houses abutting on the high road to Beckenham, as well as the four wooden cottages at the top of the hill next to Park House which have but recently been pulled down in order to widen the road.

Originally no doubt the road to Beckenham crossed the river here by a ford or water-splash; in fact, on an old plan of the Lammas Lands in Bromley by T. Proudlove, dated 1764, a water-splash is shown, but a bridge of some sort was there at the beginning of the nineteenth century.

Probably this was reconstructed in brick and stone later. The great flood in 1878 did damage to it, but it was not demolished until 1886, when the present bridge was built. The keystone of the old one is preserved in the Municipal Buildings.

On the other side of the road opposite Frogs' Island was a meadow known as the " ten-acres " or, on the Lammas Plan, " the Upper Common Mead." A stile and footpath led from the bridge straight across this meadow to the foot of Martin's Hill. Through this meadow the Ravensbourne took a very meandering course, in one place coming within three feet of its previous flow. On converting this land into building property the windings of the river were remorselessly reduced to a straight line.

From the valley we now ascend to the height once more—to the church, Church Road, and Glassmill Lane.

The piece of land between Ilott's surgery and the lych gate had always been vested in the incumbent of the Parish Church, but by what tenure is not known. A portion of it is occupied by a little shop and yard. The rest of the ground was let off as a kitchen-garden to the hotel near by, hence it came to be known as the Bell Garden. In April 1865, the churchyard required enlarging, overtures were made to Mr. R. Longsdon of Church House to give up a portion of his meadow, so that the southern boundary fence of the existing churchyard might be continued down the slope. This addition, together with the Bell Garden, would, it was said, meet all requirements. At first Mr. Longsdon agreed, but later he refused. The Rev. J. E. Newell, then Vicar, readily agreed to the sale of the Bell Garden, but shortly afterwards he resigned, and was succeeded by the Rev. A. G. Hellicar, who agreed to accept £200 in lieu of the incumbent's rights on condition that the purchase money was applied to ecclesiastical purposes. The money was invested and used towards the building of the vicarage. The land was fenced in at an additional cost of £150, Miss Ilott giving the wall abutting on the road as far as the lych gate.

This new portion of the churchyard was consecrated in November 1866 by Archbishop Longley. The lych gate, designed by Mr. St. Aubyn, was erected in 1855 at a cost of about £70. It is of heart-oak, and entirely fastened together with wooden pins.

The corresponding land on the other side of Church Road, including the wooden cottages, round the very awkward corner, has been dealt with in the High Street portion of this Itinerary.

The section from the lych gate to Glassmill Lane and Martin's Hill on the south side comprises the Parish Church and churchyard, also the demesne known now as Church House, but formerly the Rectory.

The living of Bromley was up to 1537 a rectory, thus in 1287 it was rated at thirty marks, or about £20, and in 1534 at £39 12s. In 1557, however, the rectory with the tithes of the parish were, by order of Henry VIII, transferred to the Bishops of Rochester, who were to appoint, ordain, and endow perpetual vicars. In the reign of Charles I, Hasted says, the living consisted of

" a manor and good mansion house with a gate house, a large tithe barn of eleven bays, two small barns and 51 acres of glebe."

The glebe land was worth in 1650 £50, the quit rents 8s. 9d., and the tithes £130 yearly, and a small tenement £2 per annum, £182 8s. 9d. in all. These were always leased for twenty-one years, renewable every seven years, at a rent of £60 per annum, plus forty quarters of oats (valued at £40 in 1850) with a fine at each renewal ; thus when they were so leased by Dr. John Warner in 1639 the whole was said to be worth to a tenant £183 per annum.

Lysons says that John Yonge was lessee in 1646, but the lease passed to the Emmett family soon after the Restoration, and in 1706 William Emmett's granddaughter brought it to Mr. John Innocent, whose daughter, Eleonora, by marriage brought it to Mr. James Norman, by whose son, George Norman, it was resigned in 1828.

In 1832 Church House was rebuilt by Mr. Gould, agent to the Bishop's trustees, who found, on restoring it, on the south side material of the same nature as that with which the church was built, which seems to show that that part at all events was coeval with the church.

It was held on lease then by Abel Moysey, who added very much to the beauty of the place by lawns, shrubberies, and fishponds, and a new carriage-way to the house, which opened out on to the road just opposite the entrance to Martin's Hill. At that time the Tithe Barn stood east of this entrance drive and abutted on to Church Road. East of this again, that is nearer the town, on a strip of the estate adjoining the churchyard, was, near the road, a granary about fourteen or fifteen feet square, then a range of farm-buildings, and at the rear two cottages, a line of chestnut trees marking the boundary of the churchyard.

In January 1843, as the churchyard wanted enlarging, this strip was offered by the then occupant, Rev. James King, in conjunction with the Bishop, to the Vestry, and accepted by it. The granary, farm-buildings, and cottages were removed, under tender, by Mr. Charman, who also erected the new fence bounding Church House property.

The new wall abutting on to Church Road was built by Mr. Wm. Rawlinson for £28. Some of the chestnut trees, planted in 1793, still remain to mark the old boundary.

Concerning the Tithe Barn, Hasted, as we have seen, says it was one of eleven bays, and the Rectorial Manor Roll of 1650 confirms his statement. According to Mr. Ford of Shortlands, born in 1837, it was a building about sixty by eighteen feet. It was burnt down one hot July morning in 1853, when Mr. Ford was sixteen years old. He remembered it quite well, and that Mr. Pawley of the White Hart rented it and the farm-buildings, as well as the hop garden at the foot of Martin's Hill. Mr. Alexander the butcher certainly had it in the thirties. This destruction of the Barn opened the way for the building of the present lodge and entrance gates and drive down to the house.

From 1849 to 1863 Church House was the home of a lady who was highly esteemed on account of her Christian charity and benevolence, namely, Mrs. Scott, widow of Dr. John Scott the London surgeon, and son of the noted Bromley surgeon Mr. James Scott. She was the daughter of J. F. S. Fleming St. John, Canon of Worcester. She died January 15th, 1863, aged sixty-nine, and is buried with her husband in the Parish Church.

One of the later occupants of Church House was Mr. R. Longsdon, whose family resided there from 1865 till 1889. This gentleman was associated with Henry Bessemer in bringing out the celebrated process (1856–8) for manufacturing steel, which revolutionised that industry throughout the world. Longsdon seems to have acted chiefly in the capacity of financier.

In 1889 Mr. Paul Henwood, a retired South African merchant, took the house, made additions to it, and lived there until his death. His widow remained there until her death. They were the last private occupants. The Town Council purchased the property in 1926.

On the north side of Church Road the first range of cottages was built from 1877 onwards, being known as Kingston Terrace, but originally there was a field here, the playground of Rawes' school.

The next three houses, red-tiled, with steps up to the doorways, are very old, and constitute a picturesque row. In the Vestry Minute Books they are referred to as Gould's Cottages. Mr. George Smith of Bromley Common, who had given some study to brick-courses, thought, after careful examination, that these houses may be Caroline.

The next two houses are of more recent origin. The first one, now the Church Committee Room, was once the residence of Mr. Charles Freeman, clerk to Messrs. Latter's, and one of the historians of Bromley. There

THE LODGE, BECKENHAM LANE.
Designed by Lady Farnborough.

COTTAGES, CHURCH ROAD.

is, however, a persistent tradition that Thomas Paine (1737–1809), the author of the *Age of Reason and the Rights of Man*, came to Bromley and lodged at this house, and that his favourite walk was out across the palace grounds, where he seated himself under an oak, now cut down, the site of which was near the Palace farm.   If this is so, then it would probably have been between 1761 and 1774.   There were certainly Paines in the town—Anne, John, and William Paine.

The rest of the ground as far as Martin's Hill was originally a field until Stoberry House was built, when part of it was absorbed into its garden.   In 1869–70, Church House being still on lease, the vicarage was built, and occupied by the Rev. A. G. Hellicar.

Martin's Hill, that glorious recreation ground, which is the pride of Bromley, was originally rectorial land, and was a good deal larger than when it was acquired from the Ecclesiastical Commissioners by the Local Board on June 20th, 1878.

At present there is only one dip between the two hills, and even this has been filled up to some extent.   Before 1792, where the War Memorial and the path on the south side of it now are, there was another dip, which was filled up by the material dug out from the vaults under the north aisle of the church in 1792.   The Borough engineer, Mr. Stanley Hawkings, had ample proof when the foundations of the War Memorial were being laid that it was all made-up ground.

Below Martin's Hill is the River Ravensbourne, which rises at Cæsar's Well, Keston, just outside the southern boundary of the Borough.   It has a catchment area of between forty-two to forty-three square miles, the circumference of which is twenty-eight to thirty miles.   Before entering the Borough on the south it flows through three large ponds at Keston.   Thence it flows in a north-westerly direction, skirting the western boundary of the Borough, to St. Mark's Church, Mason's Hill, whence it flows under the railway, through a pond in the grounds of Mill Vale, and then along the foot of Martin's Hill to Shortlands Bridge.   There, passing under Beckenham Lane, it continues along the foot of Bromley Hill estate, out of the Borough, through Southend, Bellingham, Catford, and Lewisham, to enter the Thames at Deptford Creek after a course of about ten and a quarter miles.

During its course it receives four tributaries, namely : the Bourne Water, an intermittent stream at Hayes Lane ; an unnamed stream, which comes from the lakes in Holwood Park at Keston, joins it at St. Mark's Church ; nearing Catford it receives the combined Chaffinch and Beck Rivers, rising in Shirley Woods, and at Lewisham comes in its longest tributary, namely, the Quaggy River or Kyd Brook, which rises in Darrick Wood, Orpington, and itself receives several small streams : in fact, this tributary is longer than the Ravensbourne itself, running a course of eleven miles before its junction with the parent stream.

Formerly the Ravensbourne was of greater volume than it is to-day. Even in the youth of many now living, trout were sometimes taken from it. As late as 1869 a salmon trout of three-and-a-half pounds was caught by one Harry Budgeon.   Kingfishers, too, were quite an everyday sight, flitting under the bridge up to a small waterfall from the mill-dam.   Mr. D. Crowhurst saw a pair as late as 1920.

Dunkin, in his *History of Deptford* (p. 207), records the occurrence of floods.   On April 11th–12th, 1878, there was a great flood here in Bromley. The whole of the Shortlands Valley was one sheet of water, covering the hedges, fences, and even the railway, which became insecure after the passing of the early business trains in the morning.   Shortlands Bridge was damaged, Beckenham Lane was impassable to pedestrians, the gas works were flooded, and there was consequently no light to be had in the houses for one day, and none in the streets for three days.

The following lines, one set taken from Hone's *Table Book*, 1837, the other from Nathaniel Daw's *History of Deptford*, point the contrast between what the Ravensbourne once was and what it has become :

> On Keston Heath wells up the Ravensbourne
> A crystal rillet, scarce a palm in width
> And crossing meads and footpaths gathering tribute,
> Wanders in Hayes and Bromley, Beckenham Vale
> To Deptford Bridge when on, to swell
> The master current of the ' mighty heart '
>   Of England.

> The Ravensbourne once called the Brome
> But oh ! how changed with changing years,
> 'Tis now the vilest stream on earth,
> Polluted from its place of birth.
> The Kent and Surrey Hills no more
> Can show their limpid rills of yore.
>   JOHNSON.

At the foot of the hill Glassmill Lane crosses the river by a bridge and then turns sharply to the left, skirting the left bank of the river and the backwater from the Mill Dam.   Formerly the river-bank was open ground, but for many years past it has been enclosed by high iron railings.   The lane ended at a footpath which crossed the railway by a level crossing, this footpath eventually joining another which led to South Hill.

The mill which gave its name to the lane was situated in the grounds of Mill Vale, its dam forming a considerable piece of ornamental water, six hundred feet long by sixty feet broad.   This mill is mentioned in Domesday, when it was used to grind corn, the entry being :

" Ibi j mold de IV sold."   (There one mill at 4*s*.)

THE MILLPOND, 1909.
From a photograph by Mr. Albert S. Hicks

445]

In the latter end of Henry III's reign it is again referred to as " 1 mill from which were received 2 marks per annum."

In 20th of Edward I (1291) two mills are mentioned " worth 40s. per annum."

In or about the year 1449 Lord Saye purchased the mill and converted it into a paper mill. Jack Cade said of him :

" Contrary to the King, his crown and dignity, thou has built a paper mill."

From 1795 to 1800 it was used by Mr. Thomas Ribright, an eminent oculist and artist in the Poultry, London, the owner being Lord Gwydir. In 1811 it belonged to Messrs. Fentham of the Strand, London, and was used for grinding and polishing mirrors and lenses, these being one to five feet in diameter, and both convex and concave. Then it was used by a Mr. Thickpenny for blanket making, afterwards by Waters & Company, who are stated by Lysons to have manufactured " Cloth without weaving," probably implying the making of felt. Their lease expired in 1825. In 1829 it was again a glass mill, run by Mr. Bradley, who, among other things, made fancy glass articles, for Mr. Allen Barrell of Bromley had a glass walking-stick that was made there. In 1832 it ceased to be a mill, Mr. E. Bilke having taken it as a family residence.

In 1795 the Vestry, held on July 12th,

" Agreed that the embankment near the Paper Mill be immediately repaired, and that the Bridge, near by, be surveyed by Messrs. Staples & Page subject to the determination of a future Vestry."

Upon the question being put whether the road was a " highway," the answer given was in the affirmative.

The land bordering the lane is now built upon, and contains Gwydir and Ridley Roads, Bromley Crescent, and Bromley Gardens, and a foot-bridge has been placed over the railway. On the west side of the lane nearest the town are two or three wooden cottages and the house known as The Valley.

About 1865 this house was the residence of Mr. William Mortimer, his son William living at Stoberry House on Martin's Hill. Both were members of a firm of Chancery brokers, and in private life were equally distinguished by their enthusiasm for fox-hunting, and for their jovial characteristics. Mr. Mortimer, senior, is buried in the parish churchyard, and is commemorated also on the family vault at Eastbourne Old Church.

The piece of water known as the Mill Pond is not associated with the mill described above, but lies just outside the Borough in a field, beyond the railway to the west end of Durham Road, at the foot of the rise to South

Hill. This pond was the favourite resort of youth and equally a source of admiration to their elders. It was encompassed on three sides by fine trees as well as by alders and willows. It was full of perennial springs, and proved an attractive and picturesque scene for artists and photographers. Some years ago, however, it was in contemplation to continue Durham Road right through the valley to Shortlands, and accordingly the trees were cut down and the place despoiled.

The rest of the land with which this section is concerned was occupied by the Simpson's Place estate, to which a special chapter is devoted.

A LIST OF THE RECTORS AND VICARS OF
BROMLEY FROM A.D. 1226

ALL previously published lists of the Rectors and Vicars of Bromley have been avowedly incomplete, and in several cases speculative.

The list here given is the result of exhaustive research in the Rochester Registers (Reg. Roff.), in the Acta Curia Consistoria (Act. Cur. Consist.), in the Harleian MSS., in the Close Rolls, and in old wills and other ancient documents.

It has therefore been thought proper to give against the various names the authorities on the strength of which those names are included.

RECTORS

Previous to 1226 no information.

1226–1238.	Richard de Wendover .	Papal Letters, 1235, and Weever's Monumental Inscriptions. Afterwards Bishop of Rochester. *d.* 1250.
Gap of 52 years.		
1290–1292.	Elya . . .	Mentioned in a grant of land. See Reg. Roff. and Cant. and York Soc.
1292–1296.	Abel de Sancto Martino.	"persona de Bromley," temp. Thoma Epis., 21 Edw. I, Reg. Roff., p. 193.
Gap of 20 years.	(? William de Bliburgh).	Patent Rolls, 4 Edw. II, Pt. 1, m. 17, 26 Aug., 1310. He was, however, a *clerk* in Chancery, not necessarily a cleric. His right to appear in this list is very doubtful.
1316–1329.	John de Frendsburie .	See Will of Thos. de Wouldam, 1316, Reg. Roff., p. 113. At variance with Bishop Hamo over property left by this will. He it was who actually excommunicated his Bishop. Deprived 18 Feb. 1329.
1329–1333.	Hugh de Penebregge .	Reg. Roff., p. 128. Appointed 6 Kal. Jun. 1329.
1333–1349.	Wm. de Wycklewoode, or de Boyleston .	Harleian MSS., 112, A 54; Close Rolls, 6 May 1342.
1349–1360.	Walter de Hethe .	Appointed 9 Kal. May 1349. Buried in Bromley Parish Church.
1361.	Robert Carey, S.T.P. .	Resigned 9 Kal. Mar. 1361. Exchanged to Chislehurst with Jno. Verieu.
1361.	John Verieu . .	Exchanged with Carey. Resigned and went to Sevenoaks. Buried at Saltwood (brass).
1361–1362.	Thomas Bay (clerk) .	Instituted on resignation of John Verieu, 6 Kal. Apl. 1361.
1362–1365.	John Salthorn . .	Exchanged with Thos. Bay, 18 Kal. July 1362, from Calistoke, Oxford.

1365.	Adam Pykeman.	Exchanged with J. Salthorn 8 Kal. Nov. 1365 from Islip, Ox. Reg. Roff., vol. i, p. 324.

(These 3 Exchanges are all recorded in Reg. Roff., vol. i,—no explanation is given for them, however.)

Gap of some 20 years.

1389–1391.	John Scharynton	Act. Cur. Consist. Named by Fielding. No. ref. in Reg. Roff.
1391–1402.	Richard de Sudbury	Named as Rector of the Par. Ch. of Bromley in Reg. Roff., vol. ii, p. 16.
1402–1405.	Roger-atte-cherch	Exchanged with R. de Sudbury, 2 Oct. 1402. Reg. Roff., p. 179. Executor to the will of John Bottlesham, Bp. of Rochester, who died 1407. See Pat. Rolls, 11 Feb. 1407.
1405.	Henry Hamonde	Arundel, i, 34. ⎫ These are taken by Fielding from the Canterbury Registers. No
1406.	Richard Braunch	Arundel, i, 312. ⎬ mention of them in Reg. Roff.
—.	Thomas Pellycan	⎭
1421–1424.	Thomas Gyles .	Chichele, i, 130 "Thos. Gyles died as Rector of Bromleygh."
1424–1431.	John Pye (Chaplain)	Appointed 12 Mar. 1424. Reg. Roff., vol. iii, p. 44.
1431.	John Wirkworth	Exchanged with Jno. Pye, 20 June 1431, from Abbechurch. Reg. Roff., vol. iii.
–1439.	Thomas Lewisham	No notice except that he exchanged with J. Boner to Melford.
1439–1440.	John Boner	Reg. Roff. Bishop of Enachdune or Annagh-down, co. Galway, in 1421. Before coming here he was Rector of Melford. In 1440 he exchanged with William Middleton.
1440–1448.	William Middleton	Came from the Chantry of Milton, Roch. diocese.
1448–1453.	William Fryston.	Appointed 15 Nov. 1448; then only a notary, but was ordained Sept. 1450.
1453–1457.	Richard Fryston.	Exchanged with Wm. Fryston. Resigned in July 1457.
1457–	John Chamberlayne	Reg. Rof.
1465–	Richard Wymando	Hasted. No other ref. Reg. Roff. here missing for 30 years.
1470–	Robert Somersby	Fielding quotes Papal Bull, 23 May.
1471–	William Shelton.	Fielding, but not found in Act. Cur. Consist., 1471, 35 as Fielding asserts.
1483–4	John Richardson	Mentioned in 2 wills, Roch. Archy, No. 6 : (1) John Juner, 1483, where he is styled Rector. (2) Margt. Lemans, 1484, where he is styled Priest.

1500–1501.	Sir Harry —— . .	Mentioned in 2 wills, Roch. Archy., No. 5 : (1) Rich. Shott, Oct. 1500, as Parson. (2) John Coleman, Jan. 1501, as Parson.
1502.	Robert Sandys . .	Died at Bromley, 1502. Reg. Roff.
1502–1524.	William Horsey, LL.D.	Appointed Rector, 5 May 1502. Styled in Reg. Roff., vol. v, " decretorium doctor." Resigned.
1524–1528.	Richard Sharpe, S.T.B.	Appointed 23 Sept. 1524. In 1520 he is described in Reg. Roff., vol. v, as " in sacra theologia, bacharlaureus." In 1524, " in sacra theologia profesori (D.D.)." Died at Bromley, 1528.
1530–1533.	John Adeson, D.D. .	Appointed 13 Mar. 1530. Reg. Roff., vol. v.
1533–1537.	Emery Tukfold, or Tuffelde.	Appointed May 1533, apparently to supervise survey of Church property. Called " King's Rector." Reg. Roff., vol. v.

In 1537 the rectory, by order of Henry VIII, was transferred to the Bishops of Rochester, who were to " appoint, ordain, and sufficiently endow perpetual vicars," etc. (Patent Rolls, Henry VIII).

The incumbents therefore lost their rectorial status, and were, from 1537, Vicars or Perpetual Curates.

VICARS OR PERPETUAL CURATES

1537–1548.	Ralph Tylney . .	He was Curate for at least twenty years before he was appointed as the first Perpetual Vicar under the order of Henry VIII. His name appears more frequently than any other in wills, not only as witness, but also as executor, or as overseer, so he was evidently a man most intimately associated with his people. He died in office 1548, and was buried at the Parish Church.
1551–1553.	Edmund Trevell. .	These names appear in wills of the dates mentioned and in intermediate years, and there is nomination of their appointments. David Curson has been named often as Vicar. He was domestic chaplain and tutor in Robert Knight's Great House in the High Street, and Rich. Wolston, " *Vicar of Bromley*," witnessed his will, 1554.
1554–1556.	Richard Wolston .	
1557–1566.	Thomas Hatherstole .	
1570– .	John Hughes . .	See will of John Wright, 3 Sept. 1570. Reg. Roff.

1576–1585.	Christofer Hills .	. Vicar and a notary mentioned in the will of John Wybarne of Bromley ; mentioned in the will of Symon Bedle, 1579.
1588–1603.	Richard Wallis .	. Ordained at Dartford, where he was then Vicar. Reg. Roff.
1603–	. James Dyer .	. In Par. Reg. called " Curate of Bromley." Reg. Roff.
1607–	. Stephen Constantine .	Hasted.
1607–	. John Preston .	. Signs in Parish Registers.
1611–	. Joseph Greene .	. Reg. Roff.
1620–	. Jasper Carrow .	. Par. Reg.
–1624.	William Wallis .	. Hasted. Died at Bromley, 1624. Reg. Roff.
1627.	John Hodges .	. Hasted.
1628.	Noah Webb .	. Hasted.
1630.	Robert Rainsford .	. Hasted.
1634.	Richard Rathbone, or Rathborne.	Par. Reg.
1639.	Thomas Smith .	. Hasted.
1640.	William Thomas	. Reg. Roff. Styled Vicar.
1640–1646.	Robert Antrobus	. Additl. MSS., Brit. Mus. 15670, 15671.
18 *April,* 1646.	John Harvey.	
9 *May,* 1646.	Walter Artson .	. Discharged 17 Sept. 1646.
18 *Sept.* 1646– 22 *Aug.* 1648	Joseph Jackson .	. Hasted. Lambeth Pal. Survey.
1648–1662.	Henry Arnold. .	. Par. Reg. Elected at a Vestry to be Parish Minister, 1653.
1663.	Richard Marsh .	. e lib. Subscrip.
1666.	Thomas Pike .	. Hasted.
1667.	Daniel Baston, or David Burton.	Hasted.
1669.	—— Stenning.	
1670.	Edmund Lee, or Lees	Hasted.
1678–1681.	Stephen Grasscombe .	Par. Reg.
1682.	George Wilson .	. Par. Reg.
1684.	Thomas Johnson .	. Hasted.
1686.	Edward Roman .	. Par. Reg.
1690.	Henry Maundrell	. Alumni Oxon. Fellow Exeter Coll., Oxon. Chaplain to Factory at Aleppo. Lysons, 1796, says, p. 317, he was appointed Curate 1680.
1695.	Samuel Bowles .	. Par. Reg.
1698–1739.	Harington Bagshaw .	Par. Reg. Styled Vicar. Chaplain Bromley College, 1696–1734. Rector of Woolwich.
1739–1744.	Joseph Sims .	. Reg. Roff.
1744–1785.	Thomas Bagshaw, M.A.	Reg. Roff. Vicar, Chap. Br. Coll. 1734–1787. Rector of Southfleet.

1785–1818.	Henry Smith, D.D. .	Par. Reg. Vicar. Rector of Headley, Hants.
1818–Oct. 1819.	John Baker, M.A. .	Reg. Roff.; Par. Reg. *d.* 1824. "Many years Lecturer of this Parish," on tablet at W. end of Par. Ch. Resigned.
Dec. 1819– 1826.	James Edward Newell	Par. Reg. Seems to have acted as *Curate* only during this period, and so signs in Par. Reg. Licensed 1826, when he signs Par. Reg. as "*Minister* of Bromley."
1826–1865.	James Edward Newell.	Par. Reg. Retired. *d.* 1880. Last entry in Par. Reg., 8 Mar. 1865.
1865–1904.	Arthur Gresley Hellicar, M.A.	Par. Reg. Came in 1861 as Curate. *d.* 1904. Buried Par. Ch. Memorial Window at W. end.
1904–1915.	Donald Tait, M.A. .	Par. Reg. Appointed Archdeacon and Canon Residentiary of Rochester in 1915, and Vice-Dean in 1924.
1915– .	Joseph Kershaw Wilson, M.A.	Par. Reg. Canon of Rochester, and Rural Dean, 1924.

The names which follow are sometimes referred to as Rectors of Bromley. They did not hold that position. They were Curates, occasional helpers, and were distinguished by the courtesy title of 'Sir.'

circ. 1147.	Hugh, Priest of Bromley	Reg. Roff.
1446.	Sir John Haryngton .	Roch. Wills.
1449.	Sir Hugh Haryngton .	Roch. Wills.
1455–1466.	Sir Thos. Rose . .	Son of John Rose, of Bromley, a monk of St. Saviour's Monastery, Bermondsey.
1471–1473.	Sir Robert ―― .	Roch. Wills.
1473–1475.	Stephen Heyward .	Roch. Wills.
1476–1479.	Thomas Inglesche .	Roch. Wills.
1480–1484.	John Wale . .	Act. Cur. Consist.; Roff.
1494–1498.	William Quynton .	Died at Bromley. Described in his will as Parish Priest of Bromley.
1500.	Richard Dudston .	Roch. Wills.
1500–1509.	William Thomlynson .	Roch. Wills.

Appendix B

THE following Inventory of church goods made in 1553 is an indication of the wealth and importance of Bromley Church in the days before the Reformation.

It has been carefully copied from the original in the Record Office by the late Mr. E. G. Atkinson, a member of the Bromley History Committee, and is here accurately transcribed from this copy.

INVENTORIES OF CHURCH GOODS—EDWARD VI, 1553

KENT, $\frac{3}{43}$, MEMBRANE 7. RECORD OFFICE

THE HUNDRED OF BROMELEYE AND BECKYNHAM
BROMELEY

KENT. The Inventorie indented, made the xii^th days of Novembre, in the sixt yeare of the reigne of our sovereigne lorde Edwarde the sixte, by the grace of God king of Englande Fraunce and Irelande, defender of the faithe, and in earthe of the Churche of Englande and also of Irelande supreme heade, Betwene Sir Parcy-vall Harte and Sir Marten Bowes, knyghtes, John Browne, and Thomas Lovelace, Esquiers, Commyssyoners, amongste others, auctorysede by vertue of his gracis Commyssyon, beryng Teste at Westm^r the xvi^th days of Maye in the sixte yeare of his moste gracyous reigne, for the viewe, presentmente, and certificate of all the goodes, plate, juelles, Bells and ornamentes to everye Churche and Chapell within the saide Countie of Kente belonging or in enye wise apperteynyng, to them and others directede and állotted to the hundredes of Blakeheathe, Bromeley and Bekenham, Litle and Leosnes, Rookysley and Axton, within the saide Countye, of the one partye, And William Momforde and Richarde Mathewe, Churchewardens of the parishe Churche of Bromeley aforesaide, of the other partie, Wittnessith that the saide Comyssioners have delyvered by thies presentes to the saide Churche-wardens all the parcells herafter particularlye written,

vz.

FIRST, one Chrismatorye of silver, being hole, weying xii ounces quarter.

Item, one pix of silver, being hole, xi ounces iii quarters.

Item, ii Cruettes of silver, being hole, x ounces.

Item, one pax of silver, being hole, vi ounces quarter.

Item, one Chalys of silver, with his patent all gilte, being hole as it is, weying xxii ounces di. [and a half].

Item, one other Chalys, with the patente of sylver, parcell gilte, being hole as it is, waying xvi ounces di.

Item, one other Chalys, with his patente of silver, parcell gilte, being hole as it is, waying ix ounces.

Item, ii crosses of Copper, with one foote of Copper to the same.

Item, one pix Clothe, of Clothe of golde.

Item, one Canapie clothe of grene Saten of Bridges [Bruges].

Item, one Cope of Blewe velvett embrothered with aungells and Starres of Clothe of golde, and one sute of vestmentes to the same.

Item, one Cope of purple velvett, imbrothered with aungels, spledegles and flowers.

Item, one Cope of Chaungeable Bawdekyn.

Item, one Cope of White Satten of Bridges, imbrodered with flowers.

Item, one vestmente of Blew velvett, imbrodered with flowers lakkyng an ames.

Item, on cope of Bawdekyn, with a sute of vestmentes belonging to yᵉ same, lakkyng an albe and a stole.

Item, on vestmente of Blewe dammaske embrodred with flowers.

Item, one vestment of white satten.

Item, on olde vestmente of dornyx [made at Dornick, or Tournay] with an albe.

Item, one vestmente and an albe of Blake satten of Bridges, imbrodered with flowers.

Item, one frunte Clothe of Tawney velvett, with a border of clothe of golde and velvett perlede.

Item, one frunt Cloth of redd damaske, embrodered with Bawdekyn.

Item, one herse clothe of Blake Satten of Bridges, with one crosse of redd Satten of Bridges.

Item, one frunt cloth of redd damaske.

Item, ii frunt Clothes of Canvas paynted.

Item, ii Corpraxes & iii Corprax casis [altar cloth of white linen].

Item, v Crosse and Banner Clothes of paynted lynnen clothe.

Item, one holywater Stokke of Brasse.

Item, iii olde latten [superior brass] Basens, one dishe & iiii cruettes of powder.

Item, ii Sencers of copper & one shippe [incense holder] of the same.

Item, ii Crosse Staves half plated with copper.

Item, iii latten Candlestikes & ii litle candlestikes of latten.

Item, one pix of Copper.

Item, ii pix Clothes, thone of nedle worke, thother of olde redd silke.

Item, one paire of organs.

Item, ii curtens of yelowe and red saye for the Quere.

Item, ii Towels, thone of diaper, thother of playne clothe.

Item, v surplesses of lynnen clothe.

Item, ii greate Standardes of Brasse.

Item, one Brasen lampe & one hanging basen for the pascall.

Item, one funt [front] clothe of lynnen.

Item, xxᵗⁱ litle bolles of peweder, whiche did serve in the rode lofte.

Item, one bible and six alter clothes of lynnen.

Item, iiii greate Bells suted in the Steple, one Santes bell, and iii lytle sacoryng Bells, one hand bell, & ii olde alter pillowes.

Item, one paraphrasis of Erasmus.

Item, one lenten vaile of lynnen clothe.

Item, one Booke of the homalies and iii englishe processioners.

Item, xxxix *s.* ii *d.* remaynyng of a crosse of silver sold by the saide Church-wardens.

To be safelie kepte and preserved by the saide Churchewardens, and the same & everye parcell therof to be forth commyng at all tymes herafter when it shalbe of them required.   In wittnes wherof aswell the saide Commyssioners as the saide Churchewardens have subscribed theire names on the daye and yeare above-wrytten.

PERCYVALL HART.   MARTYN BOWES.

JOHN BROWNE.   THOMAS LOVELACE.

Endorsed :—

Apud Estgrenewich, xvi^to die Novembris, Anno RR.
E. vi^tlvi^to.

MEMORANDUM, that all the parcelles of goodes, plate, Juelles, Belles, & ornamentes apperteynyng to the parishe churche within written, mencyoned in thinventorye made in the third yeare of the Reigne of oure saide sovereigne lorde, ar conteyned within this presente Inventorye, and bene delyvered by the withinnamed Commyssioners to the within named Churchwardens, to aunswere the same, Excepte v olde Banner clothes and one crosse of silver and gilte, weying lvi ounces, presented unto the saide Commyssioners by thothes of the saide Churchwardens, to be solde by the saide Churchwardens with the consent of the parishoners there, for the some of xiiii L. 6s. 9d., and that all the saide some of money was employed upon the necessarie Reparacions of the saide parishe churche, excepte xxxix s. ii d., parcell of the saide some remaynying in the possession of the saide Churchwardens to be lykewse aunswered.

LISTS OF BENEFACTIONS TO BROMLEY COLLEGE —OF CHAPLAINS—AND OF TREASURERS

THE record of benefactions to Bromley College is contained, in part, on four large Tablets which used to be affixed to the walls of the chapel. The entries are here completed and brought up to date.

		£	s.	d.
1666.	Dr. John Warner, Founder	8,500	0	0
	Dr. John Warner, by will, the yearly sum of	450	0	0
	His heir, for repairs	5	0	0
1666.	Sir Orlando Bridgeman, for repairs, yearly	10	0	0
1704.	Dr. Thomas Plume, Archdeacon of Rochester	100	0	0
1716.	Dr. Thomas Tenison, Archbishop of Canterbury	52	10	0
1737.	Archdeacon Clark, of Norwich	5	5	0
1757.	Mr. Wilcocks, for building east wall	112	0	0
1757.	Mrs. Swift, for repairs	10	0	0
1764.	Mrs. Wolfe, mother of General Wolfe	500	0	0
1767.	Rev. A. Jephson, Rector of Crayke, Durham	200	0	0
1768.	Dr. Thomas Secker, Archbishop of Canterbury	500	0	0
1770.	Rev. W. Hetherington, of North Cray	2,000	0	0
1773.	Earl of Thanet, through his daughter Lady Gower	500	0	0
1774.	Dr. Zachary Pearce, Bishop of Rochester	5,000	0	0
1782.	William Pearce, yearly, for the Chaplain	20	0	0
1784.	Mrs. Rogers, for repairs	120	0	0
1787.	Rev. Thomas Bagshaw, Interest on	200	0	0
1793.	Dr. John Thomas, Bishop of Rochester, Interest from	300	0	0
	and	100	0	0
1794.	Mrs. Helen Bettenson, for extension	10,000	0	0
	William Pearce, brother of the Bishop, for extension	12,000	0	0
1821.	Mrs. Goodwin, of Huddleston, Yorks	500	0	0
1821.	Miss Jane Brooke, of Norwich, for water supply	230	0	0
1822.	Mrs. Carpenter, " for Bible and Prayer Book "	10	0	0
1823.	Dr. Walker King, Bishop of Rochester, for out-pensions, interest on	3,000	0	0
1824.	Mrs. Rose, for the Widows	8,000	0	0
1827.	Magdalen College, Oxford, for College Grove	20	0	0
1829.	George Norman	500	0	0
1838.	Lord Farnborough	500	0	0
1844.	Sons of the Clergy and Cholmondely Charities, for medical attendance, yearly	100	0	0
1854.	Rev. J. T. B. Landon, collected for turret and clock	126	0	0
1860.	Peter Sutton	100	0	0
1861.	Mrs. Green, of Southampton	100	0	0
1893.	Rev. J. E. Newell	1,000	0	0
1907.	Donations from Trustees and others	615	0	0

		£	s.	d.
1907 to 1925.	Legacy from Mrs. Elizabeth Tunstall Smith . .	2,577	10	0
1909.	Legacy from Miss A. E. Younghusband . . .	200	0	0
1921.	Miss Catherine Crewe Beynon, legacy to found one out-pension	520	13	0
1925.	Donation, Rev. W. C. Parr	25	0	0
1925.	Donation, H.M. Queen Mary	10	0	0
1925.	Donation, Anonymous	500	0	0
1926. 1927.	}Donation, Anonymous, for New Endowment Fund . .	30,000	0	0
1928.	Ditto, from over 500 contributors	3,000	0	0

For Sheppard College

		£	s.	d.
1840.	Mrs. Sheppard	7,650	0	0
1842.	Mrs. Sheppard	2,000	0	0
1843.	Mrs. Sheppard, for two out-pensions . . .	2,000	0	0
1907.	Executors of Mrs. Finnie of Malvern Wells . .	3,000	0	0
1921.	Rev. A. H. Soames, legacy to found two out-pensions .	1,043	3	10
	Anonymous donation supplementing the above . .	120	0	0
1925.	Miss Edith F. Slater, legacy	20	0	0

Bromley College
Chaplains

1675–82. Thomas Leigh.
1683–86. Henry Dobson.
1687. Thomas Goodwin.
1696. Thomas Brabourn, ejected from office shortly after appointment.
1696. Harington Bagshaw, Vicar of Bromley.
1734. Thomas Bagshaw, Vicar of Bromley.
1787–8. William Partridge, deputising for A. Price.
1788. Andrew Price.
1800. James J. Talman.
1820. George Booth.
1820. Edward George Ambrose Beckwith.
1821. Thomas Scott, B.D., J.P.
1846. Charles Urquhart.
1846. James Timothy Bainbridge Landon.
1855. Henry Cadwallader Adams, author of *The Cherry Stones, Schoolboy Honour*, etc.
1868. Mark D. French.
1873. John Henry Worsley.
1884. Walter Octavius Peile.
1890. Edward Frank Cornwallis Van der Noot.
1891. James White, Executor to General Gordon.
1915. Willoughby Chase Parr.
1925. Arthur S. Hichens, B.D., elder brother of the novelist, Canon of Jerusalem.

Treasurers

1695–1698. Sir John Morden, founder of Morden's College, Blackheath.

1698–1719. Sir John Shaw.

1719–1720. Rowland Tryon.

1720–1742. William

1742–1747. Thomas Tryon.

1747–1768. Jones Raymond.

1768–1776 (Jan.) Peter Burrell.

1776 (Feb.)–1787 (Sept.) James Norman.

1788–1829. George Norman.

1829–1853 (?) John Wells of Widmore.

1855–1860 (?) Bishop George Murray.

1860–1881. George Warde Norman.

1881–1889. Charles Loyd Norman.

1889–present day. Archibald Cameron Norman.

A CHRONOLOGICAL LIST OF THE PARLIAMENTARY ELECTIONS IN WHICH BROMLEY WAS CONCERNED, FROM 1832, WITH THE NAMES OF THE CANDIDATES AND THE NUMBER OF VOTES POLLED

WEST KENT. TWO MEMBERS

1832.	T. L. Hodges	L.	3,365
	T. Rider	L.	3,099
	Sir W. R. P. Geary	C.	2,519
1835.	Sir W. R. P. Geary	C.	2,558
	T. L. Hodges	L.	2,092
	T. Rider	L.	2,007
1837.	Sir W. R. P. Geary	C.	3,584
	Sir T. L. Hodges	L.	3,334
	Sir E. Filmer, Bt.	C.	3,229

1838.   Sir W. Geary accepted Chiltern Hundreds.
      Sir E. Filmer returned unopposed.

1841.   Sir E. Filmer . . . . . C. ⎫
      Viscount Marsham . . . C. ⎬ unopposed.

1845.   Lord Marsham succeeded to Peerage as Earl of Romney.
      Colonel T. Austen . . . . P. unopposed.

1847.	Sir E. Filmer	P.	3,222
	T. L. Hodges	L.	3,133
	Colonel T. Austen	P.	3,087

(NOTE.—P. signifies Protectionist.)

1852.	Sir E. Filmer	C.	3,247
	W. M. Smith	C.	3,193
	T. L. Hodges	L.	2,652

On the death of Sir E. Filmer—
1857 (February 16).

	C. Wykeham Martin	L.	3,557
	Sir W. B. Riddell	C.	3,149

1857 (April 3).

	C. Wykeham Martin	L.	3,896
	J. Whatman	L.	3,578
	W. M. Smith	C.	3,171
1859.	Viscount Holmesdale	C.	3,769
	Sir E. Filmer	C.	3,684
	C. Wykeham Martin	L.	3,584
	J. Whatman	L.	3,460
1865.	Viscount Holmesdale	C.	4,133
	W. Hart Dyke	C.	4,054
	Sir J. Lubbock, Bt.	L.	3,896
	W. Angerstein	L.	3,861

1868.   C. H. Mills . . . . . C.   3,440
       J. G. Talbot . . . . . C.   3,378
       Sir J. Lubbock . . . . L.   3,323
       W. Angerstein . . . . L.   3,196
1874.   Sir C. H. Mills, Bt. . . . . C.   5,298
       J. G. Talbot . . . . . C.   5,227
       A. Hamilton . . . . . L.   3,391
       E. Marjoribanks . . . . L.   3,348
       Mr. Talbot having accepted Chiltern Hundreds to stand
         for Oxford University.
1878.   Viscount Lewisham . . . . C. unopposed.
1880.   Sir C. H. Mills . . . . C.   6,412
       Viscount Lewisham . . . . C.   5,998
       H. M. Bompas, Q.C.. . . . L.   4,859
       J. May . . . . . . I.C.   980
       Viscount Lewisham appointed Vice-Chamberlain.
1885 (July 4).
       Rt. Hon. Viscount Lewisham . . C. unopposed.

SEVENOAKS DIVISION. ONE MEMBER

1885.   C. W. Mills . . . . . C.   4,651
       P. Nickalls . . . . . L.   3,956
1886.   Hon. C. W. Mills . . . . C. unopposed.
1892.   H. W. Forster . . . . . C.   6,036
       T. Johnston . . . . . G.L.   3,908
       (NOTE.—G.L. signifies Gladstonian Liberal.)
1895.   H. W. Forster . . . . . C. unopposed.
1900.   H. W. Forster . . . . . C.   6,604
       M. S. Richardson . . . . L.   1,792
       Mr. Forster appointed a Lord of the Treasury.
1902.   H. W. Forster . . . . . C.   5,333
       B. Morice . . . . . L.   4,442
1906.   H. W. Forster . . . . . C.   7,219
       B. Morice . . . . . L.   6,855
       M. S. Richardson . . . . I.L.   44
1910   (January).
       H. W. Forster . . . . . C.   10,421
       Sir F. S. P. Lely . . . . L.   6,351
1910 (December).
       H. W. Forster . . . . . C. unopposed.

PARLIAMENTARY BOROUGH OF BROMLEY. ONE MEMBER

1918.   Rt. Hon. H. W. Forster . . . Co. U. 16,840
       Holford Knight . . . . L.   4,339
1919 (December 17).   Mr. Forster created a Peer (Lord Forster).
       Lt.-Col. Hon. C. James . . . Co. U. 11,148
       F. P. Hodes . . . . . Lab.   10,077

1922.	Lt.-Col. Hon. C. James	.	.	.	U.	16,803
	F. K. Griffith	.	.	.	L.	9,128
	F. P. Hodes	.	.	.	Lab.	4,735
1923.	Lt.-Col. Hon. C. James	.	.	.	U.	13,495
	F. K. Griffith	.	.	.	L.	12,612
	W. G. Hall	.	.	.	Lab.	3,992
1924.	Lt.-Col. Hon. C. James	.	.	.	C.	20,272
	F. K. Griffith	.	.	.	L.	11,580
	H. J. Wallington	.	.	.	Lab.	5,876

VALEDICTORY

"AND here will I make an end.
And if I have done well, and as is fitting the story, it is that which I desired : but if slenderly and meanly, it is that which I could attain unto.

For as it is hurtful to drink wine or water alone : and as wine mingled with water is pleasant, and delighteth the taste : even so speech finely framed delighteth the ears of them that read the story. And here shall be an end."

2 Maccabees xv. 37–9.

INDEX

Aitken, C. H., Esq.
Allen, Mrs. G.
Alston, Miss.
Arnaud, J. F., Esq.
Arnold, E., Esq.
Ashton, P. J., Esq.
Asser, Mrs.
Avebury, Rt. Hon. Lord.
Ayling, B., Esq.

Bain, D., Esq.
Balfour, Mrs. G.
Barker, Rev. Canon P.
Barnes, Miss E.
Bartrum, Mrs. D.
Bassett, W. C., Esq.
Batchelor, Mrs. J. B.
Baxter, Wm., Esq.
Beeby, Mrs. C. E.
Beer, Miss.
Beer, R., Esq.
Bennett, J. A., Esq.
Bennett, Thos., Esq.
Berry, G. R. C., Esq.
Bevan, Cosmo, Esq.
Bibby, Miss M.
Blatherwick, Miss L.
Boothroyd, E., Esq.
Boys Behrens, Mrs. L.
Britton, W. K., Esq.
Bromley Education Committee.
Bromley Literary Institute.
Bromley Public Library.
Brooker, H. T., Esq.
Brown, S. J., Esq.
Brown, Mrs. T. H.

Browne, T. G. C., Esq.
Bruce, Sir Robert, M.A., C.B., J.P.
Bryce, Rev. W. Kirk.
Bumsted, Miss E. C.
Burrett, Miss A.
Bush, H. C., Esq.
Burt, Miss K. E.

Campbell, E. T., Esq., M.P.
Carey, Mrs. H.
Carnegie, Mrs.
Chalmers, Miss C. M.
Chalmers, Mrs. Kenneth.
Child, Sir Coles, Bart., D.L., J. P.
Chitty, C., Esq.
Churchill, Miss I. J.
Cobb, Mrs. Candler.
Collins, F. H., Esq.
Coulson, A. G., Esq.
Courtney, Claude, Esq.
Cowing, Miss J. K.
Coxwell, Mrs. M.
Crossley, W. L., Esq.
Crouch, J. Morton, Esq.
Crowhurst, S., Esq.

Davis, Miss E.
Dawson, H. J., Esq.
de Greeff, R. W., Esq.
Dewey, The Rev. Sir Stanley, Bart.
Duffield, F. H., Esq.
Duncanson, E. Ford, Esq., J.P.
Duncanson, Miss.
Dunn, E. G. A., Esq.
Dunn, H. G., Esq.

Edlmann, Col. F. J. F., D.S.O., J.P.

Edmunds, Mrs. H. M.
Elliott, A. H., Esq.
Ellis, H. O., Esq.
Evans, E. F., Esq.
Everett, R., Esq.

Ferrup, H. B., Esq.
Filby, B., Esq.
Flower-Ellis, H. T., Esq.
Fordham, E. W., Esq.
Forster, Rt. Hon. Lord.
Foss, S. H., Esq.
Fox, W. A., Esq.
Frampton, A., Esq.

Ganderton, E. W., Esq.
Gatton, Edgar V., Esq.
Gelshenen, Mrs. Carpenter.
Gibbs, W. J., Esq.
Glanvill, B. A., Esq.
Goodyear, Mrs.
Grant-Wilson, Dr. C. W.
Greenwich Public Library.
Gretton, H. C., Esq.
Grout, A., Esq.
Guildhall Library, London.
Gunton, C. H., Esq.

Hall, A. J., Esq.
Hannen, the Hon. Henry.
Harris, A. T., Esq.
Hay, J. Y., Esq.
Hay, W. R. G., Esq.
Heming, F. C., Esq.
Hewett, A. H., Esq.
Hewett, Miss E. A.
Hicks, Albert S., Esq.
Hill, Mrs. M. K.
Hill, T. W., Esq.

Hodgson, S., Esq.

Ilott, H. J., Esq., M.D.
Isard, E., Esq.
Isard, F. W., Esq.
Isard, Miss.

James, R. W., Esq., J.P.
Jayes, G. H., Esq.
Jenkin Jones, Mrs. M.
Jewson, Miss E. E.
Jones, Geo., Esq.
Jupp, J. A., Esq.

Kent Archæological Society.
King, Mrs. E.
King, L. D., Esq.
Kirby, G. E., Esq.

Lamb, Thos., Esq.
Latter, A., Esq.
Latter, A. H., Esq.
Latter, E., Esq.
Leishmann, Miss.
Leonard, A. G., Esq.
Levin, Mrs.
Lewin, H. C., Esq.
Lewis, C. E. M., Esq., M.A., M.D.
Lewis, Miss.
Lewisham Public Library.
Lindley-Jones, W., Esq., O.B.E., C.C.,
    F.R.G.S.
Littlewood, Miss K. D. B., M.A.
Lucas, Miss.
Lyle, Dr. H. Willoughby.

Maconachie, Mrs. D.
McQueen, Miss.
Mann, Mrs. A. G., B.A., J.P.
Marchant, Miss A.

Marks, Mrs.

Marsh, H. T., Esq.

Mathieson, Mrs. A.

Medhurst, F., Esq.

Miller-Hallett, G., Esq.

Milstead, H. H., Esq.

Mimpriss, S. T., Esq.

Moore, A., Esq.

Nash, A. J., Esq.

Neame, Stuart, Esq.

Newland, H. G., Esq.

Norman, A. C., Esq., M.A., J.P.

Norman, F. H., Esq.

Norman, Mrs. Gerard.

Norman, P., Esq., LL.D., F.S.A.

Norman-Butler, Mrs.

Nussey, Miss H. G.

Page, F. Spurgeon, Esq.

Parks, Geo., Esq.

Parr, Mrs. Chase.

Parr, Miss E. O.

Parr, Rev. W. C., M.A.

Parsons, H., Esq., J.P.

Payne, Mrs. D.

Perkins, B. Ward, Esq.

Platt, Mrs. S.

Pott, Rev. A. P.

Pott, G. S., Esq.

Pring, W., Esq.

Pritt, W. G., Esq.

Quick, Mrs.

Reaney, Dr. M. Jane.

Richardson, W. Ridley, Esq., M.A.

Rochester, The Right Rev. the Lord Bishop of.

Rochester, The Venerable the Archdeacon of.

Rogers, Miss H. G.

Romer, Mrs.

Rouch, Mrs. E. L.

Rush, S. H., Esq.

Salt, Miss L. Godwin, M.A.

Salter, Mrs. H. J.·

Sandle, H. J., Esq.

Sandle, S. J., Esq.

Satterthwaite, Col. E., C.B., V.D., J.P.

Saunders, F. G., Esq.

Schooling, F., Esq.

Scott, Sir Samuel, Bart.

Selby, Miss D. B.

Selby, E. H., Esq.

Sherriff, Mrs. F. F.

Sherriff, F. H., Esq.

Shillcock, S., Esq.

Simpson, Miss J.

Smith, Mrs. Geo.

Smith, Mrs. J. Wilson.

Smith, W. H., Esq.

Smith, W. M., Esq.

Soames, Miss A. C.

Soames, E., Esq.

Soans, C. H., Esq.

Sprang, F. H., Esq.

Stamp, Sir Josiah C., G.B.E.

Sturgeon, Miss J. E.

Sykes, W. N., Esq.

Taylor, R. S., Esq.

Theobald, H. W., Esq.

Thomas, Dr. H. Wynne, L.R.C.P., M.R.C.S.

Thoms, H. J., Esq.

Tilling, E. W., Esq.

Titford, H. J., Esq.
Tylor, Mrs.

Unwin, E., Esq.
Uridge, I., Esq.

Ward, F.
Weeks, Miss A. A.
Weeks, Mrs. Fred.
Weeks, Geo., Esq.
Weeks, H. T., Esq.
Weeks, Miss J. S.
Weeks, Miss K. S.
Weeks, Miss M. E.
Weller, W. G., Esq.
Wells, H. G., Esq.

Wheeler-Bennett, Mrs. J. W.
White, W. B., Esq.
Wigram, Rev. E. F. E., M.A.
Willett, J. W., Esq.
Williams, Miss E. M.
Williams, Mrs. Howard.
Williams, Mrs. J.
Willis, E. W., Esq.
Willis, J., Esq.
Willis, T. M., Esq.
Wilson, Rev. Canon J. K., M.A.
Withers, Mrs.
Woolwich Public Library.

Yeatman, E. V., Miss.
Yeatman, F. P. S., Esq.